Oracle® Solaris 11 System Administration

Oracle® Solaris 11 System Administration

Bill Calkins

PRENTICE HALL

Upper Saddle River, NJ • Boston • Indianapolis • San Francisco
New York • Toronto • Montreal • London • Munich • Paris • Madrid
Capetown • Sydney • Tokyo • Singapore • Mexico City

The publisher offers excellent discounts on this book when ordered in quantity for bulk purchases or special sales, which may include electronic versions and/or custom covers and content particular to your business, training goals, marketing focus, and branding interests. For more information, please contact:

U.S. Corporate and Government Sales
(800) 382-3419
corpsales@pearsontechgroup.com

For sales outside the United States, please contact:

International Sales
international@pearson.com

Visit us on the Web: informit.com/ph

Library of Congress Cataloging-in-Publication Data

Calkins, Bill.
Oracle Solaris 11 system administration / Bill Calkins.
pages cm
Includes index.
ISBN 978-0-13-300710-7 (paperback : alkaline paper)
1. Operating systems (Computers) 2. Solaris (Computer file) I. Title.
QA76.774.S65C35 2013
005.4'32—dc23 2013010583

ISBN-13: 978-0-13-300710-7
ISBN-10: 0-13-300710-3

Text printed in the United States on recycled paper at Edwards Brothers Malloy in Ann Arbor, Michigan.
First printing, June 2013

Editor-in-Chief
Mark L. Taub

Acquisitions Editor
Greg Doench

Development Editor
Chris Zahn

Managing Editor
John Fuller

Project Editor
Elizabeth Ryan

Copy Editor
Stephanie Geels

Indexer
Dick Evans, Infodex

Proofreader
Geneil Breeze

Technical Reviewer
John Philcox

Cover Designer
Alan Clements

Compositor
diacriTech

Thank you to my family for putting up with the time I spend writing. Although I was there physically, I was away most of the time mentally. Writing this book took away valuable family time, and I will try to make it up now that I'm finally finished (writing, that is).

Kids, it's ok to come into my office and play your games again!

Contents

Preface

This book covers all of the topics necessary to effectively install and administer an Oracle Solaris 11 system. When used as a study guide, this book will save you a great deal of time and effort searching for information you will need to administer Oracle Solaris 11 on SPARC and x86-based systems. This book covers each topic in enough detail for inexperienced administrators to learn about Oracle Solaris 11 and apply the knowledge to real-life scenarios. Experienced readers will find the material complete and concise, making it a valuable reference for everyday tasks. Drawing from my years of experience as a senior Oracle Solaris administrator and consultant, you'll find new ideas and see some different approaches to system administration that probably were not covered in your Oracle Solaris administration training courses.

You might be familiar with my Oracle Solaris certification training guides and exam prep books that have been published over the past 15 years. I am a Solaris Subject Matter Expert for Oracle. I participate in the development of the Oracle Solaris 11 certification exams, and I have made certain that the topics covered on the exam are covered in this book. But, rather than stopping at simply an exam prep book, I have gone to great effort to ensure that all tasks that you need to perform are covered beyond what is simply required to pass the exam.

Experienced administrators will find many welcome enhancements in Oracle Solaris 11, but they will also find that Oracle Solaris 11 is vastly different from previous versions of the operating system. Oracle has added new features and, in some cases, has completely redesigned some of the functions you may have used on a daily basis. To eliminate the frustration of learning a new environment, I describe new solutions for performing familiar tasks.

Welcome to the Oracle Solaris 11 community, and don't forget to visit my blog at `http://www.unixed.com/blog` where I answer your questions and discuss various topics related to Oracle Solaris administration.

What's New in Oracle Solaris 11

Oracle Solaris 11 was first introduced in November 2010 as Oracle Solaris 11 Express. With Oracle Solaris 11 Express, Oracle provided a fully tested, fully supported, production-ready package that allowed customers to have access to the latest technology and hundreds of new features. Most administrators used Oracle Solaris 11 Express to test the new features and to provide feedback to the manufacturer.

The first production release of Oracle Solaris 11 was made available in November 2011 and is referred to as Oracle Solaris 11 11/11. In October 2012, Oracle introduced Oracle Solaris 11.1, the first major release of Oracle Solaris 11. This book covers features found in both versions of Oracle Solaris 11. For those of you currently running Oracle Solaris 10, you may be wondering, "What are the real benefits of moving to Oracle Solaris 11?" Throughout this book, I provide unbiased coverage of each feature to help you make an informed decision on the benefits of moving to Oracle Solaris 11.

Chapter 1 describes how to install the Oracle Solaris 11 operating system using the Live Media and text installers, and I guide you through each step of the installation process. During the installation, I help you make decisions that will affect the final installation and help you understand which configuration options may or may not be recommended for a secure production environment.

Chapter 2 discusses the new Image Packaging System (IPS). This new method of installing and updating software packages eliminates the traditional software package and patching commands that many administrators have used for years. IPS can be a complex and confusing topic, and I have created many real-life examples to guide you through the complete software lifecycle, including creating and maintaining an up-to-date IPS repository, installing and managing software packages, and using boot environments when updating the operating system.

Chapter 3 details the entire boot process on both the SPARC and x86 platforms. Where many textbooks skip the hardware-level discussion, I cover everything from powering on the server to accessing the console through the ALOM and ILOM interface and monitoring hardware faults through the fault management architecture. I describe the OpenBoot and GRUB2 environments in detail. The entire boot process, including managing multiple boot environments (BEs), booting a BE, loading the kernel, specifying run levels and milestones, and starting the Service Management Facility (SMF), is described in detail. I am aware that most problems are encountered during the boot process, and I have made an effort to describe every scenario I have encountered on both the SPARC and x86 platforms. You'll also gain a complete understanding of kernel tunables, SMF, and services. You'll learn how to create and manage custom SMF profiles and manifests. You'll learn about managing system messages using the new `rsyslog` feature and the legacy `syslog` facility.

Chapter 4 describes the hardware components and begins with attaching new hardware, identifying hardware components, configuring device drivers, and configuring and formatting storage devices.

ZFS storage pools and file systems are the topic of Chapter 5. You'll find more information on ZFS in this chapter than in entire books that have been published on the topic. I describe key concepts in creating redundant and nonredundant storage pools. I go on to describe how to create ZFS file systems, manage properties to control file system characteristics, encrypt file systems, and back up and restore ZFS file systems. I use examples to describe problems and failures with storage components and finally ZFS monitoring, troubleshooting, and recovery techniques that I have used in production environments.

Chapter 6 discusses the virtualization environment, Oracle Solaris zones. You'll be guided through the creation of the different types of non-global and immutable zones. You'll learn how to boot and manage zones, set resources on a zone, delegate ZFS storage, and monitor, clone, back up, and recover zones.

In Chapter 7, I describe techniques used to harden an Oracle Solaris system beginning with securing and monitoring user accounts, controlling system and file access, delegating administrative tasks, and controlling network security.

Chapter 8 describes how to monitor and manage system processes on a multiprocessor system. You'll also learn how to manage and configure core files and crash dumps.

Chapter 9 is a discussion of the Oracle Solaris 11 network environment. Readers with experience on previous versions of Oracle Solaris will appreciate the detail and the step-by-step examples provided in the explanation of the complex topic of virtual networking. I describe how to configure reactive and fixed network configurations. I outline the new methods used to configure network parameters and services. I illustrate how to create a virtual network between non-global zones. And I describe network monitoring and troubleshooting techniques that I use in production environments.

Chapter 10 describes Network File Systems (NFS) and begins with a thorough explanation of NFS and where NFS is used in a production environment. Again, for those with experience on previous versions of Oracle Solaris, I detail how to configure NFS in Oracle Solaris 11. Using step-by-step examples, I explain the new process of sharing file systems on Oracle Solaris 11/11 and how it changed again in Oracle Solaris 11.1. You'll learn how to mount and manage NFS file systems manually and using AutoFS. I conclude the chapter with techniques I use for monitoring and troubleshooting NFS.

Enjoy the book, keep it close by, and may the material in this book help you better your skills, enhance your career, and achieve your goals.

Conventions Used in This Book

Commands: In the steps and examples, the commands you type are displayed in a special monospaced bold font.

```
# ls -l<cr>
```

<cr> indicates pressing the Enter/Return key.

The use of the hash symbol (#), dollar sign ($) or ok, when prefixed to the command, indicates the system prompt as shown in the examples:

```
ok boot<cr>
# ls -l<cr>
$ ls -l<cr>
```

The prompt is not to be typed in as part of the command syntax.

Arguments and Options—In command syntax, command options and arguments are enclosed in < >. (The italicized words within the < > symbols stand for what you will actually type. Don't type the "< >.")

```
# ls -l <directoryname><cr>
```

Code Continuation Character—When a line of code is too long to fit on one line, it is broken and continued to the next line. The continuation is preceded by a backslash (\), for example:

```
# useradd -u 3000 -g other -d /export/home/bcalkins -m -s /usr/bin/bash \
-c "Bill Calkins, ext. 2345" bcalkins<cr>
```

The backslash is not to be typed as part of the command syntax. Type the command as one continuous line. When the text gets to the end of the line, it will automatically wrap to the next line.

Commands are case sensitive in Oracle Solaris, so make sure you use upper and lowercase as specified. Make sure that you use spaces, hyphens (-), double quotes (") and single quotes (') exactly as indicated in the examples that are provided.

Audience

This book is designed for anyone who has a basic understanding of UNIX or Linux and wants to learn more about administering an Oracle Solaris 11 system. Whether or not you plan to become certified, this book is the starting point to becoming an Oracle Solaris system administrator. It contains the same training material that I use in my Oracle Solaris System Administration classes. This book covers the basic as well as the advanced system administration topics you need to know before you begin administering the Oracle Solaris 11 operating system. The goal was to present the material in an easy-to-follow format, with text that is easy to read and understand. The only prerequisite is that you have used UNIX or Linux, you have attended a fundamental UNIX or Linux class for users, or you have studied equivalent material so that you understand basic UNIX commands and syntax. Before you begin administering Oracle Solaris, it's important that you have actually used UNIX or Linux.

This book is also intended for experienced system administrators who want to become certified, update their current Oracle Solaris certification, or simply learn about the Oracle Solaris 11 operating environment.

Acknowledgments

I would like to thank Greg Doench and Prentice Hall for giving me the opportunity to write another book on Oracle Solaris. I appreciate that you recognize the value in having a single author write an entire technical book to keep the material consistent and smooth. I also thank them for letting me take my time to get it right. Oracle Solaris 11 has gone through many changes since the initial release. At the last minute, I wanted to make sure that this book was up to date with Oracle Solaris 11.1, which meant delaying the release of this book from its original publication date.

I also want to thank John Philcox once again for coming on board as a technical editor. John has worked on most of my books, and we are of the same mind when it comes to publishing an Oracle Solaris textbook. I look forward to working with you again, John.

I also want to thank Oracle for allowing me to be part of the certification team and actively involved in the creation of the Oracle Solaris 11 certification exams. Oracle is very particular with the contractors with whom they work, and I feel privileged that they consider me as part of their team of experts.

That's it! I don't want to bore you with a long list of names when it's John, myself, and the team of editors at Prentice Hall who put this book together. A small, tight group is an efficient and successful group, and I would like to extend my sincere thanks to all of you who edited the text, laid out the pages, and shipped the books. My efforts would be lost if it weren't for your hard work.

About the Author

About the Author

Bill Calkins is an Oracle Solaris 11 Certified Professional, works as a Solaris Subject Matter Expert for Oracle Corporation, and participates in the development of the Oracle Solaris 11 certification exams. Bill is the owner and president of UnixEd and Pyramid Consulting Inc., IT training and consulting firms located near Grand Rapids, Michigan, specializing in the implementation and administration of UNIX, Linux, and Microsoft Windows–based systems. He has more than twenty years of experience in UNIX system administration, consulting, and training at more than 300 companies. Bill is known worldwide for the Oracle Solaris textbooks he's authored, which have always been best sellers and used by universities and training organizations worldwide. It began with the *Oracle Solaris 2.6 Training Guide* in 1999 and subsequent books for Oracle Solaris 7, 8, 9, and 10.

Many of you have written with your success stories, suggestions, and comments. Your suggestions are always welcome and are what keep making these textbooks better with each new release. Drop me a note at wcalkins@unixed.com, introduce yourself, and tell me what you think.

About the Technical Editor

John Philcox currently works as a Technical Specialist at Atos IT Services UK. He is based in Cheltenham, Gloucestershire, in the United Kingdom and specializes in

UNIX systems and networks. He has more than 30 years' experience in IT, 25 of those with the SunOS and Oracle Solaris environments. He is a certified Oracle Solaris system and network administrator and has worked in a number of large, multi-vendor networks in both the public and private sectors of business.

John was the author of *Solaris System Management*, published by New Riders, and *Solaris 9 Network Administrator Certification (Exam Cram 2),* published by QUE Publishing. John has acted as technical editor or contributing author to most of Bill Calkins' books.

1

Installing Oracle Solaris 11

The installation process for Oracle Solaris 11 consists of three phases: system preparation and configuration, system installation, and post-installation tasks such as setting up printers, users, and networking. This chapter describes how to install the operating system (OS) on the SPARC and x86-based hardware platforms using the Live Media and text installers. I'll begin this chapter describing how to perform a new installation, and later I'll describe the process of upgrading from a previous version of Oracle Solaris.

The last section of this chapter will describe how to log in after the software is installed and verify the system and storage configuration.

Preparation for Installing the OS

You have several decisions to make prior to installing the OS.

- Which build of Oracle Solaris 11 do you want to install?
- On which platform do you want to install Oracle Solaris: SPARC or x86?
- Where do you want the OS to reside: on a local disk or on a removable device such as a DVD or USB drive?
- Will you be upgrading from a previous version of Oracle Solaris, or will this be a new installation?

You will also need to choose a method of installing the OS. The following methods are available for installing Oracle Solaris 11:

- The Oracle Solaris Live Media installer
- The Oracle Solaris text installer using local media
- The Oracle Solaris text installer using media provided from a server
- The Automated Installer (AI) for installing multiple clients using media provided from a server

For the last two options, you will need access to a package repository on the network to complete the installation. The package repository is described in Chapter 2, "Managing and Updating Software with IPS."

In this chapter, I'll be describing the graphical Live Media installer and the interactive text installer using local media.

Oracle Solaris Versions

As of this writing, Oracle Solaris 11 has already gone through several updates and one major version. Support Repository Updates (SRUs) are released approximately every month. Major versions are less frequent. The most recent version of Oracle Solaris 11 was released in October 2012 and is referred to as Oracle Solaris 11.1. SRUs are described in Chapter 2.

You'll obtain Oracle Solaris 11.1 by downloading an ISO image from the Oracle Technology Network, also called the Oracle Software Delivery Cloud. An Internet search using the keywords "Oracle Solaris 11 download" will display the URL of the current Oracle Solaris download site and will contain the most recent version of Oracle Solaris 11.

Selecting the Platform

Oracle Solaris 11 will run on the SPARC and x86-based hardware platforms. If you plan to use the SPARC platform, your system must meet Oracle's minimum requirements. These requirements are listed in detail in the Oracle Solaris 11 Hardware Compatibility List, which can be found online at `www.oracle.com`. This list contains information for both the SPARC and x86-based platforms.

Hardware requirements are typically described in terms of disk space, memory, and architecture. Oracle provides a summary of the Oracle Solaris 11 hardware requirements displayed in Table 1-1. These requirements vary slightly, depending on the type of installation that you choose. These requirements also change quite

Table 1-1 Oracle Solaris 11 Hardware Requirements

Hardware	Requirements
Disk space	Recommended minimum: 13GB
Memory	Recommended minimum: 1GB
Architectures	X86: 64 bit only SPARC: Oracle Solaris M-series and T-Series systems only

Table 1-2 Installation System Requirements

Installer	Minimum Memory	Minimum Disk Space	Recommended Disk Space
Live media	1GB	5GB	7GB
Text installer	1.5GB	2.9GB	4.9GB
Automated Installer	1GB	2.5GB	13GB

often as new features are added, so I recommend that you review the Oracle Solaris 11 Release Notes located online in the Oracle Solaris 11 Information Library to obtain the most up-to-date requirements for the version of the OS that you will be installing.

Depending on the method of installation, Table 1-2 provides some additional system installation requirements.

Updating the Firmware

The Oracle Solaris 11 release notes specify that some SPARC systems require updating their firmware to boot the OS. Without this update, an error message might be displayed when the system is booted. Other systems might just hang during the boot process with no indication of the problem. It is recommended that you update your system's firmware to at least version 6.7.11 before you install Oracle Solaris 11 onto a SPARC system. Refer to the Oracle Solaris 11 Release Notes for your server's firmware requirements.

Determine the system's current firmware revision by typing the `showsc` and `showhost` commands at the system controller (SC) console command line prompt as follows:

```
sc> showsc version -v<cr>
```

The following is displayed:

```
Advanced Lights Out Manager CMT v1.7.3
SC Firmware version: CMT 1.7.3
SC Bootmon version: CMT 1.7.3

VBSC 1.7.0
VBSC firmware built Dec 11 2008, 13:51:17

SC Bootmon Build Release: 01
SC bootmon checksum: F1D4A5D4
SC Bootmon built Apr 1 2009, 11:17:55

SC Build Release: 01
SC firmware checksum: 01584CEF

SC firmware built Apr 1 2009, 11:18:00
SC firmware flashupdate FRI JUN 05 13:40:40 2009

SC System Memory Size: 32 MB
SC NVRAM Version = 14
SC hardware type: 4

FPGA Version: 4.2.4.7
```

and

```
sc> showhost<cr>
```

The following is displayed:

```
Sun-Fire-T2000 System Firmware 6.7.3 2009/04/01 11:21

Host flash versions:
  OBP 4.30.0 2008/12/11 12:15
  Hypervisor 1.7.0 2008/12/11 13:43
  POST 4.30.0 2008/12/11 12:41
```

This system is at firmware version 6.7.3, so I need to update it. The Oracle Solaris 11 Release Notes specify that the T2000 system needs to be at version 6.7.11 at a minimum.

Log in to the Oracle support site, search for firmware updates for the T2000 platform, and download the 6.7.12 update. This update is downloaded as a zip file, and it's been uncompressed in the `/var/tmp` directory on an FTP server. The `install.info` file that accompanies the update describes how to update the firmware. To update the firmware, issue the `flashupdate` command at the ALOM prompt:

```
sc> flashupdate -s 192.168.1.27 -f /var/tmp/139434-09/Sun_System_Firmware-6_7_12-\
Sun_Fire_T2000.bin
Username: root
Password: *******
```

```
SC Alert: System poweron is disabled.
.............................................................................
.............................................................................
...........

Update complete. Reset device to use new software.

SC Alert: SC firmware was reloaded
```

After the update is finished, reset the server.

```
sc>resetsc<cr>
```

Verify the update.

```
sc> showsc version -v<cr>

Advanced Lights Out Manager CMT v1.7.11
SC Firmware version: CMT 1.7.11
SC Bootmon version: CMT 1.7.11

VBSC 1.7.3.d
VBSC firmware built Jul 6 2011, 19:27:17

SC Bootmon Build Release: 01
SC bootmon checksum: 4CB78FC8
SC Bootmon built Jul 6 2011, 19:37:05

SC Build Release: 01
SC firmware checksum: C41F3325

SC firmware built Jul 6 2011, 19:37:18
SC firmware flashupdate SUN JAN 20 17:29:54 2013

SC System Memory Size: 32 MB
SC NVRAM Version = 14
SC hardware type: 4

FPGA Version: 4.2.4.7
```

Verify the update as follows.

```
sc> showhost<cr>
Sun-Fire-T2000 System Firmware 6.7.12 2011/07/06 20:03

Host flash versions:
  OBP 4.30.4.d 2011/07/06 14:29
  Hypervisor 1.7.3.c 2010/07/09 15:14
  POST 4.30.4.b 2010/07/09 14:24
```

Updating Via the NET MGT Port

The flash update process uses the NET MGT port to connect to the remote FTP server. The IP address is set on the NET MGT port using the `setupsc` command. The `showsc` command will display the current network settings on this port. Verify the IP address (netsc_ipaddr), the subnet mask (netsc_ipnetmask), and the gateway (netsc_ipgateway).

The other server network ports are disabled at this time. When specifying the path to the update file, use the absolute path to the `.bin` file.

Notice that when I updated the firmware, the OpenBoot version was also updated from 4.30.0 to version 4.30.4.d.

You can also update the firmware using the `sysfwdownload` command from the Oracle Solaris command prompt. This command is distributed with the update and can be found in the directory in which the update was uncompressed. You'll find instructions in the `install.info` file that accompanies the update.

Methods of Installation

There are two interactive methods of installing the OS: the graphical Live Media installer and the text installer. In addition, there is one automated method: the AI. The choice of hardware platform will determine the method of installation, as is displayed in Table 1-3.

Note

The installers cannot upgrade your OS. However, after you have installed the Oracle Solaris 11 release, you can update all of the packages on your system that have available updates by using the Image Packaging System (IPS). Updating the OS using the IPS is described in Chapter 2.

On the SPARC platform, you can install the OS using the text installer or the AI, but you cannot use the Live Media installer.

On the 64-bit x86-based platform, you can install the OS using the Live Media graphical user interface (GUI) installer, the text installer, or the AI.

Note

Before you install the OS, verify that your system has the appropriate drivers required to manage each of its devices. If necessary, use the hardware compatibility list provided on Oracle's Web site, which I described earlier.

Table 1-3 Methods of Installing Oracle Solaris 11

	Interactive		Automated
	Live Media GUI	Text Installer	Automated Installer (AI)
SPARC		X	X
x86	X	X	X
Single system	X	X	X
Multiple systems			X

Both the Live Media and text installers allow you to select, create, or modify disk partitions during the installation.

Live Media GUI Installer

Note

The Live Media installer is for 64-bit x86 platforms only. This installer was originally called the "LiveCD" Installer, but as of this writing, Live Media is Oracle's official name for the graphical installer.

The Live Media installation is the easiest method of installing Oracle Solaris 11 on x86-based systems. It is named "Live Media" because Oracle Solaris 11 can be booted directly from the DVD into RAM with no impact on the existing OS. After it is loaded into RAM, you can explore Oracle Solaris 11 without installing it on a system. If you would like to install Oracle Solaris 11 on your system, start the installer from this booted image.

The system will boot directly from the DVD or USB drive containing Live Media. To run Oracle Solaris 11 directly from Live Media, follow these steps:

1. Download the Live Media ISO image and burn it to a DVD.
2. Insert the DVD and boot the system from the DVD.

The system will boot to a desktop version of Oracle Solaris 11. When booting Oracle Solaris directly from Live Media, understand that any changes made to the system are lost when the system is shut down. For long-term use, you should install Oracle Solaris 11 onto the local disk.

The Live Media installation is available on the Live Media ISO image and utilizes a GUI. After booting Live Media as described earlier, you can begin the installation by clicking on the *Install Oracle Solaris* icon located on the desktop.

When installing Oracle Solaris 11 from the Live Media installer, many of the installation options are chosen for you, so there is less customization and interaction than with the text installer. Specifically, the Live Media installation performs the following tasks automatically:

- Default network and security settings are used.
- Oracle Solaris is automatically networked by using Dynamic Host Configuration Protocol (DHCP), with Domain Name System (DNS) resolution.
- The DNS domain and server IP addresses are retrieved from the DHCP server.
- IPv6 autoconfiguration is enabled on active interfaces.
- The NFSv4 domain is dynamically derived.

A few additional items are well worth noting:

- The Live Media installer requires more memory to run than the text installer.
- The root user is always configured as a role.
- The Live Media installer installs a desktop-based set of packages that may not be adequate for a server.

Text Installer

The text installer is an interactive installer and can be used on SPARC and x86-based systems. The text installer requires a different ISO image than what was used with the Live Media installer. The text installer provides the most flexibility for customizing your system during the installation.

The text installer can perform an initial installation on the whole disk, an Oracle Solaris x86 partition, or a SPARC slice. If you are installing Oracle Solaris on an x86-based system that will have more than one OS installed on it, you can partition your disk with a fixed disk partitioning utility (`fdisk` partition) during the installation process. `fdisk` is a utility that is used to prepare and partition a new hard drive on the x86-based platform.

Whereas the Live Media installer will install a set of software that is appropriate for a desktop or a laptop, the text installer media contains a smaller set of software that is more appropriate for a server environment.

> **Note**
>
> The text installer does not install the GNOME desktop, but the GNOME package can be installed after the installation.

Whereas the Live Media installer is more automated, the text installer has the following advantages:

- The text installer can perform an initial installation on the whole disk, an Oracle Solaris x86 partition, or a SPARC slice.
- The text installer enables you to install the OS on either SPARC or x86-based systems.
- The text installer can be used on systems that do not have, or do not require, a graphics card.
- The text installer requires less memory than the GUI-based Live Media installer.
- The text installer enables manual configuration of the network and naming services and even allows you to skip the network setup options.

- In addition to modifying partitions, the text installer enables you to create and modify slices within the Oracle Solaris partition and save the slice information to a volume table of contents (VTOC).

The package set installed by the text installer is the `solaris-large-server` package set, which is described in Chapter 2.

Automated Installer

The AI provides a hands-free installation on both SPARC and x86-based systems. To use AI you must first configure an AI server on the network. When the client boots, the system gets installation specifications from the server, retrieves software packages from an Oracle Solaris package repository, and installs the software packages on the client system. Because AI utilizes the network for the installation, each system must be connected to the network.

AI involves advanced knowledge of networking and system configuration and is not covered in this book.

Obtaining the Installation Media

Obtain the Oracle Solaris 11 installation media by downloading an ISO image from the Oracle Technology Network, also called the Oracle Software Delivery Cloud. Currently, the Delivery Cloud can be accessed at `https://edelivery.oracle.com`.

Sign in to the Oracle Software Delivery Cloud, agree to the terms and conditions, and click on the *Continue* button.

The Media Pack Search window will open. Select the Product Pack named *Oracle Solaris* and select the platform: SPARC or x86-64 as shown in Figure 1-1.

For the examples in this book, I'll select *Oracle Solaris on x86-64 (64-bit)*.

Make your selection and click *Go*. The results will be displayed as shown in Figure 1-2.

Select the *Oracle Solaris 11.1 Media Pack* and click on the *Continue* button.

The Oracle Solaris 11.1 Media Pack results will be displayed as shown in Figure 1-3.

Download the media for the method of installation that you plan to use and the type of media from which you will be booting.

Select the first option, *Oracle Solaris 11.1 Live Media (x86)*, to download an ISO to be burned to a DVD. This media will be used in the examples described in the section titled "Using the Live Media Installer."

Select the third option, *Oracle Solaris 11.1 Interactive Text Install (x86)*, to download an ISO for use in the section titled "Using the Interactive Text Installer: x86."

Select the ninth option, *Oracle Solaris 11.1 Live Media USB (x86)*, if you want to store the Live Media image on a USB flash drive. You'll download the image and use the `usbcopy` utility to copy the image to a USB flash drive.

Media Pack Search

Instructions

1. Review the License List to determine which Product Pack or Packs you need to download.
2. Select the Product Pack and Platform and click "Go".
3. If there is only one result, you will see the download page. If there are multiple results, select one and click "Continue".

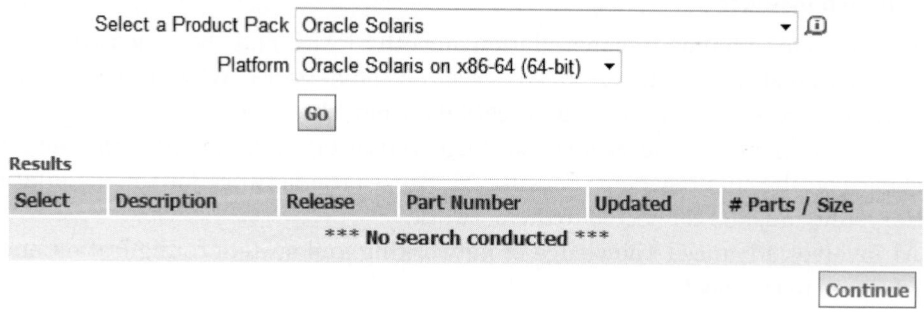

Figure 1-1 Oracle Solaris Delivery Cloud

Results

Select	Description	Release	Part Number	Updated	# Parts / Size
◉	Oracle Solaris 11.1 Media Pack	11.1.0.0.0	B70675-01	OCT-26-2012	11 / 14G
○	Oracle Solaris Cluster 4.0 Media Pack	4.0.0.0.0	B65499-02	JAN-18-2012	1 / 63M
○	Oracle Solaris Cluster 3.3 Media Pack	3.3.1.0.0	B60327-02	JAN-03-2012	3 / 293M
○	Solaris Cluster Advanced Edition for Oracle Real Application Cluster Media Pack	n/a	B62150-01	DEC-29-2011	2 / 1.5G
○	Oracle Solaris 10 8/11 Operating System Multi-Language Media Pack	n/a	B64517-01	SEP-15-2011	2 / 4.3G
Total: 5					

Continue

Figure 1-2 Oracle Media Packs

Oracle Solaris 11.1 Media Pack v1

Readme | View Digest

Select	Name	Part Number	Size (Bytes)
Download	Oracle Solaris 11.1 Live Media (x86)	V35095-01	965M
Download	Oracle Solaris 11.1 Automated Install (x86)	V35096-01	309M
Download	Oracle Solaris 11.1 Interactive Text Install (x86)	V35097-01	585M
Download	Oracle Solaris 11.1 Automated Install (SPARC)	V35098-01	379M
Download	Oracle Solaris 11.1 Interactive Text Install (SPARC)	V35099-01	678M
Download	Oracle Solaris 11.1 IPS Repository Part 1 of 2 and README (SPARC, x86)	V35100-01	3.7G
Download	Oracle Solaris 11.1 IPS Repository Part 2 of 2 (SPARC, x86)	V35101-01	3.3G
Download	Oracle Solaris 11.1 IPS Pre-Upgrade Repository and README (SPARC, x86)	V35102-01	2.6G
Download	Oracle Solaris 11.1 Live Media USB (x86)	V35103-01	952M
Download	Oracle Solaris 11.1 Automated Install USB (x86)	V35104-01	293M
Download	Oracle Solaris 11.1 Interactive Text Install USB (x86)	V35105-01	569M
Total: 11			

Figure 1-3 Oracle Solaris 11 Media Pack

Using the Live Media Installer

Begin the Live Media installation by booting to the Live Media DVD or ISO. After booting to the DVD, the Live Media GNU GRand Unified Bootloader (GRUB) menu will appear briefly as shown in Figure 1-4.

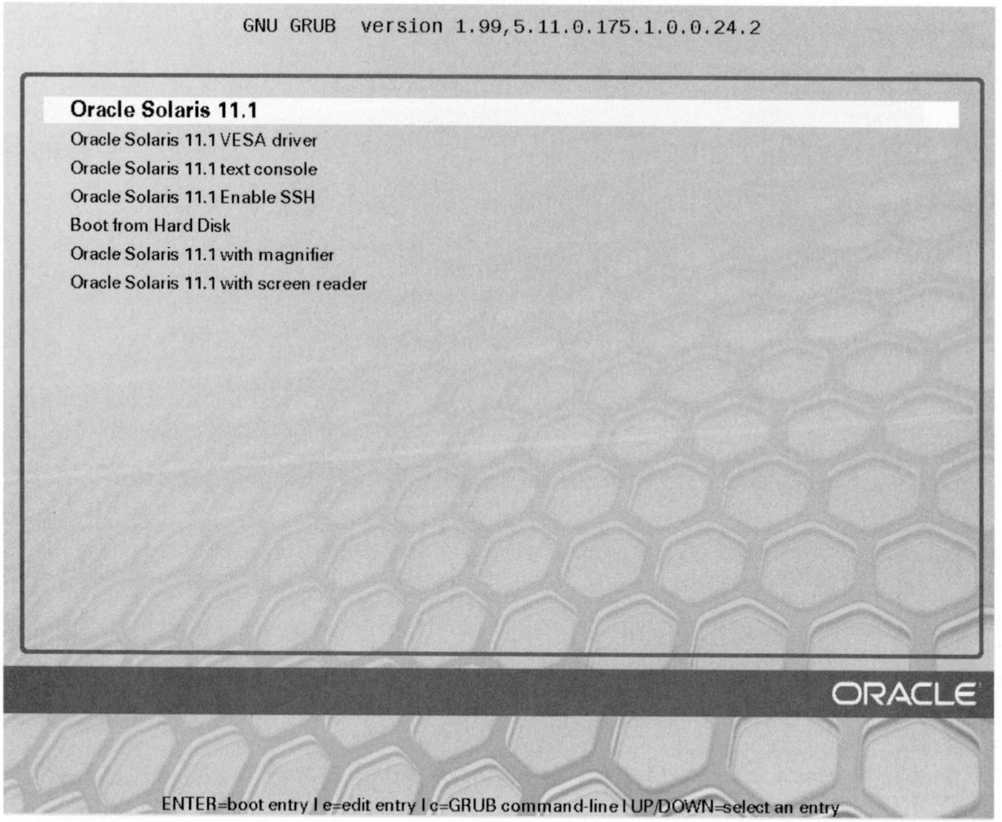

Figure 1-4 Live Media GRUB menu

Booting to an ISO Image

An ISO image is a disc image of an optical disc. It is used mainly when booting a virtual machine or when creating a USB image. For a virtual machine, the host DVD can be directed to an ISO image file to emulate a DVD. A USB image can only be used on an x86-based system. A SPARC system cannot boot from an ISO image nor an external USB drive.

The default boot environment (first option listed) will be used if you do not interrupt the GRUB menu and choose an alternate boot environment. For this example, I'll use the default, so there is no need to interrupt the boot process.

Note

The Live Media GRUB menu provides alternate boot environments that are separate bootable instances of Oracle Solaris. Boot environments are described in Chapter 2. By default, GRUB will choose the first instance after 10 seconds and the boot process will continue. By using the arrow key on your keyboard, you can stop the boot process and select an alternate instance from the GRUB menu. These alternate instances provide alternative methods of installing the OS. The GRUB menu is described in Chapter 3, "Boot and Shutdown Procedures for SPARC and x86-Based Systems."

The first screen, shown in Figure 1-5, prompts you to select the keyboard layout that you will be using. Note that the information at the top of the screen describes the version of Oracle Solaris being installed. Verify that this is the version that you intended to install.

Select the keyboard layout and press *Enter.* I will be using "US-English," so I pressed *Enter* to choose the default value.

The next screen, shown in Figure 1-6, prompts you to enter the language that you wish to use.

```
SunOS Release 5.11 Version 11.1 64-bit
Copyright (c) 1983, 2012, Oracle and/or its affiliates. All rights reserved.
Remounting root read/write
Probing for device nodes ...
Preparing image for use
Done mounting image
USB keyboard
 1. Arabic                              15. Korean
 2. Belgian                             16. Latin-American
 3. Brazilian                           17. Norwegian
 4. Canadian-Bilingual                  18. Portuguese
 5. Canadian-French                     19. Russian
 6. Danish                              20. Spanish
 7. Dutch                               21. Swedish
 8. Dvorak                              22. Swiss-French
 9. Finnish                             23. Swiss-German
10. French                              24. Traditional-Chinese
11. German                              25. TurkishQ
12. Italian                             26. UK-English
13. Japanese-type6                      27. US-English
14. Japanese
To select the keyboard layout, enter a number [default 27]:
```

Figure 1-5 Keyboard selection

```
 1. Chinese - Simplified
 2. Chinese - Traditional
 3. English
 4. French
 5. German
 6. Italian
 7. Japanese
 8. Korean
 9. Portuguese - Brazil
10. Spanish
To select the language you wish to use, enter a number [default is 3]:
```

Figure 1-6 Select the language

Make your selection and press *Enter*, or simply press *Enter* to choose "English" (the default).

The Live Media installer will boot the system, configure devices, and launch the desktop GUI as shown in Figure 1-7.

Note

Even though the command line login prompt may appear, wait a few minutes for the desktop GUI to start up.

The system is booted from the DVD and you can start using Oracle Solaris; however, Oracle Solaris is running in RAM and is not installed on the local disk. While booted from the Live Media, any changes made will be lost when the system is rebooted.

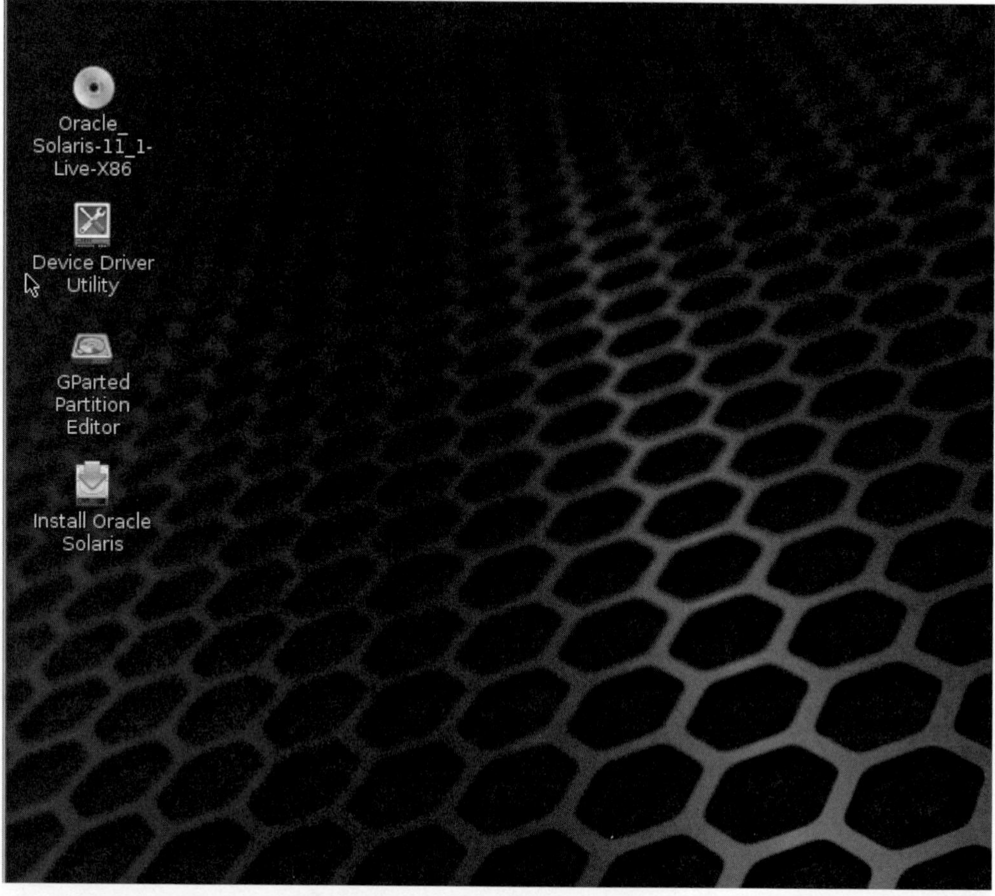

Figure 1-7 Desktop GUI: icons

Table 1-4 Desktop Icons

ICON	Description
Oracle_Solaris-11_1-Live_x86	Click on this icon to view the contents of the Live Media DVD.
Device Driver Utility	Click on this to launch the Device Driver Utility and begin searching for missing device drivers. If the utility locates any missing drivers, a notification will be displayed on the desktop.
GParted Partition Editor	This icon launches GNOME Partition Editor, which is used for creating, reorganizing, and deleting disk partitions. Use this editor to customize the root disk layout before installing the OS.
Install Oracle Solaris	Clicking this icon initiates the Oracle Solaris installation utility.

There are four icons on the desktop that are described in Table 1-4.

Click on the *Device Driver Utility* to view the status of the devices on your system as shown in Figure 1-8. If you are prompted for a password, enter **`solaris`**. It will take a few minutes for the system to gather the device information before it will display the Device Driver Utility.

The Device Driver Utility will report any device issues. It is important to resolve any device issues before continuing with the installation. The system reports zero driver problems in Figure 1-8, so it is okay to click on the *Close* button to close the Device Driver Utility.

The Device Driver Utility is only available on the x86 platform and will indicate which Oracle Solaris driver supports the various x86 components. If the utility detects a device that does not have a driver attached, that device is selected on the device list. You can choose to display more information about the device and install the missing driver. You can specify an Oracle Solaris IPS package or a file/URL path to the driver.

Begin the installation by clicking on the *Install Oracle Solaris* icon. The Welcome screen will open as shown in Figure 1-9.

The list on the left side of the window lists the steps that you will follow to configure the system before installing the OS. You will need to configure the root disk, set the time zone, create a user login account, and, finally, begin the installation.

Note

The root disk is also called the boot disk. This is the disk where the OS will be installed.

To advance to the first step, click on the *Next* button and the Disk Discovery window will appear as shown in Figure 1-10.

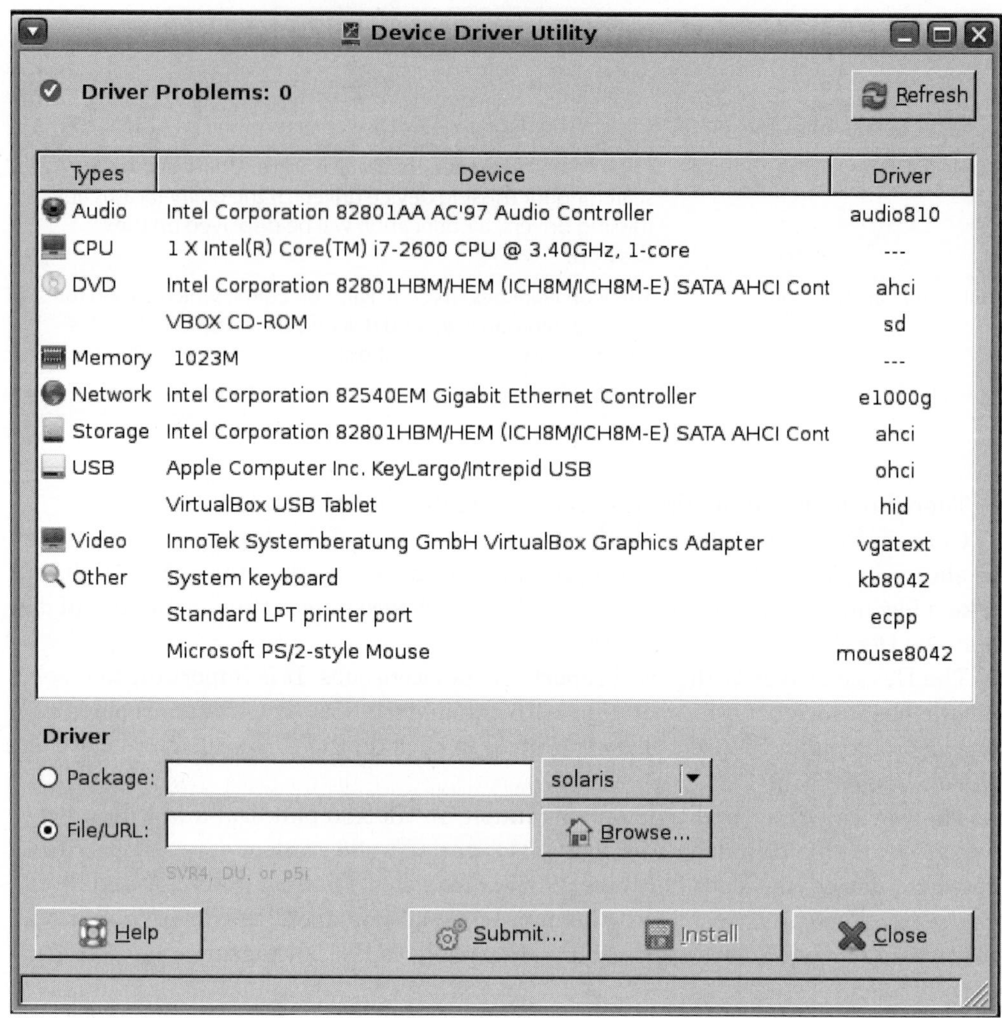

Figure 1-8 Desktop GUI: Device Driver Utility

Select whether you will be installing the OS onto a local disk (internal or external disk) or an Internet Small Computer System Interface (iSCSI) disk accessible over the network using the iSCSI protocol. I will be installing onto an internal disk, so I selected "Local Disks."

Click on the *Next* button and the Disk Selection window will appear as shown in Figure 1-11.

I will be using the whole disk for the Oracle Solaris OS, so I make my selection and click *Next*.

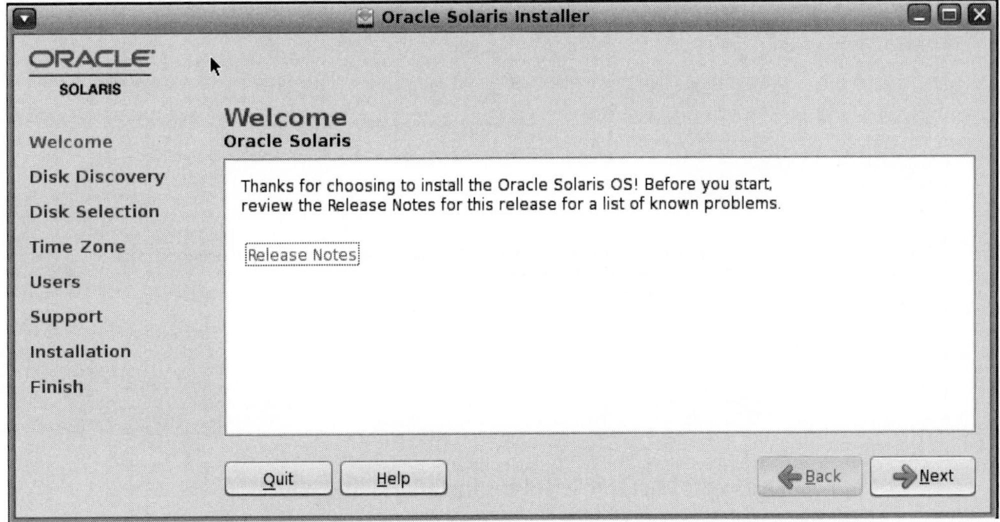

Figure 1-9 Oracle Solaris Live Media Installer: Welcome

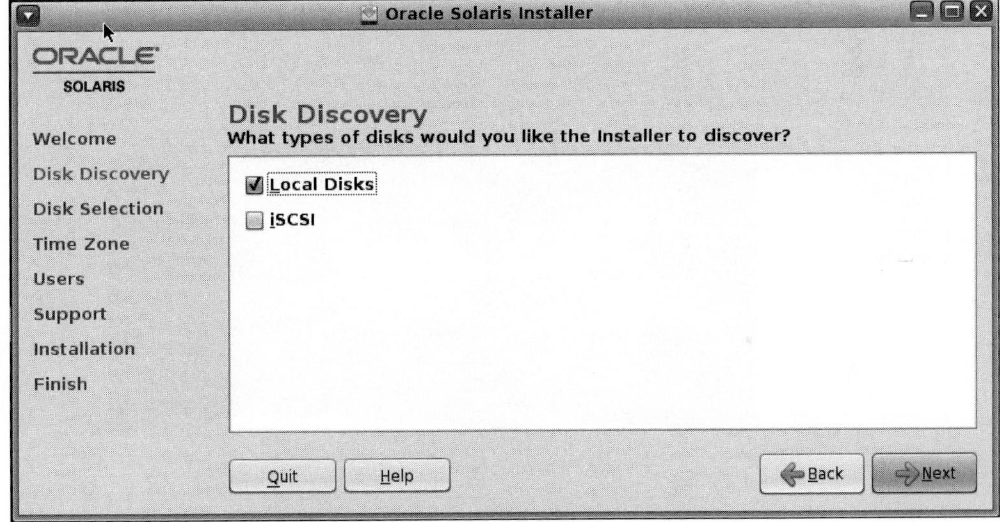

Figure 1-10 Oracle Solaris Installer: Disk Discovery

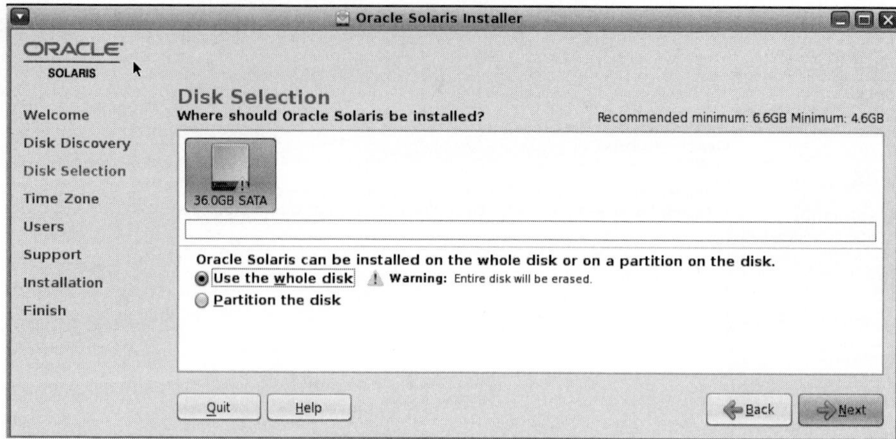

Figure 1-11 Oracle Solaris Installer: Disk Selection

Warning

This procedure will erase everything on the disk.

The Time Zone screen appears as shown in Figure 1-12.

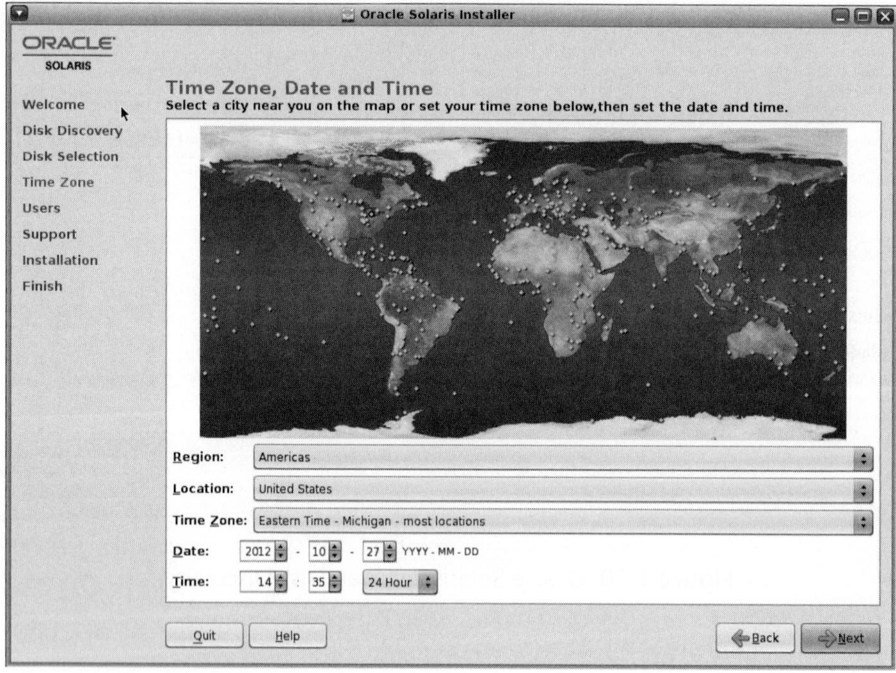

Figure 1-12 Oracle Solaris Installer: Time Zone, Date and Time

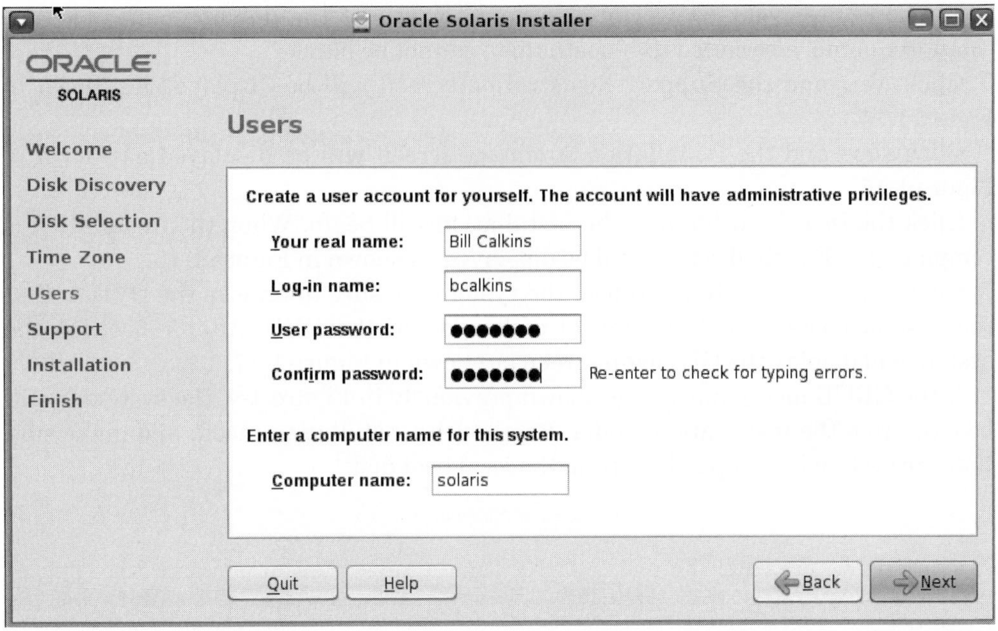

Figure 1-13 Oracle Solaris Installer: Create user login account

Set the correct region, location, time zone, date, and time, then click *Next*. The Users screen will appear as shown in Figure 1-13.

On this screen, you will create a user account and enter a computer name for this system. When installing the OS using the Live Media installer, you must create a user account. This will be your primary login account. After the installation, you will not be allowed to log in directly as root.

Note

After the installation using Live Media is complete and the system has been rebooted, the default behavior is to not allow root to log in from the login screen. You will first log in using the user account that was created during installation (see Figure 1-13) and then switch to the root account when root privileges are required. The first time that you assume the root role, you will authenticate using the password that you specified for the user account. At that point, you will receive a message that the password has expired, and you will be required to set a new password for the root account. This behavior can be changed by switching the root account from a role account to a normal account.

When creating a user account, follow these rules:

- The username cannot be root.
- The username must start with a letter.
- The username may contain alphabetical characters, numbers, underscore (_), period (.), or hyphen (-).

You can enter your own computer name or accept the default, `solaris`. The computer name, also called the "hostname," cannot be blank.

Click *Next* and the Support Registration screen will be displayed as shown in Figure 1-14.

Click *Next* and the installation summary screen will be displayed as shown in Figure 1-15.

Click the *Install* button and the installation will begin. When the installation is complete, the Finished screen will be displayed as shown in Figure 1-16.

Click the *Reboot* button to reboot the system. Be sure to remove the DVD so that the system boots from the internal disk and not the DVD. After rebooting, the system will display the GUI login screen as shown in Figure 1-17.

If the GRUB menu appears as shown previously in Figure 1-4, the system is still booting from the installation media. Remove the installation media and make sure that the system is set up to boot from the local boot disk.

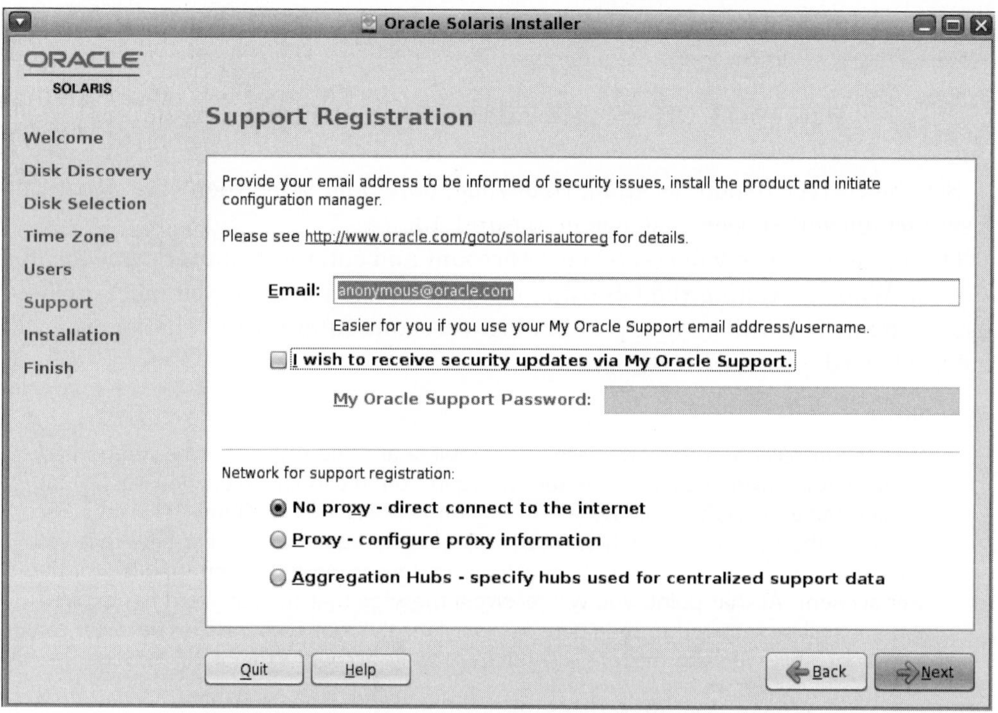

Figure 1-14 Oracle Solaris Installer: Support Registration

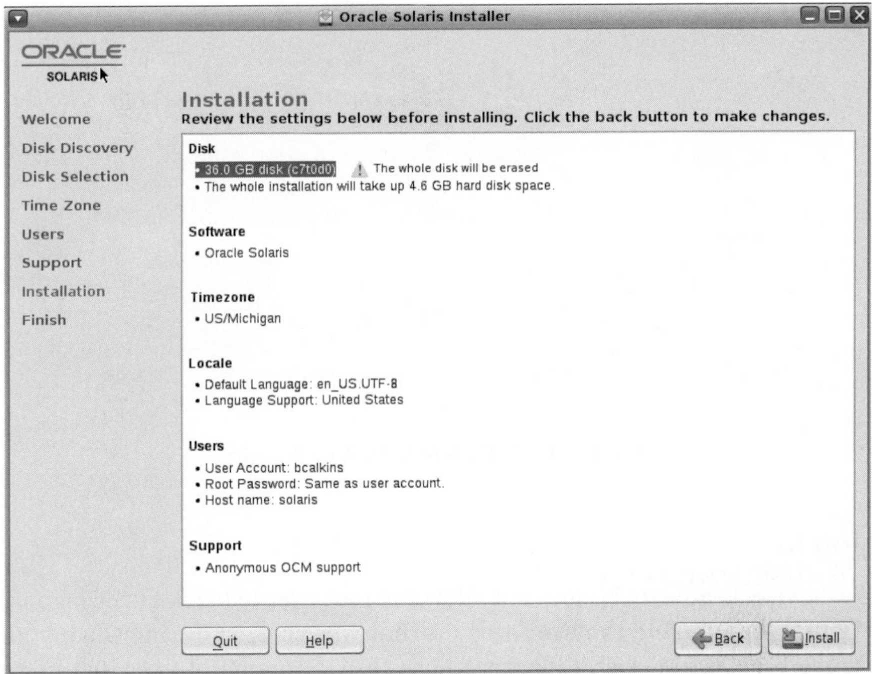

Figure 1-15 Oracle Solaris Installer: Installation summary

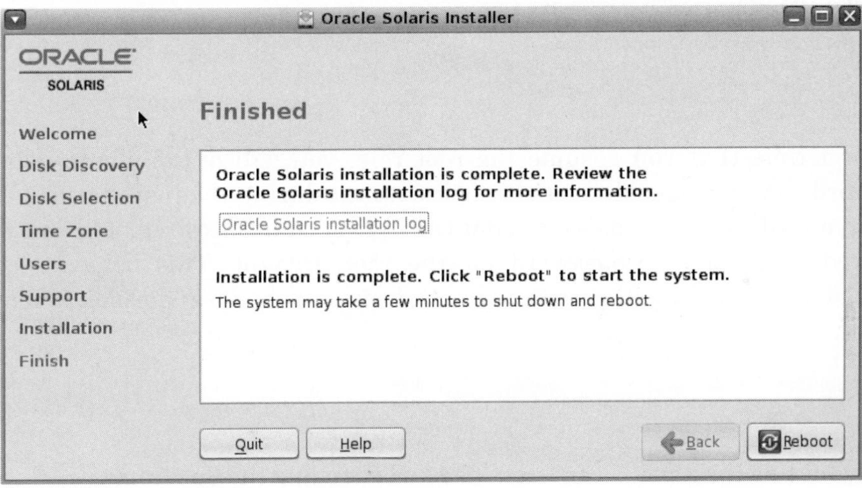

Figure 1-16 Oracle Solaris Installer: Finished

Figure 1-17 Oracle Solaris GUI login

Logging In

By default, Oracle Solaris 11 does not allow the root user to log in at the login screen. You will first log in using the user account that was created during the installation (see Figure 1-13). After you've logged in, use the `su` command to switch to the root account when root privileges are required.

```
# su root<cr>
Password:<enter the user password>
Su: Password for user 'root' has expired
New Password:<enter new password>
Re-enter new Password:<enter new password>
su: password successfully changed for root
```

The first time that you assume the root role, you will authenticate using the password that you specified for the user account during the installation. At that point, you will receive a message that the password has expired, and you will be required to set a new password for the root account. This behavior can be changed by switching the root account from a role to a normal account as follows:

```
# rolemod -K type=normal root<cr>
```

or by editing the `/etc/user_attr` file and changing the line from

```
root::::type=role
```

to

```
root::::type=normal
```

Using the Interactive Text Installer: x86

Begin running the text installer by booting to the DVD containing the text installer media. After booting to the text installation media, the text installer will prompt you to select the keyboard layout that you will be using, as shown in Figure 1-18. Notice that the information at the top of the screen describes the version of Oracle Solaris being installed. Verify that this is the version that you intended to install.

In the following example, I'll use the text installer to install an x86-based system. In the next section, I will perform the installation on the SPARC platform. Installing using the text-based installer is very similar on both the x86 and SPARC platforms.

```
SunOS Release 5.11 Version 11.1 64-bit
Copyright (c) 1983, 2012, Oracle and/or its affiliates. All rights reserved.
Remounting root read/write
Probing for device nodes ...
Preparing image for use
Done mounting image
USB keyboard
 1. Arabic                          15. Korean
 2. Belgian                         16. Latin-American
 3. Brazilian                       17. Norwegian
 4. Canadian-Bilingual              18. Portuguese
 5. Canadian-French                 19. Russian
 6. Danish                          20. Spanish
 7. Dutch                           21. Swedish
 8. Dvorak                          22. Swiss-French
 9. Finnish                         23. Swiss-German
10. French                          24. Traditional-Chinese
11. German                          25. TurkishQ
12. Italian                         26. UK-English
13. Japanese-type6                  27. US-English
14. Japanese
To select the keyboard layout, enter a number [default 27]:
```

Figure 1-18 Text installer, x86: Keyboard selection

Select the keyboard layout and press *Enter.* I will be using "US-English" in this example, so I pressed *Enter* to choose the default value.

The next screen prompts you to enter the language that you wish to use, as shown in Figure 1-19.

Make your language selection and press *Enter*, or simply press *Enter* to choose "English" (the default).

The text installer will boot the system and display the Installation Menu as shown in Figure 1-20.

Press *Enter* to select the default, *Item 1: Install Oracle Solaris.*

The Welcome screen will appear as shown in Figure 1-21.

Press *F2* and the Discovery Selection screen will be displayed as shown in Figure 1-22.

Select whether you will be installing the OS onto a local disk (internal or external disk) or an iSCSI disk accessible over the network using the iSCSI protocol. I will be installing onto an internal disk, so I selected Local Disks and pressed *F2* to continue. The Disks screen will be displayed as shown in Figure 1-23.

If multiple disks are listed, select the disk that you will be using as the root disk. In the example, I selected c7t0d0.

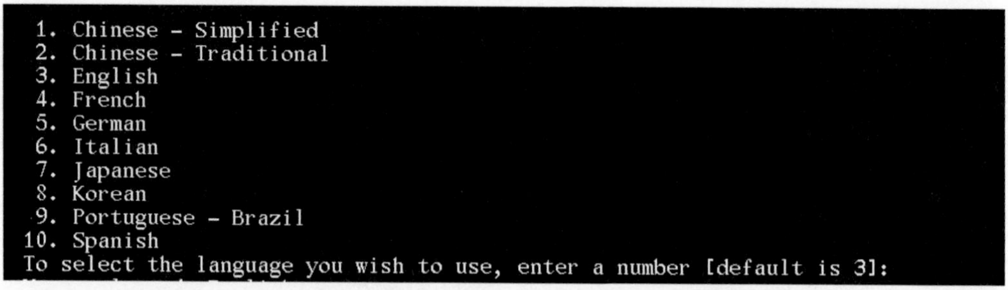

```
 1. Chinese - Simplified
 2. Chinese - Traditional
 3. English
 4. French
 5. German
 6. Italian
 7. Japanese
 8. Korean
 9. Portuguese - Brazil
10. Spanish
To select the language you wish to use, enter a number [default is 3]:
```

Figure 1-19 Text installer, x86: Select the language

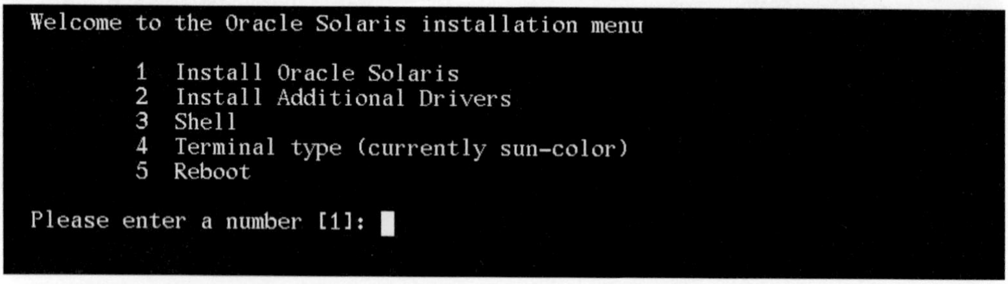

```
Welcome to the Oracle Solaris installation menu

        1  Install Oracle Solaris
        2  Install Additional Drivers
        3  Shell
        4  Terminal type (currently sun-color)
        5  Reboot

Please enter a number [1]: █
```

Figure 1-20 Text installer, x86: Installation menu

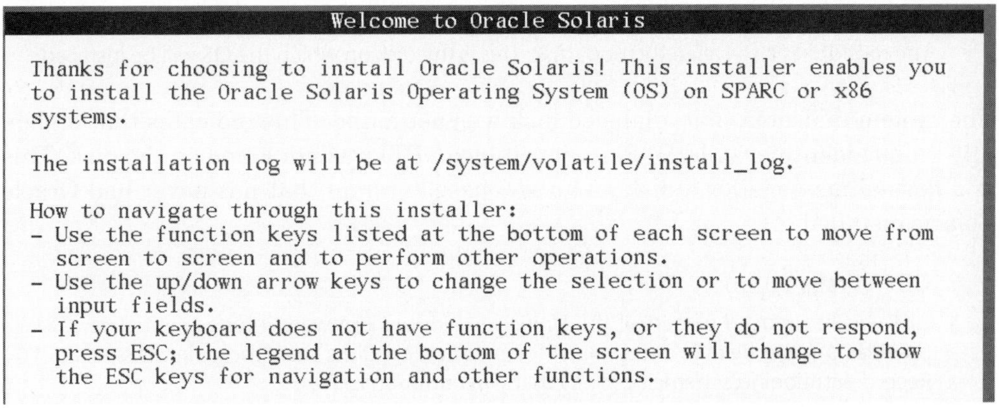

```
                        Welcome to Oracle Solaris

Thanks for choosing to install Oracle Solaris! This installer enables you
to install the Oracle Solaris Operating System (OS) on SPARC or x86
systems.

The installation log will be at /system/volatile/install_log.

How to navigate through this installer:
- Use the function keys listed at the bottom of each screen to move from
  screen to screen and to perform other operations.
- Use the up/down arrow keys to change the selection or to move between
  input fields.
- If your keyboard does not have function keys, or they do not respond,
  press ESC; the legend at the bottom of the screen will change to show
  the ESC keys for navigation and other functions.
```

Figure 1-21 Text installer, x86: Welcome to Oracle Solaris

```
                          Discovery Selection

 Select discovery method for disks

  Local Disks               Discover local disks

  iSCSI                     Discover iSCSI LUNs
```

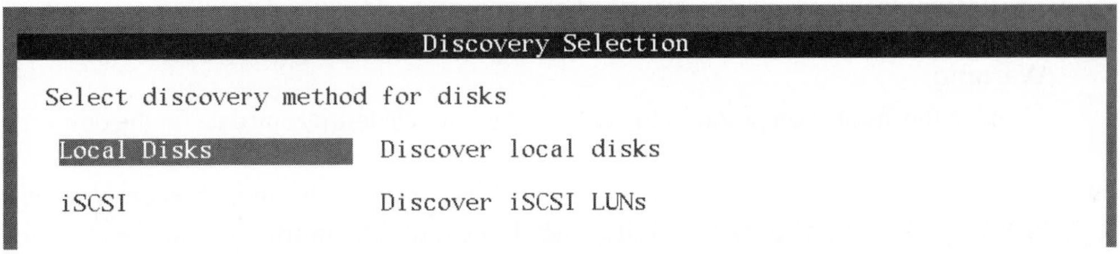

Figure 1-22 Text installer, x86: Discovery Selection

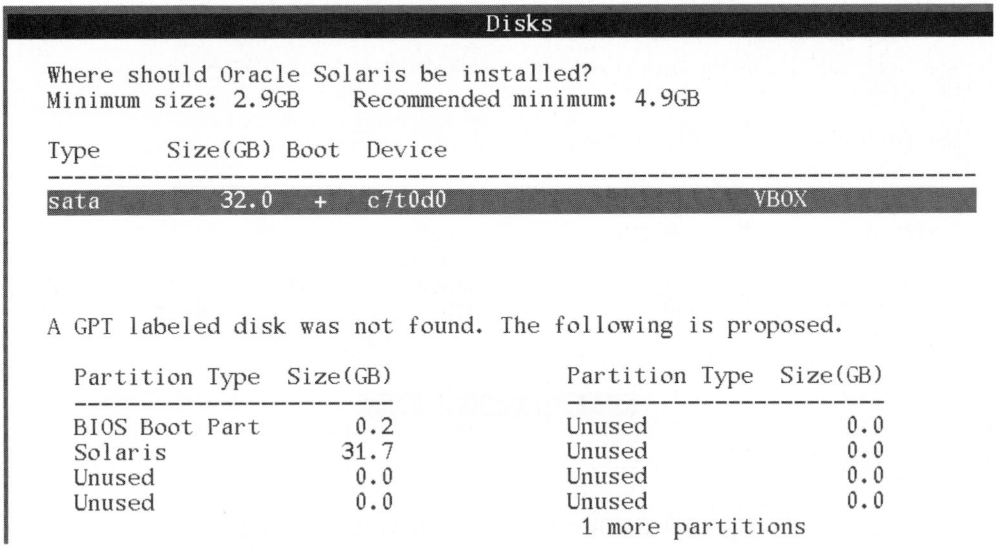

```
                                Disks

 Where should Oracle Solaris be installed?
 Minimum size: 2.9GB    Recommended minimum: 4.9GB

 Type     Size(GB) Boot  Device
 ------------------------------------------------------------------------
 sata         32.0    +   c7t0d0                            VBOX



 A GPT labeled disk was not found. The following is proposed.

   Partition Type  Size(GB)            Partition Type  Size(GB)
   ------------------------            ------------------------
   BIOS Boot Part       0.2            Unused               0.0
   Solaris             31.7            Unused               0.0
   Unused               0.0            Unused               0.0
   Unused               0.0            Unused               0.0
                                        1 more partitions
```

Figure 1-23 Text installer, x86: Disks

Note

The root disk is also called the boot disk. This is the disk on which the OS will be installed.

The system indicates that a labeled disk was not found. This indicates that a globally unique identifier (GUID) Partition Table (GPT) was not found on the disk. This is a normal message for a disk on an x86-based system that has never had Oracle Solaris installed.

GPT Versus `fdisk`

GPT was introduced as part of the Unified Extensible Firmware Interface initiative. GPT provides a more flexible mechanism for partitioning disks than the older Master Boot Record partitioning scheme (`fdisk`) that was common to PCs.

You must create a GPT partition on this disk before you install the OS on an x86-based system. The installation program will create the GPT partition for you during the installation, but you need to initiate the process as described next.

Warning

Allowing the installation program to partition the disk will destroy any data on the disk.

After making your disk selection, press the *F2* button. On the next screen, you will specify how you want the disk partitioned. I recommend using the entire disk for Oracle Solaris as shown in Figure 1-24.

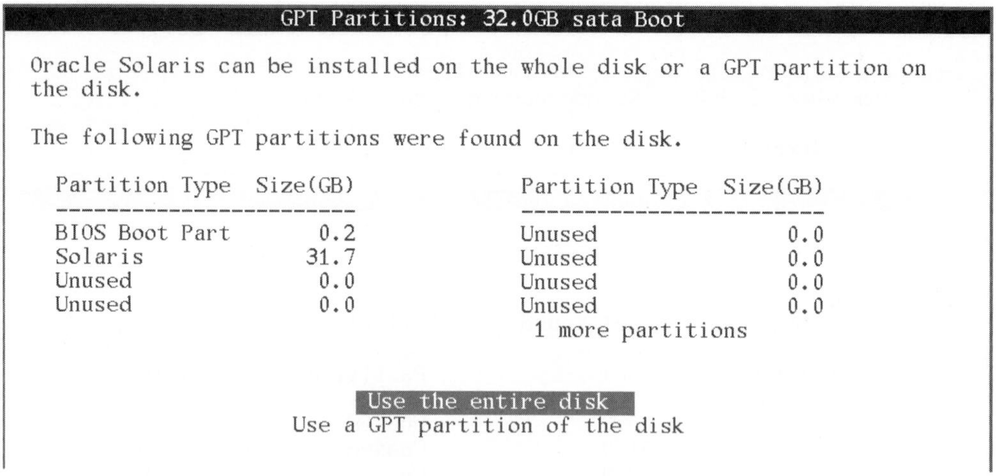

```
                    GPT Partitions: 32.0GB sata Boot

 Oracle Solaris can be installed on the whole disk or a GPT partition on
 the disk.

 The following GPT partitions were found on the disk.

   Partition Type  Size(GB)              Partition Type  Size(GB)
   ------------------------              ------------------------
   BIOS Boot Part       0.2              Unused               0.0
   Solaris             31.7              Unused               0.0
   Unused               0.0              Unused               0.0
   Unused               0.0              Unused               0.0
                                          1 more partitions

                            Use the entire disk
                          Use a GPT partition of the disk
```

Figure 1-24 Text installer, x86: GPT Partitions

Note

Oracle Solaris slices are also called partitions. Do not confuse Oracle Solaris slices with GPT partitions. Disk partitions and slices are described in Chapter 4, "Administering Storage Devices."

After making your disk selection press *F2*, and the GPT Partitions window will be displayed as shown in Figure 1-24.

In the GPT Partitions window, specify the partition information. I selected to "Use the entire Disk" and pressed *F2* to continue. The Network window is displayed as shown in Figure 1-25.

On the Network screen, you will provide the computer name. The default computer name is **`solaris`**. When entering a computer name, follow these rules:

- The computer name must be at least two characters.
- The computer name can contain letters, numbers, and minus signs (–).

I selected the default computer name and used the *arrow* key to move down to the network configuration section. You have the following options when configuring the network:

- Automatically: Use DHCP to configure the network connection. The IP address, netmask, and router will automatically be assigned. In addition, the DNS servers and Name Service will also be automatically assigned.
- Manually: Configure the network connection manually. Additional screens will be displayed where you will be prompted to enter the IP address, DNS server

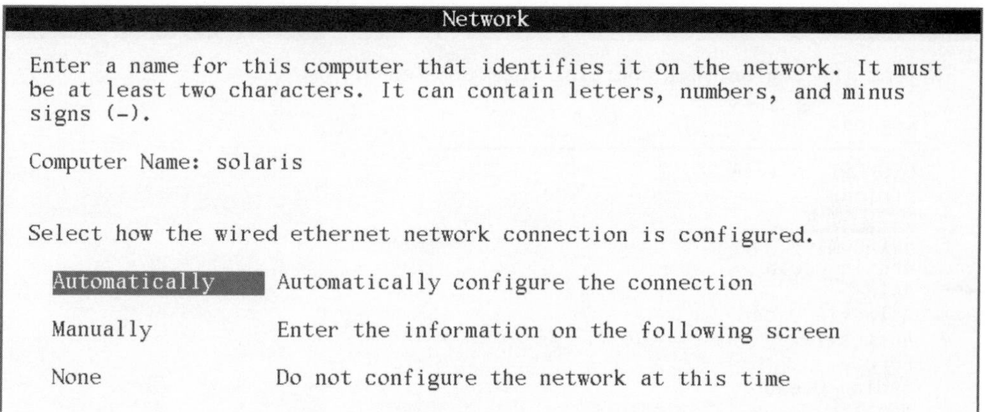

Figure 1-25 Text installer, x86: Network

IP addresses, DNS search list, and Name Service for the selected network connection.

- None: Do not configure the network connection during the installation.

To select one of these network options, use the *arrow* key to navigate down to "Automatically," "Manually," or "None." When you have the desired option highlighted, press *F2* to continue. For this example, I opted to have the network automatically configured. After pressing *F2*, you will be prompted to enter your time zone information beginning with the Time Zone: Regions screen shown in Figure 1-26.

Use the *arrow* key to scroll through the list and select your time zone region. Press *F2* and the Time Zone: Locations screen will be displayed as shown in Figure 1-27.

Select your time zone location and press *F2*. The Time Zone screen will be displayed as shown in Figure 1-28.

Select your time zone and press *F2* to continue. The Date and Time screen will be displayed as shown in Figure 1-29.

Enter the correct date and time and press *F2*. The Users screen will be displayed as shown in Figure 1-30.

Enter a password for the root account. The root password is required, and creating a user account is optional.

Note

Figure 1-30 presents a difference between the Live Media and text installers. The Live Media installer requires the creation of a user account, and the root account gets created as a role. By default, root is not allowed to log in. The text installer does not require a user account and creates the root account as a normal login account.

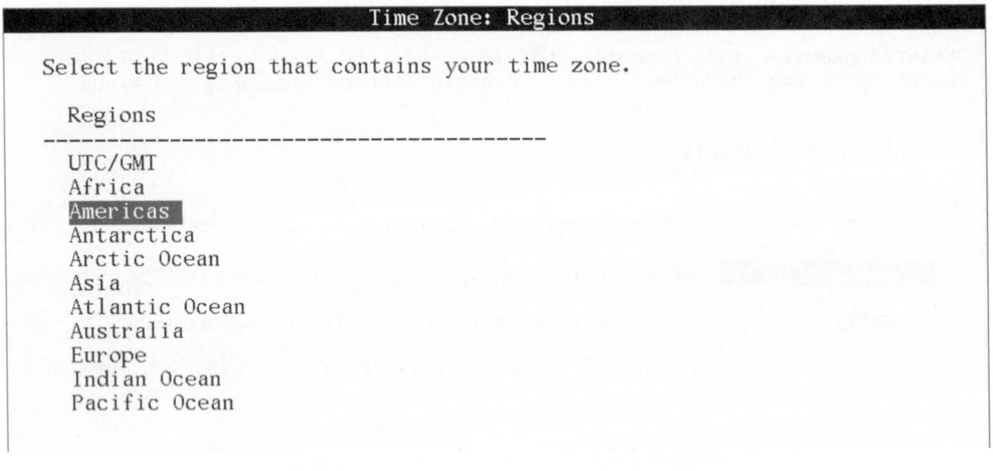

```
                         Time Zone: Regions

 Select the region that contains your time zone.

   Regions
 -----------------------------------------
   UTC/GMT
   Africa
   Americas
   Antarctica
   Arctic Ocean
   Asia
   Atlantic Ocean
   Australia
   Europe
   Indian Ocean
   Pacific Ocean
```

Figure 1-26 Text installer, x86: Time Zone, Regions

```
                    Time Zone: Locations

  Select the location that contains your time zone.

    Locations
  ---------------------------------------------
  ^ Jamaica
  | Martinique
  | Mexico
  | Montserrat
  | Nicaragua
  | Panama
  | Paraguay
  | Peru
  | Puerto Rico
  | Sint Maarten
  | St Barthelemy
  | St Kitts & Nevis
  | St Lucia
  | St Martin (French part)
  | St Pierre & Miquelon
  | St Vincent
  | Suriname
  | Trinidad & Tobago
  | Turks & Caicos Is
  | United States
  | Uruguay
  | Venezuela
```

Figure 1-27 Text installer, x86: Time Zone, Locations

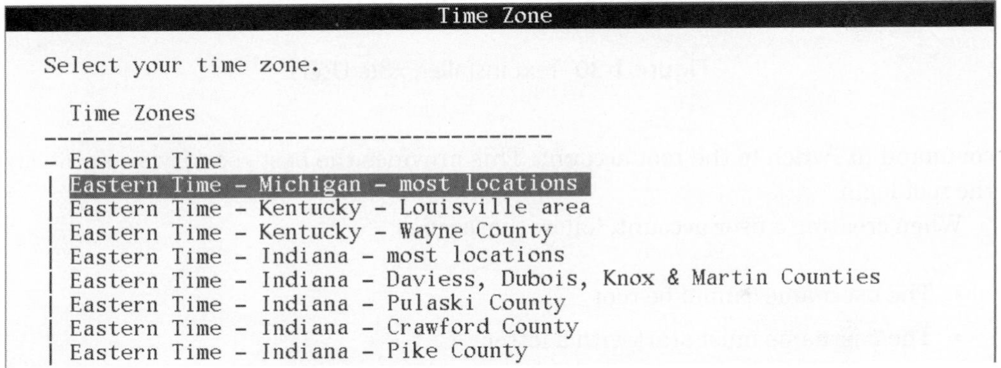

Figure 1-28 Text installer, x86: Time Zone

For security purposes, it's recommended that you create a user account by specifying a username and password. The root account is then created as a role. The user that is created is then given the root role. After the installation, and after the system reboots, you will not be able to log in as root; rather, you will log in using the username that you have provided. Once logged in, you can use the `su` or the `sudo`

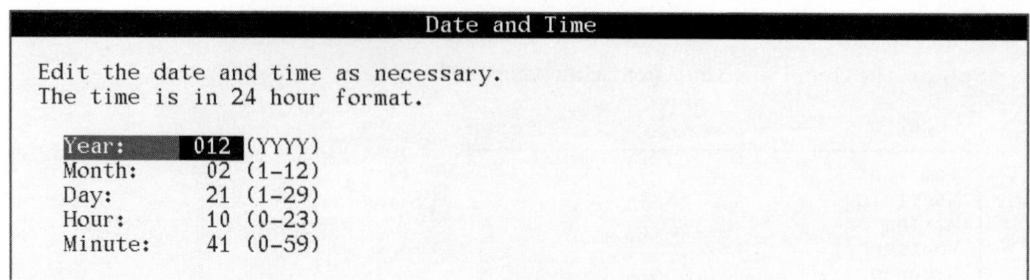
Date and Time

Edit the date and time as necessary.
The time is in 24 hour format.

Year: 012 (YYYY)
Month: 02 (1-12)
Day: 21 (1-29)
Hour: 10 (0-23)
Minute: 41 (0-59)

Figure 1-29 Text installer, x86: Date and Time

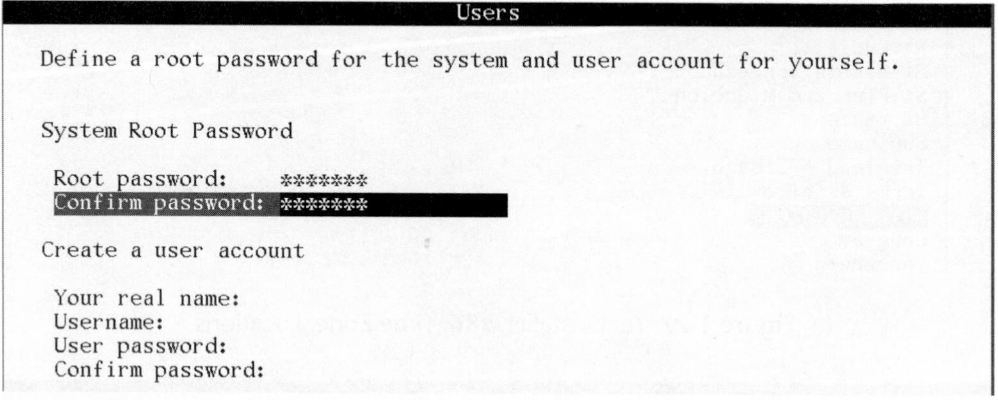
Users

Define a root password for the system and user account for yourself.

System Root Password

Root password: *******
Confirm password: *******

Create a user account

Your real name:
Username:
User password:
Confirm password:

Figure 1-30 Text installer, x86: Users

command to switch to the root account. This provides the best security and protects the root login.

When creating a user account, follow these rules:

- The username cannot be root.
- The username must start with a letter.
- The username may contain alphabetical characters, numbers, underscore (_), period (.), or hyphen (-).

If you do not create a user account, root is an account rather than a role.

When finished, press the *F2* key to continue. The Support—Registration window will be displayed as shown in Figure 1-31.

Press the *F2* key and the Support—Network Configuration page will be displayed as shown in Figure 1-32.

```
                    Support - Registration

  Provide your email address to be informed of security issues,
  install the product and initiate configuration manager.

  Please see http://www.oracle.com/goto/solarisautoreg for details.

    Email: anonymous@oracle.com
           Easier for you if you use your My Oracle Support email
           address/username.

    Please enter your password if you wish to receive security
    updates via My Oracle Support.

           My Oracle Support password:
```

Figure 1-31 Text installer, x86: Support—Registration

```
                 Support - Network Configuration

  To improve products and services, Oracle Solaris relays
  configuration data to the Oracle support organization.

  Select an internet access method for OCM and ASR.

    No proxy           Use system Internet connection parameters

    Proxy              Enter proxy information on the next screen

    Aggregation Hubs   Enter hubs information on the next screen

Esc-2_Continue Esc-3_Back Esc-6_Help Esc-9_Quit
```

Figure 1-32 Text installer, x86: Support—Network Configuration

Press the *F2* key to continue. The Installation Summary screen will be displayed as shown in Figure 1-33.

Review the information in the summary screen. If you need to make changes, press the *F3* key to go back. To start the installation, press *F2* and a status screen will be displayed as shown in Figure 1-34.

When the installation is finished, the Installation Complete window will be displayed as shown in Figure 1-35.

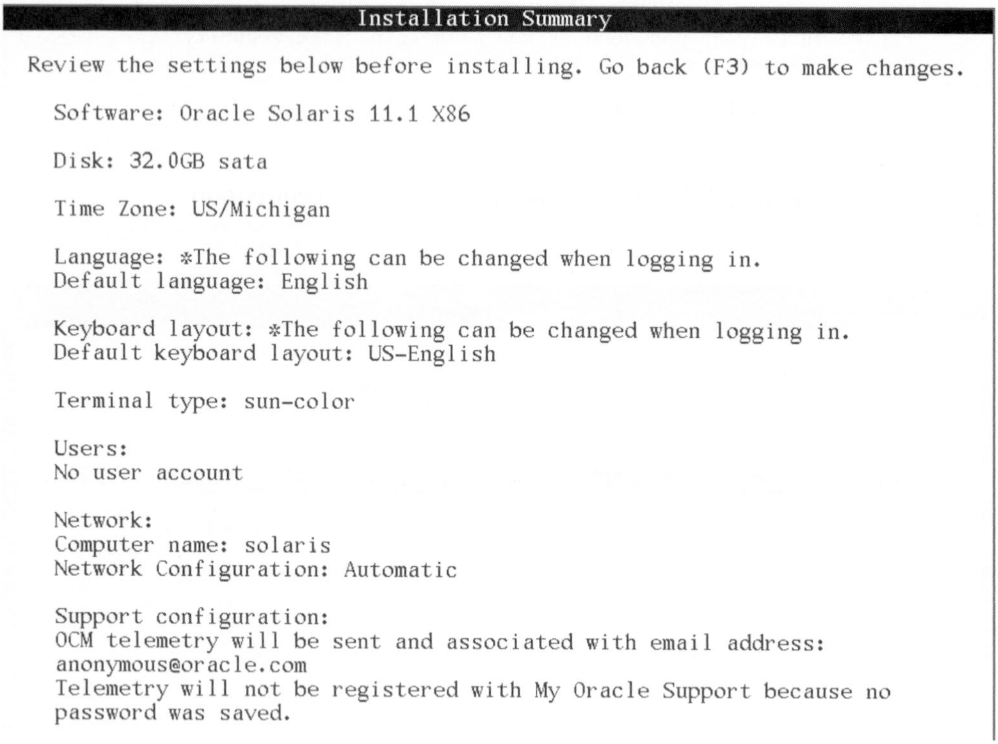

```
                         Installation Summary
Review the settings below before installing. Go back (F3) to make changes.

  Software: Oracle Solaris 11.1 X86

  Disk: 32.0GB sata

  Time Zone: US/Michigan

  Language: *The following can be changed when logging in.
  Default language: English

  Keyboard layout: *The following can be changed when logging in.
  Default keyboard layout: US-English

  Terminal type: sun-color

  Users:
  No user account

  Network:
  Computer name: solaris
  Network Configuration: Automatic

  Support configuration:
  OCM telemetry will be sent and associated with email address:
  anonymous@oracle.com
  Telemetry will not be registered with My Oracle Support because no
  password was saved.
```

Figure 1-33 Text installer, x86: Installation Summary

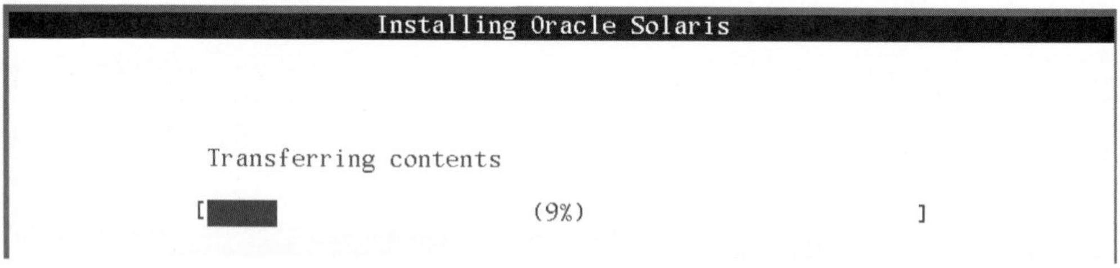

```
                      Installing Oracle Solaris



        Transferring contents

       [####                 (9%)                        ]
```

Figure 1-34 Text installer, x86: Installation status

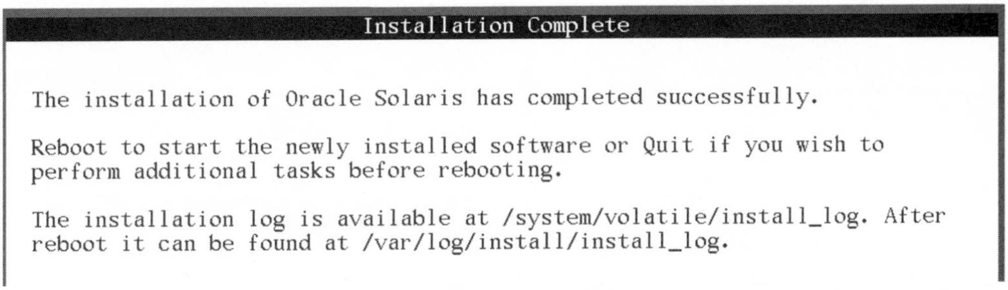

```
                         Installation Complete

 The installation of Oracle Solaris has completed successfully.

 Reboot to start the newly installed software or Quit if you wish to
 perform additional tasks before rebooting.

 The installation log is available at /system/volatile/install_log. After
 reboot it can be found at /var/log/install/install_log.
```

Figure 1-35 Text installer, x86: Installation Complete

```
SunOS Release 5.11 Version 11.1 64-bit
Copyright (c) 1983, 2012, Oracle and/or its affiliates. All rights reserved.
Hostname: solaris

solaris console login:
```

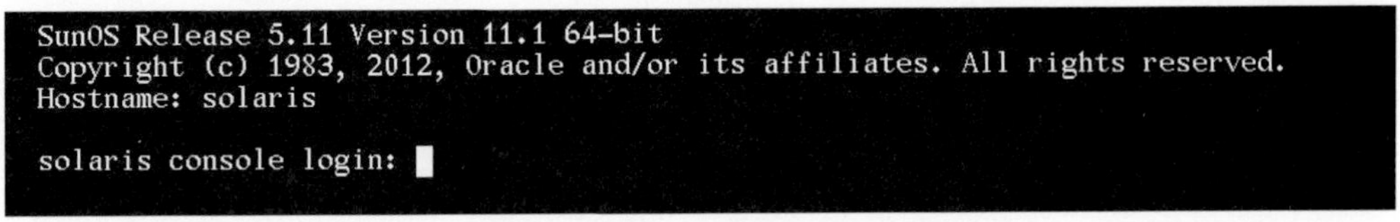

Figure 1-36 Oracle Solaris login

During the installation, a log file was created at `/system/volatile/install_log`. This file gets moved to `/var/sadm/system/logs/install_log` after the first reboot. Review this log file for any messages that were generated during the installation.

You can reboot the system by pressing the *F8* key. Be sure to remove the DVD so that the system boots from the internal disk and not the DVD. After rebooting, the system will display the login screen as shown in Figure 1-36.

If the Keyboard Selection menu appears as shown previously in Figure 1-18, the system is still booting from the installation media. Remove the installation media and make sure that the system is set up to boot from the local boot disk.

Unlike the Live Media installer, the text installer does not require a user account and creates the root account as a normal login account. Log in using the username root and the password that was provided during the installation (see Figure 1-30).

Using the Interactive Text Installer: SPARC

In the previous section, I installed Oracle Solaris using the text installer on an x86-based system. A SPARC system can only be installed using the text-based installer. The following example describes how to boot from a DVD and install Oracle Solaris 11.1 on a SPARC T2000 server.

At the OpenBoot ok prompt, boot from the DVD as follows:

```
ok boot cdrom<cr>
screen not found.
keyboard not found.
Keyboard not present. Using /virtual-devices/console for input and output.
Sun Fire T200, No Keyboard
Copyright (c) 1998, 2011, Oracle and/or its affiliates. All rights reserved.
OpenBoot 4.30.4.d, 3968 MB memory available, Serial #84994072.
Ethernet address 0:21:28:10:e8:18, Host ID: 8510e818.

Boot device: /pci@7c0/pci@0/pci@1/pci@0/ide@8/cdrom@0,0:f File and args:
SunOS Release 5.11 Version 11.1 64-bit
Copyright (c) 1983, 2012, Oracle and/or its affiliates. All rights reserved.
Remounting root read/write
Probing for device nodes ...
Preparing image for use
Done mounting image
```

After the system boots from the DVD, you'll be prompted for the keyboard language as follows:

```
USB keyboard
 1. Arabic
 2. Belgian
 3. Brazilian
 4. Canadian-Bilingual
 5. Canadian-French
 6. Danish
 7. Dutch
 8. Dvorak
 9. Finnish
10. French
11. German
12. Italian
13. Japanese-type6
14. Japanese
15. Korean
16. Latin-American
17. Norwegian
18. Portuguese
19. Russian
20. Spanish
21. Swedish
22. Swiss-French
23. Swiss-German
24. Traditional-Chinese
25. TurkishQ
26. UK-English
27. US-English

To select the keyboard layout, enter a number [default 27]:<cr>

 1. Chinese - Simplified
 2. Chinese - Traditional
 3. English
 4. French
 5. German
 6. Italian
 7. Japanese
 8. Korean
 9. Portuguese - Brazil
10. Spanish
To select the language you wish to use, enter a number [default is 3]:<cr>
```

After entering the Keyboard information, the installation menu appears as shown in Figure 1-37.

Press *Enter* to start the installation. The welcome message will be displayed as shown in Figure 1-38.

```
Welcome to the Oracle Solaris installation menu

        1  Install Oracle Solaris
        2  Install Additional Drivers
        3  Shell
        4  Terminal type (currently sun)
        5  Reboot

Please enter a number [1]: 1
```

Figure 1-37 Text installer, SPARC: Oracle Solaris installation menu

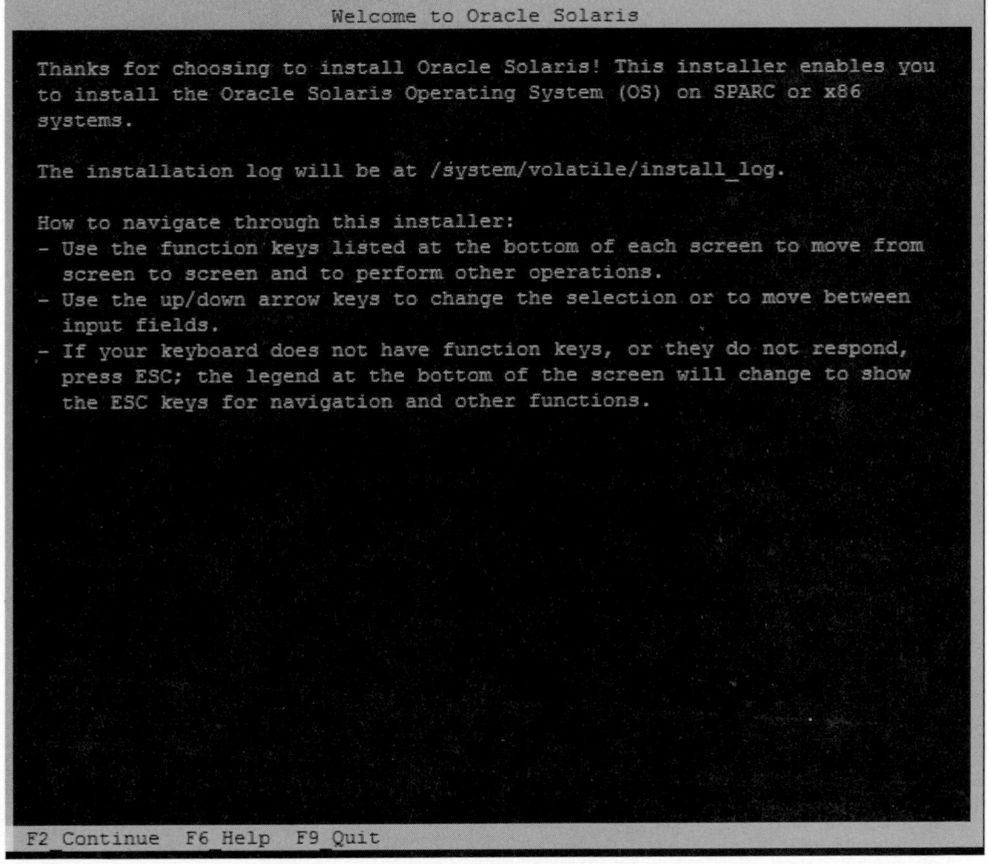

Figure 1-38 Text installer, SPARC: Welcome

Press *F2* to continue. The Disk Discovery menu will be displayed as shown in Figure 1-39.

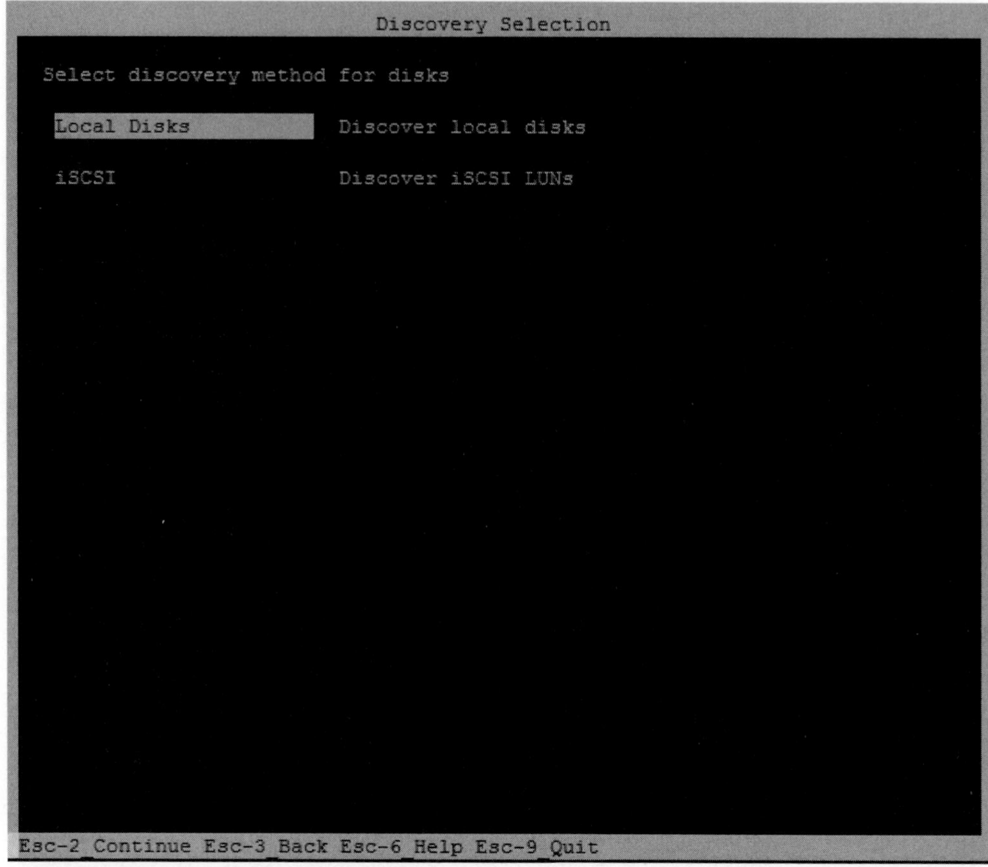

Figure 1-39 Text installer, SPARC: Disk Discovery Selection

I will be installing Oracle Solaris on the local disk, so I selected Local Disks and pressed *F2*. The Disks menu will be displayed as shown in Figure 1-40.

Obtaining Help

You can view additional documentation during the installation by pressing *F6* to obtain Help. Documentation describing the current menu will be displayed. Press *F3* to exit the Help screen and return to the current menu.

I selected to install Oracle Solaris on the primary disk, c2t0d0. Only one disk may be selected. After making the selection, press *F2* and the Solaris Slices menu is displayed as shown in Figure 1-41.

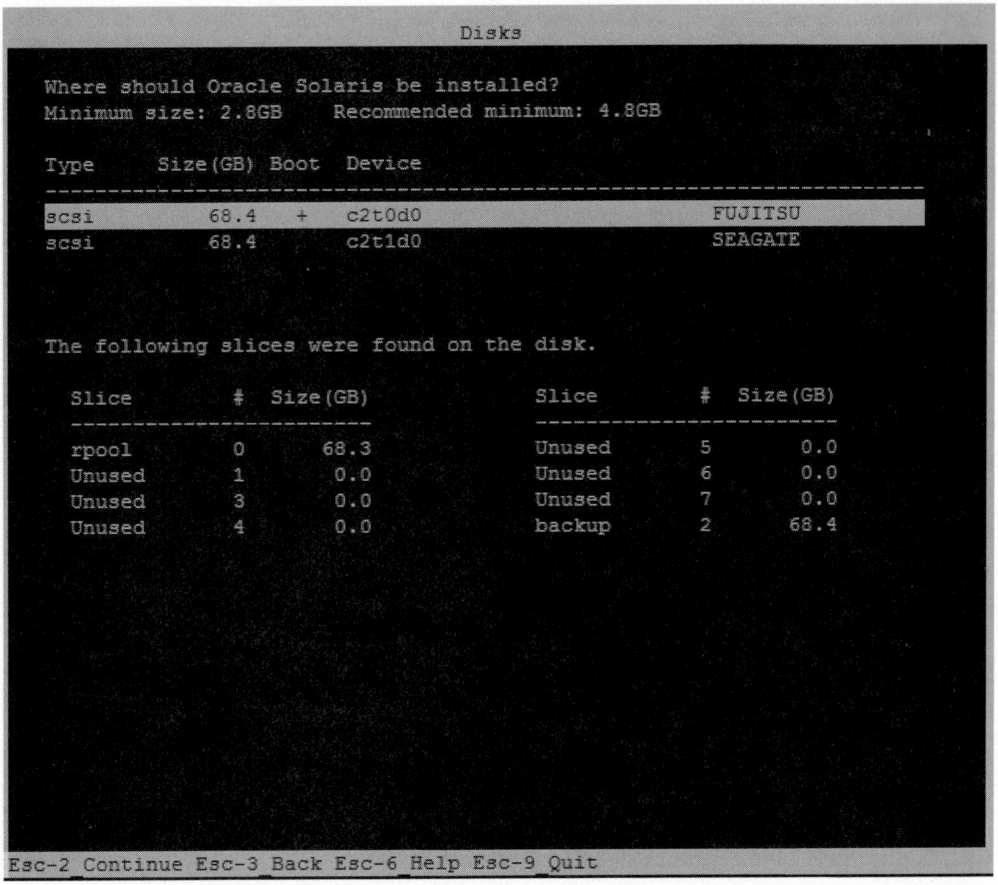

```
                                    Disks

  Where should Oracle Solaris be installed?
  Minimum size: 2.8GB    Recommended minimum: 4.8GB

  Type      Size(GB) Boot  Device
  ----------------------------------------------------------------------
  scsi           68.4    +    c2t0d0                          FUJITSU
  scsi           68.4         c2t1d0                          SEAGATE


  The following slices were found on the disk.

    Slice         #  Size(GB)               Slice        #  Size(GB)
    ------------------------               ------------------------
    rpool         0      68.3               Unused       5       0.0
    Unused        1       0.0               Unused       6       0.0
    Unused        3       0.0               Unused       7       0.0
    Unused        4       0.0               backup       2      68.4

Esc-2_Continue Esc-3_Back Esc-6_Help Esc-9_Quit
```

Figure 1-40 Text installer, SPARC: Disks

I will not be partitioning the disk into slices and will be using the entire disk. I made the selection to use the whole disk and pressed *F2*. The Network menu is displayed as shown in Figure 1-42.

I am installing Oracle Solaris on a server and I want to use a static IP address, so I selected the option to configure the network interface manually. I press *F2* to continue, and the Manual Network Configuration menu is displayed as shown in Figure 1-43 on page 40.

The following six menus are only displayed when the Manual configuration is selected. If you make the selection to Automatically configure the network, the next six menus will be skipped (after you press *F2*) and you will be prompted to enter the time zone as displayed in Figure 1-49 on page 46.

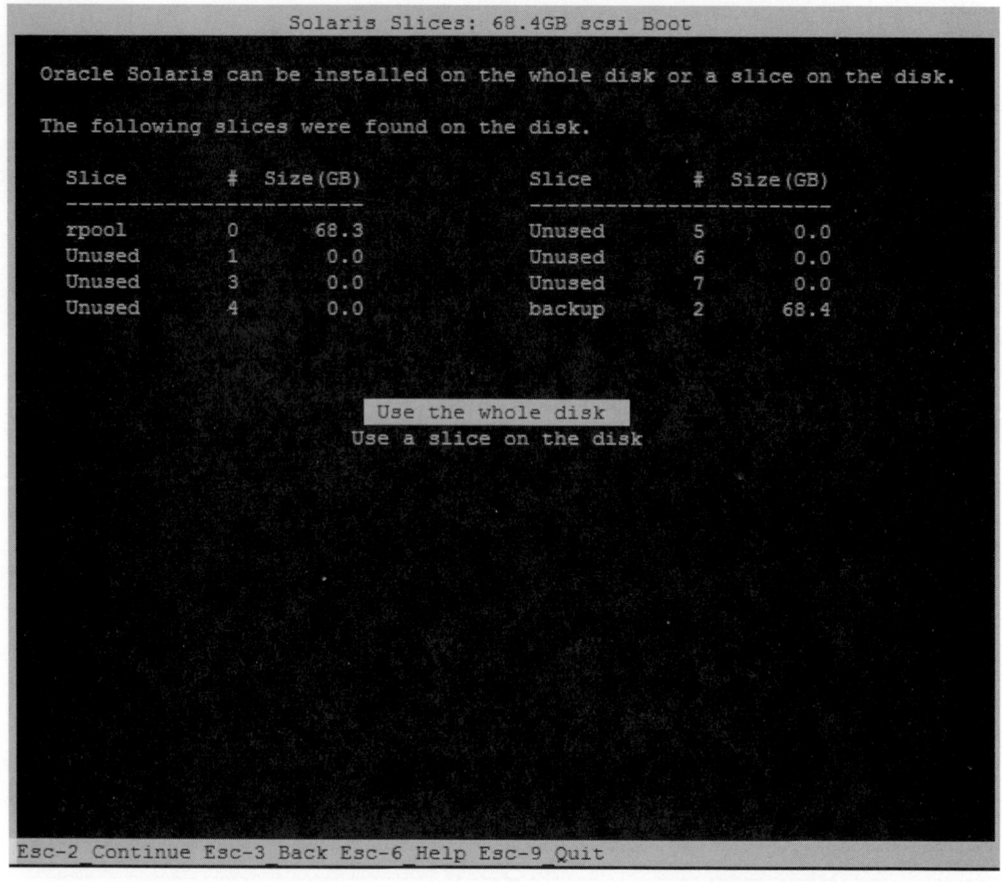

Figure 1-41 Text installer, SPARC: Solaris Slices

This server has four physical network interfaces. I selected the first interface, net0, and pressed *F2* to continue. The configuration window for net0 is displayed as shown in Figure 1-44 on page 41.

Enter the IP address, the network mask, and the router. Press *F2* when finished, and the DNS Name Service window will be displayed as shown in Figure 1-45 on page 42.

Select the option to configure DNS. Optionally, you can configure DNS after the installation. Press *F2* after making your selection, and the DNS Server Addresses menu appears as shown in Figure 1-46 on page 43.

Enter the IP address for the primary and secondary DNS servers. After entering the IP address for each server, press *F2*. The DNS Search List menu is displayed as shown in Figure 1-47 on page 44.

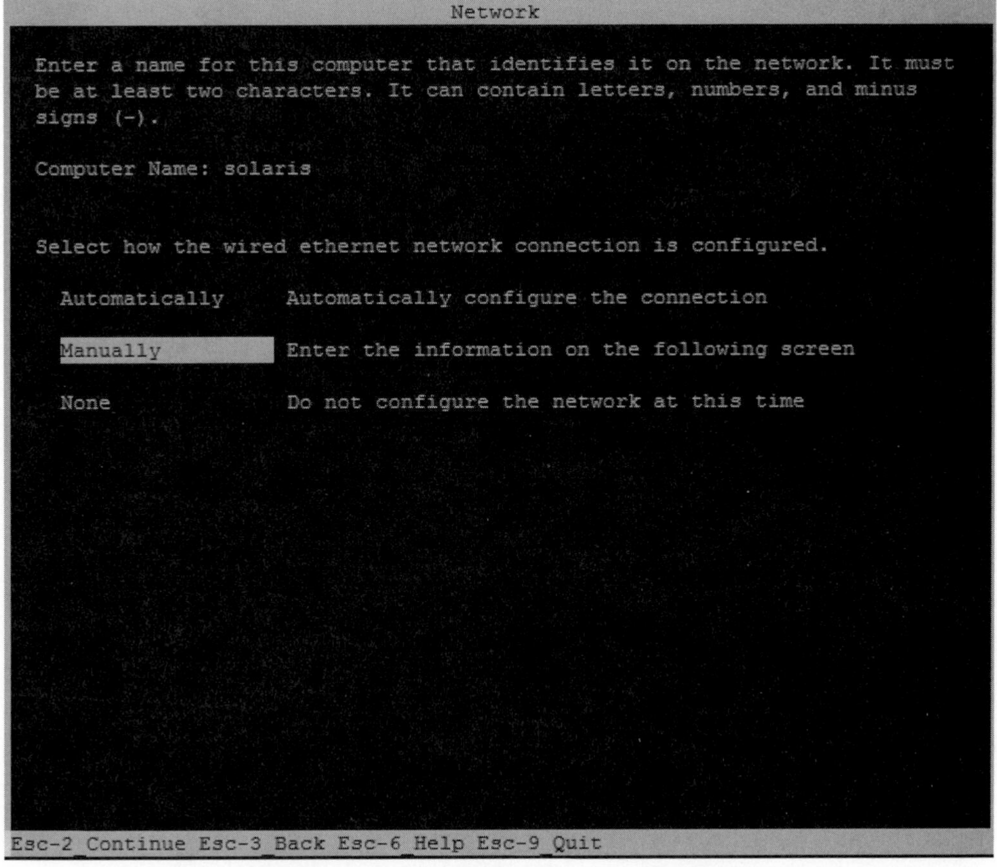

Figure 1-42 Text installer, SPARC: Network

Enter the DNS search domain and press *F2* to continue. The Alternate Name Service menu is displayed as shown in Figure 1-48 on page 45.

If you are using a Name Service, select "LDAP" or "NIS" here. If not, select "None" and press *F2*. If you select "LDAP" or "NIS," make sure that you have the name server information available to enter when prompted on the next screen. This server is not using a Name Service, so I selected "None." I will not be prompted to enter additional information regarding the Name Service server, and I progress to the time zone information as displayed in Figure 1-49 on page 46.

Enter your time zone region and press *F2*. The time zone locations menu is displayed as shown in Figure 1-50 on page 47.

Enter your location and press *F2*. The time zone menu is displayed as shown in Figure 1-51 on page 48.

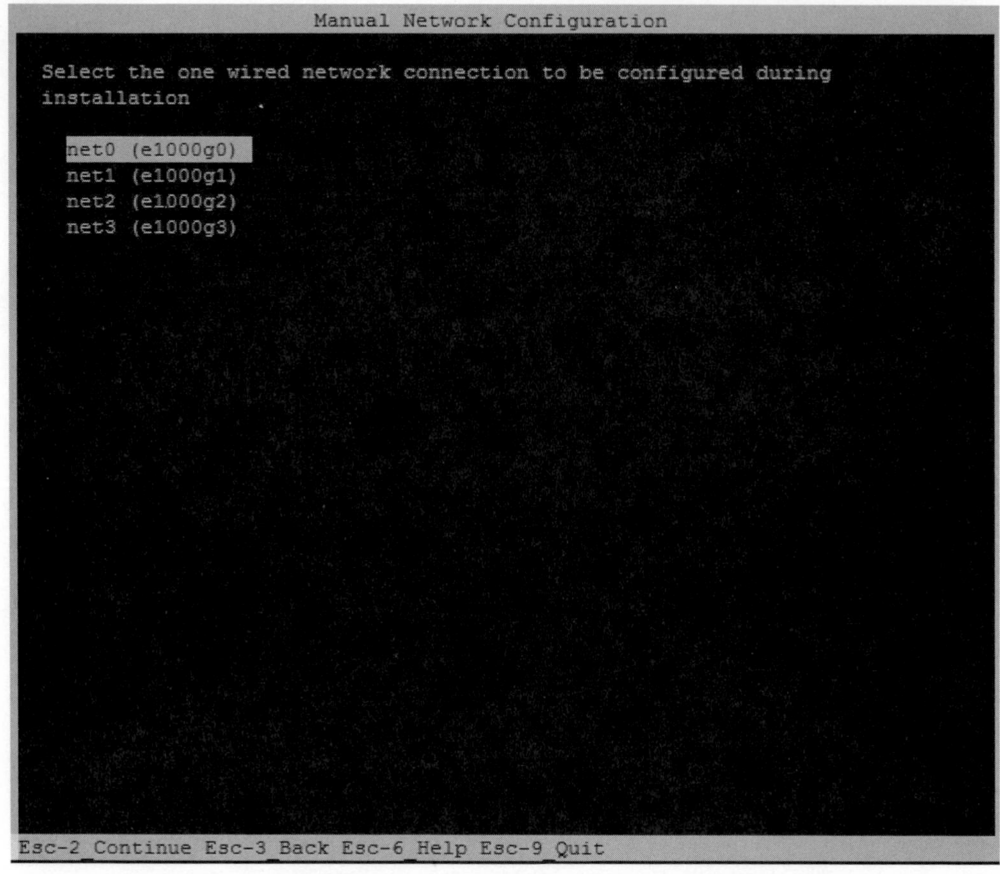

Figure 1-43 Text installer, SPARC: Manual Network Configuration

Enter your time zone and press *F2*. The Date and Time screen is displayed as shown in Figure 1-52 on page 49.

Enter the current date and time and press *F2*. The Users screen is displayed as shown in Figure 1-53 on page 50.

Enter the root password. You can also create a user account as described earlier in this chapter. When creating a user account, the root account becomes a role, and you will not be able to log in directly from the login prompt using the root account. Press *F2* when you have completed your entries, and the Support—Registration menu will be displayed as shown in Figure 1-54 on page 51.

After completing the Support—Registration form, press *F2* to continue. The Support—Network Configuration screen is displayed as shown in Figure 1-55 on page 52.

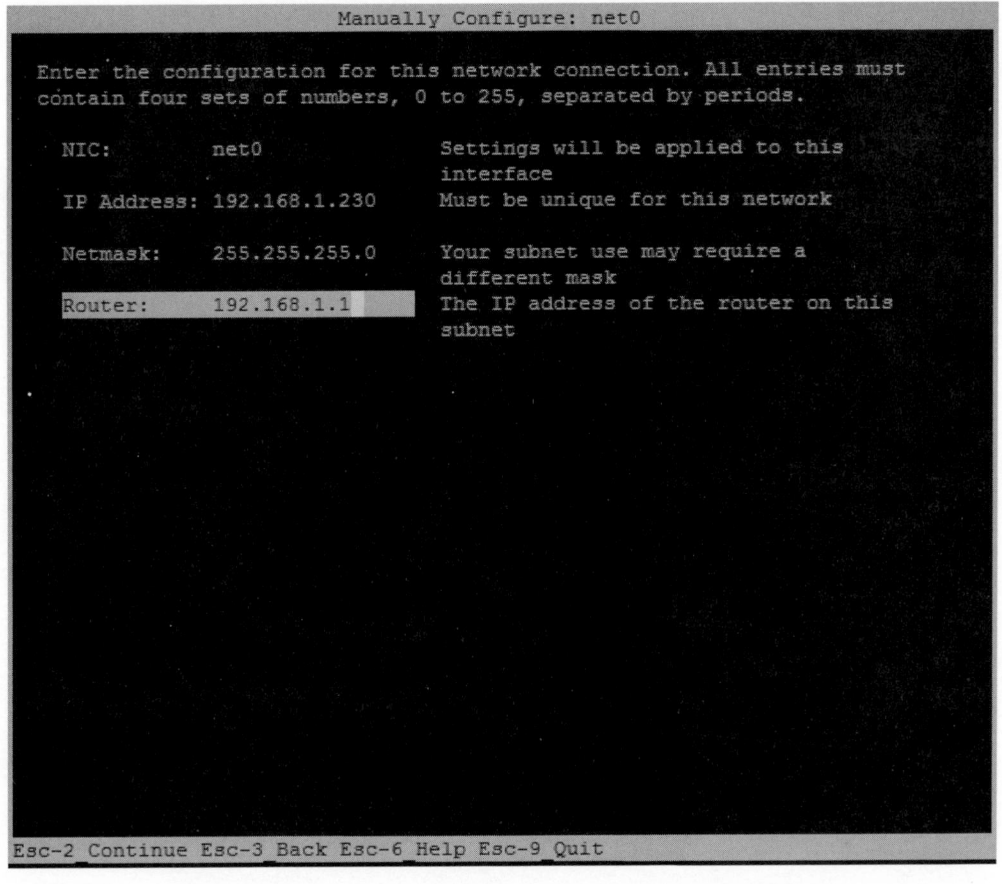

Figure 1-44 Text installer, SPARC: Manually Configure, net0

Select the method used to relay the registration information over the Internet to Oracle and press *F2*. The installation summary is displayed as shown in Figure 1-56 on page 53.

Review the installation summary and press *F2* to begin the installation. If you need to modify the installation information, press *F3* (or *ESC-3*) to go back. When the installation begins, a status bar will display the progress as shown in Figure 1-57 on page 53.

When the installation is finished, the Installation Complete message will be displayed as shown in Figure 1-58 on page 54.

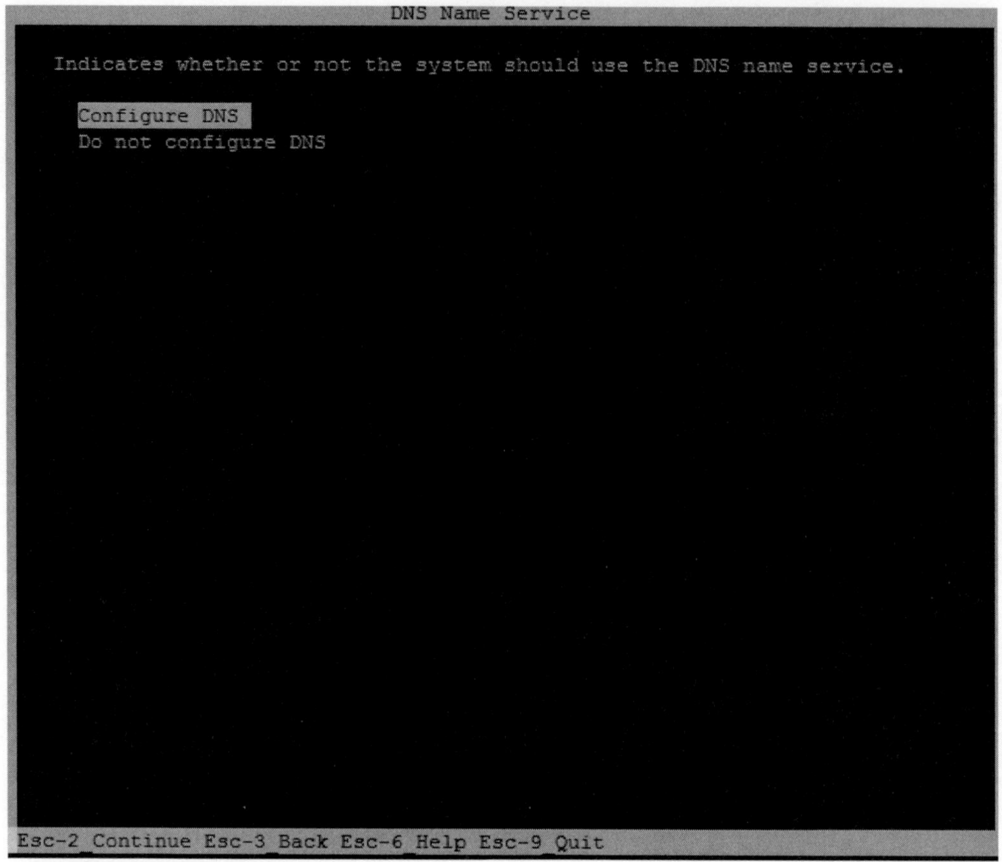

Figure 1-45 Text installer, SPARC: DNS Name Service

Press *F8* (or *ESC-8*) to reboot the system. If the Installation menu is displayed, as shown previously in Figure 1-37, select option 5 from the menu to reboot the system. The DVD can be removed after the system begins to boot.

Verifying the Operating Environment

If the OS was installed using the text installer, you'll be presented with a login screen as shown previously in Figure 1-36. If it was installed using the Live Media installer, you'll be presented with a login screen as shown previously in Figure 1-17.

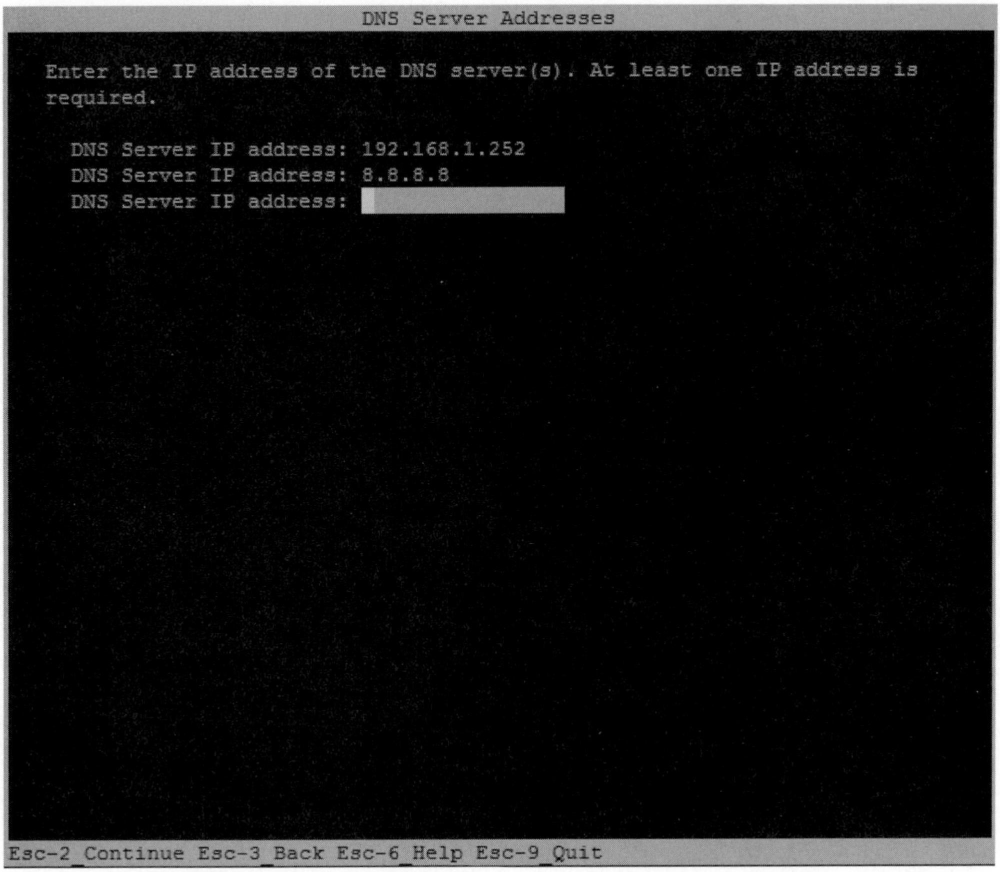

```
                         DNS Server Addresses

  Enter the IP address of the DNS server(s). At least one IP address is
  required.

    DNS Server IP address: 192.168.1.252
    DNS Server IP address: 8.8.8.8
    DNS Server IP address:

Esc-2_Continue Esc-3_Back Esc-6_Help Esc-9_Quit
```

Figure 1-46 Text installer, SPARC: DNS Server Addresses

Log in to the system and, if using the Java Desktop, open a terminal window to access the command line. The default behavior is to not allow root to log in directly, and the root account is not required to run the commands described in this section. Table 1-5 on page 55 provides a list of commands that can be used to display information about your system.

From the command line, issue the `hostname` command to verify the system name as follows.

```
$ hostname<cr>
solaris
```

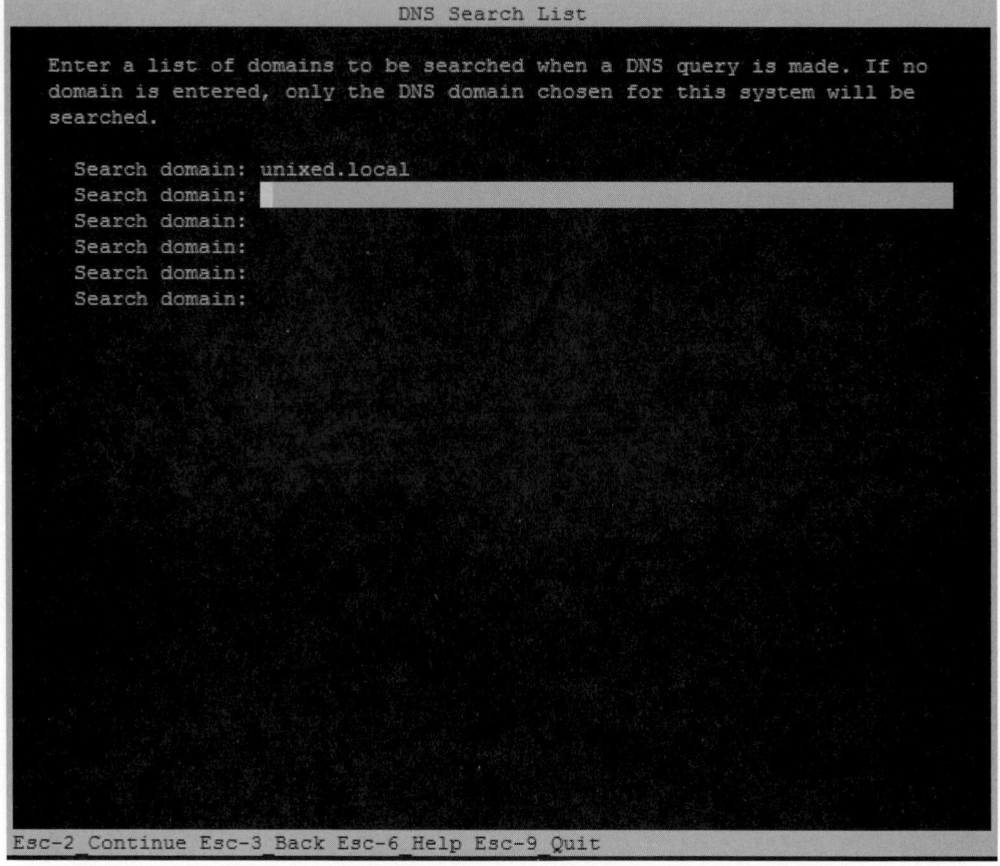

Figure 1-47 Text installer, SPARC: DNS Search List

After verifying the hostname, use the `uname(1)` command to display information about the current system. The syntax for the `uname` command is as follows:

```
uname [-aimnprsvX]
```

The commonly used options with the `uname` command are

- `-a` Print basic information currently available from the system.
- `-i` Print the name of the platform.
- `-m` Print the machine hardware name.

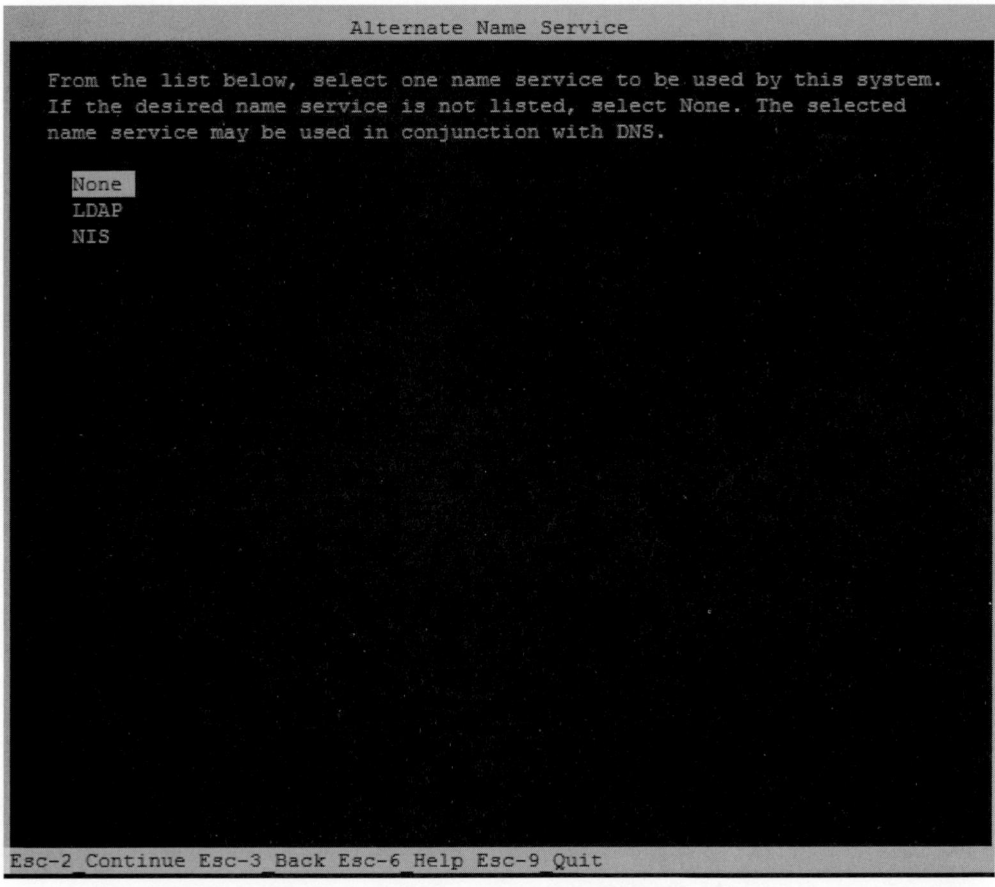

Figure 1-48 Text installer, SPARC: Alternate Name Service

`-n`	Print the note name.
`-p`	Print the processor type.
`-r`	Print the OS level.
`-s`	Print the name of the OS.
`-s` *`nodename`*	Change the *nodename* by specifying a system name as an argument. The *nodename* is the name by which the system is known to a communications network.
`-v`	Print the OS version.

Use the `-a` option to display all information as follows:

```
# uname -a<cr>
```

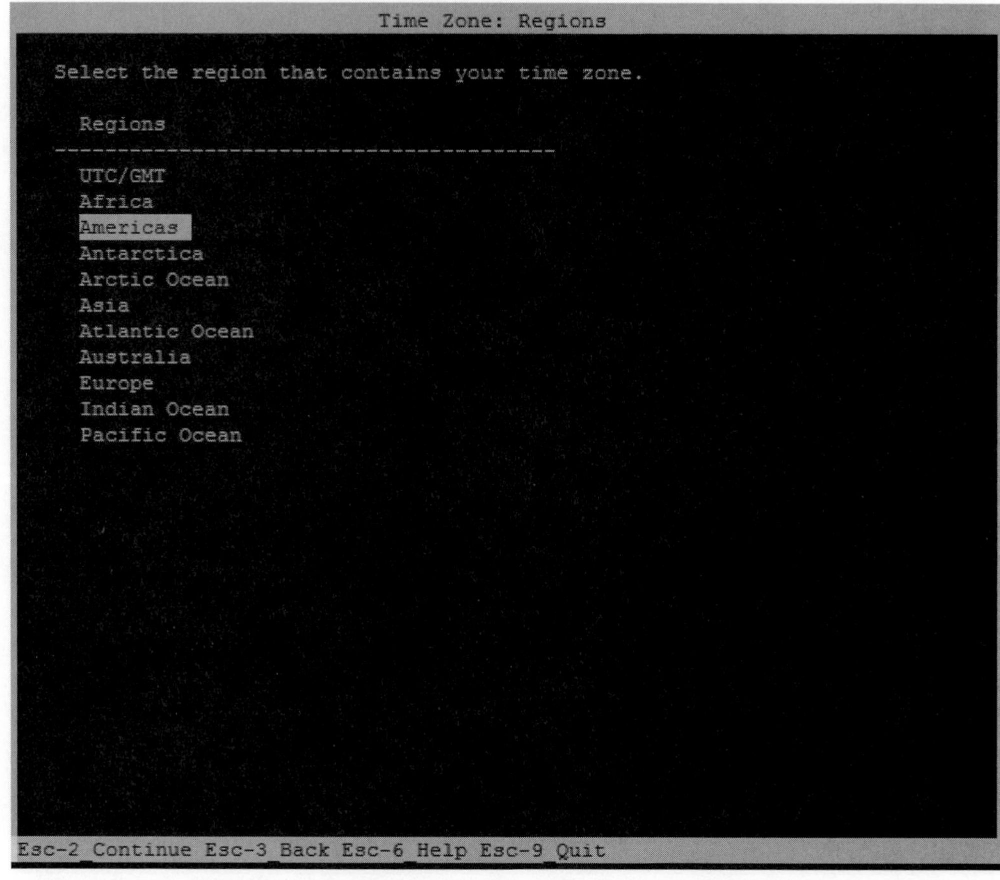

Figure 1-49 Text installer, SPARC: Time Zone, Regions

The system responds with the following output:

```
SunOS solaris 5.11 11.1 i86pc i386 i86pc
```

The information presented is as follows:

OS: `SunOS`
Hostname: `solaris`
OS release: `5.11`
OS version: `11.1`
Hardware name: `i86pc i386`
Processor type: `i386`

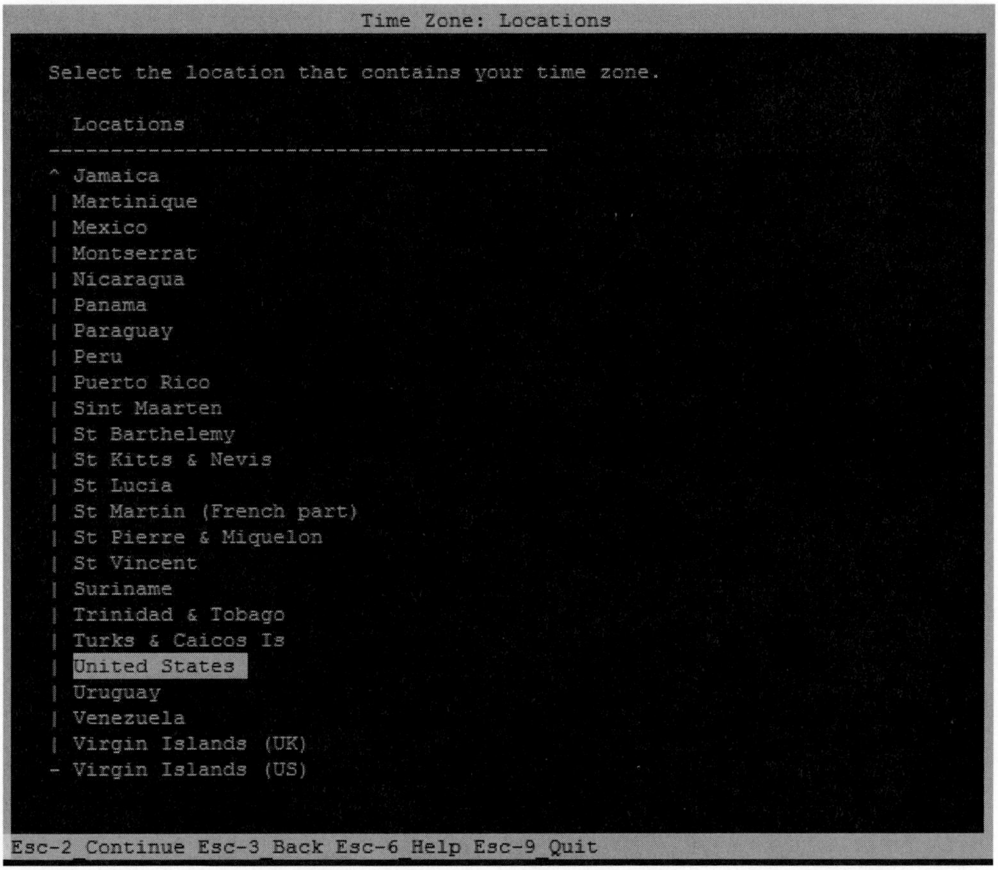

```
                         Time Zone: Locations

  Select the location that contains your time zone.

    Locations
  ----------------------------------------
  ^ Jamaica
  | Martinique
  | Mexico
  | Montserrat
  | Nicaragua
  | Panama
  | Paraguay
  | Peru
  | Puerto Rico
  | Sint Maarten
  | St Barthelemy
  | St Kitts & Nevis
  | St Lucia
  | St Martin (French part)
  | St Pierre & Miquelon
  | St Vincent
  | Suriname
  | Trinidad & Tobago
  | Turks & Caicos Is
  | United States
  | Uruguay
  | Venezuela
  | Virgin Islands (UK)
  - Virgin Islands (US)

Esc-2 Continue Esc-3 Back Esc-6 Help Esc-9 Quit
```

Figure 1-50 Text installer, SPARC: Time Zone, Locations

To display the OS release information, view the contents of the `/etc/release` file as follows:

```
$ cat /etc/release<cr>
```

The system responds with the following output:

```
            Oracle Solaris 11.1 X86
Copyright (c) 1983, 2012, Oracle and/or its affiliates. All rights reserved.
                         Assembled 19 October 2012
```

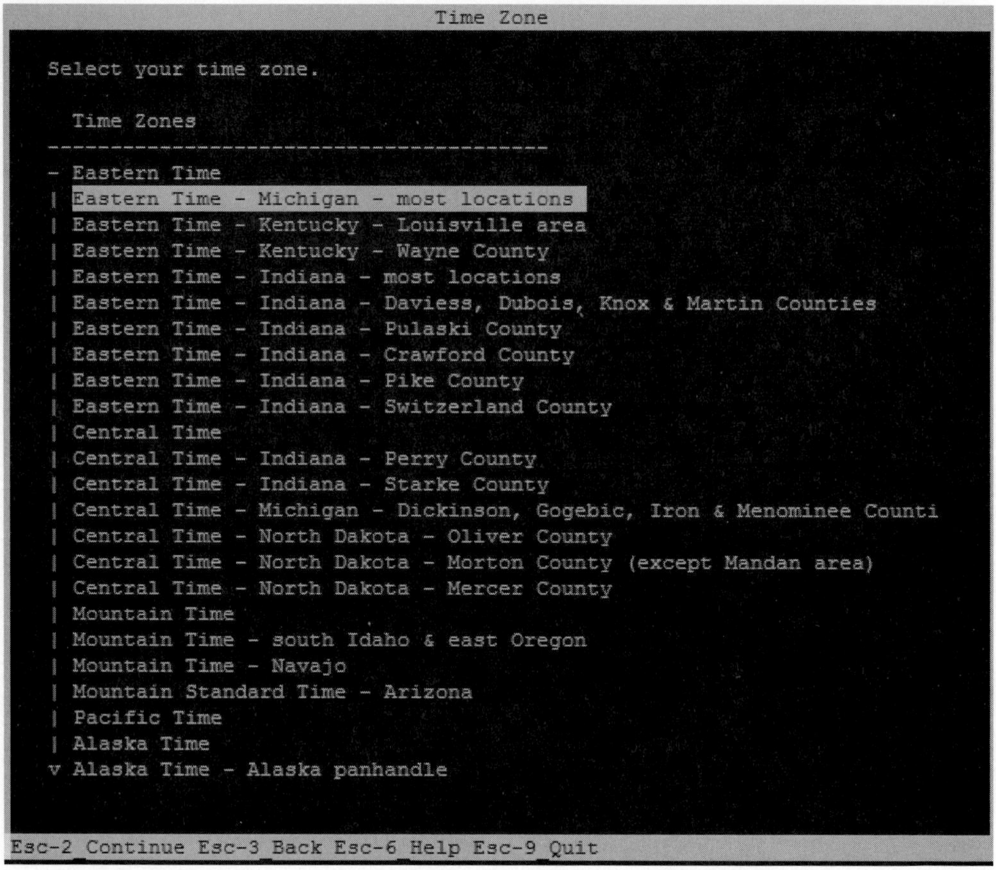

```
                                Time Zone

  Select your time zone.

    Time Zones
  ----------------------------------------
  - Eastern Time
  | Eastern Time - Michigan - most locations
  | Eastern Time - Kentucky - Louisville area
  | Eastern Time - Kentucky - Wayne County
  | Eastern Time - Indiana - most locations
  | Eastern Time - Indiana - Daviess, Dubois, Knox & Martin Counties
  | Eastern Time - Indiana - Pulaski County
  | Eastern Time - Indiana - Crawford County
  | Eastern Time - Indiana - Pike County
  | Eastern Time - Indiana - Switzerland County
  | Central Time
  | Central Time - Indiana - Perry County
  | Central Time - Indiana - Starke County
  | Central Time - Michigan - Dickinson, Gogebic, Iron & Menominee Counti
  | Central Time - North Dakota - Oliver County
  | Central Time - North Dakota - Morton County (except Mandan area)
  | Central Time - North Dakota - Mercer County
  | Mountain Time
  | Mountain Time - south Idaho & east Oregon
  | Mountain Time - Navajo
  | Mountain Standard Time - Arizona
  | Pacific Time
  | Alaska Time
  v Alaska Time - Alaska panhandle

Esc-2 Continue Esc-3 Back Esc-6 Help Esc-9 Quit
```

Figure 1-51 Text installer, SPARC: Time Zone

The `/etc/release` file contains the following information about the system:

- The full OS name
- The version of the release
- The hardware architecture
- The copyright notice
- The date on which the release was assembled

Where the `uname` command displays the operating release level, the `/etc/release` file contains the date on which the release was assembled. In the example, the OS was assembled on 19 October 2012.

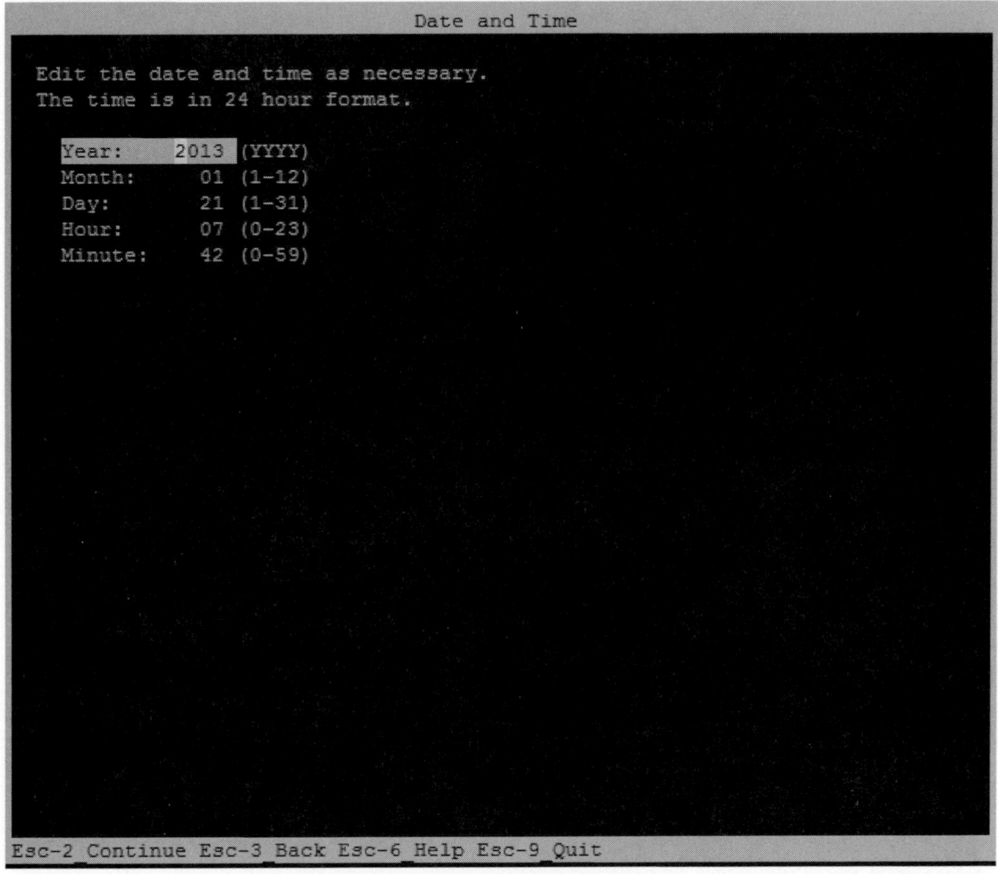

Figure 1-52 Text installer, SPARC: Date and Time

The pkg command can also be used to display information about the OS and software packages installed on your system. The pkg command is part of the IPS and is described in Chapter 2.

The commands listed in Table 1-5 on page 55 can be used to display information about the physical devices on the system.

Execute the prtconf command to display the total amount of physical memory installed on the system as follows:

```
$ prtconf| grep -i memory<cr>
     Memory size: 2048 Megabytes
```

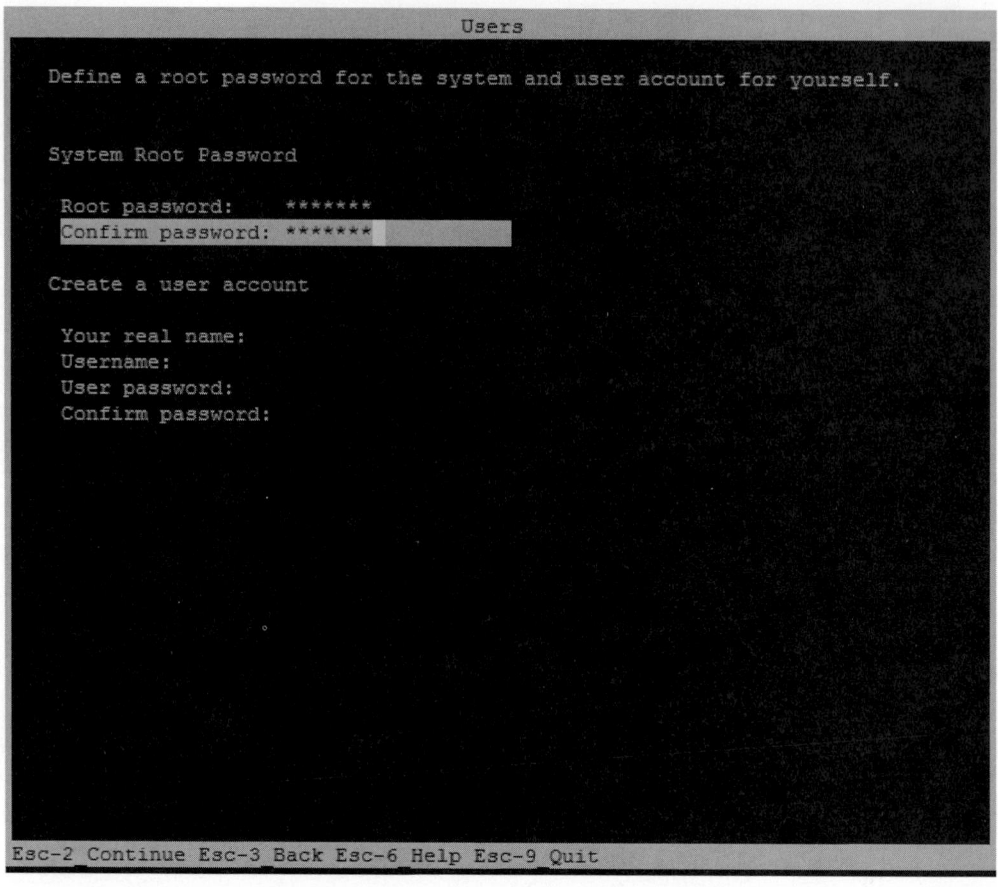

Figure 1-53 Text installer, SPARC: Users

Execute the `svcs` command to display information about the network connection configuration as follows:

```
$ svcs network/physical<cr>
STATE          STIME    FMRI
disabled       10:34:18 svc:/network/physical:nwam
online         10:34:28 svc:/network/physical:upgrade
online         10:34:43 svc:/network/physical:default
```

In this example, the output verifies that the `svc:/network/physical:default` service is online. The `svcs` command is described in detail in Chapter 3 and the `svc:/network/physical:default` service is described in Chapter 9, "The Oracle Solaris Network Environment."

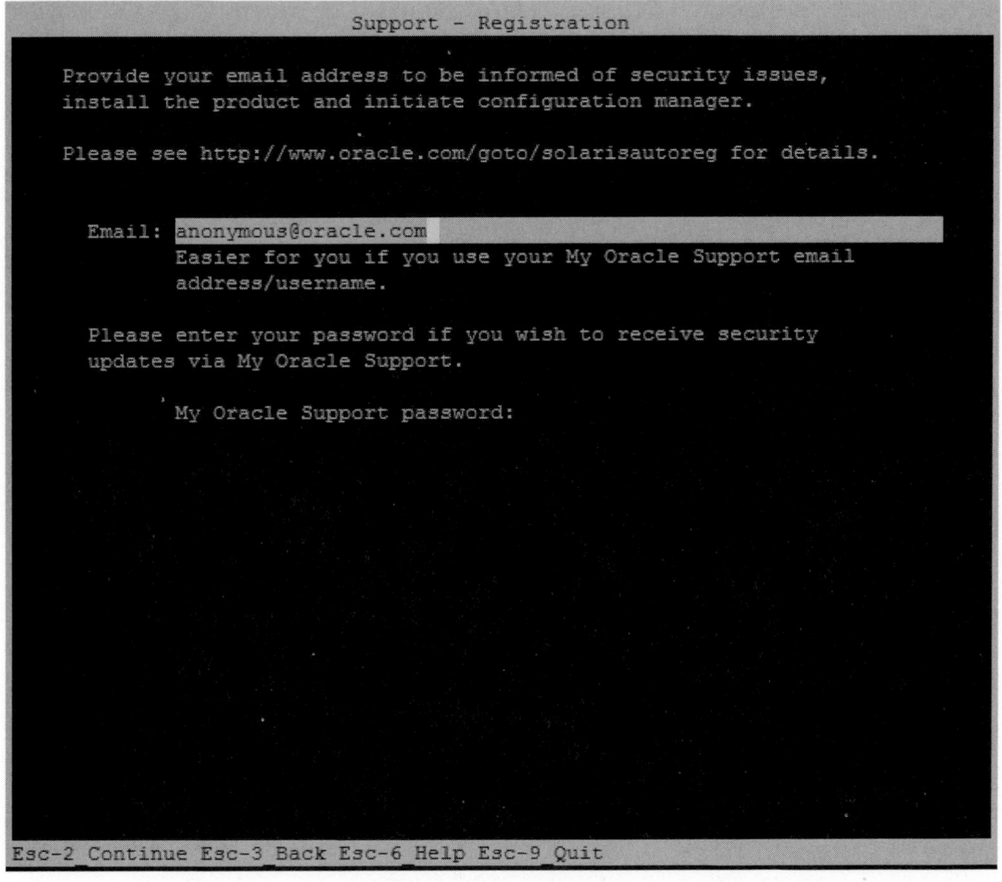

Figure 1-54 Text installer, SPARC: Support—Registration

Execute the `ipadm` command to display the configuration of the primary network interface as follows:

```
$ ipadm show-addr<cr>
ADDROBJ          TYPE       STATE       ADDR
lo0/v4           static     ok          127.0.0.1/8
net0/_b          dhcp       ok          10.0.2.15/24
lo0/v6           static     ok          ::1/128
net0/_a          addrconf   ok          fe80::a00:27ff:fe8e:c0d4/10
```

The `ipadm` command is a tool used for all IP interface configuration administration tasks and is described in Chapter 9.

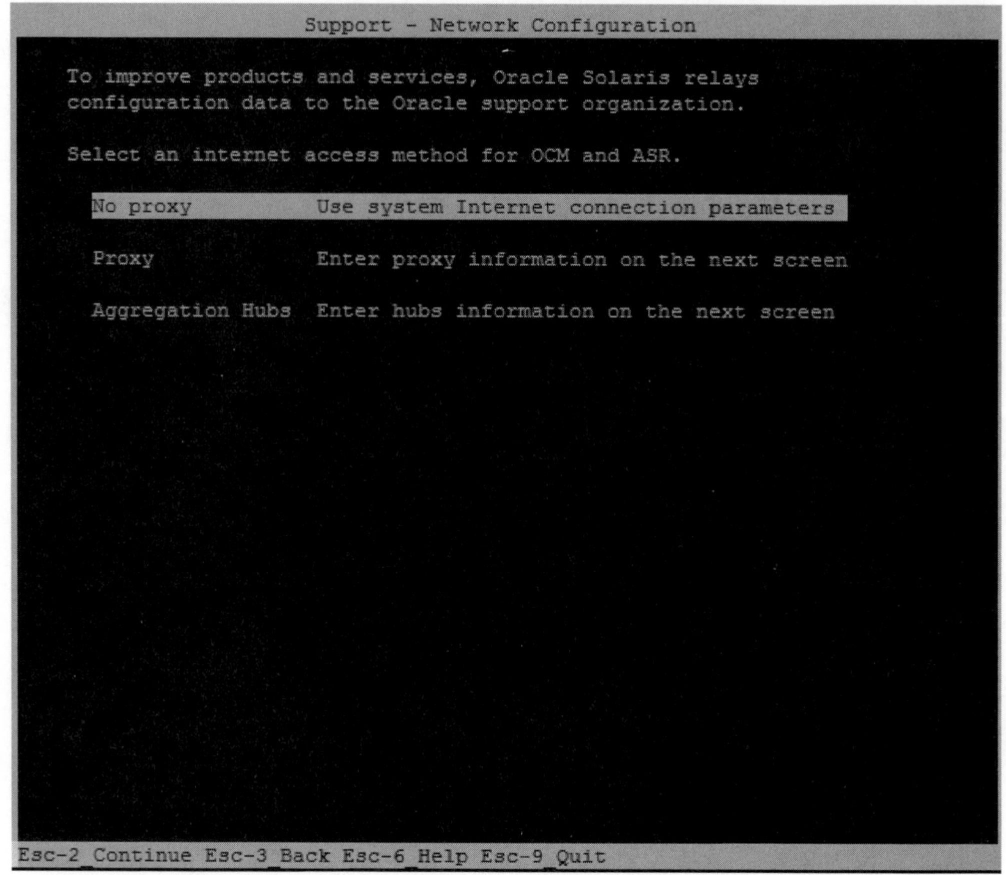

Figure 1-55 Text installer, SPARC: Support—Network Configuration

Use the `sysdef` utility to list all hardware devices, as well as pseudo devices, system devices, loadable modules, and the values of selected kernel tunable parameters. Execute the `sysdef` utility as follows:

```
$ sysdef|more<cr>
*
* Hostid
*
  0087bfbb
*
* i86pc Configuration
*
*
* Devices
<output from the sysdef command has been truncated>
```

```
                        Installation Summary

 Review the settings below before installing. Go back (F3) to make changes.

 - Software: Oracle Solaris 11.1 SPARC
 |
 | Disk: 68.4GB scsi
 | Slice 0: 68.3GB rpool
 |
 | Time Zone: US/Michigan
 |
 | Language: *The following can be changed when logging in.
 | Default language: English
 |
 | Keyboard layout: *The following can be changed when logging in.
 | Default keyboard layout: US-English
 |
 | Terminal type: vt100
 |
 | Users:
 | No user account
 |
 | Network:
 | Computer name: solaris
 | Manual Configuration: net0 (e1000g0)
 | IP Address: 192.168.1.230
 | Netmask: 255.255.255.0
 | Router: 192.168.1.1
 | Name service: DNS
 | DNS servers: 192.168.1.252 8.8.8.8
 v DNS Domain search list: unixed.local

Esc-2_Install Esc-3_Back Esc-6_Help Esc-9_Quit
```

Figure 1-56 Text installer, SPARC: Installation Summary

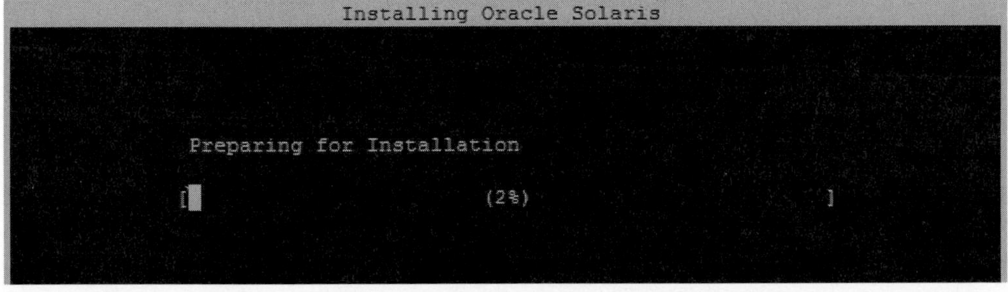

Figure 1-57 Text installer, SPARC: Installation progress

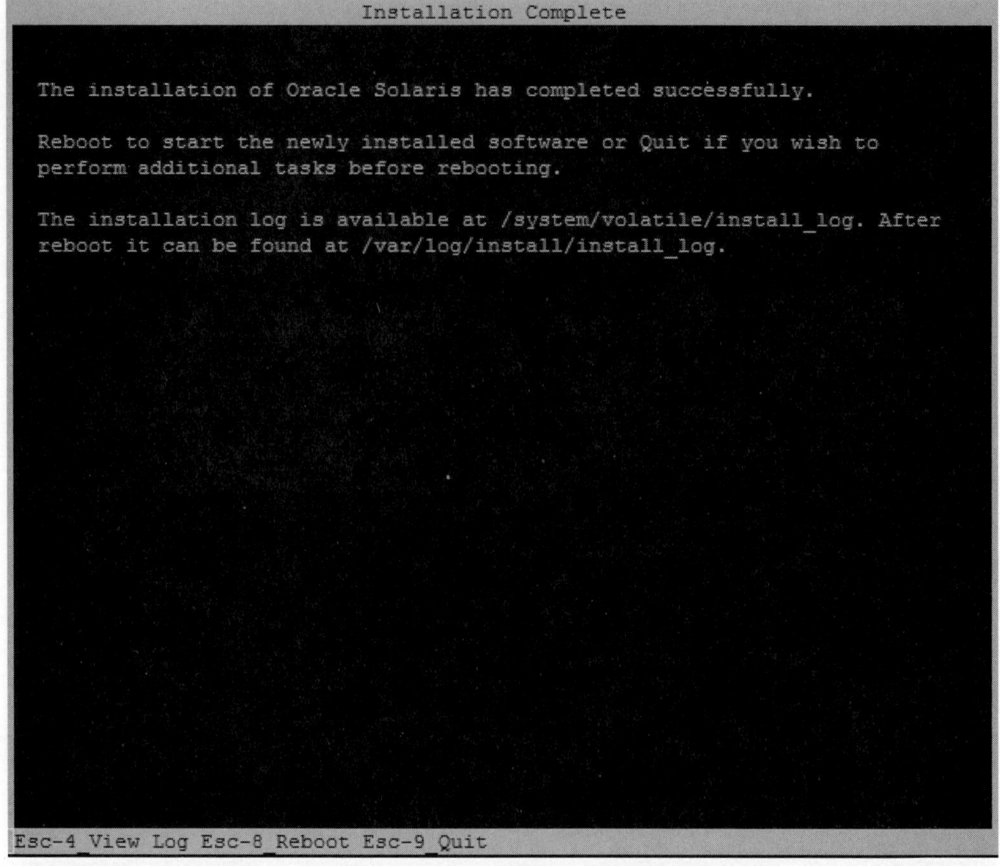

Figure 1-58 Text installer, SPARC: Installation Complete

The system will display several pages of output.

Finally, use the `format` utility to display disk information. The `format` utility is a disk partitioning and maintenance utility that allows you to format, label, repair, analyze, and scrub data from a disk. You must have root privileges to use this utility. In the following example, I'll use the `su` command to switch to the root account and then execute the `format` command to begin using the utility.

```
$ su root<cr>
Password:<enter the root password>
# format<cr>
```

Table 1-5 Device Information Commands

Command	Description
`prtconf`	Displays system configuration information, including the total amount of memory and the device configuration, as described by the system's hierarchy. This useful tool verifies whether a device has been seen by the system.
`svcs`	Reports the status of a service.
`ipadm`	Configure Internet Protocol network interfaces and TCP/IP tunables.
`sysdef`	Displays device configuration information, including system hardware, pseudo devices, loadable modules, and selected kernel parameters.
`format`	The `format` command displays both physical and logical device names for all available disks.

The format utility displays the system disks as follows:

```
Searching for disks…done

AVAILABLE DISK SELECTIONS:
     0. c3t0d0 <ATA-VBOX HARDDISK-1.0 cyl 2085 alt 2 hd 255 sec 63>
        /pci@0,0/pci8086,2829@d/disk@0,0
     1. c3t2d0 <ATA-VBOX HARDDISK-1.0-16.00GB>
        /pci@0,0/pci8086,2829@d/disk@2,0
     2. c3t3d0 <ATA-VBOX HARDDISK-1.0 cyl 2086 alt 2 hd 255 sec 63>
        /pci@0,0/pci8086,2829@d/disk@3,0
     3. c3t4d0 <ATA-VBOX HARDDISK-1.0-16.00GB>
        /pci@0,0/pci8086,2829@d/disk@4,0
Specify disk (enter its number):<ctrl+d>
```

Press `ctrl+d` to exit the utility. The `format` utility is described in Chapter 4.

Upgrading from a Previous Version of Oracle Solaris

It is not possible to upgrade a prior release of Oracle Solaris to Oracle Solaris 11. The only option is to migrate an existing Oracle Solaris 10 system (version 10/09 or later) into a `solaris10` brand non-global zone on a Solaris 11 system. To perform this migration, you will use the physical-to-virtual (P2V) function in Oracle Solaris 11 as follows:

1. Create an archive of the existing Oracle Solaris 10 system using one of the following methods:
    Flar image
    `cpio`

`gzip` compressed `cpio` archive
`bzip2` compressed `cpio` archive
`pax` archive
`ufsdump` level 0 backup

2. Prepare a `solaris10` brand zone on an Oracle Solaris 11 system.
3. Move the Oracle Solaris 10 archive to the Oracle Solaris 11 system.
4. Migrate the Oracle Solaris 10 archive into a `solaris10` brand non-global zone on an Oracle Solaris 11 system.

You can also migrate an Oracle Solaris 10 non-global zone into a `solaris10` brand non-global zone using the virtual-to-virtual (V2V) function in Oracle Solaris 11.

The process of migrating an Oracle Solaris 10 system to a `solaris10` brand zone is covered in Chapter 6, "Administering Zones."

Changing an Oracle Solaris Instance

The Live Media and text installers create an Oracle Solaris instance, also referred to as a "boot environment." The installation process created a boot environment in a global zone. Boot environments are described in Chapter 2, and global and non-global zones are described in Chapter 6.

During the installation, several configuration parameters were specified for the instance. Oracle Solaris 11 introduces a new installation architecture where the installation and configuration have been separated. Oracle Solaris 11 uses the Service Management Facility (SMF) for system configuration, where the configuration of the system is specified as a set of configuration parameters provided in a file called the system configuration profile. The system configuration profile is an SMF profile.

The situation may occur in which you need to reconfigure an existing Oracle Solaris instance. For example, you may need to change the time zone, naming services, system identity, or network parameters. The `sysconfig` utility is the interface for unconfiguring and reconfiguring the instance.

Note

The `sysconfig` command replaces the `sys-unconfig` command that was available in previous releases of Oracle Solaris.

Three operations can be performed using the `sysconfig` utility: configuration, unconfiguration, and profile creation. In addition, the command can be run in either of two modes: interactively or noninteractively. This section will describe how to use the command in the interactive mode.

Reconfigure an Oracle Solaris Instance

To reconfigure an Oracle Solaris instance, you must be logged in as root and execute the `sysconfig configure` command as follows:

> **Caution**
>
> This command will unconfigure your system. It will reset the system name, time zone, user and root accounts, and network configuration.

```
# sysconfig configure<cr>
```

The system will respond with

```
This program will re-configure your system.
Do you want to continue (y/[n])?y<cr>
```

Enter "y" to continue and the system responds with

```
Interactive configuration requested.
System Configuration Interactive (SCI) tool will be launched on console.
Since you are currently not logged on console,
you may not be able to navigate SCI tool.
Would you like to proceed with re-configuration (y/[n])? y<cr>
```

Enter "y" to continue, and the system will begin the System Configuration utility as shown in Figure 1-59.

Press the *F2* key to continue, and the Network screen will be displayed as shown in Figure 1-60.

The remaining screens presented by the system configuration utility are the same screens described in the earlier sections on using the interactive text installer. Refer to those sections for more details.

In the Network screen, you can choose to keep the default computer name, `solaris`, or change it. You can select how to configure the network connection: automatically, manually, or none (not at all). After making your selection, press *F2* to continue, and the following screens will be displayed in the order listed:

1. Time Zone, Regions
2. Time Zone, Locations
3. Time Zone
4. Date and Time
5. Users (set the root password and create a user account)
6. System Configuration Summary

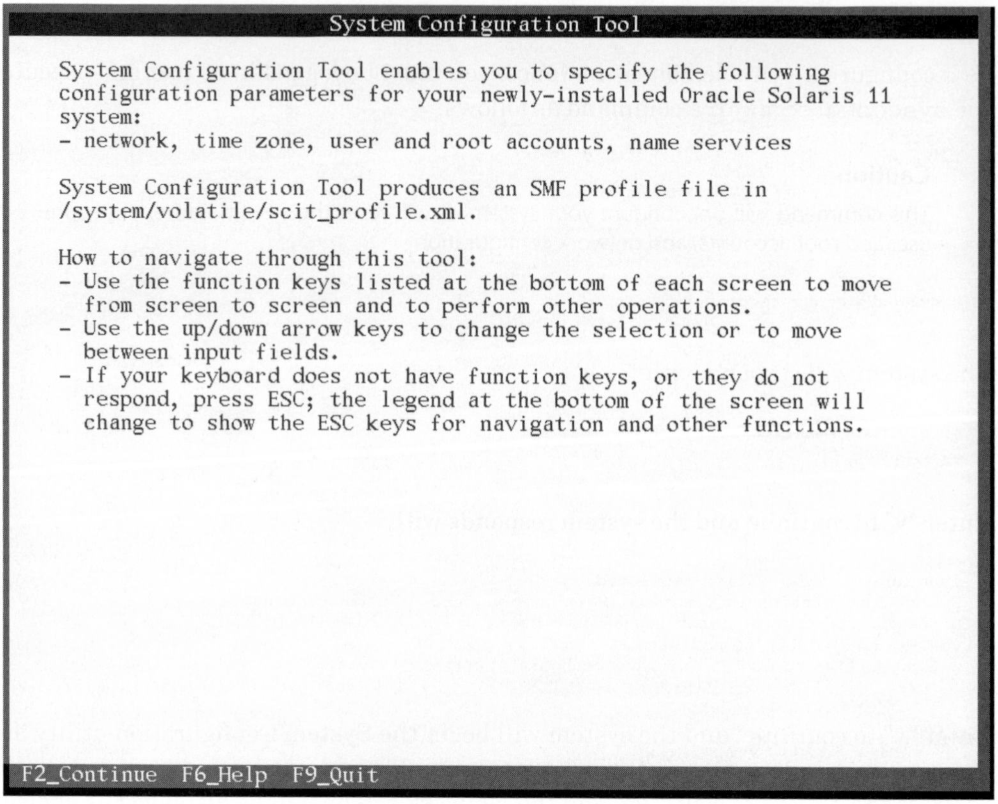

```
                      System Configuration Tool

  System Configuration Tool enables you to specify the following
  configuration parameters for your newly-installed Oracle Solaris 11
  system:
  - network, time zone, user and root accounts, name services

  System Configuration Tool produces an SMF profile file in
  /system/volatile/scit_profile.xml.

  How to navigate through this tool:
  - Use the function keys listed at the bottom of each screen to move
    from screen to screen and to perform other operations.
  - Use the up/down arrow keys to change the selection or to move
    between input fields.
  - If your keyboard does not have function keys, or they do not
    respond, press ESC; the legend at the bottom of the screen will
    change to show the ESC keys for navigation and other functions.

F2_Continue  F6_Help  F9_Quit
```

Figure 1-59 System Configuration Tool

```
                               Network

Enter a name for this computer that identifies it on the network. It must
be at least two characters. It can contain letters, numbers, and minus
signs (-).

Computer Name: solaris

Select how the wired ethernet network connection is configured.

  Automatically       Automatically configure the connection

  Manually            Enter the information on the following screen

  None                Do not configure the network at this time
```

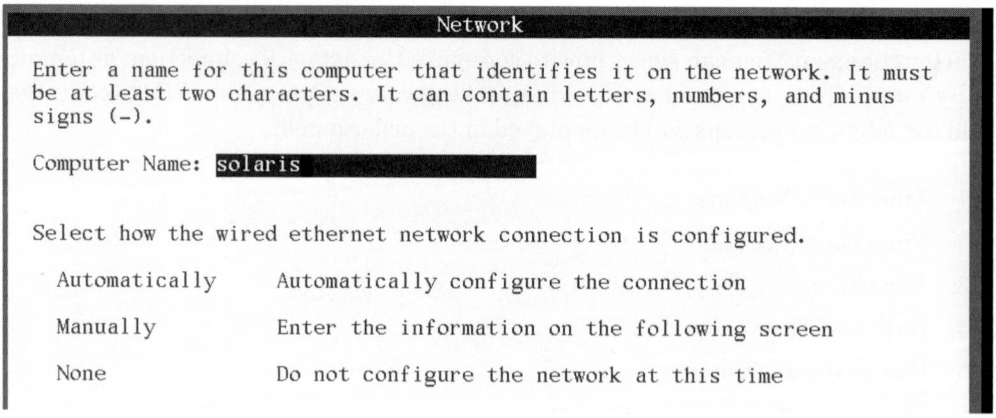

Figure 1-60 Network

Again, refer to the earlier sections on using the interactive text installers, where I described the information that is entered in each of these screens.

When the System Configuration Summary screen is presented, review the information and press *F2*. The system will exit the system configuration tool and boot back into the default run level. Any messages that were generated during the reconfiguration can be reviewed in the `/var/tmp/install/sysconfig.log` file.

During a reconfiguration, the system is transitioned through dedicated SMF milestones that allow the system configuration to be changed without the need to reboot. These transition milestones are as follows:

1. The first milestone (`svc:/milestone/unconfig:default`) takes care of the unconfiguration step where the existing configuration is removed. During this step, almost all SMF services are temporarily disabled, which ensures that the system is in a sane state after the unconfiguration is complete.
2. The next transition milestone (`svc:/milestone/config:default`) handles configuration, invoking the system configuration tool if an interactive configuration is required.
3. During the final phase, SMF services apply the new configuration to the system.

Use the `-c` option with the `sysconfig` command to specify an existing configuration profile. This XML file specifies a set of configuration parameters and provides the configuration specifications to the `sysconfig` command automatically. The following example specifies that the system is to be configured using an existing profile named `sysprofile.xml`:

```
# sysconfig configure -c sysprofile.xml<cr>
```

You can create a system configuration profile from the command line. This profile can be used to reconfigure a system in a noninteractive mode and is useful for cloning Oracle Solaris instances and for use with the AI. The `sysprofile.xml` profile can be generated from an existing Oracle Solaris system as follows:

```
# sysconfig create-profile -o sysprofile.xml<cr>
```

The file named `sysprofile.xml` is created in the current working directory. You can then modify this file and use it to configure another system, perhaps a clone. For example, I could use this profile during the configuration on another system by typing

```
# sysconfig configure -c ./sysprofile.xml<cr>
```

A sample profile is also available at this location: /usr/share/auto_install/sc_profiles/sc_sample.xml. The ability to generate a configuration profile simplifies cloning zones as well as providing templates for use with the AI. Configuration profiles are also described in Chapter 6.

Unconfigure an Oracle Solaris Instance

To unconfigure an Oracle Solaris instance, you must be logged in as root and execute the sysconfig unconfigure command as follows:

> **Caution**
>
> This command will unconfigure your system. It will reset the system identity, location, user and root accounts, network configuration, and kbd_layout.

```
# sysconfig unconfigure<cr>
```

The system will respond with

```
This program will unconfigure your system.
The system will be reverted to a "pristine" state.
It will not have a name or know about other systems or networks.
Do you want to continue (y/[n])? y<cr>
```

Enter "y" to continue and the system responds with

```
Exiting system configuration tool. Log is available at: /var/tmp/install/sysconfig.log
System is unconfigured.
Login as root user at the prompt for system maintenance.
To configure the system, reboot.
Requesting System Maintenance Mode
Enter user name for system maintenance (control-d to bypass):
```

The system is now in an unconfigured state. It no longer has a hostname, time zone, or network configured. To configure the system, log in as root and reboot the system. After the system has rebooted, log in and the system will automatically start the system configuration tool as described in the previous section.

Alternately, you can instruct the system to reboot automatically after unconfiguring the system by typing

```
# sysconfig unconfigure -s<cr>
```

The `-s` option shuts down the system after the configuration process is finished. This is useful when the system will be migrated and configured in a new environment. Without the `-s` option, the configuration and reconfiguration take place immediately.

Updating the OS

Oracle Solaris 11 utilizes the IPS framework to simplify software maintenance. In previous releases of Oracle Solaris, individual software packages were patched, and patching was a complex manual process.

IPS packaging is the default packaging technique used in Oracle Solaris 11. IPS is a comprehensive software delivery framework that addresses software installation, software updates, system upgrades, and the removal of software packages. Furthermore, IPS eliminates the need for patching. With a single IPS command, you will be able to update your system to a new OS release. IPS is described in more detail in Chapter 2.

Summary

This chapter described how to prepare for and install the Oracle Solaris operating environment on a SPARC or x86-based system. You have learned how to install the Oracle Solaris 11 operating environment using the Live Media and text installers. Whereas the Live Media provides a more automated installation, the text installer provides a more interactive interface and provides for more customization.

Now that you understand how to install the Oracle Solaris operating environment, the next chapter will describe how to use the IPS to add, update, and manage software packages and boot environments.

2

Managing and Updating Software with IPS

The IPS is a new software delivery system used in the Oracle Solaris 11 OS. Previous versions of Oracle Solaris used the SVR4 software packaging model, but in order to accommodate the new technologies such as Oracle Solaris zones, the ZFS file system, and the SMF, a new software delivery system was implemented.

The design goals with IPS are

- Minimize planned downtime by making software updates possible while systems are in production.
- Automate the installation of new software or updates to existing software.
- Resolve space restrictions with distribution media. DVDs no longer have enough space to hold all of the distribution media.
- Provide a reliable and secure method of verifying that a package is correctly installed as defined by the publisher of that package.
- Facilitate the virtualization of zones.
- Provide a mechanism for third-party software publishers to create and publish Oracle Solaris packages.
- Provide a mechanism that allows users to create their own software packages.
- Leverage ZFS snapshots, cloning, and boot environments (BEs) to minimize downtime and provide a failback mechanism for software installation and upgrades.

IPS is the framework that you will use in Oracle Solaris 11 to

- Create and manage Oracle Solaris images.
- Search and list the software packages installed on your system.
- Search for new software packages.
- Copy, mirror, create, and administer package repositories.
- Create and publish packages to a package repository.
- Republish the content of an existing package.
- Install new software packages.
- Update and verify software packages.
- Remove software packages.

This chapter provides an introduction to IPS and describes the fundamentals of managing installed software packages.

Understanding IPS

IPS introduces new terms and concepts with which you need to become familiar. The following are terms that are used in the IPS environment.

Package

An IPS package is a collection of directories, files, links, drivers, groups, users, dependencies, and license information in a defined format. Every package will have a name and description. Each package name is represented by a Fault Management Resource Identifier (FMRI) consisting of a publisher, a name, and a version. For example, the following information pertains to the Secure Shell (`ssh`) package:

```
          Name: network/ssh
       Summary: SSH Client and utilities
   Description: Secure Shell protocol Client and associated Utilities
      Category: System/Security
         State: Installed
     Publisher: solaris
       Version: 0.5.11
 Build Release: 5.11
        Branch: 0.175.0.0.0.2.1
Packaging Date: October 19, 2011 06:16:15 AM
          Size: 1010.84 kB
          FMRI: pkg://solaris/network/ssh@0.5.11,5.110.175.0.0.0.2.1:
                20111019T061615Z
```

FMRI

Package names are now FMRIs, similar to what has been used for SMF service names beginning with Oracle Solaris 10. FMRIs are used to identify both hardware and software resources. All package FMRIs include an indication of the FMRI scheme to which the package adheres.

Note

The SUNW prefix, which was used in previous versions of Oracle Solaris, is still seen in Oracle Solaris 11 because some software is still only available in the SVR4 format. The SUNW prefix will eventually be eliminated. Since Oracle Solaris is capable of executing binaries that are decades old, it shouldn't be surprising that some useful software may only be available in the old package format.

FMRI schemes exist for `svc`, `pkg`, `cpu`, `hc`, `dev`, and a number of others. In IPS, the FMRI includes descriptive information about the package. For example, the FMRI for the `ssh` package is

```
pkg://solaris/network/ssh@0.5.11,5.11-0.175.0.0.0.2.1:20111019T061615Z
```

The information contained in the FMRI is presented in this order:

- Scheme: `pkg`
- Publisher: `solaris`
- Category: `network`
- Package name: `ssh`
- Version (the package version has four parts):
  - Component version: `0.5.11`

    For OS components, this is usually the value of `uname -r` for that version of the OS.
  - Build version: `5.11`

    The build version must follow a comma (,). The build version specifies the version of the OS on which the contents of the package was built.
  - Branch version: `0.175.0.0.0.2.1`

    The branch version must follow a hyphen (-). The branch version provides vendor-specific information.
  - Time stamp (when the package was published): `20111019T061615Z`

    The time stamp is the time the package was published in ISO-8601 basic format: YYYYMMDDTHHMMSSZ.

Note

Whenever an FMRI name is preceded with `pkg://`, the FMRI name includes the publisher name. For example, `pkg://solaris/network/ssh@0.5.11,5.11-0.175.0.0.0.2.1:20111019T061615Z` specifies that the publisher is `solaris`. The package name may also be expressed as `network/ssh`, or simply `ssh` without the publisher name or version information. Review the `pkg(5)` manual (man) page for details.

Publisher

A publisher identifies a person or organization that provides the package. Publishers distribute packages using package repositories or package archives. In IPS, publishers can be configured into a preferred search order. When installing a package, if a package publisher is not specified, the first publisher in the search order is searched for that package. If the package is not found, the second publisher is searched and so on until the package is found or until all publishers have been searched.

Repository

A repository is the location to which packages are published and from which packages are retrieved. A depot server (`pkg.depotd`) is a collection of one or more package repositories. The depot server is run as a service on the system by `pkg.depotd(1m)` and is managed by SMF under the service `svc:/application/pkg/server`.

The path to a repository is specified by a URI. For example, the default Oracle Solaris repository is `http://pkg.oracle.com/solaris/release`. For `http://pkg.oracle.com/solaris/release`, the publisher is `solaris`. A repository contains packages from a single publisher, but a publisher can publish to multiple repositories.

The Oracle Solaris default repository is configured when you install or upgrade to the Oracle Solaris 11 release. The default Oracle Solaris repository is a network repository because it can only be accessed across the Internet from Oracle's server.

Every repository has an origin that contains both package metadata and package content (files). (Refer to the terms: "catalog" and "package manifest" for examples of package metadata.) A repository can also have one or more mirrors. The mirror is the location of a package repository that contains only package content.

The system administrator can create a private local package repository if your system does not have access to the Internet. It's beneficial to set up a local repository for the following reasons:

- Performance: A local package repository allows your systems to access software packages more quickly on a local network.
- Security: Your systems may not have access to the Internet.
- Replication: A local repository ensures that software versions and installations are consistent across your network of systems.

Whereas the default Oracle Solaris repository provides a complete archive of Oracle software packages, your local repository may contain packages that are specific to your organization, including third-party packages.

A repository has an origin and can also be mirrored. In the "Update the OS" section of this chapter, I describe how to configure a local repository.

Catalog

The catalog is a listing of all of the packages in a repository. The packages in a catalog are associated with a specific publisher.

Package Archive

A package archive is a file that contains publisher information and one or more packages provided by that publisher.

Package Manifest

A manifest describes the components and attributes that make up a package.

Mirror

A mirror provides a subset of the data that the origin provides. A mirror can only be used for downloading package files. The package metadata is downloaded from the origin. IPS clients access the origin to obtain a publisher's catalog when the client downloads package contents from a mirror.

Origin

An origin is a package repository that contains both package metadata and package content.

Search Index

A search index enables clients to search for packages in a repository.

Image

An image is a location where packages can be installed. For example, the Oracle Solaris instance that was installed using an installer in Chapter 1, "Installing Oracle Solaris 11," is an image.

BE

A BE is a bootable instance of an image. Think of a BE as a copy of the OS, but with ZFS file systems, a BE doesn't necessarily take up much disk space. A BE can be an exact duplicate of the OS, a different version of the OS, or a different configuration of the OS. It's not uncommon to maintain several BEs on a system.

If your system maintains more than one BE, when you boot the system, you have the option to select the BE from which to boot. You'll begin with one BE after initially installing the OS. Additional BEs will be created automatically as a result of package operations such as adding, updating, and removing software packages. New BEs can also be created on demand by the system administrator.

It's common for system administrators to create a backup BE before making changes to a system. By creating a backup BE, updating software becomes a low-risk operation. If something goes wrong during the update, you always have the option of booting to the backup BE.

Distribution Constructor

Associated with the IPS packaging model is the distribution constructor tool, which allows sites to create installation images, also called "golden images." The distribution constructor will build an ISO image (disc image). The distribution constructor can be used to create your own version of the Oracle Solaris Live Media or text installation image.

Package Lifecycle

Software packages go through various states that are collectively referred to as the "package lifecycle." Table 2-1 lists each state of the package lifecycle.

Package Dependencies

Dependencies define how packages are related. In IPS, a package cannot be installed unless all package dependencies are satisfied. Table 2-2 is a list of dependencies.

Consolidation

A collection of source files and the resulting binaries are built together as a group.

Table 2-1 States of the Package Lifecycle

State	Description
Creation	Packages can be created by anybody.
Publication	Packages are published to an IPS repository.
Installation	Packages can be installed on the system from a repository or from a package archive.
Updates	Updates are published to an IPS repository or delivered as a new package archive. The updates are used to update packages installed in an image.
Renaming	A package can be renamed at any time.
Obsolescence	When a package reaches its end of life, any package upgraded to an obsolete version is automatically removed from the system.
Removal	A package can be removed from the system if no other packages have dependencies on it.

Table 2-2 Package Dependencies

Dependency	Description
Require	A package requires the installation of another package to satisfy a functional requirement before it can be installed.
Require-any	If more than one package will satisfy a functional requirement, IPS will pick one of the packages to install (if the dependency is not already satisfied).
Optional	The optional dependency is similar to the require dependency except that the specified package may or may not be installed.
Conditional	The conditional dependency is similar to the require dependency. It specifies the require dependency if a particular condition is present during the installation.
Group	The group dependency is used to construct groups of packages.
Origin	The origin dependency is used to resolve package upgrade issues.
Parent	The parent dependency is used for zones or other child images.
Incorporate	The incorporate dependency is used to ensure that compatible versions of software are installed together. This dependency is heavily used in Oracle Solaris.
Exclude	The exclude dependency allows the containing package to preclude installation with the specified package at the specified version or higher.

Incorporation

Oracle Solaris is delivered by a set of packages with each group of packages constrained by an incorporation. Each incorporation roughly represents the organization that developed each group of packages. A sample of these incorporation packages includes

```
pkg:/consolidation/SunVTS/SunVTS-incorporation
pkg:/consolidation/X/X-incorporation
pkg:/consolidation/admin/admin-incorporation
pkg:/consolidation/cacao/cacao-incorporation
pkg:/consolidation/cde/cde-incorporation
pkg:/consolidation/desktop/desktop-incorporation
pkg:/consolidation/desktop/gnome-incorporation
```

Oracle includes a special incorporation called `entire`. The `entire` incorporation constrains all of the individual corporations together to the same build by including both `require` and `incorporate` dependencies on each incorporation package. The `entire` incorporation ensures that all packages of Oracle Solaris get upgraded as a single group or not at all.

Authority

An authority is a location containing one or more repositories, accessed via a URL.

Installing and Managing Packages

This chapter describes how to install and manage software packages using an existing repository. The chapter also describes how to manage repositories and BEs.

The system administrator has three options for creating and managing software packages:

- The command line interface. See Table 2-3 for a description of the commands.
- Two GUI options:
  - `packagemanager`
  - `updatemanager`

Because the command line provides the most flexibility, I will focus mainly on that option.

Table 2-3 Package Management Commands

IPS Command	Description
`pkg install`	Install a package (if not installed) and update packages that are already installed.
`pkg list`	Display the package state and version information.
`pkg verify`	Validate installation of packages in the current image.
`pkg info`	Display package information in a human-readable form.
`pkg contents`	Display the contents (action attributes) of a package.
`pkg search`	Search a repository for a package.
`pkg uninstall`	Remove installed packages.
`pkg update`	Update installed packages.
`pkg fix`	Fix package installation errors reported by the `pkg verify` command.
`pkg revert`	Restore a package to its "as delivered" condition.
`pkg publisher`	Display the current package publishers.
`pkg history`	View all package operations that have been performed on an image.

Package Management Commands (Command Line)

The `pkg` facility is the IPS retrieval client. `pkg` is used with its subcommands to install, list, verify, search, and update software packages from the command line. The fundamental `pkg` subcommands are listed in Table 2-3.

IPS replaces the SVR4 packaging model used in previous versions of Oracle Solaris. The older SVR4 model used the `pkgadd, pkginfo, pkgchk, and pkgrm` commands to manage software packages. These commands still exist in Oracle Solaris 11 but are only used to manage legacy SVR4 packages and have been replaced by the commands listed in Table 2-3.

The following sections will describe how to use the commands listed in Table 2-3 to manage the software on your Oracle Solaris image.

List Package Install State

Use the `pkg list` command to display package install state information. The command will tell you whether a package is installed in the current image and whether an update is available. The syntax for the `pkg list` command is as follows:

```
pkg list [-Hafnsuv] [-g path_or_uri . . . ] [--no-refresh] [pkg_fmri_pattern . . . ]
```

Descriptions of the more common options that can be used with the `list` subcommand are as follows:

- `-H` Omit the headers in the output.
- `-a` List the installed packages and the newest version of packages that are available for the package specified.
- `-f` List all versions of all packages for all variants regardless of incorporation constraints or installed state. May only be used with the `-a` option.
- `-g` Use the specified package repository or archive as the source of package data for the operation. This option can be specified multiple times. The use of `-g` implies `-a` if `-n` is not specified.
- `-n` Display the newest versions of all known packages, regardless of installed state.
- `-u` List only packages with newer versions available. This option cannot be used with `-g`.
- `-v` Show full package FMRIs, including publisher and complete version, all in the first column (the VERSION column disappears). This option can be used with `-a`, `-n`, or `-u`.

The information displayed using the `list` subcommand includes the package name, version, and state. For example, to list information about the `gzip` package, type

```
# pkg list gzip<cr>
```

The system displays the following information:

```
NAME (PUBLISHER)              VERSION                                   IFO
compress/gzip                 1.3.5-0.175.0.0.0.2.537                   i--
```

The package state information is displayed in the last column under the IFO header. The package state is represented by the following set of flags, which are as follows:

- `i` In the first position (under the I header), shows that the package is installed.
- `f` In the second position (under the F header), shows that the package is frozen.
- `o` In the third position (under the O header), shows that the package is obsolete.
- `r` In the third position (under the R header), shows that the package has been renamed.

Help Option to Display pkg Command Usage

Use the `-?` or `--help` option with the `pkg` command or any of the `pkg` subcommands as follows:

`pkg -?` Displays all of the `pkg` subcommands that can be used

`pkg list --help` Displays the command syntax and options for the `list` subcommand

You can also use the `-v` option to display the full `pkg` FMRI as follows:

```
# pkg list -v compress/gzip<cr>
FMRI                                                                      IFO
pkg://solaris/compress/gzip@1.3.5,5.11-0.175.0.0.0.2.537:20111019T091246Z i--
```

In the previous example, the system shows the "`i`" flag, which indicates that the `gzip` package is installed. It also shows that the `gzip` package is part of the category named `compress`. To see all of the packages that make up the `compress` category, type

```
# pkg list compress/*<cr>
NAME (PUBLISHER)                       VERSION                        IFO
compress/bzip2                         1.0.6-0.175.0.0.0.2.537        i--
compress/gzip                          1.3.5-0.175.0.0.0.2.537        i--
compress/p7zip                         9.20.1-0.175.0.0.0.2.537       i--
compress/unzip                         6.0-0.175.0.0.0.2.537          i--
compress/xz                            6.0-0.175.0.0.0.2.537          i--
compress/zip                           3.0-0.175.0.0.0.2.537          i--
```

All of the compression packages are displayed, and the state indicates that they are installed.

When using the `pkg list` command with no options, the command will list all packages that are installed in the current image as follows:

```
# pkg list|more<cr>
NAME (PUBLISHER)                       VERSION                        IFO
SUNWcs                                 0.5.11-0.170                   i-r
archiver/gnu-tar                       1.26-0.173.0.0.0.0.487         i--
audio/audio-utilities                  0.5.11-0.173.0.0.0.0.17656     i--
benchmark/x11perf                      1.5.4-0.173.0.0.0.0.1190       i--
codec/flac                             1.2.1-0.173.0.0.0.0.0          i--
codec/libtheora                        1.1.1-0.173.0.0.0.0.0          i--
codec/ogg-vorbis                       2.30.0-0.173.0.0.0.0.0         i--
codec/speex                            1.2-0.173.0.0.0.0.0            i--
     <output has been truncated>
```

I can narrow the results by providing either a package category or name. For example, to list an installed package named `pkg`, type

```
# pkg list pkg<cr>
NAME (PUBLISHER)                          VERSION                          IFO
package/pkg                               0.5.11-0.173                     i--
```

To list all installed packages that have the category `pkg` in the FMRI, use the asterisk (*) as a wildcard in the package name as follows:

```
# pkg list *pkg*<cr>
NAME (PUBLISHER)                          VERSION                          IFO
package/pkg                               0.5.11-0.173                     i--
package/pkg/package-manager               0.5.11-0.173                     i--
package/pkg/system-repository             0.5.11-0.173                     i--
package/pkg/update-manager                0.5.11-0.173                     i--
package/pkg/zones-proxy                   0.5.11-0.173                     i--
```

Specify the `-f` option to list all packages, including packages that cannot be installed in this image because of version constraints. The `-f` option can only be used in combination with the `-a` option as follows:

```
# pkg list -af pkg<cr>
NAME (PUBLISHER)                          VERSION                          IFO
package/pkg                               0.5.11-0.175.0.0.0.2.2576        ---
package/pkg                               0.5.11-0.173                     i--
package/pkg                               0.5.11-0.151.0.1.13              ---
package/pkg                               0.5.11-0.151.0.1                 ---
package/pkg                               0.5.11-0.134.0.2                 ---
```

The results show five versions of `package/pkg` available from the publisher. Version 0.173 is currently installed, but a newer version, 0.175.0.0.0.2.2576, is available. I cannot install this newer version because my entire image is constrained by the "`entire`" incorporation, which I will explain later in this chapter.

When listing a package that is not installed, the following message will be displayed:

```
# pkg list gzip<cr>
pkg list: no packages matching 'gzip' installed
```

Use the `-u` option to list all packages in the image `that` have newer versions available from the publisher:

```
# pkg list -u<cr>
NAME (PUBLISHER)                          VERSION                          IFO
archiver/gnu-tar                          1.26-0.173.0.0.0.0.487           i--
audio/audio-utilities                     0.5.11-0.173.0.0.0.0.17656       i--
benchmark/x11perf                         1.5.4-0.173.0.0.0.0.1190         i--
codec/flac                                1.2.1-0.173.0.0.0.0.0            i--
codec/libtheora                           1.1.1-0.173.0.0.0.0.0            i--
codec/ogg-vorbis                          2.30.0-0.173.0.0.0.0.0           i--
```

Notice that the `archiver/gnu-tar` package is listed.

Next, use the `-af` option to show the updates that are available for the `archiver/gnu-tar` package:

```
# pkg list -af gnu-tar<cr>
NAME (PUBLISHER)                    VERSION                         IFO
archiver/gnu-tar                    1.26-0.175.0.0.0.2.537          ---
archiver/gnu-tar                    1.26-0.173.0.0.0.0.487          i--
archiver/gnu-tar                    1.23-0.151.0.1                  ---
```

Three different versions (updates) are available. Use the `-n` option to display only the newest version of the package as follows:

```
# pkg list -n gnu-tar<cr>
NAME (PUBLISHER)                    VERSION                         IFO
archiver/gnu-tar                    1.26-0.175.0.0.0.2.537          ---
```

Packages can be packaged together into groups. These group packages, or meta-clusters, define lists of IPS packages that will be installed from the publisher. For example, when the text installer is used to install the OS, it installs the `solaris-large-server` group package by default. This is why the GNOME desktop is not installed; the GNOME desktop is part of the `solaris-desktop` group.

To list which package group is currently installed on your system, use the `pkg list` command as follows:

```
# pkg list -a group/*<cr>
NAME (PUBLISHER)                          VERSION                         IFO
group/feature/amp                         0.5.11-0.175.0.0.0.2.2576       ---
group/feature/developer-gnu               0.5.11-0.175.0.0.0.2.2576       ---
group/feature/multi-user-desktop          0.5.11-0.175.0.0.0.2.2576       ---
group/feature/storage-avs                 0.5.11-0.175.0.0.0.2.1          ---
group/feature/storage-nas                 0.5.11-0.175.0.0.0.2.1          ---
group/feature/storage-server              0.5.11-0.175.0.0.0.2.1          ---
group/feature/trusted-desktop             0.5.11-0.175.0.0.0.2.2576       ---
group/system/solaris-auto-install         0.5.11-0.175.0.0.0.2.2576       ---
group/system/solaris-desktop              0.5.11-0.175.0.0.0.2.2576       i--
group/system/solaris-large-server         0.5.11-0.175.0.0.0.2.2576       ---
group/system/solaris-small-server         0.5.11-0.175.0.0.0.2.2576       ---
```

The information displayed indicates that the `group/system/solaris-desktop` is installed as indicated by the `i` in the IFO column. The command was run on a system that was installed using the Live Media installer, and this package group was installed by default. This system has access to a publisher from which all of the software packages are available. The software groups listed are available from the publisher and are installable in this image.

Compare the output from the previous example to a system that was installed using the text installer:

```
# pkg list -a group/*<cr>
NAME (PUBLISHER)                              VERSION                          IFO
group/feature/amp                             0.5.11-0.175.0.0.0.2.2576        ---
group/feature/developer-gnu                   0.5.11-0.175.0.0.0.2.2576        ---
group/feature/multi-user-desktop              0.5.11-0.175.0.0.0.2.2576        ---
group/feature/storage-avs                     0.5.11-0.175.0.0.0.2.1           ---
group/feature/storage-nas                     0.5.11-0.175.0.0.0.2.1           ---
group/feature/storage-server                  0.5.11-0.175.0.0.0.2.1           ---
group/feature/trusted-desktop                 0.5.11-0.175.0.0.0.2.2576        ---
group/system/solaris-auto-install             0.5.11-0.175.0.0.0.2.2576        ---
group/system/solaris-desktop                  0.5.11-0.175.0.0.0.2.2576        ---
group/system/solaris-large-server             0.5.11-0.175.0.0.0.2.2576        i--
group/system/solaris-small-server             0.5.11-0.175.0.0.0.2.2576        ---
```

The text installer does not install the GNOME desktop; it installs the `solaris-large-server` group of packages. The `solaris-small-server` group package is an alternative you can use to install a smaller set of packages on a server. Some of the tools installed by `solaris-large-server` that are not installed by `solaris-small-server` include the following:

- `make` command
- `top` command
- Some GNU utilities, including the GNU version of the `tar` command
- CD and DVD writing tools
- Dynamic reconfiguration

In the next section, I'll describe how to use the `pkg search` command to list the packages that make up the package groups.

Search for a Software Package

Use the `pkg search` command to search for software packages. You can either search for a package installed in the current image or search for the package in the configured publisher. The syntax for the `pkg info` command is as follows:

```
pkg search [-HIaflpr] [-o attribute, … ] [-s repo_uri] query
```

Descriptions of the options that can be used with the `search` subcommand are as follows:

`-H` Omit headers from the results.

`-I` Perform a case-sensitive search.

- `-o` Control the results with the specified attribute.
- `-p` Display packages that have some actions that match each query term.
- `-r` Search the repositories corresponding to the image's publishers.
- `-s` Search the `pkg` repository located at the given URI. The option can be specified multiple times. Package archives are not supported.
- `-l` Perform a local search. `-r` and `-s` can be specified with this option.

To search for a package named `gzip`, type

```
# pkg search gzip<cr>
```

The package is located in the installed image, and the command displays the following information:

```
INDEX          ACTION VALUE          PACKAGE
basename       dir                   usr/perl5/5.12/lib/IO/Compress/Gzip\
                                     pkg:/runtime/perl-512@5.12.3-0.175.0.0.0.2.537
basename       file                  usr/bin/gzip\
                                     pkg:/compress/gzip@1.3.5-0.175.0.0.0.2.537
pkg.fmri       set                   solaris/compress/gzip\
                                     pkg:/compress/gzip@1.3.5-0.175.0.0.0.2.537
```

The information indicates that the `gzip` ELF file is part of the package named `pkg:/compress/gzip`. If the package is not located in the installed image, the publishers are searched. By default, the currently installed or newer package version is displayed. If you use the `-f` option, all matched versions will be displayed. The output contains the following fields:

- `Index` The *Index* field contains the location in the data where the match was found.
- `Action` Also known as action attributes, this field specifies which kind of action matched the query. In the example, the action `set`, `file`, and `dir` matched the query.
- `Value` The *Value* field is the directory in which the match was found.
- `Package` The *Package* field contains the FMRI for the package that matched the query.

The *Action* field specifies a delivery unit; the data needed to create this software component. The action types are: `file`, `directory`, `link`, `user`, `group`, `driver`, `set`, `depend`, `license`, `legacy`, and `signature`. These action types are all defined in the `pkg(5)` man page.

In this example, I'll check to see whether the `wireshark` package is installed using `pkg list` as described earlier:

```
# pkg list wireshark<cr>
pkg list: no packages matching 'wireshark' installed
```

The system confirms that the `wireshark` package is not installed. Next, I'll use the `pkg search` command to check whether the package is available for installation from the package publisher. I'll use the `-p` option to restrict the results to package names only and not all of the other items in the package as follows:

```
# pkg search -p wireshark<cr>
PACKAGE                                                                 PUBLISHER
pkg:/diagnostic/wireshark/wireshark-common@1.8.2-0.175.1.0.0.24.0       solaris
pkg:/diagnostic/wireshark@1.8.2-0.175.1.0.0.24.0                        solaris
```

In this next example, I'll search the image for the installed package group `solaris-desktop` as follows:

```
# pkg search */solaris-desktop<cr>
INDEX        ACTION   VALUE                             PACKAGE

incorporate  depend   group/system/solaris-desktop@     pkg:/consolidation/solaris_re/
                      0.5.11-0\.175.1.0.0.24.3          solaris_re-incorporation@0.5.11-\
                                                        0.175.1.0.0.24.3

require      depend   group/system/solaris-desktop\     pkg:/slim_install@0.1-0.166

pkg.fmri     set      solaris/group/system/solaris-     pkg:/group/system/solaris-desktop
                      desktop                           @0.5.11-0.175.1.0.0.24.3
```

I'll use the `pkg search` command, with a wildcard, to display all of the packages that make up the `group/system/solaris-desktop` group. The `-o fmri` option limits the output to the FMRI name of the package group specified, and the `-H` eliminates the header. The query will return packages that are specified in the `solaris-desktop` package as group type dependencies:

```
# pkg search -o fmri -H '*/solaris-desktop:depend:group:'<cr>
FMRI
archiver/gnu-tar
audio/audio-utilities
codec/flac
codec/libtheora
codec/ogg-vorbis
codec/speex
communication/im/pidgin
  <output has been truncated>
```

Display Package Information

The `pkg info` command displays detailed information (metadata) about a package including the name, installed state, version, packaging date, package size, and the full FMRI. The syntax for the `pkg info` command is as follows:

```
/usr/bin/pkg info [-lr] [-g path_or_uri … ] [--license] [pkg_fmri_pattern … ]
```

Descriptions of the more common options that are used with the `info` subcommand are as follows:

- `-g` Use the specified package repository or archive as the source of package data for the operation. This option can be specified multiple times. Use of `-g` implies `-r`.
- `-l` Only display information for installed packages. This is the default.
- `-r` Match packages based on the newest available versions, retrieving information for packages not currently installed (if necessary) from the repositories of the image's configured publishers. At least one package must be specified when using this option. Without `-r`, only installed packages are displayed by default.

To view detailed information about the `gzip` package, do not specify any options and `-l` will be used by default as follows:

```
# pkg info gzip<cr>
          Name: compress/gzip
       Summary: GNU Zip (gzip)
   Description: The GNU Zip (gzip) compression utility
      Category: Applications/System Utilities
         State: Installed
     Publisher: solaris
       Version: 1.4
 Build Release: 5.11
        Branch: 0.175.1.0.0.24.0
Packaging Date: September 4, 2012 05:06:03 PM
          Size: 395.17 kB
          FMRI: pkg://solaris/compress/gzip@1.4,5.11-0.175.1.0.0.24.0:20120904T170603Z
```

Because the package was installed in this image, the package information is displayed. The information indicates that `solaris` is the publisher, and `compress/gzip` is the package name. We also see detailed information about the version, build release, and branch. This information is all described in the earlier section "FMRI."

If the package was not installed in this image, an error message would be displayed. For example, the `wireshark` package is not installed in this image. Therefore, when issuing issue the `pkg info` command as follows:

```
# pkg info wireshark<cr>
```

the following error message is displayed:

```
pkg: info: no packages matching the following patterns you specified are installed on
the system. Try specifying -r to query remotely: Use the -r option to display
information about a package that is not installed and the system will search the pkg
publisher as follows:
```

Now, use the `-r` option to query the `pkg` publisher for information about the `wireshark` package:

```
# pkg info -r wireshark<cr>
          Name: diagnostic/wireshark
       Summary: Graphical network protocol analyzer
      Category: Applications/Internet
         State: Not installed
     Publisher: solaris
       Version: 1.4.8
 Build Release: 5.11
        Branch: 0.175.0.0.0.2.537
Packaging Date: October 19, 2011 10:05:41 AM
          Size: 2.47 MB
          FMRI: pkg://solaris/diagnostic/wireshark@1.4.8,5.11-\
                0.175.0.0.0.2.537:20111019T100541Z
```

In this next example, I'll use the `info` subcommand with the `-r` option and a wildcard to display information about the `solaris-large-server` package group as follows:

```
# pkg info -r */solaris-large-server<cr>
          Name: group/system/solaris-large-server
       Summary: Oracle Solaris Large Server
   Description: Provides an Oracle Solaris large server environment
      Category: Meta Packages/Group Packages
         State: Installed
     Publisher: solaris
       Version: 0.5.11
 Build Release: 5.11
        Branch: 0.175.1.0.0.24.3
Packaging Date: September 19, 2012 06:53:18 PM
          Size: 5.46 kB
          FMRI: pkg://solaris/group/system/solaris-large-\
                server@0.5.11,5.11-0.175.1.0.0.24.3:20120919T185318Z
```

Earlier in the "Understanding IPS" section, I described an incorporation named `entire`, which represents all of the Oracle Solaris packages. The `entire` incorporation constrains all of the individual Oracle Solaris packages to the same build. To view information about this incorporation, type the following:

```
# pkg info entire<cr>
          Name: entire
       Summary: Incorporation to lock all system packages to the same build
   Description: This package constrains system package versions to the same build.
                WARNING: Proper system update and Correct package selection depend on
                the presence of this incorporation. Removing this package will result
                in an unsupported system.
      Category: Meta Packages/Incorporations
         State: Installed
     Publisher: solaris
       Version: 0.5.11
 Build Release: 5.11
        Branch: 0.175.1.0.0.24.2
Packaging Date: September 19, 2012 07:01:35 PM
          Size: 5.46 kB
          FMRI: pkg://solaris/entire@0.5.11,5.11-\
                0.175.1.0.0.24.2:20120919T190135Z
```

Because all OS packages are constrained by the `entire` incorporation, the information presented provides a good description of the build of the OS currently installed on your system.

Display the Contents of a Package

Use the `pkg contents` command to display the contents (action attributes) of a package. The action attributes, shown in the *Action* field, were described earlier in the "Search for a Software Package" section. Actions are also described in the `pkg(5)` man page. The syntax for the `pkg contents` command is as follows:

```
contents [-Hmr] [-a attribute=pattern … ] [-g path_or_uri … ] \
[-o attribute,… ] [-s sort_key] [-t action_type … ] [pkg_fmri_pattern … ]
```

Descriptions of the options that can be used with the `contents` subcommand are as follows:

- `-a` Limit the output to those actions that have an attribute named in the attribute argument.
- `-g` Display information for packages that could be installed in this image from the specified package repository or archive.
- `-m` Display all attributes of all actions in the specified packages, including actions that could not be installed in this image.

- `-o` Display the listed attributes sorted according to the values of the first attribute listed. This option can be specified multiple times.
- `-r` Display information for the newest available versions of packages that could be installed in this image from the repositories of the publishers configured in this image.
- `-s` Sort actions by the specified action attributes. If this option is not provided, the default is to sort by path or by the first attribute specified by the `-o` option.
- `-t` Only list actions of the type specified. Multiple types can be specified in a comma separated list.
- `-H` Omit the headers from the listing.

Whereas the `pkg search` command is used to return the names of packages that match a query, the `pkg contents` command returns the contents of a particular package. Therefore, the commands go hand in hand.

Note

It's common to use the `pkg contents` command to show the contents of a specified package and to use the `pkg search` command to show packages that match a query. If you know which package delivers the content in which you are interested, use the `pkg contents` command.

In the previous section, the information for the `wireshark` package was displayed as follows:

```
# pkg info -r wireshark<cr>
          Name: diagnostic/wireshark
       Summary: Graphical network protocol analyzer
      Category: Applications/Internet
         State: Not installed
     Publisher: solaris
       Version: 1.4.8
 Build Release: 5.11
        Branch: 0.175.0.0.0.2.537
Packaging Date: October 19, 2011 10:05:41 AM
          Size: 2.76 MB
          FMRI: pkg://solaris/diagnostic/wireshark@1.4.8,5.11-\
                0.175.0.0.0.2.537:20111019T100541Z
```

Use the `contents` subcommand to display the file system contents of the `wireshark` package as follows:

```
# pkg contents -r wireshark<cr>
```

The system displays all of the files making up the `wireshark` package:

```
PATH
etc
etc/security
etc/security/exec_attr.d
etc/security/exec_attr.d/diagnostic:wireshark
usr
usr/sbin
usr/sbin/wireshark
usr/share
usr/share/applications
usr/share/applications/wireshark.desktop
usr/share/man
usr/share/man/man1
usr/share/man/man1/wireshark.1
usr/share/pixmaps
usr/share/pixmaps/wireshark.png
```

Use the `contents` subcommand with the `-r`, `-o`, and `-t` options to display dependencies for a package as follows:

```
# pkg contents -r -o fmri -t depend wireshark<cr>
```

The `wireshark` package depends on the installation of these packages as well:

```
FMRI
pkg:/diagnostic/wireshark/wireshark-common@1.4.8-0.175.0.0.0.2.537
pkg:/library/desktop/gtk2@2.20.1-0.175.0.0.0.0.0
pkg:/library/desktop/pango@1.28.3-0.175.0.0.0.0.0
pkg:/library/glib2@2.28.6-0.175.0.0.0.0.0
pkg:/library/zlib@1.2.3-0.175.0.0.0.0.525
pkg:/system/library/libpcap@1.1.1-0.175.0.0.0.0.525
pkg:/system/library/math@0.5.11-0.174.0.0.0.0.0
pkg:/system/library@0.5.11-0.175.0.0.0.0.0
```

The `solaris-desktop` package was described earlier. Use the `contents` subcommand to display the set of packages that are included in each group that makes up `solaris-desktop`:

```
# pkg contents -o fmri -H -rt depend -a type=group solaris-desktop<cr>
archiver/gnu-tar
audio/audio-utilities
codec/flac
codec/libtheora
codec/ogg-vorbis
codec/speex
communication/im/pidgin
  <output has been truncated>
```

Install a Package

Use the pkg install command to install a software package from an IPS package repository. To install a software package, you must send a request from the client system to an IPS repository. IPS will look for the software package from the pkg publisher. When the software package is located, IPS performs a dependency check on each package by checking the manifest that is included with the package.

The manifest describes the components and attributes that make up the software package. IPS will locate all of the packages in the list of dependencies, download these packages along with the package that you requested, and install them.

Before you attempt to install a software package, you should first make sure that you have access to the package repository and that the repository contains the package that you want to install. Issue the pkg publisher command to list the preferred publisher and the location of the repository for a particular image. If there is more than a single publisher, they will all be listed along with their origin URIs in order of search preference. When you install a new package, the preferred publisher will be the first repository that is searched. If the package is not found in the preferred publisher's repository, the additional repositories will be searched in their listed order.

In the following example, I list the publishers that are available for this image:

```
# pkg publisher<cr>
PUBLISHER        TYPE         STATUS       URI
solaris          origin       online       http://pkg.oracle.com/solaris/release/
```

The system lists a single publisher.

Note

The Oracle Solaris 11 system has only one publisher configured: the solaris publisher. The system can be configured to support multiple publishers.

When there are multiple publishers, they will all be listed with the pkg publisher command as follows:

```
# pkg publisher<cr>
PUBLISHER        TYPE         STATUS       URI
solaris          origin       online       file:///repo/Solaris11/repo/
solaris          origin       online       http://pkg.oracle.com/solaris/release/
```

Two publishers are listed in the order in which they are searched. The same publisher, solaris, has published to two different repositories. They can both contain identical packages or each can contain different versions of the same package. When I install a package, if I do not specify the publisher as part of the package FMRI, the publishers will be searched in the order listed until the package is located. The publisher search order can be modified using the -g option with the pkg install command as described later in this section.

When installing a software package, by default, the newest version of the package that is compatible with the rest of the image is installed from the preferred publisher. If the package is already installed, the package is updated by installing the newest version of the package that is compatible with the rest of the image using the publisher that provided the currently installed version.

If you have more than one publisher configured, you can control which publisher provides a package by setting publisher stickiness and search order or by specifying the publisher in the package FMRI. Publisher stickiness controls whether a package installed by one publisher can be updated from another publisher. You can also specify the version you want to install in the package FMRI.

The syntax for the pkg install command is as follows:

```
/usr/bin/pkg install [-nvq] [-g path_or_uri … ] [--accept] [--licenses] [--no-be-activate]
[--no-index] [--no-refresh] [--no-backup-be | --require-backup-be] [--backup-be-name name]
[--deny-new-be | --require-new-be] [--be-name name] [--reject pkg_fmri_pattern … ]
pkg_fmri_pattern …
```

Descriptions of the options that can be used with the install subcommand are as follows:

-g	Temporarily add the specified package repository or archive to the list of sources and image from which to retrieve package data. If the specified package repositories are available, the client will retrieve content for those packages from the specified sources only. When deciding which version of a package to use, package repositories configured in the image—but not specified as a source with -g—take precedence. When a package is installed or updated using the -g option, any packages provided by the repository not found in the image are added to the image configuration without an origin.
-n	Perform a trial "dry run" of the operation with no package changes made.
-q	Initiate quiet mode. Hide progress messages during the operation.
-v	Initiate verbose mode. Show verbose progress messages during the requested operation.
--accept	Indicate that you agree to and accept the terms of the licenses of the packages that are updated or installed.

`--licenses`	Display all of the licenses for the packages that are installed or updated.
`--no-index`	Do not update the search indexes after the operation is completed successfully.
`--no-refresh`	Do not attempt to contact the repositories for the image's publishers to retrieve the newest list of available packages and other metadata.
`--reject`	Prevent packages with names matching the given pattern from being installed. If matching packages are already installed, they are removed as part of this operation. Rejected packages that are the target of group dependencies are placed on the avoid list.

The following options pertain to BEs, which are described later in this section.

`--no-backup`	Do not create a backup BE.
`--no-be-activate`	If a BE is created, do not set it as the active BE on the next boot.
`--backup-be-name`	Name the created backup BE using the given argument.
`--be-name`	Rename the newly created a BE using the given argument.
`--require-backup-be`	Always create a BE if a new BE would not other-wise be created. Without this option, a backup BE is created based on the image policy.
`--require-new-be`	Always create a new BE. Without this option, a backup BE is created based on the image policy.
`--deny-new-ne`	Do not create a new BE. This operation is not performed if a new BE is required.

The best practice is to use the `-nv` options to perform a dry-run installation. This allows you to review the effects of the command without actually installing the package. For example, the following command shows the installation information for installing the `distribution-constructor` package without actually installing the package:

```
# pkg install -nv distribution-constructor<cr>
           Packages to install:         3
     Estimated space available:   2.17 GB
Estimated space to be consumed:  16.44 MB
       Create boot environment:        No
Create backup boot environment:        No
          Rebuild boot archive:        No

Changed packages:
solaris
```

```
  install/distribution-constructor
    None -> 0.5.11,5.11-0.175.0.0.0.2.1482:20111019T122622Z
  service/storage/media-volume-manager
    None -> 0.5.11,5.11-0.173.0.0.0.1.0:20110826T161917Z
  system/extended-system-utilities
  None -> 0.5.11,5.11-0.170:20110719T015321Z
```

A few things to note from the output of the previous command:

- Three packages need to be installed.
- The `distribution-constructor` package requires 16.44MB of space for installation.
- The package policy does not require a BE to be created.
- The package policy does not require a backup BE to be created.
- The package policy does not require the boot archive to be rebuilt.
- A list of packages would be changed if this package is installed.

In the next example, I will install the `distribution-constructor` package from the preferred publisher (`solaris`) using the `pkg install` command as follows:

```
# pkg install distribution-constructor<cr>
Creating Plan /
           Packages to install:   3
       Create boot environment:  No
Create backup boot environment:  No

DOWNLOAD                              PKGS     FILES     XFER (MB)
Completed                              3/3     65/65       0.2/0.2

PHASE                                        ACTIONS
Install Phase                                127/127

PHASE                                          ITEMS
Package State Update Phase                       3/3
Image State Update Phase                         2/2
```

Just because a package is available in a package repository does not mean that the package can be installed in the image. Incorporation and package group constraints determine whether a package is installable in an image. Use the `pkg list` command described earlier to display packages that are installable as follows:

```
# pkg list -a distribution-constructor<cr>
NAME (PUBLISHER)                       VERSION                          IFO
install/distribution-constructor       0.5.11-0.175.0.0.0.2.1482        ---
```

The output indicates that the package is not currently installed, but because it was listed with no errors, it could be installed in this image.

If the package is not installable, a message would be displayed as shown in the next example:

```
# pkg list -a wireshark<cr>
pkg list: no packages matching 'wireshark' allowed by installed incorporations, or
image variants that are known or installed
Use -af to allow all versions.
```

In the previous example, the `wireshark` package cannot be installed. By using the `-f` option, I can force the display of all available packages as follows:

```
# pkg list -af wireshark<cr>
NAME (PUBLISHER)                          VERSION                            IFO
diagnostic/wireshark                      1.4.8-0.175.0.0.0.2.537            ---
diagnostic/wireshark                      1.2.10-0.151.0.1                   ---
```

The information indicates that two versions of the `wireshark` package are available: one for build 175 and one for build 151. The installation of these packages is being denied because the "entire" incorporation is at build 173 as shown:

```
# pkg list entire<cr>
NAME (PUBLISHER)                          VERSION                            IFO
entire                                    0.5.11-0.173                       i–
```

The `entire` incorporation constrains all of the individual corporations together to the same build on each incorporation package. The `entire` incorporation ensures that all packages of Oracle Solaris get upgraded as a single group or not at all.

Verify a Package

Use the `pkg verify` command to validate the installation of packages in the current image. For example, to verify the `gzip` pkg, type

```
# pkg verify gzip<cr>
```

If there are no problems, the system will return to the command prompt. If a file was tampered with, you will receive a message. In the next example, it was determined that the `gzcmp` file was missing:

```
# pkg verify gzip<cr>
PACKAGE                                        STATUS
pkg://solaris/compress/gzip                    ERROR
                                               file: usr/bin/gzcmp
                                                    Missing: regular file does not exist
```

To fix the problem, type

```
# pkg fix gzip<cr>
Verifying: pkg://solaris/compress/gzip        ERROR
Created ZFS snapshot: 2012-11-27-22:44:42     file: usr/bin/gzcmp
Repairing: pkg://solaris/compress/gzip               Missing: regular file does not exist
Creating Plan (Evaluating mediators): \

DOWNLOAD                                    PKGS        FILES    XFER (MB)    SPEED
Completed                                    1/1          1/1      0.0/0.0   2.8k/s

PHASE                                          ITEMS
Updating modified actions                        1/1
Updating image state                            Done
Creating fast lookup database                   Done
```

Update a Package

Use the `pkg update` or `pkg install` command to update an installed software package to the newest version to be compatible with the rest of the image from the publisher that provided the current installed version. Although both subcommands `update` and `install` will perform an update, the best practice is to use the `pkg update` command to update packages. This will prevent unintentional installation of a package that was not already installed.

The syntax for the `pkg update` command is as follows:

```
/usr/bin/pkg update [-fnvq] [-g path_or_uri …] [--accept] [--licenses] \
[--no-index] [--no-refresh] [--no-be-activate] [--no-backup-be | \
--require-backup-be] [--backup-be-name name] [--deny-new-be | --require-new-be] \
[--be-name name] [--reject pkg_fmri_pattern …] [pkg_fmri_pattern …]
```

Refer to the description of options for the `pkg install` command.

To check whether an update is available, use the `pkg update` command with the `-nv` options to list updates, but not install them. You must have access to a publisher repository providing package updates.

For this example, the system is running Oracle Solaris 11, Build 175, as shown with the following `pkg list` command:

```
# pkg list entire<cr>
NAME (PUBLISHER)                            VERSION                         IFO
entire                                      0.5.11-0.175.0.0.0.2.0          i--
```

For the update, I downloaded the SRU ISO image for Oracle Solaris 11 from Oracle's Web site. This ISO image contains the IPS packages that have been added or changed since the initial release of Oracle Solaris 11 build 175. At the time of this writing, Oracle was publishing these SRU images approximately every 30 days. You must have an active Oracle support plan to have access to the support package repository so that you can routinely update your Oracle Solaris 11 systems. These SRUs take the place of maintenance updates or patch bundles that are available for Oracle Solaris 10 and earlier releases.

The system has two repositories. The `pkg publisher` command displays both publishers' repositories as follows:

```
# pkg publisher<cr>
PUBLISHER         TYPE            STATUS          URI
solaris           origin          online          file:///SRU/repo/
solaris           origin          online          http://pkg.oracle.com/solaris/release/
```

I describe how to download an SRU and make it available as a local repository in the "Update the OS" section later in this chapter.

Issue the `pkg update` command to list any available updates. Use the `-nv` option to perform a dry-run installation in verbose mode:

Caution

It's important to use the `-n` option to perform the update in trial mode and not to actually install the updates. This allows you to review the effects of the command and view the updates that will be installed without actually updating the package. The `-v` option will provide a complete listing of the packages that will be updated along with the BE policy.

```
# pkg update -nv<cr>
            Packages to update:        27
     Estimated space available:   2.15 GB
Estimated space to be consumed: 482.29 MB
       Create boot environment:       Yes
     Activate boot environment:       Yes
Create backup boot environment:        No
          Rebuild boot archive:       Yes

Changed packages:
solaris
  consolidation/SunVTS/SunVTS-incorporation
    0.5.11,5.11-0.172.0.0.0.0.0:20110816T071310Z ->
0.5.11,5.11-0.175.0.1.0.4.0:20111108T154138Z
  consolidation/desktop/desktop-incorporation
    0.5.11,5.11-0.175.0.0.0.2.0:20111019T132128Z -
0.5.11,5.11-0.175.0.2.0.2.0:20111118T053231Z
  consolidation/desktop/gnome-incorporation
  <27 packages are listed…output has been truncated>
```

The information displays each package to be updated, its current version, and the version to which it will be updated. For example:

consolidation/SunVTS/SunVTS-incorporation is currently at version: 0.5.11,5.11-0.172.0.0.0.0.0:20110816T071310Z and will be upgraded to version: 0.5.11,5.11-0.175.0.1.0.4.0:20111108T154138Z.

When an image has more than one publisher enabled, you can control which publisher provides the package by setting publisher stickiness and search order or by specifying the publisher in the package FMRI.

By specifying the package FMRI, you can specify the version you want to install. You can even specify a package version older than the version that is currently installed to perform an in-place downgrade.

When there is more than one publisher, specify which publisher will provide the update by specifying the -g option. For example, earlier I showed a system with two publishers:

```
solaris         origin        online        file:///SRU/repo/
solaris         origin        online        http://pkg.oracle.com/solaris/release/
```

Both publishers are named solaris, so when updating a package, the publishers will be searched in the order they are listed.

To apply an update to a specific package, specify that package FMRI with the pkg update command. For example, to update the wireshark package, type

```
# pkg update -nv *wireshark@latest<cr>
```

I used the latest keyword after the @ sign to explicitly request the latest version of the package. The system responds with the following message:

```
pkg update: No matching version of diagnostic/wireshark can be installed:
  Reject: pkg://solaris/diagnostic/wireshark@1.4.10,5.11-0.175.0.2.0.2.0:20111118T053353Z
  Reason: This version is excluded by installed incorporation pkg://solaris/
consolidation/userland/userland-incorporation@0.5.11,5.11-
0.175.0.0.0.2.537:20111019T091357Z
```

The package cannot be updated because it is constrained by the userland-incorporation. In other words, the userland-incorporation needs to be updated, and this will in turn update the wireshark package.

To update the entire image to the current SRU, I will issue the following command:

```
# pkg update<cr>
```

The following message is displayed during the update:

```
            Packages to update:  29
       Create boot environment: Yes
Create backup boot environment:  No
DOWNLOAD                                  PKGS         FILES    XFER (MB)
Completed                                29/29     2259/2259  102.9/102.9

PHASE                                        ACTIONS
Removal Phase                                317/317
Install Phase                                283/283
Update Phase                               2945/2945

PHASE                                          ITEMS
Package State Update Phase                     58/58
Package Cache Update Phase                     29/29
Image State Update Phase                         2/2

PHASE                                          ITEMS
Reading Existing Index                           8/8
Indexing Packages                              29/29
Optimizing Index...

PHASE                                          ITEMS
Indexing Packages                            806/806
```

When the update completes, the following message is displayed:

```
A clone of newBE exists and has been updated and activated.
On the next boot the Boot Environment newBE-1 will be
mounted on '/'. Reboot when ready to switch to this updated BE.

---------------------------------------------------------------------------
NOTE: Please review release notes posted at:

http://www.oracle.com/pls/topic/lookup?ctx=E23824&id=SERNS
```

When you reboot the system, the system will boot to the new BE and start using the new image. If the system does not function as expected, reboot the system to the previous BE. Refer to the section titled "BEs" later in this chapter for more information on managing BEs.

Package Manager

If your system has a bitmap display, you can use the Package Manager GUI to install and manage software packages on your system. You can access the Package Manager from the menu bar on the desktop of the Oracle Solaris OS as shown in Figure 2-1.

The Package Manager does not provide the full range of options for managing your system; the full range of options is only available from the command line. In addition, there are many times when you may not have access to a bitmap display and must manage software packages from the command line. Therefore, I recommend the use of the command line over the Package Manager GUI.

Figure 2-1 Package Manager GUI

BEs

A BE is a bootable instance of the OS image. System administrators can maintain multiple BEs on their systems, and each BE can contain a different version or configuration of the OS. When booting, you have the option to select and boot into any of the BEs that are available on the system.

BEs were introduced in Oracle Solaris 10 with the Live Upgrade technology. In Oracle Solaris 11, BEs have evolved even further. In both Oracle Solaris 10 and 11, BEs are designed to minimize downtime and provide a fallback mechanism. In Oracle Solaris 10 you had the option of creating BEs, but in Oracle Solaris 11 a new BE is automatically created after the first boot. Additional BEs are created when modifying an image using IPS `pkg` commands.

BEs have become a core element in Oracle Solaris 11 and are integrated into the core OS. BEs are used to manage Oracle Solaris 11 OS upgrades and software package updates. Utilizing ZFS snapshots and clones, BEs are designed to take up very little storage space. Refer to Chapter 5, "Administering ZFS File Systems," for more information on ZFS snapshots and clones.

Before I describe BEs, there are a few terms that you need to understand:

- BE: A BE is a bootable Oracle Solaris environment that consists of a root dataset. It may also contain other datasets mounted under the root dataset. Only one BE can be active at a time.
- Dataset: A ZFS dataset is described in more detail in Chapter 5. "Dataset" is a generic name for ZFS entities such as clones, file systems, or snapshots. When describing BEs, "dataset" refers to the file system specifications for a particular BE or snapshot.

- Snapshot: A snapshot is a read-only ZFS file system and is also described in Chapter 5. It is a read-only image of a dataset or BE at a given point in time. A snapshot is not bootable.
- Clone: A clone of a BE is created by copying one BE to another. A cloned BE is bootable.
- Shared datasets: Shared datasets are user-defined file systems such as `/export` or `/data` that contain the same mountpoint shared between all BEs. These shared file systems are located outside of the root dataset area for each BE.
- Critical datasets: Critical datasets are file systems that are included within the root dataset area for that particular BE.

BEs are integrated with the new IPS. IPS manages BEs transparently when packages are installed or updated. Updating a system's core operating files using the `pkg update` command will automatically create a new BE in the background, update the packages in the new BE, and wait for a reboot into the new BE. This allows packages to be updated without affecting the current running environment (i.e., the active BE). The updated packages become available after the system is booted to the new BE and the old BE is available as a backup containing the previous version of the software packages. Should the new modified BE not fulfill expectations, you can boot any of the previously created backup BEs. In addition, should the active BE become damaged, you can revert to a backup BE with a reboot.

The advantages of using BEs include

- If you're modifying a BE (Oracle Solaris image), you can create a copy of the environment at any stage during the modifications. The copy uses the ZFS snapshot technology and is created in seconds using very little disk space.
- You can mount an inactive BE at any time and make modifications to the interactive BE. The modifications can include adding or removing software, software updates, or system configuration changes.
- The new BE can be an unmodified copy of the current BE used for failback purposes.

Note

BEs use ZFS snapshots that, by default, are stored in the same storage pool as the current BE. A BE that is stored in the same pool and not copied to either tape or a remote location should not be relied upon as a backup for disaster recovery purposes.

- You can list all BEs at any time on a running system. You can activate any BE to become the default BE on the next boot. In addition, any BE can be listed and booted to from the OpenBoot boot menu on the SPARC platform or from the GRUB menu on the x86 platform.

To illustrate how a BE operates, when you first installed the Oracle Solaris OS, a new BE was automatically created. This is also referred to as your current BE, and the system automatically boots to this BE at startup. Later when you decide to update some of the installed software packages, the `pkg update` command creates a new BE. This new BE is also referred to as an alternate BE, and it is a ZFS clone of the current BE. When the `pkg update` command completes the software update, the alternate BE is designated as the default boot choice the next time the system is booted. The current BE remains available as an alternate boot choice.

The system now has two BEs. The new BE contains the most current version of the OS, and the alternate BE contains an older version of the OS. Having the alternate BE enables you to return to that version of the OS if the new version does not fulfill expectations.

Manage BEs

BEs can be managed from the command line using the `beadm` utility or by using the Package Manager GUI interface, which was explained in the previous section. Because the Package Manager must be used on a bitmap display and does not provide the full range of options for managing your BEs, I recommend using the `beadm` utility from the command line. For those of you who have used the Live Upgrade facility on previous versions of Oracle Solaris, all of the `lu` commands have been replaced by the `beadm` utility.

The `beadm` utility enables the system administrator to perform the following tasks:

- Create a new BE based on the active BE.
- Create a new BE based on an inactive BE.
- Create a snapshot of an existing BE.
- Create a new BE based on an existing snapshot.
- Create a new BE and copy it to a different ZFS storage pool (zpool).
- Create a new BE and add a custom title to the x86 GRUB menu or the SPARC boot menu.
- Activate an existing, inactive BE.
- Mount or unmount a BE.
- Destroy a BE.
- Rename an existing, inactive BE.
- Display information about BEs on your system.

The `beadm` utility handles all of the administrative tasks in setting up the BE including

- Aggregating all datasets in a BE and performing actions on the entire BE at once.
- Managing the ZFS dataset structures within BEs.
- Enabling you to perform administrative tasks on your BEs in a global zone or a non-global zone.
- Automatically managing and updating the GRUB menu for x86 systems or the boot menu on SPARC systems.

The `beadm` command must be used with a subcommand to perform the various BE functions. The subcommands are as follows:

`create`	Create a BE.
`destroy`	Destroy a BE.
`list`	List information about an existing BE.
`mount`	Mount a BE.
`unmount`	Unmount a BE.
`rename`	Rename a BE.
`activate`	Activate a BE on the next reboot.

When used with no subcommand, the `beadm` command displays the command usage.

List the BEs

Before creating a new BE, you should first determine the name of the active BE. In addition, list any inactive BEs currently available on the system. The syntax for the `beadm list` command is as follows:

```
beadm list [-a | [-ds] [-H] [BeName]
```

where the options are

`-a`	List all of the available information about the BE including subordinate ZFS datasets and ZFS snapshots.
`-d`	List information about all subordinate datasets that belong to the BE.
`-s`	List information about the snapshots of the BE.
`-H`	Prevent listing header information and present the information in a machine-parsable format.

List all of the BEs on the system using the `beadm list` command as follows:

```
# beadm list<cr>
BE       Active  Mountpoint  Space  Policy  Created
--       ------  ----------  -----  ------  -------
solaris  NR      /           4.91G  static  2011-11-14 20:21
```

The current BE is named `solaris`. This is the default BE that was created after the OS was installed. There are no other BEs listed on this system. The information displayed with the `beadm list` command is as follows:

- `BE` Name of the BE
- `Active` The status of the BE. The values for the Active column are as follows:
  - `R` Active on reboot
  - `N` Active now
  - `NR` Active now and active and reboot
  - `-` Inactive
  - `!` Unbootable BE in a non-global zone
- `Mountpoint` The directory where the BE is mounted
- `Space` Size of the BE
- `Policy` Static or volatile
- `Created` Date the BE was created

Specify the BE name to list information about a specific BE. For example, to display information describing the BE named `test`, type the following:

```
# beadm list test<cr>
BE    Active Mountpoint Space   Policy Created
--    ------ ---------- -----   ------ -------
test  -      -          156.0K  static 2012-03-26 16:55
```

List all available information about the BE named `solaris` by specifying the `-a` option as follows:

```
# beadm list -a solaris<cr>
BE/Dataset/Snapshot                  Active  Mountpoint  Space    Policy Created
-------------------                  ------  ----------  -----    ------ -------
solaris
  rpool/ROOT/solaris                 NR      /           4.07G    static 2011-11-14 20:21
  rpool/ROOT/solaris/var             -       /var        589.87M  static 2011-11-14 20:21
  rpool/ROOT/solaris/var@install -           -           149.73M  static 2011-11-14 20:33
  rpool/ROOT/solaris@install         -       -           104.97M  static 2011-11-14 20:33
```

The -a option displays the full list of information for a specified BE or all BEs, including all ZFS dataset and ZFS snapshot information as shown in the previous example. The Active column indicates that the solaris BE is active, and the Mountpoint column indicates it is mounted. Two ZFS snapshots are listed. These are the initial snapshots for the solaris BE that was created after the OS was installed.

The -H option will suppress the header and display the information in a machine-parsable format. For example, to display the test BE, type the following:

```
# beadm list -H test<cr>
test;067c1355-3705-c4c1-b0b3-afd649309e1d;;;159744;static;1332795301
```

The information is displayed using the following delimiters:

; (semicolon) Delimits BEs, datasets, zones, and snapshots
: (colon) Delimits attributes for BEs, datasets, zones, and snapshots
, (comma) Delimits multiple datasets, zones, and snapshots
Multiple BEs are delimited with a blank line.

The -s option displays information for any ZFS snapshots that exist for the BE as follows:

```
# beadm list -s solaris<cr>
BE/Snapshot                   Space     Policy Created
-----------                   -----     ------ -------
solaris
  solaris@2012-03-26-20:55:01 29.5K     static 2012-03-26 16:55
  solaris@install             104.97M   static 2011-11-14 20:33
```

Each ZFS snapshot for the solaris BE is displayed. The information displayed includes a time stamp indicating the date and time when that snapshot was taken.

Create a New BE

Use the beadm create command to create a new BE. The syntax for the beadm create command is as follows:

```
beadm create [-a] [-d description] [-e non-activeBeName | BeName@snapshot] \
[-o property=value]…[-p zpool] BeName
```

where the options for the `beadm` utility are as follows:

`-a`	Activate the newly created BE upon creation. The default is to not activate the newly created BE.
`-d` *description*	Enter a custom description as the title in the GRUB menu (x86) or OpenBoot menu (SPARC) to describe the BE. The default name used is *BeName*, which is specified as an argument.
`-e` *bename*	Create a new BE from a specified existing but inactive BE.
`-e` *bename@snapshot*	Create a new BE from a specified existing snapshot of the BE.
`-o` *property =value*	Create the datasets for a new BE with specific ZFS properties and values *<property =value>*. Multiple `-o` options can be specified. For a list of options, refer to the `zfs(1M)` man page.
`-p` *zpool*	Create the datasets for a new BE within the specified `zpool`. If the option is not provided, the default behavior is to create a new BE in the same pool as the original BE. This option can be combined with the other options.

As described earlier, the system automatically creates a new BE as part of an update operation using the `pkg update` command if the software packages that are being installed affect the core OS files.

There are also times when you will need to manually create a new BE, for example, before making OS configuration changes such as kernel modifications or adding a new application. The `beadm create` command creates a new BE that is a clone of your active BE. This clone is an inactive BE and can be mounted and modified while the active BE is running.

To create a new BE, run the `beadm create` command with the name of the new BE as follows:

```
# beadm create test<cr>
```

A new BE named `test` is created in less than 10 seconds, and it can be listed as follows:

```
# beadm list -a<cr>
BE/Dataset/Snapshot                                  Active Mountpoint Space    Policy Created
-------------------                                  ------ ---------- -----    ------ -------
solaris
  rpool/ROOT/solaris                                 NR     /          4.07G    static 2011-11\
                                                                                       -14 20:21
  rpool/ROOT/solaris/var                             -      /var       589.87M  static 2011-11\
                                                                                       -14 20:21
  rpool/ROOT/solaris/var@2012-03-27-14:57:19 -       -                 0        static 2012-03\
                                                                                       -27 10:57
  rpool/ROOT/solaris/var@install                     -      -          149.73M  static 2011-11\
                                                                                       -14 20:33
  rpool/ROOT/solaris@2012-03-27-14:57:19             -      -          0        static 2012-03\
                                                                                       -27 10:57
  rpool/ROOT/solaris@install                         -      -          104.97M  static 2011-11\
                                                                                       -14 20:33
test
  rpool/ROOT/test                                    -      -          110.0K   static 2012-03\
                                                                                       -27 10:57
  rpool/ROOT/test/var                                -      -          38.0K    static 2012-03\
                                                                                       -27 10:57
```

As I stated earlier, BEs utilize ZFS snapshots. I recommend that you become familiar with ZFS file systems, snapshots, and properties to help you better understand BEs. These topics are covered in Chapter 5.

When you compare the output from the previous `beadm list` command to the output from the `beadm list -a solaris` command in the previous section, you'll see the addition of the ZFS snapshot `@2012-03-27-14:57:19`. The `test` BE relies on this snapshot as its "origin" as shown when I display the ZFS properties for the `rpool/ROOT/test` file system:

```
# zfs get origin rpool/ROOT/test<cr>
NAME              PROPERTY   VALUE                                   SOURCE
rpool/ROOT/test   origin     rpool/ROOT/solaris@2012-03-27-14:57:19  -
```

Just as the `beadm create` command created a ZFS snapshot, you can manually create a ZFS snapshot of an existing BE. This snapshot is a read-only image of the existing BE at a given point in time. It's helpful to create a custom name for this snapshot to better describe what the snapshot contains or when it was created. You can then copy that snapshot to an off-site location using the `zfs send` command.

When creating a snapshot of an existing BE, the snapshot name must use the format *`BeName@snapshotdescription`*, where *`BeName`* is the name of an existing BE. The *`@snapshotdescription`* is used to identify the date or purpose of the snapshot.

The following example creates a snapshot of the existing BE named `test` and a snapshot name of `march30`:

```
# beadm create test@march30<cr>
```

I have just created a snapshot of the `test` BE. The BE and its snapshot can be listed as follows:

```
# beadm list -a test<cr>
BE/Dataset/Snapshot              Active  Mountpoint  Space   Policy  Created
-------------------              ------  ----------  -----   ------  -------
test
  rpool/ROOT/test                -       -           110.0K  static  2012-03-27 10:57
  rpool/ROOT/test/var            -       -           38.0K   static  2012-03-27 10:57
  rpool/ROOT/test/var@march30    -       -           0       static  2012-03-27 11:48
  rpool/ROOT/test@march30        -       -           0       static  2012-03-27 11:48
```

I can also list the snapshot using the `zfs list` command as follows:

```
# zfs list -t snapshot -r rpool/ROOT/test<cr>
NAME                              USED        AVAIL        REFER      MOUNTPOINT
rpool/ROOT/test@march30           0           -            3.39G      -
rpool/ROOT/test/var@march30       0           -            440M       -
```

It's important to note that I did not create another BE. A snapshot of a BE is not bootable, but I could create a new BE from a snapshot. I could then activate that BE as shown in the next series of steps:

Create a BE from a ZFS Snapshot

1. Create a BE named `BE1` as follows:

```
# beadm create BE1<cr>
```

2. Create a snapshot of the BE as follows:

```
# beadm create BE1@0430<cr>
```

3. List the BE and snapshot as follows:

```
# beadm list -a BE1<cr>
BE/Dataset/Snapshot         Active  Mountpoint  Space   Policy  Created
-------------------         ------  ----------  -----   ------  -------
BE1
  rpool/ROOT/BE1            -       -           110.0K  static  2012-03-27 12:26
  rpool/ROOT/BE1/var        -       -           38.0K   static  2012-03-27 12:26
  rpool/ROOT/BE1/var@0430   -       -           0       static  2012-03-27 12:26
  rpool/ROOT/BE1@0430       -       -           0       static  2012-03-27 12:26
```

4. Create a second BE named BE2 from the snapshot of BE1 as follows:

```
# beadm create -e BE1@0430 BE2<cr>
```

5. List all of the BEs as follows:

```
# beadm list -a<cr>
BE/Dataset/Snapshot         Active  Mountpoint   Space    Policy      Created
-------------------         ------  ----------   -----    ------      -------
BE1
  rpool/ROOT/BE1              -         -        192.0K   static   2012-03-27 12:26
  rpool/ROOT/BE1/var          -         -        38.0K    static   2012-03-27 12:26
  rpool/ROOT/BE1/var@0430     -         -        0        static   2012-03-27 12:26
  rpool/ROOT/BE1@0430         -         -        63.0K    static   2012-03-27 12:26
BE2
  rpool/ROOT/BE2              -         -        58.0K    static   2012-03-27 12:27
  rpool/ROOT/BE2/var          -         -        1.0K     static   2012-03-27 12:27
solaris
  rpool/ROOT/solaris          NR        /        4.07G    static   2011-11-14 20:21
  rpool/ROOT/solaris/var      -         /var     590.02M  static   2011-11-14 20:21
  rpool/ROOT/solaris/var
@2012-03-27-16:26:00          -         -        94.5K    static   2012-03-27 12:26
  rpool/ROOT/solaris/var
@install                      -         -        149.73M  static   2011-11-14 20:33
  rpool/ROOT/solaris
@2012-03-27-16:26:00          -         -        0        static   2012-03-27 12:26
  rpool/ROOT/solaris@install  -         -        104.97M  static   2011-11-14 20:33
```

Change the Default BE

Only one BE can be active at a time. The following beadm list command displays which BE is active now and at the next reboot:

```
# beadm list<cr>
BE          Active     Mountpoint    Space     Policy     Created
--          ------     ----------    -----     ------     -------
BE1         -          -             293.0K    static     2012-03-27 12:26
BE2         -          -             59.0K     static     2012-03-27 12:27
solaris     NR         /             4.89G     static     2011-11-14 20:21
```

The solaris BE is active now and active on the next reboot as indicated by the "NR" in the Active column.

When you activate a BE, that BE becomes the default BE at the next reboot. Use the beadm activate command to activate a BE. For example, to activate a BE named BE1, type the following command:

```
# beadm activate BE1<cr>
```

Now, list the BEs as follows:

```
# beadm list<cr>
BE          Active      Mountpoint      Space       Policy      Created
--          ------      ----------      -----       ------      -------
BE1         R           -               4.89G       static      2012-03-27 12:26
BE2         -           -               59.0K       static      2012-03-27 12:27
solaris     N           /               4.83M       static      2011-11-14 20:21
```

Now, `BE1` is active on reboot as indicated by the "`R`" in the Active column. The `solaris` BE is active now as indicated by the "`N`."

In the following steps, I'll create a new BE, activate it, and boot to it.

Activating a BE

1. Create a new BE named `BE1` as follows:

```
# beadm create BE1<cr>
```

2. List all of the BEs:

```
# beadm list<cr>
BE          Active      Mountpoint      Space       Policy      Created
--          ------      ----------      -----       ------      -------
BE1         -           -               156.0K      static      2012-03-27 13:05
solaris     NR          /               4.89G       static      2011-11-14 20:21
```

3. Activate the BE:

```
# beadm activate BE1<cr>
```

4. List all of the BEs as follows:

```
# beadm list<cr>
BE          Active      Mountpoint      Space       Policy      Created
--          ------      ----------      -----       ------      -------
BE1         R           -               4.89G       static      2012-03-27 13:05
solaris     N           /               82.0K       static      2011-11-14 20:21
```

5. Reboot:

```
# init 6<cr>
```

6. On an Oracle Solaris x86 system, the new BE is listed and highlighted in the GRUB menu as shown in Figure 2-2.

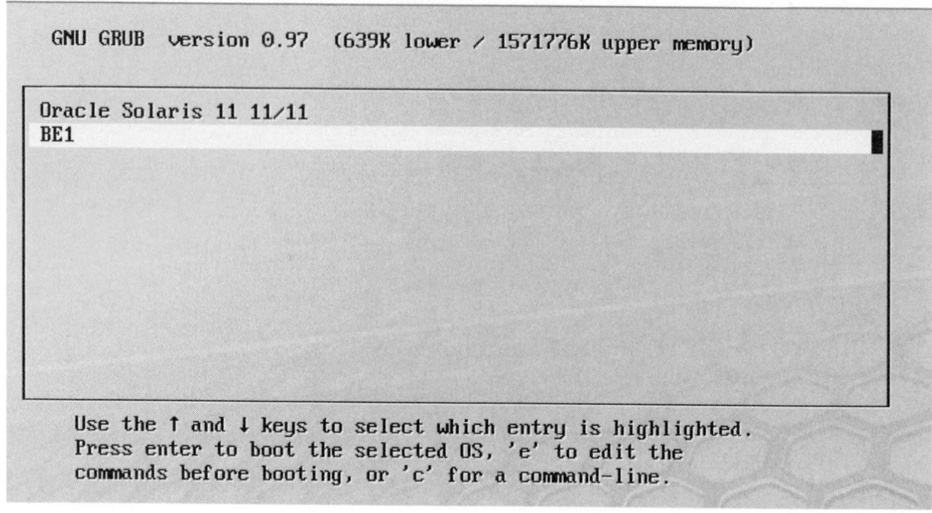

Figure 2-2 GRUB menu

On an x86-based system, the `beadm activate` command sets `BE1` as the default by changing `Default 0` to `Default 1` in the `/rpool/boot/grub/menu.lst` file as follows:

```
# default menu entry to boot
default 1
```

In addition, whenever a new BE is created, regardless of whether it is active or inactive, a new entry is made at the end of the `menu.lst` file. For example, the `BE1` BE was added as follows:

```
title BE1
bootfs rpool/ROOT/BE1
kernel$ /platform/i86pc/kernel/amd64/unix -B $ZFS-BOOTFS,console=graphics
module$ /platform/i86pc/amd64/boot_archive
```

On a SPARC system, an entry is made in the boot menu, which is stored in `/rpool/boot/menu.lst`. All of the existing BEs can be listed using the `boot -L` command from the OpenBoot PROM as follows:

```
ok boot -L<cr>
```

Issuing the `boot` command with no options will boot the system to the default BE; however, you can specify an alternate BE with the `boot -Z` command. For more information on booting an x86 or SPARC system, refer to Chapter 3, "Boot and Shutdown Procedures for SPARC and x86-Based Systems."

7. After the system boots, log in and verify that the system is booted to `BE1` as follows:

```
# beadm list<cr>
BE          Active     Mountpoint      Space     Policy     Created
--          ------     ----------      -----     ------     -------
BE1         NR         /               4.95G     static     2012-03-27 13:05
solaris     -          -               85.96M    static     2011-11-14 20:21
```

Mount an Inactive BE

An existing BE can be mounted and accessed even while it is inactive. Suppose you create a new BE to install a new application. After creating the BE, you can mount the BE using the `beadm mount` command. You can then access files in the mounted file systems associated with that BE. The syntax for the `beadm mount` command is as follows:

```
beadm mount BeName mountpoint
```

For example, to mount an existing BE named `BE1` on the mountpoint named `/bemount`, type the following command:

```
# beadm mount BE1 /bemount<cr>
```

Note

The mountpoint must be an empty directory that is not currently mounted. You can also specify a mountpoint that does not exist, and the **beadm** utility will create the directory for you.

To display the mounted BE, type

```
# beadm list<cr>
BE                Active     Mountpoint      Space       Policy      Created
--                ------     ----------      -----       ------      -------
BE1               -          /bemount        111.71M     static      2012-03-27 13:05
solaris           NR         /               5.10G       static      2011-11-14 20:21
```

`BE1` is not active, but it is mounted on `/bemount`.

Use the `zfs mount` command to list the mounted ZFS file systems that are associated with `BE1`:

```
# zfs mount<cr>
rpool/ROOT/solaris                          /
rpool/ROOT/solaris/var                      /var
rpool/export                                /export
rpool/export/home                           /export/home
rpool                                       /rpool
rpool/ROOT/BE1                              /bemount
rpool/ROOT/BE1/var                          /bemount/var
```

When mounting an inactive BE, the zones in that BE are also mounted relative to the mountpoint that was specified.

Rename a BE

Use the `beadm rename` command to rename an existing BE. The syntax for the command is as follows:

```
beadm rename BeName newBeName
```

For example, to rename the `BE1` BE to `BE2`, use the following command:

```
# beadm rename BE1 BE2<cr>
```

You cannot rename a BE that is currently active, and you cannot rename a mounted BE.

Uninstall a BE

Use the `beadm destroy` command to uninstall a BE. The syntax is as follows:

```
beadm destroy [-fF] BeName | BeName@snapshot
```

Where the options are as follows:

- `-f` Forces the destruction of the BE even if it is mounted. You will be prompted to confirm the destruction of the BE.
- `-F` Forces the destruction of the BE, without prompting for confirmation. The BE will not be destroyed if a BE is mounted.

Before destroying a BE, consider the following requirements:

- An active BE cannot be destroyed.
- The entry in the x86 GRUB menu or SPARC boot menu is automatically removed.
- When destroying a BE, the non-global zones in that BE are also destroyed.
- Only the critical or non-shared datasets of the BE are destroyed. Shared datasets, those file systems located outside of the BE, are not affected when a BE is destroyed.

For example, destroy `BE1` as follows:

```
# beadm destroy BE1<cr>
Are you sure you want to destroy BE1? This action cannot be undone(y/[n]): y<cr>
```

If the inactive BE is mounted, the following message is displayed:

```
be_destroy: BE1 is currently mounted at /bemount, cannot destroy
Unable to destroy BE1.
It is currently mounted and must be unmounted before it can be destroyed.
Use 'beadm unmount BE1' to unmount the BE before destroying it or 'beadm destroy
-fF BE1'.
```

To force the removal of the BE without first unmounting it, use the `-f` option as follows:

```
# beadm destroy -f BE1<cr>
```

Manage Software Packages in an Inactive BE

Software packages can be installed, updated, or removed from an inactive BE. The BE just needs to be mounted as described in the previous section. After mounting that BE, use the `pkg` command to manage the software packages in that BE.

To install the `distribution-constructor` software package in an inactive BE named `BE1`:

1. Mount the BE as follows:

```
# beadm mount BE1 /bemount<cr>
```

2. Install the distribution-constructor package in the BE1 BE by specifying the -R option and the mountpoint as follows:

```
# pkg -R /bemount install distribution-constructor<cr>
```

The system responds with:

```
Packages to install: 3

DOWNLOAD                              PKGS        FILES       XFER (MB)       SPEED
Completed                              3/3        65/65        0.2/0.2       19.0k/s

PHASE                                                     ITEMS
Installing new actions                                    128/128
Updating package state database                           Done
Updating image state                                      Done
Creating fast lookup database                             Done
```

3. List the software package in the BE1 BE as follows:

```
# pkg -R /bemount list distribution-constructor<cr>
NAME (PUBLISHER)                     VERSION                                  IFO
install/distribution-constructor     0.5.11-0.175.1.0.0.24.1736               i--
```

To update the distribution-constructor software package in an inactive BE, the procedure is very much like installing a software package described in the previous section.

Update the distribution-constructor software package in an inactive BE named BE1, as follows:

1. Mount the BE as follows:

```
# beadm mount BE1 /bemount<cr>
```

2. Update the distribution-constructor package in the BE1 BE as follows:

```
# pkg -R /bemount update distribution-constructor<cr>
```

The system responds with:

```
Creating Plan /
No updates available for this image.
```

To remove the software package from an inactive BE, use the `pkg uninstall` command. For example, to uninstall the `distribution-constructor` software package from the `BE1` BE, follow these instructions:

1. Mount the BE as follows:

```
# beadm mount BE1 /bemount<cr>
```

2. Uninstall the `distribution-constructor` package in the `BE1` BE as follows:

```
# pkg -R /bemount uninstall distribution-constructor<cr>
Packages to remove: 3

PHASE                                        ACTIONS
Removing old actions                         114/114
Updating package state database              Done
Updating package cache                       3/3
Updating image state                         Done
Creating fast lookup database                Done
```

Update the OS

After installing the OS, the default software repository is set to `http://pkg.oracle.com/solaris/release`. This repository will never change until a new major release of Oracle Solaris is available. A major release typically occurs every 12 months.

Oracle Solaris Version Names

Oracle has changed the naming convention of update releases from a date-based format such as "Oracle Solaris 10 8/11" to the simpler "dot" version numbering. The initial release of Oracle Solaris 11 is referred to as "11.0," the first major update is "11.1," and so on. In between each major OS release, Oracle will create update SRUs. For example, SRU 9 will be named Oracle Solaris 11.0.9.

The following system's OS was installed from the installation DVD labeled "Oracle Solaris 11 11/11." This was the first production release of Oracle Solaris 11, and it is referred to as Oracle Solaris 11 build 175. Display the current OS build using the `pkg info entire` command as follows:

```
# pkg info entire<cr>
          Name: entire
       Summary: Incorporation to lock all system packages to the same build
   Description: This package constrains system package versions to the same
                build. WARNING: Proper system update and correct package
                selection depend on the presence of this incorporation.
                Removing this package will result in an unsupported system.
      Category: Meta Packages/Incorporations
         State: Installed
     Publisher: solaris
       Version: 0.5.11
 Build Release: 5.11
        Branch: 0.175.0.0.0.2.0
Packaging Date: October 20, 2011 02:38:22 PM
          Size: 5.45 kB
          FMRI: pkg://solaris/entire@0.5.11,5.11-0.175.0.0.0.2.0:20111020T143822Z
```

The FMRI information indicates the OS revision is at 0.175.0.0.0.2.0.

Periodic OS updates are distributed through Oracle SRUs, which are described in the next section. These updates occur approximately every month and are not considered major OS revisions. The OS in this example system has been updated to SRU 12.4 (approximately 12 months later), and the OS version has changed as follows:

```
# pkg info entire<cr>
          Name: entire
       Summary: entire incorporation including Support Repository Update (Oracle
                Solaris 11 11/11 SRU 12.4).
   Description: This package constrains system package versions to the same
                build. WARNING: Proper system update and correct package
                selection depend on the presence of this incorporation.
                Removing this package will result in an unsupported system. For
                more information see https://support.oracle.com/CSP/main/article?
                cmd=show&type=NOT&doctype=REFERENCE&id=1372094.1.
      Category: Meta Packages/Incorporations
         State: Installed
     Publisher: solaris
       Version: 0.5.11 (Oracle Solaris 11 SRU 12.4)
 Build Release: 5.11
        Branch: 0.175.0.12.0.4.0
Packaging Date: October 2, 2012 04:17:28 PM
          Size: 5.45 kB
          FMRI: pkg://solaris/entire@0.5.11,5.11-0.175.0.12.0.4.0:20121002T161728Z
```

The FRMI now indicates that the OS is at SRU 12.4 (0.175.0.12.0.4.0).

The FMRI contains the build and branch version information.

The OS release will also be displayed with the `uname -v` command as follows:

```
# uname -v<cr>
11.0
```

Where the `-v` option displays the OS version.

Periodic SRUs

Periodic OS updates are distributed through Oracle SRUs. In order to access the SRUs on Oracle's support Web site, you'll need an Oracle support contract, a login ID, and a password. These SRUs are typically released every month but can be released at any time. To update the OS and software packages to these SRUs, you'll need to access an SRU containing the updates.

Each SRU is a single unit of change that you can use to update your OS, but the SRU contains updates to many different packages installed and not installed on a given system. Although this might represent a little less flexibility in terms of what changes can be applied to the system compared to patching in Oracle Solaris 10, it means the updates have been thoroughly tested by Oracle as a single unit. The SRUs are known to work well rather than being an arbitrary selection of patches that are applied in an arbitrary order.

You can view the current Oracle Solaris update SRUs by logging in to Oracle's support Web site at `https://support.oracle.com`. Search the knowledge base with the following keywords: "Oracle Solaris 11 Support Repository Updates Index." As of this writing, the SRU index contains the SRUs shown in Figure 2-3.

SRU	Release Date	ISO Image	Readme	Version
2011.11 SRU12.4	11 October 2012	14739763 ISO Image	Readme	0.5.11-0.175.0.12.0.4.0
2011.11 SRU11.4	14 September 2012	14618843 ISO Image	Readme	0.5.11-0.175.0.11.0.4.1
2011.11 SRU10.5	16 August 2012	14498553 ISO Image	Readme	0.5.11-0.175.0.10.0.5.0
2011.11 SRU9.5	16 July 2012	14325388 ISO Image	Readme	0.5.11-0.175.0.9.0.5.0
2011.11 SRU8.5	22 June 2012	14163824 ISO Image	Readme	0.5.11-0.175.0.8.0.5.0
2011.11 SRU7.5	17 May 2012	14050126 ISO Image	Readme	0.5.11-0.175.0.7.0.5.0
2011.11 SRU6.6	16 April 2012	13952102 ISO Image	Readme	0.5.11-0.175.0.6.0.6.0
2011.11 SRU5.5	21 March 2012	13872850 ISO Image	Readme	0.5.11-0.175.0.5.0.5.0
2011.11 SRU5	16 March 2012	13856538 ISO Image	Readme	0.5.11-0.175.0.5.0.4.0
* 2011.11 SRU4a	05 March 2012	13810641 ISO Image	Readme	0.5.11-0.175.0.4.0.6.0
2011.11 SRU4	20 February 2012	13723034 ISO Image	Readme	0.5.11-0.175.0.4.0.5.0
2011.11 SRU3	17 January 2012	13578624 ISO Image	Readme	0.5.11-0.175.0.3.0.4.0
* 2011.11 SRU2b	06 April 2012	13936249 ISO Image	Readme	0.5.11-0.175.0.2.0.4.0
* 2011.11 SRU2a	12 December 2011	13478131 ISO Image	Readme	0.5.11-0.175.0.2.0.3.0
2011.11 SRU2	01 December 2011	13454271 ISO Image	Readme	0.5.11-0.175.0.2.0.3.0
* 2011.11 SRU1a	16 March 2012	14110235 ISO Image	Readme	0.5.11-0.175.0.1.0.5.0
2011.11 SRU1	16 November 2011	13399198 ISO Image	Readme	0.5.11-0.175.0.1.0.4.0

Figure 2-3 Oracle Solaris 11 SRUs

To update the OS, you'll need to point your system's default publisher to the Oracle support repository URI. You can check your default publisher by using the `pkg publisher` command as follows:

```
# pkg publisher<cr>
PUBLISHER        TYPE      STATUS      URI
solaris          origin    online      http://pkg.oracle.com/solaris/release/
```

Check for updates by using the `pkg update` command. This system is still pointed to the default publisher URI, which does not contain any updates as shown:

```
# pkg update -nv entire<cr>
No updates available for this image.
```

Preview an Operation

The `-n` option allows you to review the effects of the `pkg` commands before executing the command without the `-n` option.

I'll need to create a repository for the SRU, described in the next section, and then change the default publisher URI to point to the SRU. The URI can be local or on the network.

Configure a Network-Based Support Repository

A software package repository can be configured locally or on the network. To access the update SRU over the Internet, you could simply point your default publisher's repository URI to Oracle's Web site and access the SRU at `https://pkg.oracle.com/solaris/support`. To accomplish this, you will

- Log in to the Oracle support site.
- Download the provided key and certificate files and store them on the system.
- Add the publisher.

Instructions for the installation of the SRU are included in each Readme file that accompanies each SRU, as shown in Figure 2-3. The Readme file contains instructions on how to point the default repository to the SRU over the Internet.

Configure a Local Support Repository

Many servers do not have direct access to the Internet, and many system administrators would rather use a local SRU repository rather than access the repository across the Internet. A local repository performs better and is more convenient. In the following steps, I'll describe how to download the SRU ISO file, create a local repository on the system, point the default publisher repository to this repository, and update the OS.

Create a ZFS File System for the Repository

Create a ZFS file system for the SRU ISO image as follows:

```
# zfs create rpool/repo<cr>
```

Although 10GB of free disk space should be enough to store the SRU, Oracle recommends 15GB of free space.

Download the Update SRU ISO Image

Download the SRU from Oracle's support Web site by signing in to `https://support.oracle.com` with a username and password that is linked to an Oracle support contract. For this example, I searched the "Patches and Updates" section of Oracle's support Web site to obtain a current list of the Oracle Solaris 11 SRUs (refer to Figure 2-3).

I downloaded the Oracle Solaris 11 SRU 12.4 Repo ISO image, which is an incremental repository. It contains only the latest revision of packages that have been added or changed since the initial release of Oracle Solaris 11 11/11. The SRU is a compressed ISO file named `p14739763_1100_Generic.zip`, and I stored it in the `/rpool/repo` file system that I created earlier.

Extract the SRU ISO

Extract the ISO image into the `/rpool/repo` file system as follows:

```
# unzip p14739763_1100_Generic.zip<cr>
Archive: p14739763_1100_Generic.zip
  inflating: readme.html
  inflating: readme.txt
  inflating: sol-11-1111-sru12-04-incr-repo.iso
```

Mount the SRU ISO

Mount the ISO image as a file system as follows:

```
# mount -F hsfs /rpool/repo/sol-11-1111-sru12-04-incr-repo.iso /sru12_repo<cr>
```

Add an additional origin to the existing package publisher as follows:

```
# pkg set-publisher -g file:///sru12_repo/repo solaris<cr>
```

The repository *origin* is the location of a package repository that contains both package metadata (package manifests and catalogs) and package content (package files). Verify the package publisher as follows:

```
# pkg publisher<cr>
PUBLISHER           TYPE          STATUS        URI
solaris             origin        online        file:///sru12_repo/repo/
solaris             origin        online        http://pkg.oracle.com/solaris/release/
```

Notice that the default publisher now has two different repositories in two different locations. One is local and the other is remote. It's important that your system still has access to the full repository in addition to the SRU repository. In this case, the full repository is located at `http://pkg.oracle.com/solaris/release/`. The update SRU will not install properly without the full repository being accessible.

Check which SRUs are now available to the system:

```
# pkg list -af entire<cr>
NAME (PUBLISHER)        VERSION                          IFO
entire                  0.5.11-0.175.0.12.0.4.0          ---
entire                  0.5.11-0.175.0.0.0.2.0           i--
entire                  0.5.11-0.151.0.1                 ---
```

0.5.11-0.175.0.12.0.4.0 is the latest version available in the repository.

0.5.11-0.175.0.0.0.2.0 is the level at which the OS currently is (indicated by the `i` in the IFO column).

A third (0.5.11-0.151.0.1) is also listed because the `http://pkg.oracle.com/solaris/release` URI has two repositories, each representing a different release of the OS.

List Package Updates

Before installing the updates, it's a good idea to first list the packages that will be updated. Use the `pkg list` command with the `-u` option to list all packages in the current installed image that have newer versions available from the publisher as follows:

```
# pkg list -u<cr>
NAME (PUBLISHER)                                  VERSION                           IFO
codec/ogg-vorbis                                  2.30.0-0.175.0.0.0.0.0            i--
communication/im/pidgin                           2.10.0-0.175.0.0.0.0.0            i--
consolidation/SunVTS/SunVTS-incorporation         0.5.11-0.172.0.0.0.0.0            i--
consolidation/X/X-incorporation                   0.5.11-0.175.0.0.0.0.1215         i--
consolidation/cacao/cacao-incorporation           0.5.11-0.174.0.0.0.0.0            i--
consolidation/cns/cns-incorporation               0.5.11-0.175.0.0.0.1.0            i--
consolidation/desktop/desktop-incorporation       0.5.11-0.175.0.0.0.2.0            i--
...<output has been truncated>...
```

Update the OS to an SRU

The update operation updates the packages on the system with the latest package versions by first creating a new BE and then installing those updates into the new BE. The current BE is left untouched. Update the entire OS by typing

```
root@solaris:/rpool/repo# pkg update --accept entire<cr>
            Packages to remove:   1
           Packages to install:   7
            Packages to update: 274
           Mediators to change:   1
       Create boot environment: Yes
Create backup boot environment:  No

DOWNLOAD                PKGS              FILES             XFER (MB)
Completed               282/282           9776/9776         272.0/272.0

PHASE                                         ACTIONS
Removal Phase                                 2474/2474
Install Phase                                 3146/3146
Update Phase                                  13230/13230

PHASE                                         ITEMS
Package State Update Phase                    556/556
Package Cache Update Phase                    275/275
Image State Update Phase                      2/2

A clone of solaris exists and has been updated and activated.
On the next boot the Boot Environment solaris-1 will be mounted on '/'. Reboot when
ready to switch to this updated BE.
```

Display the new BE that was created:

```
# beadm list<cr>
BE              Active       Mountpoint     Space      Policy      Created
--              ------       ----------     -----      ------      -------
solaris         N            /              302.0K     static      2012-10-23 10:03
solaris-1       R            -              5.53G      static      2012-10-24 10:01
```

The solaris-1 BE contains the package updates and is set as the default BE on the next reboot (as indicated by the R in the Active column). The solaris BE does not contain the updates. Boot to the solaris-1 BE by typing

```
# shutdown -y -g0 -r<cr>
```

The system will boot to the solaris-1 BE containing the updated version of the OS.

If you need to back out of the updates, reboot the system to the solaris BE.

Verify the OS Update

After the system boots to the solaris-1 BE, verify that the SRU 12.4 updates are installed by typing

```
# pkg info entire<cr>
          Name: entire
       Summary: entire incorporation including Support Repository Update (Oracle
                Solaris 11 11/11 SRU 12.4).
   Description: This package constrains system package versions to the same build.
WARNING: Proper system update and correct package selection depend on the presence of
this incorporation.
Removing this package will result in an unsupported system. For more information see
https://support.oracle.com/CSP/main/article?cmd=show&type=NOT&doctype=REFERENCE&
id=1372094.1.
      Category: Meta Packages/Incorporations
         State: Installed
     Publisher: solaris
       Version: 0.5.11 (Oracle Solaris 11 SRU 12.4)
 Build Release: 5.11
        Branch: 0.175.0.12.0.4.0
Packaging Date: October 2, 2012 04:17:28 PM
          Size: 5.45 kB
          FMRI: pkg://solaris/entire@0.5.11,5.11-0.175.0.12.0.4.0:20121002T161728Z

# pkg list -af entire<cr>
NAME (PUBLISHER)                  VERSION                          IFO
entire                            0.5.11-0.175.0.12.0.4.0          i--
entire                            0.5.11-0.175.0.0.0.2.0           ---
entire                            0.5.11-0.151.0.1                 ---
```

The OS is currently at level 0.5.11-0.175.0.12.0.4.0 as indicated by the i in the IFO column.

Update Oracle Solaris to a New Release

A major Oracle Solaris release includes fixes that were delivered in previous SRUs along with enhancements and new features that are typically not delivered in an SRU. When Oracle releases a new major release of Oracle Solaris, the company will update the default `solaris` release repository at `http://pkg.oracle.com/solaris/release`. As of this writing, the `solaris` repository contains four different repositories, each representing a different branch release of the OS:

```
0.5.11-0.175.1.0.0.24.2       Release 5.1,       Branch 0.175.1.0.0.24.2
0.5.11-0.175.0.10.10.0.0      Release 5.1,       Branch 0.175.0.10.10.0.0
0.5.11-0.175.0.0.0.2.0        Release 5.1,       Branch 0.175.0.0.0.2.0
0.5.11-0.151.0.1              Release 5.1,       Branch 0.151.0.1
```

You can list all of the releases by using an Internet browser and visiting `http:/pkg.oracle.com/solaris/release/en/index.shtml` as shown in Figure 2-4.

You can also display the Oracle Solaris update releases by typing the `pkg list` at the command line as follows:

```
# pkg list -af entire<cr>
NAME (PUBLISHER)          VERSION                          IFO
entire                    0.5.11-0.175.1.0.0.24.2          ---
entire                    0.5.11-0.175.0.12.0.4.0          i--
entire                    0.5.11-0.175.0.10.1.0.0          ---
entire                    0.5.11-0.175.0.0.0.2.0           ---
entire                    0.5.11-0.151.0.1                 ---
```

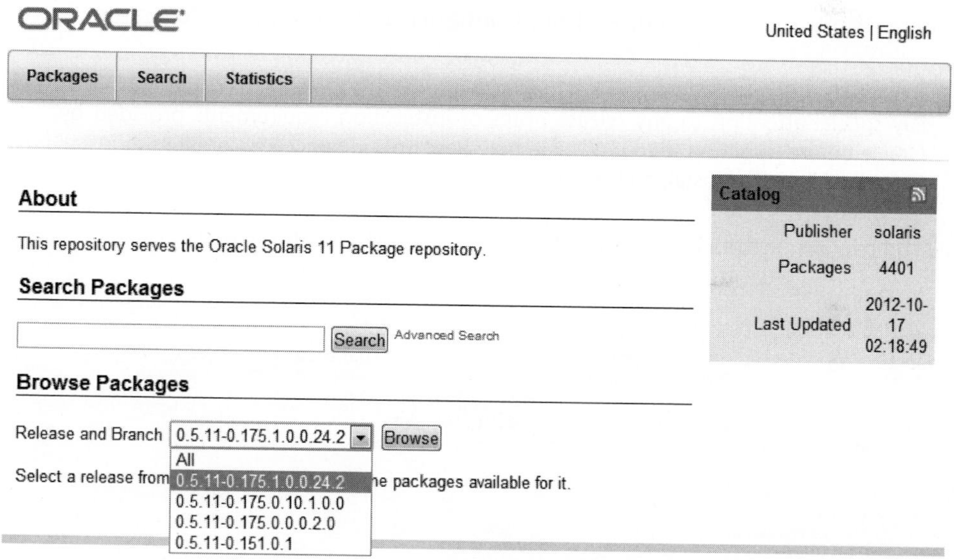

Figure 2-4 Oracle Solaris releases

Executing the `pkg list` command from the command line displays network and local repositories and also indicates the currently installed version (indicated by the `i` in the IFO column).

Typically, a new major release will be announced publicly, at which time you can update to the new release through the Oracle Solaris release repository using the `pkg update` command without a service contract. Those with a service contract will update through the Oracle Solaris support repository. Complete instructions for updating the OS will be provided at the Oracle repository site.

In this example, I will view any updates from the default `solaris` publisher by typing the `pkg list` command as follows:

```
# pkg list -af entire<cr>
NAME (PUBLISHER)                        VERSION                              IFO
entire                                  0.5.11-0.175.1.0.0.24.2              ---
entire                                  0.5.11-0.175.0.12.0.4.0              i--
entire                                  0.5.11-0.175.0.10.1.0.0              ---
entire                                  0.5.11-0.175.0.0.0.2.0               ---
entire                                  0.5.11-0.151.0.1                     ---
```

Five different OS releases are listed at the publisher's repositories. The OS on this system is at release 0.5.11-0.175.0.12.0.4.0 as indicated by the `i` in the IFO column.

You do not need to download the Oracle Solaris release repository; you can update your system across the network by using the `pkg update` command. However, you may want to download the new repository ISO from Oracle's download site and create a local repository on your own network. To download the release repository, follow the instructions in the previous section "Configure a Local Support Repository."

Caution

Pay special attention to any release notes or installation requirements provided by Oracle before updating the OS. Oracle may have specific packages or SRUs to install (or uninstall) before installing the update.

Once the repository has been created, you can view the updates by typing

```
# pkg update -nv<cr>
------------------------------------------------------------
Package: pkg://solaris/consolidation/osnet/osnet-incorporation@0.5.11,5.
11-0.175.1.0.0.24.2:20120919T184141Z
License: usr/src/pkg/license_files/lic_OTN
Oracle Technology Network Developer License Agreement
  <the Oracle license information has been truncated to save space>
. . . . .
            Packages to remove:  2
           Packages to install:  43
            Packages to updatwe:  733
           Mediators to change:  2
     Estimated space available:  10.46 GB
Estimated space to be consumed:  3.39 GB
       Create boot environment:  Yes
```

```
     Activate boot environment:  Yes
Create backup boot environment:  No
          Rebuild boot archive:  Yes

Changed mediators:
  mediator java:
      version: 1.6 (system default) -> 1.7 (system default)

  mediator python:
      version: None -> 2.6 (vendor default)

Changed packages:
solaris
  SUNWcs
    0.5.11,5.11-0.170:20110718T234908Z -> None
  web/browser/firefox/plugin/firefox-flashplayer
    11.2.202.223,5.11-0.175.0.7.0.2.0:20120421T002442Z -> None
  compress/xz
    None -> 5.0.1,5.11-0.175.1.0.0.24.0:20120904T170609Z
  data/docbook

  ..<The output listing all of the pkg updates has been truncated>…
```

Update the entire OS by typing

```
# pkg update --be-name s11.1ga -accept<cr>
------------------------------------------------------------
Package: pkg://solaris/consolidation/osnet/osnet-incorporation@0.5.11,5.
11-0.175.1.0.0.24.2:20120919T184141Z
License: usr/src/pkg/license_files/lic_OTN

Oracle Technology Network Developer License Agreement
<the Oracle license information has been truncated to save space>
….
installing and using this OTN software download.
           Packages to remove:   2
          Packages to install:  43
           Packages to update: 733
          Mediators to change:   2
      Create boot environment: Yes
Create backup boot environment:  No

DOWNLOAD          PKGS            FILES             XFER (MB)
Completed         778/778         33653/33653       647.6/647.6

PHASE                                       ACTIONS
Removal Phase                             9072/9072
Install Phase                           19452/19452
Update Phase                            27519/27519

PHASE                                         ITEMS
Package State Update Phase                1509/1509
Package Cache Update Phase                  734/734
Image State Update Phase                        2/2

A clone of solaris-1 exists and has been updated and activated.
On the next boot the Boot Environment s11.1ga will be
mounted on '/'. Reboot when ready to switch to this updated BE.
```

continues

```
-----------------------------------------------------------------------------
NOTE: Please review release notes posted at:

https://support.oracle.com/CSP/main/article?cmd=show&type=NOT&doctype=REFERENCE&
id=1372094.1
-----------------------------------------------------------------------------
```

The `s11.1ga` BE is created, and the updates are applied to that BE. Reboot, and the system will boot to the updated BE by default.

```
# shutdown -y -g0 -r<cr>
```

When the system has booted, log in and verify the OS version:

```
# pkg list -af entire<cr>
NAME (PUBLISHER)                    VERSION                         IFO
entire                              0.5.11-0.175.1.0.0.24.2         i--
entire                              0.5.11-0.175.0.10.1.0.0         ---
entire                              0.5.11-0.175.0.0.0.2.0          ---
entire                              0.5.11-0.151.0.1                ---

# uname -v<cr>
11.1
```

The system has been updated from Oracle Solaris 11/11 to Oracle Solaris 11.1. Test the new Oracle Solaris release. If needed, you can always reboot to the previous BE to undo the entire update.

Summary

This chapter introduced you to the concepts of IPS in the fundamentals of using the packaging system for installing, listing, updating, and removing software packages in the Oracle Solaris image. It also described how the IPS uses BEs to minimize downtime and provide more flexibility to the system administrator for updating or reconfiguring a production server.

This chapter also described how to update the OS by downloading an SRU, creating a local repository, and updating the OS using the local repository. I also described how to update to a new major release of Oracle Solaris.

The next chapter describes the boot process, the SMF, and how to properly shut down an Oracle Solaris system.

3

Boot and Shutdown Procedures for SPARC and x86-Based Systems

System startup requires an understanding of the hardware and the OS functions that are required to bring the system to a running state. This chapter discusses the operations that the system must perform from the time that you turn on power to the system until you receive a system login prompt. In addition, it covers the steps required to properly shut down a system.

Because of the difference in hardware, the kernel initialization phase of the boot process differs between the SPARC and x86 platforms. This chapter describes the boot process on both the SPARC and x86 platforms as described in Figure 3-1.

Once the kernel is loaded, the kernel starts the `init` process and brings the system up to the default run level using SMF, also described in this chapter.

Finally, the last part of this chapter describes how to shut down Oracle Solaris on both platforms.

The Boot Process: SPARC

Bootstrapping is the process a computer follows to load and execute the bootable OS. The term comes from the phrase "pulling yourself up by your bootstraps." The instructions for the bootstrap procedure are stored in the boot programmable read-only memory (PROM).

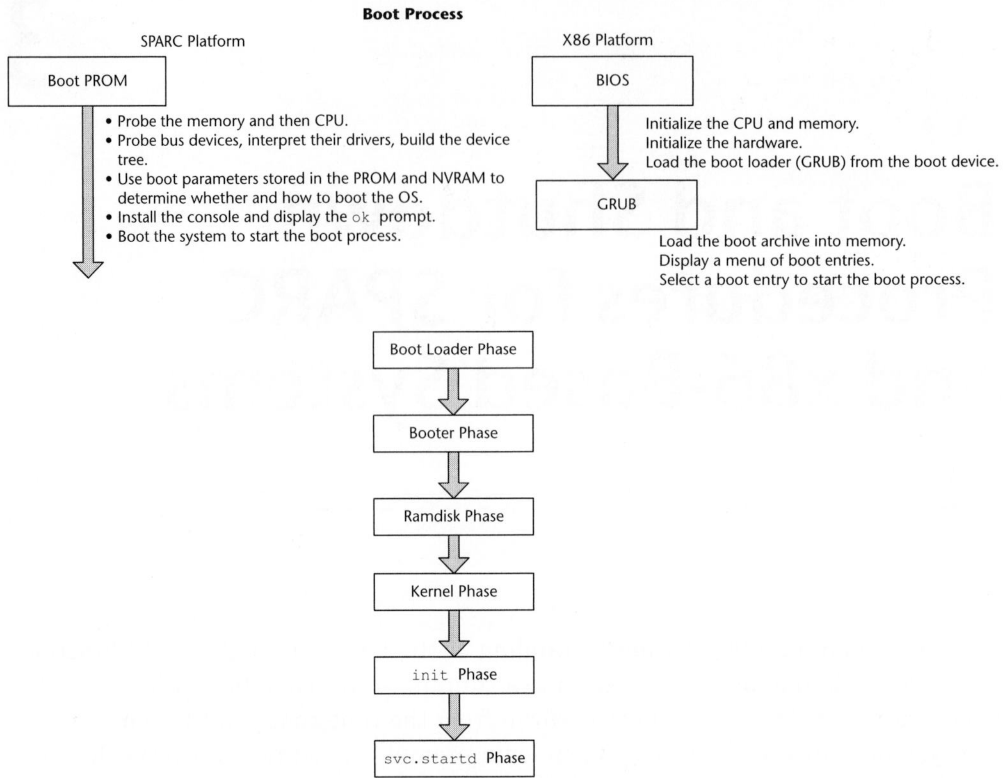

Figure 3-1 SPARC and x86 boot process

The boot process goes through the following phases:

1. OpenBoot PROM phase: After you turn on power to the system, the PROM displays system identification information and runs self-test diagnostics to verify the system's hardware and memory.

   The primary task of the OpenBoot firmware is to test the hardware and to boot the OS either from a mass storage device or from the network. OpenBoot contains a program called the monitor that controls the operation of the system before the kernel is available and before the OS has been booted. When a system is turned on, the monitor runs a power-on self-test (POST) that checks such things as the hardware and memory on the system.

   If no errors are found, the automatic boot process begins. The firmware attempts to autoboot, if the OpenBoot `auto-boot?` flag has been set to `true`. OpenBoot contains a set of parameters and instructions that locate the system boot disk and start up the system's boot program and eventually start up the OS.

Using the location provided by the OpenBoot `boot-device` parameter, the boot-device containing the boot partition is accessed and the boot blocks are retrieved from blocks 1-15. The boot program is stored in a predictable area (blocks 1 to 15) on the system hard drive, CD-ROM, or other bootable device and is referred to as the bootblock (`bootblk`). The bootblock contains a standalone booter that usually contains a file system–specific reader capable of reading the boot archive. The boot archive is described later in this chapter.

2. Boot loader phase: During this phase, the root file system boot archive is loaded from the default ZFS dataset, which is located on the media (DVD or boot disk), into RAM. The default dataset selected for booting is the dataset identified by the pool's `bootfs` property on the boot device.
3. Booter phase: During this phase, the boot archive is read and executed. Both SPARC-based and x86-based systems boot with a boot archive, which is a file system image that contains the files required for booting. When booting from a ZFS root file system, the path names of both the boot archive and the kernel file are resolved in the root file system that is selected for booting. It's at this phase that the boot process requires knowledge of the root file system format. The default format used in Oracle Solaris 11 is ZFS.
4. Ramdisk phase: The ramdisk extracts the kernel image from the boot archive and executes it. The boot archive contains a file system image that is mounted using an in-memory disk. On SPARC platforms, the file system reader mounts and opens the RAM disk image, then reads and executes the kernel that is contained within it. On x86 platforms, GRUB loads the kernel file and the boot archive into memory, then transfers control to the kernel.
5. Kernel phase: Oracle Solaris is initialized and a minimal root file system is mounted on the ramdisk that was constructed from the boot archive. In some environments, such as when booting from an installer, the ramdisk is used as the root (`/`) file system and remains mounted. The ramdisk contains a set of kernel files and drivers that are sufficient to mount the root file system on the specified root device. The kernel extracts the remaining primary modules from the boot archive, initializes itself, mounts the root file system on the local disk, and discards the boot archive. Finally, the kernel runs the `/sbin/init` program to start up the `init` phase.
6. `init` phase: The kernel creates a user process and starts the `/sbin/init` process. The `/sbin/init` process reads the `/etc/inittab` file for instructions on starting other processes, initializes stream modules, sets up the system for a correct response to a power-fail shutdown, and finally, starts up the `svc.startd` daemon (`/lib/svc/bin/svc.startd`).

7. `svc.startd` phase: The `svc.startd` daemon starts the system services and boots the system to the appropriate milestone. Specifically, `svc.startd` performs the following tasks:
   – Checks and mounts file systems
   – Configures the network and devices
   – Initiates various startup processes and performs system maintenance tasks
   – Executes the legacy run control (RC) scripts for compatibility

Powering On the System

Before you turn on power to the system, you need to make sure everything is plugged in properly. Check the small computer system interface (SCSI) and storage area network cables that connect any external devices to the system to make sure they are properly connected. Check your network connection. Also make sure that the keyboard and monitor are connected properly. Loose cables can cause your system to fail during the startup process.

Note

Connect cables with the power turned off. Always connect your cables before turning on the hardware; otherwise, you could damage your system.

The correct sequence for powering on your equipment is first to turn on any peripherals (that is, external disk drives or tape drives) and then turn on power to the system.

The OpenBoot Environment

The hardware-level user interface that you see before the OS starts is called the OpenBoot PROM (OBP). OpenBoot is based on an interactive command interpreter that gives you access to an extensive set of functions for hardware and software development, fault isolation, and debugging. The OBP firmware is stored in the system's PROM chip and on the system memory card. The card contains the values for the system's ID PROM (i.e., host ID, MAC address, date, and cyclic redundancy check value).

SPARC systems use a programmable boot PROM that allows new boot program data to be loaded into the PROM by "flashing" the PROM with software. This type of PROM is called a flash PROM (FPROM).

The nonvolatile RAM (NVRAM) chip stores user-definable system parameters, also referred to as “NVRAM variables” or “EEPROM parameters.” The parameters allow administrators to control variables such as the default boot device and boot command. The NVRAM also contains writeable areas for user-controlled diagnostics, macros, and device aliases. NVRAM is where the system identification information is stored, such as the host ID, Ethernet address, and time-of-day clock. SPARC systems contain a nonremovable serial electronically erasable programmable read-only memory (SEEPROM) chip socketed to the motherboard that does not require a battery. Some systems may contain a removable system configuration card to hold the system configuration information. Many software packages use the host ID for licensing purposes; therefore, it is important that the NVRAM chip (or memory card) can be removed and placed in any replacement system. Because NVRAM contains unique identification information for the machine, Oracle sometimes refers to it as the identification programmable read-only memory (ID PROM).

OpenBoot is currently at version 5, but this version is available only on high-end SPARC servers. Depending on the age of your system, you could have PROM version 3, 4, or 5 installed. The original boot PROM firmware, version 1, was introduced on the Sun SPARCstation 1. The first version of the OpenBoot PROM was version 2, and it first appeared on the SPARCstation 2 system. OpenBoot version 4 is the version that is currently available on the SPARC T-Series systems and Enterprise servers and is the minimum version required for running Oracle Solaris 11. Versions 4 and 5 of the OpenBoot architecture provide a significant increase in functionality over the boot PROMs in earlier Sun systems. One notable feature of the OpenBoot firmware is a programmable user interface based on the interactive programming language Forth. In Forth, sequences of user commands can be combined to form complete programs. This capability provides a powerful tool for debugging hardware and software. Another benefit of versions 4 and 5 is the flash update feature. You can update the version 4 and 5 firmware without replacing the PROM chip. I described how to update the firmware in Chapter 1, “Installing Oracle Solaris 11.”

To determine the version of the OpenBoot PROM, type

```
$ /usr/sbin/prtdiag -v<cr>
```

The system outputs several lines of diagnostic information. At the end of the output, the PROM revision is displayed as follows:

```
System PROM revisions:
----------------------
OBP 4.30.0 2008/12/11 12:15
```

Or type

```
$ prtconf -V<cr>
OBP 4.30.0 2008/12/11 12:15
```

You can also verify the OpenBoot version from the OpenBoot prompt with the `.version` command as follows:

```
ok .version<cr>
Release 4.30.4.d created 2011/07/06 14:29
```

and from the Advanced Lights Out Manager (ALOM) prompt, check the version with the `showhost` command as follows:

```
sc> showhost<cr>
Sun-Fire-T2000 System Firmware 6.7.12 2011/07/06 20:03

Host flash versions:
  OBP 4.30.4.d 2011/07/06 14:29
  Hypervisor 1.7.3.c 2010/07/09 15:14
  POST 4.30.4.b 2010/07/09 14:24
```

The OpenBoot is updated by updating the firmware. The firmware upgrade process is described in Chapter 1.

Accessing the OpenBoot Environment

When a SPARC server is at run level 0, the `ok` prompt appears indicating that you are at the OpenBoot environment. On most modern SPARC systems with multiple CPUs installed, the `ok` prompt is preceded by a number that is enclosed in curly braces. This number indicates the active CPU in the system. For example,

```
{0} ok
```

indicates that CPU 0 is the active CPU. For debugging purposes, you may switch the active CPU. At the OpenBoot prompt, use the `switch-cpu` command to selectively switch from the currently active CPU to different CPUs. For example, to switch from CPU #0 to CPU #1, type the following command:

```
{0} ok 1 switch-cpu<cr>
```

The ok prompt is now preceded by the number of the CPU to which you switched:

```
{1} ok
```

You can get to the OpenBoot environment by using any of the following methods:

- From the ALOM system controller prompt (sc>), type break -y followed by console as follows:

  ```
  sc> break -y<cr>
  sc> console<cr>
  {0} ok
  ```

  ALOM and the system controller are described in the following "System Console" section.
- Halting the OS as described at the end of this chapter.
- When the system is initially powered on. If the auto-boot? OpenBoot variable is set to false, the system will not start automatically and stops at the user interface (the ok prompt). If the auto-boot? variable is set to true, automatic startup is configured and you can make the system stop at the user interface by pressing *Stop+A* after the display console banner is displayed, but before the system begins starting the OS.
- The system hardware detects an error from which it cannot recover. (This is known as a watchdog.)

Halting the system, or otherwise stopping the OS, must be performed properly and is described later in this chapter.

Consult the user and administration guides that came with your server for more information on accessing the OpenBoot environment on your particular model of hardware.

System Console

Depending on the type of system you have, the console connection could vary. Some servers have a graphics card and keyboard connected to them. Although it's not recommended, the system console can be redirected to the graphics frame buffer. You cannot use a local graphics monitor to perform initial system installation, nor can you use a local graphics monitor to view POST messages. In most data centers, the console is connected to either the serial management (SER MGT) port or the network management (NET MGT) port on the server. Modern SPARC servers have a connection labeled "SER MGT" or "NET MGT," which is an RJ45 connection, and the console is connected to this port. When the system is powered on, and if a keyboard is not detected, the console defaults to this port. This port provides access to the system console, also called the system control facility. The system control facility enables you to remotely manage and administer your server.

Depending on the SPARC hardware, the connection to the system control facility will differ. All T1000 and T2000 servers use the ALOM. The T3, T4, T5xx, and T6xxx series servers use Integrated Lights Out Manager (ILOM). The M-series Enterprise servers use the eXtended System Control Facility (XSCF). All three system control facilities are different from one another, and I recommend that you refer to the documentation for your specific server. For the examples used in this book, I'll be covering ALOM and ILOM.

For more information on using ALOM, refer to "Advanced Lights Out Management (ALOM) CMT v1.4 Guide," part number 819-7991-10, available at Oracle's online technical library at `http://docs.oracle.com`.

For more information on ILOM, refer to "Oracle Integrated Lights Out Manager 3.1 Documentation," part number E24707-01, available at Oracle's online technical library at `http://docs.oracle.com`. These documents are located in the "Systems Management and Diagnostics" section.

For more information on using XSCF, refer to "SPARC Enterprise M3000/M4000/M5000/M8000/M9000 Servers XSCF User's Guide," part number E25381-01, and the XSCF Reference Manual for the hardware platform with which you are working. These documents are available at Oracle's online technical library at `http://docs.oracle.com`. These documents are located in the "SPARC Enterprise Servers" documentation section.

ALOM and the System Controller

The T1000 and T2000 series SPARC servers come preconfigured to allow input and output only by means of the ALOM system controller. The system controller's circuitry runs independently of the server, using the server's standby power. Therefore, ALOM firmware and software continue to function when the server OS goes offline or when the server is powered off. The ALOM system controller is accessed through either the SER MGT port or the NET MGT port.

Accessing the ALOM system console through the SER MGT port is the default configuration on most systems. Connect an ASCII terminal using a null modem serial cable with an RJ45 connector to the SER MGT port. The default configuration is

- 9,600 BAUD
- 8 bits

- No parity
- 1 stop bit
- No handshaking (set hardware flow control to none)

By default, the NET MGT port is configured to retrieve its IP address and other network configuration information using a local Dynamic Host Configuration Protocol (DHCP) server and allows connections using the Secure Shell (SSH). Most system administrators use the NET MGT port for connecting to the system console. This port can be configured to accept connections from a telnet client or SSH clients, but not both.

The network configuration for the NET MGT port can be modified by connecting to the NET MGT port using either an SSH or telnet client (or connecting to the SER MGT port) and modifying the network configuration manually on the system controller. The IP address for connecting to the NET MGT port is a unique IP address separate from the main server IP address. Refer to the documentation that came with your server or refer to the "Sun Advanced Lights Out Manager (ALOM) Administration Guide" for more information. This document is available at Oracle's online technical library at `http://docs.oracle.com`. See the "SPARC Enterprise Servers" documentation section.

When you have successfully connected to the system controller through either the SER MGT or the NET MGT port, you'll see the ALOM login prompt:

```
Sun(tm) Advanced Lights Out Manager CMT v1.7.3
Please login:
```

Enter the login name and you'll be prompted to enter a password.

```
Please Enter password:
```

The login and password is set up by the system administrator the first time the ALOM console is accessed.

After you enter the correct password, the system controller command prompt is displayed as follows:

```
sc>
```

From the system controller prompt, access the console by typing

```
sc> console<cr>
```

The OpenBoot prompt will appear as follows:

```
ok
```

At any time, you can switch back to the system controller prompt from the OpenBoot prompt by typing the pound key (#) followed by a period (.) as follows:

```
ok #.
```

Note

When typing `#.` at the OpenBoot prompt, characters are not echoed to the screen.

On a new server, when connecting to the ALOM system controller for the first time using the SER MGT port, there is no default password. When connecting to the system controller using the NET MGT port for the first time, the default password is the last eight digits of the chassis serial number. You must assign a password during the initial system configuration, and the password should be documented in a safe location. If you forget the password, you'll need to reset the ALOM NVRAM as documented in "Advanced Lights Out Manager (ALOM) CMT v1.4 Guide," part number 819-7991-10, available at Oracle's online technical library at `http://docs.oracle.com`.

The ALOM system controller runs independently of the service regardless of the system power state. As long as AC power is connected to the system and you have a physical connection to either the NET MGT or SER MGT port, you can connect to the system controller at any time. You can then power on the server from the ALOM system controller by typing `poweron` at the `sc>` prompt as follows:

```
sc> poweron<cr>
```

Refer to the "Sun Advanced Lights Out Manager (ALOM) Administration Guide" for more information on the commands that can be issued at the ALOM system controller prompt.

More than one user can access the console, but only one can have write privileges; the others have read-only access. In other words, several users can view the console, but only one user can enter commands. To gain write access to the console, use the `-f` option as follows:

```
sc> console -f<cr>

Warning: User <admin> currently has write permission to this console and forcibly
removing them will terminate any current write actions and all work will be lost. Would
you like to continue? [y/n]y

Enter #. to return to ALOM.
```

Answer "y" when prompted, and you'll take over the console and be granted write access. All other users will have read-only access.

ILOM and the Service Processor

The T3, T4, T5xx, and T6xxx series servers come preconfigured to allow input and output only by means of the ILOM service processor. The ILOM service processor is accessed through either the SER MGT or the NET MGT.

You can access the ILOM service processor through the SER MGT. Connect an ASCII terminal using a null modem serial cable with an RJ45 connector to the SER MGT port. The default configuration is

- 9,600 baud
- 8 bits
- No parity
- 1 stop bit
- No handshaking (set hardware flow control to none)

By default, the NET MGT port is configured to retrieve its IP address and other network configuration information using a local DHCP server and allows connections using an SSH client. Most system administrators use the NET MGT port for connecting to the system console. This port can be configured to accept connections from an SSH client or Web browser based network management connection.

The network configuration for the NET MGT port can be modified by connecting to the NET MGT port using an SSH client (or connecting to the SER MGT port) and modifying the network configuration manually on the system controller. The IP address for connecting to the NET MGT port is a unique IP address separate from the main server IP address. Refer to the documentation that came with your server or refer to the "Oracle Integrated Lights Out Manager (ILOM) 3.0: Daily Management—Concepts Guide" (part number E21447-02) for more information.

Connect to the NET MGT port using SSH as follows:

```
$ ssh root@<system-ip-address><cr>
```

When you have successfully connected to the service processor through either the SER MGT or the NET MGT port, you'll see the ILOM login prompt:

```
Version 3.0.0.0 r46636
Copyright 2009 Sun Microsystems, Inc. All Rights reserved.
Use is subject to license terms.
```

Enter the login name: The default login name is `root`.

```
Please login:root<cr>
```

Enter a password: The default password is `changeme`.

```
Please Enter password:changeme<cr>
```

The login name and password are set up by the system administrator the first time the ILOM console is accessed. After entering the correct password, the ILOM command prompt is displayed as follows:

```
->
```

When you see the `->` prompt, you are on the service processor, not the system console. Start the system console as follows:

```
-> start /SP/console<cr>
Are you sure you want to start /SP/console (y/n)? y<cr>

Serial console started. To stop, type #.
```

The OpenBoot prompt will appear as follows:

```
ok
```

At any time, you can switch back to the service processor prompt from the OpenBoot prompt by typing the pound key (#) followed by a period (.) as follows:

```
ok #.
```

Note

When typing `#.` at the OpenBoot prompt, characters are not echoed to the screen.

The ILOM service processor runs independently of the service regardless of the system power state. As long as AC power is connected to the system and you have a physical connection to either the NET MGT or SER MGT port, you can connect to the service processor at any time. You can then turn on power to the server from the ILOM service processor by typing `start /SYS` at the `->` prompt as follows:

```
-> start /SYS<cr>
```

For more information on the commands that can be issued at the ILOM service processor prompt, refer to "Oracle Integrated Lights Out Manager 3.1 Documentation," part number E24707-01, available at Oracle's online technical library at `http://docs.oracle.com`.

More than one user can access the console, but only one can have write privileges; the others have read-only access. In other words, several users can view the console, but only one user can enter commands. To gain write access to the console, use the `-force` option as follows:

```
-> start -force /SP/console<cr>
```

OpenBoot Firmware Tasks

The IEEE Standard 1275, "IEEE Standard for Boot (Initialization Configuration) Firmware: Core Requirements and Practices," defines the OpenBoot architecture, and the primary tasks of the OpenBoot firmware are as follows:

- Test and initialize the system hardware.
- Determine the hardware configuration.
- Start the OS from either a mass storage device or a network.
- Provide interactive debugging facilities for configuring, testing, and debugging.
- Allow modification and management of system startup configuration, such as NVRAM parameters.
- Servers such as the SunFire provide environmental monitoring and control capabilities at both the OS level and the OpenBoot firmware level to monitor the state of the system power supplies, fans, and temperature sensors. If it detects any voltage, current, fan speed, or temperature irregularities, the monitor generates a warning message to the system console, and ultimately it initiates an automatic system shutdown sequence.

Specifically, the following tasks are necessary to initialize the OS kernel:

1. OpenBoot displays system identification information and then runs self-test diagnostics to verify the system's hardware and memory. These checks are known as POSTs.
2. OpenBoot then probes system bus devices, interprets their drivers, builds a device tree, and installs the console. After initializing the system, OpenBoot displays a banner on the console.
3. OpenBoot checks parameters stored in NVRAM to determine how to boot the OS.

4. OpenBoot loads the primary startup program, bootblk, from the default boot device (`boot-device`).
5. The bootblk program finds and loads the root file system boot archive.

The OpenBoot Architecture

The OpenBoot architecture provides an increase in functionality and portability in contrast to the proprietary systems of some other hardware vendors. Although this architecture was first implemented by Sun Microsystems as OpenBoot on SPARC (Scalable Processor Architecture) systems, its design is processor independent. The following are some notable features of OpenBoot firmware:

- Plug-in device drivers: A device driver can be loaded from a plug-in device such as a peripheral component interconnect (PCI) card. The plug-in device driver can be used to boot the OS from that device or to display text on the device before the OS has activated its own software device drivers. This feature lets the input and output devices evolve without changing the system PROM.
- The FCode interpreter: Plug-in drivers are written in a machine-independent interpreted language called "FCode." Each OpenBoot system PROM contains an FCode interpreter. This enables the same device and driver to be used on machines with different CPU instruction sets.

  Nodes with children usually represent buses and their associated controllers, if any. Each such node defines a physical address space that distinguishes the devices connected to the node from one another. Each child of that node is assigned a physical address in the parent's address space. The physical address generally represents a physical characteristic that is unique to the device (such as the bus address or the slot number where the device is installed). The use of physical addresses to identify devices prevents device addresses from changing when other devices are installed or removed.
- The device tree: Devices called "nodes" are attached to a host computer through a hierarchy of interconnected buses on the device tree. A node representing the host computer's main physical address bus forms the tree's root node. Both the user and the OS can determine the system's hardware configuration by viewing the device tree.
- The programmable user interface: The OpenBoot user interface is based on the programming language Forth, which provides an interactive programming environment. It can be quickly expanded and adapted to special needs and different hardware systems. Forth is used not only by Oracle but is also used in the OpenFirmware boot ROMs provided by IBM, Apple, and Hewlett-Packard.

The OpenBoot Interface

The OpenBoot firmware provides a command-line interface for the user at the system console called the Forth Monitor.

The Forth Monitor is an interactive command interpreter that gives you access to an extensive set of functions for hardware and software diagnosis. These functions are available to anyone who has access to the system console.

The Forth Monitor prompt is `ok`. When you enter Forth Monitor mode, the following line displays:

```
Type help for more information
(0) ok
```

Getting Help in OpenBoot

At any time, you can obtain help on the various Forth commands supported in OpenBoot by using the `help` command. The `help` commands from the `ok` prompt are listed in Table 3-1.

Because of the large number of commands, help is available only for commands that are used frequently.

The following example shows the `help` command with no arguments:

```
{0} ok help<cr>
```

The system responds with the following:

```
ok help<cr>
Enter 'help command-name' or 'help category-name' for more help
(Use ONLY the first word of a category description)
Examples: help select  -or-  help line
    Main categories are:
Breakpoints (debugging)
Repeated loops
Defining new commands
Numeric output
Radix (number base conversions)
Arithmetic
Memory access
Line editor
System and boot configuration parameters
Select I/O devices
eject devices
Power on reset
Diag (diagnostic routines)
Resume execution
File download and boot
nvramrc (making new commands permanent))
(0) ok
```

Table 3-1 OpenBoot `help` Commands

Command	Description
`help`	The `help` command displays instructions for using the help system and lists the available help categories.
`help` *<category>*	This command shows help for all commands in the category. You use only the first word of the category description.
`help` *<command>*	This command shows help for an individual command.

If you want to see the help messages for all commands in the category `diag`, for example, type the following:

```
{0} ok help diag<cr>
```

The system responds with this:

```
test  <device-specifier>  Run selftest method for specified device
  Examples:
    test floppy        - test floppy disk drive
    test net           - test net
    test scsi          - test scsi
test-all         Execute test for all devices with selftest method
watch-clock      Show ticks of real-time clock
watch-net        Monitor network broadcast packets
watch-net-all    Monitor broadcast packets on all net interfaces
probe-scsi       Show attached SCSI devices
probe-scsi-all   Show attached SCSI devices for all host adapters
{0} ok

{0} ok help boot<cr>
```

The system responds with this:

```
boot <specifier>  ( - )    boot kernel ( default ) or other file
  Examples:
    boot                    - boot kernel from default device.
                              Factory default is to boot
                              from DISK if present, otherwise from NET.
    boot net                - boot kernel from network
    boot cdrom              - boot kernel from CD-ROM
    boot disk1:h            - boot from disk1 partition h
    boot tape               - boot default file from tape
    boot disk myunix -as    - boot myunix from disk with flags "-as"
dload <filename>  ( addr - )    debug load of file over network at address
  Examples:
    4000 dload /export/root/foo/test
    ?go          - if executable program, execute it
                   or if Forth program, compile it
```

PROM Device Tree (Full Device Pathnames)

OpenBoot deals directly with the hardware devices in the system. Each device has a unique name that represents both the type of device and the location of that device in the device tree. This is also referred to as the full device pathname. The OpenBoot firmware builds a device tree for all devices from information gathered at the POST. Oracle Solaris uses the device tree to organize devices that are attached to the system. The device tree is loaded into memory, to be used by the kernel during boot to identify all configured devices. The paths built in to the device tree by OpenBoot vary depending on the type of system and its device configuration. The following example shows a full device pathname for an internal Integrated Drive Electronics (IDE) DVD on a PCI bus system such as a SPARC Enterprise server:

```
/pci@7c0/pci@0/pci@1/pci@0/ide@8/cdrom
```

Typically, the OBP uses `disk` and `cdrom` for the boot disk and DVD drive.

The following example from a SPARC Enterprise Server shows the internal Serial Attached SCSI (SAS) disk device at port 0:

```
/pci@780/pci@0/pci@9/scsi@0/disk@0
```

A device tree is a series of node names separated by slashes (/). The top of the device tree is the root device node. Following the root device node, and separated by a leading slash, is a list of bus devices and controllers.

In this example,

```
/pci@780/pci@0/pci@9/scsi@0/disk@0
```

the path points to an onboard PCI 1064E controller where

`pci@780` represents the Fire I/O Bridge Bus A on a T2000 Enterprise server.
`pci@0` represents a PLX 8532 PCI-E Switch A (U0901).
`pci@9` represents the LSI 1064-E SAS Controller (U3401).

The disk device is attached to a SAS controller at target 0, and the disk is connected on port 0 of the SAS bus.

Use the OpenBoot command `show-devs` to obtain information about the device tree and to display device pathnames. This command displays all the devices known to the system directly beneath a given device in the device hierarchy. `show-devs` used by itself shows the entire device tree. The syntax is as follows:

```
ok show-devs<cr>
```

The system outputs the entire device tree:

```
/os-io
/ramdisk-root
/pci@7c0
/pci@780
/cpu@f
/cpu@e
/cpu@d
/cpu@c
/cpu@b
/cpu@a
/cpu@9
<Output has been truncated>
```

Use the `scsi` argument to display only SCSI devices as follows:

```
ok show-devs scsi<cr>
/pci@780/pci@0/pci@9/scsi@0/disk
/pci@780/pci@0/pci@9/scsi@0/tape
```

Commands that are used to examine the device tree are listed in Table 3-2. You can examine the device path from a shell prompt by typing the following:

```
# prtconf -p<cr>
System Configuration: Oracle Corporation sun4v
Memory size: 3968 Megabytes
System Peripherals (PROM Nodes):

Node 'SUNW,Sun-Fire-T200'
    Node 'packages'
        Node 'SUNW,builtin-drivers'
        Node 'deblocker'
        Node 'disk-label'
        Node 'terminal-emulator'
        Node 'dropins'
        Node 'SUNW,asr'
        Node 'kbd-translator'
        Node 'obp-tftp'
        Node 'zfs-file-system'
        Node 'hsfs-file-system'
<Output has been truncated>
```

Table 3-2 Commands for Browsing the Device Tree

Command	Description
`.properties`	Displays the names and values of the current node's properties.
`dev` *<device-path>*	Chooses the specified device node and makes it the current node.
`dev` *<node-name>*	Searches for a node with the specified name in the subtree below the current node and chooses the first such node found.
`dev ..`	Chooses the device node that is the parent of the current node.
`dev /`	Chooses the root machine node.
`cd /`	Same as `dev /`.
`device-end`	Leaves the device tree.
<device-path> `find-device`	Chooses the specified device node, similar to `dev`.
`ls`	Displays the names of the current node's children.
`pwd`	Displays the device pathname that names the current node.
`see` *<wordname>*	Decompiles the specified word.
`show-devs` *<device-path>*	Displays all the devices known to the system directly beneath a given device in the device hierarchy; `show-devs` used by itself shows the entire device tree.
`show-disks`	Displays only the disk devices currently connected to the system.
`show-nets`	Displays only the network interface devices currently connected to the system.
`words`	Displays the names of the current node's methods.
<device-path> `select-dev`	Selects the specified device and makes it the active node.

OpenBoot Device Aliases

Device pathnames can be long and complex. Device aliases, like UNIX file system aliases, allow you to substitute a short name for a long name. An alias represents an entire device pathname, not a component of it. For example, the alias `disk0` might represent the following device pathname:

```
/pci@780/pci@0/pci@9/scsi@0/disk@0
```

OpenBoot provides the predefined device aliases listed in Table 3-3 for commonly used devices, so you rarely need to type a full device pathname. Be aware, however, that device aliases and pathnames can vary on each platform. The device aliases shown in Table 3-3 are from an Oracle T2000 Enterprise server.

Specifying the Slice as Part of the Device Pathname

Sometimes you may see the slice specified as part of the device pathname, as shown with the cdrom: /pci@7c0/pci@0/pci@1/pci@0/ide@8/cdrom@0,0:f.

Other times you'll see it specified for the boot-device as follows:

/pci@780/pci@0/pci@9/scsi@0/disk@0:a. The letter after the colon specifies the slice on that particular disk, so the letter a indicates slice 0, and the letter f indicates slice 5. If the letter is not specified, slice 0 is assumed.

If you add disk drives or change the target of the startup drive, you might need to modify these device aliases. Table 3-4 describes the devalias commands, which are used to examine, create, and change OpenBoot aliases.

Table 3-3 Predefined Device Aliases

Alias	Device Pathname
disk	/pci@780/pci@0/pci@9/scsi@0/disk@0
disk3	/pci@780/pci@0/pci@9/scsi@0/disk@3
disk2	/pci@780/pci@0/pci@9/scsi@0/disk@2
disk1	/pci@780/pci@0/pci@9/scsi@0/disk@1
disk0	/pci@780/pci@0/pci@9/scsi@0/disk@0
cdrom	/pci@7c0/pci@0/pci@1/pci@0/ide@8/cdrom@0,0:f
net	/pci@780/pci@0/pci@1/network@0

Table 3-4 devalias Commands

Command	Description
devalias	Displays all current device aliases
devalias_*<alias>*	Displays the device pathname that corresponds to alias
devalias_*<alias>* *<device-path>*	Defines an alias that represents device-path

Caution When Using Existing devalias Names

If an alias with the same name already exists, you see two aliases defined: a devalias with the old value and a devalias with the new value. It gets confusing as to which `devalias` is the current `devalias`. The device alias with the old value will be deleted after the next reset or power cycle.

The following example creates a device alias named `bootdisk`, which represents a SAS disk with a target ID of 0 on a T2000 Enterprise server:

```
bootdisk        /pci@780/pci@0/pci@9/scsi@0/disk@0
```

To confirm the alias, type `devalias` as follows:

```
{0} ok devalias<cr>
```

The system responds by printing all of the aliases:

```
ttya                     /pci@7c0/pci@0/pci@1/pci@0/isa@2/serial@0,3f8
nvram                    /virtual-devices/nvram@3
net3                     /pci@7c0/pci@0/pci@2/network@0,1
net2                     /pci@7c0/pci@0/pci@2/network@0
net1                     /pci@780/pci@0/pci@1/network@0,1
net0                     /pci@780/pci@0/pci@1/network@0
net                      /pci@780/pci@0/pci@1/network@0
ide                      /pci@7c0/pci@0/pci@1/pci@0/ide@8
cdrom                    /pci@7c0/pci@0/pci@1/pci@0/ide@8/cdrom@0,0:f
disk3                    /pci@780/pci@0/pci@9/scsi@0/disk@3
disk2                    /pci@780/pci@0/pci@9/scsi@0/disk@2
disk1                    /pci@780/pci@0/pci@9/scsi@0/disk@1
disk0                    /pci@780/pci@0/pci@9/scsi@0/disk@0
disk                     /pci@780/pci@0/pci@9/scsi@0/disk@0
scsi                     /pci@780/pci@0/pci@9/scsi@0
virtual-console          /virtual-devices/console@1
name                     aliases
```

Viewing Device Aliases

You can also view device aliases from a shell prompt by using the `prtconf -vp` command.

User-defined aliases are lost after a system reset or power cycle unless you create a permanent alias. If you want to create permanent aliases, you can either manually store the `devalias` command in a portion of NVRAM called `NVRAMRC` or you can use the `nvalias` and `nvunalias` commands. The following section describes how to configure permanent settings in the NVRAM on a SPARC system.

OpenBoot NVRAM

System configuration variables are stored in system NVRAM and OpenBoot variables. These OpenBoot variables determine the startup machine configuration and related communication characteristics. If you modify the values of the configuration variables, any changes you make remain in effect even after a power cycle. Configuration variables should be adjusted cautiously, however, because incorrect settings can prevent a system from booting.

Table 3-5 describes some of the more common OpenBoot NVRAM configuration variables, their default values, and their functions.

Table 3-5 NVRAM Variables

Variable	Default	Description
`auto-boot?`	`true`	The system starts up automatically after power-on or reset if `auto-boot?` is `true`. If it is set to `false`, the system stops at the OpenBoot prompt (`ok`) after power-on or reset.
`boot-command`	`boot`	The command is executed if `auto-boot?` is `true`.
`boot-device`	`disk` or `net`	This variable is the device from which to start up.
`boot-file`	Empty string	Arguments passed to the started program.
`diag-switch?`	`false`	This variable determines whether to run in diagnostic mode. Set to `true` for POST diagnostics to run automatically when the server is powered on.
`fcode-debug?`	`false`	This variable determines whether name fields are included for plug-in device FCodes.
`input-device`	`keyboard`	A console input device (usually keyboard, ttya, or ttyb).
`nvramrc`	Empty	The contents of NVRAMRC.
`oem-banner`	Empty string	A custom original equipment manufacturer (OEM) banner (enabled with `oem-banner? true`).
`oem-banner?`	`false`	If `true`, use a custom OEM banner.
`oem-logo`	No default	A byte array custom OEM logo (enabled with `oem-logo? true`). Displayed in hexadecimal.
`oem-logo?`	`false`	If `true`, use a custom OEM logo; otherwise, use the Sun logo.
`output-device`	`screen`	A console output device (usually screen, ttya, or ttyb).
`screen-#columns`	`80`	The number of onscreen columns (characters per line).
`screen-#rows`	`34`	The number of onscreen rows (lines).

Variable	Default	Description
security-#badlogins	No default	The number of incorrect security password attempts.
security-mode	none	The firmware security level (options: none, command, or full).
security-password	No default	The firmware security password (which is never displayed).
use-nvramrc?	false	If true, execute commands in NVRAMRC during system startup.

Table 3-6 Commands for Viewing and Modifying Configuration Variables

Command	Description
password	Sets the security password.
printenv	Displays the current value and the default value for each variable. To show the current value of a named variable, type the following: printenv <*parameter-name*>.
setenv <*variable*> <*value*>	Sets <*variable*> to the given decimal or text <*value*>. Changes are permanent, but they often take effect only after a reset.
set-default <*variable*>	Resets the value of a specified <*variable*> to the factory default.
set-defaults	Resets all OpenBoot variable values to the factory defaults.

Any OpenBoot parameter that ends with a ?, is set to true or false.

OpenBoot Man Pages

Although there is not a man page for OpenBoot, refer to the online man page for monitor(1M), boot(1M), and eeprom(1M). Many of the OpenBoot configuration parameters and commands are described in those online man pages.

OpenBoot Versions

Because some SPARC systems may use older or newer versions of OpenBoot, they might use different defaults or different configuration variables from those shown in Table 3-5. This text describes OpenBoot version 4.

You can view and change the NVRAM configuration variables by using the commands listed in Table 3-6.

The following examples illustrate the use of the commands described in Table 3-6. All commands are entered at the ok OpenBoot prompt.

You use the printenv command at the OpenBoot prompt, with no argument, to display the current value and the default value for each variable as follows:

```
{0} ok printenv<cr>
```

The system responds with

```
Variable Name           Value          Default Value

ttya-rts-dtr-off        false          false
ttya-ignore-cd          true           true
keyboard-layout
reboot-command
security-mode           none           No default
security-password                      No default
<output has been truncated>
```

The printenv Command

Depending on the version of OpenBoot that you have on your system, the printenv command might show slightly different results. This example uses a system running OpenBoot version 4.30.0.

To set the auto-boot? variable to false, type the following:

```
ok setenv auto-boot? false<cr>
```

The system responds with this:

```
auto-boot? = false
```

Verify the setting by typing the following:

```
ok printenv auto-boot?<cr>
```

The system responds with this:

```
auto-boot? =  false
```

To reset the variable to its default setting, type the following:

```
{0} ok set-default auto-boot?<cr>
{0} ok
```

The system does not respond with a message—only another OpenBoot prompt. You can verify the setting by typing the following:

```
{0} ok printenv auto-boot?<cr>
```

The system responds with this:

```
auto-boot? =  true
```

To reset all variables to their default settings, type the following:

```
{0} ok set-defaults<cr>
```

The system responds with this:

```
Setting NVRAM parameters to default values.
```

It's possible to set device aliases and OpenBoot variables from the UNIX command line by issuing the `eeprom` command. `eeprom` displays or changes the values of parameters in the EEPROM. You must be logged in as root to issue this command, and although anyone can view a parameter, only root can change the value of a parameter. For example, to set the `auto-boot?` variable to `true`, type the following at the UNIX prompt (note the use of quotes to escape the `?` from expansion by the shell):

```
# eeprom 'auto-boot?=true'<cr>
```

Any nonroot user can view the OpenBoot configuration variables from a UNIX prompt by typing the following:

```
# /usr/sbin/eeprom<cr>
```

eeprom Command on the x86-Based Platform

The eeprom command is available on the x86 platform, even though the x86 platform does not support OpenBoot. EEPROM storage is simulated using a file residing in the platform-specific boot area. The /boot/solaris/bootenv.rc file simulates EEPROM storage.

For example, to change the OpenBoot parameter security-password on a SPARC system from the command line, you must be logged in as root and issue the following from the command line:

```
# eeprom security-password=
Changing PROM password:
New password:
Retype new password:
```

Setting the OpenBoot Security Mode

Setting the security mode and password can be dangerous: If you forget the password, the system is unable to boot. It is nearly impossible to break in without sending the CPU to Oracle to have the PROM reset. These security issues are discussed more in the section "OpenBoot Security" later in this chapter.

Because x86-based systems implement password protection in the system's basic input/output system (BIOS), there is no support for password protection. Although it is possible to set the security-mode, security-password, and security-#badlogins properties on x86-based systems, these properties have no special meaning or behavior on x86-based systems.

The security mode password that you assign must have between zero and eight characters. Any characters after the eighth are ignored. You do not have to reset the system after you set a password; the security feature takes effect as soon as you type the command.

You can also use the eeprom command to add or modify device aliases from the command line as follows:

```
# eeprom "nvramrc=devalias bootdisk /pci@780/pci@0/pci@9/scsi@0/disk@0"<cr>
```

This doesn't change the devalias yet. The preceding command creates an nvramrc script that contains a series of OBP commands that are executed during the boot sequence. If the use-nvramrc? configuration variable is true, the script is evaluated during the OpenBoot startup sequence, and the bootdisk alias gets created automatically at the next system reset.

With no parameters, the eeprom command displays all the OpenBoot configuration settings, similar to the OpenBoot printenv command.

Use the `prtconf` command with the `-vp` options to view OpenBoot parameters from the shell prompt as follows:

```
# prtconf -vp<cr>
```

The system responds with a great deal of output, but you see the following OpenBoot information embedded in the output:

```
. . . .<output truncated>
oem-banner?:  'false'
ansi-terminal?:  'true'
screen-#columns:  '80'
screen-#rows:  '34'
ttya-mode:  '9600,8,n,1,-'
output-device:  'screen'
input-device:  'keyboard'
auto-boot-on-error?:  'false'
load-base:  '16384'
auto-boot?:  'true'
network-boot-arguments:
boot-command:  'boot'
boot-file:
boot-device:  '/pci@780/pci@0/pci@9/scsi@0/disk@0,0:a disk'
multipath-boot?:  'false'
cdrom:  '/pci@7c0/pci@0/pci@1/pci@0/ide@8/cdrom@0,0:f'
disk3:  '/pci@780/pci@0/pci@9/scsi@0/disk@3'
disk2:  '/pci@780/pci@0/pci@9/scsi@0/disk@2'
disk1:  '/pci@780/pci@0/pci@9/scsi@0/disk@1'
disk0:  '/pci@780/pci@0/pci@9/scsi@0/disk@0'
disk:   '/pci@780/pci@0/pci@9/scsi@0/disk@0'
scsi:   '/pci@780/pci@0/pci@9/scsi@0'. . .
<output truncated>
```

Resetting NVRAM Variables

On systems with USB keyboards, turn on power to the system and wait for the front-panel power button light-emitting diode (LED) to blink. You will hear an audible beep. Quickly press the front-panel power button twice (similar to double-clicking a mouse). The console displays a screen that says you have successfully reset the NVRAM contents to their default values. At this point, some NVRAM configuration parameters are reset to their defaults, and others are not. Only parameters that are more likely to cause problems, such as TTYA terminal settings, are changed to the default. If you do nothing other than reset the machine at this point, the values are not permanently changed. Only settings that you change manually at this point become permanent. All other customized NVRAM settings are retained.

You can use the NVRAM commands listed in Table 3-7 to modify device aliases so that they remain permanent, even after a restart.

Table 3-7 NVRAM Commands

Command	Description
`nvalias <alias> <device-path>`	This command stores the command `devalias <alias> <device-path>` in NVRAMRC. (The alias persists until the `nvunalias` or `set-defaults` command is executed.) This command turns on `use-nvramrc?`.
`nvunalias <alias>`	This command deletes the corresponding *alias* from NVRAMRC.

For example, to permanently create a device alias named `bootdisk` that represents a SAS disk on port 0, type the following:

```
ok nvalias bootdisk /pci@780/pci@0/pci@9/scsi@0/disk@0<cr>
```

Because disk device pathnames can be long and complex, the `show-disks` command is provided to assist you in creating device aliases. Type the `show-disks` command, and you will see a list of disk devices:

```
{0} ok show-disks<cr>
a) /ramdisk-root
b) /pci@7c0/pci@0/pci@1/pci@0/ide@8/cdrom
c) /pci@7c0/pci@0/pci@1/pci@0/ide@8/disk
d) /pci@780/pci@0/pci@9/scsi@0/disk
q) NO SELECTION
Enter Selection, q to quit:
```

Type “d” to select a SAS disk. The system responds with the following message:

```
/pci@780/pci@0/pci@9/scsi@0/disk has been selected.
Type ^Y ( Control-Y ) to insert it in the command line.
e.g. ok nvalias mydev ^Y
   for creating devalias mydev for /pci@780/pci@0/pci@9/scsi@0/disk
{0} ok
```

Now create a device alias named `bootdisk` and press *Ctrl+Y:*

```
{0} ok nvalias bootdisk ^Y<cr>
```

The system pastes the selected device path:

```
{0} ok nvalias bootdisk /pci@780/pci@0/pci@9/scsi@0/disk
```

Now all you need to do is add the target number @0 to the end of the device name and press *Enter*:

```
ok nvalias bootdisk /pci@780/pci@0/pci@9/scsi@0/disk@0<cr>
```

Specifying the Disk Slice

If the boot slice of the disk device that you want to boot to is not slice 0, you need to add the disk slice letter to the end of the device name:

```
{0} ok nvalias bootdisk /pci@1f,0/pci@1/scsi@8/disk@0,0:b<cr>
```

In this example, the letter b was used, which corresponds to disk slice 1. This is one area where you'll find disk slices identified by an alpha character and not a number. The letter a corresponds to slice 0, b is slice 1, and so on. If no letter is specified, a for slice 0 is assumed. For example, /pci@780/pci@0/pci@9/scsi@0/disk@0 is the same as specifying /pci@780/pci@0/pci@9/scsi@0/disk@0:a.

To remove an alias, type nvunalias *<aliasname>*. For example, to remove the devalias named bootdisk, type

```
{0} ok nvunalias bootdisk<cr>
```

The alias named bootdisk will no longer be listed after the next OpenBoot reset.

OpenBoot Security

Anyone who has access to the system console can access OpenBoot and modify parameters unless you set up the security variables. These variables are listed in Table 3-8.

Table 3-8 OpenBoot Security Variables

Variable	Description
security-mode	This variable restricts the set of operations that users are allowed to perform at the OpenBoot prompt.
security-password	Records the firmware security password. (It is never displayed.) You should not set this variable directly; you set it by using password.
security-#badlogins	This variable specifies the number of incorrect security password attempts.

Setting the OpenBoot Security Mode

It is important to remember your security password and to set it before setting the security mode. If you later forget this password, you cannot use your system; you must call your vendor's customer support service to make your machine bootable again.

If you can get to a UNIX prompt as root, you can use the eeprom command to either change the security-mode parameter to "none" or reset the security password.

To set the security password, type the password command at the ok prompt, as shown in the following:

```
{0} ok password<cr>
New password (only first 8 chars are used): <enter password><cr>
Retype new password: <enter password><cr>
```

Earlier in this chapter you learned how to change the OpenBoot parameter security-password from the command line.

After you assign a password, you can set the security variables that best fit your environment.

Use security-mode to restrict the use of OpenBoot commands. When you assign one of the three values shown in Table 3-9, access to commands is protected by a password. The syntax for setting security-mode from the OpenBoot prompt is as follows:

```
{0} ok setenv security-mode <value><cr>
```

The following example sets the OpenBoot environment so that all commands except boot and go require a password:

```
{0} ok setenv security-mode command<cr>
```

Table 3-9 OpenBoot Security Values

Value	Description
full	This value specifies that all OpenBoot commands except go require a password. This security mode is the most restrictive.
command	This value specifies that all OpenBoot commands except boot and go require a password.
none	This value specifies that no password is required. This is the default.

With security-mode set to command, a password is not required if you enter the boot command by itself or if you enter the go command. Any other command requires a password, including the boot command with an argument.

Table 3-10 lists examples of when a password might be required in OpenBoot when security-mode is set to command.

The Password Is Not Displayed

Note that with password, the password is not echoed as it is typed.

If you enter an incorrect security password, there is a delay of about 10 seconds before the next startup prompt appears. The number of times that an incorrect security password can be typed is stored in the security-#badlogins variable, but you should not change this variable.

OpenBoot Diagnostics

You can run various hardware diagnostics in OpenBoot to troubleshoot hardware and network problems. The diagnostic commands are listed in Table 3-11.

Table 3-10 Restricted OpenBoot Commands

Example	Description
boot	No password is required.
go	No password is required.
reset-all	You are prompted to enter a password.

Table 3-11 OpenBoot Diagnostic Commands

Command	Description
.env	On servers, this command is used to obtain status information about the system's power supplies, fans, and temperature sensors.
probe-scsi	This command identifies devices attached to the internal SCSI bus.
probe-scsi-all	This command identifies devices attached to any SCSI bus.
probe-ide	This command identifies IDE devices attached to the PCI bus.
probe-fcal-all	This command identifies devices on all Fibre Channel loops.
reset-all	This command resets the entire system, similar to a power cycle.
test *<device-specifier>*	This command executes the specified device's self-test method. For test net, this command tests the network connection.

(*continues*)

Table 3-11 OpenBoot Diagnostic Commands *(Continued)*

Command	Description
`test-all <device-specifier>`	This command tests all devices that have built-in self-test methods below the specified device tree node. If `<device-specifier>` is absent, all devices beginning from the root node are tested.
`watch-clock`	This command tests the clock function.
`watch-net`	This command monitors the primary network connection.
`watch-net-all`	This command monitors the primary network connection and any additional network interfaces.

The OpenBoot parameter named `diag-level` can be set to specify the extent of diagnostic coverage performed by diagnostic commands. Some system administrators set the `diag-level` to `low` just to make the bootup process quicker. Understand that to ensure maximum coverage of testing, the `diag-level` needs to be set to `max`.

There are several open boot commands that can be used to probe devices. These commands can be viewed with the `sifting probe` command as follows:

```
{0} ok sifting probe<cr>
   In vocabulary forth
(f026493c) probe-all     (f0263e74) probe-ide     (f0263c64) probe-scsi-all
(f0263b78) probe-scsi    (f02639d4) probe-all     (f0263984) probe-io
(f0263780) probe-usb-all          (f02345a0) probe
(f0234460) probe-virtual          (f022fe98) xprobe        (f022fe70) lprobe
(f022fe48) wprobe        (f022fe20) cprobe
```

The OpenBoot `sifting` command, also called a `sifting` dump, searches OpenBoot commands to find every command name that contains the specified string.

This first example uses the OpenBoot probe command, `probe-scsi-all`, to identify all the SCSI devices attached to every SCSI bus:

```
{0} ok probe-scsi-all<cr>
/pci@780/pci@0/pci@9/scsi@0

MPT Version 1.05, Firmware Version 1.09.00.00

Target 0
Unit 0  Disk  FUJITSU MAY2073RCSUN72G 0401  143374738 Blocks, 73 GB
  SASAddress 500000e011988932 PhyNum 0
Target 1
Unit 0  Disk  SEAGATE ST973402SSUN72G 0603  143374738 Blocks, 73 GB
  SASAddress 5000c5000a66f535 PhyNum 1
```

If the system has not been reset before the `probe-scsi-all` command is issued, the following message is displayed:

```
This command may hang the system if a Stop-A or halt command has been executed.
Please type reset-all to reset the system before executing this command.
Do you wish to continue? (y/n) n<cr>
```

If you choose to continue, the system hangs and requires a power reset. Type n to abort the probe-scsi-all command. Before proceeding, it's best to have the auto-boot? value set to false so that the system does not try to boot after performing a reset. Next, type reset-all to reset the system. After the system resets, it's acceptable to use the probe-scsi-all command.

OpenBoot Probe Commands

The OpenBoot probe commands probe-scsi and probe-scsi-all are used to obtain a free open SCSI target ID number before adding a SCSI tape unit, a CD-ROM drive, a disk drive, or any other SCSI peripheral. Only devices that are powered on will be located, so you need to make sure everything is turned on. You can use this command after installing a SCSI device to ensure that it has been connected properly and that the system can see it. You can also use this command if you suspect the presence of a faulty cable or connection. The probe-scsi command only checks drives connected to the onboard SCSI controller. If you have more than one SCSI bus, you use the probe-scsi-all command.

Table 3-12 describes other OpenBoot commands you can use to gather information about the system.

The following example uses the banner command to display the CPU type, the installed RAM, the Ethernet address, the host ID, and the version and date of the startup PROM:

```
{0} ok banner<cr>
```

Table 3-12 System Information Commands

Command	Description
banner	This command displays the power-on banner.
show-sbus	This command displays a list of installed and probed SBus devices.
.enet-addr	This command displays the current Ethernet address.
.idprom	This command displays ID PROM contents, formatted.
.traps	This command displays a list of SPARC trap types.
.version	This command displays the version and date of the startup PROM.
show-devs	This command displays all installed and probed devices.

The system responds with the following:

```
Sun Fire T200, No Keyboard
Copyright 2008 Sun Microsystems, Inc. All rights reserved.
OpenBoot 4.30.0, 3968 MB memory available, Serial #84994072.
Ethernet address 0:21:28:10:e8:18, Host ID: 8510e818.
```

This example uses the `.version` command to display the OpenBoot version and the date of the startup PROM:

```
{0} ok .version<cr>
```

The system responds with the following:

```
Release 4.30.0 created 2008/12/11 12:15
```

You can display the OpenBoot version from a shell prompt using the `prtdiag` command as follows:

```
# /usr/sbin/prtdiag -v<cr>
```

The system displays system diagnostic information for the CPUs, physical memory, input/output (I/O) configuration, OpenBoot PROM revision, all of the hardware sensors, and LEDs. The following example prints out the diagnostic information on a T2000 Enterprise server. Some of the output has been removed to save space:

```
# prtdiag -v<cr>
System Configuration: Oracle Corporation sun4v Sun Fire T200
Memory size: 3968 Megabytes

================================ Virtual CPUs ================================

CPU ID Frequency Implementation      Status
------ --------- ---------------------- -------
0     1000 MHz SUNW,UltraSPARC-T1  on-line
1     1000 MHz SUNW,UltraSPARC-T1  on-line
2     1000 MHz SUNW,UltraSPARC-T1  on-line
3     1000 MHz SUNW,UltraSPARC-T1  on-line
. . . .
====================== Physical Memory Configuration ======================
Segment Table:
------------------------------------------------------------------
Base            Segment      Interleave   Bank      Contains
Address         Size         Factor       Size      Modules
------------------------------------------------------------------
0x0             4 GB         4            2 GB      MB/CMP0/CH1/R0/D0
                                                    MB/CMP0/CH1/R0/D1
```

```
                                    2 GB     MB/CMP0/CH2/R0/D0
                                             MB/CMP0/CH2/R0/D1
. . . .
========================= IO Configuration =========================

       IO

Location  Type Slot Path                                          Name
           Model
----------- ----- ---- ------------------------------------------------ -----------
-------------- ----------
IOBD/NET0  PCIE IOBD          /pci@780/pci@0/pci@1/network@0  network-
pciex8086,105e
. . . .
========================= HW Revisions ========================================

System PROM revisions:
----------------------
OBP 4.30.0 2008/12/11 12:15
. . . .
============================ Environmental Status ============================
Fan sensors:
-------------------------------------------------------------------
Location                     Sensor       Status
-------------------------------------------------------------------
0841NNN03L:CH/FT0/FM0        RS           ok
. . . .
```

This example shows how to use the `.enet-addr` command to display the Ethernet address:

```
{0} ok .enet-addr<cr>
```

The system responds with the following:

```
0:21:28:10:e8:18
```

Booting a SPARC System

Up to this point, this chapter describes the OpenBoot diagnostic utilities, variables, and parameters. At the OpenBoot PROM, the OS is not yet running. In fact, the OpenBoot PROM works fine if the OS is not even loaded. The primary function of the OpenBoot firmware is to start up the system. Starting up is the process of loading and executing a standalone program (for example, the OS or the diagnostic monitor). In this discussion, the standalone program that is being started is the OS kernel. After the kernel is loaded, it starts the Oracle Solaris system, mounts the necessary file systems, and runs `/sbin/init`, which in turn starts the `svc.startd` daemon and SMF to bring the system to its default run level. This process is described in the section "The `init` Phase" later in this chapter.

Starting up can be initiated either automatically or with a command entered at the user interface. On most SPARC-based systems, the bootstrap process consists of the following basic phases:

1. The system hardware is powered on.
2. The system firmware (the PROM) executes a POST. (The form and scope of POSTs depend on the version of the firmware in the system.)
3. After the tests have been completed successfully, the firmware attempts to autoboot if the appropriate OpenBoot configuration variable (`auto-boot?`) has been set to *true*.

The OpenBoot startup process is initiated from the console via the NET MGT port and is shown here:

```
{0} ok boot
SC Alert: Host System has Reset
screen not found.
keyboard not found.
Keyboard not present. Using /virtual-devices/console for input and output.

Sun Fire T200, No Keyboard
Copyright (c) 1998, 2011, Oracle and/or its affiliates. All rights reserved.
OpenBoot 4.30.4.d, 3968 MB memory available, Serial #84994072.
Ethernet address 0:21:28:10:e8:18, Host ID: 8510e818.

Boot device: /pci@780/pci@0/pci@9/scsi@0/disk@0,0:a File and args:
SunOS Release 5.11 Version 11.1 64-bit
Copyright (c) 1983, 2012, Oracle and/or its affiliates. All rights reserved.

Hostname: solaris

solaris console login:
```

The startup process is controlled by a number of OpenBoot configuration variables, as described in Table 3-13.

Table 3-13 Boot Configuration Variables

Variable	Description
`auto-boot?`	This variable controls whether the system automatically starts up after a system reset or when the power is turned on. The default for this variable is `true`. When the system is powered on, the system automatically starts up to the default run level.
`boot-command`	This variable specifies the command to be executed when `auto-boot?` is true. The default value of `boot-command` is `boot`, with no command-line arguments.
`diag-switch?`	The variable causes the system to run in diagnostic mode if the value is `true`. This variable is `false` by default.

Variable	Description
boot-device	The variable contains the name of the default startup device used when OpenBoot is not in diagnostic mode.
boot-file	The variable contains the default startup arguments used when OpenBoot is not in diagnostic mode. The default is no arguments.
diag-device	The variable contains the name of the default diagnostic mode startup device. The default is net.
diag-file	The variable contains the default diagnostic mode startup arguments. The default is no arguments.

Table 3-14 boot Command Arguments and Options

Argument	Description
<device specifier>	The full device name or devalias of the boot device. Typically this boot device is *<full device name>*. For example, /pci@780/pci@0/pci@9/scsi@0/disk@0 indicates a SCSI disk (sd) on port 0, lun0 on the SCSI bus, with the pci host adapter plugged in to slot 0. If a devalias is used for the <device specifier> such as cdrom, the system is instructed to boot from a DVD in the DVD/CD-ROM drive. If the devalias specified is disk, the system is instructed to boot from the hard drive defined by the devalias. If the devalias specified is net, the system is instructed to boot from the network.
[*arguments*]	The system will boot using the specified arguments.
[*options*]	The system will boot using the specified options.

Typically, auto-boot? is set to true, boot-command is set to boot, and OpenBoot is not in diagnostic mode. Consequently, the system automatically loads and executes the program and arguments described by boot-file from the device described by boot-device when the system is first turned on or after a system reset.

The boot Command

The boot command has the following syntax:

```
boot <device specifier> [arguments] [options]
```

All arguments and options are optional.

The boot command and its options are described in Table 3-14.

Table 3-15 boot Options

Option	Description
-a	The startup program interprets this flag to mean "Ask me," so it prompts interactively for the name of the standalone program to load. The -a flag is then passed to the standalone program where you will be asked to enter the boot device, the name of the system file, and the retire store location. See the example of a boot -a interactive boot later in this section.
-F	Boot using the named object. The primary use is to boot the failsafe or wanboot boot archive.
-L	List the bootable datasets within a ZFS pool. This option is supported only when the boot device contains a ZFS storage pool.
-m <*smf_option*>	Specify the SMF option to control the boot behavior of SMF. *smf_option* can be debug, quiet, or verbose. quiet is the default, debug controls SMF message logging, and verbose displays more detailed messages during the boot process.
-m milestone= <*level*>	Allows the operator to decide which milestone to enter upon bootup. The <*level*> can be "none", "single-user", "multi-user", "multi-user-server", or "all".
-r	Triggers device reconfiguration during startup.
-s	Boot to the single-user milestone.
-v	Boot in verbose mode. When this option is set, all system messages are displayed.
-Z	Boot from the root file system in the specified ZFS dataset.
<*flags*>	The boot program passes all startup flags to [*argument*]. The startup flags are not interpreted by boot but are passed on to the kernel.

Table 3-15 lists the options that control the behavior of the boot command. The previous list of options represents the more common options used with the boot command. A complete list of options is provided in the kernel (1M) man page. Refer to the online manual pages for boot (1M), monitor (1M), and the eeprom (1M) commands for more information on the boot command and options.

A noninteractive boot (boot with no options) automatically boots the system using default values for the boot path. You can initiate a noninteractive boot by typing the following command from the OpenBoot prompt:

```
{0} ok boot<cr>
```

The system boots without requiring any additional interaction.

An interactive boot (`boot -a`) stops and asks for input during the boot process. The system provides a dialog box in which it displays the default boot values and gives you the option of changing them. You might want to boot interactively to make a temporary change to the system file or kernel. Booting interactively enables you to test your changes and recover easily if you have problems. To do this, follow the process outlined in the next section "The Interactive Boot Process."

The `boot` command can be used to boot the system from a disk, an iSCSI disk, or from the network. In this section, I will describe how to boot from a disk.

The Interactive Boot Process

1. At the `ok` prompt, type `boot -a` and press *Enter*. The `boot` program prompts you interactively.
2. Press *Enter* to use the default `/etc/system` file as prompted, or type the name of the system file and then press *Enter*.

A Missing `/etc/system` File

If the `/etc/system` file is missing at bootup, you will see this message:

```
Warning cannot open system file!
```

The system still boots, however, using all "default" kernel parameters. Because by default the lines in the `/etc/system` file are all commented by the asterisk (*) character, `/etc/system` is actually an "empty" file. The kernel doesn't use anything from this file until you edit this file and enter an uncommented line. You can specify `/dev/null` (an empty file) for the system filename, and the system will still boot. In fact, if the `/etc/system` file gets corrupted and the system won't boot from the `/etc/system` file, you can specify a file named `/dev/null` to get the system to boot.

3. Press *Enter* to select the default Retire store.
4. Press *Enter* to use the default root file system type as prompted (that is, `zfs` for local disk booting or `nfs` for diskless clients).
5. Press *Enter* to use the default physical name of the root device as prompted or type the device name.

The following output shows an example of an interactive boot session:

```
{0} ok boot -a<cr>

SC Alert: Host System has Reset
screen not found.
keyboard not found.
Keyboard not present. Using /virtual-devices/console for input and output.
```

```
Sun Fire T200, No Keyboard
Copyright (c) 1998, 2011, Oracle and/or its affiliates. All rights reserved.
OpenBoot 4.30.4.d, 3968 MB memory available, Serial #84994072.
Ethernet address 0:21:28:10:e8:18, Host ID: 8510e818.

Boot device: /pci@780/pci@0/pci@9/scsi@0/disk@0,0:a File and args: -a
Name of system file [/etc/system]:<cr>
SunOS Release 5.11 Version 11.1 64-bit
Copyright (c) 1983, 2012, Oracle and/or its affiliates. All rights reserved.

Retire store [/etc/devices/retire_store] (/dev/null to bypass):<cr>

 [/pci@780/pci@0/pci@9/scsi@0/disk@0,0:a]:<cr>
Hostname: solaris

solaris console login:
```

When you specify an explicit device alias such as `disk3` with the `boot` command, the machine starts up from the specified startup device, using no startup arguments. Here's an example:

```
{0} ok boot disk3<cr>
```

In this case, the system boots from the disk drive defined by the device alias named `disk3`. OpenBoot then loads the root file system boot archive from the default ZFS dataset located on that device.

Various options affect the behavior of the `boot` command. You can use the following syntax to specify any of the options listed in Table 3-14 with the following `boot` command:

```
boot [options]
```

When you specify options with the `boot` command, but you specify no device, the machine starts up from the default startup device. Here's an example:

```
{0} ok boot -a<cr>
```

The `-a` option instructs the `boot` command to "ask" for the following information during the boot process and allows you to override the defaults:

- System file
- Retire store
- Root file system type
- Physical name of the root device

The system starts the boot process:

```
{0} ok boot -a

screen not found.
keyboard not found.
Keyboard not present. Using /virtual-devices/console for input and output.

Sun Fire T200, No Keyboard
Copyright (c) 1998, 2011, Oracle and/or its affiliates. All rights reserved.
OpenBoot 4.30.4.d, 3968 MB memory available, Serial #84994072.
Ethernet address 0:21:28:10:e8:18, Host ID: 8510e818.

Retire store [/etc/devices/retire_store] (/dev/null to bypass):
Invalid store path: . Using default
root filesystem type [zfs]:
Enter physical name of root device
[/pci@780/pci@0/pci@9/scsi@0/disk@0,0:a]:
Hostname: solaris

solaris console login:
```

You can mix options and arguments with the `boot` command by using the following syntax:

```
boot [argument]<program filename> -<flags>
```

When you specify the `boot` command with an explicit startup device and option, the machine starts up from the specified device using the specified option. Here's an example:

```
{0} ok boot disk3 -a<cr>
```

This gives the same prompts as the previous example, except that you are specifying the boot device and not using the default boot device. The system starts up the bootblock from the disk drive defined by the device alias named `disk3`. The system then loads the root file system boot archive from the default ZFS dataset located on `disk3`.

Installing a ZFS Bootblock

On an Oracle Solaris 11/11 SPARC system, to install a ZFS bootblock on slice 0 of target 1 on controller 1, use the following command:

```
# installboot -F zfs /usr/platform/'uname -i'/lib/fs/zfs/bootblk \
/dev/rdsk/c1t1d0s0<cr>
```

You cannot see the bootblock because it resides outside the file system area. It resides in a protected area of the disk and will not be overwritten by a file system.

The `installboot` command uses the `uname -i` command to determine your system's platform name. For example, on a T2000 Enterprise server, the path is `/platform/SUNW,Sun-Fire-T200`. You use the command uname `-m` to find a system's hardware class name; for a T2000 Enterprise server, the hardware class name is `sun4v`.

Beginning with Oracle Solaris 11.1, the `installboot` utility has been discontinued. The `bootadm install-bootloader` command replaces the `installboot` command. The `bootadm install-bootloader` command is described in Chapter 5, "Administering ZFS File Systems," in the section titled "The ZFS Root File System."

The following example shows how to specify the standalone startup program from the OpenBoot `ok` prompt:

```
{0} ok boot disk5 -s<cr>
```

In this example, the PROM looks for the primary boot program (bootblk) on disk5 (`/pci@780/pci@0/pci@9/scsi@0/disk@5,0`). The `-s` option will boot the system into the single-user run level (single-user mode).

Booting from a ZFS Boot Disk

ZFS is the default file system used on the boot disk in Oracle Solaris 11. When booting from ZFS, a device specifier identifies a storage pool, not a single root file system. A storage pool can contain multiple bootable datasets (boot environments). Boot environments were described in Chapter 2, "Managing and Updating Software with IPS." When booting from ZFS, it's not sufficient to simply specify a boot device as it was in previous versions of Oracle Solaris using UFS boot drives. A zpool and a root file system within the zpool must also be identified. The following two options of the `boot` command support identifying a boot environment and booting to that environment from a ZFS root file system on SPARC based systems:

`-L`	Displays a list of available boot environments within a ZFS pool.
`-Z` *`<dataset>`*	Boots the root file system for the specified ZFS dataset (boot environment). This option overrides the default dataset specified by the pool's `bootfs` property.

By default, the dataset selected for booting is the one identified by the pool's `bootfs` property. This default selection can be overridden by specifying an alternate bootable dataset with the -Z option. Use the -L option to list the bootable datasets within a ZFS pool.

When booting a system from a ZFS root file system, first use the boot command with the -L option from the OpenBoot prompt to print a list of the available boot environments on the system as follows:

```
{0} ok boot -L<cr>
```

One bootable dataset (boot environment) is found on the default boot device and is listed:

```
Boot device: /pci@780/pci@0/pci@9/scsi@0/disk@0,0:a File and args: -L
1 Oracle Solaris 11.1SPARC
Select environment to boot: [ 1 - 1 ]:1<cr>
```

I entered 1 to select the Oracle Solaris 11.1SPARC boot environment, and the following message is displayed:

```
To boot the selected entry, invoke:
boot [<root-device>] -Z rpool/ROOT/solaris
```

To boot to that dataset, use the -Z option to boot the specified boot environment as follows:

```
{0} ok boot -Z rpool/ROOT/solaris<cr>
```

A storage pool can contain multiple bootable ZFS root file systems, also called boot environments. Boot environments were described in Chapter 2. When booting from ZFS, you must specify a boot device and a root file system within the pool that was identified by the boot device. A storage pool can contain multiple bootable ZFS root file systems.

Booting from an Alternate Disk in a Mirrored ZFS Root Pool

One of the advantages of using ZFS for the boot disk is that you can mirror the ZFS root files system across multiple disk drives. This operation can be performed during the installation of the OS or after the OS has been installed.

The following indicates that rpool is a mirror:

```
# zpool status rpool<cr>
  pool: rpool
state: ONLINE
  scan: none requested
config:

        NAME            STATE     READ  WRITE  CKSUM
        rpool           ONLINE       0      0      0
          mirror-0      ONLINE       0      0      0
            c2t0d0s0    ONLINE       0      0      0
            c2t1d0s0    ONLINE       0      0      0
```

Mirrored pools are described in Chapter 5.

You can boot from different devices in a mirrored ZFS root pool. For example, if the root file system is mirrored across c2t0d0s0 and c2t1d0s0, you can boot from either disk in the pool. If the default boot device is /pci@780/pci@0/pci@9/scsi@0/disk@0,0:a (c2t0d0s0) and the secondary disk in the mirror is /pci@780/pci@0/pci@9/scsi@0/disk@1,0:a (c2t1d0s0), boot to the secondary disk by specifying that device with the boot command as follows:

```
{0} ok boot /pci@780/pci@0/pci@9/scsi@0/disk@1,0:a<cr>
```

Or use the OpenBoot device alias as follows:

```
{0} ok boot disk1<cr>
```

After the system is booted, confirm the active boot device using the prtconf command as follows:

```
# prtconf -vp | grep bootpath<cr>
        bootpath: '/pci@780/pci@0/pci@9/scsi@0/disk@1,0:a'
```

Display Boot Messages

To view more detailed information during the boot process, you use the boot -v or boot -m verbose options to the boot command as follows:

```
{0} ok boot -v<cr>
```

The system displays more detailed boot messages as shown:

```
<only the last few messages are shown to save space>
. . . .
```

```
Apr 19 14:04:03 solaris pseudo: pseudo-device: mdesc0
Apr 19 14:04:03 solaris genunix: mdesc0 is /pseudo/mdesc@0
Apr 19 14:04:03 solaris pseudo: pseudo-device: ntwdt0
Apr 19 14:04:03 solaris genunix: ntwdt0 is /pseudo/ntwdt@0
Apr 19 14:04:03 solaris pseudo: pseudo-device: fssnap0
Apr 19 14:04:03 solaris genunix: fssnap0 is /pseudo/fssnap@0
Apr 19 14:04:03 solaris pseudo: pseudo-device: bpf0
Apr 19 14:04:03 solaris genunix: bpf0 is /pseudo/bpf@0

solaris console login:
```

With the `-v` option (lowercase "v"), you'll see messages for all of the devices that are being initialized. Messages from the SMF services that are being started will not be displayed. To display SMF service messages during the boot process, use the `-m verbose` option as follows:

```
{0} ok boot -m verbose<cr>
```

Each service will be displayed as it is booting. Device initialization will not be displayed:

```
SC Alert: Host System has Reset
screen not found.
keyboard not found.
Keyboard not present. Using /virtual-devices/console for input and output.

Sun Fire T200, No Keyboard
Copyright (c) 1998, 2011, Oracle and/or its affiliates. All rights reserved.
OpenBoot 4.30.4.d, 3968 MB memory available, Serial #84994072.
Ethernet address 0:21:28:10:e8:18, Host ID: 8510e818.

Boot device: /pci@780/pci@0/pci@9/scsi@0/disk@0,0:a File and args: -m verbose
SunOS Release 5.11 Version 11.1 64-bit
Copyright (c) 1983, 2012, Oracle and/or its affiliates. All rights reserved.
 [ network/socket-config:default starting (socket configuration) ]
[ network/netcfg:default starting (Network configuration data management) ]
[ network/sctp/congestion-control:cubic starting (TCP-style congestion control) ]
[ network/sctp/congestion-control:highspeed starting (TCP-style congestion control) ]
[ network/sctp/congestion-control:newreno starting (TCP-style congestion control) ]
[ network/tcp/congestion-control:cubic starting (TCP-style congestion control) ]
. . . .
. . . .
[ network/smtp:sendmail starting (sendmail SMTP mail transfer agent) ]
[ system/auditd:default starting (Solaris audit daemon) ]
[ network/sendmail-client:default starting (sendmail SMTP client queue runner) ]
[ system/console-login:default starting (Console login) ]
[ milestone/multi-user:default starting (multi-user milestone) ]

solaris console login:
```

If you are not at the system console to watch the boot information, you can use the UNIX `dmesg` command to display information from the boot process. Type it at the command prompt as follows:

```
# dmesg<cr>
```

`dmesg` looks in a system buffer for recently printed diagnostic messages and prints them on the standard output. The `dmesg` command displays the contents of a fixed-size buffer. Therefore, if the system has been up for a long time, the initial boot messages may have been overwritten with other kernel log entries.

You can also view system-generated messages in the `/var/adm/messages` file. These messages get stored there by `syslogd`, which is covered in the "`syslog`" section later in this chapter.

SMF also has tools for viewing system startup messages and allows you to monitor all of the services that are started at boot time. Refer to the "SMF" section of this chapter for additional information.

Booting an x86-Based System

The procedure used to boot x86-based systems differs from that for SPARC-based systems. An x86 system is any Intel or AMD processor–based system that is listed under Oracle's Hardware Compatibility List. The x86-based platform has boot subsystems used to boot and control the system before the kernel is loaded. In the previous section, I described how the OpenBoot environment controls the system startup after the power is turned on. On an x86-based system, the system startup is controlled by the BIOS. After the system starts to boot, control is transferred from the BIOS to GRUB. GRUB then controls how the OS is started.

GRUB Versus GRUB 2

The original GRUB (GRUB Legacy) continues to be the default boot loader on x86 platforms that run Oracle Solaris 10 and the original release of Oracle Solaris 11 11/11. GRUB 2 was introduced with Oracle Solaris 11.1.

Figure 3-1 on page 122 illustrates the boot process on the x86/x64-based platform compared with the boot process on the SPARC platform.

The BIOS

Before the kernel is started, the x86-based system is controlled by the read-only-memory (ROM) BIOS, the firmware interface on the x86 platform.

Hardware adapters can also have an onboard BIOS that displays the physical characteristics of the device and can be used to access the device.

During the startup sequence, the system's BIOS checks for the presence of any adapter BIOS and, if found, loads and executes each one. Each individual adapter's BIOS runs self-test diagnostics and displays device information. An example is a redundant array of independent disks (RAID) disk controller. Before booting the OS, you'll be given the opportunity to access the RAID configuration utility.

When powered on, the system's BIOS initializes the CPU, memory, and platform hardware. When the BIOS completes its tasks, it loads the initial bootstrap software (boot loader) from the configured boot device and hands control to the boot loader (i.e., GRUB).

It might be necessary to modify the BIOS settings before installing the Oracle Solaris OS. For example, the system's BIOS must be configured to boot from the DVD in order to install the OS from a DVD. Entering the BIOS setup screen is performed by pressing a key early in the startup process. This keystroke may vary depending on the manufacturer. On some systems, you press the *F1* or *F2* key after powering on the system. On other systems, it may be the *Escape* key or the *Delete* key. Most times, the instructions to enter the BIOS setup are provided on the screen shortly after powering on the system.

GRUB

Oracle Solaris 11 uses an open-source boot loader called GRUB. Beginning with Oracle Solaris 11.1, GRUB was updated to GRUB 2. In this section, I'll still refer to GRUB 2 as simply "GRUB."

GRUB is responsible for loading a boot archive into the system's memory. The boot archive is described later in this chapter. GRUB provides the following:

- GRUB displays a menu with the list of boot options that can be selected when booting the system.
- GRUB contains a command line interface where kernel and boot options can be modified.
- GRUB can be used to boot a multitude of OSs, making it possible for the OS to coexist with other OSs on the same disk.

After you turn on power to the system and after the initialization phase is complete, the BIOS loads GRUB, and the GRUB main menu is displayed as shown in Figure 3-2.

A single boot option is shown on the main menu. The boot options listed in this menu are predefined in a configuration file named `/rpool/boot/grub/grub.cfg`.

`grub.cfg` Versus `menu.lst`

Previous versions of Oracle Solaris, including the Oracle Solaris 11 11/11, used the `menu.lst` file. The `menu.lst` file that is used by GRUB Legacy has been replaced by a new configuration file, `grub.cfg`. Unlike the `menu.lst` file, the `grub.cfg` file is automatically regenerated by boot management commands. Therefore, this file should never be directly edited because any edits are immediately destroyed when the `grub.cfg` file is regenerated.

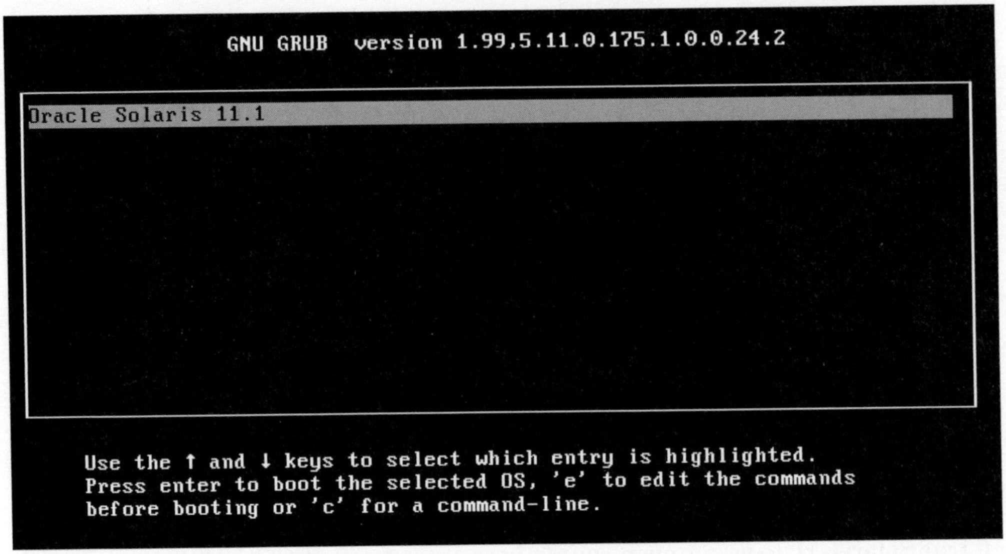

```
GNU GRUB  version 1.99,5.11.0.175.1.0.0.24.2

Oracle Solaris 11.1

Use the ↑ and ↓ keys to select which entry is highlighted.
Press enter to boot the selected OS, 'e' to edit the commands
before booting or 'c' for a command-line.
```

Figure 3-2 Oracle Solaris 11 GRUB menu

The boot option displayed on the main menu is the default boot option you see after installing the Oracle Solaris 11 OS. You can use this option to boot the system from disk into either single-user or multi-user mode.

By default, the GRUB main menu appears, and booting continues after 30 seconds. To stop the autoboot process, use the arrow key to highlight a boot entry in the GRUB main menu. Type `b` to boot the system. To override the default boot behavior, type `e` to edit the startup command.

Keep the System Bootable

To ensure that the system remains bootable, the GRUB boot blocks, the GRUB menu, and the boot archive must be up to date. The GRUB boot blocks reside in the partition. If the boot blocks become corrupt, they should be reinstalled. In previous versions of GRUB, the `installgrub` command was used to reinstall the boot loader. The `installgrub` command is no longer used for GRUB 2. Beginning with Oracle Solaris 11.1, use the `bootadm install-bootloader` command.

On the x86 platform, GRUB loads the kernel file (`/platform/i86pc/kernel/amd64/unix`) and the boot archive into memory and then transfers control to the kernel.

Modifying the Boot Behavior

When the GRUB main menu appears, you can press `b` or `<cr>` to begin the boot process, or you can type `e` to display the GRUB edit menu. Press `e` when you want to

```
GNU GRUB  version 1.99,5.11.0.175.1.0.0.24.2

setparams 'Oracle Solaris 11.1'

insmod part_msdos
insmod part_sunpc
insmod part_gpt
insmod zfs
search --no-floppy --fs-uuid --set=root f28bbe2ba2a4337e
zfs-bootfs /ROOT/solaris/@/ zfs_bootfs
set kern=/platform/i86pc/kernel/amd64/unix
echo -n "Loading ${root}/ROOT/solaris/@$kern: "
$multiboot /ROOT/solaris/@/$kern $kern -B console=graphics -B $zfs_bootfs
set gfxpayload="1024x768x32;1024x768x16;800x600x16;640x480x16;640x480x15;640x48\
0x32"
insmod gzio
echo -n "Loading ${root}/ROOT/solaris/@/platform/i86pc/amd64/boot_archive: "
$module /ROOT/solaris/@/platform/i86pc/amd64/boot_archive

Minimum Emacs-like screen editing is supported. TAB lists completions.
Press Ctrl-x or F10 to boot, Ctrl-c or F2 for a command-line or ESC to
discard edits and return to the GRUB menu.
```

Figure 3-3 GRUB edit menu

temporarily modify the default boot behavior. In Figure 3-3, I used the arrow key to select the first entry and then typed `e` to edit that entry.

Line 11, beginning with `$multiboot`, specifies the path to the kernel on the root file system. This line in the GRUB menu executes the `kernel` command, which determines the boot behavior of the OS. The last line is responsible for assembling core kernel modules in memory by reading the boot archive (described later) and passing boot-related information to the kernel. To temporarily modify the boot process, use the arrow key to go to the line that begins with `$multiboot` and edit the end of the line.

For example, to boot the system to single-user mode, edit the line as follows:

```
$multiboot /ROOT/solaris/@/$kern $kern -B console=graphics -B $zfs_bootfs -s
```

Press *Ctrl-x* or *F10* to load the kernel and boot the system using this argument. If I press *Esc*, I'm returned to the main menu, and the changes are not saved.

The kernel command supports several options and arguments that let you modify the boot behavior. In the GRUB menu, the kernel is loaded using the following string:

```
$multiboot /ROOT/solaris/@/$kern
```

Where $kern is the path to the kernel: $kern=/platform/i86pc/kernel/amd64/unix.

The following are a few of the more common kernel arguments:

- kernel$ /platform/i86pc/kernel/amd64/<kernelname>, where <kernelname> specifies the alternate kernel from which to boot.
- $multiboot /ROOT/solaris/@/$kern $kern -B console=graphics -B \ $zfs_bootfs -a, where -a performs an interactive boot and prompts for user configuration information during the boot process.
- Set the console property to ttya so that the system uses the serial port for the console:
  $multiboot /ROOT/solaris/@/$kern $kern -B console=ttya -B \
  $zfs_bootfs
- $multiboot /ROOT/solaris/@/$kern $kern -B console=graphics -B \ $zfs_bootfs -s, where -s boots the system into single-user mode.
- $multiboot /ROOT/solaris/@/$kern $kern -B console=graphics -B \ $zfs_bootfs -r, where -r specifies a reconfiguration boot. The system probes all attached hardware devices and then assigns nodes in the file system to represent only those devices that are actually found.
- $multiboot /ROOT/solaris/@/$kern $kern -B console=text-B \ $zfs_bootfs -v, where -v boots with verbose messages enabled.

Note

I changed the console from graphics to text when setting the -v option. Boot messages are displayed on a text-based console only.

- $multiboot /ROOT/solaris/@/$kern $kern -B console=graphics -B \ $zfs_bootfs -m <*smf-options*>, where -m <*smf-options*> controls the boot behavior of SMF.
- kernel$ /platform/i86pc/kernel/amd64/unix -B *prop=value*, where -B *prop=value* specifies kernel boot parameters.

The -B option can be used to specify kernel boot parameters. For example:

-B console=force-text: Specifies that the console should use video graphics array (VGA) text mode for booting

-B console=graphics: Specifies that the console should use graphics mode for booting, which enables a high-resolution state
-B console=text: Specifies that the console use text mode for booting
-B console=ttya: Redirects the console to ttya
-B acpi-user-options=0x2: Disables Advanced Configuration and Power Interface (ACPI) entirely
-B $zfs_bootfs: Specifies that the root file system is a ZFS dataset

bootfs

There can be multiple bootable datasets (that is, root file systems) within a root pool. The default root file system in a pool is identified by the pool's bootfs property. If a specific bootfs is not specified (by means of the zfs-bootfs command in a GRUB menu entry block in the grub.cfg), the default bootfs root file system is used. Each GRUB menu entry may specify the bootfs to use, enabling the administrator to select from many bootable Oracle Solaris instances in a pool.

For example, to specify that the console uses text mode for booting from the ZFS root disk and also to set the boot messages to verbose, the following entry would be used:

```
$multiboot /ROOT/solaris/@/$kern $kern -B console=text -B $zfs_bootfs -v
```

Another method for modifying the boot behavior is to use the eeprom command at the shell prompt. On the SPARC system, the eeprom command changes the OpenBoot NVRAM. On the x86-based system, the eeprom command modifies boot variables stored in the /boot/solaris/bootenv.rc file. Changes made using the eeprom command persist over each system reboot. You can still temporarily override eeprom settings for a single boot cycle if you boot the system by specifying options and arguments to the kernel command in the GRUB edit menu.

The following is an example of entries in the /boot/solaris/bootenv.rc file:

```
setprop keyboard-layout Unknown
setprop ata-dma-enabled 1
setprop atapi-cd-dma-enabled 1
setprop ttyb-rts-dtr-off false
setprop ttyb-ignore-cd true
setprop ttya-rts-dtr-off false
setprop ttya-ignore-cd true
setprop ttyb-mode 9600,8,n,1,-
setprop ttya-mode 9600,8,n,1,-
setprop lba-access-ok 1
setprop console text
```

To change the console parameter permanently in the bootenv.rc file, use the eeprom command to direct the console to run on ttya:

```
# eeprom console=ttya<cr>
```

Autoboot

Before Oracle Solaris 11.1, you could modify the boot process so that the system does not automatically boot (stopping at the GRUB menu) by changing the auto-boot? parameter to false. With Oracle Solaris 11.1 or later, this is handled through the bootadm command and setting the timeout value to -1 as follows:
bootadm set-menu timeout=-1<cr>.

Now, instead of the GRUB menu appearing for 10 seconds and automatically booting the system, the GRUB menu waits for user input.

By default, the Oracle Solaris menu file resides in /rpool/boot/grub/menu.lst. The contents of this file dictate what is displayed in the GRUB menu when you boot the system. The GRUB menu file contains entries for all of the OS instances that are installed on your system, as well as other important boot directives.

bootadm Command

Use the bootadm command to manage the GRUB menu and the /rpool/boot/grub/grub.cfg file. The bootadm command is used with the subcommands that are listed in Table 3-16.

Table 3-16 bootadm Subcommands

Subcommand	Description
set-menu	Maintain the GRUB menu. Set the entry number, timeout, or serial parameters for a serial console. Set quiet mode to true or false (default). Specify the splash image file, or set the foreground and background colors.
list-menu	List the current GRUB menu entries.
generate-menu	Create a new menu configuration that contains only the entries currently installed on the system.
add-entry	Create a new entry in the menu with a given entry title.
change-entry	Modify the contents of a given entry or a comma-separated list of entries.
remove-entry	Remove a given entry or a comma-separated list of entries.
install-bootloader	Install the system boot loader.
update-archive	Update the current boot archive if required.
list-archive	List the files and directories to be included in the boot archive.

The following examples demonstrate some of the subcommands listed in Table 3-16. For example, to view the GRUB menu entries, type

```
# bootadm list-menu<cr>
the location of the boot loader configuration files is: /rpool/boot/grub
default 0
console graphics
timeout 30
0 Oracle Solaris 11.1
```

There is one entry in the menu: `0 Oracle Solaris 11.1`.

To list details for the entry, use the `-i` option followed by the entry number as follows:

```
# bootadm list-menu -i 0<cr>
the location of the boot loader configuration files is: /boot/grub
title: Oracle Solaris 11.1
kernel: /platform/i86pc/kernel/amd64/unix
kernel arguments: -B console=graphics
boot archive: /platform/i86pc/amd64/boot_archive
bootfs: rpool/ROOT/solaris
```

If other OSs are installed on this system, a boot entry for each OS would appear in the GRUB main menu. If you install another OS after the Oracle Solaris OS is installed, you would make an entry for the new OS in the `/rpool/boot/grub/grub.cfg` file using the `bootadm add-entry` command. The following example adds a menu entry with the title "New Solaris Entry" at position 1 in the GRUB menu:

```
# bootadm add-entry -i 1 "New Solaris Entry"<cr>
```

Verify the change as follows:

```
# bootadm list-menu<cr>
the location of the boot loader configuration files is: /rpool/boot/grub
default 0
console graphics
timeout 30
splashimage /boot/grub/splash.jpg
foreground ff0000
background 0000ff
0 Oracle Solaris 11.1
1 New Solaris Entry
```

Notice that the default entry is 0. When the system is rebooted, it will automatically boot to the default entry after the default timer expires.

Now you can change the default boot entry so that entry 1 boots by default as follows:

```
# bootadm set-menu default=1<cr>
```

Change the timeout value as follows:

```
# bootadm set-menu timeout=45<cr>
```

Change the title of a boot entry using the `change-entry` subcommand as follows:

```
# bootadm change-entry "New Solaris Entry" title="Oracle Solaris 11-patched"<cr>
```

Remove an entry using the `remove-entry` subcommand as follows:

```
# bootadm remove-entry -i 1<cr>
1 entry removed.
```

GRUB `custom.cfg` Files

An additional, editable GRUB configuration file named `custom.cfg` can be used if you want to add more complex constructs, for example, menu entries or other scripting, to the GRUB configuration. This file does not exist on the system by default. You must create the file, and it must reside in the same location as the `grub.cfg` and `menu.conf` files, which are located in the `/<pool-name>/boot/grub/` directory. GRUB processes the commands and any customizations that are in the `custom.cfg` file through the following code that is located at the end of the `grub.cfg` file:

```
if [ -f $prefix/custom.cfg ]; then
        source $prefix/custom.cfg;
fi
```

The Boot Archive

When Oracle Solaris is installed on both the SPARC and x86 platforms, the `bootadm` command creates the boot archive on the system. The boot archive is a subset of the root file system and contains core kernel modules, including drivers and configuration files that are needed to initialize the OS kernel. After the I/O subsystem is initialized, the files in the boot archive are read by the kernel before the root file system is mounted. The boot archive contains a file system image that is mounted using an in-memory disk. The image is self-describing, specifically containing a file system reader in the boot block. This file system reader mounts and opens the RAM disk image, then reads and executes the kernel contained within it. By default, this kernel is located in the /platform/<*machine name*> directory of the ZFS dataset that was selected for booting. For example, on the x86 platform, the boot archive is located in the /platform/i86pc/amd64/archive_cache directory, and for the SPARC T2000 platform it is located in the /platform/sun4v/archive_chache directory.

The kernel initialization continues loading the necessary drivers and modules from the in-memory file system until I/O can be turned on and the root file system mounted. Once the root file system is mounted, the boot archive is no longer needed and is discarded from memory by the kernel.

The OS updates the boot archive from files on the root (/) file system whenever necessary. This update typically occurs when a kernel patch is applied or when a driver package is added. To detect any file updates that were performed manually, the shutdown process compares the boot archive's contents with the root file system. If any updates have been made to the system such as drivers or configuration files, the boot archive is rebuilt to include these changes so that, at the next reboot, the boot archive and root file system are synchronized.

The boot archive is located in the /platform/<machine name> directory of the ZFS dataset that was selected for booting. For example, on the x86 platform, the boot archive is located in the /platform/i86pc/amd64/archive_cache directory and the /platform/'uname -m'/archive_chache directory on a SPARC-based system. For example, on the SPARC T2000 platform, it is located in the /platform/sun4v/archive_chache directory.

The bootadm command, described earlier, manages the boot archive. The bootadm command handles the details of the boot archive update and verification. During an installation or upgrade, the bootadm command creates an initial boot archive. During the process of a normal system shutdown, the shutdown process compares the boot archive's contents with the root file system. If there were updates to the system driver or configuration files, the boot archive is rebuilt to include the changes so that, on reboot, the boot archive and the root file system are synchronized. At any time, you can update the boot archive using the bootadm command as follows:

```
# bootadm update-archive<cr>
```

Support for EFI (GPT) Labeled Disks: x86

Oracle Solaris 11.1 includes support for booting from Extensible Firmware Interface (EFI) (GPT) labeled disks on the x86-based platform. Booting from an EFI (GPT) labeled disk is slightly different than booting from a disk that uses the conventional MS-DOS partitioning (fdisk) scheme. On the x86-based platform, the introduction of GRUB 2 enables this support. On systems with BIOS firmware, the master boot record (MBR) is still the first chunk of code that the firmware loads to initiate the boot process. There is no longer a volume table of contents (VTOC) on EFI (GPT) labeled disks, only discrete partitions. GRUB now has direct support for reading and interpreting the EFI (GPT) partitioning scheme, which enables the boot loader to locate the kernel and the boot archive inside the root pool that is hosted in a ZFS EFI (GPT) partition.

The files and directories to be included in the boot archive can be listed using the `bootadm` command with the `list-archive` subcommand as follows:

```
# bootadm list-archive<cr>
```

When the command is issued on the x86 platform, the following list of files is displayed:

```
boot/acpi/tables
boot/solaris/bootenv.rc
boot/solaris/devicedb/master
boot/solaris/boot-images
etc/cluster/nodeid
etc/dacf.conf
etc/devices/devid_cache
etc/devices/mdi_ib_cache
etc/devices/mdi_scsi_vhci_cache
etc/devices/retire_store
< list of files has been truncated >
```

When the command is issued on the SPARC platform, the following list of files is displayed:

```
platform/sun4u-us3/kernel
platform/sun4v/kernel
platform/SUNW,A70/kernel
platform/SUNW,Netra-210/kernel
platform/SUNW,Netra-240/kernel
platform/SUNW,Netra-440/kernel
platform/SUNW,Netra-CP2300/kernel
platform/SUNW,Netra-CP3010/kernel
platform/SUNW,Netra-CP3060/kernel
< list of files has been truncated >
```

The boot archive is managed by SMF. The service instance is named `svc:/system/boot-archive:default`. It's important to maintain the integrity of the boot archive, and SMF performs this function as long as the service is enabled. To verify that the service is enabled, issue the `svcs` command as follows:

```
# svcs boot-archive<cr>
STATE      STIME    FMRI
online      9:50:41 svc:/system/boot-archive:default
```

If the service is offline, enable it using the following command:

```
# svcadm enable boot-archive<cr>
```

Immediately after you perform a system upgrade or apply a patch, you can manually rebuild the boot archive by running the following command as root:

```
# bootadm update-archive<cr>
```

Failsafe Mode Is Obsolete in Oracle Solaris 11

Although booting to failsafe mode was supported on Oracle Solaris 10, failsafe mode is not supported on SPARC or x86 platforms in Oracle Solaris 11. Depending on the error condition, boot to single-user mode or perform the system recovery steps described later in this chapter.

If a system failure, power failure, or kernel panic occurs immediately after a kernel file update, the boot archive and the root (/) file system might not be synchronized. This would be indicated by the following message at bootup:

```
WARNING: Automatic update of the boot archive failed.
Update the archives using 'bootadm update-archive' command and then reboot the system
from the same device that was previously booted.
```

Although the system might still boot with the old boot archive, you should boot the system in single-user mode (`boot -s`) or the `none` milestone (`boot -m milestone=none`) and rebuild the boot archive manually. The boot archive is updated or rebuilt manually by using the `bootadm` command as follows:

```
# bootadm update-archive<cr>
```

The Kernel

The OS kernel is the collection of software comprising the image files and the modules loaded into memory at boot time. The kernel is stored on the bootable ZFS dataset but can also be loaded from a DVD or over the network. The kernel and kernel files are located in several directories:

- `/platform/`*`<machine hardware name>`*`/kernel` contains the kernel components specific to the particular hardware class.
- `/platform/`*`<platform name>`*`/kernel` contains the kernel components specific to a particular platform.

- /usr/kernel and /kernel directories contain kernel components common to all platforms within a particular instruction set that are needed for booting the system.

Platform Name and Machine Hardware Name

The platform name and hardware name are specific to the type of hardware being used. Display the *<platform name>* using the uname -i command, and display the *<machine hardware name>* using the uname -m command.

The core of the kernel is two pieces of static code called genunix and unix. genunix is the platform-specific "generic" portion of the kernel, and unix is the machine-specific kernel file. genunix and unix, along with the loadable modules, are combined to form the running kernel. Although many kernel modules are loaded automatically at boot time, for efficiency, others—such as device drivers—are loaded from the disk as needed by the kernel.

Loadable Modules

A kernel module is a software component that is used to perform a specific task on the system. An example of a loadable kernel module is a device driver that is loaded when the device is accessed. Drivers, file systems, STREAMS modules, and other modules are loaded automatically as they are needed, either at startup or at runtime. This is referred to as "autoconfiguration," and the kernel is referred to as a "dynamic kernel." After these modules are no longer in use, they can be unloaded. Modules are kept in memory until that memory is needed. This makes more efficient use of memory and allows for simpler modification and tuning.

After the boot archive has loaded enough modules to mount the root file system and the boot archive is discarded from memory, the kernel continues using its own resources. The kernel creates a user process and starts the /sbin/init daemon, which starts other processes by reading the /etc/inittab file. (The /sbin/init process is described in the section "The init Phase" later in this chapter.)

The modinfo command provides information about the modules that are currently loaded on a system:

```
# modinfo<cr>
Id Loadaddr    Size     Info     Rev     Module Name
  0  1000000  21944a      -        0       unix()
  1  10e2678  27a298      -        0       genunix ()
  2  1306ae8     210      -        0       platmod ()
  3  1306d00    2e70      -        0       SUNW,UltraSPARC-T1 ()
  5  130a000    5030      1        1       specfs (filesystem for specfs)
  6  130ef90    39f0      3        1       fifofs (filesystem for fifo)
  7  7b200000  17ec8      6        1       dtrace (Dynamic Tracing)
  8  13128c8    4260     16        1       devfs (devices filesystem)
  9  13168e0   1be58      5        1       procfs (filesystem for proc)
 12  1333a38    3d38      1        1       TS (time sharing sched class)
```

```
 13  1336f80     8e0        -        1        TS_DPTBL (Time sharing dispatch table)
 14  1337030   b8648        8        1        zfs (ZFS filesystem version 33)
 14  1337030   b8648      228        1        zfs (ZFS storage pool)
. . .<output has been truncated to save space>. . .
```

The modules that make up the kernel typically reside in the directories /kernel and /usr/kernel. Platform-dependent modules reside in the /platform/'uname -m'/kernel and /platform/'uname -i'/kernel directories.

When the kernel is loading, it reads the /etc/system file where system configuration information is stored. This file is only read once during the boot process. Any modification to this file will not be used until the next reboot. This file modifies the kernel's parameters and treatment of loadable modules. It specifically controls the following:

- The search path for default modules to be loaded at boot time as well as the search path for modules not to be loaded at boot time
- The root file system type and device
- The modules to be forcibly loaded at boot time rather than at first access
- The modules that are excluded from loading automatically at boot time
- The new values to override the default kernel parameter values

More information on the system(4) file is available in the online manual page by typing

```
# man -s4 system<cr>
```

Modifying the /etc/system File

A system administrator modifies the /etc/system file to modify the kernel's behavior. By default, the contents of the /etc/system file are completely commented out, and the kernel uses all default values. A default kernel is adequate for average system use, and you should not modify the /etc/system file unless you are certain of the results. A good practice is to always make a backup copy of any system file you modify in case the original needs to be restored. Incorrect entries could prevent your system from booting. If a boot process fails because of an unusable /etc/system file, you should boot the system by using the interactive option boot -a. When you are asked to enter the name of the system file, you should enter the name of the backup system filename, or /dev/null. /dev/null acts as an empty system file, and the system will attempt to boot using its default settings.

The /etc/system file contains commands that have the following form:

```
set <parameter>=<value>
```

For example, the setting for the kernel parameter `nfs:nfs4_nra` is set in the `/etc/system` file with the following line:

```
set nfs:nfs_nra=4
```

This parameter controls the number of read-ahead operations that are queued by the Network File System (NFS) version 4 client.

Commands that affect loadable modules have this form:

```
set <module>:<variable>=<value>
```

Editing the `/etc/system` File

A command must be 80 or fewer characters in length, and a comment line must begin with an asterisk (*) and end with a hard return.

For the most part, the OS is self-adjusting to system load and demands minimal tuning. In some cases, however, tuning is necessary. Making changes in the `/etc/system` file modifies the kernel on a system wide basis, which is not always optimal. Many of the options that in the past were set in the `/etc/system` file are now controlled by the Oracle Solaris Resource Manager. The Resource Manager allows the system administrator to modify system parameters and tunables at the project and task level rather than system wide.

If you need to change a tunable parameter in the `/etc/system` file, you can use the `sysdef` command or the `mdb` command to verify the change. `sysdef` lists all hardware devices, system devices, loadable modules, and the values of selected kernel-tunable parameters. The following is the output that is produced from the `sysdef` command on a SPARC-based system:

```
# sysdef<cr>
*
* Hostid
*
  8510e818
*
* sun4v Configuration
*
*
* Devices
*
scsi_vhci, instance #0
packages (driver not attached)
    SUNW,builtin-drivers (driver not attached)
    deblocker (driver not attached)
    disk-label (driver not attached)
    terminal-emulator (driver not attached)
. . . . .
```

```
<output has been truncated to save space>
. . . .

* System Configuration
*
  swap files
swapfile       dev  swaplo  blocks  free
/dev/zvol/dsk/rpool/swap 228,2    16 2097136 2097136
*
* Tunable Parameters
*
81469440          maximum memory allowed in buffer cache (bufhwm)
   30000          maximum number of processes (v.v_proc)
      99          maximum global priority in sys class (MAXCLSYSPRI)
   29995          maximum processes per user id (v.v_maxup)
      30          auto update time limit in seconds (NAUTOUP)
      25          page stealing low water mark (GPGSLO)
       1          fsflush run rate (FSFLUSHR)
      25          minimum resident memory for avoiding deadlock (MINARMEM)
      25          minimum swapable memory for avoiding deadlock (MINASMEM)
*
* Utsname Tunables
*
   5.11  release (REL)
solaris  node name (NODE)
  SunOS  system name (SYS)
   11.1  version (VER)
*
* Process Resource Limit Tunables (Current:Maximum)
*
0x0000000000000100:0x0000000000010000  file descriptors
*
* Streams Tunables
*
    9  maximum number of pushes allowed (NSTRPUSH)
65536  maximum stream message size (STRMSGSZ)
 1024  max size of ctl part of message (STRCTLSZ)
*
* IPC Messages module is not loaded
*
*
* IPC Semaphores module is not loaded
*
*
* IPC Shared Memory module is not loaded
*
*
* Time Sharing Scheduler Tunables
*
60   maximum time sharing user priority (TSMAXUPRI)
SYS  system class name (SYS_NAME)
```

The `mdb` command is used to view or modify a running kernel and must be used with extreme care. The use of `mdb` is beyond the scope of this book; however, more information can be obtained from "Oracle Solaris Modular Debugger Guide," available online at the Oracle Solaris 11 Information Library.

Kernel Tunable Parameters in Oracle Solaris 11

In Oracle Solaris 11, you'll find that many tunable parameters that were previously set in `/etc/system` have been removed. For example, inter-process communication (IPC) facilities were previously controlled by kernel tunables, where you had to modify the /etc/system file and reboot the system to change the default values for these facilities. Because the IPC facilities are now controlled by resource controls, their configuration can be modified dynamically while the system is running. Many applications that previously required system tuning to function might now run without tuning because of increased defaults and the automatic allocation of resources.

Configuring the kernel and tunable parameters is a complex topic and requires more space than just a few sections of a chapter. I describe the resource controls in Chapter 6, "Administering Zones," where I explain how to use resource controls when configuring zones. If you are interested in learning more about the kernel and tunable parameters, refer to "Oracle Solaris 11.1 Administration: Oracle Solaris Zones, Oracle Solaris 10 Zones, and Resource Management," part number E29024–03, and "Oracle Solaris 11.1 Tunable Parameters Reference Manual," part number E29022–03, available online at the Oracle Solaris 11.1 Information Library.

The `init` Phase

After control of the system is passed to the kernel, the system begins the last stage of the boot process—the `init` phase. In this phase of the boot process, the `init` daemon (`/sbin/init`) reads the `/etc/default/init` file to set any environment variables for the shell that `init` invokes. By default, the `CMASK` and `TZ` variables are set. These values get passed to any processes that `init` starts. Then, `init` reads the `/etc/inittab` file and executes any process entries that have `sysinit` in the action field so that any special initializations can take place before users log in. `Init`'s main function is to initiate core components of SMF, `svc.startd` and `svc.configd`, and to restart these components if they fail.

After reading the `/etc/inittab` file, `init` starts the `svc.startd` daemon, which is responsible for starting and stopping other system services such as mounting file systems and configuring network devices. In addition, `svc.startd` starts the `svc.configd` daemon and also executes legacy RC scripts, which are described later in this chapter.

The `/sbin/init` command sets up the system based on the directions in `/etc/inittab`. Each entry in the `/etc/inittab` file has the following fields:

```
id:rstate:action:process
```

Table 3-17 Fields in the `inittab` File

Field	Description
`id`	Serves as a unique identifier
`rstate`	Defines the run level in which this entry is to be processed
`action`	Uses keywords to specify how the process is to be run
`process`	Gives the name of the command to execute

Table 3-17 describes each field.

The following example shows a default `/etc/inittab` file:

```
ap::sysinit:/usr/sbin/autopush -f /etc/iu.ap
smf::sysinit:/lib/svc/bin/svc.startd  >/dev/msglog 2<>/dev/msglog </dev/console
p3:s1234:powerfail:/usr/sbin/shutdown -y -i5 -g0 >/dev/msglog 2<>/dev/msglog
```

The `init` process performs the following tasks based on the entries found in the default `/etc/inittab` file:

Line 1: Initializes the STREAMS modules used for communication services
Line 2: Configures the socket transport providers for network connections
Line 3: Initializes the `svc.startd` daemon for SMF
Line 4: Describes the action to take when the `init` daemon receives a power fail shutdown signal

SMF eliminates the need to edit the `/etc/inittab` file. Most actions that, in the past, required entries in this file can now be handled through SMF services.

SMF

The `svc.startd` daemon is also referred to as the master process starter and restarter. In earlier versions of Oracle Solaris and other flavors of UNIX, `init` would start all processes and bring the system to the appropriate “run level” or “init state.” In Oracle Solaris 11, SMF—or, more specifically, the `svc.startd` daemon—assumes the role of starting system services.

SMF Services

A service can be described as an entity that provides a resource or list of capabilities to applications and other services. This entity can be running locally or remote, but at this phase of the boot process the service is running locally.

A service does not have to be a process; it can be a system state, a software state of a device, or a mounted file system. Also, a system can have more than one instance of a service, such as with multiple network interfaces, multiple Web services, or a set of other services.

There are advantages to using SMF to manage system services over the traditional UNIX startup scripts that, in the past, were run by the `init` process. These advantages are as follows:

- SMF automatically restarts failed services in the correct order, whether they failed as the result of administrator error or a software bug or were affected by an uncorrectable hardware error. The restart order is defined by dependency statements within SMF.
- The system administrator can view and manage services as well as view the relationships between services and processes.
- SMF allows the system administrator to back up, restore, and undo changes to services by taking automatic snapshots of service configurations.
- SMF allows the system administrator to interrogate services and determine why a service may not be running.
- SMF allows services to be enabled and disabled either temporarily or permanently.
- SMF allows the system administrator to delegate tasks to nonroot users, giving these users the ability to modify, enable, disable, or restart system services.
- Large systems boot and shut down faster because services are started and stopped in parallel according to dependencies set up in SMF.
- SMF allows customization of output sent to the boot console either to be as quiet as possible, which is the default, or to be verbose by using `boot -m verbose` from the OpenBoot prompt.
- SMF provides compatibility with legacy RC scripts.

The `svc.startd` daemon obtains information about services from the service configuration repository. This daemon can also delegate responsibility for services to other delegated restarter daemons such as the `inetd` daemon. The `svc.startd` daemon uses information in the repository to start services for a given milestone by processing the manifests located in the `/var/svc/manifest` directory.

The service instance is the fundamental unit of administration in the SMF framework, and each SMF service has the potential to have multiple versions of itself configured. A service instance is either enabled or disabled with the `svcadm` command described later in this chapter. An instance is a specific configuration of a service, and multiple instances of the same service can run in the same Oracle Solaris instance. For example, a Web server is a service. A specific Web server daemon that is configured to listen on port 80 is an instance. Another instance of the Web server service could have different configuration requirements listening on port 8080. The service has systemwide configuration requirements, but each instance can override specific requirements as needed.

Services are represented in the SMF framework as service instance objects, which are children of service objects. These instance objects can inherit or override the configuration settings of the parent service object. Multiple instances of a single service are managed as child objects of the service object.

Services are not just the representation for standard long-running system services such as `httpd` or `nfsd`. Services also represent varied system entities that include third-party applications, such as Oracle software. In addition, a service can include less traditional entities such as the following:

- A system `init` state, referred to as a milestone
- A physical network device
- A configured IP address
- Kernel configuration information

The services started by `svc.startd` are referred to as milestones. The milestone concept is much like the traditional run levels that were used in previous versions of Oracle Solaris. It's important to note that milestones do not replace run levels. A milestone is a special type of service that represents a specific state of system readiness. Services that depend on the milestone service will have their dependency satisfied and can start after other dependencies are satisfied. A milestone is made up of several SMF services. For example, the services that constituted run levels S, 2, and 3 in the previous version of Oracle Solaris are also represented by the following milestone services:

```
milestone/single-user (equivalent to run level S)
milestone/multi-user (equivalent to run level 2)
milestone/multi-user-server (equivalent to run level 3)
```

Other milestones are available in the Oracle Solaris 11 OS:

```
online    14:10:02 svc:/milestone/unconfig:default
online    14:10:02 svc:/milestone/config:default
online    14:10:02 svc:/milestone/devices:default
online    14:10:13 svc:/milestone/network:default
online    14:10:32 svc:/milestone/name-services:default
online    14:10:32 svc:/milestone/self-assembly-complete:default
```

An SMF manifest is an Extensible Markup Language (XML) file that contains a complete set of properties that are associated with a service or a service instance. The properties are stored in files and subdirectories located in `/var/svc/manifest`. Manifests should not be edited directly to modify the properties of a service. Services should only be manipulated using the SMF commands listed in Table 3-19 on page 191. These commands are used to modify a service via the service configuration repository.

The Service Configuration Repository

The service configuration repository is the authoritative source of the service configuration information. It can only be manipulated or queried using SMF interfaces, which are command-line utilities described later in this section.

The repository database stores state and configuration information for each service instance. The repository provides a per-service snapshot at the time that each service is successfully started so that fallback is possible. In addition, the repository provides a consistent and persistent way to enable or disable a service, as well as a consistent view of service states. This capability can be helpful when debugging service configuration problems.

The repository database is distributed among local memory and local files and is named `/etc/svc/repository.db`. It is managed by the `svc.configd` daemon. This daemon is the interface between the repository and the user, and it ensures that a consistent picture of the repository is presented to the user. A service known as the manifest-import service takes a backup of the repository during reboot. This backup ensures that a failback is possible. The `svc.configd` daemon backs up the repository before any changes are applied from the SMF commands and utilities. You'll find copies of the database in the `/etc/svc` directory:

```
# ls /etc/svc<cr>
profile
repository-boot
repository-boot-20121231_093442
repository-boot-20130120_064245
repository-boot-20130120_071059
repository-boot-20130121_095104
repository-manifest_import
repository-manifest_import-20121207_113824
repository-manifest_import-20121207_113903
```

```
repository-manifest_import-20121213_104246
repository.db
volatile
```

The backup databases are named based on their type and the time they were taken. Those that contain the word `boot` are made before the first change after a system boot. Those that contain the phrase `manifest_import` are made after `svc:/system/early-manifest-import:default` or `svc:/system/manifest-import:default` finishes its processing. On a system that has been in operation for several months, four backups of each type are maintained by the system.

The system deletes the oldest backup when necessary. The backups are stored as `/etc/svc/repository-type-YYYYMMDD_HHMMSWS`, where `YYYYMMDD` (year, month, day) and `HHMMSS` (hour, minute, second) are the date and time when the backup was taken.

Repair a Corrupt Repository

When `svc.configd` is started, it performs an integrity check of the configuration repository and stores it as `/etc/svc/repository.db`. The repository can become corrupted for various reasons. A corrupt repository database keeps the system from booting, resulting in the following error:

```
svc.configd: smf(5) database integrity check of:

    /etc/svc/repository.db

  failed. The database might be damaged or a media error might have
  prevented it from being verified. Additional information useful to
  your service provider is in:

    /system/volatile/db_errors

The system will not be able to boot until you have restored a working
database. svc.startd(1M) will provide a sulogin(1M) prompt for recovery
purposes. The command:

    /lib/svc/bin/restore_repository

  can be run to restore a backup version of your repository. See
  http://sun.com/msg/SMF-8000-MY for more information.
```

You can repair the corrupt database by logging in as `root` and running the `/lib/svc/bin/restore_repository` command.

A list of the backups will be displayed from oldest to newest:

```
manifest_import-20121207_113824
manifest_import-20121207_113903
manifest_import-20121213_104246
boot-20121231_093442
boot-20130120_064245
boot-20130120_071059
boot-20130121_095104
```

The list of backups is followed by a menu of options:

```
CHOICE               ACTION
---------------      -------------------------------------------
boot                 restore the most recent post-boot backup
manifest_import      restore the most recent manifest_import backup
-seed-               restore the initial starting repository (All
                     customizations will be lost, including those
                     made by the install/upgrade process.)
-quit-               cancel script and quit
Enter response [boot]:<cr>
```

I pressed *Enter* without specifying a backup to restore, the default response, and `boot` is selected. Selecting `-quit-` exits the `restore_repository` script, returning you to the shell prompt.

> **Note**
>
> Selecting `-seed-` restores the seed repository. This repository is designed for use during initial installation and upgrades. Using the seed repository for recovery purposes should be a last resort.

After the backup to restore has been selected, it is validated and an integrity check is performed. If there are any problems, the `restore_repository` command prints error messages and prompts you for another selection. Once a valid backup is selected, the following information is printed, and you are prompted for final confirmation.

```
After confirmation, the following steps will be taken:

svc.startd(1M) and svc.configd(1M) will be quiesced, if running.
/etc/svc/repository.db
  -- renamed --> /etc/svc/repository.db_old_20130123_101612
/etc/svc/repository-boot
  -- copied --> /etc/svc/repository.db

Proceed [yes/no]? yes<cr>
```

The system displays the following message and reboots the system:

```
Quiescing svc.startd(1M) and svc.configd(1M): done.
/etc/svc/repository.db
  -- renamed --> /etc/svc/repository.db_old_20130123_101612
/etc/svc/repository-boot
  -- copied --> /etc/svc/repository.db

The backup repository has been successfully restored.

Rebooting in 5 seconds.

Quiescing svc.startd(1M) and svc.configd(1M): done.
/etc/svc/repository.db
```

```
  -- renamed --> /etc/svc/repository.db_old_20130123_101612
/etc/svc/repository-boot
  -- copied --> /etc/svc/repository.db

The backup repository has been successfully restored.

Rebooting in 5 seconds.
```

Service FMRI

Each service instance is named with an FMRI. The FMRI includes the service name and the instance name. For example, the FMRI for the `ftp` service is `svc:/network/ftp:default`, where the `svc` prefix indicates that the service is managed by SMF. The category of the service is `network`. `ftp` identifies the service name, and `default` identifies the service instance.

You may see various forms of the FMRI that all refer to the same service instance:

```
svc://localhost/network/inetd:default
svc:/network/inetd:default
network/inetd:default
```

An FMRI for a legacy service has the following format:

```
lrc:/etc/rc2_d/S47pppd
```

where the `lrc` (legacy run control) prefix indicates that the service is not managed by SMF. The pathname `/etc/rc2_d` refers to the directory where the legacy script is located, and `S47pppd` is the name of the RC script. See the section titled "Using the RC Scripts to Stop or Start Services" later in this chapter for information on RC scripts.

The service names include a general functional category that includes the following:

- Application
- Device
- Legacy
- Milestone
- Network
- Platform
- Site
- System

Service Dependencies

In earlier versions of Oracle Solaris, processes were started at bootup by their respective shell scripts, which ran in a predetermined sequence. Sometimes, one of these shell scripts failed for various reasons. Perhaps it was an error in the script, or one of the daemons did not start. When a script failed, the other scripts were started regardless, and sometimes these scripts failed because a previous process failed to start. Tracking down the problem was difficult for the system administrator.

To remedy the problem with sequencing scripts, Oracle uses SMF to manage the starting and stopping of services. SMF understands the dependencies that some services have on other services. If an SMF-managed service fails or is terminated, all dependent processes are taken offline until the required process is restarted. The interdependency is started by means of a service contract. This contract is maintained by the kernel and describes the process interdependency, restarter process, and startup methods.

Most service instances have dependencies on other services or files. Those dependencies control when the service is started and automatically stopped. When the dependencies of an enabled service are not satisfied, the service is kept in the offline state. When the service instance dependencies are satisfied, the service is started or restarted by the `svc.startd` daemon. If the start is successful, the service is transitioned to the online state. There are four types of service instance dependencies:

- `require_all`: The dependency is satisfied when all cited services are running (online or degraded) or when all indicated files are present.
- `require_any`: The dependency is satisfied when one of the cited services is running (online or degraded) or when at least one of the indicated files is present.
- `optional_all`: The dependency is satisfied when all cited services are running (online or degraded), disabled, or in the maintenance state or when cited services are not present. For files, this type is the same as `require_all`.
- `exclude_all`: The dependency is satisfied when all cited services are disabled or in the maintenance state or when cited services or files are not present.

Each service or service instance must define a set of methods that start, stop, and optionally refresh the service. These methods can be listed and modified for each service using the `svccfg` command described later in this chapter.

A service instance is satisfied and started when its criteria, for the type of dependency, are met. Dependencies are satisfied when cited services move to the online state. After it is running (online or degraded), if a service instance with a `require_all`, `require_any`, or `optional_all` dependency is stopped or refreshed, SMF considers why the service was stopped and uses the `restart_on` attribute of the dependency to decide whether to stop the service. Table 3-18 defines the `restart_on` attributes.

Table 3-18 `restart_on` Values

Event	None	Error	Restart	Refresh
stop due to error	no	yes	yes	yes
non-error stop	no	no	yes	yes
refresh	no	no	no	yes

Table 3-19 SMF Command-Line Utilities

Command	Description
`inetadm`	Used to configure and view services controlled by the `inetd` daemon
`svcadm`	Used to perform common service management tasks such as enabling, disabling, or restarting service instances
`svccfg`	Used to display and manipulate the contents of the service configuration repository
`svcprop`	Used to retrieve property values from the service configuration repository with output that is appropriate for use in shell scripts
`svcs`	Used to obtain a detailed view of the service state of all service instances in the configuration repository
`svcbundle`	Used to generate SMF manifests

A service is considered to have stopped due to an error if the service has encountered a hardware error or a software error such as a core dump. For `exclude_all` dependencies, the service is stopped if the cited service is started and the `restart_on` attribute is not `none`.

You can use the `svcs` command (described later in this chapter) to view service instance dependencies and to troubleshoot failures. You'll also see how to use the `svccfg` command to modify service dependencies.

SMF Command-Line Administration Utilities

SMF provides a set of command-line utilities used to administer and configure SMF. Table 3-19 describes these utilities.

Displaying Information about Services

Use the `svcs` command to display information about service instances. Some of the more common options to the `svcs` command are as follows:

- `-a` Shows all services, even the disabled ones. Services are sorted by state and time.

- `-d` Shows dependencies. Lists the services or service instances upon which the given service instances depend.
- `-D` Shows dependents. Lists the service instances that depend on the given services or service instances.
- `-l` Displays all available information.
- `-p` Lists processes associated with a service.
- `-R` Displays service instances that use the specified service instance as their restarter.
- `-v` Displays verbose output. When used with the `-x` option, this displays extra information for each explanation.
- `-x` Explains the status of services that might require maintenance, or explains the status of the specified service(s).
- `-?` Displays information on how to use the command.

To report the status of all enabled service instances and to get a list of the various services that are running, use the `svcs` command with no options:

```
# svcs | more<cr>
```

The `svcs` command obtains information about all service instances from the service configuration repository and displays the state, start time, and FMRI of each service instance:

```
STATE          STIME    FMRI
legacy_run     8:18:59 lrc:/etc/rc2_d/S47pppd
legacy_run     8:18:59 lrc:/etc/rc2_d/S81dodatadm_udaplt
legacy_run     8:18:59 lrc:/etc/rc2_d/S89PRESERVE
disabled       8:18:27 svc:/ldoms/agents:default
disabled       8:18:38 svc:/network/ipsec/policy:default
disabled       8:18:49 svc:/network/dns/client:default
disabled       8:19:00 svc:/system/console-login:vt2
disabled       8:19:00 svc:/system/console-login:vt3
. . . .
<output has been truncated to save space>
online         8:19:22 svc:/system/fm/smtp-notify:default
online         8:19:22 svc:/system/fm/asr-notify:default
online         8:19:26 svc:/system/devchassis:daemon
online         8:20:34 svc:/application/texinfo-update:default
online         8:20:57 svc:/network/ilomconfig-interconnect:default
```

Listing Legacy Services

You'll notice that the list includes legacy scripts that were used to start up processes. Legacy services can be viewed, but they cannot be administered with SMF.

The state of each service is one of the following:

`degraded`	The service instance is enabled but is running at a limited capacity.
`disabled`	The service instance is not enabled and is not running.
`legacy_run`	The legacy service is not managed by SMF, but the service can be observed. This state is only used by legacy services that are started with RC scripts.
`maintenance`	The service instance has encountered an error that must be resolved by the administrator.
`offline`	The service instance is enabled, but the service is not yet running or available to run.
`online`	The service instance is enabled and has successfully started.
`uninitialized`	This state is the initial state for all services before their configuration has been read.

Running the `svcs` command without options displays the status of all enabled services. Use the `-a` option to list all services, including disabled services:

```
# svcs -a<cr>
```

The result is a listing of all services, including all disabled services:

```
STATE          STIME    FMRI
legacy_run     8:18:59 lrc:/etc/rc2_d/S47pppd
legacy_run     8:18:59 lrc:/etc/rc2_d/S81dodatadm_udaplt
legacy_run     8:18:59 lrc:/etc/rc2_d/S89PRESERVE
disabled       8:17:47 svc:/system/device/mpxio-upgrade:default
disabled       8:17:50 svc:/network/install:default
disabled       8:17:52 svc:/network/nis/domain:default
disabled       8:17:52 svc:/network/ipsec/manual-key:default
disabled       8:17:52 svc:/network/ipsec/ike:default
disabled       8:17:53 svc:/system/name-service-cache:default
disabled       8:17:54 svc:/network/ldap/client:default
disabled       8:17:55 svc:/network/nis/client:default
disabled       8:17:55 svc:/network/inetd-upgrade:default
disabled       8:17:56 svc:/network/nfs/status:default
disabled       8:17:56 svc:/network/nfs/nlockmgr:default
disabled       8:17:56 svc:/network/nfs/cbd:default
. . .<output has been truncated>
```

To display information on selected services, you can supply the FMRI as an argument to the `svcs` command:

```
# svcs -l network<cr>
```

With the `-l` option, the system displays detailed information about the network service instance. The `network` FMRI specified in the previous example is a general functional category and is also called the network milestone. The information displayed by the previous command is as follows:

```
fmri         svc:/milestone/network:default
name         Network milestone
enabled      true
state        online
next_state   none
state_time   January 23, 2013 02:15:18 PM EST

fmri         svc:/milestone/network:default
name         Network milestone
enabled      true
state        online
next_state   none
state_time   January 23, 2013 02:15:18 PM EST
logfile      /var/svc/log/milestone-network:default.log
restarter    svc:/system/svc/restarter:default
manifest     /lib/svc/manifest/milestone/network.xml
manifest     /lib/svc/manifest/network/ipsec/ipsecalgs.xml
manifest     /lib/svc/manifest/network/ipsec/ike.xml
manifest     /lib/svc/manifest/network/ipsec/policy.xml
manifest     /lib/svc/manifest/network/ipsec/manual-key.xml
manifest     /lib/svc/manifest/network/ipfilter.xml
dependency   require_all/none svc:/network/loopback (online)
dependency   require_all/none svc:/network/physical:default (online)
dependency   optional_all/none svc:/network/ipsec/ipsecalgs (online)
dependency   optional_all/none svc:/network/ipsec/ike (disabled)
dependency   optional_all/none svc:/network/ipsec/policy (online)
dependency   optional_all/none svc:/network/ipsec/manual-key (disabled)
dependency   optional_all/restart svc:/network/ipfilter (disabled)
```

Use the -d option to view which services are started at the `network:default` milestone:

```
# svcs -d milestone/network:default<cr>
```

The system displays the following:

```
disabled     8:17:52 svc:/network/ipsec/manual-key:default
disabled     8:17:52 svc:/network/ipsec/ike:default
disabled     8:18:38 svc:/network/ipsec/policy:default
online       8:18:19 svc:/network/ipsec/ipsecalgs:default
online       8:18:19 svc:/network/loopback:default
online       8:18:37 svc:/network/physical:default
online       8:18:52 svc:/network/ipfilter:default
```

Another milestone is the `multi-user` milestone, which is displayed as follows:

```
# svcs -d milestone/multi-user<cr>
```

The system displays all the services started at the `multi-user` milestone:

```
STATE        STIME    FMRI
disabled     8:17:57  svc:/network/nfs/client:default
disabled     8:17:59  svc:/platform/sun4u/sf880drd:default
disabled     8:18:00  svc:/system/rcap:default
online       8:18:17  svc:/system/resource-controls:default
online       8:18:26  svc:/system/utmp:default
online       8:18:27  svc:/system/rmtmpfiles:default
online       8:18:39  svc:/milestone/single-user:default
online       8:18:40  svc:/system/filesystem/local:default
online       8:18:40  svc:/system/filesystem/ufs/quota:default
online       8:18:53  svc:/network/rpc/bind:default
online       8:18:56  svc:/system/cron:default
online       8:18:56  svc:/network/inetd:default
online       8:18:57  svc:/network/iscsi/initiator:default
online       8:18:57  svc:/milestone/name-services:default
online       8:18:58  svc:/system/name-service/cache:default
online       8:18:58  svc:/system/filesystem/autofs:default
online       8:18:58  svc:/system/system-log:default
online       8:18:58  svc:/system/system-log:default
online       8:18:59  svc:/network/smtp:sendmail
online       8:18:59  svc:/system/auditd:default
```

Many of these services have their own dependencies, services that must be started before they get started. We refer to these as subdependencies. For example, one of the services listed is the `svc:/network/inetd:default` service. You can see a listing of the subdependencies for this service by typing

```
# svcs -d network/inetd<cr>
```

The system displays the following dependencies:

```
STATE        STIME    FMRI
disabled     8:17:55  svc:/network/inetd-upgrade:default
online       8:18:19  svc:/network/loopback:default
online       8:18:39  svc:/milestone/network:default
online       8:18:40  svc:/system/filesystem/local:default
online       8:18:53  svc:/network/rpc/bind:default
online       8:18:57  svc:/milestone/name-services:default
```

The `-d` option in the previous example lists the services or service instances upon which the `multi-user` service instance depends. These are the services that must be running before the `multi-user` milestone is reached. The `-D` option shows which other services depend on the `milestone/multi-user` service:

```
# svcs -D milestone/multi-user<cr>
```

The system displays the following output, displaying all of the services that are dependent on the `multi-user` service:

```
STATE         STIME    FMRI
disabled      8:18:00 svc:/application/management/net-snmp:default
disabled      8:18:09 svc:/network/dhcp/relay:ipv4
disabled      8:18:09 svc:/network/dhcp/relay:ipv6
disabled      8:18:09 svc:/network/dhcp/server:ipv4
disabled      8:18:09 svc:/network/dhcp/server:ipv6
disabled      8:18:18 svc:/system/rad:remote
online        8:19:00 svc:/system/intrd:default
online        8:19:00 svc:/system/rad:local
online        8:19:00 svc:/application/man-index:default
online        8:19:00 svc:/system/boot-config:default
online        8:19:02 svc:/milestone/multi-user-server:default
```

To view processes associated with a service instance, use the `-p` option as follows:

```
# svcs -p svc:/network/inetd:default<cr>
```

The system displays processes associated with the `svc:/network/inetd:default` service. In this case, information about the `inetd` process is shown:

```
STATE         STIME    FMRI
online        8:18:56 svc:/network/inetd:default
              8:18:56 579 inetd
```

Viewing processes using `svcs -p` instead of the traditional `ps` command makes it easier to track all of the processes associated with a particular service.

Each service is managed by a restarter. For example, the `ssh` service is managed and started by the `svc:/system/svc/restarter:default` service. This is shown by viewing the `ssh` service using the `-l` option as follows:

```
# svcs -l ssh<cr>
fmri          svc:/network/ssh:default
name          SSH server
enabled       true
state         online
next_state    none
state_time    January 23, 2013 02:15:29 PM EST
logfile       /var/svc/log/network-ssh:default.log
restarter     svc:/system/svc/restarter:default
contract_id   95
manifest      /etc/svc/profile/generic.xml
manifest      /lib/svc/manifest/network/ssh.xml
dependency    require_all/none svc:/system/filesystem/local (online)
dependency    optional_all/none svc:/system/filesystem/autofs (online)
dependency    require_all/none svc:/network/loopback (online)
dependency    require_all/none svc:/network/physical:default (online)
dependency    require_all/none svc:/system/cryptosvc (online)
```

```
dependency    require_all/none svc:/system/utmp (online)
dependency    optional_all/error svc:/network/ipfilter:default (disabled)
dependency    require_all/restart file://localhost/etc/ssh/sshd_config (online)
```

If a service fails for some reason and cannot be restarted, you can list the service using the -x option:

```
# svcs -x ftp<cr>
```

The system displays the following:

```
svc:/network/ftp:default (FTP server)
 State: disabled since January 23, 2013 02:14:52 PM EST
Reason: Disabled by an administrator.
   See: http://support.oracle.com/msg/SMF-8000-05
   See: proftpd(1M)
   See: file://usr/share/doc/proftpd/
Impact: This service is not running.
```

The example shows that the ftp service is not running and explains that the service has been disabled by the system administrator.

It's helpful to use the -v and -x options together when troubleshooting a service because it displays more verbose output:

```
# svcs -vx ftp<cr>
svc:/network/ftp:default (FTP server)
 State: disabled since January 23, 2013 02:14:52 PM EST
Reason: Disabled by an administrator.
   See: http://support.oracle.com/msg/SMF-8000-05
   See: man -M /usr/share/man -s 1M proftpd
   See: file://usr/share/doc/proftpd/
Impact: This service is not running.
```

Modifying the Service Configuration Repository

Use the svccfg command to manipulate data in the service configuration repository. The svccfg command interacts with the svc.configd daemon, which is started at system startup by the svc.startd daemon and is the repository daemon for SMF. The repository can be manipulated from the command line or in interactive mode using the svccfg command. For example, to view and manipulate the properties for the network/ftp service, you could use the svccfg command in interactive mode, as shown in the next example.

Manipulating the Service Configuration Repository

In this example, I'll use the svccfg command to enable FTP logging by modifying the start property for the ftp service.

1. From the command line, type the following command to enter interactive mode:

```
# svccfg<cr>
```

The system displays the following prompt:

```
svc:>
```

2. Type the list command to view all services:

```
svc:> list<cr>
```

The system displays all the services:

```
system/boot-archive
system/device/local
milestone/devices
. . .<Output has been truncated>
```

3. Select the FTP service by typing the following:

```
svc:> select network/ftp<cr>
```

The prompt changes as follows:

```
svc:/network/ftp>
```

4. Type the `listprop` command to list all the properties associated with the FTP service:

```
svc:/network/ftp> listprop<cr>
```

The following is displayed:

```
firewall_config                    com.sun,fw_configuration
firewall_config/apply_to          astring
firewall_config/exceptions        astring
firewall_config/policy            astring      use_global
```

```
firewall_config/value_authorization astring     solaris.smf.value.firewall.config
firewall_context                     com.sun,fw_definition
firewall_context/ipf_method         astring     "/lib/svc/method/svc-ftp
ipfilter"
net-loopback                         dependency
net-loopback/entities               fmri        svc:/network/loopback
net-loopback/grouping               astring     require_any
net-loopback/restart_on             astring     none
net-loopback/type                   astring     service
net-service                          dependency
net-service/entities                fmri        svc:/network/service
net-service/grouping                astring     require_all
net-service/restart_on              astring     none
net-service/type                    astring     service
net-physical                         dependency
net-physical/entities               fmri        svc:/network/physical
net-physical/grouping               astring     require_all
net-physical/restart_on             astring     none
net-physical/type                   astring     service
filesystem-local                     dependency
filesystem-local/entities           fmri
svc:/system/filesystem/local
filesystem-local/grouping           astring     require_all
filesystem-local/restart_on         astring     none
filesystem-local/type               astring     service
name-service-cache                   dependency
name-service-cache/entities         fmri        svc:/system/name-service/cache
name-service-cache/grouping         astring     require_all
name-service-cache/restart_on       astring     none
name-service-cache/type             astring     service
manifestfiles                        framework
manifestfiles/etc_svc_profile_generic_xml       astring
/etc/svc/profile/generic.xml
manifestfiles/lib_svc_manifest_network_ftp_xml  astring
/lib/svc/manifest/network/ftp.xml
general                              framework
general/action_authorization        astring     solaris.smf.manage.ftp
general/single_instance             boolean     true
general/value_authorization         astring     solaris.smf.manage.ftp
startd                               framework
startd/duration                     astring     contract
startd/ignore_error                 astring     core,signal
start                                method
start/exec                          astring     /usr/lib/inet/proftpd
Output has been truncated -
The output shows that the start method (the startup script) for the ftp service is
/usr/lib/inet/proftpd.
```

5. I will add the `-d` option to the `proftpd` command to enable logging. I will modify the start method for the FTP service so that it starts up with the `-d` option. Set the start method using the `setprop` command:

```
svc:/network/ftp> setprop start/exec=astring: "/usr/lib/inet/proftpd -d 10"<cr>
```

6. Exit the session by typing `end`:

```
svc:/network/ftp> end<cr>
```

An alternative is to change the `start` property for the FTP service using the default editor. Issue the following command at the shell prompt:

```
# svccfg -s network/ftp editprop<cr>
```

After setting the property, use the `svcprop` command to verify the change:

```
# svcprop -p start/exec network/ftp<cr>
```

The system displays the following:

```
/usr/lib/inet/proftpd\ -d10
```

Now, the manifest needs to be reloaded as follows:

```
# svcadm refresh network/ftp<cr>
```

List SMF service customizations using the `listcust` subcommand as follows:

```
# svccfg -s ftp listcust<cr>
start/exec                astring     admin       "/usr/lib/inet/proftpd -d10"
```

Delete the service customization using the `delcust` subcommand as follows:

```
# svccfg -s ftp delcust<cr>
Deleting customizations for service: network/ftp
```

Refresh the service and view the property to confirm that the customization has been deleted as follows:

```
# svcadm refresh ftp<cr>
# svcprop -p start/exec ftp<cr>
/usr/lib/inet/proftpd
```

Starting and Stopping Services Using SMF

To disable services in previous versions of Oracle Solaris, the system administrator had to search for and rename the relevant RC script(s) or comment out statements in a configuration file, such as modifying the `inetd.conf` file when disabling FTP.

SMF makes it much easier to locate services and their dependencies. To start a particular service using SMF, the service instance must be enabled using the `svcadm enable` command. By enabling a service, the status change is recorded in the service configuration repository. The enabled state persists across reboots as long as the service dependencies are met. The following example demonstrates how to use the `svcadm` command to enable the FTP server:

```
# svcadm enable network/ftp:default<cr>
```

To disable the FTP service, use the `disable` option as follows:

```
# svcadm disable network/ftp:default<cr>
```

To verify the status of the service, type

```
# svcs network/ftp<cr>
```

The system displays the following:

```
STATE          STIME    FMRI
disabled       16:07:08 svc:/network/ftp:default
```

The `svcadm` command allows the following subcommands:

- `enable`: This subcommand enables the service instances.
- `disable`: This subcommand disables the service instances.
- `delegate`: This subcommand changes the delegated restarter.
- `mark`: This subcommand forces a service to a certain state.
- `restart`: This subcommand requests that the service instances be restarted.
- `refresh`: For each service instance specified, `refresh` requests that the assigned restarter update the service's running configuration snapshot with the values from the current configuration. Some of these values take effect immediately (for example, dependency changes). Other values do not take effect until the next service restart.
- `clear`: For each service instance specified, if the instance is in the maintenance state, this subcommand sends a signal to the assigned restarter indicating that the service has been repaired. If the instance is in the degraded state, this subcommand requests that the assigned restarter take the service to the online state.

In the following example, users cannot telnet into the server, so I check on the telnet service using the `svcs -x` command:

```
# svcs -x telnet<cr>
```

The results show that the service is not running:

```
svc:/network/telnet:default (Telnet server)
 State: disabled January 23, 2013 10:18:28 AM EST
Reason: Temporarily disabled by an administrator.
   See: http://sun.com/msg/SMF-8000-1S
   See: in.telnetd(1M)
   See:  telnetd(1M)
Impact: This service is not running.
```

I enable the service using the `svcadm` command:

```
# svcadm enable svc:/network/telnet:default<cr>
```

After enabling the service, check the status using the `svcs` command:

```
# svcs -x telnet<cr>
```

The system responds with the following:

```
svc:/network/telnet:default (Telnet server)
  State: online since January 23, 2013 10:18:28 AM EST
   See: in.telnetd(1M)
   See: telnetd(1M)
Impact:  None.
```

Also, if a service that has been running stops, try restarting the service using the `svcadm restart` command as follows:

```
# svcadm restart svc:/network/telnet:default<cr>
```

The `svcadm` command can also be used to change milestones. In the next example, I'll use the `svcadm` command to determine my current system state (milestone) and then change the system default milestone to single-user.

Changing Milestones

1. I begin by checking which milestone the system is currently running:

```
# svcs | grep milestone<cr>
```

   The system responds with

```
disabled      16:16:36 svc:/milestone/multi-user-server:default
online        16:16:36 svc:/milestone/name-services:default
online        16:16:43 svc:/milestone/devices:default
online        16:16:45 svc:/milestone/network:default
online        16:16:57 svc:/milestone/single-user:default
online        16:17:03 svc:/milestone/sysconfig:default
online        16:17:16 svc:/milestone/multi-user:default
```

   From the output, I see that `multi-user-server` is not running, but `multi-user` is running.

2. To start the transition to the single-user milestone, type

```
# svcadm milestone single-user<cr>
```

   The system responds with the following, prompting for the root password and finally entering single-user mode:

```
Root password for system maintenance (control-d to bypass):<enter root password>
```

3. Verify the current milestone with the following command:

```
# svcs -a | grep milestone<cr>
```

   The system responds with the following:

```
disabled      16:16:36 svc:/milestone/multi-user-server:default
disabled      17:21:37 svc:/milestone/multi-user:default
disabled      17:21:37 svc:/milestone/sysconfig:default
disabled      17:21:39 svc:/milestone/name-services:default
online        16:16:43 svc:/milestone/devices:default
online        16:16:45 svc:/milestone/network:default
online        16:16:57 svc:/milestone/single-user:default
```

The output indicates that the multi-user and multi-user-server milestones are disabled, and the single-user milestone is currently online.
Notice that when I check the run level:

```
# who -r<cr>
```

the system responds with the following:

```
.    run-level 3 Mar 18 16:09    3    0 S
```

That's because, although changing milestones may disable or enable selected services, changing a milestone does not change the run level reported by the `who -r` command. Only the `init` process changes the current run level. The `svcadm milestone` command does not communicate directly with the `init` process.

4. Finally, I bring the system back up to the multi-user-server milestone:

```
# svcadm milestone milestone/multi-user-server:default<cr>
```

Issuing the `svcs` command again shows that the multi-user-server milestone is back online:

```
# svcs -a |grep milestone<cr>
online  16:16:43 svc:/milestone/devices:default
online  16:16:45 svc:/milestone/network:default
online  16:16:57 svc:/milestone/single-user:default
online  17:37:06 svc:/milestone/name-services:default
online  17:37:12 svc:/milestone/sysconfig:default
online  17:37:23 svc:/milestone/multi-user:default
online  17:37:31 svc:/milestone/multi-user-server:default
```

The SMF Master Restarter Daemon

At bootup, `svc.startd`, referred to as the "master restarter daemon," retrieves the information in the service configuration repository and starts services when their dependencies are met. This daemon is responsible for starting services, restarting services, and shutting down services. The `svc.startd` daemon is responsible for restarting services that have failed and for shutting down services whose dependencies are no longer satisfied. The `svc.startd` daemon ensures that the system boots to the correct milestone. All service instances in SMF must be managed by a restarter.

In some cases, an alternate restarter may be designated for a particular service instance. For example, `inetd(1M)` is a delegated restarter that provides its service instances with an initial environment. The restarter for each service instance is assigned by the restarter property. If you want to know the restarter for a particular service, list that service with the `-l` option as follows:

```
# svcs -l  svc:/network/telnet:default<cr>
fmri         svc:/network/telnet:default
name         Telnet server
enabled      false
state        disabled
next_state   none
state_time   January 23, 2013 10:18:28 AM EST
restarter    svc:/network/inetd:default
manifest     /etc/svc/profile/generic.xml
manifest     /lib/svc/manifest/network/telnet.xml
```

Notice that the restarter is `svc:/network/inetd:default`. If the restarter property is not set, it defaults to `svc:/system/svc/restarter:default`. Many networking services use `inetd` as a restarter as shown with the `svcs -R` command:

```
# svcs -R svc:/network/inetd:default<cr>
STATE        STIME    FMRI
disabled     19:22:41 svc:/network/rpc/rstat:default
disabled     19:22:41 svc:/application/cups/in-lpd:default
disabled     19:22:42 svc:/network/finger:default
disabled     19:22:42 svc:/network/rexec:default
disabled     19:22:42 svc:/network/talk:default
disabled     19:22:42 svc:/network/telnet:default
disabled     19:22:42 svc:/network/stlisten:default
disabled     19:22:42 svc:/network/tftp/udp6:default
. . .<output has been truncated>
```

In the past, many of these network services appeared in the `/etc/inetd.conf` file and were managed by `inetd`. Now they use `inetd` as a starter.

The `svc.startd` daemon is managed by the `svc:/system/svc/restarter:default service`. All of the services that use `svc.startd` as the starter/restarter are listed as follows:

```
# svcs -R svc:/system/svc/restarter:default<cr>
STATE        STIME    FMRI
disabled     19:21:31 svc:/system/device/mpxio-upgrade:default
disabled     19:21:34 svc:/network/install:default
disabled     19:21:35 svc:/network/nis/domain:default
disabled     19:21:36 svc:/network/ipsec/manual-key:default
. . .<output has been truncated>
```

The `svc.startd` daemon is not configured by command line options. Instead, the configuration is read from the service configuration repository. You can use svccfg(1M) to set all options and properties for svc.startd by modifying the svc:/system/svc/restarter:default service. For example, to turn on verbose logging by svc.startd, type the following:

```
# svccfg -s system/svc/restarter:default<cr>
svc:/system/svc/restarter:default> addpg options application
svc:/system/svc/restarter:default> setprop options/logging = astring: verbose
svc:/system/svc/restarter:default> exit
```

Service State Transition Notifications

SMF has a built-in notification feature that sends an e-mail message whenever a service state transitions or when a fault management event occurs. The notification feature uses the SMTP service to send an e-mail notification when a service changes states.

To use this feature, make sure that the smtp-notify package is installed using the pkg info smtp-notify command. If it needs to be installed, install it as follows:

```
# pkg install service/fault-management/smtp-notify<cr>
```

After verifying that the package is installed, you will need to enable the service that controls the notification daemon as follows:

```
# svcadm enable svc:/system/fm/smtp-notify:default<cr>
```

This will start up the smtp-notify process, which can be verified as follows:

```
# ps -ef|grep smtp-notify<cr>
root       2073  2045  0 06:52:46 pts/1      0:00 grep smtp-notify
noaccess  1416     1  0 06:26:49 ?          0:00 /usr/lib/fm/notify/smtp-notify
```

The next step is to configure the transition notifications for all services using the svccfg command. To configure the transition notification for all services, issue the following command:

```
# svccfg -s svc:/system/svc/global:default setnotify -g from-online \
mailto:root@localhost<cr>
```

The above command will set the notification level to "from-online," which will notify you whenever a service transitions from the online state to any other state. To verify the notification setting, type

```
# svccfg -s global listnotify<cr>
    Event: from-online (source: svc:/system/svc/global:default)
        Notification Type: smtp
            Active: true
            to: root@localhost
```

To configure a notification for a single service only, issue the `svccfg` command for that particular service. For example, configure notifications for the `ssh` service as follows:

```
# svccfg -s svc:/network/ssh:default setnotify -g from-online mailto:root@localhost<cr>
```

To verify the notification setting, type

```
# svccfg -s ssh listnotify<cr>
    Event: from-online (source: svc:/network/ssh)
        Notification Type: smtp
            Active: true
            to: root@localhost
```

The following command creates a notification that sends an e-mail message when transactions go into the maintenance state:

```
# /usr/sbin/svccfg setnotify -g maintenance maito:root@localhost<cr>
```

You can also set up notifications for fault management architecture (FMA) events as follows:

```
# svccfg setnotify problem-diagnosed,problem-updated mailto:root@localhost snmp:<cr>
```

Verify the settings by typing the following:

```
# svccfg listnotify problem-diagnosed,problem-updated<cr>
    Event: problem-diagnosed (source: svc:/system/fm/notify-params:default)
        Notification Type: smtp
            Active: true
            reply-to: root@localhost
            to: root@localhost

        Notification Type: snmp
            Active: true

        Notification Type: syslog
            Active: true
```

```
    Event: problem-updated (source: svc:/system/fm/notify-params:default)
        Notification Type: smtp
            Active: true
            to: root@localhost
```

Set up a notification to receive a message when an FMA problem has been repaired:

```
# /usr/sbin/svccfg setnotify problem-repaired snmp:<cr>
```

When a service experiences a transition, such as when the ssh service is disabled, the following message is sent to root:

```
# mail<cr>
From noaccess@solaris Wed Jan 23 08:52:11 2013
Date: Wed, 23 Jan 2013 08:52:11 -0400 (EDT)
From: No Access User <noaccess@solaris>
Message-Id: <201207261252.q6QCqBMn002180@solaris>
Subject: solaris: svc:/network/ssh:default online->disabled
To: root@solaris
Content-Length: 229

HOSTNAME: solaris
TIMESTAMP: Wed Jan 23 08:51:11 2013
FMRI: svc:/network/ssh:default
FROM-STATE: online
TO-STATE: disabled
DESCRIPTION: The indicated service has transitioned to the disabled state
REASON: a disable was requested
```

To stop service state transition notifications, use the delnotify subcommand, as follows:

```
# svccfg -s svc:/system/svc/global:default delnotify -g all<cr>
```

The previous command stops all notifications.

For additional information on the smtp-notify feature, refer to the smtp-notify(1M) man page.

Fault Management Architecture

The Oracle Solaris Fault Management feature provides an architecture for building resilient error handlers, structured error telemetry, automated diagnostic software, response agents, and structured messaging. Many parts of the software stack participate in Fault Management, including the CPU, memory and I/O subsystems, Oracle Solaris ZFS, an increasing set of device drivers, and other management stacks. Refer to the fmd(1M) and fmadm(1M) man pages for more information.

Starting Services during Boot

Under SMF, the boot process is much quieter than previous versions of Oracle Solaris. This was done to reduce the amount of uninformative "chatter" that could obscure any real problems that might occur during boot.

Some new boot options have been added to control the verbosity of boot. One that you may find particularly useful is `-m verbose`, which prints a line of information when each service attempts to start up. This is similar to previous versions of Oracle Solaris in which the boot messages were more verbose.

You can also boot the system using one of the milestones using the OpenBoot `boot` command followed by the `-m` option:

```
{0} ok boot -m milestone=single-user<cr>
```

The system boots into single-user mode, where only the basic services are started, as shown when the `svcs` command is used to display services:

```
# svcs<cr>
STATE     STIME    FMRI
disabled  17:10:27 svc:/system/filesystem/local:default
disabled  17:10:27 svc:/system/identity:domain
disabled  17:10:27 svc:/system/sysidtool:net
disabled  17:10:28 svc:/system/cryptosvc:default
disabled  17:10:28 svc:/network/initial:default
disabled  17:10:28 svc:/network/rpc/bind:default
disabled  17:10:28 svc:/system/sysidtool:system
disabled  17:10:28 svc:/milestone/sysconfig:default
Output has been truncated. . . . .
```

This method of booting is slightly different than using the `boot -s` command. When the system is explicitly booted to a milestone, exiting the console administrative shell does not transition the system to multi-user mode, as `boot -s` does. To move to multi-user mode after `boot -m milestone=single-user`, use the following command:

```
# svcadm milestone milestone/multi-user-server:default<cr>
```

If no milestone is specified at bootup, `svc.startd` boots to the built-in milestone `all`, which includes all the system-enabled services.

The milestones that can be specified at boot time are as follows:

```
none
single-user
multi-user
multi-user-server
all
```

If you boot a system using one of the milestones and you do not include the `-s` option, the system stays in the milestone state in which you booted it. The system does not go into multi-user state automatically when you press *Ctrl+D*. You can, however, get into the multi-user state by using the following command, and all services will be restored:

```
# svcadm milestone all<cr>
```

To boot the system without any milestones, type

```
{0} ok boot -m milestone=none<cr>
```

The `boot` command instructs the `svc.startd` daemon to temporarily disable all services except for the master restarter named `svc:/system/svc/restarter:default` and start `sulogin` on the console. The "none" milestone can be very useful in troubleshooting systems that have failures early in the boot process.

To bring the system back down to single-user mode from multi-user mode, type

```
# svcadm milestone milestone/single-user<cr>
```

The `-d` option can be used with the previous example to cause `svcadm` to make the given milestone the default boot milestone, which persists across reboots. This would be the equivalent of setting the default run level in the `/etc/inittab` file on previous versions of Oracle Solaris.

Other options that can be used with `svcadm` include

- `-r` This option enables each service instance and recursively enables its dependencies.
- `-s` This option enables each service instance and then waits for each service instance to enter the online or degraded state. `svcadm` returns early if it determines that the service cannot reach these states without administrator intervention.
- `-t` This option temporarily enables or disables each service instance. Temporary enable or disable only lasts until reboot.

Changing Run Levels

Run levels have not disappeared and are described later in this chapter. You should still use the `init` command to change run levels. In fact, `init` is still the best command for changing the system state because it changes the run level as well as the milestone. init informs svc.startd that the run level is changing, and svc.startd restricts the system to the set of services for that corresponding milestone. The svcadm command does not change run levels, although it does change the set of services that are running. Using milestones to change the system state can be confusing and can lead to unexpected behavior. For example, running svcadm milestone svc:/milestone/single-user:default won't change the system's run level (as described by who -r). Running init s will. Also, you can continue to use boot -s if you want to; it works just fine.

So, if you're still confused about when to use milestones (svcadm milestone) and when to use run levels (the init command), note that most people still use run levels to transition between system states. In fact, Oracle recommends this method. Oracle states that "using milestones to change the system state can be confusing and can lead to unexpected behavior" (from Oracle's "System Administration Guide: Basic Administration," available at http://docs.oracle.com).

A milestone is nothing more than a service that aggregates several other services and dependencies. It declares a specific state of readiness that other services can depend on. Other than occasionally using the boot -m milestone=none command to boot a system for recovery or troubleshooting purposes, most people typically use the boot -s command to bring the system into single-user mode and the init command to transition to the desired run level.

Troubleshooting SMF Boot Problems

The following is an example of the steps to follow when a particular service is not starting properly. I'll begin by booting the system to milestone none, and I'll work my way up to the point where the service is started.

1. Boot the system as follows:

   ```
   {0} ok boot -m milestone=none<cr>
   ```

   The none milestone starts the system with all services disabled except the master restarter (svc:/system/svc/restarter:default). The system boots and asks you to enter the root password to enter system maintenance:

   ```
   Root password for system maintenance (control-d to bypass):
   ```

2. After you log in, run svcs, and you'll notice that all services are disabled or uninitialized. Next, step through the milestones as follows:

```
# svcadm milestone svc:/milestone/single-user:default<cr>
# svcadm milestone svc:/milestone/multi-user:default<cr>
# svcadm milestone svc:/milestone/multi-user-server:default<cr>
```

3. As you troubleshoot your system, follow these steps if a service fails to start:
   a. Is the service in maintenance mode? Issue the following command to check the state:

```
# svcs -l <FMRI><cr>
```

   b. Check the log file. This file is specified in output from the svcs -l command as follows:

```
# svcs -l svc:/network/inetd:default<cr>
```

The system responds with the following:

```
fmri          svc:/network/inetd:default
name          inetd
enabled       true
state         online
next_state    none
state_time    January 23, 2013 10:18:28 AM EST
logfile       /var/svc/log/network-inetd:default.log
restarter     svc:/system/svc/restarter:default
contract_id   93
manifest      /etc/svc/profile/generic.xml
manifest      /lib/svc/manifest/network/inetd.xml
dependency    require_any/error svc:/network/loopback (online)
dependency    require_all/error svc:/system/filesystem/local (online)
dependency    optional_all/error svc:/milestone/network (online)
dependency    optional_all/refresh svc:/network/rpc/bind (online)
dependency    optional_all/none svc:/network/inetd-upgrade (disabled)
dependency    require_all/none svc:/milestone/name-services (online)
```

   c. Check the service dependencies with svcs -d <FMRI>. The output from svcs -l distinguishes between optional and mandatory dependencies.
   d. Check the startup properties with svcprop -p start <FMRI>.

SMF Message Logging

In addition to the system logging methods described earlier in this chapter, each service has a log file in the /var/svc/log directory (or the /etc/svc/volatile directory for services started before the single-user milestone) indicating when and how the system was started, whether it started successfully, and any messages it may have printed during its initialization. If a severe problem occurs during boot, you can log in on the console in maintenance mode, and you can use the `svcs` command to help diagnose the problem, even for problems that would have caused boot to hang. Finally, the `boot -m boot` option allows the system administrator to configure the boot process to be more verbose, printing a simple message when each service starts.

Create SMF Manifest and Profiles

Prior to Oracle Solaris 11.1, creating an SMF manifest was a complex task because these manifests had to be created in XML using a text editor. The service manifest, also called a "service bundle," is an XML file that describes a service and instances of a service along with properties associated with those services. It also stores the relationship and dependency information between software services on an Oracle Solaris system. This file describes the conditions under which failed services may be automatically restarted. A separate service manifest is required per service. Service bundles are used to deliver services into Oracle Solaris.

There are two types of service bundles used in SMF: manifests and profiles.

- Manifests, as I've already described, are usually located in `/lib/svc/manifest` and they are automatically imported into the SMF configuration repository during system reboot, or they can be manually imported by restarting the `svc:/system/manifest-import:default` service.
- Profiles are similar to manifests, but they are typically used to provide customization of a service or service instance from what was provided in the manifest. Customizations include whether an instance of a service should be enabled or disabled, or they include any modifications to service configuration properties. Profiles are usually located in `/etc/svc/profiles` and applied during system reboot, or they can be applied again manually by restarting the `svc:/system/manifest-import:default` service.

The following section describes how to create an SMF manifest from scratch using the `vi` editor. After I create the manifest manually, I'll describe a much easier way to create an SMF manifest using the new `svcbundle` command, which was introduced in Oracle Solaris 11.1.

Create New Service Scripts

As you customize your system, you'll create custom scripts to start and stop processes or applications on your system. You have two options for starting and stopping applications and processes during the boot and shutdown process. These are 1) using SMF to start and stop the application via a service instance; or 2) using a conventional RC script located in the /etc/init.d directory.

This section describes how to create a service manifest to start and stop an application in Oracle Solaris using SMF. You'll follow these steps as you plan how SMF will manage your application:

1. Determine the process for starting and stopping your service.
2. Establish a name for the service and the category into which this service falls.
3. Determine whether your service runs multiple instances.
4. Identify any dependency relationships between this service and any other services. Practically every service has a dependency so that the service does not start up too soon in the boot process.
5. If a script is required to start and stop the process, create the script and place it in a local directory such as /lib/svc/method.
6. Create a service manifest file for your service in the /var/svc/manifest/site directory. This XML file describes the service and any dependency relationships. Service manifests are incorporated into the repository either by using the svccfg command or at boot time. See the service_bundle(4) manual page for a description of the contents of SMF manifests.
7. Incorporate the script into SMF using the svccfg utility.

In this example, I'll take an existing legacy RC script and place it under SMF control as a service. Although they are still used in Oracle Solaris 11, RC scripts were used extensively in earlier versions of Oracle Solaris to start and stop services before the introduction of SMF in Oracle Solaris 10. RC scripts are described in the "Legacy Services" section found later in this chapter.

Taking the time to convert an RC script to a service managed by SMF allows me to take advantage of automated restart capabilities such as when an application may stop as the result of a hardware failure, unexpected service failure, or administrative error. SMF also provides better control of when the application starts and stops as well as the relationship and dependency between other processes on which this application may depend. Furthermore, SMF also brings enhanced visibility with svcs and ease of management with svcadm and other management tools. The task requires the creation of a short XML file and a few simple modifications to the service RC script.

This RC script is named /etc/init.d/legacy and has the following entries:

```
#!/sbin/sh
case "$1" in
'start')
```

```
    /usr/local/legacyprog
    ;;

'stop')
    /usr/bin/pkill -x -u 0 legacyprog
    ;;

*)
    echo "Usage: $0 { start | stop }"
    exit 1
    ;;

esac
exit 0
```

I'll move this script to `/lib/svc/method/legacyservice`. The `legacyprog` script is already in place in the `/usr/local` directory.

The most complex part of this procedure is writing the SMF manifest in XML. The service manifest is an XML file that stores the relationship and dependency information between software services on an Oracle Solaris system. This file describes the conditions under which failed services may be automatically restarted. A separate service manifest is required for each service.

These manifests are created with an editor such as `vi`. The `service_bundle(4)` man page describes this XML-based file, but you need to be familiar with the XML programming language, and that is beyond the scope of this book. Here's a copy of my manifest for the service we will implement; I named it `/var/svc/manifest/site/legacyservice`, and I'll describe the contents of the file in this section.

```
<?xml version="1.0"?>
<!DOCTYPE service_bundle SYSTEM
"/usr/share/lib/xml/dtd/service_bundle.dtd.1">
<!–
ident "@(#)newservice.xml 1.2 04/09/13 SMI"
–>
<service_bundle type='manifest' name='OPTnew:legacyservice'>

<service
    name='site/legacyservice'
    type='service'
    version='1'>

<single_instance/>

<dependency
    name='usr'
    type='service'
    grouping='require_all'
    restart_on='none'>
    <service_fmri value='svc:/system/filesystem/local' />
</dependency>

<dependent
    name='newservice'
    grouping='require_all'
    restart_on='none'>
```

```
    <service_fmri value='svc:/milestone/multi-user' />
</dependent>

<exec_method
    type='method'
    name='start'
    exec='/lib/svc/method/legacyservice start'
    timeout_seconds='30' />

<exec_method
    ntype='method'
    name='stop'
    exec='/lib/svc/method/legacyservice stop'
    timeout_seconds='30' />

<property_group name='startd' type='framework'>
<propval name='duration' type='astring' value='transient'
/>
</property_group>

<instance name='default' enabled='true' />

<stability value='Unstable' />

<template>
    <common_name>
        <loctext xml:lang='C'>
        New service
        </loctext>
    </common_name>
</template>
</service>
</service_bundle>
```

Now let's take a closer look at the XML-based manifest file and the steps I took to create it.

1. My file starts out with a standard header. After the header, I specify the name of the service, the type of service, the package providing the service, and the service name:

    ```
    <?xml version="1.0"?>
    <!DOCTYPE service_bundle SYSTEM
    "/usr/share/lib/xml/dtd/service_bundle.dtd.1">
    <!–
    ident "@(#)newservice.xml 1.2 04/09/13 SMI"
    –>

    <service_bundle type='manifest' name='OPTnew:legacyservice'>
    ```

2. I specify the service category, type, name, and version. These categories aren't used by the system, but they help the administrator to identify the general use of the service. These category types are

`application:` Higher-level applications, such as apache
`milestone:` Collections of other services, such as name-services
`platform:` Platform-specific services, such as Dynamic Reconfiguration daemons
`system:` Oracle Solaris system services, such as coreadm
`device:` Device-specific services
`network:` Network/Internet services, such as protocols
`site:` Site specific descriptions

The service name describes what is being provided. It includes both the category identifier and the actual service name, separated by /. Service names should identify the service being provided. In this example, the entry I'll make to my manifest file is as follows:

```
<service
  name='site/legacyservice'
  type='service'
  version='1'>
```

3. Identify whether your service will have multiple instances. The instance name describes any specific features about the instance. Most services deliver a "default" instance. Some (such as Oracle) may want to create instances based on administrative configuration choices. This service will have a single instance, so I'll make the following entry in the manifest:

```
<single_instance />
```

4. Define any dependencies for this service. I added the following entry to the manifest:

```
<dependency
  name='usr'
  type='service'
  grouping='require_all'
  restart_on='none'>
  <service_fmri value='svc:/system/filesystem/local' />
</dependency> <
```

The first entry states that the `legacyservice` requires the `filesystem/local` service.

5. Now we need to identify dependents. If I want to make sure that my service is associated with the multi-user milestone and that the multi-user milestone requires this service, I add the following entry to the manifest:

```
<dependent
  name='testservice'
  grouping='require_all'
  restart_on='none'>
  <service_fmri value='svc:/milestone/multi-user' />
 <dependent>
```

   Because I can identify dependents, I can deliver a service that is a dependency of another service (`milestone/multi-user`) that I don't deliver. I can specify this in my `legacyservice` manifest without modifying the `milestone/multi-user` manifest, which I don't own. It's an easy way to have a service run before a default service.

   If all the dependent services have not been converted to SMF, you will need to convert them because there is no way to specify a dependent on a legacy script.

   To avoid conflicts, it is recommended that you preface the dependent name with the name of your service. For example, if you're delivering a service (`legacyservice`) that must start before `syslog`, use the following entry:

```
<dependent
 name='legacyservice_syslog'
```

6. Specify how the service will be started and stopped. SMF interacts with your service primarily by its methods. The stop and start methods must be provided for services managed by `svc.startd`. They can directly invoke either a service binary or a script to achieve this. The refresh method is optional for `svc.startd`-managed services. I'll use the following start and stop methods:

```
<exec_method
  type='method'
  name='start'
  exec='/lib/svc/method/legacyservice start'
  timeout_seconds='30' />

<exec_method
  type='method'
  name='stop'
exec='/lib/svc/method/legacyservice stop'
timeout_seconds='30' />
```

   Timeouts must be provided for all methods. The timeout should be defined to be the maximum amount of time in seconds that your method might take to run on a slow system or under a heavy load. A method that exceeds its timeout is killed. If the method could potentially take an unbounded amount of time, such as a large file system `fsck`, an infinite timeout may be specified as 0.

7. Identify the service model. Will it be started by `inetd` or `svc.startd`? My service will be started by `svc.startd`. `svc` provides three models of service:
   - `Transient` services: These are often configuration services, which require no long-running processes to provide service. Common transient services take care of boot-time cleanup or load configuration properties into the kernel. `Transient` services are also sometimes used to overcome difficulties in conforming to the method requirements for contract or wait services. This is not recommended and should be considered a stopgap measure.
   - `Wait` services: These services run for the lifetime of the child process and are restarted when that process exits.
   - `Contract` services: These are the standard system daemons. They require processes that run forever after they are started to provide service. Death of all processes in a contract service is considered a service error, which causes the service to restart.

   The default service model is contract, but it may be modified. For this example, I'll start the service with `svc.startd`. As a transient service, it will be started once and not restarted by adding the following lines to the manifest:

```
<property_group name='startd' type='framework'>
<propval name='duration' type='astring' value='transient'
/>
</property_group>
```

8. The next step is to create the instance name for the service by making the following entry:

```
<instance name='default' enabled='true' />
```

9. Finally, create template information to describe the service providing concise detail about the service. I'll assign a common name in the C locale. The common name should
   Be short (40 characters or less).
   Avoid capital letters (aside from trademarks like Oracle Solaris).
   Avoid punctuation.
   Avoid the word "service" (but do distinguish between client and server).

I make the following entry in the manifest to describe my service as "New service":

```
<template>
  <common_name>
    <loctext xml:lang='C'>
    New service
    </loctext>
  </common_name>
</template>
```

10. When the manifest is complete, save it and change the permission to 555 as follows:

```
# chmod 555 /var/svc/manifest/site/legacyservice<cr>
```

11. It is a good idea to verify the syntax using the `xmllint` program:

```
# xmllint –valid /var/svc/manifest/site/legacyservice<cr>
```

The `xmllint` program parses the XML file and identifies any errors in the code before you try to import it into SMF. The `svccfg` program also can validate your file as follows, but the output is not as verbose as with the `xmllint` command:

```
# svccfg validate /var/svc/manifest/site/legacyservice<cr>
```

12. After you've validated the syntax of your XML file, you need to import the new service into SMF by issuing the `svccfg` command:

```
# svccfg import /var/svc/manifest/site/legacyservice<cr>
```

13. The service should now be visible using the `svcs` command:

```
# svcs legacyservice<cr>
STATE  STIME  FMRI
-     svc:/site/legacyservice:default
```

14. You can also see on which services the `legacyservice` depends on by using the `svcs -d` command:

```
# svcs -d legacyservice<cr>
STATE   STIME   FMRI
online  Sep_20  svc:/system/filesystem/local:default
```

15. As a final step, enable the service using the `svcadm` command:

```
# svcadm -v enable legacyservice<cr>
svc:/site/legacyservice:default enabled.
```

I used the `-v` option in this example because I wanted to see the message that says the service was enabled. Without the `-v` option, the result is silent.

16. At any time, I can view the properties of the service using the `svccfg` command:

```
# svccfg -v -s legacyservice<cr>
```

The system responds with the following prompt:

```
svc:/site/legacyservice>
```

Use the `listprop` subcommand at the `svccfg` prompt to list the service properties:

```
# svc:/site/legacyservice> listprop<cr>
usr              dependency
usr/entities         fmri  svc:/system/filesystem/local
usr/grouping         astring require_all
usr/restart_on       astring none
usr/type         astring service
general          framework
general/entity_stability astring Unstable
general/single_instanc  boolean true
dependents          framework
dependents/newservice  astring svc:/milestone/multi-user
startd           framework
startd/duration        astring transient
start            method
start/exec          astring "/lib/svc/method/legacyservice start"
start/timeout_seconds     count   30
start/type          astring method
stop            method
```

```
stop/exec              astring "/lib/svc/method/legacyservice stop"
stop/timeout_seconds        count 30
stop/type            astring method
tm_common_name          template
tm_common_name/C         ustring "New service"
svc:/site/legacyservice>
```

Create an SMF Manifest: svcbundle

In this example, I'll create the same SMF manifest for the legacy service that I created earlier, but this time using the `svcbundle` command. The `svcbundle` command is available in Oracle Solaris 11.1 and was not available in previous versions of Oracle Solaris. It is designed to simplify the process.

`svcbundle` allows you to create an SMF manifest from scratch or convert an existing RC script to an SMF service. In the next example, I'll use `svcbundle` to convert the existing RC script that is named `/etc/init.d/legacy` (see previous section) to an SMF service. This example assumes that the RC script runs at the multi-user level and does not start a daemon. `svcbundle` makes a number of simple assumptions when creating the manifest to deal with common scenarios:

- Generated manifests are intended to be used with the master restarter, `svc.startd`.
- An automatic dependency on the `svc:/milestone/multi-user` service ensures that the service is not started too early in the system boot process.
- The timeout for the `start` and `restart` exec methods defaults to 60 seconds.

Type the following command to convert the RC script:

```
# svcbundle -i -s service-name=legacy -s rc-script=/etc/init.d/legacy:2<cr>
Waiting for legacy to reach online state.
It is safe to interrupt.
```

- The `-i` option automatically saved the generated manifest in the `/lib/svc/manifest/site` directory.
- The `-s service-name` option results in the service name being called `svc:/legacy:default`.
- The `-s rc-script` option specifies the path to the existing RC script. It is used to generate the `start` and `stop` exec method elements in the manifest. The path is followed by the run level at which the RC script currently starts. The run level is used to generate dependencies so that the script runs at the appropriate time during booting.

Verify the service as follows:

```
# svcs -l legacy<cr>
fmri         svc:/legacy:default
enabled      true
state        online
next_state   none
state_time   January 23, 2013 10:18:28 AM EST
logfile       /var/svc/log/legacy:default.log
restarter    svc:/system/svc/restarter:default
contract_id
manifest     /lib/svc/manifest/site/legacy.xml
dependency   require_all/none svc:/milestone/multi-user (online)
```

For more information on using the `svcbundle` command to create SMF services, refer to the `svcbundle(1M)` man page.

Legacy Services

Before SMF, previous versions of Oracle Solaris used RC scripts. Oracle Solaris still supports RC scripts, and they are referred to as legacy RC scripts. RC scripts are located in the `/etc/init.d` directory and linked to the `/etc/rc#.d` directory, also called the sequencer directory. These RC scripts are started by SMF and are identified by their unique FMRI prefix: `lrc`. Legacy run scripts are not initialized until all SMF services are up and running. When the system shuts down, these legacy scripts are the first to be run before the SMF services are stopped. Therefore, another reason for converting these scripts to SMF services would be to have better control over when these services start and stop. Legacy run scripts cannot be manipulated with the `svcadm` command, and no error diagnosis or restart is done for these services. The following lists the legacy control scripts currently configured on the system:

```
 # svcs |grep lrc:<cr>
legacy_run     10:18:29 lrc:/etc/rc2_d/S47pppd
legacy_run     10:18:29 lrc:/etc/rc2_d/S81dodatadm_udaplt
legacy_run     10:18:29 lrc:/etc/rc2_d/S89PRESERVE
```

For those readers who are experienced on Oracle Solaris versions 9 and older, you are accustomed to starting and stopping services via RC scripts. For instance, to stop and start the `sshd` daemon, you would type

```
# /etc/init.d/sshd stop<cr>
# /etc/init.d/sshd start<cr>
```

In SMF, the correct procedure to start sshd is to type

```
# svcadm enable network/ssh:default<cr>
```

To temporarily stop sshd, you would type

```
# svcadm disable -t network/ssh:default<cr>
```

Or simply type

```
# svcadm restart network/ssh:default<cr>
```

to stop and restart the sshd daemon.

Prior to Oracle Solaris 10, to send a HUP signal to the ssh daemon, you would have typed

```
# kill -HUP 'cat /var/run/sshd.pid'<cr>
```

In Oracle Solaris 11, the correct procedure is to type

```
# svcadm refresh network/ssh:default<cr>
```

Using the RC Scripts to Stop or Start Services

Although it is recommended that you use SMF to start and stop services as described in the previous section "Create New Service Scripts," functionality still exists to allow the use of RC scripts to start and stop system services at various run levels. RC scripts were used in previous versions of Oracle Solaris to start and stop system services before SMF was introduced, and they are still used.

A run level is a system state (run state), represented by a number or letter that identifies the services and resources that are currently available to users. The who -r command can still be used to identify a system's run level:

```
# who -r<cr>
```

The system responds with the following, indicating that run-level 3 is the current run state:

```
.     run-level 3  Jan 23 10:18    3    0  S
```

Since the introduction of SMF in Oracle Solaris 10, some administrators refer to run levels as if they are the same as milestones; however, that's not necessarily true.

Run levels can be compared to milestones, but they are not the same as milestones. As I described earlier in this chapter, run levels refer to specific run states that are achieved by running the `init` command. Milestones simply describe a specific state of system readiness. Sometimes, milestones are compared to run levels based on the processes and services that are started. Table 3-20 describes how the various legacy run states coincide with the Oracle Solaris 11 milestones.

Table 3-20 System Run Levels

Run State (Milestone)	Description
`0`	Stops system services and daemons. Terminates all running processes. Unmounts all file systems.
`S, s (single-user)`	Single-user (system administrator) state. This is the only run level that does not require the existence of a properly formatted `/etc/inittab` file. If this file does not exist, then the system will enter single-user mode. Only root is allowed to log in at the console, and any logged-in users are logged out when you enter this run level. Only critical file systems are mounted and accessible. All services except the most basic OS services are shut down in an orderly manner.
`1`	Single-user (system administrator) state. If the system is booted into this run level, all local file systems are mounted and all files are accessible. All services except the most basic kernel services are running. No users will be allowed to log on.
`2 (multi-user)`	Normal multi-user operation, without NFSs shared: has directories; locks interfaces and starts processes; starts the `cron` daemon; cleans up the `uucp tmp` files; starts the `lp` system; and starts the `sendmail` daemon and `syslog`.
`3 (multi-user-server)`	Normal multi-user operation of a file server, with NFS shared. Completes all the tasks in run state 2 and starts the NFS daemons.
`4`	Alternative multi-user state (not configured, but available for use).
`5`	Power-down state. Shuts down the system so that it is safe to turn off power to the system. If possible, automatically turns off system power on systems that support this feature.
`6`	Reboot state. The service `svc:/system/boot-config:default` is enabled by default. When the `config/fastreboot_default` property is set to `true`, `init 6` will bypass certain firmware initialization and test steps, depending on the specific capabilities of the system.
`a,b,c`	Process only those `/etc/inittab` entries having the a, b, or c run level set. These are pseudo-states, which may be defined to run certain commands, but which do not cause the current run level to change.
`Q,q`	Instruct `init` to re-examine the `/etc/inittab` file.

With RC scripts, each `init` state has a corresponding series of RC scripts—which are located in the `/sbin` directory—to control each run state. These RC scripts are as follows:

- `rc0`
- `rc1`
- `rc2`
- `rc3`
- `rc5`
- `rc6`
- `rcS`

RC Scripts

Startup scripts can be identified by their `rc` prefix or suffix, which means "run control."

Use the `init` command to transition between the various run states. The `init` daemon simply passes the required run state to the `svc.startd` daemon for execution. SMF executes the `/sbin/rc<n>` scripts, which in turn execute a series of other scripts that are located in the `/etc/init.d` directory. For each RC script in the `/sbin` directory, a corresponding directory named `/etc/rc<n>.d` contains scripts to perform various actions for that run state. For example, `/etc/rc3.d` contains files that are used to start and stop processes for run state 3.

The run levels operate as follows:

`s/S` Read `/etc/rcS.d/README` for details. This run level corresponds to the milestone `svc:/milestone/single-user:default`.

`0/5/6` All `/etc/rc0.d/K*` scripts are run, followed by all `/etc/rc0.d/S*` scripts. The `S*` scripts should only be used for cleanup during shutdown.

1. If the system was in a higher run level, all `/etc/rc1.d/K*` scripts are run. Regardless of the previous run level, all `/etc/rc1.d/S*` scripts are run.
2. This run level corresponds to the milestone `svc:/milestone/multi-user:default`. After all its dependencies have been satisfied, the start method of the SMF major milestone `svc:/milestone/multi-user:default` executes each `S` script within `/etc/rc2.d` with the argument `start`. All start scripts in the directory `/etc/rcS.d` will have been run as part of the earlier single-user milestone. Any warnings, errors, or output from the scripts in `/etc/rc2.d` are logged to the file: `/var/svc/log/milestone-multi-user:default.log`.
   If the system is changing from a higher run level (for example, executing the `init 2` command), SMF executes all `K` scripts within `/etc/rc2.d`

with the argument stop. Any warnings, errors, or output from these scripts are logged to the file /var/svc/log/rc2.log.

3. This run level corresponds to the milestone svc:/milestone/multi-user-server:default. When moving to run level 3, via executing the init 3 command or the SMF major milestone svc:/milestone/multi-user-server:default, /usr/sbin/rc3 executes each S script within /etc/rc3.d with the argument start. All start scripts in the directories /etc/rcS.d and /etc/rc2.d will have been run as part of the earlier major milestones. Any warnings, errors, or output from the scripts in /etc/rc3.d are logged to the file: /var/svc/log/milestone-multi-user-server:default.log.

Legacy Scripts

Legacy scripts are run last—after the infrastructure services that are managed by SMF are started.

The /etc/rc<n>.d scripts are always run in ASCII sort order shown by the ls command and have names of the following form:

```
[K,S][#][filename]
```

A file that begins with “K” is referred to as a stop script and is run to terminate (kill) a system process. A file that begins with “S” is referred to as a “start script” and is run to start a system process. Each of these start and stop scripts is called by the appropriate /sbin/rc# script. For example, the /sbin/rc0 script runs the scripts located in the /etc/rc0.d directory. The /sbin/rc# script passes the argument start or stop to each script based on its prefix.

All RC scripts are located in the /etc/init.d directory, and all scripts must be /sbin/sh scripts. These files are hard-linked to corresponding RC scripts in the /etc/rc<n>.d directories.

These RC scripts can also be run individually to start and stop services. For example, you can turn off sendmail functionality by typing

```
#/etc/init.d/sendmail stop<cr>
```

After you have changed the system configuration, you can restart the sendmail service by typing

```
# /etc/init.d/sendmail start<cr>
```

Notice, however, many of these RC scripts simply have svcadm commands embedded in them to perform the task of stopping and starting the service.

In addition to the svcs -p command, you can still use the pgrep command to verify whether a service has been stopped or started:

```
# pgrep -f <service><cr>
```

The pgrep utility examines the active processes on the system and reports the process IDs. See Chapter 8, "Managing System Processes," for details on this command.

Adding Scripts to the RC Directories

If you add a script to the RC directories, you put the script in the /etc/init.d directory and create a hard link to the appropriate rc<n>.d directory. You need to assign appropriate numbers and names to the new scripts so that they will be run in the proper ASCII sequence, as described in the previous section.

To add a new RC script to a system, follow these steps:

1. Become the superuser.
2. Add the RC script to the /etc/init.d directory:

```
# cp <filename> /etc/init.d<cr>
# cd /etc/init.d<cr>
# chmod 744 <filename><cr>
# chown root:sys <filename><cr>
```

3. Create hard links to the appropriate rc<n>.d directory:

```
# ln <filename> /etc/rc2.d/S<nnfilename><cr>
# ln <filename> /etc/rc<n>.d/K<nnfilename><cr>
```

4. Use the ls command to verify that the script has links in the specified directories:

```
# ls -li /etc/init.d/<filename> /etc/rc?.d/[SK]*<filename><cr>
```

The following example creates an RC script named program that starts up at run level 2 and stops at run level 0. Note the use of hard links versus soft links:

```
# cp program /etc/init.d<cr>
# cd /etc/init.d<cr>
# chmod 744 program<cr>
```

```
# chown root:sys program<cr>
# ln /etc/init.d/program /etc/rc2.d/S99program<cr>
# ln /etc/init.d/program /etc/rc0.d/K01program<cr>
```

You can verify the links by typing the following:

```
# ls -li /etc/init.d/program /etc/rc?.d/[SK]*program<cr>
```

The system displays the following:

```
389928 -rwxr-r-  3 root  sys   69 Oct 26 23:31 /etc/init.d/program
389928 -rwxr-r-  3 root  sys   69 Oct 26 23:31 /etc/rc0.d/K01program
389928 -rwxr-r-  3 root  sys   69 Oct 26 23:31 /etc/rc2.d/S99program
```

Disabling an RC Script

If you do not want a particular script to run when the system is entering a corresponding `init` state, you can change the uppercase prefix (`S` or `K`) to some other character; I prefer to prefix the filename with an underscore or the word "no." Only files beginning with uppercase prefixes of `S` or `K` are run. For example, you could change `S99mount` to `_S99mount` to disable the script.

System Shutdown

Oracle Solaris has been designed to run continuously—seven days a week, 24 hours a day. Occasionally, however, you need to shut down the system to carry out administrative tasks. Very seldom, an application might cause the system to go awry, and the OS must be stopped to kill off runaway processes and then be restarted.

You can shut down the system in a number of ways, using various commands. With Oracle Solaris, taking down the OS in an orderly fashion is important. When the system boots, several processes are started; they must be shut down before you power off the system. In addition, information that has been cached in memory and has not yet been written to disk will be lost if it is not flushed from memory and saved to disk. The process of shutting down the OS involves shutting down processes, flushing data from memory to the disk, and unmounting file systems.

Improper Shutdown Can Corrupt Data

Shutting down a system improperly can result in loss of data and the risk of corrupting the file systems.

Protecting against Power Loss

To avoid having your system shut down improperly during a power failure, you should use an uninterruptible power supply (UPS) that can shut down the system cleanly before the power is shut off. Be sure to follow the UPS manufacturer's recommendations for maintenance to eliminate the risk of the UPS becoming the cause of an improper shutdown.

Commands to Shut Down the System

When you're preparing to shut down a system, you need to determine which of the following commands is appropriate for the system and the task at hand:

`/usr/sbin/shutdown`
`/sbin/init`
`/usr/sbin/halt`
`/usr/sbin/reboot`
`/usr/sbin/poweroff`
Stop+A

Aborting the OS

Using the *Stop+A* key sequence (or *L1+A*) abruptly breaks execution of the OS and should be used only as a last resort to restart the system.

The first three commands—`/usr/sbin/shutdown`, `/sbin/init`, and `/usr/sbin / halt`—initiate shutdown procedures, kill all running processes, write data to disk, and shut down the system software to the appropriate run level. The `/usr/sbin/reboot` command does all these tasks as well, and it then boots the system back to the default milestone. The `/usr/sbin/poweroff` command is equivalent to `init` state 5.

The `halt` and `poweroff` utilities do not cleanly shut down SMF services, they do not execute the scripts in `/etc/rc<n>.d`, and they do not execute shutdown actions in `/etc/inittab`.

The `/usr/sbin/shutdown` Command

You use the `shutdown` command to shut down a system that has multiple users. The `shutdown` command sends a warning message to all users who are logged in, waits for 60 seconds (by default), and then shuts down the system to single-user state. The command option `-g` lets you choose a different default wait time. The `-i` option lets you define the `init` state to which the system will be shut down. The default is `S`.

The `shutdown` command performs a clean system shutdown, which means that all system processes and services are terminated normally, and file systems are synchronized. You need superuser privileges to use the `shutdown` command.

When the `shutdown` command is initiated, all logged-in users and all systems mounting resources receive a warning about the impending `shutdown`, and then they get a final message. For this reason, the `shutdown` command is recommended over the `init` command on a server with multiple users.

Sending a Shutdown Message

When using either `shutdown` or `init`, you might want to give users advance notice by sending an e-mail message about any scheduled system shutdown.

Follow these steps for shutting down the system:

1. As superuser, type the following to find out whether users are logged in to the system:

```
# who<cr>
```

2. A list of all logged-in users is displayed. You might want to send an e-mail message or broadcast a message to let users know that the system is being shut down.
3. Shut down the system by using the `shutdown` command:

```
# shutdown -i<init-state> -g<grace-period> -y<cr>
```

Table 3-21 describes the options available for the `shutdown` command.

For example, to broadcast a message to all logged-in users and shut down the system in 15 minutes, issue the following command:

```
# shutdown -i0 -g900 "System is going down for maintenance"<cr>

Shutdown started.  Wednesday, January 23, 2013 03:45:12 PM EST

Broadcast Message from root (pts/1) on solaris Wed Jan 23 15:45:12. . .
The system solaris will be shut down in 15 minutes
System is going down for maintenance
. . . .
Broadcast Message from root (pts/1) on solaris Wed Jan 23 15:45:42. . .
The system solaris will be shut down in 1 minute
System is going down for maintenance
. . . . .<output has been truncated>. . .
```

Table 3-21 Options for the `shutdown` Command

Option	Description
`-i`<*init-state*>	Brings the system to an `init` state that is different from the default, `S`. The choices are `0`, `S`, `1`, `2`, `5`, and `6`.
`-g`<*grace-period*>	Indicates a time (in seconds) before the system is shut down. The default is 60 seconds.
`-y`	Continues to shut down the system without intervention; otherwise, you are prompted to continue the shutdown process after 60 seconds. If you use the `shutdown -y` command, you are not prompted to continue; otherwise, you get the message, "Do you want to continue? (y or n)."

The warning message is output 2 minutes, 1 minute, and 30 seconds before the final confirmation message, and then the following prompt will appear:

```
Do you want to continue?  (y or n):
```

Answer "Y" to reboot or "N" to cancel. If you enter "N", the following message is displayed:

```
False Alarm: The system solaris will not be brought down.
```

Answer "Y" and the system will be shut down as follows:

```
Do you want to continue? (y or n):  y<cr>
Broadcast Message from root (pts/1) on server Wed Jan 23 15:49:50. . .
THE SYSTEM server IS BEING SHUT DOWN NOW ! ! !
Log off now or risk your files being damaged
going down
showmount: server: RPC: Program not registered
Changing to init state 0 - please wait
```

The `/sbin/init` Command

You can use the `init` command to shut down a single-user system or to change its run level. The `init` command communicates with the `init` process, which was described earlier in this chapter. The syntax is as follows:

```
init <run-level>
```

`<run-level>` is any run level described in Table 3-20. In addition, `<run-level>` can be `a`, `b`, or `c`, which tells the system to process only `/etc/inittab` entries that have the `a`, `b`, or `c` run level set. These are pseudo-states, which can be defined to run certain commands but that do not cause the current run level to change. `<run-level>` can also be the keyword `Q` or `q`, which tells the system to reexamine the `/etc/inittab` file. Use this option if you've modified the `/etc/inittab` file and need to notify `init` of the change.

The `init` command is slightly faster than the `shutdown` command because `init` does not take the time to notify users of the impending shutdown.

Use the `init` command to change system run levels such as to place the system in power-down state (`init` state 5) or in single-user state (`init` state 1). For example, to bring the system down to run level 1 from the current run level, type the following:

```
# init 1<cr>
```

The system responds with the following:

```
svc.startd: Changing to state 1.
Jan 23 15:39:17 solaris syslogd: going down on signal 15
svc.startd: Killing user processes.
svc.startd: The system is ready for administration.
Requesting System Maintenance Mode
(See /lib/svc/share/README for more information.)

Enter user name for system maintenance (control-d to bypass):root<cr>
Enter root password (control-d to bypass):
```

Log in as root and enter the root password as prompted.

The `/usr/sbin/halt` Command

You can use the `halt` command when the system must be stopped immediately and it is acceptable not to warn current users. The `halt` command writes any pending information to the disks and then shuts down the system without delay and does not warn other users on the system of the shutdown. The `halt` command logs the system shutdown to the system log daemon- `syslogd(1M)`.

Note

The `halt` and `reboot` commands do not perform a graceful shutdown.

Options to the `halt` command include

- `-d` Force a system crash dump before rebooting.
- `-l` Suppress sending a message to the system log daemon, `syslogd`, about who executed the `halt` command.
- `-n` Prevent a `sync` (updating of the file system superblock) before stopping.
- `-q` Quick halt. No graceful shutdown attempted.
- `-y` Halt the system, even from a dial-up terminal.

The `/usr/sbin/reboot` Command

Use the `reboot` command to shut down a single-user system and bring it into multi-user state. `reboot` does not warn other users on the system of the shutdown.

The `reboot` command provides the capability to pass arguments to OpenBoot, which can be useful. For example, the following command reboots the system into run level `s` and reconfigures the device tables:

```
# reboot -- -rs
```

Notice the use of the double hyphen (`--`), which is used to pass options onto the OpenBoot `boot` command.

The following are options to the `reboot` command:

- `-d` Force a system crash dump before rebooting.
- `-e` If `-f` is present, reboot to the specified boot environment. This option is only available on the x86 platform.
- `-l` Suppress sending a message to the system log daemon, `syslogd`, about who executed the `halt` command.
- `-n` Prevent a `sync` (updating of the file system superblock) before stopping.
- `-q` Quick halt. No graceful shutdown attempted.
- `-y` Halt the system, even from a dial-up terminal.

The `/etc/nologin` File

When a system will be unavailable for an extended time, you can create an `/etc/nologin` file to prevent users from logging in to it. When a user logs in to a system that has an `/etc/nologin` file, the message in the `/etc/nologin` file is displayed, and the user login is terminated. Superuser logins are unaffected by the `/etc/nologin` file.

The `/usr/sbin/poweroff` Command

The `poweroff` command is equivalent to the `init 5` command. As with the `reboot` and `halt` commands, the `poweroff` command synchronizes the disks and immediately shuts down the system. Users are not notified of the shutdown. If the hardware supports it, the `poweroff` command also turns off power.

The `init` and `shutdown` Commands

Using `init` and using `shutdown` are the most reliable ways to shut down a system, because these commands communicate directly with `init` to shut down services in a clean, orderly fashion. The `halt` and `reboot` commands do not shut down services and processes gracefully, but simply flush the disk cache (sync) and bring the system to run level 0 as quickly as possible by sending a signal 9 to all processes. Therefore, `halt` and `reboot` are not the preferred methods of shutting down the system.

Fastboot

New in Solaris Solaris 11 is the option to perform a fast reboot and minimize system downtime. A fast reboot allows ths OS to restart without resetting the motherboard and bypassing the BIOS and POST. The Fast Reboot feature behaves differently on SPARC-based systems than it does on an x86-based system. The SMF service property `boot-config` is set for a fast reboot by default on x86 systems. On the SPARC-based systems, fast reboot is not enabled by default.

To initiate a fast reboot on the SPARC platform, use the -f option with the reboot command as follows:

```
# reboot -f<cr>
```

On the x86 platform, where fast reboot is already enabled, type

```
# init 6<cr>
```

Administrators can enable a fast reboot on SPARC by modifying the config/fastreboot_default property for the boot-config service as follows:

```
# svccfg -s system/boot-config:default setprop config/fastreboot_default=true<cr>
# svcadm refresh system/boot-config:default<cr>
```

Setting the config/fastreboot_default property value to true enables the fast reboot process, which bypasses certain POST tests. When this property is set to true, you do not have to use the -f option with the reboot command to initiate a fast reboot of the system.

To reboot a system that has the Fast Reboot feature enabled, without having to reconfigure the properties of the boot-config service, use the -p option with the reboot command, as follows:

```
# reboot -p<cr>
```

To check whether the fast reboot option is enabled (config/fastreboot_default true), type

```
# svccfg -s system/boot-config:default listprop config/fastreboot_default<cr>
```

The system responds with the following indicating that the value is set to true:

```
  config/fastreboot_default boolean      true
```

Stopping the System for Recovery Purposes: SPARC

Occasionally, a SPARC system might not respond to the `init` commands described earlier in this chapter. A system that doesn't respond to anything, including `reboot` or `halt`, is called a "crashed" or "hung" system. If you try to use the commands discussed in the previous sections but get no response, your system may be hung. The steps to break out of an unresponsive SPARC system are as follows:

1. Refer to the section titled "Accessing the OpenBoot Environment" earlier in the chapter to get the system to the OpenBoot `ok` prompt from the system console.
2. After the system displays the `ok` PROM prompt, type the `sync` command to manually synchronize the file systems:

   ```
   {0} ok sync<cr>
   ```

   The sync procedure synchronizes the file systems and is necessary to prevent corruption to the file systems. During the sync process, the system panics, synchronizes the file systems, performs a crash dump by dumping the contents of kernel memory to disk, and finally performs a system reset to start the boot process.
3. After you receive the `login:` message, log in and type the following to verify that the system is booted to the specified run level:

   ```
   # who -r<cr>
   ```

4. The system responds with the following:

   ```
   .  run-level 3 Jan 23 09:38    3    1 1
   ```

Stopping the System for Recovery Purposes: x86

If your x86-based system is unresponsive, follow these steps:

1. If the system is running, become the superuser and type `init 0` to stop the system. After the `Press any key to reboot` prompt appears, press any key to reboot the system.
2. If the system is running, become the superuser and type `init 6` to reboot the system.
3. If the system doesn't respond to any input from the mouse or keyboard, press the *Reset* key on the system tower, if it exists, to reboot the system. Or you can use the power switch to reboot the system.

Turning Off the Power to the Hardware

Only after shutting down the file systems should you turn off the power to the hardware. You can turn off power to all devices after the system is shut down. If necessary, you should also unplug the power cables. When power can be restored, follow these steps to turn on the system and devices.

1. Plug in the power cables.
2. Turn on all peripheral devices, such as disk drives, tape drives, and printers.
3. Turn on the CPU and monitor.

syslog

A critical part of the system administrator's job is monitoring the system. Oracle Solaris uses the `syslog` message facility to do this. `syslogd` is the daemon responsible for capturing system messages. The messages can be warnings, alerts, or simply informational messages. As the system administrator, you customize `syslog` to specify where and how system messages are to be saved.

The `syslogd` daemon receives messages from applications on the local host or from remote hosts and then directs messages to a specified log file. To each message that `syslog` captures, it adds a time stamp, the message type keyword at the beginning of the message, and a new line at the end of the message. For example, the following messages were logged in the `/var/adm/messages` file:

```
Jan 23 20:23:21 solaris mac: [ID 736570 kern.info] NOTICE: e1000g3 unregistered
Jan 23 20:23:24 solaris pseudo: [ID 129642 kern.info] pseudo-device: bmc0
Jan 23 20:23:24 solaris genunix: [ID 936769 kern.info] bmc0 is /pseudo/bmc@0
Jan 23 20:23:36 solaris pseudo: [ID 129642 kern.info] pseudo-device: devinfo0
Jan 23 20:23:36 solaris genunix: [ID 936769 kern.info] devinfo0 is /pseudo/devinfo@0
Jan 23 20:23:38 solaris vnex: [ID 367333 kern.info] virtual-device: glvc0
Jan 23 20:23:38 solaris genunix: [ID 936769 kern.info] glvc0 is /
virtual-devices@100/fma@9
```

`syslog` enables you to capture messages by facility (the part of the system that generated the message) and by level of importance. Facility is considered to be the service area generating the message or error (such as printing, e-mail, or network), whereas the level can be considered the level of severity (such as notice, warning, error, or emergency). `syslog` also enables you to forward messages to another machine so that all of your messages can be logged in one location. The `syslogd` daemon reads and logs messages into a set of files described by the configuration file `/etc/syslog.conf`. When the `syslogd` daemon starts up, it preprocesses the `/etc/syslog.conf` file through the m4 macroprocessor to get the correct information for specific log files. `syslogd` does not read the `/etc/syslog.conf` file directly. `syslogd` starts m4, which parses the `/etc/syslog.conf` file for `ifdef` statements that can be interpreted by m4. The function `ifdef` is an integral part of m4 and identifies the system designated as LOGHOST. The macro can then evaluate whether log files are to be held locally, on a remote system, or a combination of both.

If m4 doesn't recognize any m4 commands in the `syslog.conf` file, output is passed back to `syslogd`. `syslogd`, then uses this output to route messages to appropriate destinations. When m4 encounters `ifdef` statements that it can process, the statement is evaluated for a true or false condition and the message is routed relative to the output of the test.

An entry in the `/etc/syslog.conf` file is composed of two fields:

```
selector    action
```

Separate with Tabs

The separator between the two fields must be a tab character. Spaces do not work and give unexpected results. This is a very common mistake.

The selector field contains a semicolon-separated list of priority specifications of this form:

```
facility.level [ ; facility.level ]
```

The action field indicates the facilities to which the message should be forwarded. Many defined facilities exist.

The facilities are described in Table 3-22.

Table 3-23 lists recognized values for the `syslog` level field. They are listed in descending order of severity.

Levels Include All Higher Levels, Too

When you specify a `syslog` level, it means the specified level and all higher levels. For example, if you specify the `err` level, this includes `crit`, `alert`, and `emerg` levels as well.

Values for the action field can have one of four forms:

1. A filename, beginning with a leading slash. This indicates that messages specified by the selector are to be written to the specified file. The file is opened in append mode and must already exist. `syslog` does not create the file if it doesn't already exist.

Table 3-22 Recognized Values for Facilities

Value	Description
user	Messages generated by user processes. This is the default priority for messages from programs or facilities not listed in this file.
kern	Messages generated by the kernel.
mail	The mail system.
daemon	System daemons, such as in.ftpd.
auth	The authorization system, such as login, su, getty, and others.
lpr	The line print spooling system.
uucp	Reserved for the UUCP system. It does not currently use the syslog mechanism.
news	Reserved for the Usenet network news system.
cron	The cron/at facility, such as crontab, at, cron, and others.
audit	The audit facility, such as auditd.
local0-7	Reserved for local use.
mark	For time stamp messages produced internally by syslogd.
*	Indicates all facilities except the mark facility.

Table 3-23 Recognized Values for Level

Value	Description
emerg	Panic conditions that would normally be broadcast to all users.
alert	Conditions that should be corrected immediately, such as a corrupted system database.
crit	Warnings about critical conditions, such as hard device errors.
err	Other errors.
warning	Warning messages.
notice	Conditions that are not error conditions but might require special handling, such as a failed login attempt. A failed login attempt is considered a notice and not an error.
info	Informational messages.
debug	Messages that are normally used only when debugging a program.
none	Does not send messages from the indicated facility to the selected file. For example, the entry *.debug;mail.none in /etc/syslog.conf sends all messages except mail messages to the selected file.

2. The name of a remote host, prefixed with a @. An example is @server, which indicates that messages specified by the selector are to be forwarded to syslogd on the named host. The hostname loghost is the hostname given to the machine that will log syslogd messages. Every machine is its own loghost by default. This is specified in the local /etc/hosts file. It is also possible to specify one machine on a network to be loghost by making the appropriate host table entries. If the local machine is designated as loghost, syslogd messages are written to the appropriate files. Otherwise, they are sent to the machine loghost on the network.
3. A comma-separated list of usernames, which indicates that messages specified by the selector are to be written to the named users if they are logged in.
4. An asterisk, which indicates that messages specified by the selector are to be written to all logged-in users.

Blank lines are ignored. Lines in which the first non-whitespace character is a # are treated as comments.

All of this becomes much clearer when you look at sample entries from an /etc/syslog.conf file:

```
*.err                                  /dev/console
*.err;daemon,auth.notice;mail.crit     /var/adm/messages
mail.debug                             /var/log/syslog
*.alert                                root
*.emerg                                *
kern.err                               @server
*.alert;auth.warning                   /var/log/auth
```

The information in each line of the sample /etc/syslog.conf file can be described as follows:

1. The first line prints all errors on the console.
2. The second line sends all errors, daemon and authentication system notices, and critical errors from the mail system to the file /var/adm/messages.
3. The third line sends mail system debug messages to /var/log/syslog.
4. The fourth line sends all alert messages to user root.
5. The fifth line sends all emergency messages to all users.
6. The sixth line forwards kernel messages of err (error) severity or higher to the machine named server.
7. The last line logs all alert messages and messages of warning level or higher from the authorization system to the file /var/log/auth.

The level none may be used to disable a facility. This is usually done in the context of eliminating messages. For example:

```
*.debug;mail.none      /var/adm/messages
```

This selects debug messages and above from all facilities except those from mail. In other words, mail messages are disabled. The mail system, sendmail, logs a number of messages. The mail system can produce a large amount of information, so some system administrators disable mail messages or send them to another file that they clean out frequently. Before disabling mail messages, however, remember that sendmail messages come in very handy when you're diagnosing mail problems or tracking mail forgeries.

The mechanism for stopping, starting, and refreshing syslogd is under the control of SMF. syslogd is controlled by the svc:/system/system-log:default service. To stop or start syslogd, use the svcadm command with the appropriate parameter, enable or disable:

```
# svcadm enable -t system-log<cr>
# svcadm disable -t system-log<cr>
```

The syslog facility reads its configuration information from /etc/syslog.conf whenever it receives a refresh command from the service administration command, svcadm, and when the system is booted. You can make your changes to /etc/syslog.conf and then run the following command to cause the file to be reread by the syslogd daemon:

```
# svcadm refresh system-log<cr>
```

Make sure you remember that the kill -HUP facility should no longer be used to try to cause a daemon process to reread its configuration file, even though it still works. The svcadm refresh command is now the recommended way of achieving this.

The first message in the log file is logged by the syslog daemon itself to show when the process was started.

syslog logs are automatically rotated on a regular basis. Log rotation is handled by logadm, a program normally run as a root-owned cron job. A configuration file /etc/logadm.conf is used to manage log rotation and allows a number of criteria to be specified. See the logadm(1M) and logadm.conf(4) manual pages for further details.

Table 3-24 `logger` **Options**

Option	Description
`-i`	Logs the process ID (PID) of the logger process with each line written to a log file.
`-f` *<file>*	Uses the contents of file as the message to be logged.
`-p` *<priority>*	Lists the message priority. This can be defined as a numeric value or as a `facility.level` pair, as described in Tables 3-21 and 3-22. The default priority is `user.notice`.
`-t` *<tag>*	Marks each line with the specified tag.
`message`	One or more string arguments, separated by a single-space character, comprising the text of the message to be logged.

Using the `logger` Command

The `logger` command provides the means of manually adding one-line entries to the system logs from the command line. This is especially useful in shell scripts.

The syntax for the `logger` command is as follows:

```
logger [-i] [-f file] [-p priority] [-t tag] [message] . . .
```

Options to the `logger` command are described in Table 3-24.

For example, perhaps you have a simple shell script that backs up files:

```
#/bin/ksh
tar cvf /tmp/backup .
logger -p user.alert "Backups Completed"
```

The last line of the script uses the `logger` command to send a “Backups Completed” message to the default system log (`/var/adm/messages`). After running the script, the following message is appended to the end of the log file:

```
Jan 23 14:02:52 sunfire root: [ID 702911 user.alert] Backups Completed
```

`rsyslog`

The `rsyslog` utility is an enhanced `syslogd` and is available beginning with the Oracle Solaris 11.1 release. It has always been available for Oracle Solaris as open-source material but was never included as part of the OS distribution.

The rsyslog utility provides several enhancements over traditional syslog logging such as

- More precise logging of messages and more flexibility to format and manage these messages
- Capability to filter messages on any part of the log message rather than just on the priority of the message or the originating facility
- Capability to create a per-host logging file on the logging server
- Use of templates to choose the exact logging format of messages created by rsyslog
- More precise time stamps on messages

Check to see whether the rsyslog package is installed on your system by typing

```
# pkg list rsyslog<cr>
NAME (PUBLISHER)                  VERSION                    IFO
system/rsyslog                    6.2.0-0.175.1.0.0.24.0     i--
```

If rsyslog is not installed, install it using the pkg install command as follows:

```
# pkg install rsyslog<cr>
```

Before enabling rsyslog, disable the syslogd service by typing

```
# svcadm disable svc:/system/system-log:default<cr>
```

Then, enable the rsyslog service as follows:

```
# svcadm enable svc:/system/system-log:rsyslog<cr>
```

The rsyslog utility uses the rsyslogd daemon. The rsyslogd configuration file is /etc/rsyslog.conf. Modify this file to instruct rsyslogd how to handle messages that are received from the system and kernel. For example, to configure rsyslog to log all debug messages to the file /var/log/misc.log, add the following line to the /etc/rsyslog.conf file:

```
*.info;mail.none;auth.none;cron.none          /var/log/misc.log
```

`rsyslog` will log anything except messages coming from `auth`, `cron`, and `mail` of level `info` or higher.

For more information on `rsyslog`, refer to the `rsyslogd(1M)` and `rsyslogd.conf(4)` man pages. The complete documentation can be found online at `http://www.rsyslog.com/doc`.

Summary

This chapter described the OpenBoot environment, the PROM, NVRAM, and the kernel. It described how to access OpenBoot and the various commands that are available to test and provide information about the hardware.

This chapter described the OpenBoot architecture, and it explained how OpenBoot controls many of the hardware devices. By using the programmable user interface available in OpenBoot, you can set several parameters that control system hardware and peripherals.

The device tree and OpenBoot device names were explained. This book mentions various device names used in Oracle Solaris. It's important that you understand each of them and how they differ between the SPARC and x86/x64-based platforms. Along with device names, this chapter explained how to set temporary and permanent device aliases.

The system startup phases were described, and you learned how Oracle Solaris processes and services are started, from bootup to loading and initializing the two-part kernel, to continuing to the multi-user milestone. You can further control these services through SMF. You need to understand the startup process and boot-related configuration files on both the SPARC and x86/x64-based platforms.

This chapter described how important it is to shut down the system properly because the integrity of the data can be compromised if the proper shutdown steps are not performed. All of the various commands used to shut down a system in an orderly manner were outlined.

Chapter 4, "Administering Storage Devices," describes how to configure the disks and file systems on your server.

4

Administering Storage Devices

It's important that you understand how Oracle Solaris views the disk drives and various other hardware components on your system. In particular, you need to understand how the storage devices are configured and named before you can create a file system on them or install the Oracle Solaris operating environment.

Device management in the Oracle Solaris 11 environment includes adding and removing from system peripheral devices such as tape drives, printers, and disk drives. Device management sometimes also involves adding a third-party device driver to support a device if the device driver is not available in Oracle's distribution of the Oracle Solaris operating environment.

System administrators need to know how to specify device names when using commands to manage disks, file systems, and other devices. This chapter describes disk device management in detail. It also describes disk device naming conventions as well as adding, configuring, and displaying information about disk devices attached to your system.

Device Drivers

A computer typically uses a wide range of peripheral and mass-storage devices such as a serial attached SCSI disk drive, a keyboard, a mouse, and some kind of magnetic backup medium. Other commonly used devices include CD/DVD-ROM drives, printers, and various USB devices. Oracle Solaris communicates with peripheral devices through device files or drivers. A "device driver" is a low-level program that allows the kernel to communicate with a specific piece of hardware. The driver serves as the OS's "interpreter" for that piece of hardware. Before Oracle Solaris can communicate with a device, the device must have a device driver.

When a system is started for the first time, the kernel creates a device hierarchy to represent all of the devices connected to the system. This is the autoconfiguration process, which is described later in this chapter. If a driver is not loaded for a particular peripheral device, that device is not functional. In Oracle Solaris, each disk device is described in three ways, using three distinct naming conventions:

- Physical device name: Represents the full device pathname in the device information hierarchy
- Instance name: Represents the kernel's abbreviation name for every possible device on the system
- Logical device name: Used by system administrators with most file system commands to refer to devices

System administrators need to understand these device names when using commands to manage disks and file systems. We discuss these device names throughout this chapter.

Physical Device Name

Before the OS is loaded, the system locates a particular device through the device tree, also called the full device pathname. Full device pathnames are described in the "PROM Device Tree (Full Device Pathnames)" section of Chapter 3, "Boot and Shutdown Procedures for SPARC and x86-Based Systems." After the kernel is loaded, however, a device is located by its physical device pathname. Physical device names represent the full device pathname for a device. Note that the two names have the same structure. For example, the full device pathname for a SCSI disk at target 0 on a SunFire T2000 system is as follows:

```
/pci@780/pci@0/pci@9/scsi@0/disk@0
```

SAS Disk Drives

SCSI drives come in two types: parallel and serial. The serial attached SCSI (SAS) drive delivers better performance than its parallel predecessor. Both drives show up as SCSI drives in the OS.

Intel-based systems commonly use IDE or Serial AT Attachment (SATA) disk drives. On the x86 platform, the SATA disk (target 0) looks like this:

```
/pci@0,0/pci8086,2829@d/disk@0,0
```

Now let's look at the corresponding physical device name from the OS level. Use the dmesg command, described later in this section, to obtain information about devices connected to your system. By viewing information displayed by the dmesg command, you'll receive the following information about the SunFire T2000's SAS disk 0:

```
# dmesg |grep scsi<cr>
Jan 23 16:02:42 server rootnex: [ID 349649 kern.info] scsi_vhci0 at root
Jan 23 16:02:42 server genunix: [ID 936769 kern.info] scsi_vhci0 is /scsi_vhci
Jan 23 16:02:45 server scsi: [ID 583861 kern.info] sd0 at ahci0: target 0 lun 0
Jan 23 16:02:45 server scsi: [ID 583861 kern.info] sd1 at ahci0: target 1 lun 0
Jan 23 16:03:04 server rootnex: [ID 349649 kern.info] iscsi0 at root
Jan 23 16:03:04 server genunix: [ID 936769 kern.info] iscsi0 is /iscsi
```

This same information is also available in the /var/adm/messages file.

As you can see, the physical device name listed above and the full device name seen at the OpenBoot PROM are the same. The difference is that the full device pathname is simply a path to a particular device. The physical device is the actual driver used by Oracle Solaris to access that device from the OS.

Physical device files are found in the /devices directory. The content of the /devices directory is controlled by the devfs file system. The entries in the /devices directory dynamically represent the current state of accessible devices in the kernel and require no administration. New device entries are added when the devices are detected and added to the kernel. The physical device files for SAS disks 0 and 1 connected to the primary SCSI controller would be

```
/devices/pci@780/pci@0/pci@9/scsi@0/sd@0,0:<#>
/devices/pci@780/pci@0/pci@9/scsi@0/sd@1,0:<#>
```

for the block device and

```
/devices/pci@780/pci@0/pci@9/scsi@0/sd@0,0:<#>,raw
/devices/pci@780/pci@0/pci@9/scsi@0/sd@1,0:<#>,raw
```

for the character (raw) device, where <#> is a letter representing the disk slice. Block and character devices are described later in this chapter in the section titled "Block and Raw Devices."

Table 4-1 Device Information Commands

Command	Description
`prtconf`	The `prtconf` command displays system configuration information, including the total amount of memory and the device configuration, as described by the system's hierarchy. This useful tool verifies whether a device has been seen by the system.
`sysdef`	The `sysdef` command displays device configuration information, including system hardware, pseudo devices, loadable modules, and selected kernel parameters.
`dmesg`	The `dmesg` command displays system diagnostic messages as well as a list of devices attached to the system since the most recent restart.
`format`	The `format` command displays both physical and logical device names for all available disks.

The system commands used to provide information about physical devices are described in Table 4-1.

`prtconf` Output

The output produced by the `prtconf` command can vary depending on the version of the system's PROM.

Type the `prtconf` command:

```
# prtconf<cr>
System Configuration: Oracle Corporation sun4v
Memory size: 3968 Megabytes
System Peripherals (Software Nodes):

SUNW,Sun-Fire-T200
    scsi_vhci, instance #0
    packages (driver not attached)
        SUNW,builtin-drivers (driver not attached)
        deblocker (driver not attached)
        disk-label (driver not attached)
  <Output has been truncated.>
```

Use the `-v` option to display detailed information about devices.

The `sysdef` command can also be used to list information about hardware devices, pseudo devices, system devices, loadable modules, and selected kernel tunable parameters as follows:

```
# sysdef<cr>
*
* Hostid
```

```
*
  8510e818
*
* sun4v Configuration
*
*
* Devices
*
scsi_vhci, instance #0
packages (driver not attached)
        SUNW,builtin-drivers (driver not attached)
        deblocker (driver not attached)
        disk-label (driver not attached)
        terminal-emulator (driver not attached)
        dropins (driver not attached)
        SUNW,asr (driver not attached)
        kbd-translator (driver not attached)
        obp-tftp (driver not attached)
        zfs-file-system (driver not attached)

*Output has been truncated.
* System Configuration
*
  swap files
swapfile              dev    swaplo  blocks  free
/dev/zvol/dsk/rpool/swap 228,2       16 2097136 2097136
*
* Tunable Parameters
*
81469440        maximum memory allowed in buffer cache (bufhwm)
   30000        maximum number of processes (v.v_proc)
      99        maximum global priority in sys class (MAXCLSYSPRI)
   29995        maximum processes per user id (v.v_maxup)
      30        auto update time limit in seconds (NAUTOUP)
      25        page stealing low water mark (GPGSLO)
       1        fsflush run rate (FSFLUSHR)
      25        minimum resident memory for avoiding deadlock (MINARMEM)
*Output has been truncated
```

Use the output of the `prtconf` command to identify which disk, tape, and CD/DVD-ROM devices are connected to the system. As shown in the preceding `prtconf` and `sysdef` examples, some devices display the `driver not attached` message next to the device instance. This message does not always mean that a driver is unavailable for this device. It means that no driver is currently attached to the device instance because there is no device at this node or the device is not in use. The OS automatically loads drivers when the device is accessed, and it unloads them when it is not in use.

The system determines which devices are attached to it at startup. This is why it is important to have all peripheral devices powered on at startup, even if they are not currently being used. During startup, the kernel configures itself dynamically, loading needed modules into memory. Device drivers are loaded when devices, such as disk and tape devices, are accessed for the first time. This process is called "autoconfiguration" because all kernel modules are loaded automatically if needed. As described in Chapter 3, the system administrator can customize the way in which kernel modules are loaded by modifying the `/etc/system` file.

Device Autoconfiguration

Autoconfiguration offers many advantages over the manual configuration method used in earlier versions of SunOS, in which device drivers were manually added to the kernel, the kernel was recompiled, and the system had to be restarted. Now, with autoconfiguration, the administrator simply connects the new device to the system and performs a reconfiguration startup. To perform a reconfiguration startup, follow these steps:

1. Create the `/reconfigure` file with the following command:

   ```
   # touch /reconfigure<cr>
   ```

   The `/reconfigure` file causes the Oracle Solaris software to check for the presence of any newly installed devices the next time you turn on or start up your system.
2. Shut down the system using the shutdown procedure described in Chapter 3.

   If you need to connect the device, turn off power to the system and all peripherals after Oracle Solaris has been properly shut down.
3. After the new device is connected, restore power to the peripherals first and then to the system. Verify that the peripheral device has been added by attempting to access it.

Automatic Removal of `/reconfigure`

The file named `/reconfigure` automatically gets removed during the bootup process.

An optional method of performing a reconfiguration startup is to type “boot -r” at the OpenBoot prompt.

On an x86-based system, perform a reconfiguration reboot by editing the `boot` command in the GRUB menu as described in Chapter 3.

Specify a Reconfiguration Reboot

As root, you can also issue the `reboot -- -r` command from the shell prompt. The `-- -r` passes the `-r` to the `boot` command.

During a reconfiguration restart, a device hierarchy is created in the `/devices` file system to represent the devices connected to the system. The kernel uses this to associate drivers with their appropriate devices.

Autoconfiguration offers the following benefits:

- Main memory is used more efficiently because modules are loaded as needed.
- There is no need to reconfigure the kernel if new devices are added to the system. When you add devices such as disks or tape drives other than USB and hot-pluggable devices, the system needs to be shut down before you connect the hardware so that no damage is done to the electrical components.
- Drivers can be loaded and tested without having to rebuild the kernel and restart the system.

`devfsadm`

Another option used to automatically configure devices on systems that must remain running at all times, and one that does not require a reboot, is the `devfsadm` command.

Occasionally, you might install a new device for which Oracle Solaris does not have a supporting device driver. Always check with the manufacturer to make sure any device you plan to add to your system has a supported device driver. If a driver is not included with the standard Oracle Solaris release, the manufacturer should provide the software needed for the device to be properly installed, maintained, and administered.

USB Removable Devices

USB devices were developed to provide a method to attach peripheral devices such as keyboards, printers, cameras, and disk drives using a common connector and interface. Furthermore, USB devices are "hot-pluggable," which means they can be connected or disconnected while the system is running. The OS automatically detects when a USB device has been connected and automatically configures the operating environment to make it available.

The Oracle Solaris 11 operating environment supports USB devices. When hot-plugging a USB device, the device is immediately displayed in the device hierarchy. For example, a full device pathname for a USB thumb drive connected to a SunFire T2000 system would appear as follows:

```
/devices/pci@7c0/pci@0/pci@1/pci@0/usb@6/hub@1/storage@2/disk@0,0
```

A printer would look like this:

```
/pci@1f,4000/usb@5/hub@3/printer@1
```

The steps to add a USB mass storage device are as follows:

1. Insert a USB thumb drive into the USB port on your server. For this example, the device already contains a file system.
2. Verify that the USB device is mounted by entering the `rmformat` command as follows:

```
# rmformat<cr>
Two devices are listed as follows:
Looking for devices ...
     1. Logical Node: /dev/rdsk/c3t0d0s2
        Physical Node: /pci@7c0/pci@0/pci@1/pci@0/ide@8/sd@0,0
        Connected Device: TEAC  DW-224SL-R    1.0B
        Device Type: DVD Reader
        Bus: IDE
        Size: 525.9 MB
        Label: <None>
        Access permissions: Medium is not write protected.
     2. Logical Node: /dev/rdsk/c5t0d0s2
        Physical Node: /pci@7c0/pci@0/pci@1/pci@0/usb@6/hub@1/storage@2/disk@0,0
        Connected Device: Generic Flash Disk    8.07
        Device Type: Removable
        Bus: USB
        Size: 981.0 MB
        Label: <None>
        Access permissions: Medium is not write protected.
```

Note

If the device does not contain a file system, use the `rmformat` command to format the device. The `rmformat` command is described later in this section.

The first device listed is the removable DVD, and the second device listed is the removable USB thumb drive.

3. Verify that the device has been automatically mounted by typing

```
# mount<cr>
```

The mounted device is displayed as follows:

```
/media/NO NAME on /dev/dsk/c5t0d0s2:1 read/write/nosetuid/nodevices/rstchown/
hidden/nofoldcase/clamptime/noatime/timezone=18000/owner=0/group=0/mask=077/
dev=32c102a on Thu Jan 24 12:09:11 2013
```

4. The nickname for the mounted device can also be listed by typing

```
# rmmount -l<cr>
/dev/dsk/c5t0d0s2:1 rmdisk,rmdisk0,THUMBDRIVE,/media/THUMBDRIVE
/dev/dsk/c3t0d0s2  cdrom,cdrom0,cd,cd0,sr,sr0,Oracle_Solaris-11_1-Text-\
SPARC,/media/Oracle_Solaris-11_1-Text-SPARC
```

Notice the path to each device. Access the removable DVD media through this path:

```
/media/Oracle_Solaris-11_1-Text-SPARC
```

Access the USB thumb drive media through this path:

```
/media/THUMBDRIVE
```

The `rmformat` command is used to format, list, eject, partition, and protect removable rewritable media. If the USB device already has a file system, the device is automatically mounted. To unmount the device, type

```
# rmmount -u /dev/dsk/c5t0d0s2<cr>
/dev/dsk/c5t0d0s2 unmounted
```

To format the device, type

```
# rmformat -F quick /dev/rdsk/c5t0d0s2<cr>
Formatting will erase all the data on disk.
Do you want to continue? (y/n)y<cr>
```

The `rmformat` command has three formatting options:

1. `quick`: This option formats the media without certification or with limited certification of certain tracks on the media.
2. `long`: This option completely formats the media.
3. `force`: This option formats completely without user confirmation.

Create a file system on the device as follows:

```
# mkfs -F pcfs -o nofdisk,size=9800 /dev/rdsk/ c5t0d0s2<cr>
```

The `mkfs` command constructs a file system on a raw device. I specified `-F pcfs` to create a file allocation table (FAT) file system.

Be careful when removing USB devices. If the device is being used when it is disconnected, you will get I/O errors and possible data errors. When this happens, you'll need to plug the device back in, stop the application that is using the device, and then unplug the device.

USB mass storage devices and DVD-ROMs can be inserted and automatically mounted by using the removable media services. These services are started by default and can be enabled or disabled as follows.

To prevent removable volumes from automatically mounting, disable the `rmvolmgr` service as follows:

```
# svcadm disable rmvolmgr<cr>
```

To disable all of the volume management media services, disable the `dbus`, `hal`, and `rmvolmgr` services as follows:

```
# svcadm disable rmvolmgr<cr>
# svcadm disable dbus<cr>
# svcadm disable hal<cr>
```

Disabling the volume management services means that you would have to mount all media manually using the `mount` command.

Enable removable media services:

```
# svcadm enable rmvolmgr<cr>
# svcadm enable dbus<cr>
# svcadm enable hal<cr>
```

When disconnecting a USB device such as a USB thumb drive, eject the device as follows:

1. List the removable devices as follows:

```
# rmmount -l<cr>
/dev/dsk/c3t0d0s2 cdrom,cdrom0,cd,cd0,sr,sr0,Oracle_Solaris_Text_SPARC,\
/media/Oracle_Solaris_Text_SPARC
/dev/dsk/c5t0d0s2:1 rmdisk,rmdisk0,NO NAME the devices currently mounted:
```

2. Unmount the device as follows:

```
# rmmount -u rmdisk0<cr>
```

3. Eject the device as follows:

```
# eject rmdisk0<cr>
```

Instance Names

The instance name represents the kernel's abbreviated name for every possible device on the system. A few examples of instance names are

- sd0: The instance name for a SCSI disk
- e1000g: The instance name for a type of network interface

Instance names are mapped to a physical device name in the /etc/path_to_inst file. The following shows the contents of a path_to_inst file:

```
# more /etc/path_to_inst<cr>
#
#    Caution! This file contains critical kernel state
#
#
#    Caution! This file contains critical kernel state
#
"/fcoe" 0 "fcoe"
"/iscsi" 0 "iscsi"
"/pseudo" 0 "pseudo"
"/scsi_vhci" 0 "scsi_vhci"
"/options" 0 "options"
"/pci@780" 0 "px"
"/pci@780/pci@0" 0 "pcieb"
"/pci@780/pci@0/pci@1" 1 "pcieb"
"/pci@780/pci@0/pci@1/network@0" 0 "e1000g"
"/pci@780/pci@0/pci@1/network@0,1" 1 "e1000g"
"/pci@780/pci@0/pci@2" 2 "pcieb"
"/pci@780/pci@0/pci@8" 3 "pcieb"
"/pci@780/pci@0/pci@9" 4 "pcieb"
"/pci@780/pci@0/pci@9/scsi@0" 0 "mpt"
"/pci@780/pci@0/pci@9/scsi@0/sd@0,0" 2 "sd"
"/pci@780/pci@0/pci@9/scsi@0/sd@1,0" 3 "sd"
 ... <output has been trunctated> ...
```

Although instance names can be displayed using the commands dmesg, sysdef, and prtconf, the only command that shows the mapping of the instance name to the physical device name is the dmesg command. For example, you can determine the mapping of an instance name to a physical device name by looking at the dmesg output, as shown in the following example from a T2000 SPARC system:

```
Jan 24 12:31:02 solaris genunix: [ID 936769 kern.info] sd2 is\
 /pci@780/pci@0/pci@9/scsi@0/sd@0,0
Jan 24 12:32:03 solaris genunix: [ID 936769 kern.info] sd3 is\
 /pci@780/pci@0/pci@9/scsi@0/sd@1,0
```

In the first example, sd2 is the instance name and /pci@780/pci@0/pci@9/scsi@0/sd@0,0 is the physical device name. In the second example, sd3 is the instance name and /pci@780/pci@0/pci@9/scsi@0/sd@1,0 is the physical device name. After the instance name has been assigned to a device, it remains mapped to that device. To keep instance numbers consistent across restarts, the system records them in the /etc/path_to_inst file. This file is only read at startup, and it is updated by the devfsadmd daemon described later in this section.

Devices already existing on a system are not rearranged when new devices are added, even if new devices are added to pci slots that are numerically lower than those occupied by existing devices. In other words, the /etc/path_to_inst file is appended to, not rewritten, when new devices are added.

It is generally not necessary for the system administrator to change the path_to_inst file because the system maintains it. The system administrator can, however, change the assignment of instance numbers by editing this file and doing a reconfiguration startup. However, any changes made in this file are lost if the devfsadm command is run before the system is restarted.

Resolving Problems with /etc/path_to_inst

If you can't start up from the startup disk because of a problem with the /etc/path_to_inst file, you should start up from the CD/DVD (boot cdrom -s) and remove the /etc/path_to_inst file from the startup disk. To do this, start up from the DVD using boot cdrom -s at the OpenBoot prompt. Use the rm command to remove the file named /a/etc/path_to_inst. The path_to_inst file will automatically be created the next time the system boots.

You can add new devices to a system without requiring a reboot. It's all handled by the devfsadmd daemon that transparently builds the necessary configuration entries for those devices capable of notifying the kernel when the device is added (such as USB, FC-AL, disks, and so on). An example of when to use the devfsadm command would be if the system had been started but the power to the tape drive was not turned on. During startup, the system did not detect the device; therefore, its drivers were not installed.

To gain access to the device, you could halt the system, turn on power to the tape drive, and start the system back up, or you could simply turn on power to the tape drive and issue the following command at the command prompt:

```
# devfsadm<cr>
```

When used without any options, devfsadm will attempt to load every driver in the system and attach each driver to its respective device instances. You can restrict devfsadm to only look at specific devices using the -c option as follows:

```
# devfsadm -c tape<cr>
```

This restricts the `devfsadm` command to devices of class *tape*.

You can also use the `devfsadm` command to configure only the devices for a specific driver such as "st" by using the `-i` option as follows:

```
# devfsadm -i st<cr>
```

The `devfsadm` command will only configure the devices for the driver named "st."

Major and Minor Device Numbers

Each device has a major and minor device number assigned to it. These numbers identify the proper device location and device driver to the kernel. This number is used by the OS to key into the proper device driver whenever a physical device file corresponding to one of the devices it manages is opened. The major device number maps to a device driver such as sd, st, or e1000g. The minor device number indicates the specific member within that class of devices. All devices managed by a given device driver contain a unique minor number. Some drivers of pseudo devices (software entities set up to look like devices) create new minor devices on demand. Together, the major and minor numbers uniquely define a device and its device driver.

Physical device files have a unique output when listed with the `ls -l` command, as shown in the following example:

```
# cd /devices/pci@780/pci@0/pci@9/scsi@0<cr>
# ls -l<cr>
```

The system responds with the following:

```
total 4
drwxr-xr-x   2 root     sys         2 Jan 24 13:25 sd@0,0
brw-r-----   1 root     sys    203, 16 Jan 24 12:32 sd@0,0:a
crw-r-----   1 root     sys    203, 16 Jan 24 12:32 sd@0,0:a,raw
brw-r-----   1 root     sys    203, 17 Jan 24 12:32 sd@0,0:b
crw-r-----   1 root     sys    203, 17 Jan 24 12:32 sd@0,0:b,raw
brw-r-----   1 root     sys    203, 18 Jan 24 12:32 sd@0,0:c
crw-r-----   1 root     sys    203, 18 Jan 24 12:32 sd@0,0:c,raw
brw-r-----   1 root     sys    203, 19 Jan 24 12:32 sd@0,0:d
crw-r-----   1 root     sys    203, 19 Jan 24 12:32 sd@0,0:d,raw
brw-r-----   1 root     sys    203, 20 Jan 24 12:32 sd@0,0:e
crw-r-----   1 root     sys    203, 20 Jan 24 12:32 sd@0,0:e,raw
```

continues

```
brw-r-----   1 root     sys     203, 21 Jan 24 12:32 sd@0,0:f
crw-r-----   1 root     sys     203, 21 Jan 24 12:32 sd@0,0:f,raw
brw-r-----   1 root     sys     203, 22 Jan 24 12:32 sd@0,0:g
crw-r-----   1 root     sys     203, 22 Jan 24 12:32 sd@0,0:g,raw
brw-r-----   1 root     sys     203, 23 Jan 24 12:32 sd@0,0:h
crw-r-----   1 root     sys     203, 23 Jan 24 12:32 sd@0,0:h,raw ...
<output has been truncated> ...
```

This long listing includes columns showing major and minor numbers for each device. The sd driver manages all of the devices listed in the previous example that have a major number of 203. Minor numbers are listed after the comma.

During the process of building the /devices directory, major numbers are assigned based on the kernel module attached to the device. Each device is assigned a major device number by using the name-to-number mappings held in the /etc/name_to_major file. This file is maintained by the system and is undocumented. The following is a sample of the /etc/name_to_major file:

```
# more /etc/name_to_major<cr>
... <output has been truncated> ...
sckmdrv 199
scsa1394 200
scsa2usb 201
scsi_vhci 202
sd 203
sdpib 204
sdt 205
seeprom 206
ses 207
... <output has been truncated> ...
```

To create the minor device entries, the devfsadmd daemon uses the information placed in the dev_info node by the device driver. Permissions and ownership information are kept in the /etc/minor_perm file.

Logical Device Names

The final stage of the autoconfiguration process involves the creation of the logical device name to reflect the new set of devices on the system. Both SPARC and x86 systems use logical device names, but they differ slightly on each platform. To see a list of logical device names for the disks connected to a SPARC system, execute a long listing on the /dev/dsk directory as follows:

```
# ls -l /dev/dsk<cr>
total 96
lrwxrwxrwx   1 root     root          54 Jan 21 07:59 c1t0d0s0 ->\
 ../../devices/pci@0,600000/pci@0/pci@0/scsi@0/sd@0,0:a
```

```
lrwxrwxrwx   1 root     root          54 Jan 21 07:59 c1t0d0s1 ->\
 ../../devices/pci@0,600000/pci@0/pci@0/scsi@0/sd@0,0:b
lrwxrwxrwx   1 root     root          54 Jan 21 07:59 c1t0d0s2 ->\
 ../../devices/pci@0,600000/pci@0/pci@0/scsi@0/sd@0,0:c
lrwxrwxrwx   1 root     root          54 Jan 21 07:59 c1t0d0s3 ->\
 ../../devices/pci@0,600000/pci@0/pci@0/scsi@0/sd@0,0:d
 ... <output has been truncated> ...
```

On the second line of output from the `ls -l` command, notice that the logical device name `c1t0d0s0` is linked to the physical device name, as shown in the following:

```
../../devices/pci@0,600000/pci@0/pci@0/scsi@0/sd@0,0:a
```

On SPARC systems, you'll see an eight-string logical device name (`c#t#d#s#`) for each disk slice that contains the following:

- Controller number (`c#`): Identifies the host bus adapter, which controls communications between the system and disk unit. The controller number is assigned in sequential order, such as c0, c1, c2, and so on.
- Target number (`t#`): Target numbers, such as t0, t1, t2, and t3 correspond to a unique hardware address that is assigned to each disk, tape, or DVD-ROM. Some external disk drives have an address switch located on the rear panel. Some internal disks have address pins that are jumpered to assign that disk's target number.
- Disk number (`d#`): The disk number is also known as the logical unit number (LUN). This number reflects the number of disks at the target location. The disk number is always set to 0 on embedded SCSI controllers.
- Slice number (`s#`): A slice number ranging from 0 to 7.

On the x86 platform, IDE and SATA disk drives do not use target controllers. Device names of these types of disks represent the controller (`c3`), disk (`d#`), and slice (`s#`). Because IDE disks do not use target controllers, these disks use a t# value to represent the identity of the disks on its primary and secondary IDE buses. Target values on these systems are as follows:

- t0: Master device on the primary IDE bus
- t1: Slave device on the primary IDE bus
- t2: Master device on the secondary IDE bus
- t3: Slave device on the secondary IDE bus

The following is an example of IDE disks on an x86-based server:

```
# ls -l /dev/dsk<cr>
total 48
lrwxrwxrwx    1 root      root            45 Jan 23 18:11 c0t0d0s0 ->\
 ../../devices/pci@1f,0/pci@1,1/ide@d/sd@0,0:a
lrwxrwxrwx    1 root      root            45 Jan 23 18:11 c0t0d0s1 ->\
 ../../devices/pci@1f,0/pci@1,1/ide@d/sd@0,0:b
lrwxrwxrwx    1 root      root            44 Jan 23 18:11 c1t1d0s0 ->\
 ../../devices/pci@1f,0/pci@1/scsi@8/sd@1,0:a
lrwxrwxrwx    1 root      root            44 Jan 23 18:11 c1t1d0s1 ->\
 ../../devices/pci@1f,0/pci@1/scsi@8/sd@1,0:b
```

x86-based Oracle Solaris systems have a different disk-naming convention, but before describing the logical device name for a disk on an x86-based system, it's worth pointing out a fundamental difference between disk slicing on a SPARC system and disk slicing on an x86-based system. Disk partitioning on Oracle Solaris for the x86 platform has one more level than that of Oracle Solaris for SPARC. On Oracle Solaris for SPARC, slices and partitions are one and the same; on Oracle Solaris for x86, slices are "subpartitions" of a fixed disk (`fdisk`) partition table. This was done to allow Oracle Solaris to coexist with other x86-based OSs, such as for dual-boot configurations.

This difference in slicing brings some differences in the naming of disk devices on an x86-based system. Slices are created in the first partition on a drive and, for SCSI disks, are named the same as with Oracle Solaris for SPARC (`c#t#d0s#`). However, because slices are within an `fdisk` partition table, the x86 partitions have their own device names. The entire drive is named `c#t#d0p0`, and the `fdisk` partitions (maximum of 4) are `c#t#d0p1` through `c#t#d0p4`. To support the x86 environment, the `format` utility also has an added command called `fdisk` to deal with the `fdisk` partitions.

Oracle Solaris x86-based systems have 16 slices (numbered 0-15) versus 8 for SPARC. On the x86 system, slice 8 is used to hold boot code and contains the GRUB `stage1` program in sector 0, the disk label, the VTOC in sectors 1 and 2, and GRUB `stage2` program beginning at sector 50. GRUB is described in Chapter 3. Slice 8 also occupies the first cylinder (cylinder 0) of the `fdisk` partition.

On IDE and SATA disk drives, slice 9 is used for alternate sectors and contains blocks used to store bad block information. Higher slices are available for use but are not supported by `format` at this time, and the `format` utility will only allow you to modify slices 0–7. The major differences between the logical device names used on SPARC-based systems versus x86-based systems are as follows:

c is the controller number.
t is the SCSI target number.
s is the slice number ranging from 0 to 15.

p represents the `fdisk` partition (not slice partition). This number ranges from `p0` to `p4`. `p0` represents the entire disk.
d is the LUN or IDE drive number.

If an IDE drive is used, `d` is used to determine MASTER or SLAVE, and the `t` is not used for IDE drives. For example, two controllers are installed on an x86 PC:

c0 is an IDE controller.
c1 is a SCSI controller.

On an x86-based system, the following devices are listed in the `/dev/dsk` directory for a SATA disk, target 0:

```
c1t0d0p0        c1t0d0s1        c1t0d0s15       c1t0d0s7
c1t0d0p1        c1t0d0s10       c1t0d0s2        c1t0d0s8
c1t0d0p2        c1t0d0s11       c1t0d0s3        c1t0d0s9
c1t0d0p3        c1t0d0s12       c1t0d0s4
c1t0d0p4        c1t0d0s13       c1t0d0s5
c1t0d0s0        c1t0d0s14       c1t0d0s6
```

Examples of logical device names are the following:

- `c1t0d0s0`: A SCSI, SAS, or SATA disk device name that specifies controller 1, target 0, disk 0, and slice 0
- `c1d0p0`: An IDE disk name on an x86-based system that specifies controller 1, disk 0, and `fdisk` partition 0
- `c1d0s0`: An IDE disk name that specifies controller 1, disk 0, and slice 0
- `c2t11d0p0`: A SCSI, SAS, or SATA disk device name on an x86 system that specifies controller 2, target 11, disk 0, and `fdisk` partition 0
- `c2t11d0s0`: A SCSI, SAS, or SATA disk device name that specifies controller 2, target 11, disk 0, and slice 0
- `c3t266000C0FFF7C140d31s2`: A Fibre Channel attached LUN name that specifies controller 3, WWN 266000C0FFF7C140, LUN 31, and slice 2

On both SPARC-based and x86-based systems, the logical device name is the name that the system administrator uses to refer to a particular device when running various file system commands.

For example, if running the `mount` command, use the logical device name `/dev/dsk/c0t0d0s7` to mount the file system `/home`:

```
# mount /dev/dsk/c0t0d0s7 /home<cr>
```

Table 4-2 Device Directories

Directory	Description of Contents
`/dev/dsk`	Block interface to disk devices
`/dev/rdsk`	Raw or character interface to disk devices
`/dev/rmt`	Tape devices
`/dev/term`	Serial line devices
`/dev/cua`	Dial-out modems
`/dev/pts`	Pseudo terminals
`/dev/fbs`	Frame buffers
`/dev/sad`	STREAMS administrative driver
`/dev/md`	Metadevices managed by Oracle Solaris Volume Manager (SVM)

Logical device files in the `/dev` directory are symbolically linked to physical device files in the `/devices` directory. Logical device names are used to access disk devices if you do any of the following:

- Add a new disk to the system.
- Move a disk from one system to another.
- Access (or mount) a file system residing on a local disk.
- Back up a local file system.
- Repair a file system.

Logical devices are organized in subdirectories under the `/dev` directory by their device types, as shown in Table 4-2.

Block and Raw Devices

Disk drives have an entry under both the `/dev/dsk` and `/dev/rdsk` directories. The `/dsk` directory refers to the block or buffered device file, and the `/rdsk` directory refers to the character or raw device file. The "r" in `rdsk` stands for "raw." You may even hear these devices referred to as "cooked" and "uncooked" devices.

The `/dev/dsk` directory contains the disk entries for the block device nodes in `/devices`, as shown in the following command output:

```
# ls -l /dev/dsk<cr>
total 96
lrwxrwxrwx  1 root      root          54 Jan 21 07:59 c1t0d0s0 ->\
```

```
 ../../devices/pci@0,600000/pci@0/pci@0/scsi@0/sd@0,0:a
lrwxrwxrwx   1 root     root            54 Jan 21 07:59 c1t0d0s1 ->\
 ../../devices/pci@0,600000/pci@0/pci@0/scsi@0/sd@0,0:b
lrwxrwxrwx   1 root     root            54 Jan 21 07:59 c1t0d0s2 ->\
 ../../devices/pci@0,600000/pci@0/pci@0/scsi@0/sd@0,0:c
lrwxrwxrwx   1 root     root            54 Jan 21 07:59 c1t0d0s3 ->\
 ../../devices/pci@0,600000/pci@0/pci@0/scsi@0/sd@0,0:d
 ... <Output has been truncated> ...
```

The /dev/rdsk directory contains the disk entries for the character device nodes in /devices, as shown in the following command:

```
# ls -l /dev/rdsk<cr>
total 96
lrwxrwxrwx   1 root      root            58 Jan 21 07:59 c1t0d0s0 ->\
 ../../devices/pci@0,600000/pci@0/pci@0/scsi@0/sd@0,0:a,raw
lrwxrwxrwx   1 root      root            58 Jan 21 07:59 c1t0d0s1 ->\
 ../../devices/pci@0,600000/pci@0/pci@0/scsi@0/sd@0,0:b,raw
lrwxrwxrwx   1 root      root            58 Jan 21 07:59 c1t0d0s2 ->\
 ../../devices/pci@0,600000/pci@0/pci@0/scsi@0/sd@0,0:c,raw
lrwxrwxrwx   1 root      root            58 Jan 21 07:59 c1t0d0s3 ->\
 ../../devices/pci@0,600000/pci@0/pci@0/scsi@0/sd@0,0:d,raw

 ... <Output has been truncated> ...
```

A File System Defined

A file system is a collection of files and directories stored on disk in a standard UNIX file system (UFS) format. All disk-based computer systems have a file system. In UNIX, file systems have two basic components: files and directories. A file is the actual information as it is stored on the disk, and a directory is a list of the filenames. In addition to keeping track of filenames, the file system must keep track of a file's access date, permissions, and ownership. Managing file systems is one of the system administrator's most important tasks. Administration of the file system involves the following:

- Ensuring that users have access to data. This means that systems are up and operational, file permissions are set up properly, and data is accessible.
- Protecting file systems against file corruption and hardware failures. This is accomplished by checking the file system regularly and maintaining proper system backups.
- Securing file systems against unauthorized access. Only authorized users should have access to files.
- Providing users with adequate space for their files.

- Keeping the file system clean. In other words, data in the file system must be relevant and not wasteful of disk space. Procedures are needed to make sure that users follow proper naming conventions and that data is stored in an organized manner.

You'll see the term "file system" used in several ways. Usually, "file system" describes a particular type of file system (disk based, network based, or virtual). It might also describe the entire file tree from the root directory downward. In another context, the term "file system" might be used to describe the structure of a disk slice, which is described later in this chapter.

Creating and administering ZFS file systems is described in the next chapter.

Defining a Disk's Geometry

Before creating a file system on a disk, you need to understand the basic geometry of a disk drive. Disks come in many shapes and sizes. The number of heads, tracks, and sectors and the disk capacity vary from one model to another. Basic disk terminology is described in Table 4-3.

A hard disk consists of several separate disk platters mounted on a common spindle. Data stored on each platter surface is written and read by disk heads. The circular path that a disk head traces over a spinning disk platter is called a "track."

Table 4-3 Disk Terminology

Disk Term	Description
Track	A concentric ring on a disk that passes under a single stationary disk head as the disk rotates.
Cylinder	The set of tracks with the same nominal distance from the axis about which the disk rotates.
Sector	Section of each disk platter. A sector holds 512 bytes.
Block	A data storage area on a disk. A disk block is 512 bytes.
Disk controller	A chip and its associated circuitry that control the disk drive.
Disk label	The first sector of a disk (block 0) that contains disk geometry and partition information. Also referred to as the VTOC. To label a disk means to write slice information onto the disk. You usually label a disk after you change its slices using the `format` command.
Device driver	A kernel module that controls a hardware or virtual device.

Each track is made up of a number of sectors laid end to end. A sector consists of a header, a trailer, and 512 bytes of data. The header and trailer contain error-checking information to help ensure the accuracy of the data. Taken together, the set of tracks traced across all the individual disk platter surfaces for a single position of the heads is called a "cylinder."

Disk Controllers

Associated with every disk is a controller, an intelligent device responsible for organizing data on the disk. Some disk controllers are located on a separate circuit board, such as SCSI. Other controller types are integrated with the disk drive, such as SATA and IDE.

Defect List

Disks might contain areas where data cannot be written and retrieved reliably. These areas are called "defects." The controller uses the error-checking information in each disk block's trailer to determine whether a defect is present in that block. When a block is found to be defective, the controller can be instructed to add it to a defect list and avoid using that block in the future. The last two cylinders of a disk are set aside for diagnostic use and for storing the disk defect list.

Disk Labels

A special area of every disk is set aside for storing information about the disk's controller, geometry, and slices. This information is called the disk's label or VTOC.

To label a disk means to write slice information onto the disk. You usually label a disk after defining its slices. If you fail to label a disk after creating slices, the slices will be unavailable because the OS has no way of knowing about them.

Oracle Solaris supports two types of disk labels:

- SMI: The traditional VTOC disk label used for boot disks and disks smaller than two terabytes (2TB)
- EFI: The Extensible Firmware Interface label for disks larger than 2TB

The advantages of the EFI disk label over the SMI disk label are as follows:

- Provides support for disks greater than 2TB in size.
- Provides usable slices 0–6, where slice 2 is just another slice.

- Partitions (or slices) cannot overlap with the primary or backup label, nor with any other partitions. The size of the EFI label is usually 34 sectors, so partitions start at sector 34. This feature means that no partition can start at sector zero (0).
- No cylinder, head, or sector information is stored in the EFI label. Sizes are reported in blocks.
- Information that was stored in the alternate cylinders area, the last two cylinders of the disk, is now stored in slice 8.
- If you use the `format` utility to change partition sizes, the `unassigned` partition tag is assigned to partitions with sizes equal to zero. By default, the `format` utility assigns the `usr` partition tag to any partition with a size greater than zero. You can use the partition change menu to reassign partition tags after the partitions are changed.
- Oracle Solaris ZFS file systems use EFI labels by default when the entire disk is selected.

The following are restrictions of the EFI disk label:

- A disk with an EFI label may not be recognized on systems running older releases.
- Up until Oracle Solaris 11.1, the x86- and SPARC-based systems could not boot from a disk with an EFI disk label. In Oracle Solaris 11.1, x86-based systems can now boot to an EFI (GPT) labeled disk using GRUB2 (an updated version of GRUB). As of this writing, this feature is not currently available on SPARC-based systems. A boot disk on a SPARC-based system is installed with a legacy VTOC (SMI) label.
- The EFI specification prohibits overlapping slices. The entire disk is represented by c#t#d#.
- The EFI disk label provides information about disk or partition sizes in sectors and blocks, but not in cylinders and heads.
- The following `format` options are either not supported or are not applicable on disks with EFI labels:
  - The `save` option is not supported because disks with EFI labels do not need an entry in the `format.dat` file.
  - The `backup` option is not applicable because the disk driver finds the primary label and writes it back to the disk.

It may be necessary to change a disk label from SMI to EFI or vice versa. Use the `format` command with the `-e` option as described in the section titled, "Using the `format` Utility to Create Slices: SPARC" later in this chapter.

Partition Tables

An important part of the disk label is the partition table, which identifies a disk's slices, the slice boundaries (in cylinders), and the total size of the slices. A disk's partition table can be displayed by using the `format` utility described in the "Disk Slices" section that follows.

Disk Slices

Disks are divided into regions called "disk slices" or "disk partitions." A slice is composed of a single range of contiguous blocks. It is a physical subset of the disk (except for slice 2, which represents the entire disk). A UFS or the swap area is built within these disk slices. The boundaries of a disk slice are defined when a disk is partitioned using the `format` utility, and the slice information for a particular disk can be viewed by using the `prtvtoc` command. Each disk slice appears to the OS (and to the system administrator) as though it were a separate disk drive.

Disk Slices and ZFS

With ZFS file systems, disk slicing has become unnecessary except for configuring the boot disk. ZFS file systems are described in Chapter 5, "Administering ZFS File Systems." Previous versions of Oracle Solaris used disk slices, and you should be familiar with the concept in case you encounter disk slices on other Oracle Solaris systems.

Disk slicing differs between the SPARC and x86 platforms. On the SPARC platform, the entire disk is devoted to the OS; the disk can be divided into 8 slices, numbered 0 to 7. On the x86 platform, the disk is divided into `fdisk` partitions using the `fdisk` command. The `fdisk` partition is divided into 10 slices, numbered 0 to 9.

Slices Versus Partitions

Oracle Solaris device names use the term "slice" (and the letter "s" in the device name) to refer to the slice number. Slices were called partitions in SunOS 4.x. This book attempts to use the term "slice" whenever possible; however, certain interfaces, such as the `format` and `prtvtoc` commands, refer to slices as partitions.

A physical disk consists of a stack of circular platters. Data is stored on these platters in a cylindrical pattern called "cylinders" as illustrated in Figure 4-1. Cylinders can be grouped and isolated from one another. A group of cylinders is referred to as a slice. A slice is defined with start and end points, starting from the outside of the platters to the center of the stack of platters, which is called the "spindle."

For example, a 73GB SCSI disk has 14,087 cylinders, numbered 0 to 14,086. Cylinder 0 is on the outside edge of the platters, and cylinder 14,086 is the closest to the spindle. Disk slices are defined by an offset and a size in cylinders. The offset is

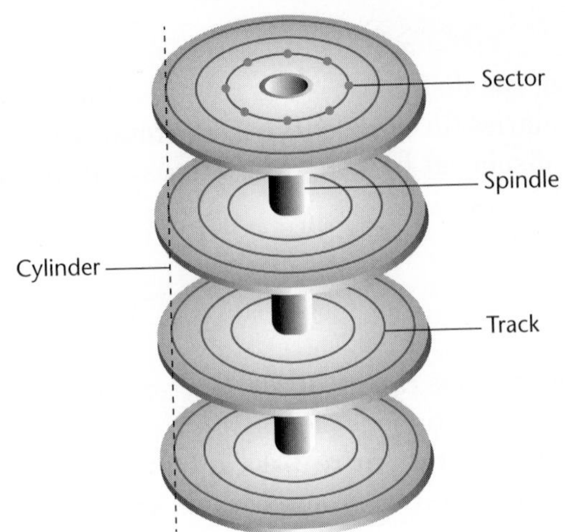

Figure 4-1 Disk platters and cylinders

the distance from cylinder 0. To define a slice, the administrator provides a starting cylinder and an ending cylinder. A slice spanning from cylinder 0 to 14,086 would use the entire disk and is typical of the slicing scheme used on a ZFS boot disk.

When setting up slices, remember these rules:

- Each disk slice holds only one file system.
- No file system can span multiple slices without the use of a volume manager such as ZFS or SVM.
- After a file system is created, its size cannot be increased or decreased without repartitioning and possibly destroying the partition directly before or after it.
- Slices cannot span multiple disks; however, multiple swap slices on separate disks are allowed.

When we discuss ZFS in Chapter 5, you'll learn how to get around some of these limitations in file systems.

Displaying Disk Configuration Information

As described earlier, disk configuration information is stored in the disk label. If you know the disk and slice number, you can display information for a disk by using the print volume table of contents (`prtvtoc`) command. You can specify the volume by specifying any slice defined on the disk (for example, /dev/rdsk/c0t3d0s2 or /dev/rdsk/c0t3d0s*). Regardless of which slice you specify, all slices defined on the disk will be displayed. If you know the target number of the disk but do not know how it is divided into slices, you can show information for the entire disk by specifying either slice 2 or s*. The following steps show how you can examine information stored on a disk's label by using the prtvtoc command.

1. Become the superuser.
2. Type the following text and press *Enter*.

```
# prtvtoc /dev/rdsk/c2t0d0s2<cr>
```

The system responds with the following:

```
* /dev/rdsk/c2t0d0s2 partition map
*
* Dimensions:
*     512 bytes/sector
*     424 sectors/track
*      24 tracks/cylinder
*   10176 sectors/cylinder
*   14089 cylinders
*   14087 accessible cylinders
*
* Flags:
*   1: unmountable
*  10: read-only
*
* Unallocated space:
*       First     Sector    Last
*       Sector     Count    Sector
*           0     10176     10175
*
*                          First     Sector    Last
* Partition  Tag  Flags    Sector     Count    Sector  Mount Directory
       0      2    00      10176 143339136 143349311
       2      5    01          0 143349312 143349311
```

The disk described is a SAS disk, target 0 with an SMI VTOC label. The prtvtoc command shows the number of cylinders and heads, as well as how the disk's slices are arranged.

The following is an example of running the prtvtoc command on a SCSI disk with an EFI label:

```
# prtvtoc /dev/rdsk/c2t1d0s1<cr>
* /dev/rdsk/c2t1d0s1 partition map
```

continues

```
*
* Dimensions:
*      512 bytes/sector
* 8385121 sectors
* 8385054 accessible sectors
*
* Flags:
*    1: unmountable
*   10: read-only
*
*                          First     Sector     Last
* Partition   Tag  Flags  Sector      Count     Sector  Mount Directory
       0        2    01        34     41006      41039
       1        2    00     41040   8327663   8368702   /mnt
       8       11    00   8368703     16384   8385086
```

Using the `format` Utility to Create Slices: SPARC

Before you can create a file system on a disk, the disk must be formatted, and you must divide it into slices using the `format` utility. Formatting involves two separate processes:

- Writing format information to the disk
- Completing a surface analysis, which compiles an up-to-date list of disk defects

When a disk is formatted, header and trailer information is superimposed on the disk. When the `format` utility runs a surface analysis, the controller scans the disk for defects. It should be noted that defects and formatting information reduce the total disk space available for data. This is why a new disk usually holds only 90% to 95% of its capacity after formatting. This percentage varies according to disk geometry and decreases as the disk ages and develops more defects.

The need to perform a surface analysis on a disk drive has dropped as more manufacturers ship their disk drives formatted and partitioned. You should not need to perform a surface analysis within the `format` utility when adding a disk drive to an existing system unless you think disk defects are causing problems. The primary reason that you would use `format` is if you want to view or change the partitioning scheme on a disk.

Always Back Up Your Data

Formatting and creating slices is a destructive process, so make sure user data is backed up before you start.

The `format` utility searches your system for all attached disk drives and reports the following information about the disk drives it finds:

- Target location
- Disk geometry
- Whether the disk is formatted
- Whether the disk has mounted partitions

In addition, the `format` utility is used in disk repair operations to do the following:

- Retrieve disk labels
- Repair defective sectors
- Format and analyze disks
- Partition disks
- Label disks (i.e., write the disk name and configuration information to the disk for future retrieval)

The installation program partitions and labels disk drives as part of installing the Oracle Solaris release. However, you might need to use the `format` utility when doing the following:

- Displaying slice information
- Dividing a disk into slices
- Formatting a disk drive when you think disk defects are causing problems
- Repairing a disk drive
- Changing a disk label from EFI to SMI or vice versa

The following example uses the `format` utility to create disk slices on a disk.

1. Become the superuser
2. Type "code."

   The system responds with the following:

```
Searching for disks ... done

AVAILABLE DISK SELECTIONS:
       0. c0t0d0 <SUN36G cyl 24620 alt 2 hd 27 sec 107>
          /pci@1f,0/pci@1/scsi@8/sd@0,0
       1. c0t1d0 <SUN36G cyl 24620 alt 2 hd 27 sec 107>
          /pci@1f,0/pci@1/scsi@8/sd@1,0
```

3. Specify the disk (enter its number).

   The system responds with the format main menu:

```
FORMAT MENU:
    disk - select a disk
    type - select (define) a disk type
    partition - select (define) a partition table
    current - describe the current disk
    format - format and analyze the disk
    repair - repair a defective sector
    label - write label to the disk
    analyze - surface analysis
    defect - defect list management
    backup - search for backup labels
    verify - read and display labels
    save - save new disk/partition definitions
    inquiry - show vendor, product and revision
    volname - set 8-character volume name
    !<cmd> - execute <cmd>, then return
    quit
```

   Table 4-4 describes the format main menu items.

4. Type "partition" at the format prompt. The partition menu is displayed.

Using Shortcuts in the `format` Utility

It is unnecessary to type the entire command. After you type the first two characters of a command, the `format` utility recognizes the entire command.

```
format> partition<cr>
PARTITION MENU:
    0 - change '0' partition
    1 - change '1' partition
    2 - change '2' partition
    3 - change '3' partition
    4 - change '4' partition
    5 - change '5' partition
    6 - change '6' partition
    7 - change '7' partition
    select - select a predefined table
    modify - modify a predefined partition table
    name - name the current table
    print - display the current table
    label - write partition map and label to the disk
    !<cmd> - execute <cmd>, then return
    quit
```

5. Type "print" to display the current partition map.

```
partition> print<cr>
```

Table 4-4 Format Main Menu Item Descriptions

Menu Item	Description
`disk`	Lists all of the system's drives. Also lets you choose the disk you want to use in subsequent operations. This disk is referred to as the current disk.
`type`	Identifies the manufacturer and model of the current disk. Also displays a list of known drive types. Choose the *Auto configure* option for all SCSI-2 disk drives.
`partition`	Creates and modifies slices.
`current`	Describes the current disk (that is, device name, device type, number of cylinders, alternate cylinders, heads, sectors, and physical device name).
`format`	Formats the current disk using one of these sources of information in this order:
	Information that is found in the `format.dat` file.
	Information from the automatic configuration process.
	Information that you type at the prompt if no `format.dat` entry exists.
	This command does not apply to IDE disks. IDE disks are preformatted by the manufacturer.
`fdisk`	x86 platform only: Runs the `fdisk` program to create an Oracle Solaris `fdisk` partition.
`repair`	Used to repair a specific block on the current disk.
`label`	Writes a new label to the current disk. This is not the same as labeling the disk with `volname`.
`analyze`	Runs read, write, and compare tests.
`defect`	Retrieves and displays defect lists. This feature does not apply to IDE disks. IDE disks manage defects automatically.
`backup`	Searches for backup labels if the VTOC becomes corrupted or gets deleted.
`verify`	Displays information about the current disk such as device name, device type, number of cylinders, alternate cylinders, heads, sectors, and partition table.
`save`	Saves new disk and partition information.
`inquiry`	SCSI disks only: Displays the vendor, product name, and revision level of the current drive. This will also display the disk's current firmware.
`volname`	Labels the disk with a new eight-character volume name that you specify. This is not the same as writing the partition table to disk using `label`.
`quit`	Exits the format menu. Pressing *Ctrl+D* will also exit the `format` utility from the main menu or from any submenu.

The system responds with the following:

```
Current partition table (original):
Total disk cylinders available: 24620 + 2 (reserved cylinders)

Part      Tag    Flag     Cylinders         Size            Blocks
  0       root    wm     1418 -  9924      11.72GB   (8507/0/0)   24576723
  1        var    wm     9925 - 13469       4.88GB   (3545/0/0)   10241505
  2     backup    wm        0 - 24619      33.92GB   (24620/0/0) 71127180
  3       swap    wu        0 -  1417      1.95GB   (1418/0/0)   4096602
  4 unassigned    wm    13470 - 14887       1.95GB   (1418/0/0)   4096602
  5 unassigned    wm    14888 - 16112       1.69GB   (1225/0/0)   3539025
  6 unassigned    wm    16113 - 16821    1000.15MB   (709/0/0)   2048301
  7       home    wm    16822 - 23910       9.77GB   (7089/0/0)   20480121
```

The columns displayed with the partition table are

– Part: The slice number (0–7).

– Tag: This is an optional value that indicates how the slice is being used. The value can be any of the following names that best fits the function of the file system you are creating:
 `unassigned`, `boot`, `root`, `swap`, `usr`, `backup`, `stand`, `var`, `home`, `alternates`, `reserved`, `system`, `BIOS_boot`

– Flag: Values in this column can be

`wm`	The disk slice is writable and mountable.
`wu`	The disk slice is writable and unmountable (such as a swap slice).
`rm`	The disk slice is read-only and mountable.
`ru`	The disk slice is read-only and unmountable.

– Cylinders: The starting and ending cylinder number for the disk slice.

– Size: The slice size specified as

`mb`	megabytes
`gb`	gigabytes
`b`	blocks
`c`	cylinders
`b`	Blocks
`e`	Ending cylinder

Wasted Disk Space

Wasted disk space occurs during partitioning when one or more cylinders have not been allocated to a disk slice. This may happen intentionally or accidentally. If there are unallocated slices available, then wasted space can possibly be assigned to a slice at another time.

You can use the `name` and `save` commands in the partition menu to name and save a newly created partition table to a file that can be referenced by name later, when you want to use this same partition scheme on another disk. When issuing the `name` command, you'll provide a unique name for this partition scheme and then issue the `save` command to save the information to the `./format.dat` file. Normally this file is located in the `/etc` directory, so provide the full pathname for `/etc/format.dat` to update the master file.

6. After you partition the disk, you must label it by typing `label` at the partition prompt:

```
partition> label<cr>
```

You are asked for confirmation on labeling the disk as follows:

```
Ready to label disk, continue? y<cr>
```

Enter "Y" to continue.

Label Your Drive

To label a disk means to write slice information onto the disk. If you don't label the drive when exiting the `format` utility, your partition changes will not be retained. It's a good idea to get into the habit of labeling at the partition submenu, but you can also label at the `format` utility main menu as well—you get two chances to remember before exiting the utility.

7. After labeling the disk, type "quit" to exit the partition menu or press *Ctrl+D* to exit the `format` utility:

```
partition> quit<cr>
```

8. Type "quit" again to exit the format utility:

```
format> quit<cr>
```

It's important to point out a few undesirable things that can happen when defining disk partitions with the `format` utility if you're not careful. First, be careful not to waste disk space. Wasted disk space can occur when you decrease the size of one slice and do not adjust the starting cylinder number of the adjoining disk slice.

Second, don't overlap disk slices. Overlapping occurs when one or more cylinders are allocated to more than one disk slice. For example, increasing the size of one slice without decreasing the size of the adjoining slice will create overlapping partitions. The `format` utility will not warn you of wasted disk space or overlapping partitions.

The main reason a system administrator uses the `format` utility is to divide a disk into disk slices. In Oracle Solaris 11 11/11, for a bootable ZFS root pool, the disks in the pool must contain slices and must be labeled with an SMI label. The simplest configuration would be to put the entire disk capacity in slice 0 and use that slice for the root pool. Bootable ZFS root pools are discussed further in Chapter 5.

EFI Boot Disks in Oracle Solaris 11.1

Oracle Solaris 11.1 is the first release to support booting from an EFI (GPT) or SMI formatted disk on the x86-based systems using GRUB2. As of this writing, the SPARC platform still requires the boot disk to contain an SMI label.

I'll describe how to use the SMI label for SPARC-based systems. For example, on a SPARC-based system with a 72GB disk, you would need to have 68GB of usable space located in slice 0. Similarly, on an x86-based system with a 72GB disk, you would also need to allow 68GB of usable space located in slice 0. A small amount of boot information is contained in slice 8. Slice 8 requires no administration and cannot be changed.

Follow these steps to partition a disk (`c2t0d0`) to be used as a ZFS boot disk (bootable ZFS root pool) on a SPARC-based system. If the disk has an EFI label, and the firmware has not been upgraded, you must first convert it to an SMI label.

Use the `prtvtoc` command to verify the disk label as follows:

```
# prtvtoc /dev/rdsk/c2t0d0s2<cr>
```

The system displays

```
Part      Tag     Flag  Cylinders       Size            Blocks
  0       root     wm    1 - 14086    68.35GB    (14086/0/0) 143339136
  1 unassigned     wm    0              0        (0/0/0)             0
  2     backup     wu    0 - 14086    68.35GB    (14087/0/0) 143349312
  3 unassigned     wm    0              0        (0/0/0)             0
  4 unassigned     wm    0              0        (0/0/0)             0
  5 unassigned     wm    0              0        (0/0/0)             0
  6 unassigned     wm    0              0        (0/0/0)             0
  7 unassigned     wm    0              0        (0/0/0)             0
```

Notice that slice 2 is labeled "backup" and the slices are numbered 0-7. This is an SMI label.

The following shows the output that is displayed for a disk with an EFI label:

```
Part      Tag    Flag   First Sector          Size          Last Sector
  0        usr    wm              34       68.36GB           143358320
  1 unassigned    wm               0             0                   0
  2 unassigned    wm               0             0                   0
  3 unassigned    wm               0             0                   0
  4 unassigned    wm               0             0                   0
  5 unassigned    wm               0             0                   0
  6 unassigned    wm               0             0                   0
  7 unassigned    wm               0             0                   0
  8   reserved    wm       143358321        8.00MB           143374704
```

Notice there is a slice 8 and slice 2 is NOT labeled "backup." This is an EFI label and would need to be changed. Use the following steps to change the label from an EFI label to an SMI label:

1. As root, use the `format -e` command and select the disk to label as follows:

```
# format -e<cr>
```

The system displays a list of disks. In the example, I selected disk 1 (`c2t1d0`):

```
Searching for disks ... done
AVAILABLE DISK SELECTIONS:
       0. c2t0d0 <SUN72G cyl 14087 alt 2 hd 24 sec 424>
          /pci@780/pci@0/pci@9/scsi@0/sd@0,0
       1. c2t1d0 <SEAGATE-ST973402SSUN72G-0603-68.37GB>
          /pci@780/pci@0/pci@9/scsi@0/sd@1,0
Specify disk (enter its number): 1<cr>
selecting c2t1d0
[disk formatted]
```

2. The main menu is displayed. Type "label" to `label` the disk:

```
FORMAT MENU:
    disk       - select a disk
    type       - select (define) a disk type
    partition  - select (define) a partition table
    current    - describe the current disk
    format     - format and analyze the disk
    repair     - repair a defective sector
    label      - write label to the disk
    analyze    - surface analysis
    defect     - defect list management
    backup     - search for backup labels
    verify     - read and display labels
    inquiry    - show disk ID
    scsi       - independent SCSI mode selects
    cache      - enable, disable or query SCSI disk cache
    volname    - set 8-character volume name
```

continues

```
    !<cmd>  - execute <cmd>, then return
    quit
format> label<cr>
```

3. Select option 1 to label the disk with an SMI label and press *Enter* when prompted for autoconfiguration:

```
[0] SMI Label
[1] EFI Label
Specify Label type[1]: 0<cr>
Auto configuration via format.dat[no]?<cr>
Auto configuration via generic SCSI-2[no]?<cr>
format>
```

4. Exit the `format` utility.

```
format> quit<cr>
```

To slice the disk so that it can be used as a ZFS boot disk, follow these steps:

1. As root, enter the `format` utility:

```
# format<cr>
Searching for disks ... done
```

   Select the disk that is going to be sliced. In the example, I will select disk 1 (`c2t1d0`):

```
AVAILABLE DISK SELECTIONS:
       0. c2t0d0 <SUN72G cyl 14087 alt 2 hd 24 sec 424>
          /pci@780/pci@0/pci@9/scsi@0/sd@0,0
       1. c2t1d0 <SEAGATE-ST973402SSUN72G-0603-68.37GB>
          /pci@780/pci@0/pci@9/scsi@0/sd@1,0
Specify disk (enter its number): 1<cr>
```

   The system responds with

```
selecting c2t1d0
[disk formatted]
```

2. Type “partition” at the `format` prompt. The partition menu is displayed.

```
format> partition<cr>
PARTITION MENU:
```

```
0 - change '0' partition
1 - change '1' partition
2 - change '2' partition
3 - change '3' partition
4 - change '4' partition
5 - change '5' partition
6 - change '6' partition
7 - change '7' partition
select - select a predefined table
modify - modify a predefined partition table
name - name the current table
print - display the current table
label - write partition map and label to the disk
!<cmd> - execute <cmd>, then return
quit
```

3. Type "print" to display the current partition map.

```
partition> print<cr>
```

The system responds with the following:

```
partition> print<cr>
Current partition table (original):
Total disk cylinders available: 14087 + 2 (reserved cylinders)

Part      Tag    Flag     Cylinders        Size            Blocks
  0       root    wm       0 -    25      129.19MB    (26/0/0)        264576
  1       swap    wu      26 -    51      129.19MB    (26/0/0)        264576
  2     backup    wu       0 - 14086       68.35GB    (14087/0/0) 143349312
  3 unassigned    wm       0                0         (0/0/0)              0
  4 unassigned    wm       0                0         (0/0/0)              0
  5 unassigned    wm       0                0         (0/0/0)              0
  6        usr    wm      52 - 14086       68.10GB    (14035/0/0) 142820160
  7 unassigned    wm       0                0         (0/0/0)              0

partition>
```

4. Enter "modify" to change the partition table:

```
partition> modify<cr>
```

5. Select option 1 for "All Free Hog" when prompted:

```
Select partitioning base:
        0. Current partition table (original)
        1. All Free Hog
Choose base (enter number) [0]? 1<cr>

Part      Tag    Flag     Cylinders        Size            Blocks
  0       root    wm       0                0         (0/0/0)              0
```

continues

```
1       swap     wu      0              0        (0/0/0)             0
2     backup     wu      0 - 14086    68.35GB    (14087/0/0) 143349312
3 unassigned     wm      0              0        (0/0/0)             0
4 unassigned     wm      0              0        (0/0/0)             0
5 unassigned     wm      0              0        (0/0/0)             0
6        usr     wm      0              0        (0/0/0)             0
7 unassigned     wm      0              0        (0/0/0)             0
```

6. Type "yes" when asked whether to continue:

```
Do you wish to continue creating a new partition table based on above table[yes]?
yes<cr>
```

Type "0" for the Free Hog partition:

```
Free Hog partition[6]? 0<cr>
```

The Free Hog Slice

When using the `format` utility to change the size of disk slices, a temporary slice is automatically designated that expands and shrinks to accommodate the slice resizing operations. This temporary slice is referred to as the "free hog," and it represents the unused disk space on a disk drive. If a slice is decreased, the free hog expands. After the `modify` operation is complete, the remaining free hog space is allocated to the slice specified.

7. The system will prompt you to enter a size for each partition. Press *Enter* when prompted as follows, and each slice will be 0MB:

```
Enter size of partition '1' [0b, 0c, 0.00mb, 0.00gb]:<cr>
Enter size of partition '3' [0b, 0c, 0.00mb, 0.00gb]:<cr>
Enter size of partition '4' [0b, 0c, 0.00mb, 0.00gb]:<cr>
Enter size of partition '5' [0b, 0c, 0.00mb, 0.00gb]:<cr>
Enter size of partition '6' [0b, 0c, 0.00mb, 0.00gb]:<cr>
Enter size of partition '7' [0b, 0c, 0.00mb, 0.00gb]:<cr>
```

Because all of the slices have been set to "0," the free hog space is the entire disk. This space will be allocated to slice 0 as specified in step 6.

8. When prompted to make this the current partition table, press *Enter* to use the default value "yes":

```
Okay to make this the current partition table[yes]?<cr>
```

9. When prompted for a table name, enter “rootdisk.” This name is not significant and can be any name.

```
Enter table name (remember quotes): rootdisk<cr>
```

Enter “pr” to display the new partition table:

```
partition> pr<cr>
Current partition table (unnamed):
Total disk cylinders available: 14087 + 2 (reserved cylinders)
Part      Tag    Flag     Cylinders        Size           Blocks
  0       root    wm      0 - 14086       68.35GB    (14087/0/0) 143349312
  1       swap    wu      0                0         (0/0/0)             0
  2     backup    wu      0 - 14086       68.35GB    (14087/0/0) 143349312
  3 unassigned    wm      0                0         (0/0/0)             0
  4 unassigned    wm      0                0         (0/0/0)             0
  5 unassigned    wm      0                0         (0/0/0)             0
  6        usr    wm      0                0         (0/0/0)             0
  7 unassigned    wm      0                0         (0/0/0)             0

partition>
```

Notice that slice 0 is the entire disk.

10. Enter “quit” or press *Ctrl+D* to exit the `format` utility.

```
partition> quit<cr>
```

Using the `format` Utility to Create Slices: x86

As described earlier in this chapter, Oracle Solaris on the x86 platform treats disk drives slightly differently than on the SPARC-based systems. Disks on the x86 platform must have an `fdisk` partition table. The x86-based systems use the `fdisk` partition table to identify parts of the disk reserved for different OSs and to identify the partition that the system will boot from. This boot partition is referred to as the “active disk” partition. You can assign one `fdisk` partition on a disk to be used for Oracle Solaris.

On an x86-based system, once a disk drive has been physically installed and verified as working, you'll use the `format` command to slice the disk, but first an `fdisk` partition must be created on the new drive. You can create this `fdisk` partition using the `fdisk` command from the command line or through the `format` utility.

The following steps describe how to create a fixed disk partition table on a disk using the format utility:

1. As root, type "format" to get into the `format` utility.

```
# format<cr>
```

The following menu appears:

```
AVAILABLE DISK SELECTIONS:
       0. c1t0d0 <FUJITSU-M1606S-512-6234 cyl 3455 alt 2 hd 6 sec 102>
          /pci@0,0/pci9004,8178@3/cmdk@0,0
       1. c1t1d0 <IBM-DFHSS1W!e-4141 cyl 4071 alt 2 hd 4 sec 135>
          /pci@0,0/pci9004,8178@3/cmdk@1,0
       2. c1t2d0 <DEFAULT cyl 2928 alt 2 hd 6 sec 120>
          /pci@0,0/pci9004,8178@3/cmdk@2,0
Specify disk (enter its number):
```

2. Enter the number corresponding to the new drive and the following menu will be displayed:

```
FORMAT MENU:
    disk       - select a disk
    type       - select (define) a disk type
    partition  - select (define) a partition table
    current    - describe the current disk
    format     - format and analyze the disk
    fdisk      - run the fdisk program
    repair     - repair a defective sector
    label      - write label to the disk
    analyze    - surface analysis
    defect     - defect list management
    backup     - search for backup labels
    verify     - read and display labels
    save       - save new disk/partition definitions
    inquiry    - show vendor, product and revision
    volname    - set 8-character volume name5
    quit
format>
```

3. Select the `fdisk` option and the following menu appears:

```
The recommended default partitioning for your disk is:
a 100% "SOLARIS System" partition.

To select this, please type "y". To partition your disk
differently, type "n" and the "fdisk" program will let you select other
partitions.
```

4. If you wish to use the entire drive for Oracle Solaris, enter "Y." This will return you to the format menu. If "N" is entered, the `fdisk` menu will be displayed.

```
        Total disk size is 4073 cylinders
        Cylinder size is 540 (512 byte) blocks
                                              Cylinders
      Partition  Status  Type          Start  End  Length    %
      =========  ======  ======== =====  ===  ======  ===

    THERE ARE NO PARTITIONS CURRENTLY DEFINED
    SELECT ONE OF THE FOLLOWING:
            1.  Create a partition
            2.  Change Active (Boot from) partition
            3.  Delete a partition
            4.  Exit (Update disk configuration and exit)
            5.  Cancel (Exit without updating disk configuration)
    Enter Selection:
```

5. Choose `1` to create an `fdisk` partition. This is not the same as a slice.
6. After creating the partition, choose `4` to exit and save. The format menu will return.
7. Choose `partition` and follow the procedure for formatting a disk on page 272, beginning at step 4.

Disks on x86-based systems can be divided into 10 slices labeled slice 0 through slice 9. On Oracle Solaris 11/11, slices 0 through 7 are used for the same purposes as disk slices found on SPARC-based systems. Slice 2 represents all of the space within the `fdisk` partition. As stated earlier, slices 8 and 9 are used for purposes specific to x86-based hardware. You cannot modify slices 8 and 9 using the `format` utility. Beginning with Oracle Solaris 11.1, the boot disk on an x86-based system can contain an EFI label, and the partition scheme is slightly different than the SPARC system. Slice 0 is reserved for the `BIOS_boot` information. I'll describe this more in the next chapter.

Here's an example of the partition table on an IDE or SATA disk on an x86-based system running Oracle Solaris 11/11, as displayed by the `format` utility:

```
Part  Tag          Flag    Cylinders    Size        Blocks
(output omitted)
8     boot         wu      0 - 0        7.84MB      (1/0/0) 16065
9     alternates   wm      1 - 2        15.69MB     (2/0/0) 32130
```

In the previous example, notice that slice 9 is defined and tagged as the `alternates` slice.

The next example shows the partition table for a SCSI disk attached to an x86-based system. Notice that partition 8 is assigned, but slice 9 is not used:

```
Part  Tag          Flag    Cylinders    Size        Blocks
(output omitted)
8     boot         wu      0 - 0        7.84MB      (1/0/0) 16065
9     unassigned   wm      0            0           (0/0/0) 0
```

One more item of note: On standard UFSs, don't change the size of disk slices that are currently in use. When a disk with existing slices is repartitioned and relabeled, any existing data will be lost. Before repartitioning a disk, first copy all of the data to tape or to another disk.

You can also create the fixed disk partition table on an x86-based system disk from the command line using a single command as follows:

```
# fdisk -B c1t0d0<cr>
```

The -B option creates a single fixed disk partition that spans the entire disk. The following 36GB disk was formatted using the fdisk -B command:

```
Part      Tag  Flag  Cylinders    Size          Blocks
  0 unassigned  wm    0           0        (0/0/0)            0
  1 unassigned  wm    0           0        (0/0/0)            0
  2     backup  wu    0 - 4695   35.97GB (4696/0/0) 75441240
  3 unassigned  wm    0           0        (0/0/0)            0
  4 unassigned  wm    0           0        (0/0/0)            0
  5 unassigned  wm    0           0        (0/0/0)            0
  6 unassigned  wm    0           0        (0/0/0)            0
  7 unassigned  wm    0           0        (0/0/0)            0
  8       boot  wu    0 -   0     7.84MB (1/0/0)          16065
  9 unassigned  wm    0           0        (0/0/0)            0
```

The fdisk -B command can also be used to convert a disk label from an EFI to SMI.

To verify that a disk contains a fixed disk partition table, issue the following command:

```
# fdisk -v -W - /dev/rdsk/c3t0d0p<cr>
```

The system displays the fdisk table for disk c3t0d0:

```
* /dev/rdsk/c3t0d0p0 default fdisk table
* Dimensions:
*   512 bytes/sector
*   63 sectors/track
*   255 tracks/cylinder
*   2088 cylinders
*
* systid:
*       1: DOSOS12
*       2: PCIXOS
*       4: DOSOS16
*       5: EXTDOS
*       6: DOSBIG
*       7: FDISK_IFS
```

```
*       8: FDISK_AIXBOOT
*       9: FDISK_AIXDATA
*      10: FDISK_OS2BOOT
*      11: FDISK_WINDOWS
*      12: FDISK_EXT_WIN
*      14: FDISK_FAT95
*      15: FDISK_EXTLBA
*      18: DIAGPART
*      65: FDISK_LINUX
*      82: FDISK_CPM
*      86: DOSDATA
*      98: OTHEROS
*      99: UNIXOS
*     100: FDISK_NOVELL2
*     101: FDISK_NOVELL3
*     119: FDISK_QNX4
*     120: FDISK_QNX42
*     121: FDISK_QNX43
*     130: SUNIXOS
*     131: FDISK_LINUXNAT
*     134: FDISK_NTFSVOL1
*     135: FDISK_NTFSVOL2
*     165: FDISK_BSD
*     167: FDISK_NEXTSTEP
*     183: FDISK_BSDIFS
*     184: FDISK_BSDISWAP
*     190: X86BOOT
*     191: SUNIXOS2
*     238: EFI_PMBR
*     239: EFI_FS

* Id  Act  Bhead  Bsect  Bcyl  Ehead  Esect  Ecyl  Rsect  Numsect
  191 128  0      1      1     254    63     1023  16065  33527655
  0   0    0      0      0     0      0      0     0      0
  0   0    0      0      0     0      0      0     0      0
  0   0    0      0      0     0      0      0     0      0
```

When there are multiple disks of the same type (manufacturer, model, size, and geometry) to be sliced, you can save time by copying the label from a source disk over to a target disk without going through all of the steps using the `format` utility. Use the `prtvtoc` command to get the partition table from the source disk (`c0t0d0`) and write the table to the target disk (`c0t1d0`) using the `fmthard` command as follows:

```
# prtvtoc /dev/rdsk/c0t0d0s2 | fmthard -s - /dev/rdsk/c0t1d0s2<cr>
```

Administering LUNs

Many modern Oracle Solaris systems are attached directly to an external Storage Area Network (SAN) device containing several disk drives. The drives in this storage device are configured as virtual drives, and each is referred to as a logical unit. Each logical unit is identified by a number, the logical unit number or LUN. The LUN is attached to the server through a Fibre Channel connection. These LUNs appear as disk drives, just like an internal disk, but the device name is different in that it contains the device's World Wide Name (WWN). Here's an example:

```
# format<cr>
Searching for disks ... done


AVAILABLE DISK SELECTIONS:
       0. c0t0d0 <SUN146G cyl 14087 alt 2 hd 24 sec 848>
          /pci@0,600000/pci@0/pci@8/pci@0/scsi@1/sd@0,0
       1. c0t1d0 <SUN146G cyl 14087 alt 2 hd 24 sec 848>
          /pci@0,600000/pci@0/pci@8/pci@0/scsi@1/sd@1,0
       2. c3t60A98000572D577465346D3936706348d0 <NETAPP-LUN-7330-200.00GB>
          /scsi_vhci/ssd@g60a98000572d577465346d3936706348
       3. c3t60A9800043346B74635A4F4371304A66d0 <NETAPP-LUN-7330-200.00GB>
          /scsi_vhci/ssd@g60a9800043346b74635a4f4371304a66
       4. c3t60A9800043346B74635A4F4370767969d0 <NETAPP-LUN-7330-200.00GB>
          /scsi_vhci/ssd@g60a9800043346b74635a4f4370767969
       5. c3t60A9800043346B7448344F4371543378d0 <NETAPP-LUN-7330-1.27TB>
          /scsi_vhci/ssd@g60a9800043346b7448344f4371543378
       6. c3t60A9800043346B7448344F4374437666d0 <NETAPP-LUN-7330-1.22TB>
          /scsi_vhci/ssd@g60a9800043346b7448344f4374437666
Specify disk (enter its number):
```

For disks 2–6, the WWN is in place of the target ID field. On a fiber-attached device, the WWN is a unique identifier used to uniquely identify each LUN in a Fibre Channel network. In the previous example, the server is connected to a NetApp data storage system connected via Fibre Channel. The LUNs were identified and dynamically configured during the boot process. They can be displayed using the `format` command as shown in the previous example.

Use the `luxadm` command to scan the devices and present a list of all LUNs and their logical names as follows:

```
# luxadm probe<cr>
No Network Array enclosures found in /dev/es

Found Fibre Channel device(s):
  Node WWN:500a0980894b97b6 Device Type:Disk device
    Logical Path:/dev/rdsk/c3t60A98000572D577465346D3936706348d0s2
  Node WWN:500a0980894b97b6 Device Type:Disk device
    Logical Path:/dev/rdsk/c3t60A9800043346B74635A4F4371304A66d0s2
  Node WWN:500a0980894b97b6 Device Type:Disk device
    Logical Path:/dev/rdsk/c3t60A9800043346B74635A4F4370767969d0s2
  Node WWN:500a0980894b97b6 Device Type:Disk device
    Logical Path:/dev/rdsk/c3t60A9800043346B7448344F4371543378d0s2
  Node WWN:500a0980894b97b6 Device Type:Disk device
    Logical Path:/dev/rdsk/c3t60A9800043346B7448344F4374437666d0s2
```

Choose a logical name and display information about each individual LUN as follows:

```
# luxadm display /dev/rdsk/c3t60A98000572D577465346D3936706348d0s2<cr>
DEVICE PROPERTIES for disk: /dev/rdsk/c3t60A98000572D577465346D3936706348d0s2
  Vendor:                 NETAPP
  Product ID:             LUN
```

```
   Revision:                  7330
   Serial Num:                W-Wte4m96pcH
   Unformatted capacity: 204800.000 MBytes
   Read Cache:                Enabled
     Minimum prefetch:        0x0
     Maximum prefetch:        0x0
   Device Type:               Disk device
   Path(s):

   /dev/rdsk/c3t60A98000572D577465346D3936706348d0s2
   /devices/scsi_vhci/ssd@g60a98000572d577465346d3936706348:c,raw
    Controller           /devices/pci@1,700000/SUNW,emlxs@0/fp@0,0
     Device Address                500a0981894b97b6,5
     Host controller port WWN      10000000c9729bb9
     Class                         primary
     State                         ONLINE
    Controller
 /devices/pci@0,600000/pci@0/pci@9/SUNW,emlxs@0/fp@0,0
     Device Address                 500a0981994b97b6,5
     Host controller port WWN       10000000c972a675
     Class                          secondary
     State                          ONLINE
```

Provide the information obtained from the `luxadm display` command to your storage administrator so that you create the file system on the correct LUN. It's very important that you select the correct LUN when more than one LUN is available.

The next step is to configure a file system on the LUN. I'll create a ZFS file system on the LUN as follows:

```
# zpool create pool1 c3t60A98000572D577465346D3936706348d0<cr>
```

For more information on creating file systems, refer to Chapter 5.

Summary

This chapter discussed administering storage devices and the various device drivers and device names used in Oracle Solaris 11. You must understand the device naming conventions used on both the SPARC-based and x86-based systems. I described the Oracle Solaris commands and utilities used to obtain information about these devices and drivers.

Device drivers are discussed in several chapters of this book because they are used in many aspects of the system administrator's job. Devices are referenced when we install and boot the OS, when creating and mounting file systems, when setting up printers, and in general troubleshooting of system problems. It is very important that you have a good understanding of how device drivers are configured and named in the Oracle Solaris operating environment.

Now that we've discussed devices, device and driver names, and disk slices, the next chapter will introduce the creation and administration of ZFS file systems.

5

Administering ZFS File Systems

Several file system types are available for configuring storage in Oracle Solaris, but ZFS is the default file system used in Oracle Solaris 11. Before Oracle Solaris 10, the traditional type of file system used for storing data in the Oracle Solaris environment was the UFS. The ZFS file system was introduced in Oracle Solaris 10, and now ZFS is the file system of choice in Oracle Solaris 10 and 11. ZFS is used on the boot drive and all storage drives, including SAN and network-attached storage (NAS) devices.

SVM volumes and UFSs can still be created and used in Oracle Solaris 11, but Oracle is recommending that system administrators migrate these file systems to ZFS.

My previous Oracle Solaris 10 administration books go into great detail on how to create and manage legacy UFSs on both disk slices and soft partitions using SVM. However, these file systems are more cumbersome to administer when compared to ZFS. I recommend that you try to migrate any of those file system types (UFS or SVM) to ZFS as quickly as possible, and I describe how to migrate these file systems in this chapter.

This chapter describes how to create and administer ZFS file systems. I will not be covering legacy UFSs or SVM in this book. For information on UFSs, refer to my book *Solaris 10 System Administration Exam Prep (Exam CX-310-200), Part I;* see the section titled "Manage File Systems" in Chapter 1. For information on UFS and SVM, refer to my book *Solaris 10 System Administration Exam Prep (Exam CX-310-202), Part II*, Chapter 3, "Managing Storage Volumes."

Introduction to ZFS

ZFS is a 128-bit file system that was introduced in the 6/06 update of Oracle Solaris 10 in June 2006. ZFS has been associated with “Zettabyte File System,” mainly because “Zetta” is one of the largest International System of Units (SI) prefixes. The name referred to the fact that ZFS could store 256 quadrillion zettabytes of data. Since then, we simply call it “ZFS,” and it is no longer an acronym for anything.

ZFS represents an entirely new approach to managing disk storage space. It revolutionizes the traditional file systems used in previous versions of Oracle Solaris, or UNIX for that matter. ZFS does not replace those traditional file systems, nor is it an improvement on that existing technology; rather, it is a fundamental new approach to data management. ZFS was designed to be more robust, more scalable, and easier to administer than traditional Oracle Solaris file systems.

With ZFS, all metadata is allocated dynamically, so there is no need to preallocate I-nodes or otherwise limit the scalability of the file system when it is first created. All of the algorithms were written with scalability in mind. Directories can have up to 256 trillion entries, and no limit exists on the number of file systems or the number of files that can be contained within a ZFS file system.

As you learn about ZFS, it’s best to try to forget everything you know about traditional file systems and volume management. ZFS is quite different and much easier to administer.

ZFS Storage Pools

With conventional file systems, we add disks to the system and then divide those disks into one or more file systems. As we add data to a file system, the file system begins to fill up. If we need more space, we manually allocate more space to that file system. Sometimes we allocate too much space to one file system while another file system fills up. To get more free disk space, we either add another disk or take away space from another file system. Taking away space from an existing file system typically requires backing up, destroying, and rebuilding the existing file system.

With ZFS, disk space is not allocated to a file system, much as we do not worry about allocating physical memory when we add dual inline memory modules (DIMMs) to a server. When I add RAM to a server, I don’t partition it and allocate the RAM to each application one chip at a time. I simply install the DIMMs and let the kernel manage it all. That is precisely what ZFS does to the disks installed on a server. ZFS has no slices, no file system consistency checks, and no initialization or mount procedures. There is just a pool of disks, and ZFS manages how the storage gets allocated.

ZFS uses storage pools, called “zpools,” to manage physical storage. Block devices (disks or disk slices) make up the zpool. Your server may have one or more zpools.

When I create a ZFS file system, I specify to which zpool the file system belongs. I do not, however, specify the size of the file system. The file system takes data blocks from the zpool as it needs the storage space. I can limit how much space the ZFS file system takes from the zpool, or I simply let ZFS use as much as it needs. When I run out of space in the zpool, I add another block device to increase the size of the zpool. ZFS allocates the space as it is needed. ZFS file systems can span multiple devices. However, ZFS differs from conventional file systems in that we do not need to allocate blocks of storage to each file system as it is created.

ZFS Is Self-Healing

ZFS is a transactional file system that ensures that data is always consistent. Traditional file systems simply overwrite old data as data changes. ZFS uses copy-on-write semantics, in which live data is never overwritten, and any sequence of operations is either entirely committed or entirely ignored. This mechanism ensures that the ZFS file system can never be corrupted through loss of power or a system crash. In addition, there is no need for an `fsck` equivalent. The most recently written pieces of data might be lost, but the file system itself is always consistent.

ZFS File System

The ZFS transactional file system should not be confused with file system journaling. The journaling process, which is used on traditional file systems, records an action in a separate journal. The journal can be replayed if a system crash occurs. The journaling process introduces unnecessary overhead, however, because the data needs to be written twice. This often results in a new set of problems, such as when the journal can't be replayed properly.

In a ZFS file system, a checksum is computed for every block to prevent silent data corruption.

What Is a Checksum?

A checksum is a value used to ensure that data is stored without error. It is derived by calculating the binary value in a block of data using a particular algorithm and storing the calculated results with the data. When data is retrieved, the checksum is recalculated and matched against the stored checksum. If the checksums are the same, the data has not changed. If the checksums are different, the data has been changed, corrupted, or tampered with.

Furthermore, in a replicated (mirrored or RAID) configuration, if one copy is damaged, ZFS detects it and uses another copy to repair it. In a mirrored ZFS file system, ZFS checksums each block as it is returned from disk. If there's a disparity between the 256-bit checksum and the block, ZFS terminates the request and pulls the block from the other member of the mirror set, matching the checksums and delivering the valid data to the application. In a subsequent operation, the bad block seen on the first disk is replaced with a good copy of the data from the redundant copy, essentially providing a continuous file system check-and-repair operation. Performance is not negatively affected on newer systems because performance is maintained by delegating a single core of a multicore CPU to perform the checksums.

Simplified Administration

ZFS greatly simplifies file system administration as compared with traditional file systems. The system administrator will find it easy to create and manage file systems without issuing multiple commands or editing configuration files.

Two main commands are used to administer ZFS: `zpool` for administering storage pools and `zfs` for administering ZFS file systems. Using these commands, you'll find it easy to mount file systems, set disk quotas, enable file compression, and manage numerous file systems with a single command. All of these tasks are described in this chapter.

ZFS Terms

Before I describe how to manage ZFS, Table 5-1 defines some terms that you will need to understand for this chapter.

The types of virtual devices that are used in ZFS are described in Table 5-2.

Table 5-1 ZFS Terminology

Term	Definition
Checksum	A 256-bit hash of the data in a file system block.
Clone	A file system with contents that are identical to the contents of a ZFS snapshot.
Dataset	A generic name for the following ZFS entities: clones, file systems, snapshots, and volumes. Each dataset is identified by a unique name in the ZFS namespace. Datasets are identified using the following format:
	`<pool>/<path>[@<snapshot>`
	`<pool>` is the name of the storage pool that contains the dataset.
	`<path>` is a slash-delimited pathname for the dataset object.
	[`<snapshot>`] is an optional component that identifies a snapshot of a dataset.
Default file system	A file system that is created by default when using Oracle Solaris Live Upgrade to migrate from UFS to a ZFS root file system. The current set of default file systems is `/`, `/usr`, `/opt`, and `/var`.

Term	Definition
ZFS file system	A ZFS dataset that is mounted within the standard system namespace and behaves like other traditional file systems.
zpool	ZFS storage pool. A collection of devices that provide physical storage and data replication for ZFS datasets.
resilvering	The process of transferring data from one device to another. For example, when a mirror component is taken offline and then later is put back online, the data from the up-to-date mirror component is copied to the newly restored mirror component. The process is also called "mirror resynchronization" in traditional volume management products.
shared file systems	The set of file systems that are shared between the alternate boot environment and the primary boot environment. This set includes file systems, such as `/export`, and the area reserved for swap. Shared file systems might also contain zone roots.
snapshot	A read-only image of a file system or volume at a given point in time.
vdev (virtual device)	A logical device in a pool, which can be a physical device, a file, or a collection of devices. See Table 5-2 for a list of vdevs.
volume	A dataset used to emulate a physical device. For example, you can create a ZFS volume as a swap device.

Table 5-2 Types of Virtual Devices (vdevs)

Virtual Device	Description
disk	A block device, typically located in `/dev/dsk`. The device can be a particular slice or whole disk.
file	A regular file. The use of files as a backing store is strongly discouraged.
mirror	A mirror of two or more devices. Data is replicated in an identical fashion across all components of a mirror.
raidz	A variation on RAID-5 that allows for better distribution of parity. raidz specifies a single-parity `raidz` group that can sustain one device failure without losing data.
raidz2	raidz2 specifies a double-parity `raidz` group that can sustain two device failures without losing data.
raidz3	raidz3 specifies a triple-parity `raidz` group that can sustain three device failures without losing data.
spare	A special pseudo-vdev that keeps track of available hot spares for a pool.
log	A separate-intent log device.
cache	A device used to cache storage pool data.

ZFS Hardware and Software Requirements

The system must meet the following requirements before ZFS can be used:

- The machine must be a SPARC or x86-based system that is running Oracle Solaris 10 6/06 release or newer. Any version of Oracle Solaris 11 supports ZFS.
- The minimum disk size that can be used in a ZFS environment is 128MB. The minimum amount of disk space for a storage pool is approximately 64MB.
- For good ZFS performance, at least 1GB or more of memory is recommended.
- Multiple controllers are recommended for a mirrored disk configuration, but this is not a requirement.

ZFS System Process

Each ZFS storage pool has an associated process named `zpool-`*<poolname>*. Each process contains the respective pool's I/O processing threads for handling I/O tasks such as compression and checksum validation. The process can be viewed using the `ps` command as follows:

```
# ps -ef|grep zpool<cr>
    root      5      0    0     Aug 05  ?          0:13 zpool-rpool
    root   5718   5575    0   16:32:07  pts/1      0:00 grep zpool
    root   5704      0    0   16:10:11  ?          0:00 zpool-pool1
```

The above example shows two processes—one for each storage pool that is configured on this system.

ZFS RAID Configurations

ZFS supports the following RAID configurations:

- RAID-0: Data is distributed across one or more disks with no redundancy. If a single disk fails, all data is lost.
- RAID-1: Also referred to as mirroring. This configuration requires at least two disks, preferably using two separate disk controllers. Two or more disks store exactly the same data, at the same time. Data is not lost as long as one mirror set survives.
- RAID-Z: A ZFS redundancy scheme uses a copy-on-write policy, rather than writing over old data. Using a dynamic stripe width, every block of data is its own RAID-Z stripe so that every write is a full stripe write. RAID-Z is similar to RAID-5, but RAID-Z eliminates a flaw in the RAID-5 scheme called the "RAID-5 write hole."

Creating a Storage Pool

The `zpool` command is used to create and manage zpools, and the `zpool` command is always used with a subcommand. The `zpool` subcommands are listed in Table 5-3.

Table 5-3 `zpool` Subcommands

Subcommand	Description
`-?`	Displays the list of subcommands.
`help`	Displays the list of subcommands.
`add`	Adds a virtual device to an existing zpool. Adds space to a storage spool.
`attach`	Attaches a new device to an existing zpool. Used for mirroring.
`clear`	Clears device errors in a zpool.
`create`	Creates a new zpool.
`destroy`	Destroys (remove) a zpool.
`detach`	Detaches a device or spare from a mirrored zpool.
`export`	Exports a zpool from a system. Used to move devices between systems.
`get`	Retrieves a list of properties for a specified zpool.
`history`	Displays the command history of the specified zpool or all zpools when a zpool is not specified.
`import`	Imports a zpool that has been previously exported.
`iostat`	Displays I/O statistics for the specified zpool or all zpools when a zpool is not specified.
`list`	Lists the given zpools along with a health status and space usage.
`offline`	Takes a device offline. No attempt is made to read or write to the device.
`online`	Restores an offline device back to online status.
`remove`	Removes a specified device from a zpool.
`replace`	Replaces an old device with a new device in a zpool.
`scrub`	Examines all data in the specified zpools to verify that it checksums correctly.
`set`	Sets a given property on the specified zpool.
`split`	Splits off one disk from each mirrored top-level vdev in a zpool and creates a new zpool from the split-off disks.
`status`	Displays the detailed health status for the given zpools.
`upgrade`	Identifies a zpool's version, which determines available pool features in the currently running software release. Also used to upgrade a specified zpool to the latest on-disk version.

ZFS Help

If you forget the subcommand for either the `zpool` or `zfs` command, use the `help` facility to display the available subcommands as follows:

```
# zpool help<cr>
The following commands are supported:
add       attach    clear     create    destroy   detach    export    get
help      history   import    iostat    list      offline   online
remove    replace   scrub     set       split     status    upgrade
For more info, run: zpool help <command>
```

You can also get help for each subcommand by typing `zpool help` *<subcommand>* as shown in the next example:

```
# zpool help create<cr>
usage:
        create [-f] [-n [-l]] [-B] [-o property=value] ...
            [-O file-system-property=value] ...
            [-m mountpoint] [-R root] <pool> <vdev> ...
```

List property information with the `-l` option. ZFS properties are described later in this chapter. I'll display all of the `zpool` properties as follows:

```
# zpool help -l properties<cr>
PROPERTY       EDIT      VALUES
allocated       NO       <size>
altroot        YES       <path>
autoexpand     YES       on | off
autoreplace    YES       on | off
bootfs         YES       <filesystem>
...<output has been truncated>...
```

The first step in creating a ZFS file system is to create the storage pool using the `zpool create` command. This command creates the pool and the top-level ZFS file system using an unused disk (`c2t1d0`):

```
# zpool create pool1 c2t1d0<cr>
```

Pool Terminology

The terms "storage pool," "zpool," and "pool" are used interchangeably. All three terms refer to a logical group of block devices describing the layout and physical characteristics of the available storage in a ZFS file system.

Choose an unused disk when creating a storage pool. Make sure that this disk is not being used in another storage pool, as a swap or dump device, or in any other volume manager. In the previous example, I created a RAID-0 zpool named `pool1` on a 72GB disk named `c2t1d0`. Notice that I did not specify a slice, so the entire 72GB disk is assigned to the zpool.

If the disk has an existing file system, you receive the following error:

```
invalid vdev specification
use '-f' to override the following errors:
/dev/dsk/c1t1d0s0 contains a ufs filesystem.
/dev/dsk/c1t1d0s2 contains a ufs filesystem.
```

To force the system to overwrite an existing file system, type the following:

```
# zpool create -f pool1 c2t1d0<cr>
```

If the disk is being used, an error similar to this will be displayed:

```
/dev/dsk/c2t1d0s0 is part of active ZFS pool pool1. Please see zpool(1M).
```

The system returns to the prompt if the `zpool create` command is successful.

When I issue the `df -h` command, I see that the following `/pool1` file system is ready for data:

```
# df -h<cr>
Filesystem                  Size   Used   Available  Capacity    Mounted on
rpool/ROOT/solaris           67G   1.7G         62G        3%    /
/devices                      0K     0K          0K        0%    /devices
/dev                          0K     0K          0K        0%    /dev
ctfs                          0K     0K          0K        0%    /system/contract
proc                          0K     0K          0K        0%    /proc
mnttab                        0K     0K          0K        0%    /etc/mnttab
swap                        3.1G   2.3M        3.1G        1%    /system/volatile
objfs                         0K     0K          0K        0%    /system/object
sharefs                       0K     0K          0K        0%    /etc/dfs/sharetab
fd                            0K     0K          0K        0%    /dev/fd
rpool/ROOT/solaris/var       67G   218M         62G        1%    /var
swap                        3.1G     0K        3.1G        0%    /tmp
rpool/export                 67G    32K         62G        1%    /export
rpool/export/home            67G    31K         62G        1%    /export/home
rpool                        67G    73K         62G        1%    /rpool
pool1                        67G    31K         67G        1%    /pool1
```

The previous `zpool create` command created a zpool named `pool1` and a ZFS file system in that pool, also named `pool1` with a mountpoint of `/pool1`. The `/pool1` directory should be empty or, better yet, must not exist before the storage pool is created. ZFS creates this directory automatically when the pool is created. As you can see, the /pool1 ZFS file system is mounted automatically after it is created. This is the parent (top-level) ZFS file system for this storage pool. This file system will be available and mounted after each reboot.

This type of storage pool is the simplest and is called a "dynamic stripe." It has no redundancy (RAID-0), and the stripe width is a single disk.

I could have created a dynamic stripe with more than one disk as follows:

```
# zpool create pool1 c2t1d0 c2t2d0<cr>
```

This would create a nonredundant striped storage pool, and the data would be striped across two 72GB drives and would provide better performance. It would also be twice the size at 144GB. Because there is no redundancy, if one drive fails, the entire storage pool and data are lost.

Creating a ZFS File System

The zfs command is used to create and manage ZFS file systems, and the zfs command is always used with a subcommand. The zfs subcommands are listed in Table 5-4.

Table 5-4 zfs Subcommands

Subcommand	Description
-?	Display a list of zfs subcommands.
help	Display a list of zfs subcommands.
allow	Delegate ZFS file system administration permission to nonprivileged users.
clone	Create a clone of a ZFS snapshot.
create	Create a new ZFS file system.
destroy	Destroy (remove) a ZFS file system.
diff	Display a description of the differences between a ZFS snapshot and a descendant dataset.
get	Display the properties for a dataset.
groupspace	Display space consumed by, and quotas on, each group in the specified file system or snapshot.
hold	Place a hold on a ZFS snapshot. If a hold exists on a snapshot, attempt to destroy that snapshot using the zfs destroy command return EBUSY.
holds	List holds that have been placed on a given snapshot.

Subcommand	Description
inherit	Clear the specified ZFS property, causing it to be inherited from an ancestor.
key	Used to manage the wrapping key for an encrypted dataset. See the section titled "Encrypting ZFS File Systems" later in this chapter.
list	List the property information for a given dataset.
mount	Mount ZFS file systems. Also used to display mounted ZFS file systems.
promote	Promote a clone ZFS file system to no longer be dependent on its origin snapshot.
receive	Used to receive a ZFS snapshot stream that was created with `zfs send`. Create a snapshot whose contents are as specified in the stream provided on standard input.
release	Remove a hold that was placed on a ZFS dataset.
rename	Rename a dataset.
rollback	Roll back a specified dataset to a previous snapshot.
send	Create a snapshot stream (backup file) of a snapshot.
set	Set a property value on a given dataset.
share	Share a ZFS file system for NFS or SMB.
snapshot	Create a snapshot of a dataset.
unallow	Revoke ZFS file system administrative permission for nonprivileged users.
unmounts	Unmount currently mounted ZFS file systems.
unshare	Remove an NFS or SMB share for a ZFS file system.
upgrade	Upgrade a ZFS file system to a new version of ZFS. Also used to verify the version of a ZFS file system.
userspace	Display space consumed by, and quotas on, each user in the specified ZFS file system or snapshot.

If you forget the subcommand for the `zfs` command, use the `help` facility to display the available subcommands as follows:

```
# zfs help<cr>

The following commands are supported:
allow       clone     create     destroy     diff      get
groupspace  help      hold       holds       inherit   key
list        mount     promote    receive     release   rename
rollback    send      set        share       snapshot  unallow
unmount     unshare   upgrade    userspace
For more info, run: zfs help <command>
```

Get help on a subcommand by adding the subcommand after `help`. For example, to get help on the `create` subcommand, type

```
# zfs help create<cr>
usage:
  create [-p] [-o property=value] ... <filesystem>
  create [-ps] [-b blocksize] [-o property=value] ... -V <size> <volume>
```

List all of the ZFS file system properties using the `-l` option as follows:

```
# zfs help -l properties<cr>
PROPERTY          EDIT       INHERIT        VALUES
aclmode           YES            YES        discard | mask | passthrough
atime             YES            YES        on | off
available          NO             NO        <size>
...<output has been truncated>...
```

In the previous section, I created the storage pool named `pool1`, and the top level ZFS file system `/pool1` was automatically created. The `pool1` pool is 67GB, the entire size of the 72GB disk (minus 5GB for overhead). The `/pool1` file system has access to all 67GB available in the storage pool. The file system will be mounted automatically at bootup by SMF through the `svc:/system/filesystem/local:default` service instance.

`/etc/vfstab` File

If you've used the `/etc/vfstab` file in previous versions of Oracle Solaris to manage file system mountpoints at bootup, you do not need to make an entry in this file for ZFS file systems.

Now, I'll create another ZFS file system in the same storage pool as follows:

```
# zfs create pool1/data<cr>
```

I've just created a ZFS file system named `/pool1/data` in the `pool1` storage pool. The new file system is called a descendant of the /`pool1` file system; /`pool1` is its parent file system. This file system will be available and mounted after each reboot.

A `df -h` command shows the following information:

```
<df output has been truncated>
pool1                        67G    32K   67G   1%        /pool1
pool1/data                   67G    31K   67G   1%        /pool1/data
```

Again, the /pool1/data file system has 67GB available. The descendant file system also has access to all the space in the zpool. Now, I'll create a 1GB file in the /pool1/data file system:

```
# mkfile 1g /pool1/data/largefile<cr>
```

The df -h command displays the following storage information for each of the ZFS file systems:

```
<df output has been truncated>
pool1                       67G    32K   66G   1%        /pool1
pool1/data                  67G    788M  66G   2%        /pool1/data
```

Notice how the available space has decreased for each file system. The output shows that the pool1/data file system is using 788MB of disk space, and pool1 is using only 32K. The overall available space in the storage pool has decreased to 66GB. As each file system uses space, the available space decreases for the entire storage pool.

Using the Whole Disk in a Storage Pool

Although using the entire disk c0t0d0 for the storage pool is recommended, you can also create a storage pool from a portion of a disk—a disk slice—and not use the entire disk. For example, when creating a bootable ZFS root pool, the root pool must be constructed from a disk slice and not the entire disk. This is probably the only time you will use a disk slice instead of the entire disk. With ZFS, when specifying the entire disk for the storage pool as follows:

```
# zpool create pool1 c0t0d0<cr>
```

ZFS automatically formats the disk with an EFI label. EFI and SMI disk labels are described in Chapter 4, "Administering Storage Devices."

Here's the disk partition table before the zpool create command:

```
Part          Tag    Flag     Cylinders         Size            Blocks
  0    unassigned    wm        0 -  7006     34.00GB    (7007/0/0)    71303232
  1    unassigned    wu     7007 - 14086     34.35GB    (7080/0/0)    72046080
  2        backup    wu        0 - 14086     68.35GB    (14087/0/0)  143349312
  3    unassigned    wm        0              0         (0/0/0)              0
  4    unassigned    wm        0              0         (0/0/0)              0
  5    unassigned    wm        0              0         (0/0/0)              0
  6           usr    wm        0              0         (0/0/0)              0
  7    unassigned    wm        0              0         (0/0/0)              0
```

Notice that it has an SMI disk label. Now, here's the disk partition table after the `zpool create` command:

```
Part          Tag          Flag      First Sector       Size        Last Sector
  0           usr           wm                256    68.36GB          143358320
  1    unassigned           wm                  0          0                  0
  2    unassigned           wm                  0          0                  0
  3    unassigned           wm                  0          0                  0
  4    unassigned           wm                  0          0                  0
  5    unassigned           wm                  0          0                  0
  6    unassigned           wm                  0          0                  0
  8      reserved           wm          143358321     8.00MB          143374704
```

Notice that the disk has been reformatted with an EFI disk label. The pool can be listed as follows:

```
# zpool list pool1<cr>
NAME  SIZE  ALLOC   FREE  CAP  DEDUP  HEALTH  ALTROOT
pool1 68G    85K  68.0G   0%  1.00x  ONLINE  -
```

The storage pool is using the entire disk.

Using a Disk Slice in a Storage Pool

When using a disk slice to create the storage pool, you'll specify the disk (`c0t0d0`) and the disk slice (`s0`) as follows:

```
# zpool create pool1 c0t0d0s0<cr>
```

The disk retains its current disk label and partition table.

In the next example, I have a 73GB disk (`c2t1d0`) that is sliced as follows:

```
Part          Tag      Flag     Cylinders         Size            Blocks
  0    unassigned       wm       0 -  7006      34.00GB    (7007/0/0)     71303232
  1    unassigned       wu    7007 - 14086      34.35GB    (7080/0/0)     72046080
  2        backup       wu       0 - 14086      68.35GB    (14087/0/0)   143349312
  3    unassigned       wm       0               0         (0/0/0)              0
  4    unassigned       wm       0               0         (0/0/0)              0
  5    unassigned       wm       0               0         (0/0/0)              0
  6           usr       wm       0               0         (0/0/0)              0
  7    unassigned       wm       0               0         (0/0/0)              0
```

The `c2t1d0` disk has two slices. Slice 0 is 34GB, and slice 1 is 34.35GB. I'll use slice 0 for my storage pool as follows:

```
# zpool create pool1 c2t1d0s0<cr>
```

Here's the disk partition table after the zpool create command:

```
Part      Tag        Flag     Cylinders       Size            Blocks
  0  unassigned       wm       0 -  7006     34.00GB    (7007/0/0)     71303232
  1  unassigned       wu    7007 - 14086     34.35GB    (7080/0/0)     72046080
  2      backup       wu       0 - 14086     68.35GB    (14087/0/0)   143349312
  3  unassigned       wm       0              0         (0/0/0)               0
  4  unassigned       wm       0              0         (0/0/0)               0
  5  unassigned       wm       0              0         (0/0/0)               0
  6         usr       wm       0              0         (0/0/0)               0
  7  unassigned       wm       0              0         (0/0/0)               0
```

The disk is unchanged. Notice that it has retained its SMI disk label and partition table. The pool can now be listed as follows:

```
# zpool list<cr>
NAME    SIZE  ALLOC   FREE  CAP  DEDUP  HEALTH  ALTROOT
pool1  33.8G    85K  33.7G   0%  1.00x  ONLINE  -
rpool    68G  4.87G  63.1G   7%  1.00x  ONLINE  -
```

pool1 is 33.8GB, slightly less than the 34GB disk slice because a small portion is used for ZFS metadata.

For the root data pool, we typically use a slice that represents the entire disk as shown with slice 0 in the following example:

```
Part      Tag    Flag  Cylinders      Size          Blocks
  0        root   wm     1 - 14086   68.35GB   (14086/0/0) 143339136
  1  unassigned   wm     0            0        (0/0/0)             0
  2      backup   wu     0 - 14086   68.35GB   (14087/0/0) 143349312
  3  unassigned   wm     0            0        (0/0/0)             0
  4  unassigned   wm     0            0        (0/0/0)             0
  5  unassigned   wm     0            0        (0/0/0)             0
  6  unassigned   wm     0            0        (0/0/0)             0
  7  unassigned   wm     0            0        (0/0/0)             0
```

We do this so that the disk retains its SMI label, yet we are still able to use the entire disk for our root storage pool.

With the examples I've shown, I've provided quick and easy methods to create a ZFS file system. However, you may want more control over the hierarchy of the file systems, which I'll describe later.

Dry Run of Storage Pool and File System Creation

The zpool and zfs commands include the -n option, which allows a "dry run" of the command without performing the operation. The configuration is displayed without actually creating or modifying the system. For example, to perform a dry run of a `zpool create` operation, type

```
# zpool create -n pool1 c3t8d0 c3t9d0<cr>
```

The system displays the following message:

```
would create 'pool1' with the following layout:

  pool1
    c3t8d0
    c3t9d0

but with no redundancy; failure of one device will cause loss of the pool
```

Renaming a ZFS File System

You can rename a ZFS file system using the `zfs rename` command. In the following example, the `zfs rename` command is used to rename the `pool1/data` file system to `pool1/documents`:

```
# zfs rename pool1/data pool1/documents<cr>
```

To rename a file system, the file system must be inactive so that the file system can be unmounted and remounted. If the file system is busy, you will receive a message as follows:

```
cannot unmount '/pool1/data': Device busy
```

and the operation will not be performed. Refer to the `fuser` command described below to determine what user or process may be using the file system.

Listing ZFS File Systems and Storage Pools

It's important to understand how to retrieve information about the ZFS storage pools and file systems that exist on your system. You'll need to understand how to list storage pools and file systems as well as how to view the status of these components.

Displaying ZFS Storage Pool Information

You can display status information about the usage, I/O statistics, and health of your ZFS pools using the `zpool list` and `zpool status` commands. To display basic status information about all the storage pools installed on the system, type the following command:

```
# zpool list<cr>
```

The system displays the following:

```
NAME    SIZE   USED  AVAIL   CAP  HEALTH  ALTROOT
pool1  9.94G   112K  9.94G    0%  ONLINE  -
pool2  4.97G   111K  4.97G    0%  ONLINE  -
rpool  17.9G  4.27G  13.6G   23%  ONLINE  -
```

To display information about a specific pool, specify the pool name:

```
# zpool list pool1<cr>
NAME    SIZE  USED  AVAIL   CAP  HEALTH  ALTROOT
pool1  9.94G  112K  9.94G    0%  ONLINE  -
```

The information displayed includes the following:

- NAME: The pool's name.
- SIZE: The pool's total size of all top-level virtual devices.
- USED: The amount of space allocated by all the datasets.
- AVAILABLE: The unallocated space in the pool.
- CAPACITY: The space used, calculated as a percentage of total space.
- HEALTH: The pool's current health status.
- ALTROOT: The alternate root of the pool if an alternate exists. Alternate root pools are used with removable media, where users typically want a single-file system, and they want it mounted wherever they choose. Alternate pools are also used when importing a pool under a temporary directory while repairs are being made. An alternate root pool is created using the `-R` option.

`zpool list` shows the following information:

```
# zpool list<cr>
NAME  SIZE  ALLOC   FREE  CAP   DEDUP  HEALTH  ALTROOT
pool1  68G   120K  68.0G   0%   1.00x  ONLINE  -
rpool  68G  4.87G  63.1G   7%   1.00x  ONLINE  -
#
```

Instruct the system to display only specific information about the pool:

```
# zpool list -o name,size pool1<cr>
```

No Spaces between Options

Notice that there are no spaces between the comma-separated list of options.

The system displays only the name and the total size for `pool1`:

```
NAME    SIZE
pool1  9.94G
```

The following storage pool I/O statistics can also be displayed for each pool:

- USED CAPACITY: The amount of data currently stored in the pool or device
- AVAILABLE CAPACITY: The amount of space available in the pool or device
- READ OPERATIONS: The number of read I/O operations sent to the pool or device
- WRITE OPERATIONS: The number of write I/O operations sent to the pool or device
- READ BANDWIDTH: The bandwidth of all read operations (including metadata), expressed as units per second
- WRITE BANDWIDTH: The bandwidth of all write operations, expressed as units per second

Use the following command to list all the I/O statistics for each storage pool:

```
# zpool iostat<cr>
```

The system displays the following:

```
                 capacity      operations       bandwidth
pool          used    avail    read  write      read   write
------  ---  ---   --- ---     ---  ---
pool1         112K    9.94G       0      0       240   2.23K
pool2         111K    4.97G       0      0         0     270
rpool        4.27G    13.6G       2      1      183K   16.9K
------  ---  ---   --- ---     ---  ---
```

All of the statistics displayed are cumulative since the system was booted. It's best to specify an interval with the zpool command, where the first line of output is cumulative and the next lines represent activity since the previous stat. The following command displays current stats every 2 seconds until *Ctrl+C* is pressed:

```
# zpool iostat pool1 2<cr>
```

The system displays the following:

```
               capacity    operations      bandwidth
pool         used  avail  read   write   read   write
-----   ---  ---  ---  ---  ---  ---
pool1        112K  9.94G     0       0    204   1.90K
pool1        112K  9.94G     0       0      0       0
pool1        112K  9.94G     0       0      0       0
pool1        112K  9.94G     0       0      0       0
<Ctrl+C>
#
```

Last, view the health of the storage pools and devices using the zpool status command. The health of the storage pool is determined by the health of the devices that make up the pool. Use the zpool status command to obtain the health information:

```
# zpool status<cr>
```

The system displays the following:

```
  pool: pool1
 state: ONLINE
 scrub: none requested
config:
        NAME        STATE     READ WRITE CKSUM
        pool1       ONLINE       0     0     0
          c2t2d0    ONLINE       0     0     0
          c2t3d0    ONLINE       0     0     0
errors: No known data errors
```

The following two options are available with the zpool status command:

- The -v option displays verbose output. The default is to display verbose output.

- The -x option can be used to display only the status of pools that are exhibiting errors or are otherwise unavailable:

```
# zpool status -x<cr>
all pools are healthy
```

- The health status of each device falls into one of the following states:
  - ONLINE: The device is normal and in good working order. In this state, it's possible for some transient errors to still occur.
  - DEGRADED: The virtual device has experienced a failure, but the device can still function. This state is most common when a mirror or RAID-Z device has lost one or more constituent devices. The pool's fault tolerance might be compromised because a subsequent fault in another device might be unrecoverable.
  - FAULTED: The virtual device is inaccessible due to a total failure. ZFS is incapable of sending data to it or receiving data from it. If a top-level virtual device is in this state, the pool is inaccessible.
  - OFFLINE: The administrator has taken the virtual device offline.
  - UNAVAILABLE: The device or virtual device cannot be opened. In some cases, pools with UNAVAILABLE devices appear in DEGRADED mode. If a top-level virtual device is UNAVAILABLE, nothing in the pool can be accessed.
  - REMOVED: The device was physically removed while the system was running. Device removal detection is hardware dependent and might not be supported on all platforms.

The health of the storage pool is determined by the health of all its top-level virtual devices. If all virtual devices are ONLINE, the storage pool is ONLINE. If a virtual device is FAULTED, the pool is also FAULTED.

The following example displays the health status of a storage pool with a failed disk drive:

```
# zpool status -x<cr>
  pool: pool1
 state: DEGRADED
status: One or more devices could not be opened. Sufficient replicas exist
for the pool to continue functioning in a degraded state.
action: Attach the missing device and online it using 'zpool online'.
   see: http://www.sun.com/msg/ZFS-8000-2Q
 scrub: none requested
config:
```

```
        NAME          STATE         READ   WRITE CKSUM
        pool1         DEGRADED         0       0     0
        c2t2d0        ONLINE           0       0     0
        c2t3d0        UNAVAIL          0       0     0  cannot open

errors: No known data errors
```

Notice the link displayed in the output. This link (`www.sun.com/msg/ZFS-8000-2Q`) points to an online article at Oracle's Web site to visit for more information. It provides up-to-date information on the problem and describes the best recovery procedure.

Listing ZFS File Systems

List all the active ZFS file systems and volumes on a system using the `zfs list` command:

```
# zfs list<cr>
```

All the file systems and volumes on this particular system are displayed:

```
NAME                       USED  AVAIL  REFER  MOUNTPOINT
pool1                     1.00G  65.9G    32K  /pool1
pool1/documents           1.00G  65.9G  1.00G  /pool1/documents
rpool                     4.96G  62.0G  73.5K  /rpool
rpool/ROOT                1.93G  62.0G    31K  legacy
rpool/ROOT/solaris        1.93G  62.0G  1.71G  /
rpool/ROOT/solaris/var     221M  62.0G   219M  /var
rpool/dump                2.00G  62.0G  1.94G  -
rpool/export               63K  62.0G    32K  /export
rpool/export/home          31K  62.0G    31K  /export/home
rpool/swap                1.03G  62.0G  1.00G  -
```

The information displayed includes the following:

- NAME: The name of the dataset.
- USED: The amount of space consumed by the dataset and all its descendants.
- AVAIL: The amount of space available to the dataset and all its children. This space is shared with all the datasets within that pool. The space can be limited by quotas and other datasets within that pool.
- REFER: The amount of data accessible by this dataset, which might or might not be shared with other datasets in the pool.
- MOUNTPOINT: The mountpoint used by this file system. If the value is legacy, the file system is mounted manually using the `mount` command.

To recursively list only the datasets in the pool1 storage pool, use the -r option followed by the pool name:

```
# zfs list -r pool1<cr>
NAME              USED  AVAIL  REFER  MOUNTPOINT
pool1            1.00G  65.9G    32K  /pool1
pool1/documents  1.00G  65.9G  1.00G  /pool1/documents
```

ZFS Versions

ZFS has gone through several versions since being introduced in Oracle Solaris 10. As of this writing, ZFS is at version 5. Through each version, new enhancements have been added to ZFS storage pools and file systems. Therefore, ZFS storage pools and ZFS file systems each have their own versioning scheme.

Upgrading the OS does not necessarily update the versions of ZFS. This is a manual process that is completed using the zfs upgrade and zpool upgrade commands. Even though your system is running Oracle Solaris 11, a storage pool or file system that was originally created on Oracle Solaris 10 may actually still be running an old version of ZFS.

Display the version of ZFS for all storage pools using the zpool upgrade command as follows:

```
# zpool upgrade<cr>
This system is currently running ZFS pool version 33.

All pools are formatted using this version.
```

Use the -v option to display all of the previously supported versions of ZFS with an explanation of the features that are provided at each version:

```
# zpool upgrade -v<cr>
This system is currently running ZFS pool version 33.

The following versions are supported:

VER  DESCRIPTION
---  --------------------------------------------------------
 1   Initial ZFS version
 2   Ditto blocks (replicated metadata)
 3   Hot spares and double parity RAID-Z
 4   zpool history
 5   Compression using the gzip algorithm
 6   bootfs pool property
 7   Separate intent log devices
 8   Delegated administration
 9   refquota and refreservation properties
 10  Cache devices
 11  Improved scrub performance
```

```
 12  Snapshot properties
 13  snapused property
 14  passthrough-x aclinherit
 15  user/group space accounting
 16  stmf property support
 17  Triple-parity RAID-Z
 18  Snapshot user holds
 19  Log device removal
 20  Compression using zle (zero-length encoding)
 21  Deduplication
 22  Received properties
 23  Slim ZIL
 24  System attributes
 25  Improved scrub stats
 26  Improved snapshot deletion performance
 27  Improved snapshot creation performance
 28  Multiple vdev replacements
 29  RAID-Z/mirror hybrid allocator
 30  Encryption
 31  Improved 'zfs list' performance
 32  One MB blocksize
 33  Improved share support
```

Display the version of ZFS for all ZFS file systems using the `zfs upgrade` command as follows:

```
# zfs upgrade<cr>
This system is currently running ZFS filesystem version 5.
All filesystems are formatted with the current version.
```

Use the `-v` option to display all of the previously supported versions of ZFS with an explanation of the features that are provided at each version:

```
# zfs upgrade -v<cr>
The following filesystem versions are supported:

VER DESCRIPTION
--- --------------------------------------------------------
1   Initial ZFS filesystem version
2   Enhanced directory entries
3   Case insensitive and SMB credentials support
4   userquota, groupquota properties
5   System attributes
```

If you have ZFS storage pools from a previous Oracle Solaris release, you can upgrade your pools with the `zpool upgrade` command to take advantage of the pool features in the current release. In addition, the `zpool status` command notifies you when your pools are running older versions. For example:

```
# zpool status pool1<cr>
  pool: pool1
 state: ONLINE
status: The pool is formatted using an older on-disk format.  The pool can
        still be used, but some features are unavailable.
action: Upgrade the pool using 'zpool upgrade'.  Once this is done, the
        pool will no longer be accessible on older software versions.
        scrub: none requested
config:
```

```
        NAME        STATE     READ WRITE CKSUM
        pool1       ONLINE       0     0     0
          mirror-0  ONLINE       0     0     0
            c3t7d0  ONLINE       0     0     0
            c3t8d0  ONLINE       0     0     0
errors: No known data errors
```

Use the `zpool upgrade` command to upgrade the pool as follows:

```
# zpool upgrade pool1<cr>
```

To upgrade all of the pools on the system, type

```
# zpool upgrade -a<cr>
```

If your system has ZFS file systems from a previous Oracle Solaris release, you can upgrade the file systems with the `zfs upgrade` command. For example, to upgrade the `/pool1/docs` file system to the current version, type

```
# zfs upgrade pool1/docs<cr>
```

To upgrade all of the ZFS file systems on the system, type

```
# zfs upgrade -a<cr>
```

ZFS Components

The following are considered ZFS components:

- Disks
- Files
- Virtual devices

Follow these rules when naming ZFS components:

- Empty components are not permitted.
- Each component can contain only alphanumeric characters in addition to the following:
  - Underscore (_)
  - Hyphen (-)

- Colon (:)
- Period (.)

- Pool names must begin with a letter, except for the following restrictions:
  - The beginning sequence c[0-9] is not allowed.
  - The name "log" is reserved and cannot be used.
  - A name that begins with "mirror", "raidz", "raidz1", "raidz2", "raidz3", or "spare" is not allowed because these names are reserved.
  - Pool names cannot begin with a percent sign (%).
- Dataset names must begin with an alphanumeric character.
- Dataset names must not contain a percent sign (%).

Using Disks in a ZFS Storage Pool

The most basic element in a storage pool is a physical storage device, which can be either a disk or a slice on a disk. The only requirement is that the device must be at least 128MB in size.

It is recommended that an entire disk be allocated to a storage pool. Although disk slices can be used in storage pools, it makes administration more difficult, and performance could be adversely affected. When using an entire disk for ZFS, there is no need to format the disk. ZFS formats the disk for you using an EFI disk label, and slice 0 encompasses the entire disk.

For a bootable ZFS root pool, the disks in the pool must contain slices and must be labeled with an SMI label. The exception is for an x86-based system. Beginning with Oracle Solaris 11.1, a boot disk on an x86-based system may contain an EFI label. I describe this in detail later in this chapter in the section titled "The ZFS Root File System." On the SPARC platform, when slicing the boot disk, it's best to allocate the entire disk capacity to slice zero and use that slice for the root pool.

For more information on disk slices and disk labels, refer to Chapter 4.

Using Files in a ZFS Storage Pool

You can use UFS files as virtual devices in your ZFS storage pool. Use this feature for testing purposes only because any use of files relies on the underlying file system for consistency. If you create a ZFS pool backed by files on a UFS, you are relying on UFS to guarantee correctness and synchronous semantics and not fully using the benefits of ZFS.

I'll create a ZFS pool on a file located in a UFS when I don't have any physical devices; I'll do this strictly for testing purposes. In the following steps, I'll create a ZFS pool in a UFS file.

1. Use the `mkfile` command to create an empty file in the `/export/home` file system. I'll use the `-n` option, which only "reserves" the space and does not actually allocate disk blocks to the file system until data is written to the file:

```
# mkfile -n 200m /export/home/zfsfile<cr>
```

2. Create a ZFS pool and file system named "tempzfs" on the UFS file:

```
# zpool create tempzfs /export/home/zfsfile<cr>
```

3. Verify the status of the new pool:

```
# zpool status -v tempzfs<cr>
```

The system displays the following information:

```
  pool: tempzfs
 state: ONLINE
 scrub: none requested
config:

        NAME                    STATE     READ WRITE CKSUM
        tempzfs                 ONLINE       0     0     0
          /export/home/zfsfile  ONLINE       0     0     0

errors: No known data errors
```

Encrypting ZFS File Systems

ZFS file systems can be encrypted to protect data. The data in the file system is encoded for privacy, and a key is needed by the data owner to access the protected data. A few points to be aware of regarding ZFS encryption are as follows:

- ZFS encryption requires that the zpool is at version 30 or higher. Verify the version of your zpool by typing # **`zpool upgrade -v<cr>`**.
- Specific file systems within the pool can be encrypted, allowing other file systems within the same pool to be unencrypted.

- ZFS encryption is inheritable to descendant file systems.
- The root file system cannot be encrypted.
- Data is encrypted using Advanced Encryption Standard (AES) with key lengths of 128, 192, and 256 in the Counter with Cipher Block Chaining Message Authentication Code (CCM) and Galois/Counter Mode (GCM) operation modes. The encryption policy is set when the ZFS file system is created and cannot be changed.
- The default encryption policy is aes-128-ccm and is set to prompt for a passphrase, which must be a minimum of eight characters in length.

Create an Encrypted ZFS File System

The following creates an encrypted file system and sets the passphrase to "secretword":

```
# zfs create -o encryption=on pool1/protect<cr>
Enter passphrase for 'pool1/protect': <type passphrase>
Enter again: <type passphrase>
```

Confirm the file system encryption by typing

```
# zfs get encryption pool1/protect<cr>
NAME          PROPERTY    VALUE     SOURCE
pool1/protect encryption  on        local
```

The following properties were set when the encrypted file system was created (viewed using the `zfs get all` command):

```
pool1/protect  encryption   on                    local
pool1/protect  keysource    passphrase,prompt     local
pool1/protect  keystatus    available             -
pool1/protect  rekeydate    Wed Jan 23  9:03 2013 local
```

A "wrapping key" is used to encrypt the actual data encryption keys. The wrapping key is passed from the ZFS command when the file system was created. A wrapping key is either in a file or is derived from a passphrase. In the previous example, the key was derived from a passphrase and can be verified by viewing the `keysource` property.

Passphrase Keysource

When a file system's `keysource` property value is `passphrase`, then the wrapping key is derived from the passphrase using PKCS#5 PBKD2 and a per-file system randomly generated salt. This means that the same passphrase generates a different wrapping key if used on descendant file systems.

To mount an encrypted file system at boot time that has an encryption policy set to `passphrase,prompt`, you will need to either:

- Explicitly mount it after the system boots with the `zfs mount` command and specify the passphrase as follows:

```
# zfs mount pool1/protect<cr>
Enter passphrase for 'pool1/protect': <enter passphrase>
```

- Or use the `zfs key - l` command to be prompted for the key after the system is booted and then mount the file system as follows:

```
# zfs key -l pool1/protect<cr>
Enter passphrase for 'pool1/protect': <enter passphrase>
# zfs mount pool1/protect<cr>
```

Change the `keysource` Property

You can set the `keysource` property when creating the ZFS file system to change it from a passphrase to a wrapping key stored in an encrypted file. This way the key will be available during the boot process and the file system will automatically be mounted.

Follow these steps to create a new encrypted ZFS file system that will use a 256-bit AES raw key stored in a file named `/zfskey`:

1. Use the `pktool` utility to generate a 256-bit AES raw key in a `keystore` file named `/zfskey` as follows:

```
# pktool genkey keystore=file outkey=/zfskey keytype=aes keylen=256<cr>
```

2. Create an encrypted ZFS file system named `pool1/bcalkins` and specify the aes-256-ccm encryption algorithm and the key that was generated in the previous step:

```
# zfs create -o encryption=aes-256-ccm -o keysource=raw,file:///zfskey pool1/
bcalkins<cr>
```

3. Verify the file system encryption properties as follows:

```
# zfs get encryption pool1/bcalkins<cr>
NAME             PROPERTY     VALUE          SOURCE
pool1/bcalkins   encryption   aes-256-ccm    local
```

```
# zfs get keysource pool1/bcalkins<cr>
NAME            PROPERTY   VALUE               SOURCE
pool1/bcalkins keysource  raw,file:///zfskey  local
```

For more information on ZFS encryption, refer to the `zfs_encrypt(1M)` man page.

Removing a ZFS File System

Use the `zfs destroy` command to remove a ZFS file system. Understand that destroying a file system or a storage pool does not actually wipe the data from the drive. It simply removes references to the blocks of data. The only way to ensure that the data is inaccessible on a fileset that has been destroyed is to encrypt the data on that fileset and then throw away the matching key. ZFS data encryption is not described in this chapter.

Destroying Data

The `zfs destroy` and `zpool destroy` commands destroy data. You receive no confirmation prompt after the command is executed. Make certain that you are destroying the correct file system or storage pool. If you accidentally destroy the wrong file system or pool, you'll lose data. You can attempt to recover the pool using `zpool import`, but you risk losing all the data in that pool.

I'll use the `zfs destroy` command to remove the `/pool1/documents` file system created earlier:

```
# zfs destroy pool1/documents<cr>
```

Destroying a file system can fail for the following reasons:

- The file system is in use and busy.
  When a file system is busy, you can forcibly remove it using the `-f` option. In the following example, I forcibly remove the `pool1/documents` file system:

```
# zfs destroy -f pool1/documents<cr>
```

The -f Option

Use the `-f` option with caution because it will unmount, unshare, and destroy active file systems, causing unexpected application behavior. Use the `fuser` command described later in this section to determine which user or process is using the file system and causing it to be in a busy state.

- The file system has children. In other words, it is a parent file system, and other ZFS file systems are created under it:

```
pool1            33G  20K  33G  1%  /pool1
pool1/data       33G  19K  33G  1%  /pool1/data
pool1/data/app1  33G  18K  33G  1%  /pool1/data/app1
pool1/data/app2  33G  18K  33G  1%  /pool1/data/app2
```

  For a ZFS file system with children, use the `-r` option to recursively destroy the parent file system named `pool1/data` and all its descendants:

```
# zfs destroy -r pool1/data<cr>
```

- The ZFS file system has indirect dependents such as clones or snapshots associated with it.

  Use the `-R` option to destroy a file system and all its dependents, but use extreme caution when using this option. You receive no confirmation prompt, and you could remove dependents that you did not know existed. In the following example, I'll remove the file system named `pool1/data` and all its dependents:

```
# zfs destroy -R pool1/data<cr>
```

Object Sets

ZFS supports hierarchically structured object sets—object sets within other object sets. A child dataset is dependent on the existence of its parent. A parent cannot be destroyed without first destroying all children. The `-R` option to the `zfs destroy` command overrides this and automatically removes the parent and its children.

You can view a dataset's dependencies by looking at the properties for that particular dataset. For example, the `origin` property for a ZFS clone displays a dependency between the clone and the snapshot. The `zfs destroy` command lists any dependencies, as shown in the example when I try to destroy the `pool1/data@today` snapshot:

```
# zfs destroy pool1/data@today<cr>
cannot destroy 'pool1/data@today': snapshot has dependent clones
use '-R' to destroy the following datasets:
pool1/clone
```

The `fuser` Command

A file system is considered busy if a user is in a directory in the file system or if a program has a file open in that file system. If something is causing the file system to be busy, you can use the fuser command to list all of the processes that are accessing the file system and to stop them if necessary.

The syntax for fuser is as follows:

```
/usr/sbin/fuser [options] <file>|<file system>
```

Replace <file> with the filename you are checking, or replace <file system> with the name of the file system you are checking. The options that can be used with the fuser command are listed in Table 5-5.

The following example uses the fuser command to find out why /pool1/data is busy:

```
# fuser -cu /pool1/data<cr>
```

The system displays each process and user login name that is using this file system:

```
/pool1/data:    5657c(root)    5575c(root)
```

The following command stops all processes that are using the /pool1/data file system by sending a SIGKILL to each one. Don't use it without first warning the users:

```
# fuser -c -k /pool1/data<cr>
/pool1/data:    5658cKilled
```

Using the fuser command as described is the preferred method for determining who is using a file system before unmounting it.

Table 5-5 The fuser Command Options

Option	Description
-c	Reports on files that are mountpoints for file systems and on any files within that mounted file system
-f	Prints a report for the named file but not for files within a mounted file system
-k	Sends the SIGKILL signal to each process
-u	Displays the user login name in parentheses following the process ID

You can also use the fuser command to check on any device such as the system console by typing

```
# fuser /dev/console<cr>
```

The system displays the processes associated with that device as follows:

```
/dev/console:    1342o
```

Removing a ZFS Storage Pool

Use the zpool destroy command to remove an entire storage pool and all the file systems it contains. Earlier in this chapter, I created a storage pool named pool1. I'll remove pool1 using the following command:

```
# cd /<cr>
# zpool destroy pool1<cr>
```

When I destroy the storage pool, everything in that pool is also destroyed. In this example, the /pool1 and /pool1/data ZFS file systems that I created earlier have been removed.

If you accidentally destroy a pool, you can attempt to recover it by using the zpool import command. When you destroy a pool, ZFS marks that pool as destroyed, but nothing is actually erased. This space will get used over time, so the amount of time that this destroyed pool remains available for recovery will vary. List your destroyed pools using the zpool import command with the -D option:

```
# zpool import -D<cr>
```

The system responds with the following:

```
  pool: pool1
    id: 1669544482979045385
 state: ONLINE (DESTROYED)
action: The pool can be imported using its name or numeric identifier.
config:
        pool1     ONLINE
        c2t1d0    ONLINE
```

In the output produced from `zpool import`, you can identify the `pool1` pool that was destroyed earlier. To recover the pool, issue the `zpool import` command again using the `-D` and `-f` options, and specify the name of the pool to be recovered:

```
# zpool import -Df  pool1<cr>
```

The `-f` option forces the import of the pool, even if the pool has been destroyed. A message will not be displayed when the command completes.

Now, list the pool:

```
# zpool list pool1<cr>
NAME   SIZE   USED   AVAIL  CAP  HEALTH  ALTROOT
pool1  33.8G  50.2M  33.7G  0%   ONLINE  -
```

The pool has been recovered, and all the data is accessible.

You can also import a pool by its ID as follows:

```
# zpool import -Df 16695444829790453 85<cr>
```

Finally, import the deleted pool under a different name. For example, to import deleted `pool1` as `pool2`, type the following:

```
# zpool import -Df 1848894050265917313 pool2<cr>
```

In addition, pools can be imported using an alternate root. An example is a recovery situation, where the mountpoint must not be interpreted in the context of the current root directory, but under some temporary directory where repairs can be made. In the next example, I'll import `pool2`, but I'll mount the ZFS file systems under a temporary mountpoint named `/temp` (`/temp` must not exist):

```
# zpool import -Df -R /temp pool2<cr>
```

The `df -h` command shows the pool is imported and each file system has been prefixed with `/temp`:

```
# df -h<cr>
...<output has been truncated>...
pool2                  16G    32K     16G    1%    /temp/pool2
pool2/data             16G    31K     16G    1%    /temp/pool2/data
```

Adding Storage Space to a ZFS Storage Pool

Add more space to a storage pool using the zpool add command. The add subcommand adds another storage device to an existing storage pool. The additional space becomes available immediately to all datasets within the pool.

The following example shows a dynamic stripe storage pool named pool1 with a dataset named /pool1/data:

```
# zfs list -r pool1<cr>
NAME          USED   AVAIL   REFER   MOUNTPOINT
pool1        3.96G    949M     19K   /pool1
pool1/data 3.96G     949M   3.96G   /pool1/data
```

Storage pool1 currently has a single 5GB disk (c2t2d0). The storage pool only has 949MB of storage space available. Add another 5GB disk drive (c2t3d0) to the pool as follows:

```
# zpool add pool1 c2t3d0<cr>
```

Another check of the storage pool shows that the size has been increased and the available space has been increased to 5.78GB:

```
# zfs list -r pool1<cr>
NAME          USED  AVAIL  REFER  MOUNTPOINT
pool1        4.00G  5.78G    19K  /pool1
pool1/data 4.00G  5.78G  4.00G  /pool1/data
```

A check of the storage pool shows the status of the two disk drives:

```
# zpool status pool1<cr>
  pool: pool1
  state: ONLINE
  scrub: none requested
 config:
      NAME        STATE    READ WRITE CKSUM
      pool1       ONLINE      0     0     0
        c2t2d0    ONLINE      0     0     0
        c2t3d0    ONLINE      0     0     0

errors: No known data errors
```

The disk space was added while the file systems in the storage pool were active. When the additional space was added, it became available to the file systems in that storage pool immediately.

Because we added a disk to an existing dynamic stripe, we now have a concatenated stripe. The first disk (c2t2d0) is nearly full and data cannot be properly striped across both drives equally, so performance may not be the same as when a new device is created with both drives initially. As space frees up on c2t2d0, striping will improve. Rather than adding to a stripe, it's usually better to re-create the storage pool with two drives to get optimum performance. I'll describe how to add space to mirrored and RAID-Z storage pools later in this chapter.

Mirrored Storage Pools

To set up a mirrored file system (RAID-1) in ZFS, you'll begin by creating a mirrored storage pool. Mirroring is done at the storage-pool level and requires at least two disks. It's recommended that each of these disks be connected to separate disk controllers. A storage pool can contain more than one mirror. A two-way mirror consists of two disks, and a three-way mirror consists of three disks.

When creating a mirrored pool, a separate top-level virtual device (vdev) is created. Use the following command to create a two-way mirror device:

```
# zpool create pool2 mirror c3t6d0 c3t7d0<cr>
```

This pool was created using two 8GB disks. The zpool status command shows that the following zpool has been created:

```
# zpool status pool2<cr>
  pool: pool2
 state: ONLINE
  scan: none requested
config:

        NAME        STATE     READ  WRITE  CKSUM
        pool2       ONLINE       0      0      0
          mirror-0  ONLINE       0      0      0
            c3t6d0  ONLINE       0      0      0
            c3t7d0  ONLINE       0      0      0
```

mirror-0 is the name of the vdev. It consists of two disks, c3t6d0 and c3t7d0.

The size of the storage pool can be displayed as follows:

```
# zpool list pool2<cr>
NAME    SIZE  ALLOC   FREE  CAP  DEDUP  HEALTH  ALTROOT
pool2  7.94G   119K  7.94G   0%  1.00x  ONLINE  -
```

To add space to an existing mirrored vdev, you need to add another mirrored vdev using the zpool add command. Add another vdev by adding two more 8GB disks to the storage pool as follows:

```
# zpool add pool2 mirror c3t8d0 c3t9d0<cr>
```

The size of the storage pool has increased by 8GB as shown with the `zpool list` command:

```
# zpool list pool2<cr>
NAME    SIZE  ALLOC   FREE  CAP  DEDUP  HEALTH  ALTROOT
pool2  15.9G   121K  15.9G   0%  1.00x  ONLINE  -
```

The `zpool status` command shows that the storage pool now consists of two mirrored vdevs, `mirror-0` and `mirror-1`:

```
# zpool status pool2<cr>
  pool: pool2
 state: ONLINE
  scan: none requested
config:
        NAME        STATE     READ WRITE CKSUM
        pool2       ONLINE       0     0     0
          mirror-0  ONLINE       0     0     0
            c3t6d0  ONLINE       0     0     0
            c3t7d0  ONLINE       0     0     0
          mirror-1  ONLINE       0     0     0
            c3t8d0  ONLINE       0     0     0
            c3t9d0  ONLINE       0     0     0
```

Data is striped between the two vdevs, creating a striped mirror configuration. In other words, `c3t6` and `c3t7` contain the same data, and `c3t8` and `c3t9` contain the same data. When data is written to the storage pool, it is striped across `c3t6/c3t8` and across `c3t7/c3t9`.

Adding more space to a mirrored vdev is a good place to use the `-n` option to perform a dry run before actually performing the task. When learning the commands, it's best to make sure you have the correct syntax before committing to the task. For example:

```
# zpool add -n pool1 mirror c3t8d0 c3t9d0<cr>
would update 'pool1' to the following configuration:
        pool1
          mirror
            c3t6d0
            c3t7d0
          mirror
            c3t8d0
            c3t9d0
```

RAID-Z Storage Pools

RAID-Z provides a striped storage pool, but it also provides redundancy through single (raid-z), double (raid-z2), or triple parity (raid-z3) fault tolerance. Single parity is similar to RAID-5, and double-parity RAID-Z is similar to RAID-6. Like RAID 5, RAID-Z can handle a whole-disk failure, RAID-Z2 can handle two disk failures, and RAID-Z3 can handle up to three simultaneous disk failures.

RAID-Z can be more proactive than RAID-5 and actually detect and correct any corruption it encounters. When ZFS reads a RAID-Z block, ZFS compares it against its checksum. If the data disks didn't return the right answer, ZFS reads the parity and then does reconstruction to figure out which disk returned the bad data. It then repairs the damaged disk and returns good data to the application. ZFS also reports the incident through Oracle Solaris FMA so that the system administrator knows that one of the disks is silently failing.

Use the `zpool create` command to create a single RAID-Z (single-parity) device that consists of three disks. A RAID-Z vdev should not contain more than nine disk drives. When using more than nine drives, create multiple vdevs. All disks in the vdev should be of the same size and performance:

```
# zpool create pool3 raidz c2t2d0 c2t3d0 c2t4d0<cr>
```

This RAID-Z pool is created from three 5GB disks. The `df -h` command shows the following information:

```
pool3    9.8G    24K    9.8G    1%    /pool3
```

You need at least two disks for a single-parity RAID-Z configuration and at least three disks for a double-parity RAID-Z configuration. Create a double-parity RAID-Z configuration by using the `raidz2` keyword:

```
# zpool create pool1 raidz2 c3t6d0 c3t7d0 c3t8d0 c3t9d0<cr>
```

Use the `raidz3` keyword to create a triple-parity RAID-Z configuration.

A RAID-Z device is displayed with the `zpool status` command as follows:

```
# zpool status pool1<cr>
  pool: pool1
 state: ONLINE
  scan: none requested
config:

        NAME          STATE     READ WRITE CKSUM
        pool1         ONLINE       0     0     0
          raidz2-0    ONLINE       0     0     0
            c3t6d0    ONLINE       0     0     0
            c3t7d0    ONLINE       0     0     0
            c3t8d0    ONLINE       0     0     0
            c3t9d0    ONLINE       0     0     0

errors: No known data errors
```

`raidz2-0` is the name of the vdev, indicating that it is a double-parity RAID-Z vdev and it consists of four disks.

Mirrored Versus RAID-Z Storage Pools

Mirrored pools are recommended over RAID-Z pools for smaller random read/write workloads. A RAID-Z configuration maximizes disk space and generally performs well when data is written and read in large chunks (128K or more). RAID-Z pools are generally not recommended for random read workloads.

The root pool may be created as a mirrored configuration or as a single-disk configuration. A RAID-Z or a striped configuration is not supported.

You cannot add a disk to an existing RAID-Z vdev. For example, it is not possible to expand a RAID-Z group from raidz(disk1, disk2, disk3, disk4, disk5, disk6) to raidz(disk1, disk2, disk3, disk4, disk5, disk6, disk7) due to architectural reasons. You could, however, replace each disk with a larger disk as follows:

```
# zpool replace pool1 c2t1d0 c3t1d0<cr>
```

where `c2t1` is an 80GB disk and `c3t1` is a 160GB disk.

The `zpool replace` command is described later in this chapter.

You can expand a RAID-Z storage pool by adding another RAID-Z vdev as follows:

1. Create the first RAID-Z pool with three 2GB disks as follows:

   ```
   # zpool create pool1 raidz c2t0d0 c2t1d0 c2t2d0<cr>
   ```

   (3.9GB of storage space is available.)
2. Add storage space by adding a second RAID-Z vdev to `pool1` as follows:

   ```
   # zpool add pool1 raidz c2t3d0 c2t4d0 c2t5d0<cr>
   ```

   (7.8GB of storage space is now available.)

Note

The `autoexpand` property in the storage pool should be set to `on`, or you'll need to issue the `zpool online -e` command to expand the pool to fit the larger disk.

Attaching and Detaching Devices in a Storage Pool

Add another device to a storage pool using the `zpool attach` command. The `attach` subcommand will add redundancy (mirroring) to a storage pool. Data on the existing drive will automatically be mirrored to the new disk while the file systems in that storage pool are active.

`zpool add` Versus `zpool attach`

To remember which subcommand to use with `zfs`, use the `add` subcommand to add space to a storage pool. Use the `attach` subcommand to add redundancy to a storage pool (such as a mirror).

Converting a Nonredundant Pool to a Mirrored Pool

Use the `zpool attach` command to convert a nonredundant pool into a mirrored (redundant) storage pool. In the first example, I have a RAID-0 storage pool made up of a single 8GB disk (`c3t6d0`). The pool status is displayed as follows:

```
# zpool status pool1<cr>
  pool: pool1
 state: ONLINE
  scan: none requested
config:

        NAME        STATE     READ  WRITE  CKSUM
        pool1       ONLINE       0      0      0
          c3t6d0    ONLINE       0      0      0

errors: No known data errors
```

To mirror the data in this storage pool onto a second disk and convert the storage pool into a mirrored storage pool, I'll use the `zpool attach` command to add another 8GB disk (`c3t7d0`) to `pool1` as follows:

```
# zpool attach pool1 c3t6d0 c3t7d0<cr>
```

Verify the creation of the redundant storage pool:

```
# zpool status pool1
  pool:  pool1
 state:  ONLINE
  scan:  resilvered 86.5K in 0h0m with 0 errors on Wed Aug  Jan  23 17:46:27 2012
config:

        NAME        STATE     READ  WRITE  CKSUM
        pool1       ONLINE       0      0      0
          mirror-0  ONLINE       0      0      0
            c3t6d0  ONLINE       0      0      0
            c3t7d0  ONLINE       0      0      0

errors: No known data errors
```

Notice that the STATE is ONLINE and resilvering has completed without errors. A vdev has been created named `mirror-0`, indicating that the storage pool is a mirrored volume.

Resilvering

Resilvering is the syncing process that takes place where data is copied from the source drive (`c3t6d0`) to the target drive (`c3t7d0`).

ZFS only resilvers the minimum amount of necessary data. When an entire disk is replaced, the resilvering process takes time proportional to the amount of data used on disk. Adding a 500GB disk can take seconds if only a few gigabytes of used space are in the pool.

Resilvering is interruptible and safe. If the system loses power or is rebooted, the resilvering process resumes exactly where it left off, without any need for manual intervention. To view the resilvering process, use the `zpool status` command.

Adding Redundancy to a Mirrored Pool

Add another device to a mirrored storage pool using the `zpool attach` command. For example, use this to change a two-way mirror to a three-way mirror. The following example shows a two-way mirrored storage pool named `pool1` with a dataset named `/pool1/docs`:

```
# zfs list -r pool1<cr>
NAME         USED  AVAIL  REFER  MOUNTPOINT
pool1        134K  7.81G    32K  /pool1
pool1/docs    31K  7.81G    31K  /pool1/docs
```

A check of the storage pool shows the mirror's status:

```
# zpool status pool1<cr>
  pool: pool1
 state: ONLINE
  scan: resilvered 86.5K in 0h0m with 0 errors on Wed Jan  23 17:46:27 2013
config:

        NAME          STATE     READ WRITE  CKSUM
        pool1         ONLINE       0     0      0
          mirror-0    ONLINE       0     0      0
            c3t6d0    ONLINE       0     0      0
            c3t7d0    ONLINE       0     0      0

errors: No known data error
```

To convert this pool to a three-way mirror, attach another 5GB disk (`c3t8d0`) to the pool:

```
# zpool attach pool1 c3t6d0 c3t8d0<cr>
```

When attaching a disk, you'll specify two disks:

1. The source disk is the existing disk that has the data on it. It doesn't matter if you select c3t6d0 or c3t7d0; because it is a mirror they both have the same information on them.
2. The target disk (c3t8d0) is the new disk that you are attaching to the mirror.

After attaching the new disk, a check of the storage pool shows the mirror's status:

```
# zpool status pool1<cr>
  pool: pool1
 state: ONLINE
  scan: resilvered 136K in 0h0m with 0 errors on Wed Jan  23 09:36:35 2013
config:

        NAME          STATE     READ WRITE  CKSUM
        pool1         ONLINE       0     0      0
          mirror-0 ONLINE          0     0      0
            c3t6d0 ONLINE          0     0      0
            c3t7d0 ONLINE          0     0      0
            c3t8d0 ONLINE          0     0      0

errors: No known data errors
```

The three-way mirror is online, and resilvering is complete.

Detaching a Device from a Mirrored Pool

Use the zpool detach command to permanently detach a device from a mirrored storage pool. For example, earlier I created a redundant pool named pool1. The current status is as follows:

```
# zpool status pool1<cr>
  pool: pool1
 state: ONLINE
  scan: resilvered 136K in 0h0m with 0 errors on Wed Jan  23 09:36:35 2013
config:

        NAME          STATE     READ WRITE CKSUM
        pool1         ONLINE       0     0     0
          mirror-0 ONLINE          0     0     0
            c3t6d0 ONLINE          0     0     0
            c3t7d0 ONLINE          0     0     0

errors: No known data errors
```

To detach the device c3t7d0 and convert the mirror back to a nonredundant pool, issue the zpool detach command:

```
# zpool detach pool1 c3t7d0<cr>
```

A check of the storage pool shows the status:

```
# zpool status pool1<cr>
  pool: pool1
 state: ONLINE
  scan: resilvered 136K in 0h0m with 0 errors on Wed Jan  23 09:36:35 2013
config:

        NAME        STATE     READ WRITE CKSUM
        pool1       ONLINE       0     0     0
          c3t6d0    ONLINE       0     0     0

errors: No known data errors
```

Notice that the `zfs status` shows that a resilvering operation was performed. ZFS did not perform a resilvering operation when the `c3t7d0` device was detached. The message refers to the previous resilver operation that was performed when the pool was originally mirrored. The scrub message gets updated only when a ZFS scrub or resilvering operation completes. That message remains until the next operation. Because the `detach` operation did not perform a scrub, the old message still appears.

The vdev, `mirror-0`, is no longer displayed in the status information, which indicates the storage pool has no redundancy and is a RAID-0 device.

The `c3t7d0` disk has been detached, but even though it still contains data, the data cannot be mounted. If the detached drive contains sensitive data, steps should still be taken to either encrypt the data or to completely remove all data from the drives by overwriting the drives.

Note

A device cannot be detached from a nonredundant pool or a RAID-Z pool.

Split a Mirrored Pool

You can use the `zpool split` command to detach disks from a mirrored ZFS storage pool to create a new pool with the detached disks. The new pool will have identical contents to the original mirrored ZFS storage pool.

For example, this system has the following mirrored storage pool:

```
# zpool status pool1<cr>
  pool: pool1
 state: ONLINE
  scan: none requested
config:

        NAME        STATE     READ WRITE CKSUM
        pool1       ONLINE       0     0     0
          mirror-0  ONLINE       0     0     0
            c3t6d0  ONLINE       0     0     0
            c3t7d0  ONLINE       0     0     0
```

I'll split pool1 as follows and create a second pool named pool2 as follows:

```
# zpool split pool1 pool2<cr>
```

The contents of pool1 and pool2 are identical. The zpool list shows only pool1:

```
# zpool list<cr>
NAME    SIZE   ALLOC   FREE    CAP   DEDUP   HEALTH   ALTROOT
pool1 7.94G    138K  7.94G     0%   1.00x   ONLINE   -
```

By default, a zpool split operation on a mirrored pool detaches the last disk for the newly created pool.

The pool2 storage pool has been exported but can be viewed using the zpool import command as follows:

```
# zpool import<cr>
  pool: pool2
    id: 12587293052353906187
 state: ONLINE
action: The pool can be imported using its name or numeric identifier.
config:

        pool2     ONLINE
          c3t7d0  ONLINE
```

This pool can now be moved to another system, or it can be imported onto this system as follows:

```
# zpool import pool2<cr>
```

Both pools are now visible and available, and both pools contain identical information:

```
# zpool status pool1 pool2<cr>
  pool: pool1
 state: ONLINE
  scan: none requested
config:
        NAME      STATE     READ WRITE CKSUM
        pool1     ONLINE       0     0     0
          c3t6d0  ONLINE       0     0     0

errors: No known data errors
  pool: pool2
 state: ONLINE
  scan: none requested
config:

        NAME      STATE     READ WRITE CKSUM
        pool2     ONLINE       0     0     0
          c3t7d0  ONLINE       0     0     0
```

The `zfs list` command shows the identical file systems that exist in each pool:

```
# zfs list<cr>
NAME                          USED    AVAIL    REFER    MOUNTPOINT
pool1                        86.5K    7.81G      31K    /pool1
pool2                          85K    7.81G      31K    /pool2
```

Taking Devices in a Storage Pool Offline and Online

To temporarily disconnect a device from a storage pool for maintenance purposes, ZFS allows a device to be taken offline using the `zpool offline` command. Taking a device offline is not the same as detaching a device, which was described earlier. Taking a device offline is meant to be a temporary state, whereas detaching a device is a permanent state.

In the following example, a redundant storage pool named `pool1` is set up on a server. A check of the status shows the following information about that pool:

```
# zpool status pool1<cr>
  pool: pool1
 state: ONLINE
  scan: resilvered 138K in 0h0m with 0 errors on Wed Jan  23 13:32:16 2013
config:

        NAME        STATE       READ WRITE CKSUM
        pool1       ONLINE         0     0     0
          mirror-0  ONLINE         0     0     0
            c3t7d0  ONLINE         0     0     0
            c3t6d0  ONLINE         0     0     0

errors: No known data errors
```

Take the `c3t7d0` device offline using the following command:

```
# zpool offline pool1 c3t7d0<cr>
```

The pool's status has changed, as displayed by the following `zpool status` command:

```
# zpool status pool1<cr>
  pool: pool1
 state: DEGRADED
status: One or more devices has been taken offline by the administrator.
        Sufficient replicas exist for the pool to continue functioning in a degraded
        state.
action: Online the device using 'zpool online' or replace the device with
        'zpool replace'.
  scan:  resilvered 138K in 0h0m with 0 errors on Wed Jan  23 13:32:16 2013
```

```
config:

        NAME         STATE      READ WRITE CKSUM
        pool1        DEGRADED      0     0     0
          mirror-0   DEGRADED      0     0     0
            c3t7d0   OFFLINE       0     0     0
            c3t6d0   ONLINE        0     0     0

errors: No known data errors
```

The `c3t7d0` disk is labeled as OFFLINE, and the `mirror-0` vdev shows a DEGRADED state. While `c3t7d0` is in the offline state, it is not accepting read or write operations, but it is still identified as being a component in the `mirror-0` vdev. The offline state is persistent, and this device remains offline even after the system has been rebooted.

While the device is offline, data can still be written to the `pool1` storage pool. All the data gets written to the `c3t6d0` device, and there is no redundancy. When the `c3t7d0` device is brought back online, only the information that has changed on `c3t6d0` will get resilvered to `c3t7d0`. The length of time `c3t7d0` has been offline and the quantity of data that has been changed will determine how quickly `c3t7d0` is resilvered and the `mirror-0` vdev changes back to an online state.

To bring the `c3t7d0` device back online, issue the following command:

```
# zpool online pool1 c3t7d0<cr>
```

A device can be brought back online while the file system is active. When a device is brought back online, any information that was previously written to the storage pool is resynchronized to the newly available device.

Taking a Device Offline

Devices do not need to be taken offline to be replaced. Note that you cannot use the act of bringing a device online to replace a disk. If you take a device offline, replace the drive, and try to bring it online, the device remains in a faulted state.

ZFS History

The system administrator can view all of the operations that have been performed on a ZFS pool by viewing the history. Use the `zpool history` command:

```
# zpool history pool1<cr>
History for 'pool1':
2013-01-23.17:41:26 zpool create pool1 c3t6d0
2013-01-23.17:46:57 zpool attach pool1 c3t6d0 c3t7d0
2013-01-24.09:31:13 zfs create pool1/docs
```

```
2013-01-24.09:37:05 zpool attach pool1 c3t6d0 c3t8d0
2013-01-24.10:03:51 zpool detach pool1 c3t6d0
2013-01-24.13:32:15 zpool detach pool1 c3t8d0
2013-01-24.13:32:30 zpool attach pool1 c3t7d0 c3t6d0
2013-01-24.13:44:33 zpool online pool1 c3t7d0
```

Use the `-l` option to display the log records in long format:

```
# zpool history -l pool1<cr>
History for 'pool1':
2013-01-23.17:41:26 zpool create pool1 c3t6d0 [user root on solaris:global]
2013-01-23.17:46:57 zpool attach pool1 c3t6d0 c3t7d0 [user root on solaris:global]
2013-01-24.09:31:13 zfs create pool1/docs [user root on solaris:global]
2013-01-24.09:37:05 zpool attach pool1 c3t6d0 c3t8d0 [user root on solaris:global]
2013-01-24.10:03:51 zpool detach pool1 c3t6d0 [user root on solaris:global]
2013-01-24.13:32:15 zpool detach pool1 c3t8d0 [user root on solaris:global]
2013-01-24.13:32:30 zpool attach pool1 c3t7d0 c3t6d0 [user root on solaris:global]
2013-01-24.13:44:33 zpool online pool1 c3t7d0 [user root on solaris:global]
```

The `-i` option displays internally logged ZFS events in addition to user-initiated events.

ZFS Properties

When you create ZFS file systems, a default set of properties control the behavior of the file systems and storage pools. These properties are divided into two types: native and user-defined.

Native properties either export internal statistics or control ZFS file system behavior. In addition, native properties are either read-only or able to be set. User properties have no effect on ZFS file system behavior, but you can use them to annotate datasets in a way that is meaningful in your environment.

Many settable properties are inherited from the parent and are propagated to its descendants. All inheritable properties have an associated source indicating how the property was obtained. The source can have the following values:

- `default`: A value of `default` means that the property setting was not inherited or set locally. This source is a result of no ancestor having had the property as source local.
- `local`: A `local` source indicates that the property was explicitly set on the dataset using the `zfs set` command.
- `inherited from` <*dataset-name*>: <*dataset-name*> specifies where that property was inherited.

List all of the ZFS file system property information, including whether the property value is editable and inheritable and their possible values, by typing

```
# zfs help -l properties<cr>
```

The complete list of properties will be listed. Or, specify a property as follows:

```
# zfs help -l properties quota<cr>
quota (property)
Editable, Non-inheritable
Accepted values: <size> | none
(Sizes are specified in bytes with standard units such as k, m, g, etc.)
```

ZFS File System Properties

ZFS file system properties are managed using the `zfs set`, `zfs inherit`, and `zfs get` commands. Use the `zfs get` command with the `all` keyword to view all the dataset properties for the storage pool named `pool1`:

```
# zfs get all pool1<cr>
```

The system displays the list of properties:

```
NAME     PROPERTY            VALUE                      SOURCE
pool1    type                filesystem                 -
pool1    creation            Thu Jan 24 10:47 2013      -
pool1    used                85K                        -
pool1    available           15.6G                      -
pool1    referenced          31K                        -
pool1    compressratio       1.00x                      -
pool1    mounted             yes                        -
pool1    quota               none                       default
pool1    reservation         none                       default
...<output has been truncated>...
```

```
# zfs list<cr>
NAME               USED      AVAIL     REFER          MOUNTPOINT
pool1             86.5K      7.81G       31K          /pool1
pool2               85K      7.81G       31K          /pool2
<the list has been truncated>
```

Table 5-6 lists some of the more common native read-only ZFS file system properties. These properties cannot be set, nor are they inherited. For a complete set of ZFS properties, see the ZFS man pages by typing `man zfs` at the command prompt.

Table 5-7 lists the more common settable ZFS properties. These are properties whose values can be both retrieved and set. These properties are set using the `zfs set` command, described later in this section. Most of these properties are inherited from the parent, with the exception of `quota` and `reservation`.

Table 5-6 Native Read-Only ZFS Properties

Property Name	Description
`available`	The amount of space available to the dataset and all its children, assuming no other activity in the pool.
`compressratio`	A read-only property that identifies the compression ratio achieved for this dataset.
`creation`	The time when the dataset was created.
`mounted`	For file systems, indicates whether the file system is currently mounted. This property can be either `yes` or `no`.
`origin`	For cloned file systems or volumes, the snapshot from which the clone was created.
`type`	The type of dataset: `filesystem`, `volume`, `snapshot`, or `clone`.
`used`	The amount of space consumed by this dataset and all its descendants.

Table 5-7 Settable ZFS Properties

Property Name	Default Value	Description
`aclinherit`	`secure`	Controls how access control list (ACL) entries are inherited when files and directories are created.
`aclmode`	`groupmask`	Controls how an ACL is modified during `chmod`.
`atime`	`on`	Controls whether the access time for files is updated when they are read.
`canmount`	`on`	If this property is set to "off," the file system cannot be mounted using the `zfs mount` or `zfs mount -a` command.
`checksum`	`on`	Controls the checksum used to verify data integrity.
`compression`	`off`	Controls the compression algorithm used for this dataset.

Property Name	Default Value	Description
`copies`	`1`	Controls the number of copies of data stored for this dataset.
`dedup`	`off`	Controls the ability to remove duplicate data in a ZFS file system. Possible values are `on`, `off`, `verify`, and `sha256`[,`verify`]. The default checksum for deduplication is `sha256`.
`devices`	`on`	Controls whether device nodes can be opened on this file system.
`encryption`	`off`	Controls whether a file system is encrypted. An encrypted file system means that data is encoded and a key is needed by the file system owner to access the data.
`exec`	`on`	Controls whether processes can be executed from within this file system.
`groupquota`	`none`	Sets a quota on the amount of space consumed by files that are owned by a particular group.
`mountpoint`	`N/A`	Controls the mountpoint used for this file system.
`quota`	`none`	Limits the amount of space a dataset and its descendants can consume. This property enforces a hard limit on the amount of space used.
`readonly`	`off`	Controls whether this dataset can be modified.
`recordsize`	`128K`	Specifies a suggested block size for files in the file system.
`refreserva-tion`	`none`	Used to guarantee (reserve) a minimum amount of storage to a file system.
`reservation`	`none`	The minimum amount of space guaranteed to a dataset and its descendants.
`setuid`	`on`	Controls whether the set-UID bit is respected for the file system.
`sharenfs`	`off`	This property has been replaced by the `share.nfs` and `share.smb` properties in Oracle Solaris 11.1. `sharenfs` controls whether the file system is shared via Network File System (NFS) and what options are used. A file system with a `sharenfs` property of `off` is managed through traditional tools such as `share`, `unshare`, and `dfstab`.

(*continues*)

Table 5-7 Settable ZFS Properties (*Continued*)

Property Name	Default Value	Description
`share.nfs`	`off`	Controls whether a ZFS dataset is created and published as an NFS share. Additional NFS share properties are also available and are listed in the `zfs_share(1M)` man page, in the section titled "Global Share Property Descriptions." Also see Chapter 10 for more information on NFS shares.
`share.smb`	`off`	Controls whether a ZFS dataset is created and published as a Server Message Block (SMB) share. Additional SMB share properties are also available and are listed in the `zfs_share(1M)` man page, in the section titled "Global Share Property Descriptions."
`snapdir`	`hidden`	Controls whether the `.zfs` directory is hidden or visible in the root of the file system, as discussed in the "ZFS Snapshots" section later in this chapter.
`userquota`	`none`	Sets a quota on the amount of space consumed by files that are owned by a particular user.
`volsize`	`8Kbytes`	For volumes, specifies the volume's logical size.
`zoned`	`off`	Controls whether the dataset is managed from a non-global zone.

In addition to the native properties that have been described, ZFS supports arbitrary user properties. The user properties have no effect on the ZFS behavior, but they can be used to annotate datasets with meaningful information. The user properties must conform to the following rules:

- They must contain a colon (:) character to distinguish them from native properties.
- They must contain lowercase letters, numbers, and the following punctuation characters: plus (+), period (.), underscore (_).
- The maximum user property name is 256 characters.
- Typically, the property name is divided into the following two components, though this namespace is not enforced by ZFS:

```
<module>:<property>
```

- Arbitrary strings are always inherited and are never validated.
- The maximum user property value is 1,024 characters.
- Here are two examples of user properties:

```
dept:users=finance
backup:frequency=daily
```

ZFS Storage Pool Properties

ZFS storage pools also have their own set of properties that can be viewed using the `zpool get all` command as follows:

```
# zpool get all pool1<cr>
NAME   PROPERTY       VALUE                SOURCE
pool1  size           7.94G                -
pool1  capacity       0%                   -
pool1  altroot        -                    default
pool1  health         ONLINE               -
pool1  guid           4327525802158749161  -
pool1  version        33                   default
pool1  bootfs         -                    default
pool1  delegation     on                   default
pool1  autoreplace    off                  default
pool1  cachefile      -                    default
pool1  failmode       wait                 default
pool1  listsnapshots  off                  default
pool1  autoexpand     off                  default
pool1  dedupditto     0                    default
pool1  dedupratio     1.00x                -
pool1  free           7.94G                -
pool1  allocated      86.5K                -
pool1  readonly       off                  -
```

In addition, you can display zpool property information, including whether the property value is editable and their possible values, by typing

```
# zpool help -l properties<cr>
PROPERTY         EDIT   VALUES
allocated          NO   <size>
altroot           YES   <path>
autoexpand        YES   on | off
...<output has been truncated>...
```

Or specify a property as follows:

```
# zpool help -l properties version<cr>
version (property)
Editable
Accepted values: <version>
```

All zpool properties are described in the `zpool(1M)` man page.

Setting ZFS File System Properties

You can modify any of the ZFS file system settable properties using the `zfs set` command. The syntax is as follows:

```
zfs set <property>=<value>
```

Only one property can be set or modified during each `zfs set` invocation.

The following command sets the file system quota to 25GB. This prevents the `pool1/data` file system from using all of the space in the pool:

```
# zfs set quota=25G pool1/data<cr>
```

View a specific property using the following command:

```
# zfs get quota pool1/documents<cr>
```

The system displays the following:

```
NAME              PROPERTY   VALUE   SOURCE
pool1/documents   quota      25G     local
```

In this example, I'll create a user-definable property named `backup:frequency` and set the value to `daily`:

```
# zfs set backup:frequency=daily pool1/documents<cr>
```

Now I'll use the `-s` option to list the properties by source type. The valid source types are `local`, `default`, `inherited`, `temporary`, and `none`. The following example uses the `-s` option to list only properties that were set locally on `pool1`:

```
# zfs get -s local all pool1/documents<cr>
```

The system displays this:

```
NAME              PROPERTY           VALUE    SOURCE
pool1/documents   quota              25G      local
pool1/documents   backup:frequency   daily    local
```

The following illustrates how properties are inherited. In this example, I have a storage pool named pool1 and a ZFS file system in that pool named pool1/documents. I'll start by setting the compression property on the storage pool named pool1:

```
# zfs set compression=on pool1<cr>
```

Compression

In addition to reducing space usage by two to three times, compression reduces the amount of I/O by two to three times. All compression is done by the CPU and therefore results in less data being written to the disk. For this reason, enabling compression actually makes some workloads go faster. Because CPU cycles are being used for compression, CPU performance might be degraded on a system that already has high CPU utilization.

Use the -r option to recursively display the compression property for all of the children of the pool1 dataset:

```
# zfs get -r compression pool1<cr>
```

The system displays only the compression property:

```
NAME                PROPERTY      VALUE      SOURCE
pool1               compression   on         local
pool1/documents     compression   off        local
```

Notice that compression is set to on for pool1 but is set to off for pool1/documents, which was a previously created dataset.

Now, I'll create two new file systems in pool1:

```
# zfs create pool1/bill<cr>
# zfs create pool1/data<cr>
```

Check the compression property for all of the datasets in pool1:

```
# zfs get -r compression pool1<cr>
```

The system displays the following information. Notice that compression in pool1/bill and pool1/data was automatically set to on:

```
NAME              PROPERTY        VALUE    SOURCE
pool1             compression     on       local
pool1/bill        compression     on       inherited from pool1
pool1/data        compression     on       inherited from pool1
pool1/documents   compression     off      local
```

The compression property for both datasets was inherited from pool1.

When you issue the zfs inherit command, the compression property goes back to its default value for all the datasets:

```
# zfs inherit compression pool1<cr>
# zfs get -r compression pool1<cr>
```

The system displays the following:

```
NAME              PROPERTY        VALUE     SOURCE
pool1             compression     off       default
pool1/bill        compression     off       default
pool1/data        compression     off       default
pool1/documents   compression     off       local
```

Notice that compression=off for all the datasets in pool1. The use of the -r option clears the current property setting for all descendant datasets. Therefore, you can use the zfs inherit command to clear a property setting for all of the datasets in a pool.

Setting the compression property again automatically sets it for all of the datasets except pool1/documents:

```
# zfs set compression=on pool1<cr>
# zfs get -r compression pool1<cr>
```

The system displays the following:

```
NAME              PROPERTY        VALUE    SOURCE
pool1             compression     on       local
pool1/bill        compression     on       inherited from pool1
pool1/data        compression     on       inherited from pool1
pool1/documents   compression     off      local
```

Use the copies property to store multiple copies of the same data (ditto blocks) for redundancy. This is especially useful when mirroring or RAID-Z is not being used. With copies set to 1, 2, or 3, ZFS will spread the ditto blocks across the vdev or vdevs to provide spatial diversity. This reduces the possibility that a single failure, such as a drive head impact with media, could disturb both copies of the data. If the storage pool has multiple disks, ZFS will try to spread the copies across multiple disks. This is different from mirroring in subtle ways because it can be turned on and off at the file system level versus mirroring, which can be turned on and off at the storage pool level.

File system properties can be set at the time of creation. For example, to create a file system named `pool1/data` with a `mountpoint` called `/data`, and a `quota` of 500MB, issue the following command:

```
# zfs create -o mountpoint=/data -o quota=500m pool1/data<cr>
```

The results can be displayed by listing the file system as follows:

```
# zfs list -r pool1<cr>
NAME          USED      AVAIL    REFER     MOUNTPOINT
pool1         136K      7.81G      31K     /pool1
pool1/data     31K       500M      31K     /data
```

The `mountpoint` property is explained in the section titled "Mounting ZFS File Systems," which can be found later in this chapter.

Setting ZFS Storage Pool Properties

Set ZFS pool properties using the `zpool set` command. A few of the more common properties are described in Table 5-8.

Table 5-8 ZFS Storage Pool Properties

Property Name	Default Value	Description
`autoexpand`	off	Enables or disables automatic pool expansion when a dynamic LUN expansion event is received
`autoreplace`	off	Sets automatic disk drive replacement
`bootfs`	pool/dataset	Identifies the default bootable dataset (i.e., rootpool)
`deduplication`	off	The process of removing redundant data at the block-level, reducing the total amount of data stored
`listsnaps`	off	Controls whether snapshot information that is associated with this pool is displayed with the `zfs list` command

To allow the zfs list command to display snapshot information, set the listsnapshots property to on for pool1 as follows:

```
# zpool set listsnapshots=on pool1<cr>
```

Verify the setting:

```
# zpool get listsnapshots pool1<cr>
NAME   PROPERTY       VALUE      SOURCE
pool1  listsnapshots  on         local
```

Mounting ZFS File Systems

As you can see by now, a ZFS file system is automatically mounted when it is created. It is not necessary to manually mount a ZFS file system, as was required with traditional file systems. At boot time, ZFS file systems are automatically mounted by SMF via the svc://system/filesystem/local service. It is not necessary to make an entry in the /etc/vfstab file for a ZFS file system to be mounted at boot time.

Use the zfs mount command to list all currently mounted file systems that are managed by ZFS:

```
# zfs mount<cr>
rpool/ROOT/solaris              /
rpool/ROOT/solaris/var          /var
rpool/VARSHARE                  /var/share
rpool/export                    /export
rpool/export/home               /export/home
rpool                           /rpool
```

ZFS uses the value of the mountpoint property when mounting a ZFS file system. For example, the mountpoint property for the pool1/data file system can be displayed as follows:

```
# zfs get mountpoint pool1/data<cr>
NAME        PROPERTY    VALUE         SOURCE
pool1/data  mountpoint  /pool1/data   default
```

The ZFS file system is automatically mounted on /pool1/data, as shown in the output from the following df -h command:

```
pool1/data          67G   31K    67G   1%   /pool1/data
```

When the pool1/data file system was created, the mountpoint property was inherited. However, a file system's mountpoint can be changed simply by changing the mountpoint property. For example, change the mountpoint on pool1/data to /export/data:

```
# zfs set mountpoint=/export/data pool1/data<cr>
```

Whenever the mountpoint property is changed, the file system is automatically unmounted from the old mountpoint and remounted to the new mountpoint.

Now the df -h command shows the following information:

```
pool1/data          67G   31K    67G   1%   /export/data
```

Notice how I was able to change the mountpoint to /export/data without creating the /export/data directory. ZFS creates the mountpoint directories as needed and removes them when they are no longer needed.

Mounted ZFS file systems can be unmounted manually using the zfs unmount command. For example, to unmount the /export/data file system, issue the following command:

```
# zfs unmount /export/data<cr>
```

The file system can be mounted as follows:

```
# zfs mount pool1/data<cr>
```

Notice how the dataset name is specified (pool1/data) rather than the mountpoint property value /export/data.

The mountpoint property could be set to none, preventing the file system from being mounted:

```
# zfs set mountpoint=none pool1<cr>
```

Now, /pool1 does not show up when the df -h command is executed. This can be useful for the following reason. When I create a ZFS file system using the following command:

```
# zpool create pool1 c2t1d0<cr>
# zfs create pool1/data<cr>
```

Two file systems are created: /pool1 and /pool1/data. I typically don't want users putting files directly into the top-level file system named /pool1. Therefore, I simply don't mount /pool1 by setting the mountpoint property to none. With the mountpoint property set to none, the /pool1 file system does not get mounted. A listing of the system's file systems shows the following:

```
# df -h<cr>
Filesystem                 Size   Used   Available    Capacity  Mounted on
rpool/ROOT/solaris          67G   1.7G         62G          3%   /
/devices                     0K     0K          0K          0%   /devices
/dev                         0K     0K          0K          0%   /dev
ctfs                         0K     0K          0K          0%   /system/contract
proc                         0K     0K          0K          0%   /proc
mnttab                       0K     0K          0K          0%   /etc/mnttab
swap                       3.1G   2.3M        3.1G          1%   /system/volatile
objfs                        0K     0K          0K          0%   /system/object
sharefs                      0K     0K          0K          0    /etc/dfs/sharetab
fd                           0K     0K          0K          0%   /dev/fd
rpool/ROOT/solaris/var      67G   219M         62G          1%   /var
swap                       3.1G     0K        3.1G          0%   /tmp
rpool/export                67G    33K         62G          1%   /export
rpool/export/home           67G    31K         62G          1%   /export/home
rpool                       67G    73K         62G          1%   /rpool
```

The descendants of pool1 inherited the mountpoint property, so /pool1/data also was set to none:

```
# zfs get -r mountpoint pool1<cr>
NAME        PROPERTY    VALUE        SOURCE
pool1       mountpoint  none         local
pool1/data  mountpoint  none         inherited from pool1
```

Therefore, I'll change the pool1/data mountpoint property to /pool1/data:

```
# zfs set mountpoint=/pool1/data pool1/data<cr>
```

Now, /pool1 is not mounted and /pool1/data is mounted:

```
# zfs list -r pool1<cr>
NAME        USED      AVAIL        REFER     MOUNTPOINT
pool1       142K      66.9G          32K     none
pool1/data   31K      66.9G          31K     /pool1/data
```

ZFS mount properties can be changed temporarily. Temporary properties revert to their original settings when the file system is unmounted. In the following example, the readonly property is temporarily changed to on for a file system that is currently mounted:

```
# zfs mount -o remount,ro pool1/data<cr>
```

To temporarily change a property on a file system that is currently mounted, you must use the special remount option.

Display the readonly property using the following command:

```
# zfs get readonly pool1/data<cr>
```

The readonly value is displayed:

```
NAME            PROPERTY        VALUE    SOURCE
Pool1/data      readonly        on       temporary
```

Legacy Mountpoints

File systems can also be managed through the legacy mount command and the /etc/vfstab file. If you set the file system's mountpoint property to legacy, ZFS will not automatically mount and manage this file system. The file system must be managed using the legacy commands mount and umount and the /etc/vfstab file. The following steps describe how to set up a ZFS file system using a legacy mountpoint.

1. Find an unused disk that is available for use in a ZFS storage pool.

   a. Use the `format` command to find all the available disks on your system:

```
# format<cr>
Searching for disks-done

AVAILABLE DISK SELECTIONS:
    0. c2t0d0 <SUN72G cyl 14087 alt 2 hd 24 sec 424>
         /pci@780/pci@0/pci@9/scsi@0/sd@0,0
    1. c2t1d0 <SEAGATE-ST973402SSUN72G-0603-68.37GB>
         /pci@780/pci@0/pci@9/scsi@0/sd@1,0
Specify disk (enter its number):
```

   All the available disks are listed.

   b. Check which disks ZFS is using:

```
# zpool status<cr>
pool: rpool
 state: ONLINE
  scan: resilvered 1.30M in 0h0m with 0 errors on Sun Aug  5 17:40:15 2012
config:

        NAME        STATE     READ WRITE CKSUM
        rpool       ONLINE       0     0     0
          c2t0d0s0  ONLINE       0     0     0
```

   In the output, notice that `c2t0d0` is in use for `rpool`.

   c. Make sure that none of the disks are being used for traditional file systems by issuing the `df -h` command and checking for mounted slices, SVM, or Veritas volumes. Also issue the `dumpadm` and `swap -l` commands to determine which drives are being used for swap and the dump device.

2. After verifying that the disk was not being used, I chose `c2t1d0`. Create a ZFS pool and file system on that disk:

```
# zpool create pool1 c2t1d0<cr>
```

   Verify that `/pool1` is mounted by issuing the `df -h` command.

3. Change the `mountpoint` property to `legacy`:

```
# zfs set mountpoint=legacy pool1<cr>
```

   The `df -h` command verifies that the `/pool1` file system is no longer mounted.

4. Create a directory for the mountpoint:

```
# mkdir /data<cr>
```

5. Mount the ZFS file system:

```
# mount -F zfs pool1 /data<cr>
```

   Use the `df -h` command to verify that the file system is mounted as `/data`.

6. To automatically mount the ZFS file system at bootup, make the following entry in the `/etc/vfstab` file:

```
pool1   -   /data   zfs   -   yes   -
```

Legacy mountpoints must be managed through legacy tools. Any attempt to use ZFS tools will result in an error. Any mountpoint properties are set explicitly using the `mount -o` command and by specifying the required `mount` options.

Sharing ZFS File Systems

A ZFS file system is shared by creating the share by setting the appropriate properties in the ZFS file system and then publishing the share. The process used to share ZFS file systems has changed between Oracle Solaris 11 11/11 and Oracle Solaris 11.1. I've included two different sections in Chapter 10, "Network File Systems," describing how to share a ZFS file system. The method used depends on whether your storage pool is at version 33 or 34.

For more information on administering NFS, see Chapter 10.

ZFS Snapshots

A ZFS snapshot is a read-only copy of a ZFS file system. A snapshot can be created quickly, and it initially consumes no space within the pool. The snapshot simply references the data in the file system from which it was created. As the file system from which the snapshot was created changes, the snapshot grows and consumes space in the storage pool. Use the snapshot feature to create backups of live file systems.

ZFS snapshots provide the following features:

- The snapshot persists across reboots.
- The snapshot does not use a separate backing store. However, the snapshot consumes space from the same storage pool as the file system from which it was created.
- Snapshots are created almost instantly.
- Any snapshot can be used to generate a full backup, and any pair of snapshots can be used to generate an incremental backup.
- The number of snapshots that can be taken is virtually unlimited. The theoretical maximum is 2^{64}.
- Snapshots can be used to roll back a file system to a previous state.

As you'll see, snapshots are a great tool for backing up live file systems.

Creating a ZFS Snapshot

Create a snapshot using the `zfs snapshot` command followed by the name of the snapshot. The snapshot name follows this format:

```
<filesystem>@<snapname>
```

or

```
<volume>@<snapname>
```

For example, to take a snapshot of the `pool2/data` file system, the name of the snapshot could be `pool2/data@tue`.

Issue the following command to create the snapshot of the `/pool2/data` file system:

```
# zfs snapshot pool2/data@tue<cr>
```

Listing ZFS Snapshots

After creating the snapshot, list all the snapshots on the system by issuing the following command:

```
# zfs list -t snapshot<cr>
NAME                          USED      AVAIL  REFER    MOUNTPOINT
pool2/data@tue                0         -        22K    -
```

The snapshot is stored in the /pool2/data file system, but you can't see it because the snapdir property is set to hidden. Change that property to visible:

```
# zfs set snapdir=visible pool2/data<cr>
```

Now, when you list the contents of the /pool2/data file system, you see the snapshot directory named .zfs:

```
# ls -la /pool2/data<cr>
total 15
drwxr-xr-x    6 root    root    5 Dec  10  13:01.
drwxr-xr-x    3 root    root    3 Dec   9  20:14..
dr-xr-xr-x    3 root    root    3 Dec   9  20:14 .zfs
drwxr-xr-x    2 root    root    2 Dec  10  12:22 dir1
```

Change into the snapshot directory:

```
# cd /pool2/data/.zfs/snapshot/tue<cr>
```

Issue the ls -la command. You see a read-only copy of the /pool2/data file system:

```
# ls -la<cr>
total 13
drwxr-xr-x   2 root    root         2 Dec 10 12:22 dir1
drwxr-xr-x   2 root    root         2 Dec 10 12:22 dir2
drwxr-xr-x   2 root    root         2 Dec 10 12:22 dir3
-rw-r—r—     1 root    root         0 Dec 10 12:22 foo
-rw-r—r—     1 root    root         0 Dec 10 12:22 foo1
-rw-r—r—     1 root    root         0 Dec 10 12:22 foo2
-rw-r—r—     1 root    root         0 Dec 10 12:22 foo3
```

This is an exact duplicate of the /pool2/data file system, as it looked when the snapshot was taken earlier. As data is added to and changed in the /pool2/data file system, this snapshot does not change or update. Because it's a read-only snapshot, you can copy data from this directory, but you cannot modify it.

Snapshot Disk Space Accounting

When the snapshot is created, initially it takes up no space. As described in the previous section, the snapshot is created in the file system that it references. As the file system changes, disk space that was previously shared becomes unique to the snapshot and is counted in the snapshot's USED property. This property can be displayed as follows:

```
# zfs list -r pool2<cr>
NAME               USED   AVAIL   REFER          MOUNTPOINT
pool2             1.26M   66.9G     32K          /pool2
pool2/data        1.16M   66.9G   1.16M          /pool2/data
pool2/data@tue        0       -   1.16M          -
```

`listsnaps` Property

To get the listing of both file systems and snapshots when issuing the `zfs list` command, I set the `listsnaps` property to "on" for the pool as follows: `zpool set listsnaps=on pool2`.

The default behavior of the `zfs list` command is to not list snapshots.

The snapshot's USED value is initially 0, and the snapshot's REFER value for `pool2/data@tue` is the same size as `the pool2/data` file system's USED value when the snapshot was created. Although data was not copied when the snapshot was created, the REFER value is the space in `pool2/data` originally being referenced by the snapshot. As the `pool2/data` file system changes, you'll see the snapshot USED value increase as it maintains the original read-only image of `pool2/data`. The following is an example of how the USED value for the snapshot increases as `pool2/data` changes:

```
# zfs list -r pool2<cr>
NAME              USED   AVAIL    REFER    MOUNTPOINT
pool2             261M   66.7G      32K    /pool2
pool2/data        262M   66.7G     261M    /pool2/data
pool2/data@tue   1.15M       -    1.16M    -
```

Over time, the snapshot can consume a substantial amount of disk space. When the system administrator forgets about a snapshot, she may be puzzled as to why a storage pool is using so much space. The system administrator needs to monitor snapshots and the amount of space is used. A useful variation of the `zfs list` command that will provide space information on the snapshot is as follows:

```
# zfs list -o space -r pool2<cr>
NAME              AVAIL    USED    USEDSNAP    USEDDS    USEDREFRESERV    USEDCHILD
pool2             66.7G    288M           0       32K                0         288M
pool2/data        66.7G    288M       1.15M      287M                0            0
pool2/data@tue        -   1.15M           -         -                -            -
```

The values listed in each column are as follows:

AVAIL	The amount of space available
USED	The amount of space being used
USEDSNAP	The amount of space being consumed by snapshots
USEDDS	The amount of space being used by the data set itself.
USEDREFRESERV	The amount of space being used by a reservation set on the dataset
USEDCHILD	The amount of space being used by the children of this dataset

Saving and Restoring a ZFS Snapshot

A snapshot can be saved to tape or to a disk on the local system or a remote system. Use the `zfs send` command to save the snapshot to tape:

```
# zfs send pool2/data@tue > /dev/rmt/0<cr>
```

To retrieve the files from tape, use the `zfs recv` command:

```
# zfs recv pool2/data@tue < /dev/rmt/0<cr>
```

This restores the snapshot to the storage pool it came from.

Rather than saving the snapshot to tape, you can save the snapshot to disk on a remote system:

```
# zfs send pool2/data@tue | ssh host2 zfs recv newpool/data<cr>
```

The snapshot is sent to the remote host named "host2" and is saved in the `/newpool/data` file system.

Compress a ZFS snapshot stream using the following command:

```
# zfs send pool2/data@tue | gzip > backupfile.gz<cr>
```

Now the `backup.gz` file can be sent via FTP to another system for a remote backup.

Destroying a ZFS Snapshot

To remove the snapshot from the system, use the `zfs destroy` command:

```
# zfs destroy pool2/data@tue<cr>
```

Destruction

A dataset cannot be destroyed if snapshots of the dataset exist. In addition, if clones have been created from a snapshot, they must be destroyed before the snapshot can be destroyed.

Renaming a ZFS Snapshot

You can rename a snapshot within the pool and the dataset from which it came using the `zfs rename` command:

```
# zfs rename pool2/data@tue pool2/data@backup<cr>
```

List the snapshots on the system to verify the name change:

```
# zfs list -t snapshot<cr>
NAME                  USED   AVAIL   REFER   MOUNTPOINT
pool2/data@backup       0       -      22K            -
```

Rolling Back a ZFS Snapshot

Roll back a ZFS snapshot to discard all changes made to a file system since a specific snapshot was created. Using the `zfs rollback` command, the file system reverts to the state at the time the snapshot was taken. The following steps describe how to revert the /pool2/data file system to the most recent snapshot using the zfs rollback command:

1. List the snapshots currently available on the system:

```
# zfs list -t snapshot<cr>
NAME                         USED  AVAIL      REFER    MOUNTPOINT
pool1/docs@tue               0     -          18K      -
pool2/data@backup            0     -          22K      -
pool2/data@tue               0     -          22K      -
pool2/data@weds_snapshot     0     -          22K      -
```

   Four snapshots are listed.

2. List the contents of the /pool2/data file system:

```
# ls -la /pool2/data<cr>
total 12
drwxr-xr-x   5 root      root         4 Dec 10 14:31 .
drwxr-xr-x   3 root      root         3 Dec  9 20:14 ..
dr-xr-xr-x   3 root      root         3 Dec  9 20:14 .zfs
drwxr-xr-x   2 root      root         2 Dec 10 12:22 dir1
drwxr-xr-x   2 root      root         2 Dec 10 12:22 dir2
```

3. Roll back the /pool2/data file system to the data@tue snapshot:

```
# zfs rollback pool2/data@tue<cr>
cannot rollback to 'pool2/data@tue': more recent snapshots
 exist use '-r' to force deletion of the following snapshots:
  pool2/data@weds_snapshot
```

   The error indicates that there is a more recent backup named weds_snapshot. You can only revert a file system to the most recent snapshot. To use the older data@tue, you need to force ZFS to use the data@tue and remove the weds_snapshot. You do this using the -r option:

```
# zfs rollback -r pool2/data@tue<cr>
```

4. The zfs list command shows that the weds_snapshot was removed:

```
# zfs list -t snapshot<cr>
NAME                         USED    AVAIL    REFER    MOUNTPOINT
pool1/docs@tues_snapshot     0       -        18K      -
pool2/data@backup            0       -        22K      -
pool2/data@tue               0       -        22K      -
```

5. List the contents of the /pool2/data file system, and you'll see that the file system has changed:

```
# ls -la /pool2/data<cr>
total 15
drwxr-xr-x   6 root    root        5 Dec 10 13:01 .
drwxr-xr-x   3 root    root        3 Dec  9 20:14 ..
dr-xr-xr-x   3 root    root        3 Dec  9 20:14 .zfs
drwxr-xr-x   2 root    root        2 Dec 10 12:22 dir1
drwxr-xr-x   2 root    root        2 Dec 10 12:22 dir2
drwxr-xr-x   2 root    root        2 Dec 10 12:22 dir3
```

The dir3 directory, which was missing, has been restored.

Identifying ZFS Snapshot Differences

When multiple snapshots have been taken of the same dataset, you may want to compare snapshots to determine what has changed between the snapshots of a particular dataset. Use the zfs diff command to determine the ZFS snapshot differences. For example, assume that the following two snapshots are created:

```
# zfs list -t snapshot -r pool2<cr>
NAME                USED   AVAIL   REFER    MOUNTPOINT
pool2/data@tue     1.15M       -   1.16M    -
pool2/data@weds        0       -    287M    -
```

pool2/data@tue was created on Tuesday, and pool2/data@weds was created on Wednesday. Identify the difference between the two snapshots as follows:

```
# zfs diff pool2/data@tue pool2/data@weds<cr>
M       /pool2/data/
-       /pool2/data/file2
+       /pool2/data/file4
+       /pool2/data/file5
```

where

M File or directory has been modified or file or directory link has changed.

R File or directory has been renamed.

- File or directory is present in the older snapshot but not in the more recent snapshot.

+ File or directory is present in the more recent snapshot but not in the older snapshot.

ZFS Clones

A snapshot is a read-only point-in-time copy of a file system, and a clone is a writable copy of a snapshot. Clones provide an extremely space-efficient way to store many copies of mostly shared data such as workspaces, software installations, and diskless clients.

A clone is related to the snapshot from which it originated. After a clone is created, the snapshot from which it originated cannot be deleted unless the clone is deleted first.

The `zfs clone` command is used to specify the snapshot from which to create the clone. In the following example, a clone is created from the snapshot named `pool2/data@tue`:

```
# zfs clone pool2/data@tue pool2/docs<cr>
```

The `zfs list` command shows that a new ZFS file system named `/pool2/docs` has been created:

```
# zfs list -r pool2<cr>
NAME              USED    AVAIL   REFER    MOUNTPOINT
pool2             288M    66.7G     33K    pool2
pool2/data        288M    66.7G    287M    /pool2/data
pool2/data@tue   1.15M        -   1.16M    -
pool2/docs         19K    66.7G   1.16M    /pool2/docs
```

The contents are exactly the same as `/pool2/data`:

```
# ls -la /pool2/docs<cr>
total 15
drwxr-xr-x   5 root    root        5 Dec 10 13:01 .
drwxr-xr-x   4 root    root        4 Dec 10 14:46 ..
drwxr-xr-x   2 root    root        2 Dec 10 12:22 dir1
drwxr-xr-x   2 root    root        2 Dec 10 12:22 dir2
drwxr-xr-x   2 root    root        2 Dec 10 12:22 dir3
```

The clone must be created in the same storage pool that the snapshot is in. When you try to create the clone outside the `pool2` storage pool, the following error is reported:

```
# zfs clone pool2/data@tue pool1/data1<cr>
cannot create 'pool1/data1': source and target pools differ
```

Destroying a ZFS Clone

Destroy a ZFS cloned file system just like you would destroy any other ZFS file system—by using the `zfs destroy` command:

```
# zfs destroy pool2/docs<cr>
```

Because a clone is dependent on a snapshot, clones must be destroyed before the parent snapshot can be destroyed. In the following example, I'll try to destroy the `data@tue` before I destroy the file system that was cloned from that snapshot:

```
# zfs destroy pool2/data@tue<cr>
cannot destroy 'pool2/data@tue': snapshot has dependent clones
  use '-R' to destroy the following datasets: pool2/docs
```

When viewing the file system properties for the clone, we see a new property named `origin`:

```
# zfs get all pool2/docs<cr>
NAME        PROPERTY       VALUE                  SOURCE
pool2/docs  type           filesystem             -
pool2/docs  creation       Thu Aug 99:41 2012     -
pool2/docs  used           19K                    -
pool2/docs  available      66.7G                  -
pool2/docs  referenced     1.16M                  -
pool2/docs  compressratio  1.00x                  -
pool2/docs  mounted        yes                    -
pool2/docs  origin         pool2/data@tue         -
pool2/docs  quota          none                   default
pool2/docs  reservation    none                   default
...<output has been truncated>...
```

The `origin` property exposes the clone's dependency on the snapshot.

Replacing a ZFS File System with a ZFS Clone

An active ZFS file system can be replaced by a clone of that file system using the `zfs promote` command. This feature makes it possible to destroy the "original" file system—the file system from which the clone was originally created. Without clone promotion, you cannot destroy the "original" file system of an active clone.

In the preceding section, I created a clone named `/pool2/docs`. This clone was created from a snapshot of the `/pool2/data` file system. To replace the `/pool2/data` file system with the clone named `/pool2/docs`, follow these steps:

1. Create a snapshot of the /pool2/data file system:

```
# zfs snapshot pool2/data@tue<cr>
```

2. Create a clone of the snapshot:

```
# zfs clone pool2/data@tue pool2/docs<cr>
```

3. Promote the cloned file system:

```
# zfs promote pool2/docs<cr>
```

4. Rename the /pool2/data file system:

```
# zfs rename pool2/data pool2/data_old<cr>
```

5. Rename the cloned file system:

```
# zfs rename pool2/docs  pool2/data<cr>
```

6. Remove the original file system:

```
# zfs destroy pool2/data_old<cr>
```

zpool scrub

Cheap disks can fail, so ZFS provides disk scrubbing. Like error-correcting code (ECC) memory scrubbing, the idea is to read all data to detect latent errors while they're still correctable. A scrub traverses the entire storage pool to read every copy of every block, validate it against its 256-bit checksum, and repair it if necessary.

The simplest way to check your data integrity is to initiate an explicit scrubbing of all data within the pool. This operation traverses all the data in the pool once and verifies that all blocks can be read. Scrubbing proceeds as quickly as the devices allow, although the priority of any I/O remains below that of normal operations. This operation might negatively affect performance, but the file system should remain usable and nearly as responsive while the scrubbing occurs. To initiate an explicit scrub, use the `zpool scrub` command:

```
# zpool scrub pool1<cr>
```

You can stop a scrub that is in progress by using the `-s` option:

```
# zpool scrub -s pool1<cr>
```

Replacing Devices in a Storage Pool

If a drive fails and it is no longer visible to the system, the device should be treated as a damaged device. It might first appear as FAULTED in a `zpool list` as follows:

```
# zpool list<cr>
NAME    SIZE   ALLOC    FREE     CAP      DEDUP   HEALTH      ALTROOT
pool1     -       -        -       -          -   FAULTED     -
rpool  15.9G   13.9G   1.94G     87%      1.00x   ONLINE      -
```

The first step is to examine the error counts in the `zpool status` output. I'll review the status output for `pool1` as follows:

```
# zpool status -v pool1<cr>
  pool:   pool1
 state:   UNAVAIL
status:   One or more devices could not be opened.  There are insufficient
          replicas for the pool to continue functioning.
action:  Attach the missing device and online it using 'zpool online'.
   see:    http://www.sun.com/msg/ZFS-8000-3C
  scan:   none requested
 config:

          NAME           STATE     READ WRITE CKSUM
          pool1          UNAVAIL      0     0     0 insufficient replicas
            c3t6d0       ONLINE       0     0     0
            c3t7d0       ONLINE       0     0     0
            c3t8d0       UNAVAIL      0     0     0 cannot open
```

This pool is a dynamic stripe and therefore has no redundancy. The state of the storage pool is UNAVAIL. The disk, `c3t8d0`, cannot be opened. This disk needs to be replaced, and the storage pool needs to be destroyed, recreated, and restored from a backup.

Errors that happen only once are considered *transient, and do not indicate potential failure.* Errors that are persistent or severe enough to indicate potential hardware failure are considered "fatal." The system administrator should either clear the transient errors with the `zpool clear pool1 c3t8d0` command or replace the device due to fatal errors.

If a disk in a redundant storage pool fails and needs to be replaced, swap out the disk and use the `zpool replace` command to replace the disk within ZFS.

In the following example, a `zpool status` shows that `rpool` is in a DEGRADED state:

```
# zpool status -lx rpool<cr>
  pool:  rpool
 state:  DEGRADED
status:  One or more devices are unavailable in response to persistent errors.
         Sufficient replicas exist for the pool to continue functioning in a
         degraded state.
action:  Determine if the device needs to be replaced, and clear the errors using
         'zpool clear' or 'fmadm repaired', or replace the device with
         'zpool replace'. Run 'zpool status -v' to see device specific details.
scan:    resilvered 6.42G in 0h9m with 0 errors on Wed Nov 28 08:39:16 2012
config:

         NAME              STATE     READ WRITE CKSUM
         rpool             DEGRADED     0     0     0
            mirror-0       DEGRADED     0     0     0
               c7t0d0      ONLINE       0     0     0
               c7t2d0      UNAVAIL      0   104     0

errors:  No known data errors
```

Notice in the output that the storage pool is a mirror but is in a degraded state. This means that the virtual device has experienced a failure but can still function. The `zpool status` output shows that `c7t2d0` is in an UNAVAIL state, which means that the device cannot be opened. The physical disk is either disconnected or has failed. The mirror continues to operate.

You can also identify failed disks by using the `fmadm` command as follows:

```
# fmadm faulty<cr>
```

For this example, a faulty disk has been identified and the following information is displayed:

```
-------------- ------------------------------------ ------------- ------
TIME            EVENT-ID          MSG-ID           SEVERITY
-------------- ------------------------------------ ------------- -----
Nov 28 09:07:38 f81d55a6-cc2d-c213-c58b-bcbd761638f0  ZFS-8000-FD    Major

Problem Status      : solved
Diag Engine         : zfs-diagnosis / 1.0
System
    Manufacturer   : unknown
    Name           : unknown
    Part_Number    : unknown
    Serial_Number  : unknown

System Component
    Manufacturer   : innotek-GmbH
    Name           : VirtualBox
    Part_Number    : unknown
    Serial_Number  : 0
    Host_ID        : 00cf27d5

----------------------------------------
Suspect 1 of 1  :
   Fault class  : fault.fs.zfs.vdev.io
   Certainty    : 100%
   Affects      :
zfs://pool=f28bbe2ba2a4337e/vdev=de496baad5c90d32/pool_name=rpool/vdev_name=
id1,sd@SATA_____VBOX_HARDDISK____VBd338ea51-aebb117e/b
       Status        : faulted and taken out of service

  FRU
    Name           :
"zfs://pool=f28bbe2ba2a4337e/vdev=de496baad5c90d32/pool_name=rpool/vdev_name
=id1,sd@SATA_____VBOX_HARDDISK____VBd338ea51-aebb117e/b"
    Status         : faulty

Description : The number of I/O errors associated with ZFS device
              'id1,sd@SATA_____VBOX_HARDDISK____VBd338ea51-aebb117e/b' in pool
              'rpool' exceeded acceptable levels.

Response    : The device has been offlined and marked as faulted. An attempt will be made
              to activate a hot spare if available.

Impact      : Fault tolerance of the pool may be compromised.

Action      : Use 'fmadm faulty' to provide a more detailed view of this event.
              Run 'zpool status -lx' for more information. Please refer to the
              associated reference document at http://support.oracle.com/msg/ZFS-
              8000-FD for the latest service procedures and policies regarding this
              diagnosis.
```

The steps for replacing a failed disk in a ZFS pool are as follows:

1. Take the disk offline using the `zpool offline` command. You cannot unconfigure a SATA disk that is currently being used.

Unconfigure Hot Pluggable Drives

For information about hot-plugging devices on your specific hardware configuration, such as on enterprise-level systems, refer to your hardware configuration documentation. You may need to use the `cfgadm` command to unconfigure the device before replacing it.

2. Remove the disk to be replaced.
3. Insert the replacement disk.
4. Run the `zpool replace` command.

In this scenario, a mirrored storage pool named `mypool` has a failing disk drive (`c2t2d0`). A spare disk (`c2t4d0`) that is already connected to the system can be used as a replacement. Follow these steps to replace the failing disk with the replacement disk:

1. Take the failed disk offline:

```
# zpool offline mypool c2t2d0<cr>
```

2. Replace the failed disk with the good disk:

```
# zpool replace mypool c2t2d0 c2t4d0<cr>
```

3. Check the pool's status:

```
# zpool status mypool<cr>
   pool: mypool
  state: DEGRADED
  scrub: resilver completed after 0h0m with 0 errors on Wed Jan 25 10:28:51 2013
config:

        NAME          STATE     READ WRITE CKSUM
        mypool        DEGRADED     0     0     0
          mirror      DEGRADED     0     0     0
           replacing DEGRADED     0     0     0
              c2t2d0 OFFLINE      0     0     1
              c2t4d0 ONLINE       0     0     0
            c2t3d0    ONLINE       0     0     0

errors: No known data errors
```

Note that the preceding `zpool status output` shows both the new and old disks under a `replacing` heading. This heading means that the replacement process is in progress and the new disk is being resilvered.

After a few minutes, the `zpool status` command displays the following:

```
# zpool status mypool<cr>
  pool: mypool
  state: ONLINE
  scrub: resilver completed after 0h0m with 0 errors on Fri Jan 25 10:28:51 2013
 config:
```

```
        NAME            STATE     READ WRITE CKSUM
        mypool          ONLINE       0     0     0
          mirror        ONLINE       0     0     0
            c2t4d0      ONLINE       0     0     0
            c2t3d0      ONLINE       0     0     0

errors: No known data errors
```

The `c2t2d0` disk has been replaced. The physical disk can be removed from the system and replaced.

After a faulty device is replaced in a ZFS storage pool, clear the device error using the `zpool clear` command as follows:

```
# zpool clear rpool c2t2d0<cr>
```

You may also need to notify the FMA that the device is replaced. Check the status of a failed device by typing

```
# fmadm faulty<cr>
```

Obtain the field-replaceable unit (FRU) name from any device that is listed. Clear the fault after replacing the disk by typing

```
fmadm repair <FRU name>
```

For example, to clear the device that was identified as faulty earlier in this section, type

```
# fmadm repair "zfs://pool=f28bbe2ba2a4337e/vdev=de496baad5c90d32/pool_name=rpool/\
vdev_name=id1,sd@SATA_____VBOX_HARDDISK____VBd338ea51-aebb117e/b"<cr>
```

The system responds with the following message:

```
fmadm: recorded repair to zfs://pool=f28bbe2ba2a4337e/vdev=de496baad5c90d32/pool_
name=rpool/vdev_name=id1,sd@SATA_____VBOX_HARDDISK____VBd338ea51-aebb117e/bReplacing
a disk in the root pool
```

When replacing a disk in a mirrored root pool using the `zpool replace` command, the disk must be made bootable. Depending on the version of Oracle Solaris 11, you will use either the `installboot`, `installgrub`, or `bootadm install-bootloader` commands. These commands are described in the next section.

The following should be considered when replacing a failed device in a ZFS storage pool:

- If you set the `autoreplace` pool property to `on`, then any new device found in the same physical location as a device that previously belonged to the pool is automatically formatted and replaced. You are not required to use the `zpool replace` command when this property is enabled. This feature might not be available on all hardware types.
- The storage pool state REMOVED is provided when a device or hot spare has been physically removed while the system was running. A hot spare device is substituted for the removed device, if available.
- If a device is removed and then reinserted, the device is placed `online`. If a hot spare was activated when the device was reinserted, the hot spare is removed when the online operation completes.
- Automatic detection when devices are removed or inserted is hardware dependent and might not be supported on all platforms. For example, USB devices are automatically configured upon insertion. However, you might need to use the `cfgadm -c configure` command to configure a SATA drive.
- Hot spares are checked periodically to ensure that they are online and available.
- The size of the replacement device must be equal to or larger than the smallest disk in a mirrored or RAID-Z configuration. When a replacement device that is larger in size than the device it is replacing is added to a pool, it is not automatically expanded to its full size. The `autoexpand` pool property value determines whether a replacement LUN is expanded to its full size when the disk is added to the pool. By default, the `autoexpand` property is disabled. You can enable this property to expand the LUN size before or after the larger LUN is added to the pool.

Hot Spares

The hot spares feature in ZFS enables you to identify disks that could be used to replace a failed or faulted disk in a storage pool. When a hot spare is assigned to a storage pool, that disk is not an active device in the pool. When an active device in the pool fails, the hot spare automatically replaces the failed device. Devices can be designated as hot spares in the following ways:

- When the pool is created with the `zpool create` command
- After the pool is created with the `zpool add` command

The following example adds a hot spare to an existing pool named "zone." The zone pool is currently configured as follows:

```
# zpool status zone<cr>
  pool: zone
 state: ONLINE
  scan: resilvered 3.41G in 0h8m with 0 errors on Wed Jan 23 11:32:51 2013
config:

        NAME          STATE     READ WRITE CKSUM
        zone          ONLINE       0     0     0
          mirror-0    ONLINE       0     0     0
            c3t2d0    ONLINE       0     0     0
            c3t3d0    ONLINE       0     0     0
```

The active disks are 16GB disk drives. For my spare, I'll choose another 16GB drive. I'll add this drive to the pool as a hot spare as follows:

```
# zpool add zone spare c3t5d0<cr>
```

The zpool status command displays the hot spare as part of the storage pool:

```
# zpool status zone<cr>
  pool: zone
 state: ONLINE
  scan: resilvered 3.41G in 0h8m with 0 errors on Wed Jan 23 11:32:51 2013
config:

        NAME          STATE     READ WRITE CKSUM
        zone          ONLINE       0     0     0
          mirror-0    ONLINE       0     0     0
            c3t2d0    ONLINE       0     0     0
            c3t3d0    ONLINE       0     0     0
        spares
          c3t5d0    AVAIL

errors: No known data errors
```

For this next example, I'll simulate a disk fault by performing an fdisk command on one of the active disks (c3t3d0) as follows:

```
# fdisk -B c3t3d0<cr>
```

The zpool status command displays the following information, indicating a problem:

```
# zpool status zone<cr>
  pool: zone
 state: DEGRADED
status: One or more devices is currently being resilvered.  The pool will
        continue to function, possibly in a degraded state.
```

```
action: Wait for the resilver to complete.
 scan:  resilver in progress since Wed Jan 23 13:14:31 2013
   297M  scanned out of 3.41G at 2.21M/s, 0h24m to go
   296M  resilvered, 8.50% done
config:

        NAME          STATE     READ WRITE CKSUM
        zone          DEGRADED     0     0     0
          mirror-0    DEGRADED     0     0     0
            c3t2d0    ONLINE       0     0     0
            spare-1   DEGRADED     0     0     0
              c3t3d0  UNAVAIL      0     0     0  cannot open
              c3t5d0  ONLINE       0     0     0  (resilvering)
        spares
          c3t5d0      INUSE     currently in use

errors: No known data errors
```

The storage pool is in a DEGRADED state, and the hot spare is activated automatically when a fault is detected, as shown in the previous output. `c3t3d0` is in an UNAVAIL state, and `c3t5d0` is resilvering. The hot spare is in the INUSE state. After resilvering, the status of the pool will be as follows:

```
# zpool status zone<cr>
  pool: zone
 state: DEGRADED
status: One or more devices could not be opened. Sufficient replicas exist for the pool
        to continue functioning in a degraded state.
action: Attach the missing device and online it using 'zpool online'.
   see: http://www.sun.com/msg/ZFS-8000-2Q
  scan: resilvered 3.41G in 0h8m with 0 errors on Wed Jan 23 13:23:01 2013

config:

        NAME          STATE     READ WRITE CKSUM
        zone          DEGRADED     0     0     0
          mirror-0    DEGRADED     0     0     0
            c3t2d0    ONLINE       0     0     0
            spare-1   DEGRADED     0     0     0
              c3t3d0  UNAVAIL      0     0     0  cannot open
              c3t5d0  ONLINE       0     0     0
        spares
          c3t5d0      INUSE     currently in use

errors: No known data errors
```

The storage pool will remain in a degraded state until the failed drive is either replaced or detached from the storage pool. In this case, I'll detach the failed drive as follows:

```
# zpool detach zone c3t3d0<cr>
```

After detaching the faulty disk, the pool status is changed to ONLINE as shown:

```
# zpool status zone<cr>
  pool: zone
 state: ONLINE
```

```
  scan: resilvered 3.41G in 0h8m with 0 errors on Wed Jan 23 13:23:01 2013
config:

        NAME          STATE     READ WRITE CKSUM
        zone          ONLINE       0     0     0
          mirror-0    ONLINE       0     0     0
            c3t2d0    ONLINE       0     0     0
            c3t5d0    ONLINE       0     0     0
errors: No known data errors
```

The spare is automatically promoted to an active disk (submirror) and is no longer listed as a hot spare.

The `zpool remove` command is used to remove hot spares, but only when the spare is in the AVAIL state. For example, to remove the spare from the zone pool, type

```
# zpool remove zone c3t5d0<cr>
```

The ZFS Root File System

ZFS is the default file system used in Oracle Solaris 11 for the boot disk and the root file system. ZFS on the boot drive is configured automatically during software installation. It is referred to as a bootable root pool and is typically named `rpool`. A recursive list of the `rpool` storage pool shows the following:

```
# zfs list -r rpool<cr>
NAME                        USED   AVAIL   REFER   MOUNTPOINT
rpool                      5.06G   61.9G   73.5K   /rpool
rpool/ROOT                 2.03G   61.9G     31K   legacy
rpool/ROOT/solaris         2.03G   61.9G   1.81G   /
rpool/ROOT/solaris/var      221M   61.9G    219M   /var
rpool/dump                 2.00G   61.9G   1.94G   -
rpool/export                 64K   61.9G     33K   /export
rpool/export/home            31K   61.9G     31K   /export/home
rpool/swap                 1.03G   61.9G   1.00G   -
```

The disks in the root pool must meet these requirements:

- A SPARC-based system must contain a slice and must be labeled with an SMI label.

Note

In Oracle Solaris 11.1, the x86-based system can boot to a disk with an EFI label. As of this writing, the SPARC boot disk still needs to have an SMI label.

- The disk that is intended for the root pool must be less than 2 terabytes (TB) in size so that the Oracle Solaris OS can boot successfully. The exception is when using an EFI-labeled disk on the x86 platform.
- On an x86-based system, the disk must contain an `fdisk` partition. An Oracle Solaris `fdisk` partition is created automatically when the x86-based system is installed.
- The `gzip` compression algorithm is not supported on root pools.
- The `bootfs` property for the root pool identifies the bootable dataset for the root pool. For example, when I list the `bootfs` property using `zpool get bootfs rpool`, the following information is displayed:

```
rpool  bootfs  rpool/ROOT/solaris  local
```

- Do not rename the root pool after it is created by an initial installation. Renaming the root pool might result in an unbootable system.

On the SPARC platform, the simplest configuration is to put the entire disk capacity in slice 0 and use that slice for the root pool. This is how the `rpool` boot disk is formatted on a SPARC system:

```
Part          Tag    Flag      Cylinders        Size            Blocks
  0          root     wm       1 - 14086       68.35GB    (14086/0/0) 143339136
  1    unassigned     wm       0                0         (0/0/0)             0
  2        backup     wu       0 - 14086       68.35GB    (14087/0/0) 143349312
  3    unassigned     wm       0                0         (0/0/0)             0
  4    unassigned     wm       0                0         (0/0/0)             0
  5    unassigned     wm       0                0         (0/0/0)             0
  6    unassigned     wm       0                0         (0/0/0)             0
  7    unassigned     wm       0                0         (0/0/0)             0
```

As with any other storage pool, the same ZFS operations can be performed on the root pool such as snapshots, cloning, and mirroring. A bootable root pool can be either a dynamic stripe, nonredundant pool, or a mirrored pool. It cannot be a RAID-Z pool.

A nonredundant root pool on a SPARC-based system can be mirrored as follows:

```
# zpool attach rpool c2t0d0s0 c2t1d0s0<cr>
```

In the example, I have attached `c2t1d0s0` to the existing root pool disk (`c2t0d0s0`). Make certain that the new disk, `c2t1d0`, is formatted exactly like c2t0d0 and, for a SPARC-based system, is labeled with an SMI label. Also make sure that you specify the slice for each disk to preserve the SMI label.

After the resilvering is complete, the zpool status rpool command will display the following:

```
pool: rpool
  state: ONLINE
  scan: resilvered 6.42G in 0h9m with 0 errors on Wed Nov 28 08:39:16 2012
config:
```

The final step is to make the new disk bootable. On Oracle Solaris 11/11, a disk is made bootable by using the installboot(1M) command as follows:

```
# installboot -F zfs /usr/platform/'uname -i'/lib/fs/zfs/bootblk /dev/rdsk/c2t1d0s0<cr>
```

In Oracle Solaris 11.1 and newer, the bootadm command is used on both the SPARC and x86 platforms as follows:

```
# bootadm install-bootloader<cr>
```

The install-bootloader subcommand installs the system bootloader onto the boot disk. In Oracle Solaris 11.1 and newer systems, the bootadm command supersedes the functionality of the installboot(1M) command on the SPARC platform.

Finally, you should verify that you can successfully boot to the new disk.

Using an EFI-Formatted Boot Disk: x86

As of the release of Oracle Solaris 11.1, an x86-based system may use an EFI- or SMI-labeled disk. On an Oracle Solaris 11.1 boot disk with an EFI label, the disk partitioning is as follows:

```
Volume name = <        >
ascii name  = <ATA-VBOX HARDDISK-1.0-36.00GB>
bytes/sector  =  512
sectors = 75497471
accessible sectors = 75497438
Part         Tag    Flag     First Sector        Size        Last Sector
  0    BIOS_boot     wm               256     256.00MB         524543
  1          usr     wm            524544      35.74GB         75481054
  2   unassigned     wm                 0         0              0
```

```
  3   unassigned    wm                  0            0            0
  4   unassigned    wm                  0            0            0
  5   unassigned    wm                  0            0            0
  6   unassigned    wm                  0            0            0
  8     reserved    wm           75481055       8.00MB     75497438
```

Notice that slice 0 contains `BIOS_boot` information, and the OS will be installed in slice 1. The same boot disk on an earlier Oracle Solaris 11/11 x86-based system would have used an SMI label, and the disk information would have been as follows:

```
Primary label contents:

Volume name = <        >
ascii name  = <ATA-VBOX HARDDISK-1.0 cyl 2085 alt 2 hd 255 sec 63>
pcyl        = 2087
ncyl        = 2085
acyl        =    2
bcyl        =    0
nhead       =  255
nsect       =   63
Part      Tag     Flag  Cylinders    Size             Blocks
  0       root     wm    1 - 2084   15.96GB     (2084/0/0) 33479460
  1  unassigned    wm    0           0          (0/0/0)           0
  2     backup     wu    0 - 2086   15.99GB     (2087/0/0) 33527655
  3  unassigned    wm    0           0          (0/0/0)           0
  4  unassigned    wm    0           0          (0/0/0)           0
  5  unassigned    wm    0           0          (0/0/0)           0
  6  unassigned    wm    0           0          (0/0/0)           0
  7  unassigned    wm    0           0          (0/0/0)           0
  8       boot     wu    0 -    0    7.84MB     (1/0/0)       16065
  9  unassigned    wm    0           0          (0/0/0)           0
```

Notice that, on the SMI-labeled disk, the root file system will be located on slice 0.

On an x86-based system, when using an EFI label for the boot disk, the root pool can be mirrored without specifying the slice as follows:

```
# zpool attach rpool c7t0d0 c7t2d0<cr>
```

I described formatting and labeling a root pool disk for both the SPARC and the x86 platforms in Chapter 4. After the resilvering process is complete, the root disk will be mirrored but not bootable.

In addition, the `zpool` command for the x86 platform now includes a new option: `-B`. The `zpool create -B` command, when operating on a whole disk device, creates the boot partition for an x86-based system on an EFI-labeled boot disk.

Another example is when I want to change an existing root pool on an x86-based system that is running Oracle Solaris 11.1 or newer. I will convert the root pool from a nonredundant single-disk configuration into a redundant mirrored configuration. I'll begin with an unformatted disk that does not contain a label. When accessing this disk in the `format` utility, the following message is displayed:

```
selecting c7t2d0
[disk formatted]
No Solaris fdisk partition found.
```

When I verify the disk in the `format` utility, I receive the following message:

```
format> verify<cr>
WARNING - This disk may be in use by an application that has
          modified the fdisk table. Ensure that this disk is
          not currently in use before proceeding to use fdisk.
```

I could perform the `fdisk` and slicing operation in the `format` utility, but it would be a multistep operation. Instead, I'll exit the format utility, and I'll add the disk to the existing `rpool`. The formatting will take place automatically as follows:

```
# zpool attach rpool c7t0d0 c7t2d0<cr>
```

The following message is displayed as the root pool is mirrored:

```
Make sure to wait until resilver is done before rebooting.
```

After attaching the disk to the root pool, when I verify the new disk in the `format` utility, we see that the disk has been formatted with an EFI label, has been sliced, and contains a slice 0 for the boot information:

```
format> verify<cr>

Volume name = <        >
ascii name  = <ATA-VBOX HARDDISK-1.0-36.00GB>
bytes/sector  =  512
sectors = 75497471
accessible sectors = 75497438
Part      Tag    Flag     First Sector       Size       Last Sector
  0    BIOS_boot  wm              256      256.00MB       524543
  1          usr  wm           524544       35.74GB       75481054
  2   unassigned  wm                0          0           0
  3   unassigned  wm                0          0           0
  4   unassigned  wm                0          0           0
  5   unassigned  wm                0          0           0
  6   unassigned  wm                0          0           0
  8   reserved    wm         75481055        8.00MB     75497438
```

Finally, make the disk bootable as follows:

```
# /usr/sbin/bootadm install-bootloader<cr>
```

The `install-bootloader` subcommand installs the system bootloader. In Oracle Solaris 11.1, `install-bootloader` supersedes the functionality of `installgrub(1M)` on x86 and `installboot(1M)` on SPARC, as well as supporting the installation of GRUB2's bootloader on the x86 boot disk.

As a last step, you should verify that you can successfully boot to the new disk.

Creating Root Pool Snapshots

You can create root pool snapshots for recovery purposes. The best way to create root pool snapshots is to perform a recursive snapshot of the root pool.

A good practice is to create a recursive root pool snapshot and then store the snapshot as a file on a remote system. If a root pool fails, the remote dataset can be mounted using NFS, and the snapshot file can be received into the recreated pool.

The following steps describe the process of creating root pool snapshots of a local system and storing those snapshots on a remote system through an NFS mount:

1. On the remote system, share the remote file system with the local system. For example:

```
remote# zfs set sharenfs='rw=local-system,root=local-system' rpool/snaps<cr>
```

2. On the remote system, verify that the file system is shared:

```
remote# share<cr>
  -@rpool/snaps   /rpool/snaps   sec=sys,rw=local-system,root=local-system   ""
```

3. On the local system, create a recursive snapshot of the root pool as follows:

```
local# zfs snapshot -r rpool@snap1<cr>
```

4. List the snapshots to verify that they have been created:

```
local# zfs list -r rpool<cr>
```

5. Send the root pool snapshots to the remote system. For example, to send the root pool snapshots to a remote pool as a file, use the following syntax:

```
local# zfs send -Rv rpool@snap1 > /net/remote-system/rpool/snaps/rpool. snap1<cr>
```

To send the root pool snapshots to a remote pool as snapshots, use the following syntax:

```
local# zfs send -Rv rpool@snap1 | ssh remote-system \
zfs receive -Fd -o canmount=off tank/snaps<cr>
```

Validating remotely stored snapshots as files or snapshots is an important step in root pool recovery.

Snapshots should be recreated on a routine basis, such as when the pool configuration changes or when the Oracle Solaris OS is upgraded.

It's a good practice to create snapshots of the root pool before making changes to the boot drive. Use the procedure described earlier to create a recursive snapshot of the root pool. After the snapshots have been created, make the change to the root pool. If the change does not work as planned, or if the system does not operate as it should after the change, you can put the root drive back to its previous state by performing a snapshot rollback using the `zfs rollback` command.

In the example, I've already created a recursive snapshot of my root pool. I verify the snapshots using the `zfs list` command as follows:

```
# zfs list -t snapshot<cr>
NAME                              USED  AVAIL  REFER  MOUNTPOINT
rpool@snap                           0      -  73.5K  -
rpool/ROOT@snap                      0      -    31K  -
rpool/ROOT/solaris@install       8.19M      -  1.55G  -
rpool/ROOT/solaris@snap              0      -  1.81G  -
rpool/ROOT/solaris/var@install   2.33M      -   215M  -
rpool/ROOT/solaris/var@snap          0      -   219M  -
rpool/dump@snap                      0      -  1.94G  -
rpool/export@snap                    0      -    33K  -
rpool/export/home@snap               0      -    31K  -
rpool/swap@snap                      0      -  1.00G  -
```

I accidentally removed the `/etc/group` file as shown:

```
# ls -l /etc/group<cr>
/etc/group: No such file or directory
```

I need to restore the /etc/group file. My best option is to roll back the root file system to its previous state (when I took the snapshot). Use the zfs rollback command as follows:

```
# zfs rollback rpool/ROOT/solaris@snap<cr>
```

In only a few seconds, the / file system has been restored to its previous state and the file is back online:

```
# ls -l /etc/group<cr>
-rw-r--r--   1 root     sys        416 Sep 19 16:34 /etc/group
```

Use the zfs destroy command to remove the recursive snapshots of the root pool as follows:

```
# zfs destroy -r rpool@snap<cr>
```

The zfs list command shows that the snapshots have been removed:

```
# zfs list -t snapshot<cr>
NAME                               USED   AVAIL  REFER    MOUNTPOINT
rpool/ROOT/solaris@install         8.19M  -      1.55G    -
rpool/ROOT/solaris/var@install     2.33M  -      215M     -
```

Two snapshots remain: rpool/ROOT/solaris@install and rpool/ROOT/solaris/var@install. These snapshots were created automatically, immediately after the OS was installed. If required, you can use these snapshots to roll your system back to its original "installed" state. Any customization since the installation would be lost.

Monitoring ZFS

ZFS continually monitors the data within the storage pool by validating the checksum of each block of data as it's retrieved from storage. You can also instruct ZFS to check the data in the entire pool using the zpool scrub command, which was described earlier in this chapter. In addition, to persistently track errors within the storage pools, ZFS notifies syslog when events of interest occur. If ZFS detects a device error and recovers from it, no notification occurs. If an error is deemed transient and unlikely to affect the future health of the device, the error can safely be cleared using the `zpool clear` command. For example, to clear errors associated with `pool1`, issue the following command:

```
# zpool clear pool1<cr>
```

Configure the `smtp-notify` service to notify you when a faulty hardware component is diagnosed. The `smtp-notify` service is described in Chapter 3. To configure the notification, you just have to configure the target e-mail address as follows.

```
# svccfg setnotify problem-diagnosed mailto:root@localhost<cr>
```

To check the configuration, use the `listnotify` command as follows:

```
# svccfg listnotify problem-diagnosed<cr>
   Event: problem-diagnosed (source: svc:/system/fm/notify-params:default)
        Notification Type: smtp
            Active: true
            reply-to: root@localhost
            to: root@localhost

        Notification Type: snmp
            Active: true

        Notification Type: syslog
            Active: true
```

For demonstration purposes, I'll connect a USB thumb drive to the server. I'll configure a ZFS file system on the thumb drive as follows:

```
# zpool create pool2 c4t0d0<cr>
```

To generate a notification, I'll remove the thumb drive. The following message appears in the `/var/adm/messages` file and on the system console:

```
Jan  9 16:01:19 solaris scsi: [ID 107833 kern.warning] WARNING: /pci@7c0/pci@0/pci@1/
pci@0/usb@6/hub@1/storage@2/disk@0,0 (sd0):
Jan 9 16:01:19 solaris      Command failed to complete...Device is gone
Jan 9 16:01:19 solaris fmd: [ID 377184 daemon.error] SUNW-MSG-ID: ZFS-8000-HC, TYPE:
Error, VER: 1, SEVERITY: Major
Jan 9 16:01:19 solaris EVENT-TIME: Thu Aug  9 16:01:19 EDT 2012
Jan 9 16:01:19 solaris PLATFORM: SUNW,Sun-Fire-T200, CSN: -, HOSTNAME: solaris
Jan 9 16:01:19 solaris SOURCE: zfs-diagnosis, REV: 1.0
Jan 9 16:01:19 solaris EVENT-ID: ff28a96e-7b43-434b-836f-d60fdda3d629
```

```
Jan 9 16:01:19 solaris DESC: The ZFS pool has experienced currently unrecoverable I/O
Jan 9 16:01:19 solaris          failures.  Refer to http://sun.com/msg/ZFS-8000-HC for
more information.
Jan 9 16:01:19 solaris AUTO-RESPONSE: No automated response will be taken.
Jan 9 16:01:19 solaris IMPACT: Read and write I/Os cannot be serviced.
Jan 9 16:01:19 solaris REC-ACTION: Make sure the affected devices are connected, then run
Jan 9 16:01:19 solaris         'zpool clear'.
Jan 9 16:01:19 solaris sendmail[1159]: [ID 702911 mail.crit] My unqualified host name
(solaris) unknown; sleeping for retry
Jan 9 16:01:55 solaris genunix: [ID 408114 kern.info] /pci@7c0/pci@0/pci@1/pci@0/usb@6/
hub@1/storage@2 (scsa2usb0) removed
Jan 9 16:01:55 solaris genunix: [ID 408114 kern.info] /pci@7c0/pci@0/pci@1/pci@0/usb@6/
hub@1/storage@2/disk@0,0 (sd0) removed
```

An e-mail message is also sent to root that reads:

```
From noaccess@solaris Thu Aug  9 16:02:19 2012
Date: Wed, 9 Jan 2013 16:02:19 -0400 (EDT)
From: No Access User <noaccess@solaris>
Message-Id: <201208092002.q79K2J8a001159@solaris>
Subject: Fault Management Event: solaris:ZFS-8000-HC
To: root@solaris
Content-Length: 568

SUNW-MSG-ID: ZFS-8000-HC, TYPE: Error, VER: 1, SEVERITY: Major
EVENT-TIME: Wed, 9 Jan 2013 16:01:19 EDT 2013
PLATFORM: SUNW,Sun-Fire-T200, CSN: -, HOSTNAME: solaris
SOURCE: zfs-diagnosis, REV: 1.0
EVENT-ID: ff28a96e-7b43-434b-836f-d60fdda3d629
DESC: The ZFS pool has experienced currently unrecoverable I/O
           failures.  Refer to http://sun.com/msg/ZFS-8000-HC for more information.
AUTO-RESPONSE: No automated response will be taken.
IMPACT: Read and write I/Os cannot be serviced.
REC-ACTION: Make sure the affected devices are connected, then run
            'zpool clear'.
```

When I issue the `zpool status` command, the following is displayed:

```
# zpool status -v pool2<cr>
  pool: pool2
 state: ONLINE
status: One or more devices are faulted in response to IO failures.
action: Make sure the affected devices are connected, then run 'zpool clear'.
   see: http://www.sun.com/msg/ZFS-8000-HC
  scan: none requested
config:

        NAME      STATE     READ WRITE CKSUM
        pool2     ONLINE       1     6     0
          c4t0d0  ONLINE       2     0     0
```

In this scenario, the `zpool clear` command would not clear the error because of a drive failure in a nonredundant storage pool. The disk would need to be replaced, and the storage pool would need to be recreated.

Migrate Legacy File Systems to ZFS

Oracle recommends using ZFS for all file systems. Although Oracle Solaris 11 supports legacy UFS and SVM volumes, you should migrate these file systems to ZFS as quickly as possible to take advantage of the many features provided by ZFS that are not available with legacy file systems. On smaller file systems, it's easiest to simply create a ZFS file system and copy the data from the legacy file system to the new ZFS file system as described in the next set of steps.

In the following example, I have an existing legacy file system named `/data`. I'm going to create a new ZFS pool and ZFS file system (`pool1/data`) on an empty disk. I'll change the `/data` file system to read-only so that the data remains static while I copy it. I'll use the `tar` utility to copy the data to the `pool1/data` file system. When finished, I'll rename the mountpoint for the ZFS file system from `pool1/data` to `/data`.

1. Create a ZFS pool and file system on a spare drive:

```
# zpool create pool1 c3t3d0<cr>
# zfs create pool1/data<cr>
```

2. Change the source file system to read-only:

```
# umount /data<cr>
# mount -o ro /dev/dsk/c3t2d0s1 /data<cr>
```

3. Copy the data to the new ZFS file system:

```
# cd /data<cr>
# tar cf - .|(cd /pool1/data; tar xf -)<cr>
```

4. Change the mountpoint on the new ZFS file system:

```
# cd/<cr>
# umount /data<cr>
# zfs set mountpoint=/data pool1/data<cr>
```

Instead of using `tar`, I could use the `rsync` command to copy data from one file system to another. `rsync` is actually the more popular option with system administrators. `rsync` can be used to copy files locally or to a remote host. It works especially well when synchronizing data between two file systems. Whereas `tar` copies everything from the source file system, `rsync` compares the two file systems and only copies the data that is different between the two file systems, improving performance across a network. It works great for backups and mirroring because it can be used to keep file systems and directories in sync with one another after the initial copy.

In this next example, I'll use `rsync` to copy all of the data from the UFS to the new ZFS file system (don't forget to perform all of the other steps I've outlined in the previous example):

```
# rsync -avH --progress /data /pool1<cr>
sending incremental file list
data/
data/documents/
data/lost+found/
data/production/
data/production/tarfile1
   179436544 100%  10.83MB/s    0:00:15 (xfer#1, to-check=0/6)
data/public/

sent 179458668 bytes  received 51 bytes  10876286.00 bytes/sec
total size is 179436544  speedup is 1.00
```

There are several options for the `rsync` command that are documented in the `rsync(1)` man pages.

The previous examples work well on smaller file systems because they can be copied quickly. However, on large file systems, where the copy could take several hours, it may not be possible to take a file system out of production (or change it to read-only) for that length of time.

The shadow migration tool is a new feature in Oracle Solaris 11 for migrating UFSs to ZFS. It's especially beneficial on large file systems. The feature can be used to

- Copy a local or remote ZFS file system to a target ZFS file system
- Copy a local or remote UFS to a target ZFS file system

Shadow Migration

Shadow migration works this way. Suppose we have an active UFS and we want to migrate the data to a new ZFS file system. Shadow migration will allow us to migrate the data to the new file system without taking the file system offline or restricting the users to a read-only file system. There are few requirements:

- The existing file system to be migrated must be set to read-only.
- The target ZFS file system must be completely empty.

- If the system must be rebooted during the migration, the migration continues after the system is booted.
- Data that is not completely migrated is blocked until the entire content has been migrated.
- Migrating a file system over NFS is possible but can be slow depending on your network bandwidth.

During the migration, users will be pointed to the new ZFS file system, even though that file system is initially empty. The `shadow` property is set to `on` when creating the new ZFS file system. When a request comes for a file that has not yet been migrated, ZFS will automatically migrate that file to the new file system before responding to the request. This could incur some initial latency for some client requests, but once the files have been migrated all requests for that data will be to the new file system and performance will be back to normal.

The following steps outline the process of migrating the data from the UFS to the new ZFS file system.

1. Make sure that the `shadow-migration` feature is installed:

```
# pkg list shadow-migration<cr>
pkg list: no packages matching 'shadow-migration' installed
```

Install the package as follows:

```
# pkg install shadow-migration<cr>
```

2. After installing the migration package, enable the `shadowd` daemon as follows:

```
# svcadm enable shadowd<cr>
```

3. Set the existing file system to read-only as follows:

```
# umount /data<cr>
# mkdir /data_old<cr>
# mount -o ro /dev/dsk/c3t2d0s1 /data_old<cr>
```

Notice that I also changed the mountpoint from `/data` to `/data_old`. This is so I can use the `/data` mountpoint for the new ZFS file system.

4. Create an empty ZFS file system in an existing zpool and set the shadow option to the source file system name (`/data`) as follows:

```
# zfs create -o shadow=file:///data_old -o mountpoint=/data rpool/data<cr>
```

If you are migrating data from a remote server, set the `shadow` property as follows:

```
# zfs create -o shadow=nfs://hosta/data -o mountpoint=/data pool1/data<cr>
```

5. You can monitor the progress of the migration with the `shadowstat` command as follows:

```
# shadowstat<cr>
                                        EST
                              BYTES     BYTES           ELAPSED
DATASET                                 XFRD     LEFT   ERRORS     TIME
No migrations in progress
```

The `shadowstat` command will display a line of output for each migrating file system indicating bytes transferred thus far, a rough estimate of bytes left to transfer, number of migration errors, and the time elapsed since the migration was started.

Summary

This chapter has described how to administer ZFS datasets. After reading this chapter, you should understand the advantages of a ZFS file system over legacy UFSs. You also should understand how to create and remove a ZFS storage pool and file system.

Having read this chapter, you learned about the various ZFS configurations: RAID-0, mirrored, and RAID-Z storage pools. You should understand the advantages and disadvantages of each and how to create each type of storage pool.

I have described how to display the ZFS datasets installed on your system and how to identify which types of storage pools have been configured. You should now be able to identify all of the components of a ZFS file system including the properties that are associated with ZFS datasets, the purpose of these properties, and how to manage them.

The chapter also described the various health states of a ZFS dataset, how to view the current state of ZFS datasets, how to identify problems, and how to recover from problems such as a disk failure.

ZFS snapshots were described, as well as how to create a ZFS snapshot, back up and restore a snapshot, list a snapshot, roll back a snapshot, and remove a snapshot. In addition, read-only clones were described, as well as how to create a read-only clone and how to promote a clone to make it a writable ZFS file system.

I described the bootable root pool and ZFS file systems that are created during the installation of the OS.

Finally, I described how to migrate existing legacy file systems to ZFS.

There are many more topics to explore with ZFS file systems, but the topics I have covered in this chapter will get you off to a good start. Later, you may want to learn more about ZFS delegated administration, troubleshooting, tuning, and recovering ZFS file systems, including the root file system.

6

Administering Zones

Oracle Solaris provides a virtualization environment called "zones." Zones provide an isolation environment that allows virtual Oracle Solaris 11 and 10 environments to run on the same physical system. You can create Oracle Solaris 10 or 11 virtual environments on x86- or SPARC-based Oracle Solaris 11 systems.

Zones provide a virtual OS environment within a single physical instance of Oracle Solaris 11. Applications can run in an isolated and secure environment. This isolation prevents an application running in one zone from monitoring or affecting an application running in a different zone. A further important aspect of zones is that a failing application, such as one that would traditionally have leaked all available memory or exhausted all CPU resources, can be limited to affect only the zone in which it is running. This is achieved by limiting the amount of physical resources on the system that the zone can use.

The following are features provided by zones:

- Security: When a process is created in a zone, that process (and any of its children) cannot change zones or affect other zones.
- Isolation: Multiple applications can be deployed on the same machine, each in different zones. An application in one zone does not affect applications in another zone on the same system. Each zone has its own set of user accounts, root account, and passwords.

- Network isolation: Allows the zone to have an exclusive IP, allowing the zone to run on a different LAN or virtual LAN (VLAN) (when used on an exclusive network interface controller [NIC]) than the global zone.
  - Network services can be isolated to each zone so that if a network service is compromised in a zone, activities using that service affect only that zone.
- Virtualization: In a virtualized environment, each zone is administered separately. Details about the system's physical devices and primary IP address are hidden from the applications in each zone.
- Granularity: Hardware resources can be shared between several zones or allocated on a per-zone basis using Oracle Solaris resource management tools.
- Environment: Zones provide the same standard interfaces and application environment that applications expect on an Oracle Solaris system. In fact, with a `solaris10` branded zone, it is possible to run Oracle Solaris 10 binaries in an Oracle Solaris 10 environment on an Oracle Solaris 11 host. You can migrate an Oracle Solaris 10 system or zone into a `solaris10` zone on an Oracle Solaris 11 system.

Zones provide an isolated and secure environment for running applications. Each zone will have its own instance of the Oracle Solaris OS; however, all zones will share the same kernel. A zone will provide an application execution environment in which processes in a zone are isolated from the rest of the system. The isolation prevents processes that are running in one zone from monitoring or affecting processes that are running in other zones. Even the root user has a limited set of privileges in each zone and cannot review or affect the activity in other zones. With zones, it makes it possible to maintain a one-application-per-server deployment model while simultaneously sharing hardware resources.

You might be familiar with VMware, which is available on x86-compatible computers. It is used to host multiple OS instances on a single computer. Zones differ from VMware in that VMware uses large amounts of the system's CPU capacity to manage the VMware environments. With zones, the system overhead is negligible. In most cases, several dozen zones can take up less than 1% of the system's resources. The best comparison of zones to existing technology would be FreeBSD jails.

This chapter looks at the whole concept of Oracle Solaris zones, including how to configure and create a zone, how to make it operational, and then how to remove it. In addition, I'll include an introduction to Oracle Solaris resource management techniques to help put the zones containment feature in the correct context.

Zones and Containers

Some people refer to zones and containers interchangeably, as if they are the same thing. This is incorrect. Containers are a technology that combines a zone with the OS's resource management features. With containers, a system administrator can use the resource management facility to allocate resources such as memory and CPU to applications and services within each zone. Therefore, Oracle Solaris zones are a subset of containers, and the two terms should not be used interchangeably.

Oracle Solaris 11 Enhancements

If you have experience using zones in Oracle Solaris 10, the following changes have been made to zones in Oracle Solaris 11:

- Boot environments in zones: Boot environments are now integrated in Oracle Solaris 11 zones.
- IPS integration: The IPS package management tools have been integrated into Oracle Solaris 11 zones.
- Zone resource monitoring: A new resource monitoring utility, `zonestat`, is available to observe system resources consumed by zones.
- Delegated administration: Common zone administration tasks can be delegated to specific zones for different system administrators using role-based access control (RBAC).
- Oracle Solaris 10 branded zones: BrandZ technology provides a complete runtime environment for Oracle Solaris 10 applications in a non-global zone.
- Immutable zones: These provide read-only file system profiles to zones, but with more flexibility than what was available with sparse root zones in Oracle Solaris 10.

Consolidation and Resource Management

Resource management is one of the components of the Oracle Solaris containers technology. It allows you to do the following:

- Allocate specific computer resources, such as CPU time and memory.
- Monitor how resource allocations are being used and adjust the allocations when required.
- Generate more detailed accounting information. The extended accounting feature of Oracle Solaris 11 provides this facility.

- A resource capping daemon (`rcapd`) allows you to regulate how much physical memory is used by a project by "capping" the overall amount that can be used. Remember that a project can be a number of processes or users, so it provides a useful control mechanism for a number of functions.

Consolidation

The resource management feature of Oracle Solaris containers is extremely useful when you want to consolidate a number of applications to run on a single server.

Consolidation has become more popular in recent years because it reduces the cost and complexity of having to manage numerous separate systems. You can consolidate applications onto fewer, larger, more scalable servers and also segregate the workload to restrict the resources that each can use.

Previously, a number of applications would run on separate servers, with each application having full access to the system on which it was running. Using the resource management feature, multiple workloads can now be run on a single server, providing an isolated environment for each, so that one workload cannot affect the performance of another.

Resource pools can be used to group applications or functions together and control their resource usage globally, such as the maximum amount of CPU resource or memory. Additionally, the resource management feature can tailor the behavior of the Fair-Share Scheduler (FSS) to give priority to specific applications. This is very useful if you need to allocate additional resources to a group of resources for a limited period of time. An example of this would be when a company runs end-of-month reports. Before resource management was introduced, this would have meant that a larger server would be needed to accommodate the resource requirement, even though it would be used to its capacity only once a month. Now the resources can be allocated according to priority, allowing the server to be more efficiently used.

Oracle Solaris Zones

The zones technology provides virtual OS services to allow applications to run in an isolated and secure environment. A zone is a virtual environment that is created within a single running instance of the Oracle Solaris operating environment. Applications running in a zone environment cannot affect applications running in a different zone, even though they exist and run on the same physical server. Even a privileged user in a zone cannot monitor or access processes running in a different zone.

Types of Zones

The two types of zones are "global" and "non-global". Think of a global zone as the server itself, the traditional view of an Oracle Solaris system as we all know it, where you can log in as root and have full control of the entire system. The global zone is the default zone and is used for system-wide configuration and control. Every system contains a global zone, and there can only be one global zone on a physical Oracle Solaris server.

A non-global zone is created from the global zone and also managed by it. You can have up to 8,192 non-global zones on a single physical system. The only real limitation is the capability of the server itself. Applications that run in a non-global zone are isolated from applications running in a separate non-global zone, allowing multiple versions of the same application to run on the same physical server.

By default, a non-global zone has the same OS and characteristics of the global zone because they share the same kernel. Therefore, the default zone runs the Oracle Solaris 11 environment. It is also possible to run a different operating environment inside a non-global zone. This is called a branded zone (BrandZ). It allows the creation of brands, which allow an alternative runtime configuration within each zone. This brand could be used to "emulate" the Oracle Solaris 10 operating environment. Use the `solaris10` brand zone to run applications designed to run on Oracle Solaris 10.

In branded zones, the brand defines the operating environment to be installed and how the system will behave within the zone.

Other Branded Zones

In Oracle Solaris 10, branded zones could be configured to emulate Oracle Solaris 8, Oracle Solaris 9, and Linux environments. These environments are not available in Oracle Solaris 11. The `solaris10` brand zone and Oracle Solaris 11 are the only environments available in Oracle Solaris 11 zones.

Zone States

Non-global zones are referred to simply as "zones" and can be in a number of states depending on the current state of configuration or readiness for operation. You should note that "zone states" refer only to non-global zones because the global zone is always running and represents the system itself. The only time the global zone is not running is when the server has been shut down.

Table 6-1 describes the seven states in which a zone can be.

Table 6-1 Zone States

State	Description
Configured	A zone is in this state when the configuration has been completed and storage has been committed. Additional configuration that must be done after the initial reboot has yet to be done.
Incomplete	A zone is set to this state during an install or uninstall operation. Upon completion of the operation, it changes to the correct state.
Installed	A zone in this state has a confirmed configuration. The `zoneadm` command is used to verify that the zone will run on the designated Oracle Solaris system. Packages have been installed under the zone's `root` path. Even though the zone is installed, it still has no virtual platform associated with it.
Ready	The zone's virtual platform is established. The kernel creates the `zsched` process, the network interfaces are plumbed, and file systems are mounted. The system also assigns a zone ID at this state, but no processes are associated with this zone.
Running	A zone enters this state when the first user process is created. This is the normal state for an operational zone.
Shutting Down + Down	Transitional states are visible only while a zone is in the process of being halted. If a zone cannot shut down for any reason, it also displays this state.
Unavailable	This state allows `pkg` operations to work even if a zone's storage is not available. This state was added in Oracle Solaris 11.1 and is important for zones that are on Shared Storage.

Zone Features

This section describes the features of both the global zone and non-global zones. The global zone has the following features:

- The global zone is assigned zone ID 0 by the system.
- It provides the single bootable instance of the Oracle Solaris operating environment that runs on the system.
- It contains a full installation of Oracle Solaris system packages.
- It can contain additional software, packages, file, or data that was not installed through the package mechanism.
- The global zone contains a complete product database of all installed software components.
- It holds configuration information specific to the global zone, such as the global zone hostname and the file system table.
- It is the only zone that is aware of all file systems and devices on the system.
- It is the only zone that is aware of non-global zones and their configuration.

- It is the only zone from which a non-global zone can be configured, installed, managed, and uninstalled.

Non-global zones have the following features:

- The non-global zone is assigned a zone ID by the system when it is booted.
- It shares the kernel that is booted from the global zone.
- It contains a subset of the installed Oracle Solaris system packages.
- It can contain additional software packages, shared from the global zone.
- It can contain additional software packages that are not shared from the global zone.
- It can contain additional software, files, or data that were not installed using the package mechanism nor shared from the global zone.
- It contains a complete product database of all software components that are installed in the zone. This includes software that was installed independently of the global zone as well as software shared from the global zone.
- It is unaware of the existence of other zones.
- It cannot install, manage, or uninstall other zones, including itself.
- It can have a read-writable root file system or a read-only file system.
- It contains configuration information specific to itself, the non-global zone, such as the non-global zone hostname and file system table, domain name, and Network Information Service (NIS) server.
- It can have its own time zone setting.
- It can have its own customized set of services.
- It can have its own set of boot environments.
- A package installed in the global zone is no longer installed into all non-global zones. In general, the global zone's package contents no longer dictate each zone's package contents, for both IPS and SVR4 packaging.
- Zone software is minimized to start. Any additional packages the zone requires must be added.
- It can be an NFS server (a new feature in Oracle Solaris 11).

Zones

Only one kernel is running on the system, and it is running on the global zone. The non-global zones share this kernel. Therefore, all non-global zones are at the same kernel patch level as the global zone. However, for middleware applications such as Java Enterprise System, each zone can be patched on a per-zone basis.

Non-global Zone Root File System Models

In Oracle Solaris 10, a zone's root file system could be either whole root or sparse. The whole root zone provided the greatest configuration flexibility because all of the required Oracle Solaris packages were copied to the zone's private file system and the root file system was read-writable.

In Oracle Solaris 10, a sparse root zone shared parts of the root file system with the global zone. The sparse root zone implemented a read-only loopback file system from the global zone, and it installed only a subset of the system root packages locally. The majority of the root file system was shared (inherited) from the global zone, which saved a great deal of disk space. The sparse root file system provided a smaller footprint, requiring less disk space, and a read-only root file system that could not be modified. Although the read-only sparse root zone provided security against unauthorized or accidental changes, the disadvantage is that it was difficult to make authorized modification to the root file system. In addition, with advances in ZFS file systems such as ZFS data deduplication, sparse root zones are no longer required and have been discontinued and replaced with immutable zones.

Immutable zones are read-only zones but still contain "whole root" file systems. The immutable zone can be configured as a completely read-only zone, or it can be partially read-only. The immutable zone is controlled by a mandatory write access control kernel policy. This policy enforces the zone's root file system write privilege through a `zonecfg file-mac-profile` property. The policy is enabled at zone boot.

By default, the `zonecfg file-mac-profile property` is not set in a non-global zone. The default policy for a non-global zone is to have a writable root file system. In an Oracle Solaris read-only zone, the `file-mac-profile property` is used to configure a read-only zone root. A read-only root restricts access to the runtime environment from inside the zone. Through the `zonecfg` utility, the `file-mac-profile` can be set to one of the following values.

`none`	Standard, read-write, non-global zone with no additional protection beyond the existing zones boundaries. Setting the value to `none` is equivalent to not setting the `file-mac-profile` property.
`strict`	Read-only file system, no exceptions. IPS packages cannot be installed. Persistently enabled SMF services are fixed. SMF manifests cannot be added from the default locations. Logging and auditing configuration files are fixed. Data can only be logged remotely.

`fixed-configuration`	Permits updates to `/var/*` directories, with the exception of directories that contain system configuration components. IPS packages, including new packages, cannot be installed. Persistently enabled SMF services are fixed. SMF manifests cannot be added from the default locations. Logging and auditing configuration files can be local. `syslog` and the audit configuration files are fixed.
`flexible-configuration`	Permits modification of files in `/etc/*` directories, changes to root's home directory, and updates to `/var/*` directories. This configuration provides the closest functionality to the Oracle Solaris 10 native sparse root zone. IPS packages, including new packages, cannot be installed. Persistently enabled SMF services are fixed. SMF manifests cannot be added from the default locations. Logging and auditing configuration files can be local. `syslog` and the audit configuration can be changed.

All of the profiles except `none` will cause the `/var/pkg` directory and its contents to be read-only from inside the zone.

Non-global Zone `zonepath`

The zone is typically stored in its own ZFS file system that is created and managed from the global zone. This is referred to as the `zonepath`. This `zonepath` will contain the non-global zone's root (`/`) file system.

Each non-global zone will have its own `zonepath` and its own root file system. There is no limit on how much disk space a zone can use in its root file system, but the zone administrator, normally the system administrator, must ensure that sufficient local storage exists to accommodate the requirements of all non-global zones being created on the system.

The system administrator should place the `zonepath` outside of the global zone's root pool, but this is not a requirement. In addition, you can restrict the amount of space allocated to the non-global zone's `zonepath`, using ZFS dataset quotas, so that the non-global zone does not unexpectedly fill up a storage pool.

Although a non-global zone requires a minimum of 150MB of free disk space per zone, a typical zone will consume between 500MB and 1GB of disk space once the non-global zone has been installed using all of the standard Oracle Solaris packages.

Networking in a Zone Environment

On a system supporting zones, the zones can communicate with each other over the network. But even though the zones reside on the same physical system, network traffic is restricted so that applications running on a specified zone cannot interfere with applications running on a different zone.

Each zone has its own set of bindings, and zones can all run their own network daemons. As an example, consider three zones all providing Web server facilities using the `apache` package. Using zones, all three zones can host websites on port 80, the default port for `http` traffic, without any interference between them. This is because the IP stack on a system supporting zones implements the separation of network traffic between zones.

The only interaction allowed is for Internet Control Message Protocol (ICMP) traffic to resolve problems, so that commands such as `ping` can be used to check connectivity.

Of course, when a zone is running, it behaves like any other Oracle Solaris system on the network in that you can `telnet` or `ftp` to the zone, assuming that the zone has configured these network services for use.

Zones use the network virtualization feature in Oracle Solaris 11, which allows partitioning of a physical NIC. I describe network virtualization in Chapter 7, "User and Security Administration." IP networking in a zone can be configured in two different ways, depending on whether the zone has its own exclusive network interface (exclusive-IP) or shares the network interface with the global zone (shared-IP).

The exclusive-IP model is the default, and the exclusive-IP zone must have a dedicated virtual network interface controller (VNIC), a separate LAN such as bge1, or a separate VLAN such as bge2000. Typically, a VNIC is created in the global zone, and this VNIC is associated with a specific zone during the zone-configuration process. If a VNIC is not created, it will be created automatically each time the zone boots and deleted each time the zone shuts down. Creating a VNIC is covered in Chapter 9, "The Oracle Solaris Network Environment."

In Oracle Solaris 10 zones, if a dedicated network stack (exclusive-IP) for the zone's network interface was desired, a dedicated physical NIC would have been required. New with Oracle Solaris 11, a dedicated physical NIC can be divided into multiple virtual interfaces to create dedicated network stacks from the physical interface to the application.

A zone can be assigned as many VNICs as needed, and each will have its own dedicated stack whose bandwidth and CPU allocation can be managed independently. For example, a 1GB NIC on the global zone could be divided into three VNICs. Bandwidth on each VNIC could be managed to prevent one zone from using all of the bandwidth. VNIC1 could be set to a maximum bandwidth of 100Mbps, VNIC2 could be set to 300Mbps, and VNIC3 could be set to 600Mbps.

A shared-IP zone shares a data link with the global zone and shares the IP layer configuration and state with the global zone. The IP address assigned to a shared-IP zone is associated with a logical network interface created in the global zone. The shared-IP model is less flexible than the exclusive-IP model, and a DHCP address cannot be configured in a shared-IP zone.

A zone must be either an exclusive-IP or a shared-IP, but it cannot be both.

To begin this chapter, I will be discussing exclusive-IP zones. When I create the zone, the VNIC for the zone will automatically be created in the global zone. Later in the chapter, I will describe how to configure a shared-IP zone.

Planning the Zone

Before creating a zone, you'll need to make a few decisions on how to configure the zone. Use the following information as a pre-planning guide:

- Select a name for the zone. The following rules apply to zone names:
  - Each zone must have a unique name.
  - A zone name is case sensitive.
  - A zone name must begin with an alphanumeric character.
  - The name can contain alphanumeric characters, underscores (_), hyphens (-), and periods (.).
  - The name cannot be longer than 63 characters.
  - The name "global" and all names beginning with "SYS" are reserved and cannot be used.
- Select a hostname for the zone.
- Select an IP address and decide whether the zone will use the exclusive-IP or shared-IP network model.
- Determine which network interfaces should be made available on the zone.

- Determine the zone path and disk space requirements. The zone path is a ZFS file system with quotas enabled.

  The `zonepath` property specifies the path under which the zone will be installed. Each zone has a path to its root directory that is relative to the global zone's root directory. The zone path must be owned by root with the mode 700. If the zone path does not exist, it will be automatically created during installation (this is the preferred method). If the permissions are incorrect, they will be automatically corrected.

  The non-global zone's root path is one level lower. The zone's root directory has the same ownership and permissions as the root directory (/) in the global zone. The zone directory must be owned by root with the mode 755. This hierarchy ensures that unprivileged users in the global zone are prevented from traversing a non-global zone's file system.

  The zone must reside on a ZFS dataset. The ZFS dataset is created automatically when the zone is installed or attached. If a ZFS dataset cannot be created, the zone will not install or attach.
- Make the FSS the default scheduler on the system so that you can configure CPU shares for each zone. The FSS guarantees a fair allocation of CPU resources among the zones.
- Determine which additional file systems the zone will be allowed to access.
- Determine which devices should be configured in each zone.
- Determine whether you must alter the default set of non-global zone permissions.

Many additional properties can also be configured when creating the zone, but these items cover the fundamentals.

Zone Service Instances and Daemons

The zone management service is managed through SMF; the service identifier is called `svc:/system/zones:default`. The service is responsible for the autobooting of a zone when the zone's `autoboot` property is set to `true`. This service references the `/lib/svc/method/svc-zones` startup script when starting zones.

Two daemon processes are associated with zones—`zoneadmd` and `zsched`.

The `zoneadmd` (zones administration) daemon starts when a zone needs to be managed. An instance of `zoneadmd` is started for each active zone (ready, running, or shutting down), so it is not uncommon to have multiple instances of this daemon running on a single server. `zoneadmd` is started automatically by the zone management software. The daemon shuts down automatically when it is no longer in use. Unless the daemon is already running, it is automatically started by the `zoneadm` command.

The zoneadmd daemon is the primary process for managing the zone's virtual platform. The daemon is responsible for booting and shutting down the zone. During the boot process, zoneadmd performs the following actions:

- Allocates the zone ID and starts the zsched system process
- Sets zone-wide resource controls
- Prepares the zone devices as specified in the zone configuration
- Sets up network interfaces
- Mounts loopback and conventional file systems
- Instantiates and initializes the zone console device

The zsched process is started when the zone enters the ready state. During this state, a unique zone ID is assigned by the system, file systems are mounted, network interfaces are set up, and devices are configured. Transitioning into the ready state prepares the virtual platform to begin running user processes. The job of zsched is to keep track of kernel resources associated with the zone. It is also known as the "zone scheduler."

Configuring a Zone

Before a zone can be installed and booted, it has to be created and configured. This section deals with the initial configuration of a zone and describes the zone components.

A zone is configured using the zonecfg command. The zonecfg command is also used to verify that the resources and properties that are specified during configuration are valid for use on an Oracle Solaris system. zonecfg checks that a zone path has been specified and that, for each resource, all the required properties have been specified.

Create a Zone: zonecfg

The zonecfg utility is used to configure a zone. It can run interactively, on the command line, or using a command file. A command file is created by using the export subcommand of zonecfg, which is described later. zonecfg carries out the following operations:

- Create or delete a zone configuration.
- Add or remove resources in a configuration.
- Set the properties for a resource in the configuration.
- Query and verify a configuration.
- Commit (save) a configuration.

- Revert to a previous configuration.
- Exit from a zonecfg session.

Before I describe how to manage zones, it's good to understand how to create a zone. The following steps outline how to create a simple zone in only a few steps. For this exercise, the zone will be named apps, it will be created in the /zones/apps file system, and it will be running the Oracle Solaris brand zone. The brand determines the user-level environment used within the zone, as well as various behaviors for the zone when it is installed, boots, or is shut down. Once the zone is installed, the brand cannot be changed.

1. If you do not have a storage pool for the zone's file system, create a new storage pool on a separate drive as follows:

```
# zpool create zones c3t3d0<cr>
```

2. Enter the zonecfg utility in the interactive mode and specify the name of the new zone as follows:

```
# zonecfg -z apps<cr>
zonecfg:apps apps: No such zone configured
Use 'create' to begin configuring a new zone.
zonecfg:apps>
```

When you enter zonecfg in interactive mode, the prompt changes to show that you are in a zonecfg session. The message that is displayed is not an error; it's simply stating that the apps zone does not exist and that you'll need to issue the create command to begin the configuration process. The prompt indicates that you are in the *global* scope of zonecfg.

3. Enter the create command to create the zone as follows:

```
zonecfg:apps> create<cr>
create: Using system default template 'SYSdefault'
```

The system informs us that we are using the SYSdefault zone template. This template is located in the /etc/zones directory and will set default values for some of the zone resources that are not specified. Specify the -b option to use a blank template and create a blank configuration with no defaults. If you have your own template, use the -t option and specify the template name.

The prompt indicates that you are in the *global* scope of zonecfg. We will configure the new zone by configuring the zone's resources. Some resources are required; others are optional. I'll describe all of the commands available and resources that can be configured in the zonecfg utility later. For now, let's keep it simple.

4. The next step is to configure the zonepath as follows:

```
zonecfg:apps> set zonepath=/zones/apps<cr>
```

Because the /zones/apps ZFS file system does not exist, it will automatically be created and the file permissions will be set correctly.

5. Exit the zonecfg utility as follows:

```
zonecfg:apps> exit<cr>
```

The system returns to a shell prompt:

```
#
```

The zone has been configured, and a file named /etc/zones/apps.xml has been created.

6. The final step is to install the zone. It is important to understand that zones in Oracle Solaris 11 are created by using the IPS feature. You will need to ensure that the system has access to an IPS repository. In this case, I have network access to a local IPS repository, which will be much faster than copying the files from the default repository at Oracle's Web site. For more details on IPS, refer to Chapter 2, "Managing and Updating Software with IPS."

Install the zone using the zoneadm command as follows:

```
# zoneadm -z apps install<cr>
The following ZFS file system(s) have been created:
    zones/apps
Progress being logged to /var/log/zones/zoneadm.20130125T023018Z.apps.install
       Image: Preparing at /zones/apps/root.

  AI Manifest: /tmp/manifest.xml.7YaGkf
   SC Profile:  /usr/share/auto_install/sc_profiles/enable_sci.xml
     Zonename:  apps
 Installation: Starting . . .

              Creating IPS image
Startup linked: 1/1 done
              Installing packages from:
                  solaris
                      origin:  http://192.168.1.221/
DOWNLOAD                                  PKGS         FILES    XFER (MB)    SPEED
Completed                              183/183   33556/33556  222.2/222.2   337k/s
```

continues

```
PHASE                                           ITEMS
Installing new actions                    46825/46825
Updating package state database                  Done
Updating image state                             Done
Creating fast lookup database                    Done
Installation: Succeeded

        Note: Man pages can be obtained by installing pkg:/system/manual

 done.

        Done: Installation completed in 1012.006 seconds.

  Next Steps: Boot the zone, then log into the zone console (zlogin -C)

              to complete the configuration process.

Log saved in non-global zone as
/zones/apps/root/var/log/zones/zoneadm.20130125T023018Z.apps.install
```

zoneadm Command

The zoneadm command is described later in the section titled "Administering Zones: zoneadm."

You can see that the zonecfg command automatically created the zonepath that was specified in step 3:

```
# zfs list -r /zones<cr>
NAME                                     USED  AVAIL  REFER  MOUNTPOINT
zones                                    335M  15.3G    32K  /zones
zones/apps                               335M  15.3G    32K  /zones/apps
zones/apps/rpool                         335M  15.3G    31K  /rpool
zones/apps/rpool/ROOT                    334M  15.3G    31K  legacy
zones/apps/rpool/ROOT/solaris            334M  15.3G   310M  /zones/apps/root
zones/apps/rpool/ROOT/solaris/var       24.2M  15.3G  23.2M  /zones/apps/root/var
zones/apps/rpool/export                  62K   15.3G    31K  /export
zones/apps/rpool/export/home             31K   15.3G    31K  /export/home
```

This zonepath contains the root file system for the zone.

The zone is installed, but it is not running. I'll describe how to connect to the zone and boot the zone later in this chapter.

To view the zone configuration, use the zonecfg command with the info subcommand as follows:

```
# zonecfg -z apps info<cr>
zonename: apps
zonepath: /zones/apps
brand: solaris
autoboot: false
bootargs:
file-mac-profile:
pool:
```

```
limitpriv:
scheduling-class:
ip-type: exclusive
hostid:
fs-allowed:
anet:
        linkname: net0
        lower-link: auto
        allowed-address not specified
        configure-allowed-address: true
        defrouter not specified
        allowed-dhcp-cids not specified
        link-protection: mac-nospoof
        mac-address: random
        mac-prefix not specified
        mac-slot not specified
        vlan-id not specified
        priority not specified
        rxrings not specified
        txrings not specified
        mtu not specified
        maxbw not specified
        rxfanout not specified
        vsi-typeid not specified
        vsi-vers not specified
        vsi-mgrid not specified
        etsbw-lcl not specified
        cos not specified
        pkey not specified
        linkmode not specified
```

The zonecfg utility can be used in the interactive mode, or it can be executed directly from the command line in a noninteractive mode. In step 2, I ran the zonecfg utility in the interactive mode. In the previous example, I ran it directly from the command line. By running the zonecfg command from the command line (noninteractively), I could reference a command file (-f option) to build my zones automatically from a shell script.

Although I did not specify a network interface when I created the zone, net0 was used by default. When the zone was booted, the VNIC was automatically created:

```
# dladm show-vnic<cr>
LINK                OVER    SPEED   MACADDRESS          MACADDRTYPE    VID
apps/net0           net0    1000    2:8:20:98:5b:fe     random         0
```

When the zone is shut down, the VNIC is deleted.

zonecfg Subcommands

As stated in the previous section, the zonecfg utility allows you to configure the zone by specifying subcommands and zone resources. Table 6-2 describes the subcommands that are available with the interactive mode of zonecfg.

Table 6-3 lists the resource types that are applicable to the zonecfg command.

Table 6-2 `zonecfg` Subcommands

Subcommand	Description
`create`	Begins configuring a zone using the default template of `SYSdefault`. This starts a configuration in memory for a new zone.
`cancel`	Ends the resource specification and resets scope to global. Abandons any partially specified resources. `cancel` is only applicable in the resource scope.
`commit`	Commits the current configuration from memory to stable storage. Until the in-memory configuration is committed, you can remove changes with the `revert` subcommand. The `commit` operation is attempted automatically upon completion of a `zonecfg` session. Since a configuration must be correct to be committed, this operation automatically does a `verify`. A configuration must be committed before it can be used by the `zoneadm` command, described later in this chapter.
`export`	Prints the configuration to `stdout`, or to a specified file name, which can be used as a command file.
`add`	In the global scope, this command takes you to the specified resource scope. In the resource scope, it adds the specified property to the resource type.
`set`	Sets a specified property name to a specified property value.
`select`	This is applicable only in the global scope; it selects the resource of the specified type. The scope changes to the resource, but you have to enter sufficient property name-value pairs to uniquely identify the required resource as follows: `select` *`resource`* [*`propertyname=value`*].
`remove`	In the global scope, removes the specified resource type. You have to enter sufficient property name-value pairs to uniquely identify the required resource as follows: `remove` *`resource`* [*`propertyname=value`*].
`end`	This is available only in the resource scope and ends the current resource specification.
`delete`	Destroys the specified configuration. You can use the `-F` option to force deletion with this option.
`info`	Displays information about the current configuration. If a resource type is specified, it displays information about the resource type.
`verify`	Verifies the current configuration to ensure that all resources have the required properties specified.
`revert`	Reverts the configuration to the last committed state.
`exit`	Exits the `zonecfg` session. You can use the `-F` option with this subcommand to force the command to execute.
`help`	Prints general help or help about given topic. Specify the subcommand for help on that command as follows: `help` <*subcommand*>.

Table 6-3 `zonecfg` Resource Types

Resource Type	Description
`zonename`	This resource identifies the zone and must be unique. It can't be longer than 63 characters. It's case sensitive and must begin with an alphanumeric character. It can also contain underscores (_), hyphens (-), and periods (.). The name "global" and all names beginning with "SUNW" are reserved and not allowed.
`zonepath`	This is the path to the zone root in relation to the global zone's root directory (/). To restrict visibility to nonprivileged users in the global zone, the permissions on the `zonepath` directory should be set to 700.
`fs`	Each zone can mount file systems. This resource specifies the path to the file system mountpoint.
`fs-allowed`	This resource provides a comma-separated list of additional file systems that can be mounted within the zone; for example, ufs,pcfs. By default, only hsfs and network file systems can be mounted.
`net`	Each zone can have network interfaces that are plumbed when the zone transitions from the installed state to the ready state. Network interfaces are implemented as virtual interfaces.
`file-mac-profile`	This resource defines which parts of the file system are exempted from the read-only policy. `file-mac-profile` is described in an earlier section titled "Non-global Zone Root File System Models."
`autoboot`	This Boolean resource indicates that a zone should be booted automatically at system boot. Note that if the zones service is disabled, the zone will not autoboot, regardless of the setting of this property. Default is false.
`bootargs`	This resource specifies arguments (options) to be passed to the zone at bootup.
`pool`	This resource provides the name of the resource pool to which this zone must be bound when booted. This property is incompatible with the `dedicated-cpu` resource.
`brand`	This resource specifies the zone's brand type.
`anet`	This resource specifies the automatic network interface.
`device`	Each zone can have devices that are configured when the zone transitions from the installed state to the ready state.
`rctl`	This resource is used for zone-wide resource controls. The controls are enabled when the zone transitions from the installed state to the ready state. The zone-wide resource controls implemented in Oracle Solaris 11 are `zone.cpu-shares` and `zone.max-lwps`.
`cpu-shares`	This resource specifies the number of FSS shares to allocate to this zone. This property is incompatible with the `dedicated-cpu` resource.

(continues)

Table 6-3 `zonecfg` Resource Types (*Continued*)

Resource Type	Description
`hostid`	A zone can emulate a 32-bit host identifier to ease system consolidation. A zone's `hostid` property is empty by default, meaning that the zone does not emulate a host identifier. Zone host identifiers must be hexadecimal values between 0 and FFFFFFFE. A 0x or 0X prefix is optional. Both uppercase and lowercase hexadecimal digits are acceptable.
`max-processes`	This resource specifies the maximum number of process table slots simultaneously available to this zone.
`attr`	This resource is a generic type most often used for comments.
`limitpriv`	This resource provides the maximum set of privileges any process in this zone can obtain.
`scheduling-class`	This resource specifies the scheduling class used for processes running in a zone.
`capped-cpu`	This resource specifies limits for CPU usage.
`ip-type`	A zone can either have its own exclusive instance of IP (the default) or share the IP instance with the global zone. In the default zone template, `SYSdefault`, `ip-type` is set to `exclusive`. In the also-supplied `SYSdefault-shared-ip` template, `ip-type` is set to `shared`.
`capped-memory`	This resource specifies limits for physical, swap, and locked memory.
`dataset`	This resource gives the ZFS dataset.
`dedicated-cpu`	This resource lists the subset of the system's processors dedicated to this zone while it is running.
`admin`	This resource specifies the delegated administrator.

There are several more resource types that I have not listed in Table 6-3. Refer to the `zonecfg` online man pages for a complete listing and description.

During the `zonecfg` session, additional resources can be specified. Some of the resource types described in Table 6-3 also have properties that need to be configured if the resource type is to be used. The following list describes some of the resource types, their properties and the parameters, and examples of usage:

- `fs`: `dir`, `special`, `raw`, `type`, `options`
  The following code gives an example of how these properties are used. The text in bold type indicates what the user enters.

```
zonecfg:apps> add fs<cr>
zonecfg:apps:fs> set dir=/testmount<cr>
zonecfg:apps:fs> set special=/dev/dsk/c0t1d0s0<cr>
zonecfg:apps:fs> set raw=/dev/rdsk/c0t1d0s0<cr>
```

```
zonecfg:apps:fs>  set type=ufs<cr>
zonecfg:apps:fs>  add options [logging, nosuid]<cr>
zonecfg:apps:fs>  end<cr>
```

This code example specifies that `/dev/dsk/c0t1d0s0` in the global zone is to be mounted on directory `/testmount` in the non-global zone and that the raw device `/dev/rdsk/c0t1d0s0` is the device to `fsck` before attempting the mount. The file system is of type `ufs`, and a couple of mount options have been added.

For instructions on how to add a ZFS file system to a zone, refer to the section titled "Using ZFS for Oracle Solaris Zones" later in this chapter.

- `dataset:name, alias`
  This specifies the ZFS dataset to be accessed from within a zone. The dataset will be assigned an alias and will appear as a virtual ZFS pool in the zone. Refer to the section titled "Using ZFS for Oracle Solaris Zones" later in this chapter.
- `device: match`
  This specifies a device to be included in the zone. The following code example includes a tape drive, `/dev/rmt/0`:

```
zonecfg:apps>  add device<cr>
zonecfg:apps:device>  set match=/dev/rmt/0<cr>
zonecfg:apps:device>  end<cr>
```

- `attr: name, type, value`
  The `attr` resource type is mainly used for adding a comment to a zone. The following example adds a comment for the zone `apps`:

```
zonecfg:apps>  add attr<cr>
zonecfg:apps:attr>  set name=comment<cr>
zonecfg:apps:attr>  set type=string<cr>
zonecfg:apps:attr>  set value="The Application Zone"<cr>
zonecfg:apps:attr>  end<cr>
```

- `capped-memory`
  Add a memory cap to a zone as follows:

```
zonecfg:testzone>  add capped-memory<cr>
zonecfg:testzone:capped-memory>  set physical=60m<cr>
zonecfg:testzone:capped-memory>  set swap=100m<cr>
zonecfg:testzone:capped-memory>  set locked=30m<cr>
```

The `capped-memory` resource sets the limit for physical memory, swap usage, and locked memory usage (privileged processes that are held in RAM and

cannot be swapped out) for a zone. You do not have to set all three limits, but at least one must be set.
To use the `capped-memory` resource, the `pkg://solaris/service/resource-cap` package must be installed in the global zone.

There are several other zone-wide resource controls that are described later in this chapter in the "Zone Resource Controls" section; here are a few:

- `zone.cpu-shares`: The number of FSS CPU shares for this zone
- `zone.max-locked-memory`: The total amount of physical locked memory available to a zone
- `zone.max-lwps`: The maximum number of lightweight processes (LWPs) simultaneously available to this zone
- `zone.max-swap`: The total amount of swap that can be consumed by user process address space mappings and `tmpfs` mounts for this zone

The `zone.cpu-shares` and `zone.max-lwps` controls prevent the zone from exhausting resources that could affect the performance or operation of other zones.

The following example allocates 20 CPU shares to the zone. This demonstrates the use of the Oracle Solaris containers feature to manage a resource within a zone. The resource manager in Oracle Solaris is based on an FSS. FSS ensures that processes get their fair share of the processing power as opposed to a percentage. If nothing else is using the processor, this zone gets 100% of the CPU power. If other zones are contending for CPU power, the shares determine which of them gets what.

```
zonecfg:apps> add rctl<cr>
zonecfg:apps:rctl> set name=zone.cpu-shares<cr>
zonecfg:apps:rctl> set value=(priv=privileged,limit=20,action=none)<cr>
zonecfg:apps:rctl> end<cr>
```

Be sure to set the FSS as the default process scheduler in the global zone; otherwise, you'll get an error when booting the zone. To set the process scheduler to FSS, type the following in the global zone:

```
# dispadmin -d FSS<cr>
#
```

To verify the process scheduler, type the following in the global zone:

```
# dispadmin -d<cr>
FSS  (Fair Share)
```

There are no known methods of breaking into a zone from another zone. However, it is possible for an attacker to try to use up all the process IDs (PIDs) in a system by issuing a denial-of-service attack on one zone. Using up all the PIDs in a zone could essentially use up all the PIDs and virtual memory on the entire system, including the global zone. To prevent this type of attack, you could limit the number of LWPs that can be run simultaneously within a given zone:

```
zonecfg:apps> add rctl<cr>
zonecfg:apps:rctl> set name=zone.max-lwps<cr>
zonecfg:apps:rctl> add value (priv=privileged,limit=1000,action=deny)<cr>
zonecfg:apps:rctl> end<cr>
```

This prevents a zone's processes from having more than 1,000 simultaneous LWPs.

Making Corrections in `zonecfg`

While configuring the zone in the `zonecfg` utility, mistakes are common. The bash shell command history is completely functional inside the `zonecfg` utility. To reissue or edit a previous command while in `zonecfg`, use the arrow keys to move back to previous commands.

If you need to modify a global property, such as the `zonepath`, just set the property again. For example, view the current `zonepath` property value using the `info` subcommand as follows:

```
zonecfg:apps> info zonepath<cr>
zonepath: /zones/apps
```

Change the `zonepath` as follows:

```
zonecfg:apps> set zonepath=zones/newzonepath<cr>
```

To clear a property, use the `clear` subcommand to set the value back to its default value. For example, view the current value for the `autoboot` property as follows:

```
zonecfg:apps> info autoboot<cr>
autoboot: true
```

Clear the `autoboot` value:

```
zonecfg:apps> clear autoboot<cr>
zonecfg:apps> info autoboot<cr>
autoboot: false
```

If you need to make a correction to a property contained in a particular resource, such as `anet`, you'll first need to select that resource. For example, the zone has the following automatic network interface configured:

```
zonecfg:apps> info anet<cr>
anet:
        linkname: net0
        lower-link: auto
        allowed-address not specified
        configure-allowed-address: true
        defrouter not specified
        allowed-dhcp-cids not specified
        link-protection: mac-nospoof
        mac-address: random
        auto-mac-address: 2:8:20:98:5b:fe
        mac-prefix not specified
        mac-slot not specified
        vlan-id not specified
        priority not specified
        rxrings not specified
        txrings not specified
        mtu not specified
        maxbw not specified
        rxfanout not specified
```

You must select the resource by its name as follows:

```
zonecfg:apps> select anet linkname=net0<cr>
zonecfg:apps:anet>
```

Notice how the prompt has changed now that you've selected the resource.

Now, change the network interface (`linkname`) on the zone from `net0` to `net1` as follows:

```
zonecfg:apps>  select anet linkname=net0<cr>
zonecfg:apps:anet>  set linkname=net1<cr>
zonecfg:apps:anet>  set lower-link=net1<cr>
zonecfg:apps:anet>  end<cr>
```

Changing a Zone Configuration

There are times when you may need to change a resource or a resource property within a zone. Although a resource can be changed on a running zone, the change will not go into effect until the zone reboots. Therefore, it's best to shut down the zone before making modifications. I'll describe how to shut down a zone later in this chapter, but for now let's assume the zone is already shut down.

Use the zonecfg utility to modify a zone. In the example, I want to remove the dataset named pool1/docs from the zone named apps:

1. Enter the zonecfg utility as follows:

```
# zonecfg -z apps<cr>
```

2. Issue the info command to view the current zone configuration as follows:

```
zonecfg:apps> info<cr>
zonename: apps
zonepath: /zones/apps
brand: solaris
autoboot: false
bootargs:
file-mac-profile:
pool:
limitpriv:
scheduling-class:
ip-type: exclusive
hostid:
fs-allowed:
anet:
   linkname: net0
   lower-link: auto
   allowed-address not specified
   configure-allowed-address: true
   defrouter not specified
   allowed-dhcp-cids not specified
   link-protection: mac-nospoof
   mac-address: random
   auto-mac-address: 2:8:20:98:5b:fe
   mac-prefix not specified
   mac-slot not specified
   vlan-id not specified
   priority not specified
   rxrings not specified
   txrings not specified
   mtu not specified
   maxbw not specified
   rxfanout not specified
dataset:
   name: pool1/docs
   alias: documents_pool
```

3. Remove the dataset named pool1/docs as follows:

```
zonecfg:apps> remove dataset name=pool1/docs<cr>
```

4. Verify the change:

```
zonecfg:apps> info<cr>
zonename: apps
zonepath: /zones/apps
brand: solaris
autoboot: false
bootargs:
file-mac-profile:
pool:
limitpriv:
scheduling-class:
ip-type: exclusive
hostid:
fs-allowed:
anet:
   linkname: net0
   lower-link: auto
   allowed-address not specified
   configure-allowed-address: true
   defrouter not specified
   allowed-dhcp-cids not specified
   link-protection: mac-nospoof
   mac-address: random
   auto-mac-address: 2:8:20:98:5b:fe
   mac-prefix not specified
   mac-slot not specified
   vlan-id not specified
   priority not specified
   rxrings not specified
   txrings not specified
   mtu not specified
   maxbw not specified
   rxfanout not specified
```

5. Exit the utility as follows:

```
zonecfg:apps>exit<cr>
```

Creating a Zone from the Command Line

The previous section described how to create a zone using the interactive mode of `zonecfg`. We can also create a zone using the noninteractive mode called the "command file mode." In the noninteractive mode, we specify the `zonecfg` subcommands as a semicolon-separated list. For example:

```
# zonecfg -z webzone-1 "create ; set zonepath=/zones/testzone"<cr>
```

The zone is configured and can be listed as follows:

```
# zoneadm -z testzone list -v<cr>
  ID NAME             STATUS          PATH                  BRAND       IP
   - testzone         configured      /zones/testzone       solaris     excl
```

Viewing the Zone Configuration

The zone configuration data can be viewed in three ways:

- By viewing the zone configuration file
- By using the `zonecfg` command with the `info` subcommand
- By using the `zonecfg` command with the `export` subcommand

These three methods are described next.

The zone configuration file is held in the `/etc/zones` directory and is stored as an `xml` file. To view the configuration for the zone I created earlier in this chapter named `apps`, you would enter

```
# cat /etc/zones/apps.xml<cr>
```

The file contents are displayed as follows:

```
<?xml version="1.0" encoding= "UTF-8"?>
<!DOCTYPE zone PUBLIC "-//Sun Microsystems Inc//DTD Zones//EN"
"file:///usr/share/lib/xml/dtd/zonecfg.dtd.1">
<!--
     DO NOT EDIT THIS FILE. Use zonecfg(1M) instead.
-->
<zone name="apps" zonepath="/zones/apps" autoboot="false" brand="solaris"\
ip-type="exclusive">
  <automatic-network lower-link="net1" linkname="net1" configure-allowed-\
address="true" link-protection="mac-nospoof" auto-mac-address=\
"2:8:20:98:5b:fe" mac-address="random"/>
</zone>
```

Use the `zonecfg` command with the `info` subcommand to view the zone configuration as follows:

```
# zonecfg -z apps info<cr>
zonename: apps
zonepath: /zones/apps
brand: solaris
autoboot: false
bootargs:
file-mac-profile:
pool:
limitpriv:
scheduling-class:
ip-type: exclusive
hostid:
fs-allowed:
anet:
    linkname: net1
    lower-link: net1
```

continues

```
allowed-address not specified
configure-allowed-address: true
defrouter not specified
allowed-dhcp-cids not specified
link-protection: mac-nospoof
mac-address: random
auto-mac-address: 2:8:20:98:5b:fe
mac-prefix not specified
mac-slot not specified
vlan-id not specified
priority not specified
rxrings not specified
txrings not specified
mtu not specified
maxbw not specified
rxfanout not specified
```

The alternative method of viewing the configuration is to use the `zonecfg` command with the `export` option. The following example shows how to `export` the configuration data for zone `testzone`:

```
# zonecfg -z apps export<cr>
```

The system displays the following:

```
create -b
set  zonepath=/zones/apps
set  brand=solaris
set  autoboot=false
set  ip-type=exclusive
add  anet
set  linkname=net1
set  lower-link=net1
set  configure-allowed-address=false
set  link-protection=mac-nospoof
set  mac-address=random
set  auto-mac-address=2:8:20:98:5b:fe
end
```

By default, the output goes to `stdout`, but you can change this by entering a filename instead as follows:

```
# zonecfg -z apps export -f zonefile<cr>
```

If you save the configuration to a file, it can be used later, if required, as a command file input to the `zonecfg` command. This option is useful if you have to re-create the zone for any reason. For example, I'll use the `-f` option to create a zone configuration file when cloning a zone. For more information, refer to the section titled "Clone a Zone" later in this chapter.

Administering Zones: zoneadm

The zoneadm command is the primary tool used to administer non-global zones and can only be run from the global zone. Use the zoneadm command to perform the following administrative tasks:

- List a zone.
- Verify a zone.
- Install and uninstall a zone.
- Boot a zone.
- Attach and detach a zone.
- Move a zone to a new zonepath.
- Migrate a zone to a different global zone.
- Clone a zone.
- Halt, shut down, and reboot a zone.
- Delete a zone.

Table 6-4 lists the zoneadm subcommands that are used to perform administrative tasks on non-global zones.

Table 6-4 zoneadm Subcommands

Subcommand	Description
help	Prints usage message.
attach	Attaches the specified zone.
boot	Boots the specified zone.
clone	Installs a zone by copying an existing installed zone.
detach	Detaches the specified zone.
halt	Halts a zone, bypassing shutdown scripts and removing runtime resources of the zone.
install	Installs a zone onto the system.
list	Displays the name of the current zones or the specified zone.
mark	Changes the state of a zone to incomplete or unavailable.
move	Moves the zonepath to new_zonepath.

(continues)

Table 6-4 `zoneadm` Subcommands (*Continued*)

Subcommand	Description
`ready`	Prepares a zone for running applications but does not start any user processes in the zone.
`reboot`	Restarts the zone. This is equivalent to a `halt boot` sequence (shutdown scripts are not run).
`shutdown`	Cleanly shuts down the zone (equivalent to running `/usr/sbin/init 0` in the zone).
`uninstall`	Uninstalls the specified zone from the system.
`verify`	Checks to make sure the configuration of the specified zone can safely be installed on the machine.

The `zoneadm` subcommands are described in the next sections. You can always get more information about these subcommands at the command line by typing

```
# man zoneadm<cr>
```

or

```
# zoneadm help<cr>
```

List a Zone

List all of the zones installed on the system by using the `zoneadm list` subcommand as follows:

```
# zoneadm list -v<cr>
  ID NAME        STATUS      PATH            BRAND       IP
   0 global      running     /               solaris     shared
   7 apps        running     /zones/apps     solaris     excl
```

By default, only the running zones are listed. I also included the `-v` option to display verbose information about each zone that includes the zone name, ID, current state, root directory, brand type, IP type, and options.

Use the `-c` option to display all configured zones as follows:

```
# zoneadm list -cv<cr>
  ID NAME        STATUS      PATH            BRAND       IP
   0 global      running     /               solaris     shared
```

```
  7 apps        running     /zones/apps       solaris     excl
  - dbzone      installed   /export/dbzone    solaris     excl
  - dbzone2     installed   /export/dbzone2   solaris     excl
  - dbzone3     installed   /export/dbzone3   solaris     excl
```

All installed and running zones are also listed because these are also configured zones. Use the -i option to display only installed zones.

To list a specific zone, use the -z option and specify the zone name as follows:

```
# zoneadm -z apps list -v<cr>
  ID NAME       STATUS      PATH              BRAND       IP
   7 apps       running     /zones/apps       solaris     excl
```

A universally unique identifier (UUID) is assigned to a zone when it is installed. The UUID can be obtained using zoneadm with the list subcommand and the -p option as follows:

```
# zoneadm list -pc<cr>
0:global:running:/::solaris:shared:-:none
2:clonezone:running:/zones/clonezone:66442159-672e-6d15-fbe3-\
ff08cc21422c:solaris:excl:-:
-:dbzone:installed:/export/dbzone:09e92b83-cbb8-6968-edf5-\
a74a26151e54:solaris:excl:-:
-:dbzone2:installed:/export/dbzone2:fdecbfb0-8f20-c983-a55a-\
ea168386f722:solaris:excl:-:
-:apps:installed:/zones/apps:a802d0b9-77f2-e1ee-86e1-\
c09915015e23:solaris:excl:-:
```

The UUID is the fifth field of the display.

Using the UUID

For any command that requires the zone name to be specified, the zone name or the UUID may be specified. Sometimes, the UUID is more reliable.

Verify a Zone

After a zone has been configured using the zonecfg utility, it should be verified to make sure that the configuration of the specified zone is correct and that it can safely be installed on the machine. A zone can be verified in the zonecfg utility as follows:

```
zonecfg:apps> verify<cr>
zonecfg:apps>
```

Or, a zone can be verified directly from the command line using the `zoneadm verify` command as follows:

```
# zoneadm -z apps verify<cr>
#
```

If, for example, the `zonepath` does not exist or it does not have the correct permissions set, the `verify` operation generates a suitable error message. If the zone configuration is correct, nothing is displayed and the system returns to a prompt.

Install a Zone

When a zone has been configured and verified, the next step in its creation is to install it. This has the effect of copying the necessary files from the global zone and populating the product database for the zone. Install the zone as follows:

```
# zoneadm -z apps install<cr>
```

A number of status and progress messages are displayed on the screen as the files are copied and the package database is updated as shown:

```
Progress being logged to
/var/log/zones/zoneadm.20120820T214650Z.apps.install
       Image: Preparing at /zones/apps/root.

 Install Log: /system/volatile/install.21305/install_log
 AI Manifest: /tmp/manifest.xml._BayLP
  SC Profile: /tmp/apps.xml
    Zonename: apps
Installation: Starting . . .

              Creating IPS image
              Installing packages from:
                  solaris
                      origin:
http://localhost:1008/solaris/bbb612b800c4a05fe489e22179376fa4cb0b1970/
DOWNLOAD                                  PKGS       FILES    XFER (MB)
Completed                              167/167 32062/32062  175.8/175.8

PHASE                                        ACTIONS
Install Phase                            44313/44313

PHASE                                          ITEMS
Package State Update Phase                   167/167
Image State Update Phase                         2/2
Installation: Succeeded

    Note: Man pages can be obtained by installing pkg:/system/manualdone.

        Done: Installation completed in 2098.576 seconds.
```

```
   Next Steps: Boot the zone, then log into the zone console (zlogin -C)
               to complete the configuration process.

Log saved in non-global zone as
/zones/apps/root/var/log/zones/zoneadm.20120820T214650Z.apps.install
```

Notice that while the zone is installing, its state changes from *configured* to *incomplete*. The state changes to *installed* when the `install` operation has completed. These zone states are displayed with the `zoneadm list` command as follows:

```
# zoneadm -z apps list -v<cr>
ID NAME        STATUS     PATH              BRAND    IP
  7 apps       installed  /zones/apps       solaris  excl
```

This zone is not yet complete. The Oracle Solaris instance still needs to be configured the first time you boot the zone with the following information:

- Language
- Terminal type
- Hostname
- Security policy
- Name service
- Time zone
- Root password

Connect to the zone's console as described in the section titled "Log In to a Zone: `zlogin`." You will be prompted to enter the above information. To eliminate this configuration process, preconfigure the Oracle Solaris instance using a configuration profile.

The previous section described how to create a zone using the interactive mode of `zonecfg`. We can also create a zone using the noninteractive mode called the command file mode. In the noninteractive mode, we specify the `zonecfg` subcommands as a semicolon-separated list. For example:

```
# zonecfg -z webzone-1 "create ; set zonepath=/zones/testzone"<cr>
```

Before installing the zone, you can preconfigure the following zone settings that were not configured when you created the zone using the `zonecfg` command:

- Language
- Terminal type
- Hostname

- Security policy
- Name service
- Time zone
- Root password

In Oracle Solaris 10, these settings were preconfigured using a `sysidcfg` file; however, the `sysidcfg` file is no longer used. It has been replaced with a configuration profile. The configuration profile specifies the default locale and time zone, the zone's root password, the naming service, and other aspects of the application environment that may include

- The computer name of the zone
- IP address of the zone
- Netmask of the IP address

This information should be available before you begin creating the system configuration profile.

Create the system configuration profile using the `sysconfig` tool. The `sysconfig` tool is described in Chapter 1, "Installing Oracle Solaris 11." See the section titled "Reconfigure an Oracle Solaris Instance" for more information.

To create a `sysconfig` profile named `/tmp/apps.xml` for the non-global zone named `apps`, type the following:

```
# sysconfig create-profile -o /tmp/apps.xml<cr>
```

You will be presented with a series of screens where you will enter the following information:

- Computer name
- How to configure the network interface (automatically, manually, or none)
- Time zone
- Date and time
- Root password
- User account (optional)

When finished, a configuration profile is created in the directory that was specified after the `-o` option. In the previous example, the profile was named `/tmp/apps.xml`.

After creating the configuration profile, you can use this profile to install the zone using the zoneadm command as follows:

```
# zoneadm -z apps install -c /tmp/apps.xml<cr>
```

The zone is created using the information provided in the configuration profile, and you will not be prompted to configure the Oracle Solaris instance during the first boot.

Reconfigure an Oracle Solaris Instance

To reconfigure an Oracle Solaris instance for a zone, log in to the zone as follows:

```
# zlogin -z apps<cr>
```

and type

```
# sysconfig configure -g system<cr>
```

The zone will shut down, and you will be prompted to enter the Oracle Solaris instance configuration information. When complete, the zone will boot back up.

Boot a Zone

Before the boot command is issued, a zone needs to be in the installed state and transitioned to the ready state. You must be the global administrator or a user with appropriate authorizations in the global zone to boot a zone.

> **Zone Delegation**
>
> Oracle Solaris 11 allows fine-grained authorizations to allow the delegation of zone management to a user. Delegation of zone administration is not covered in this chapter.

Before booting, it's best to make certain that the zone is in the installed state as follows:

```
# zoneadm -z apps list -v<cr>
  ID NAME    STATUS     PATH                 BRAND    IP
   - apps    installed  /zones/apps          solaris  excl
```

As described earlier, the zsched process is started when the zone enters the ready state. During this state, a unique zone ID is assigned by the system, file systems are mounted, network interfaces are set up, and devices are configured. Transitioning into the ready state prepares the virtual platform to begin running user processes.

You do not need to bring the zone to the ready state manually; the zone will transition through the ready state automatically when you boot the zone. If you do not want to boot the zone, you can bring the zone to the ready state manually as follows:

```
# zoneadm -z testzone ready<cr>
```

At this point, no processes are running in the zone.

Before booting a zone, you should connect to the zone's console. Connect to the console using the zlogin -C command as follows:

```
# zlogin -C apps<cr>
```

zlogin Command

Connecting to the console using zlogin is covered in more detail later in this chapter.

To boot the zone named apps, issue the following command:

```
# zoneadm -z apps boot<cr>
```

The following message will be displayed in the zone's console window:

```
[NOTICE: Zone booting up]

OS Release 5.11 Version 11.1 64-bit
Copyright (c) 1983, 2012, Oracle and/or its affiliates. All rights reserved.

Hostname: apps
```

Confirm that the zone has booted successfully by listing the zone using the zoneadm command:

```
# zoneadm -z apps list -v<cr>
ID NAME     STATUS    PATH                BRAND    IP
  8 apps    running   /zones/apps         solaris  excl
```

The state of the zone will have changed to running if the boot operation was successful.

You can also supply other boot arguments when booting a zone:

- To boot the zone into single-user mode, issue the following command:

```
# zoneadm -z apps boot -- -s<cr>
```

- To boot a zone using the verbose option, issue the following command:

```
# zoneadm -z apps boot -- -m verbose<cr>
```

- Boot a zone into the single-user milestone as follows:

```
# zoneadm -z apps boot -- -m milestone=single-user<cr>
```

Shut Down a Zone

It's important that you shut down your zone properly and in a clean manner by running the zone's shutdown scripts. The `shutdown` subcommand will run the zone's shutdown scripts and then halt the zone. This is equivalent to typing the `init 0` command while logged in to the zone. Use the `zoneadm shutdown` command as follows to shut down the `apps` zone:

```
# zoneadm -z apps shutdown<cr>
```

The following message is displayed in the zone's console window:

```
apps console login: svc.startd: The system is coming down. Please wait.
svc.startd: 79 system services are now being stopped.
Jan 20 14:30:24 apps syslogd: going down on signal 15
svc.startd: Killing user processes.
Jan 20 14:30:28 The system is down. Shutdown took 5 seconds.

[NOTICE: Zone halted]
```

If the zone cannot be shut down using the `zoneadm shutdown` command, it may be necessary to halt the zone. A halt will forcibly halt the zone, bypassing shutdown scripts and removing the runtime resources of the zone. Halt the `apps` zone as follows:

```
# zoneadm -z apps halt<cr>
```

Rebooting the zone using the `reboot` subcommand halts the specified zone (bypassing shutdown scripts) and boots the zone (equivalent to the `zoneadm boot` sequence). Reboot the `apps` zone as follows:

```
# zoneadm -z apps reboot<cr>
```

The following message is displayed in the zone's console window:

```
[NOTICE: Zone rebooting]
```

When the zone has been successfully shut down or halted, the zone state changes from running to installed as follows:

```
# zoneadm -z apps list -v<cr>
  ID NAME          STATUS      PATH                    BRAND     IP
   - apps          installed   /zones/apps             solaris   excl
```

The `zlogin` command can also be used to reboot a zone. Refer to the section titled "Log In to a Zone: `zlogin`" later in this chapter.

Uninstall a Zone

When a zone is no longer required, it should be uninstalled before it is deleted. To uninstall a zone, it must first be shut down and in the installed state. When this has been done, issue the `zoneadm uninstall` command. For example, to uninstall the zone named `apps`, shut the zone down:

```
# zoneadm -z apps shutdown<cr>
```

Next, uninstall the zone.

```
# zoneadm -z apps uninstall<cr>
```

You'll be prompted to answer "Y" to confirm that you really want to uninstall the zone as follows:

```
Are you sure you want to uninstall zone apps (y/[n])? y<cr>
```

After answering yes, the following messages are displayed as the zone is uninstalled:

```
Progress being logged to /var/log/zones/zoneadm.20120820T185257Z.apps.uninstall
promoting 'zones/apps/rpool/ROOT/solaris-1/var'.
promoting 'zones/apps/rpool/ROOT/solaris-1'.
root@solaris:/tmp#
```

Verify that the zone is uninstalled by typing the `zoneadm list` command and checking the zone state. The zone state should be listed as `configured` when it has been uninstalled as shown in the following example:

```
# zoneadm -z apps list -v<cr>
  ID NAME          STATUS      PATH              BRAND    IP
   - apps          configured  /zones/apps        solaris  excl
```

The `-F` option can be specified to force the command to execute without confirmation as follows:

```
# zoneadm -z apps uninstall -F<cr>
```

Delete a Zone

When a zone has been successfully uninstalled, its configuration can be deleted from the system. Enter the `zonecfg` command to delete the zone `apps` from the system:

```
# zonecfg -z apps delete -F<cr>
```

The `-F` option forces the command to execute without confirmation. If you omit this option, you are asked to confirm that you want to delete the zone configuration.

Remember the Force

Unlike most other UNIX commands, `zoneadm` and `zonecfg` use an uppercase letter `F` to force the command to be executed without prompting you for confirmation. All other commands, such as `mv`, `rm`, and `umount`, for example, always use a lowercase letter `f`.

Log In to a Zone: `zlogin`

When a zone is operational and running, the normal network access commands can be used to access it, such as `telnet`, `rlogin`, and `ssh`, but a non-global zone can also be accessed from the global zone using `zlogin`. This is necessary for administration purposes and to be able to access the console session for a zone. Only the superuser (root), or a role with the RBAC profile "Zone Management" can use the `zlogin` command from the global zone.

The syntax for the `zlogin` command is as follows:

```
zlogin [-CE] [-e c] [-l <username>] <zonename>
zlogin [-ES] [-e c] [-l <username>] <zonename> <utility> [argument. . .]
```

`zlogin` works in three modes:

- Interactive: A login session is established from the global zone.
- Noninteractive: A single command or utility can be executed.
  Upon completion of the command or utility, the session is automatically closed.
- Console: A console session is established for administration purposes.

Table 6-5 describes the various options for `zlogin`.

Table 6-5 `zlogin` Options

Option	Description
`-C`	A connection is made to the zone's console device, and `zlogin` operates in console mode.
`-e c`	This option changes the escape sequence to exit from the console session. The default is the tilde dot (~.).
`-E`	This option disables the use of extended functions and also prohibits the use of the Escape sequence to disconnect from the session.
`-l` *<username>*	A different user is specified for the zone login. User root is used when this option is omitted. This option cannot be used when using `zlogin` in console mode.
`-S`	This is the "safe" login mode. This option is used to recover a damaged zone when other login forms do not work. This option cannot be used in console mode.
<zonename>	This option specifies the zone to connect to.
<utility>	This option specifies the utility or command to run in the zone.
<argument>	This option allows arguments to be specified and passed to the utility or command being executed.

Log In to the Zone Console

You can access the console of a zone by using the zlogin -C <*zonename*> command. If you are completing a hands-off configuration, connect to the console before the initial boot. You will see the boot messages appear in the console as well as the reboot after the configuration profile file has been referenced. The zone console is available as soon as the zone is in the installed state.

The following session shows what happens when the zone named apps is booted for the first time, after using a configuration profile file:

```
# zlogin -C app\s<cr>
[NOTICE: Zone booting up]

OS Release 5.11 Version 11.1 64-bit
Copyright (c) 1983, 2012, Oracle and/or its affiliates. All rights reserved.

Hostname: appszone

apps console login:
```

A shortcut is to boot the zone and connect to the zone's console as follows:

```
# zoneadm -z apps boot; zlogin -C apps<cr>
```

Break the Connection to the Zone Console

Connections to the console persist even when the zone is rebooted. To disconnect from the zone console, type "~." (tilde + period) to break the connection. Be aware that breaking the connection to the zone's console is not the same as logging out.

Initial Zone Login

If you did not install the zone using a configuration profile as described earlier, you'll need to provide the Oracle Solaris configuration information interactively the first time the system is booted. If this is not completed, the zone will not be operational, and users will be unable to connect to the zone across the network.

Before booting the zone for the first time, connect to the zone's console using the zlogin -C command. Boot the zone from another window. In the zone's console you will be prompted to configure the Oracle Solaris instance, and then the zone will reboot to implement the changes. When this reboot completes, the zone is fully operational.

Log In to a Zone

The superuser (root), or a role with the RBAC profile "Zone Management," can log directly into a zone from the global zone without having to supply a password. The system administrator uses the `zlogin` command. The following example shows a zone login to the `apps` zone:

```
# zlogin apps<cr>
[Connected to zone 'apps' pts/4]
Oracle Corporation  SunOS 5.11  11.1  September 2012
```

The command `zonename` is run to display the name of the current zone, and then the connection is closed:

```
root@appszone:~# zonename<cr>
apps
# exit<cr>

[Connection to zone 'apps' pts/4 closed]
```

Run a Command in a Zone

In the previous section, an interactive login to a zone was achieved. Here, a noninteractive login is initiated and a single command is executed. The connection is automatically disconnected as soon as the command has completed. The following example shows how this works. First, the `hostname` command is run, demonstrating that we are on the host called "global." Then a noninteractive login to the `apps` zone runs, which runs the `zonename` command and then exits automatically. Finally, the same `hostname` command is run, which shows we are back on the host called `global`:

```
global-zone # hostname<cr>
global

global-zone # zlogin apps zonename<cr>
apps

global-zone # hostname<cr>
global
```

No `-z` in `zlogin`

Be careful not to include the `-z` option on `zlogin`. It's easy to get confused with the `zoneadm` command, where the `-z` option is used.

I can also use the `zlogin` command to shut down a zone from the global zone as follows:

```
global-zone# zlogin apps shutdown -i 0<cr>
Shutdown started.  Friday, January 25, 2013 03:00:56 AM GMT
Do you want to continue? (y or n):  y<cr>
```

Using ZFS for Oracle Solaris Zones

ZFS can be used with Oracle Solaris zones, but keep in mind a few points:

- The global administrator can add a ZFS file system or a ZFS clone to a non-global zone with or without delegating administrative control.
- You can add a ZFS volume as a device to non-global zones.
- You cannot associate ZFS snapshots with zones at this time.
- A ZFS file system that is added to a non-global zone must have its `mountpoint` property set to `legacy`.
- ZFS storage pools cannot be created or modified from within a non-global zone.

Adding a ZFS Dataset to a Non-global Zone

A ZFS dataset that has been created in the global zone using the `zfs create` command can be added as a legacy file system to a non-global zone. The following steps describe how to add a ZFS file system to a zone named `testzone`.

1. Create a ZFS file system in the global zone, to be used for the `testzone`:

```
global-zone# zfs create pool1/test_data<cr>
```

2. Set the `mountpoint` property to `legacy`:

```
global-zone# zfs set mountpoint=legacy pool1/test_data<cr>
```

3. Shut down the zone, and add the new ZFS file system to the non-global zone as follows:

```
global-zone# zonecfg -z testzone<cr>
zonecfg:testzone> add fs<cr>
zonecfg:testzone:fs> set type=zfs<cr>
zonecfg:testzone:fs> set special=pool1/test_data<cr>
zonecfg:testzone:fs> set dir=/export/shared<cr>
zonecfg:testzone:fs> end<cr>
zonecfg:testzone> exit<cr>
#
```

The pool1/test_data file system has been added and will be mounted in the non-global zone as /export/shared.

4. Boot the zone:

```
global-zone# zoneadm -z testzone boot<cr>
```

5. Log in to the non-global zone (testzone), and verify that the file system has been added with the df -h command:

```
# df -h<cr>
Filesystem           size   used   avail capacity   Mounted on
/                      0K   494M    4.4G    10%     /
/dev                 4.9G   494M    4.4G    10%     /dev
pool1/test_data        0K    18K    4.4G     1%     /export/shared
    <output has been truncated>
```

6. The ZFS file system has been added as a legacy file system mounted as /export/shared. Therefore, when the zfs list command is executed, the non-global zone reports that no ZFS datasets are available:

```
# zfs list<cr>
no datasets available
#
```

Delegating a ZFS Dataset to a Non-global Zone

In the preceding section, a ZFS file system was added to the non-global zone as a legacy file system. In that scenario, the global zone administrator is responsible for setting and controlling the properties of that file system. The non-global zone administrator has no control over the ZFS properties of that dataset. In fact, to the non-global zone administrator, the dataset appears to be a traditional UFS file system.

To add a ZFS file system to a non-global zone that can then be administered within the non-global zone, the ZFS file system must be delegated to the non-global zone. The administrator of the global zone delegates the file system to the non-global zone. When the ZFS file system has been delegated, it is visible within the non-global zone via the zfs list command. The zone administrator can set ZFS file system properties as well as create children. In addition, the zone administrator can take snapshots, create clones, and otherwise control the entire file system hierarchy.

To delegate a ZFS dataset to a non-global zone, follow the procedure described in these steps:

1. Halt the non-global zone:

```
globalzone# zoneadm -z testzone halt<cr>
```

2. Create the ZFS dataset named /pool1/docs:

```
global-zone# zfs create pool1/docs<cr>
```

3. Delegate the ZFS file system to the zone:

```
# zonecfg -z testzone<cr>
zonecfg:testzone> add dataset<cr>
zonecfg:testzone:dataset> set name=pool1/docs<cr>
zonecfg:testzone:dataset> end<cr>
zonecfg:testzone> exit<cr>
```

4. Boot the testzone:

```
global-zone# zoneadm -z testzone boot<cr>
```

5. Log in to the non-global zone console, and verify that the ZFS dataset is visible within that zone:

```
global-zone# zlogin -C testzone<cr>
# zfs list<cr>
NAME                        USED  AVAIL  REFER  MOUNTPOINT
docs                         31K  7.81G    31K  /docs
rpool                       378M  15.3G    31K  /rpool
rpool/ROOT                  378M  15.3G    31K  legacy
rpool/ROOT/solaris          378M  15.3G   348M  /
rpool/ROOT/solaris/var     24.3M  15.3G  23.4M  /var
rpool/export                 63K  15.3G    32K  /export
rpool/export/home            31K  15.3G    31K  /export/home
```

Notice the alias "docs" that was created and represents the pool1/docs dataset. This name can be set using the following syntax when adding the dataset to the zone:

```
zonecfg:testzone> add dataset<cr>
zonecfg:testzone:dataset> set name=pool1/docs<cr>
zonecfg:testzone> set alias=documents_pool<cr>
zonecfg:testzone:dataset> end<cr>
```

Log in to the non-global zone console, and verify the ZFS dataset alias:

```
# zfs list<cr>
NAME                     USED  AVAIL  REFER  MOUNTPOINT
documents_pool            31K  7.81G    31K  /documents_pool
rpool                    382M  15.3G    31K  /rpool
rpool/ROOT               382M  15.3G    31K  legacy
rpool/ROOT/solaris       382M  15.3G   351M  /
rpool/ROOT/solaris/var  24.3M  15.3G  23.4M  /var
rpool/export              63K  15.3G    32K  /export
rpool/export/home         31K  15.3G    31K  /export/home
```

ZFS storage pools cannot be created or modified within a non-global zone. For example, in the preceding steps, you cannot set the quota property on the pool1/docs dataset. However, you can create a ZFS file system under the pool1/docs dataset and set the quota property on that file system:

```
# zfs create pool1/docs/personal<cr>
# zfs set quota=50m pool1/docs/personal<cr>
```

A pool-level dataset can be added to a zone, but any command that modifies the pool's physical characteristics is not allowed. This includes adding devices to or removing devices from the pool.

When a dataset is added to a non-global zone under the control of a zone administrator, its contents can no longer be trusted. setuid binaries or other questionable contents could compromise the security of the global zone. To address this issue, ZFS uses the zoned property to indicate that the dataset has been delegated to a non-global zone. By listing this property on the pool1/docs dataset, we can see that the zoned property was turned on:

```
# zfs list -o zoned pool1/docs<cr>
ZONED
   on
```

The zoned property is set when the non-global zone containing the ZFS dataset is first booted. When the zoned property is set to on, the dataset cannot be mounted or shared in the global zone. When the dataset is removed from the non-global zone, or if the zone is destroyed, the zoned property does not get reset to off. The zoned property must be manually cleared by the global administrator if you want to reuse the dataset in any way. Change this property only when you are sure that this dataset is no longer in use by a non-global zone. Before setting the zoned property to off, ensure that the mountpoint property for the dataset and all its descendants are set to reasonable values and that no setuid binaries exist, or turn off the setuid property. The following example clears the zoned property for the ZFS file system named /data so that the file system can be reused:

```
# zfs set zoned=off /data<cr>
```

Zone Resource Controls

Some administrators refer to zones and containers interchangeably as if they mean exactly the same thing, but this is not so.

Containers are a technology that combines a zone with the OS's resource management features. With containers, a system administrator can use the resource management facility to allocate resources such as memory and CPU to applications and services within each zone. Therefore, Oracle Solaris zones are a subset of containers, and the two terms should not be used interchangeably.

The resource management feature is a powerful one that can be used to allocate resources to zones such as CPU, processes, memory, and swap. In previous versions of Oracle Solaris, many of these resources could only be configured on a system-wide basis. Now, much more control is provided through resource management where hardware and kernel resources can be controlled on a zone-by-zone basis. The resource management offers resource controls (outlined in Table 6-6) that can be set on a zone-wide basis and control the total resource usage of all process entities within a zone.

Table 6-6 Zone-wide Resource Controls

Control Name	Description
zone.cpu-cap	Absolute limit on the amount of CPU resources that can be consumed by a non-global zone
zone.cpu-shares	Number of FSS CPU shares for this zone
zone.max-lofi	Maximum number of lofi devices that can be created by a zone
zone.max-locked-memory	Total amount of physical locked memory available to a zone
zone.max-lwps	Maximum number of LWPs simultaneously available to this zone
zone.max-msg-ids	Maximum number of message queue IDs allowed for this zone

(continues)

Table 6-6 Zone-wide Resource Controls (*Continued*)

Control Name	Description
`zone.max-processes`	Maximum number of process table slots simultaneously available to this zone
`zone.max-sem-ids`	Maximum number of semaphore IDs allowed for this zone
`zone.max-shm-ids`	Maximum number of shared memory IDs allowed for this zone
`zone.max-shm-memory`	Total amount of System V shared memory allowed for this zone
`zone.max-swap`	Total amount of swap that can be consumed by user process address space mappings and `tmpfs` mounts for this zone

For more information on the resource management zone-wide resource controls, refer to the `resource_controls(5)` man page. Refer to the earlier section titled "`zonecfg` Subcommands" for instructions on how to set these controls.

Monitor a Zone

Use the `zonestat` utility to monitor a zone's resource use and to report the CPU, memory, and resource control use for the non-global zones that are running on your system. Zone use is reported as a percentage of both system resources and the zone's configured limits.

The `zonestat` utility can be run from within the zone or from the global zone for a system-wide view of the zones and to identify resource bottlenecks or misbehaving applications.

System performance monitoring is an in-depth topic and beyond the scope of this book, but I just want to briefly introduce the `zonestat` utility. More information can be found by reading the `zonestat(1)` man page.

In the following example, `zonestat` is executed in the global zone to monitor the resource use of all the zones. `zonestat` will print a report every 5 seconds. After two reports, `zonestat` will exit.

```
# zonestat 5s 2<cr>

Collecting data for first interval. . .
Interval: 1, Duration: 0:00:05
```

```
SUMMARY                  Cpus/Online: 4/4  PhysMem: 3095M  VirtMem: 4119M
                    ---CPU----    --PhysMem--  --VirtMem--  --PhysNet--
               ZONE  USED %PART   USED %USED   USED %USED PBYTE %PUSE0
            [total]  0.04 1.13%  1131M 36.5%  1567M 38.0%      0 0.00%
           [system]  0.02 0.55%   371M 11.9%   912M 22.1%      -     -
             global  0.02 0.53%   536M 17.3%   428M 10.3%      0 0.00%
              sol10  0.00 0.02%   167M 5.40%   182M 4.43%      0 0.00%
              sol11  0.00 0.01%  55.8M 1.80%  44.9M 1.09%      0 0.00%

Interval: 2, Duration: 0:00:10
SUMMARY                  Cpus/Online: 4/4  PhysMem: 3095M VirtMem: 4119M
              ---CPU----  --PhysMem--  --VirtMem--  --PhysNet--
        ZONE  USED %PART   USED %USED   USED %USED PBYTE %PUSE
     [total]  0.05 1.25%  1131M 36.5%  1567M 38.0%      0 0.00%
    [system]  0.02 0.62%   371M 11.9%   912M 22.1%      -     -
      global  0.02 0.55%   536M 17.3%   428M 10.3%      0 0.00%
       sol10  0.00 0.06%   167M 5.40%   182M 4.43%      0 0.00%
       sol11  0.00 0.00%  55.8M 1.80%  44.9M 1.09%      0 0.00%
#
```

The summary line shows how many CPUs are available on the system and how many are being used: `Cpus/Online: 4/4`.

To the right, the report displays the total amount of physical memory and virtual memory configured on the system: `PhysMem: 3095M VirtMem: 4119M`.

This system has 3GB of physical memory and 1GB of swap space.

Below the summary line, CPU use, physical memory, virtual memory, and network use are displayed for the global zone and each non-global zone. This information is useful for determining the resources being consumed by each zone.

This next example monitors all zones silently in the background. It takes a sample every 10 seconds and produces a report every 10 minutes. The report will detail the highest usage of each zone during each 10-minute interval. The report will repeat every 10 minutes for 24 hours.

```
# zonestat -q -R high 10s 25h 10m<cr>
Report: High Usage
    Start: Tue Jan 8 05:09:45 EDT 2012
      End: Tue Jan 8 05:19:45 EDT 2012
  Intervals: 60, Duration: 0:10:00
SUMMARY                Cpus/Online: 4/4  PhysMem: 3095M  VirtMem: 4119M
                 ---CPU----  --PhysMem-- --VirtMem-- --PhysNet--
          ZONE  USED %PART  USED %USED  USED %USED PBYTE %PUSE
       [total]  0.27 6.86% 1139M 36.8% 1574M 38.2%   330 0.00%
      [system]  0.21 5.43%  372M 12.0%  912M 22.1%     -     -
        global  0.05 1.37%  537M 17.3%  428M 10.3%     0 0.00%
         sol10  0.00 0.05%  167M 5.40%  182M 4.43%     0 0.00%
         sol11  0.00 0.24% 55.8M 1.80% 44.9M 1.09%     0 0.00%
```

The summary indicates that 60 samples were taken over a 10-minute period (one sample per minute): `Intervals: 60, Duration: 0:10:00`

This report contains the highest usage of each zone during that 10-minute period.

This final example demonstrates how to run the zonestat utility within a non-global zone. The zonestat utility will only report information on this non-global zone:

```
# zonestat 5 2<cr>
Collecting data for first interval. . .
Interval: 1, Duration: 0:00:05
SUMMARY                   Cpus/Online: 4/4  PhysMem: 3095M  VirtMem: 4119M
              ---CPU----  --PhysMem-- --VirtMem-- --PhysNet--
           ZONE  USED %PART  USED %USED  USED %USED PBYTE %PUSE
        [total]  0.09 2.47% 1137M 36.7% 1573M 38.2%   126 0.00%
       [system]  0.09 2.46% 1077M 34.8% 1525M 37.0%     -     -
          sol11  0.00 0.00% 59.8M 1.93% 47.8M 1.16%     0 0.00%

Interval: 2, Duration: 0:00:10
SUMMARY                   Cpus/Online: 4/4  PhysMem: 3095M VirtMem: 4119M
              ---CPU----  --PhysMem-- --VirtMem-- --PhysNet--
           ZONE  USED %PART USED %USED USED %USED PBYTE %PUSE
        [total]  0.06 1.67% 1137M 36.7% 1573M 38.2%   0 0.00%
       [system]  0.06 1.66% 1077M 34.8% 1525M 37.0%   -     -
          sol11  0.00 0.01% 59.8M 1.93% 47.9M 1.16%   0 0.00%
```

Other conventional Oracle Solaris commands used to view system information in the global zone can also be used to view information on non-global zones. For example, the df -h command is normally used to display file system information. When executed in the global zone with the -Z option, it will display file system mounts in both the global and non-global zones as follows:

```
# df -hZ<cr>
Filesystem                 Size  Used  Available Capacity  Mounted on
rpool/ROOT/solaris          24G  3.8G        18G    18%    /
/devices                    0K    0K         0K     0%    /devices
/dev                        0K    0K         0K     0%    /dev
ctfs                        0K    0K         0K     0%    /system/contract
proc                        0K    0K         0K     0%    /proc
mnttab                      0K    0K         0K     0%    /etc/mnttab
swap                       1.0G  1.8M       1.0G     1%    /system/volatile
objfs                       0K    0K         0K     0%    /system/object
sharefs                     0K    0K         0K     0%    /etc/dfs/sharetab
/usr/lib/libc/libc_hwcap 1.so.1
                            22G  3.8G        18G    18%    /lib/libc.so.1
fd                          0K    0K         0K     0%    /dev/fd
rpool/ROOT/solaris/var
                            24G  494M        18G     3%    /var
swap                       1.2G  128M       1.0G    11%    /tmp
rpool/VARSHARE              24G   47K        18G     1%    /var/share
rpool/export                24G   32K        18G     1%    /export
rpool/export/home           24G   32K        18G     1%    /export/home
rpool/export/home/train
                            24G  795K        18G     1%    /export/home/train
rpool                       24G  4.9M        18G     1%    /rpool
/export/home/train          18G  795K        18G     1%    /home/train
zones                       16G   32K        15G     1%    /zones
zones/apps                  16G   33K        15G     1%    /zones/apps
zones/apps/rpool/ROOT/solaris
                            16G  397M        15G     3%    /zones/apps/root
/dev                        0K    0K         0K     0%\   /zones/apps/root/dev
zones/apps/rpool/ROOT/solaris/var
```

```
                        16G    24M          15G      1%     /zones/apps/root/var
  proc                  0K     0K           0K       0%\    /zones/apps/root/proc
  ctfs                  0K     0K           0K       0%\
      /zones/apps/root/system/contract
  mnttab                0K     0K           0K       0%\
      /zones/apps/root/etc/mnttab
  objfs                 0K     0K           0K       0%\
      /zones/apps/root/system/object
  swap                  1.0G   264K         1.0G     1%\
      /zones/apps/root/system/volatile
  sharefs               0K     0K           0K       0%\
      /zones/apps/root/etc/dfs/sharetab
  /zones/apps/root/usr/lib/libc/libc_hwcap1.so.1
                        16G    397M         15G      3%\
      /zones/apps/root/lib/libc.so.1
  fd                    0K     0K           0K       0%\
      /zones/apps/root/dev/fd
  swap                  1.0G   0K           1.0G     0%\
      /zones/apps/root/tmp
  zones/apps/rpool/VARSHARE
                        16G    38K          15G      1%\
      /zones/apps/root/var/share
```

The ps command is used to display process status information for every process on the system. Add the -Z option to also view processes that are running in both the global and non-global zones as follows:

```
# ps -eZ<cr>
  ZONE     PID  TTY          TIME  CMD
  global     0  ?            0:04  sched
  global     5  ?            0:03  zpool-rp
  global     6  ?            0:00  kmem_tas
  global     1  ?            0:00  init
   . . .<output has been truncated>. . .
  sol11  2713    ?           0:02  svc.star
  sol11  2582    ?           0:00  init
  global 1904    ?           0:00  zoneadmd
  sol11  2715    ?           0:05  svc.conf
  sol11  2743    ?           0:00  svc-dlmg
```

The -Z option is only useful when used in the global zone. When issued in a non-global zone, you do not have permission to view either the global zone or other non-global zones.

Create an Exclusive-IP Zone

Now that we have seen the technicalities of configuring a zone, let's put it all together and create a zone. The following step-by-step instructions will configure an exclusive-IP zone named testzone, install it, and boot it. This non-global zone will have its own complete network stack that will allow the system administrator to set the unique IP address and routing configuration. Finally, we will list the zone configuration data.

First, make sure you have a ZFS storage pool with enough space to store your zone. We'll create a new storage pool named zones on a separate disk (c3t3d0) as follows:

```
# zpool create zones c3t3d0<cr>
```

I'm also going to use the default template named SYSdefault, which is going to create a network resource named anet with the following properties automatically configured:

- linkname is net0.
- lower-link is auto.
- mac-address is random.
- link-protection is mac-nospoof.

Create the zone named testzone:

1. Perform the initial configuration on a zone named testzone. The zonepath will be /zones/testzone, and the IP address will be 192.168.0.43. Enter the zonecfg command to configure the new zone:

```
# zonecfg -z testzone<cr>
testzone: No such zone configured
Use 'create' to begin configuring a new zone.
zonecfg:testzone> create<cr>
create: Using system default template 'SYSdefault'
zonecfg:testzone> set zonepath=/zones/testzone<cr>
zonecfg:testzone> set autoboot=true<cr>
zonecfg:testzone> set bootargs="-m verbose"<cr>
zonecfg:testzone> add capped-memory<cr>
zonecfg:testzone:capped-memory> set physical=60m<cr>
zonecfg:testzone:capped-memory> set swap=100m<cr>
zonecfg:testzone:capped-memory> set locked=30m<cr>
zonecfg:testzone:capped-memory> end<cr>
zonecfg:testzone> add rctl<cr>
zonecfg:testzone:rctl> set name=zone.cpu-shares<cr>
zonecfg:testzone:rctl> add value (priv=privileged,limit=20,action=none)<cr>
zonecfg:testzone:rctl> end<cr>
zonecfg:testzone> add attr<cr>
zonecfg:testzone:attr> set name=comment<cr>
zonecfg:testzone:attr> set type=string<cr>
zonecfg:testzone:attr> set value="Testzone with capped memory"<cr>
zonecfg:testzone:attr> end<cr>
```

   Open a second shell before proceeding to step 2.

2. Having entered the initial configuration information, use a separate login session to check whether the zone exists using the zoneadm command:

```
# zoneadm -z testzone list -v<cr>
zoneadm: testzone: No such zone configured
```

At this point, the zone configuration has not been committed and saved to disk, so it exists only in memory and is not listed.

3. In the `zonecfg` session, verify and exit the zone configuration. The zone configuration is automatically saved when you exit.

```
zonecfg:testzone> verify<cr>
zonecfg:testzone> exit<cr>
```

4. After you exit `zonecfg`, check whether the zone exists using the `zoneadm` command as follows:

```
# zoneadm -z testzone list -v<cr>
  ID NAME            STATUS     PATH                           BRAND      IP
   - testzone        configured /zones/testzone                solaris    excl
```

Notice that the zone now exists and that it has been placed in the *configured* state. If you do not verify the zone prior to installing it, the verification is performed automatically when the zone is installed.

5. Install the zone:

```
# zoneadm -z testzone install<cr>
The following ZFS file system(s) have been created:
     zones/testzone
Progress being logged to /var/log/zones/zoneadm.20130125T135221Z.testzone.
install
       Image: Preparing at /zones/testzone/root.
  AI Manifest: /tmp/manifest.xml.gtaOhn
    SC Profile: /usr/share/auto_install/sc_profiles/enable_sci.xml
     Zonename: testzone
 Installation: Starting . . .
              Creating IPS image
Startup linked: 1/1 done
              Installing packages from:
                  solaris
                     origin: http://192.168.1.221/
DOWNLOAD                              PKGS         FILES    XFER (MB)     SPEED
Completed                          183/183   33556/33556  222.2/222.2    791k/s
PHASE                                            ITEMS
Installing new actions                     46825/46825
Updating package state database                   Done
Updating image state                              Done
Creating fast lookup database                     Done
Installation: Succeeded

     Note: Man pages can be obtained by installing pkg:/system/manual

  done.
```

continues

```
     Done: Installation completed in 529.448 seconds.

   Next Steps: Boot the zone, then log into the zone console (zlogin -C)

        to complete the configuration process.

Log saved in non-global zone as
/zones/testzone/root/var/log/zones/zoneadm.20130125T135221Z.testzone.install
```

6. Verify that the zone is in the installed state:

```
# zoneadm -z testzone list -v<cr>
  ID NAME           STATUS     PATH                        BRAND    IP
    - testzone      installed /zones/testzone              solaris  excl
```

7. Connect to the console to watch the system boot and to finish the configuration:

```
# zlogin -C testzone<cr>
[Connected to zone 'testzone' console]
```

8. Boot the zone as follows:

```
# zoneadm -z testzone boot<cr>
```

   As the system boots, messages will be displayed in the zone's console. You'll notice more messages than usual because the zone's `bootargs` was set to "`-m verbose`" in step 1.

9. We did not specify a configuration profile when we installed this zone. After the system initializes, you will be prompted to enter the system identification information, such as hostname, network information, time zone, and root password.

10. View the `testzone` configuration data as follows:

```
# zonecfg -z testzone info<cr>
zonename: testzone
zonepath: /zones/testzone
brand: solaris
autoboot: true
bootargs: -m verbose
file-mac-profile:
pool:
limitpriv:
scheduling-class:
ip-type: exclusive
hostid:
fs-allowed:
[cpu-shares: 20]
anet:
    linkname: net0
    lower-link: auto
```

```
    allowed-address not specified
    configure-allowed-address: true
    defrouter not specified
    allowed-dhcp-cids not specified
    link-protection: mac-nospoof
    mac-address: random
    mac-prefix not specified
    mac-slot not specified
    vlan-id not specified
    priority not specified
    rxrings not specified
    txrings not specified
    mtu not specified
    maxbw not specified
    rxfanout not specified
    vsi-typeid not specified
    vsi-vers not specified
    vsi-mgrid not specified
    etsbw-lcl not specified
    cos not specified
    pkey not specified
    linkmode not specified
capped-memory:
    physical: 60M
    [swap: 100M]
    [locked: 30M]
attr:
    name: comment
    type: string
    value: "Testzone with capped memory"
rctl:
    name: zone.max-swap
    value: (priv=privileged,limit=104857600,action=deny)
rctl:
    name: zone.max-locked-memory
    value: (priv=privileged,limit=31457280,action=deny)
rctl:
    name: zone.cpu-shares
    value: (priv=privileged,limit=20,action=none)
```

Zone Configuration File

You can also view the configuration file directly by viewing the /etc/zones/ <*zonename*>.xml file from the global zone. This file is created when you save the configuration using zonecfg.

Notice, in the previous output, the VNIC named anet that was created. In an exclusive-IP zone, anet was automatically configured, which gives the zone a virtual network device. The virtual network device will automatically get created in the global zone when the non-global zone is booted and will get destroyed when the non-global zone is shut down. VNICs are described in Chapter 9.

When the zone is booted, the VNIC is automatically created as shown when executing the dladm command:

```
# dladm<cr>
LINK        CLASS   MTU   STATE  OVER
net0        phys    1500  up     --
apps/net0   vnic    1500  up     net0
```

When the zone is shut down, the VNIC is destroyed as shown:

```
# dladm<cr>
LINK          CLASS    MTU  STATE  OVER
net0          phys    1500  up      --
```

From within the testzone non-global zone, the network information can also be viewed and is as follows:

```
root@testzone:~# dladm<cr>
LINK          CLASS   MTU   STATE  OVER
net0          vnic    1500  up      ?

root@testzone:~# ipadm show-addr<cr>
ADDROBJ      TYPE       STATE    ADDR
lo0/v4       static     ok       127.0.0.1/8
net0/v4      dhcp       ok       192.168.1.43/24
lo0/v6       static     ok       ::1/128
net0/v6      addrconf  ok        fe80::8:20ff:fe0b:76d6/10
```

Modify an Existing Zone

After a zone has been installed, you can still modify it. For example, suppose you want to add a ZFS file system to an existing zone. Adding a file system to a zone was described in the section above titled "Adding a ZFS Dataset to a Non-global Zone."

Perhaps you want to modify an existing resource in a zone. Start by shutting down the zone, then use the zonecfg utility to modify the resource, and then boot the zone.

In the following example, I'll modify the capped-memory resource that was set when I originally created testzone in an earlier exercise.

1. Shut down testzone as follows:

```
# zoneadm -z testzone shutdown<cr>
```

2. Use the zonecfg utility to modify testzone:

```
# zonecfg -z testzone<cr>
zonecfg:testzone>
```

3. Select the capped-memory resource:

```
zonecfg:testzone> select capped-memory<cr>
```

4. View the current settings using the `info` subcommand:

```
zonecfg:testzone:capped-memory> info<cr>
capped-memory:
  physical: 60M
  [swap: 100M]
  [locked: 30M]
```

5. Change the `locked` value to `25m` as follows:

```
zonecfg:testzone:capped-memory> set locked=25m<cr>
zonecfg:testzone:capped-memory> info<cr>
capped-memory:
  physical: 60M
  [swap: 100M]
  [locked: 25M]
```

6. Exit `zonecfg`:

```
zonecfg:testzone:capped-memory> end<cr>
zonecfg:testzone> exit<cr>
```

The next time the zone is booted, the changes will go into effect.

Move a Zone

You will move a zone when you simply want to relocate a non-global zone from one point on a system to another point. Typically, it's when you want to move a zone's path on a system from one directory to another. The new directory can be on an alternate file system, but it cannot be on an NFS mounted file system.

In this first example, the zone named `testzone` is currently installed in the `/zones/testzone` file system:

```
# zoneadm -z testzone list -v<cr>
  ID NAME           STATUS     PATH                      BRAND    IP
   - testzone       installed /zones/testzone            solaris  excl
```

Next, `testzone` is going to be moved to a new ZFS files system within the same ZFS storage pool. Data does not need to be copied; the file system is simply renamed.

```
# zoneadm -z testzone move /zones/newpath<cr>
```

No message is displayed; the change happens instantly, and listing the zone shows that the zone has been moved:

```
# zoneadm -z testzone list -v<cr>
  ID NAME           STATUS     PATH                         BRAND    IP
   - testzone     installed /zones/newpath               solaris  excl
```

When the zone is moved to a different storage pool, the data is copied and the original directory is removed. All data is copied using `cpio` to preserve all data within the zone. In this example, I'll move the zone from the `/zones/testzone` file system to the `/pool1/testzone` file system as follows:

```
# zoneadm -z testzone move /pool1/testzone<cr>
A ZFS file system has been created for this zone.
Copying from zones/newpath to pool1/testzone: please be patient
```

Listing the zone shows that the zone has been moved:

```
# zoneadm -z testzone list -v<cr>
  ID NAME           STATUS      PATH                        BRAND    IP
   - testzone     installed  /pool1/testzone            solaris  excl
```

Migrate a Zone

You migrate a zone when you want to move a zone from one system to another. Sometimes this involves moving from a host that may be running an Oracle Solaris 10 OS onto a host that is running Oracle Solaris 11. There are two types of migrations:

- One type of migration is moving a physical system (global zone) to a non-global zone, referred to as physical to virtual (P2V). An example would be to migrate an Oracle Solaris 10 physical server into a `solaris10` brand zone on an Oracle Solaris 11 global zone.
- Another type of migration involves moving a non-global zone from one global zone to another global zone, referred to as V2V (virtual to virtual). This type of migration simply moves the `zonepath` from one physical server to another. Both servers are running the same version of Oracle Solaris.

First, I'll describe how to perform a V2V migration. The following section "Migrate an Oracle Solaris 10 Global Zone to Oracle Solaris 11 (P2V)" describes how to perform a P2V migration, migrating an Oracle Solaris 10 physical server to a `solaris10` brand zone on an Oracle Solaris 11 global zone.

The following rules apply when migrating a non-global zone from one Oracle Solaris 11 host to another:

- You must remove all inactive BEs on the source system before migration.
- The global zone on the target system must be running the same Oracle Solaris 11 release as the original source host.
- To ensure that the zone will run properly, the target system must have the same or later versions of the required OS packages as those installed on the original source host.
- If the new host has later versions of the zone-dependent packages, using `zoneadm attach` with the `-u` or `-U` options updates those packages within the zone to match the new host. The update on attach software looks at the zone that is being migrated and determines which packages must be updated to match the new host. Only those packages are updated. The rest of the packages can vary from zone to zone. Any packages installed inside the zone but not installed in the global zone are ignored and left as is.

During a V2V migration, we are moving the `zonepath` from one host to another. First, halt the zone. Then, detach the zone and archive the files in the `zonepath`. You can archive the `zonepath` using your favorite backup tool, but because most zones run on a ZFS file system, a ZFS archive using `zfs send` and `zfs receive` is the best option.

Move the zone archive to the new system, extract the `zonepath` archive, reconfigure the zone on the new system, and finally attach the zone and boot it. The following steps describe the process of migrating a zone from `systemA` to `systemB`.

A zone named "`testzone`" already exists and is currently running on `systemA`. The zone's path is `/pool1/testzone`.

On the source system (`systemA`):

1. Halt the zone:

```
# zoneadm -z testzone halt<cr>
```

2. Detach the zone. Detaching a zone leaves the zone in a configured state on the original system. An XML file, called the "manifest," is generated and stored in the zone's path. The following command detaches the `testzone`:

```
# zoneadm -z testzone detach<cr>
```

The zone also goes into the configured state as shown:

```
# zoneadm -z testzone list -v<cr>
  ID NAME         STATUS     PATH                    BRAND    IP
   - testzone     configured /pool1/testzone         solaris  excl
```

3. Export testzone's zone configuration to a text file and store it in a temporary location. For the example, I created a ZFS file system named /zone/archive. I made sure this file system has 1GB of free disk space—enough to hold the data currently being stored in testzone's zonepath. Export the testzone configuration as follows:

```
# zonecfg -z testzone export > /zone/archive/testzone.cfg<cr>
```

4. Make a backup of the data in the zonepath by creating a ZFS snapshot of the zonepath, and then send the snapshot stream to a compressed archive file named testzone.gz as follows:

```
# zfs -r snapshot pool1/testzone@now<cr>
# zfs send -rc pool1/testzone@now |gzip > /zone/archive/testzone.gz<cr>
```

On the target server (systemB):

5. Transfer testzone.cfg and the testzone.gz file from systemA. You can use sftp, NFS, or removable media. Save the file in a temporary directory on systemB; I chose /zone/archive.
6. Use the zonecfg command to create the zone configuration as follows:

```
# zonecfg -z newzone -f /zone/archive/testzone.cfg<cr>
```

This zone can now be listed as follows:

```
# zoneadm -z newzone list -v<cr>
  ID NAME        STATUS      PATH                    BRAND    IP
   - newzone     configured  /pool1/testzone         solaris  excl
```

7. Make any configuration changes using the zonecfg command. I'll modify the zonepath as follows:

```
zonecfg:newzone> set zonepath=/zone/newzone<cr>
```

8. View the zone configuration:

```
zonecfg:newzone> info<cr>
zonename: newzone
zonepath: /zone/newzone
brand: solaris
autoboot: false
bootargs:
file-mac-profile:
pool:
limitpriv:
scheduling-class:
ip-type: exclusive
hostid:
fs-allowed:
```

9. Now that the configuration is correct, you can attach the zone:

```
# zoneadm -z newzone attach -a /zone/archive/testzone.gz<cr>
```

The -a option provides the path to the zone's compressed backup file that was saved in step 4. The backup does not need to be uncompressed; the zoneadm command can read the compressed ZFS archive as is.

The following messages are displayed as the archive is extracted and zone is attached:

```
A ZFS file system has been created for this zone.
Progress being logged to /var/log/zones/zoneadm.20120823T172231Z.z2.attach
Attaching. . .
    Installing: This may take several minutes. . .
      Zone BE root dataset: zone/newzone/rpool/ROOT/solaris
                     Cache: Using /var/pkg/publisher.
Updating image format
  Updating non-global zone: Linking to image /.
  Updating non-global zone: Auditing packages.
No updates necessary for this image.
  Updating non-global zone: Zone updated.
                    Result: Attach Succeeded.
Log saved in non-global zone as
/zone/testzone/root/var/log/zones/zoneadm.20120823T172231Z.z2.attach
```

10. Verify that the zone is in the installed state:

```
# zoneadm -z newzone list -v<cr>
  ID NAME          STATUS      PATH                      BRAND    IP
   - newzone       installed   /zone/newzone             solaris  excl
```

11. The zone is now ready to boot.

Clone a Zone

You clone a non-global zone when a zone is copied from its current `zonepath` to a new `zonepath`. The objective is to have two identical non-global zones running on the same global zone. However, you must reset properties and resources for the components that cannot be identical between the two zones. Cloning allows the system administrator to rapidly provision a new zone on the same system. The following describes the steps to clone a zone.

A zone named `apps` already exists and is currently running. The zone's path is `/zones/apps`, which is a ZFS file system.

Cloning with ZFS

When the source `zonepath` and the target `zonepath` both reside on ZFS and are in the same pool, the `zoneadm clone` command automatically uses ZFS to clone the zone. Override this function by using the `-m` option to force a new copy of the zone files to be created and not to use a ZFS clone.

You want to create a clone of this zone and name it "clonezone." Its `zonepath` will be in a ZFS file system (within the same zpool) named `/zones/clonezone`.

1. As root (on the global zone), shut down the `apps` zone:

```
# zoneadm -z apps shutdown<cr>
```

2. Configure the new zone, `clonezone`, by exporting the configuration from `apps`. The following procedure will create a configuration file named `/zones/master`:

```
# zonecfg -z apps export -f /zones/master<cr>
```

This is what the `/zones/master` file looks like:

```
create -b
set zonepath=/zones/apps
set brand=solaris
set autoboot=false
set ip-type=exclusive
add anet
set linkname=net1
set lower-link=net1
set configure-allowed-address=false
set link-protection=mac-nospoof
set mac-address=random
set auto-mac-address=2:8:20:94:4:61
```

```
add rctl
set name=zone.max-lwps
add value (priv=privileged,limit=6400,action=deny)
end
```

3. Use the `vi` editor to edit the `/zones/master` file that was created in the previous step. Modify the zone properties, such as `zonepath`.

   The following output is a sample `master` file that was created in the previous step. The items in bold have been modified for the new zone, `clonezone`.

```
# more /zone/master<cr>
```

   The system displays the following information:

```
create -b
set zonepath=/zones/clonezone
set brand=solaris
set autoboot=false
set ip-type=exclusive
add anet
set linkname=net0
set lower-link=auto
set configure-allowed-address=false
set link-protection=mac-nospoof
set mac-address=random
set auto-mac-address=2:8:20:94:4:62
add rctl
set name=zone.max-lwps
add value (priv=privileged,limit=6400,action=deny)
end
```

4. Create the new zone, `clonezone`:

```
# zonecfg -z clonezone -f /zones/master<cr>
```

   The zone has been created and is in the configured state as displayed next:

```
# zoneadm -z clonezone list -v<cr>
  ID NAME       STATUS     PATH                       BRAND     IP
   - clonezone  configured /zones/clonezone           solaris   excl
```

5. I'll create a configuration profile to be used for `clonezone` as follows:

```
# sysconfig create-profile -o /zones/myprofile.xml<cr>
```

I'll specify the following:

– Hostname: `clonezone`
– Network configuration: `automatically`
– Region: `Americas`
– Time zone: `Eastern Time`
– Name service: `none`
– Set root password
– Do not create a user account

6. Install the new zone by cloning `apps` and specifying the configuration profile created in the previous step:

```
# zoneadm -z clonezone clone -c /zones/myprofile.xml apps<cr>
A ZFS file system has been created for this zone.
Progress being logged to /var/log/zones/zoneadm.20120905T191155Z.clonezone.clone
Log saved in non-global zone as
/zones/clonezone/root/var/log/zones/zoneadm.20120905T191155Z.clonezone.clone
```

The zone is created in approximately 15 seconds because it was cloned to a new ZFS file system within the same zpool. Therefore, a ZFS clone was created, and very small amount of disk space is used (338K) for `clonezone` as shown with the following `zfs list` command:

```
# zfs list -r /zones<cr>
NAME                                       USED  AVAIL   REFER  MOUNTPOINT
zones                                      765M  14.9G     37K  /zones
zones/apps                                 763M  14.9G   34.5K  /zones/apps
zones/apps/rpool                           763M  14.9G     31K  /rpool
zones/apps/rpool/ROOT                      763M  14.9G     31K  legacy
zones/apps/rpool/ROOT/solaris              384M  14.9G    354M  /
zones/apps/rpool/ROOT/solaris-1            378M  14.9G    355M
/zones/apps/root
zones/apps/rpool/ROOT/solaris-1/var      23.4M  14.9G   23.4M
/zones/apps/root/var
zones/apps/rpool/ROOT/solaris/var        24.3M  14.9G   23.4M  /var
zones/apps/rpool/export                    63K  14.9G     32K  /export
zones/apps/rpool/export/home               31K  14.9G     31K  /export/home
zones/clonezone                           338K  14.9G     35K  /zones/clonezone
zones/clonezone/rpool                     303K  14.9G     31K  /rpool
zones/clonezone/rpool/ROOT                283K  14.9G     31K  legacy
zones/clonezone/rpool/ROOT/solaris-0      282K  14.9G    355M
/zones/clonezone/root
zones/clonezone/rpool/ROOT/solaris-0/var   38K  14.9G   23.4M
/zones/clonezone/root/var
zones/clonezone/rpool/export                2K  14.9G  32K      /export
zones/clonezone/rpool/export/home           1K  14.9G  31K      /export/home
```

7. List the zones on the system, and verify that both zones are installed:

```
# zoneadm list -iv<cr>
  ID NAME         STATUS     PATH                    BRAND    IP
   0 global       running    /                       solaris  shared
   - apps         installed  /zones/apps             solaris  excl
   - clonezone    installed  /zones/clonezone        solaris  excl
```

Create a Shared-IP Zone

Earlier I described how to create an exclusive-IP zone. In this next configuration, the global zone is going to share the network stack with the non-global zone. This configuration is referred to as a "shared-IP zone," and the system will not create a virtual network device, anet, as was described earlier with the exclusive-IP zone.

The advantage of a shared-IP zone is that the network can be completely configured from the global zone. The disadvantage is that its network stack is shared by other connections. It's possible to snoop other IP traffic when using a shared stack. In addition, another disadvantage is that a dedicated hardware interface is required for each shared-IP stack and can only be configured from the global zone.

Exclusive-IP zones use VNICs in Oracle Solaris 11, which provide far more flexibility and are the preferred configuration over shared-IP zones. With an exclusive-IP zone, there is no one-to-one relationship of a VNIC to a physical NIC. In an exclusive-IP zone, the network is configurable from within the non-global zone.

The following step-by-step instructions will configure a shared-IP zone named sharedzone.

First, make sure you have a ZFS storage pool with enough space to store your zone. We'll use a storage pool named zones on a separate disk (c3t3d0) as follows:

```
# zpool create zones c3t3d0<cr>
```

I'm also going to use the default template named SYSdefault-shared-ip, which will set the IP-type to shared and not the default exclusive-IP. Both the global zone and the shared-IP zone will share the net0 network interface.

Create the zone named sharedzone:

1. Perform the initial configuration on a zone named sharedzone. The zonepath will be /zones/sharedzone, and the IP address will be 192.168.1.99.
   Enter the zonecfg command to configure the new zone:

```
# zonecfg -z testzone<cr>
zonecfg:sharedzone> create -t SYSdefault-shared-ip<cr>
```

continues

```
zonecfg:sharedzone> set zonepath=/zones/sharedzone<cr>
zonecfg:sharedzone> add net<cr>
zonecfg:sharedzone:net> set physical=net0<cr>
zonecfg:sharedzone:net> set address=192.168.1.199<cr>
zonecfg:sharedzone:net> end<cr>
zonecfg:sharedzone> verify<cr>
zonecfg:sharedzone> exit<cr>
```

2. Install the zone as follows:

```
root@solaris:~# zoneadm -z sharedzone install<cr>
The following ZFS file system(s) have been created:
    zones/sharedzone
Progress being logged to
/var/log/zones/zoneadm.20130125T161435Z.sharedzone.install
       Image: Preparing at /zones/sharedzone/root.
 AI Manifest: /tmp/manifest.xml.3ZaWgx
   SC Profile: /usr/share/auto_install/sc_profiles/enable_sci.xml
    Zonename: sharedzone
Installation: Starting . . .
              Creating IPS image
Startup linked: 1/1 done
              Installing packages from:
                  solaris
                      origin: http://192.168.1.221/
DOWNLOAD                                PKGS         FILES    XFER (MB)   SPEED
Completed                            183/183  33556/33556 222.2/222.2  736k/s
PHASE          ITEMS
Installing new actions                          46825/46825
Updating package state database                        Done
Updating image state                                   Done
Creating fast lookup database                          Done
Installation: Succeeded
        Note: Man pages can be obtained by installing pkg:/system/manual
  done.
        Done: Installation completed in 519.123 seconds.
  Next Steps: Boot the zone, then log into the zone console (zlogin -C)
              to complete the configuration process.
Log saved in non-global zone as
/zones/sharedzone/root/var/log/zones/zoneadm.20130125T161435Z.sharedzone.install
```

The following configuration information is from the shared-IP zone, `sharedzone`. Compare this to the output from the exclusive-IP zone created in the previous section:

```
# zonecfg -z sharedzone info<cr>
zonename: sharedzone
zonepath: /zones/sharedzone
brand: solaris
autoboot: false
bootargs:
file-mac-profile:
pool:
limitpriv:
scheduling-class:
ip-type: shared
hostid:
fs-allowed:
net:
        address: 192.168.1.199
        allowed-address not specified
```

```
        configure-allowed-address: true
        physical: net0
        defrouter not specified
```

Before the shared-IP zone is booted, the network configuration as viewed from the global zone is as follows:

```
# dladm<cr>
LINK         CLASS   MTU   STATE  OVER
net0         phys    1500  up     --

# ipadm show-addr<cr>
ADDROBJ            TYPE             STATE        ADDR
lo0/v4             static           ok           127.0.0.1/8
net0/v4            static           ok           192.168.1.220/24
lo0/v6             static           ok           ::1/128
net0/v6            addrconf         ok           fe80::a00:27ff:fe1d:b42b/10
```

After booting the shared-IP zone, the network configuration as viewed from the global zone is as follows:

```
# dladm<cr>
LINK         CLASS   MTU   STATE  OVER
net0         phys    1500  up     --

# ipadm show-addr<cr>
ADDROBJ            TYPE             STATE        ADDR
lo0/v4             static           ok           127.0.0.1/8
lo0/zoneadmd.v4    static           ok           127.0.0.1/8
net0/v4            static           ok           192.168.1.220/24
net0/zoneadmd.v4   static           ok           192.168.1.199/24
lo0/v6             static           ok           ::1/128
lo0/zoneadmd.v6    static           ok           ::1/128
net0/v6            addrconf         ok           fe80::a00:27ff:fe1d:b42b/10
```

From within the `sharedzone` non-global zone, the network information can also be viewed and is as follows:

```
# dladm<cr>
dladm: could not open /dev/dld: object not found
```

The output from the `dladm` command indicates that the data link is not accessible or configurable from within the non-global zone.

```
root@sharedzone:~# ipadm show-addr<cr>
ADDROBJ            TYPE             STATE        ADDR
lo0/?              from-gz          ok           127.0.0.1/8
net0/?             from-gz          ok           192.168.1.199/24
lo0/?              from-gz          ok           ::1/128
```

The output indicates that the IP address is only configurable from the global zone.

Migrate an Oracle Solaris 10 Global Zone to Oracle Solaris 11 (P2V)

I stated in Chapter 1 that it was not possible to upgrade an Oracle Solaris 10 system to Oracle Solaris 11. The only path is to back up the Oracle Solaris 10 system and import that backup into an Oracle Solaris 10 brand zone on an Oracle Solaris 11 host. This is referred to as a P2V migration. An existing Oracle Solaris 10 9/10 (update 9) or later system can be directly migrated into an Oracle Solaris 10 zone on an Oracle Solaris 11 system. The next set of steps describes how to perform this operation.

Prepare an Oracle Solaris 10 Global Zone for Migration

Back up the Oracle Solaris 10 server using `cpio`, `gzip compressed cpio`, `bzip2 compressed cpio`, `pax`, or `ufsdump`. For this example, I'll create a flash archive using the Oracle Solaris 10 `flarcreate` command.

> **Note**
>
> `flarcreate` was available on Oracle Solaris 10 and is no longer used in Oracle Solaris 11. For more information on `flarcreate`, refer to *Solaris 10 System Administration Exam Prep,* written by Bill Calkins and published by QUE Publishing.

Log in to the Oracle Solaris 10 system and verify that you have a local file system large enough to store a flash archive of the server's root file system. Estimate the size by totaling the root (`/`), `/var`, `/opt`, and `/usr` file systems on your Oracle Solaris 10 host. For this example, I'll use the `/export/share` directory.

Log in to the Oracle Solaris 10 system and create a flash archive of that system as follows:

```
# flarcreate -S -n sol10-server -L cpio /export/share/sol10-server.flar<cr>
```

Copy the flash archive file to the Oracle Solaris 11 server. You could also share `/export/share` on the Oracle Solaris 10 server and access the archive from the Oracle Solaris 11 system across the network using NFS.

Create a `Solaris10` Brand Zone

Log in to the Oracle Solaris 11 system and create a `solaris10` brand non-global zone as described in the following steps.

1. Create a ZFS file system for the zone:

```
# zfs create rpool/zone1<cr>
```

2. Configure the solaris10 brand zone as follows:

```
# zonecfg -z zone1<cr>
zone1: No such zone configured
Use 'create' to begin configuring a new zone.
zonecfg:zone1> create -t SYSsolaris10<cr>
zonecfg:zone1> set zonepath=/rpool/zone1<cr>
zonecfg:zone1> set autoboot=true<cr>
zonecfg:zone1> select anet linkname=net0<cr>
zonecfg:zone1:anet> set allowed-address=192.168.1.159/24<cr>
zonecfg:zone1:anet> set configure-allowed-address=true<cr>
zonecfg:zone1:anet> end<cr>
zonecfg:zone1> set hostid=087fd976<cr>
zonecfg:zone1> verify<cr>
zonecfg:zone1> commit<cr>
zonecfg:zone1> exit<cr>
```

3. Use the zone install command to install the flash archive that was created earlier. My archive was copied into the /data file system on the Oracle Solaris 11 host. I'm using the -p option to preserve the original system identity. This will configure the zone to use the same identity as the system used to create the flash archive. Alternatively, you could use the -u option to sys-unconfig the zone and prompt for the system identification information during the first boot.

```
# zoneadm -z zone1 install -a /data/sol10-server.flar -p<cr>
Progress being logged to /var/log/zones/zoneadm.20121025T184316Z.zone1.install
     Installing: This may take several minutes. . .
Postprocessing: This may take a while. . .
   Postprocess: Updating the image to run within a zone
   Postprocess: Migrating data
   from: rpool/zone1/rpool/ROOT/zbe-0
     to: rpool/zone1/rpool/export
   Postprocess: A backup copy of
/export is stored at /export.backup.20121025T185135Z.
It can be deleted after verifying it was migrated correctly.

        Result: Installation completed successfully.
Log saved in non-global zone as /rpool/zone1/root/var/log/zones/
zoneadm.20121025T184316Z.zone1.install
```

4. The non-global zone is now complete. List the zone to verify that it is in the installed state as follows:

```
# zoneadm list -cv<cr>
  ID NAME          STATUS      PATH                 BRAND      IP
   0 global        running     /                    solaris    shared
   - zone1         installed   /rpool/zone1         solaris10  excl
```

5. Start a console for the zone:

```
# zlogin -C zone1<cr>
```

6. Boot the zone into single-user mode from the global zone:

```
# zoneadm -z zone1 boot -s<cr>
```

In the zone's console, watch the system boot. When prompted, log in to the zone console and use the root password from the migrated host:

```
NOTICE: Zone booting up]

SunOS Release 5.10 Version Generic_Virtual 64-bit
Copyright (c) 1983, 2011, Oracle and/or its affiliates. All rights reserved.
Booting to milestone "milestone/single-user:default".
Failed to plumb IPv4 interface(s): e1000g0
Failed to configure IPv4 DHCP interface(s): e1000g0
Moving addresses from missing IPv4 interface(s): e1000g0 (not moved -- not
in an IPMP group).
Loading smf(5) service descriptions: 1/1
Hostname: zone1
Requesting System Maintenance Mode
SINGLE USER MODE

Root password for system maintenance (control-d to bypass): <enter password>
single-user privilege assigned to /dev/console.
Entering System Maintenance Mode

Oct 25 15:03:07 su: 'su root' succeeded for root on /dev/console
Oracle Corporation  SunOS 5.10      Generic Patch    January 2005
#
```

During the boot process, I see an error related to e1000g0. That is because the Oracle Solaris 11 host does not have this interface configured. The non-global zone will use the net0 device that was specified when I configured the zone.

Verify that the hostid is the same as the migrated system's hostid. This is important for any applications that may be linked to the system hostid. The hostid was specified when I created the zone. I used the same hostid as the original Oracle Solaris 10 host.

```
# hostid<cr>
087fd976
```

The uname command shows that the zone is running Oracle Solaris 10 (SunOS 5.10):

```
# uname -r<cr>
5.10
```

The `ifconfig` command verifies that the IP address has been set:

```
# ifconfig net0<cr>
net0: flags=40001000863<UP,BROADCAST,NOTRAILERS,RUNNING,MULTICAST,IPv4,L3PROTECT> mtu
1500 index 2
        inet 192.168.1.159 netmask ffffff00 broadcast 192.168.1.255
        ether 2:8:20:e4:97:f
```

Back Up a Zone

Back up a zone by backing up all of the files in the `zonepath`. In addition, you should back up the zone configuration file located in `/etc/zones`.

For example, a zone named `apps` already exists and is currently running on `systemA`. The zone's path is `/zones/apps`, a ZFS file system. Follow these steps to back up this zone by creating a snapshot of the `zonepath` and then sending the snapshot stream to a remote system. The snapshot can be created on a running zone.

1. Obtain the `zonepath` for the zone:

```
# zoneadm -z apps list -v<cr>

ID NAME     STATUS     PATH                  BRAND    IP
 2 apps     running    /zones/apps           solaris  excl
```

2. Create a snapshot of the `zonepath` as follows:

```
# zfs snapshot -r zones/apps@snap<cr>
```

3. Send the snapshot stream as a compressed file to another system or disk for storage:

```
# zfs send -rc zones/apps@snap|gzip > /path/to/save/archive.gz<cr>
```

4. Destroy the snapshot as follows:

```
# zfs destroy -r zones/apps@snap<cr>
```

Creating a ZFS snapshot is described in Chapter 5, "Administering ZFS File Systems."

You should also back up the zone configuration. A good practice is to export the zone configuration and store the zone configuration file in the `zonepath` so that it is backed up with the rest of the zone. For example, I'll export the zone configuration file for the apps zone as follows:

```
# zonecfg -z apps export >/zones/apps/apps.config<cr>
```

Optionally, you could back up the entire /etc/zones directory or the individual .xml file located in /etc/zones.

Recover a Zone

In the previous section, a backup was made of the zone configuration file and the zone path. Now, we'll use those backups to recover a zone.

Recovering a zone involves re-creating the zone configuration through its zone configuration file as follows:

```
# zonecfg -z apps -f /zones/apps/apps.config<cr>
```

The apps zone should now be in the configured state.

Next, attach the zone to the compressed ZFS snapshot stream archive as follows:

```
# zoneadm -z apps attach -a /zones/archive.gz<cr>
```

The following messages are displayed as the archive is extracted and the zone is attached:

```
Progress being logged to /var/log/zones/zoneadm.20120905T232332Z.apps.attach
Attaching. . .
    Installing: This may take several minutes. . .
Jan 25 19:20:23 solaris last message repeated 1 time
     Zone BE root dataset: zones/apps/rpool/ROOT/solaris-0
                    Cache: Using /var/pkg/publisher.
Updating image format
   Updating non-global zone: Linking to image /.
   Updating non-global zone: Auditing packages.
No updates necessary for this image.
   Updating non-global zone: Zone updated.
                   Result: Attach Succeeded.
Log saved in non-global zone as
/zones/apps/root/var/log/zones/zoneadm.20120905T232332Z.apps.attach
```

The -a option provides the path to the zone's compressed backup file, which was saved in the previous section as a gzip compressed file. The archive does not need to be uncompressed; the `zoneadm` command can read the `gzip` compressed ZFS archive as is.

Finally, verify that the zone is in the installed state as follows:

```
# zoneadm -z apps list -v<cr>
  ID NAME       STATUS     PATH                BRAND    IP
   - apps       installed  /zones/apps         solaris  excl
```

Delegated Zone Administration

With Oracle Solaris 11, common administration tasks can be delegated to users or administrators on a zone-by-zone basis. Authorizations are interpreted by the appropriate command running in the global zone to allow access at the correct authorization level to a specific user or administrator. There are two basic levels of zone administration:

- Global administrator
- Zone administrator

The global administrator has full root privileges when logged in to the global zone and can monitor and control the system and all non-global zones as a whole.

The zone administrator can administer a non-global zone. The global administrator will assign the required authorizations to the zone administrator. The privileges assigned to the zone administrator are confined to a specific non-global zone.

Configuring delegated zone administration requires knowledge of RBAC and is described in Chapter 7.

Summary

The Oracle Solaris zones facility allows virtualization of OS services so that applications can run in an isolated and secure environment. One of the advantages of zones is that multiple versions of the same application can be run on the same physical system but independently of one another. Zones also protect the user from having a single application that can exhaust the CPU or memory resources when a zone encounters an error. This also allows each application to run in its own, secure environment.

This chapter described the concepts of Oracle Solaris zones and the zone components as well as the types of zone that can be configured. The root file system of each zone can be configured as fully writable or read-only.

You have seen how to configure a zone from scratch and how to install and boot a zone. You've learned how to list, view, uninstall, remove, move, migrate, and clone a zone configuration.

You've also learned how to access the zone console and log in to a zone for system administration purposes.

In Chapter 9, I will describe how to create a private virtual network between non-global zones.

For more information on Oracle Solaris zones, refer to the "System Administration Guide: Oracle Solaris Zones, Oracle Solaris 10 Containers, and Resource Management," by Oracle Corporation, all of which are available at the Oracle Technology Documentation Web site, `http://docs.oracle.com`.

7

User and Security Administration

Managing user accounts can be simple or complex, depending on the size of the network. Today, many Oracle Solaris servers are simply database servers or Web servers, and users do not log directly in to these systems. In addition, workstations may only require login accounts for one or two users. On the other hand, in a university setting, a server may hold hundreds of user login accounts. Managing these accounts is very complex because the accounts change every semester. The system administrator is not only responsible for managing user accounts but also for ensuring that system security is not compromised.

This chapter describes how to manage user accounts while maintaining a reasonable level of security on a system.

Administering User Accounts

Access to a system is allowed only through user login accounts that are set up by the system administrator. A user account includes information that a user needs to log in and use a system—a user login name, a password, the user's home directory, and login initialization files. Each of these items is described later in this chapter.

Previous versions of Oracle Solaris provided both a GUI and a command line interface for administering user accounts. The Oracle Solaris Management Console graphical tool that was used to manage users and groups has been eliminated in Oracle Solaris 11. To create and manage users and groups, use the command line tools described in this chapter.

The first step in setting up a new user account is to have the user provide the information you need in order to administer the account. You also need to set up proper permissions so that the user can share information with other members of his or her department. You need to know the user's full name, department, and any groups with which the user will be working. It's a good idea for the system administrator to develop an information sheet to pass on to users for them to complete. It's also a good idea to have the proper authorizations and signatures on this form to approve the new user addition. Table 7-1 has a sample of the information that you need to obtain from the user in advance of setting up a new user account.

When creating a user account, you will need to supply some or all of the components from Table 7-2, depending on the options selected at the command line. Table 7-2 describes the format that must be followed when entering this information.

Table 7-1 User Information Data Sheet

Item
Username:
UID:
Primary group:
Secondary groups:
Comment:
Default shell:
Password status and aging:
Home directory server name:
Home directory path name:
Mail server:
Department name:
Department administrator:
Manager:
Employee name:
Employee title:
Employee status:
Employee number:
Start date:
RBAC roles assigned to this login:

Table 7-2 User Account Components

Field	Description
Username	The username is a unique login name that is entered at the Oracle Solaris login prompt. You should choose a name that is unique to the organization. The name can contain two to eight uppercase characters (A–Z), lowercase characters (a–z), or digits (0–9). Periods, underscores, hyphens, and spaces should not be used. The first character must be a letter, and at least one character must be a lowercase letter. The system allows you to use more than eight characters for the login name, but only the first eight characters are recognized. Sometimes this username is consistent throughout the organization as a desktop login and LAN ID and is assigned to the user when he or she is hired.
User ID	The user ID is a unique identifier (UID). The system can automatically assign the next available UID; however, in a networked environment, you need to make sure this number is not duplicated by another user on another system. All UIDs must be consistent across the network. A UID is typically a number between 100 and 60,002, but it can be as high as 2,147,483,647. UIDs 0-99 are reserved for use by the OS.
Password	The password is a combination of up to 256 letters, numbers, or special characters that a user enters with the login name to gain access to a system. The first six characters of the password must contain at least two alphabetic characters and at least one numeric or special character.
Primary Group	This is the primary group name for the group to which the user will belong. This is the group that the OS will assign to files created by the user. Group 10 (staff) is a predefined group that is sufficient for most users.
Secondary Group	A user can belong to additional groups referred to as "secondary groups." Up to 1,024 secondary groups can be specified.
Full Name and Description	These are optional comment fields. You can enter any comments, such as the full username, employee number, or phone number.
Home Directory	Home directory is a field that points to an existing directory or specifies a new directory to create. This will be the location of the user's home directory and where the user's personal files will be stored. Refer to the section titled "The Home Directory" later in this chapter.
Login Shell	The login shell is the user's work environment as set up by the initialization files that are defined by the user's login shell. Typical login shells are: Bourne, C-shell, Korn, Bash, T-shell, Z-shell, or Restricted shell.

Managing User and Group Accounts from the Command Line

This section will describe how to create and manage user accounts from the command line. However, you should note that the User Manager panel available through the `pkg:/system/management/visual-panels/panel-usermgr` IPS package can also be used. This GUI is much easier to use and can be started using one of the following methods:

- From the desktop, choose System → Administration → User Manager.
- Start the User Manager GUI from the command line by typing `vp usermgr &`.

Oracle Solaris supplies the user administration commands described in Table 7-3 for setting up and managing user accounts from the command line.

Adding User Accounts from the Command Line

You can add new user accounts on the local system by using the `useradd` command. This command adds an entry for the new user into the `/etc/passwd` and `/etc/shadow` files, which are described later in this chapter in the section titled "Where User Account Information Is Stored."

The syntax for the `useradd` command is as follows:

```
useradd [-c comment] [-d dir] [-e expire]  [-f inactive]  [-g group] \
 [  -G group   [  , group. . .]] [ -m [-k skel_dir]] [-u uid  [-o]] \
 [-s shell]  [-A  authorization  [,authorization. . .]] [-P profile   [,profile. . .]] \
[-R role  [,role. . .]] [-p projname] [-K key=value] <loginname>
```

Table 7-4 describes these options.

Table 7-3 Account Administration Commands

Command	Description
`useradd`	Adds a new user account
`userdel`	Deletes a user account
`usermod`	Modifies a user account
`groupadd`	Adds a new group
`groupmod`	Modifies a group (for example, changes the group identifier [GID] or name)

Table 7-4 useradd Command Options

Option	Description
-A <*authorization*>	One or more comma-separated authorizations.
-b <*base-dir*>	This option specifies the default base directory for the system if -d is not specified.
-u <*uid*>	This option sets the unique UID for the user.
-o	The -o option allows a UID to be duplicated. The default is not to let you choose a UID that is already in use.
-g <*gid*>	This option specifies a predefined GID or name for the user that will be the user's primary group.
-G <*gid*>	This option defines the new user's secondary group memberships. You can enter multiple groups, but they must be separated by commas. A user can belong to up to 15 additional groups. The number of groups can be increased to 1,024 by changing the kernel parameter ngroups_max.
-m	The -m option creates a new home directory if one does not already exist.
-s <*shell*>	This option defines the full pathname for the shell program to be used as the user's login shell. The default is /bin/sh if a shell is not specified.
-c <*comment*>	This option specifies the user's full name, location, and phone number, in a comment.
-d <*dir*>	This option specifies the home directory of the new user. It defaults to <*base-dir*>/<*account-name*>, where <*base-dir*> is the base directory for new login home directories and <*account-name*> is the new login name.
-D	This option displays the default values for group, basedir, skel-dir, and so on. When used with the -g, -b, -f, -e, -A, -P, -p, -R, or -K options, the -D option sets the default values for the specified fields.
-e <*expiration*>	This option sets an expiration date on the user account. It specifies the date on which the user can no longer log in and access the account. After the specified date, the account is locked. Use the following format to specify the date: mm/dd/yy.
-f <*inactive*>	This option sets the number of inactive days allowed on a user account. If the account is not logged in to during the specified number of days, the account is locked.
-k <*skeldir*>	This option specifies an alternate location for the user initialization template files. Files from this directory are copied into the user's home directory when the -m option is specified to create the home directory. The default location is /etc/skel.

(*continues*)

Table 7-4 `useradd` Command Options (*Continued*)

Option	Description
-p *<project-name>*	This option specifies the name of the project with which the user is associated.
-P *<profile>*	This option specifies an execution profile for the account.
-R *<role>*	This option specifies a role for the account.
-S *<repository>*	Valid repositories are `files`, `ldap`. The repository specifies which name service will be updated.
<login-name>	This option specifies the user login name to be assigned to this account.

Many additional options are available, although most of them are not used as often as the ones in Table 7-4. You can refer to the man pages to find a listing of all the options to the `useradd(1M)` command.

The `useradd` command can be used with just one argument and no options, as follows:

```
# useradd bcalkins<cr>
```

This creates the user account named `bcalkins` using all default options. To see all of the default values, type

```
# useradd -D<cr>
```

The system responds with the following:

```
group=staff,10  project=default,3  basedir=/export/home
skel=/etc/skel  shell=/usr/bin/bash  inactive=0
expire=  auths=  profiles=  roles=  limitpriv=
defaultpriv=  lock_after_retries=
```

These defaults can be modified by using the `-D` option with the `useradd` command as follows:

```
# useradd -D -b /export/home<cr>
```

The defaults for the `useradd` command are stored in the `/usr/sadm/defadduser` file. This file does not initially exist and is created the first time the useradd command is executed using the -D option. This file can then be edited manually or modified using one of the following options along with the -D option: -g, -b, -f, -e, -A, -P, -u, -R, or -K (see the useradd command described earlier or the useradd man pages for a description of these options).

For example, to change the default group, execute the following command:

```
# useradd -D -g staff<cr>
```

You can also temporarily override the default options by specifying them on the command line when executing the useradd command. The following example creates a new login account for Bill Calkins:

```
# useradd -u 3000 -g other -d /export/home/bcalkins -m -s /usr/bin/bash \
 -c "Bill Calkins, ext. 2345" bcalkins<cr>
```

The login name is bcalkins, the UID is 3000, and the group is other. In this example, you instruct the system to create a home directory named /export/home/bcalkins. The default shell is /usr/bin/bash, and the initialization files are to be copied from the /etc/skel directory.

Use the -k option to the useradd command to copy all of the user initialization files found in the /etc/skel directory into the new user's home directory. This directory can be customized or changed by specifying an alternate directory containing the files to be copied by supplying an argument to the -k option. User initialization files are covered in the section titled "Setting Up Shell Initialization Files" later in this chapter.

Assigning a UID

If the -u option is not used to specify a UID, the UID defaults to the next available number above the highest number currently assigned. For example, if UIDs 100, 110, and 200 are already assigned to login names, the next UID that is automatically assigned is 201.

After creating the new account with the useradd command, the user account has not yet been activated and cannot be used. The next step is to set a password for the account using the passwd command as follows:

```
# passwd bcalkins<cr>
passwd: Changing password for bcalkins
New Password: <ENTER PASSWORD>
Re-enter new Password: <RE_ENTER PASSWD>
passwd: password successfully changed for bcalkins
```

Some of the more common options that can be used with the passwd command are described in Table 7-5.

Table 7-5 passwd Options

Option	Description
`-s <name>`	Shows password attributes for a particular user; when used with the `-a` option, -attributes for all user accounts are displayed.
`-d <name>`	Deletes password for name and unlocks the account; the login name is not prompted for a password.
`-e <name>`	Changes the login shell, in the `/etc/passwd` file, for a user.
`-f <name>`	Forces the user to change passwords at the next login by expiring the password.
`-h <name>`	Changes the home directory, in the `/etc/passwd` file, for a user.
`-l <name>`	Locks a user's account; use the `-d` or `-u` option to unlock the account.
`-N <name>`	Makes the password entry for `<name>` a value that cannot be used for login but does not lock the account.
`-u <name>`	Unlocks a locked account.

For a complete listing of the options, refer to the online man pages for the `passwd(1)` command.

To force a user to change his or her password at the next login, type

```
# passwd -f bcalkins<cr>
passwd: password information changed for bcalkins
#
```

To change a user's home directory, type

```
# passwd -h bcalkins<cr>
```

The system responds with the following:

```
Default values are printed inside of '[]'.
To accept the default, type <return>.
To have a blank entry, type the word 'none'.
```

Enter the new home directory when prompted:

```
Home Directory [/home/wcalkins]: /home/bcalkins<cr>
passwd: password information changed for bcalkins
```

Modifying User Accounts from the Command Line

You use the usermod command to modify existing user accounts from the command line. You can use usermod to modify most of the options that were used when the account was originally created.

The following is the syntax for the usermod command:

```
usermod [ -u uid [-o]] [-g group] [ -G group [ ,  group. . .]]
[  -d dir  [-m]]  [-s shell]  [-c comment]  [-l new_name] [-f inactive]
[-e expire]  [-A  authorization2  [,  authorization]]  [-P  profile
[,  profile]] [-R role  [, role]] [-K key=value] <loginname>
```

The options used with the usermod command are the same as those described for the useradd command, except for those listed in Table 7-6.

Additional options to the usermod command apply specifically to RBAC accounts.

The following example changes the login name for user bcalkins to wcalkins:

```
# usermod -d /export/home/wcalkins -m -s /bin/ksh -l wcalkins bcalkins<cr>
```

This example also changes the home directory to /export/home/wcalkins and the default shell to /bin/ksh.

Modifying the Home Directory

When you're changing the home directory, unless the -d and -m options are used, existing files still must be manually moved from the old home directory to the new home directory. In all cases, symbolic links, application-specific configuration files, and various other references to the old home directory must be manually updated.

To set a user's account expiration date, enter the following:

```
# usermod -e 10/15/2013 wcalkins<cr>
```

Table 7-6 usermod Command Options

Option	Description
-l <new-login-name>	Changes a user's login name on a specified account
-m	Moves the user's home directory to the new location specified with the -d option

The account is now set to expire October 15, 2013. Notice the entry made to the `/etc/shadow` file:

```
wcalkins:$5$VWZPYaFo$EVDwt4h/NVxegGOjNI0jA99G/U.6aQTlVdAOc.GGin3:15593::::15993:
```

The last field for the `wcalkins` entry in the `/etc/shadow` file is `15993`. This is an absolute date expressed as the number of days since the UNIX epoch (January 1, 1970). When this number is reached, the login is expired.

The syntax of the `/etc/shadow` file is described later in this chapter in the section titled "Where User Account Information Is Stored."

Deleting User Accounts from the Command Line

Use the `userdel` command to delete a user's login account from the system. You can specify options to save or remove the user's home directory. The syntax for the `userdel` command is as follows:

```
userdel [-r] [-S repository] <login-name>
```

`-r` removes the user's home directory from the local file system. If this option is not specified, only the login is removed; the home directory remains intact.

Caution

Make sure you know where the user's home directory is located before removing it. Some users have "/" as their home directory, and removing their home directory would remove important system files.

The following example removes the login account for `bcalkins` but does not remove the home directory:

```
# userdel bcalkins<cr>
```

Adding Group Accounts from the Command Line

You use the `groupadd` command to add new group accounts on the local system. This command adds an entry to the `/etc/group` file. The syntax for the `groupadd` command is as follows:

```
groupadd [-g gid [-o]] [-S repository] [-U user1[,user2..] ] group
```

Table 7-7 describes the `groupadd` command options.

The following example adds to the system a new group named `acct` with a GID of `1000`:

```
# groupadd -g 1000 acct<cr>
```

Assigning a GID

If the `-g` option is not used to specify a GID, the GID defaults to the next available number above the highest number currently assigned. For example, if GIDs 100, 110, and 200 are already assigned to group names, the next GID that is automatically assigned is 201.

Modifying Group Accounts from the Command Line

You use the `groupmod` command to modify the definitions of a specified group. The syntax for the `groupmod` command is as follows:

```
groupmod [-S [files | ldap]] [-U user1[,user2]] [-g gid [-o]] [-n name] group
```

Table 7-8 describes the `groupmod` command options.

Table 7-7 `groupadd` Command Options

Option	Description
`-g <gid>`	This option assigns the GID `<gid>` for the new group.
`-o`	The `-o` option allows the GID to be duplicated. In other words, more than one group with group-name can share the same GID.
`-S`	This option specifies which name service repository will be updated. When repository is not specified, the `files` repository is used. When the repository is `files`, the username and other items can be present in other name service repositories and can be assigned to a group in the `files` repository. When the repository is `ldap`, all the assignable attributes must be present in the `ldap` repository. The valid repositories are files and `ldap`.
`-u`	This option adds a list of users to the group.

Table 7-8 groupmod Command Options

Option	Description
-g <*gid*>	This option assigns the new GID <*gid*> for the group.
-o	The -o option allows the GID to be duplicated. In other words, more than one group with group-name can share the same GID.
-n <*name*>	This option specifies a new name for the group.
-S	The valid repositories are files and ldap. The repository specifies which name service will be updated. When repository is not specified, groupmod consults nsswitch.conf(4). When the repository is files, the username and other items can be present in other name service repositories and can be assigned to a group in the files repository. When the repository is ldap, all of the assignable attributes must be present in the ldap repository.
-U	The -U option updates the list of users for the group as follows: A prefix + before the list adds that list to the existing users list. A prefix - before the list removes each user in the list from the existing users list. With no prefix before the list, replaces the existing users list with the new list of users specified.

The following example changes the engrg group GID from 200 to 2000:

```
# groupmod -g 2000 engrg<cr>
```

Any files that had the group ownership of "engrg" are now without a group name. A long listing would show a group ownership of 200 on these files, the previous GID for the engrg group. The group 200 no longer exists on the system, so only the GID is displayed in a long listing.

Deleting Group Accounts from the Command Line

You use the groupdel command to delete a group account from the local system. The syntax for the groupdel command is as follows:

```
groupdel [-S repository] <group-name>
```

The -S option allows the name service to be specified. The valid repositories that can be specified are files and ldap. When the repository is not specified, groupdel consults nsswitch.conf(4).

The following example deletes the group named "acct" from the local system:

```
# groupdel acct<cr>
```

Editing User Accounts Files

When you're adding or modifying user accounts, the system automatically edits the files `/etc/passwd`, `/etc/shadow`, and `/etc/group`. These files are described later in this chapter. As root, you could edit these files directly, but that is not recommended. Errors in any of these files could cause adverse effects on the system.

Setting Up Shell Initialization Files

As a system administrator, when you're setting up a user's home directory, you need to set up the shell initialization files for the user's login shell (also called "user initialization files"). A shell initialization file is a shell script that runs automatically each time the user logs in. The initialization file sets up the work environment and customizes the shell environment for the user. The primary job of the shell initialization file is to define the user's shell environment, such as the search path, environment variables, and windowing environment. Each UNIX shell has its own shell initialization file (or files), located in the user's home directory, as described in the following sections.

C Shell Initialization Files

C shell initialization files run in a particular sequence after the user logs in to the system. For the C shell, initialization files are run in the following sequence:

1. Commands in `/etc/.login` are executed if present. This is the global initialization file for the C shell.
2. Commands from the `$HOME/.cshrc` file (located in the user's home directory) are executed. In addition, each time the user starts a new shell or opens a new window in the Common Desktop Environment (CDE), commands from `$HOME/.cshrc` are run.
3. The shell executes commands from the `$HOME/.login` file (located in the user's home directory). Typically, the `$HOME/.login` file contains commands to specify the terminal type and environment.
4. When startup processing is complete, the C shell begins reading commands from the default input device, the terminal.

Although it is not part of the initialization of the shell, when the C shell terminates, it performs commands from the `$HOME/.logout` file (if that file exists in the user's home directory).

Bourne Shell Initialization Files

Bourne shell initialization files run in a particular sequence after the user logs in to the system. For the Bourne shell, initialization files are run in the following sequence:

1. Commands in `/etc/profile` are executed if present. This is the global initialization file for the Bourne shell.
2. Commands from the `$HOME/.profile` file (located in the user's home directory) are executed. Typically, the `$HOME/.profile` file contains commands to specify the terminal type and environment.
3. When startup processing is complete, the Bourne shell begins reading commands from the default input device, the terminal.

Korn Shell Initialization Files

Korn shell initialization files run in a particular sequence after the user logs in to the system. For the Korn shell, initialization files are run in the following sequence:

1. Commands in `/etc/profile` are executed if present. This is the global initialization file for the Korn shell.
2. Commands from the `$HOME/.profile` file (located in the user's home directory) are executed. Typically, the `$HOME/.profile` file contains commands to specify the terminal type and environment.
3. If the `$HOME/.kshrc` file is present, commands located in this file are executed. In addition, this initialization file gets read (and the commands get executed) every time a new Korn shell is started after login. The `.kshrc` file name is defined by the `ENV` variable. This filename is user definable but is typically named `.kshrc` or `.kshenv`.
4. When startup processing is complete, the Korn shell begins reading commands from the default input device, the terminal.

Bash Shell Initialization Files

Bash shell initialization files run in a particular sequence after the user logs in to the system. For the Bash shell, initialization files are run in the following sequence:

1. Commands in /etc/profile are executed if present. This is the global initialization file for the Bash shell.
2. Commands from the $HOME/.bash_profile, $HOME/.bash_login, and $HOME/.profile file (located in the user's home directory) are executed. The system reads and executes commands from the first file that exists and is readable. Typically either .bash_profile or .profile is used. The file contains commands to specify the terminal type and environment.
3. When an interactive shell that is not a login shell is started (for example, a new terminal window is opened), Bash reads and executes commands from the $HOME/.bashrc file if it is present. Typically, you may see shell aliases placed in this file.
4. When startup processing is complete, the Bash shell begins reading commands from the default input device, the terminal.
5. Upon exiting the shell, Bash reads and executes $HOME/.bash_logout (if it exists).

Read the man pages for each of the shells, csh(1), sh(1), ksh(1), and bash(1) for more information.

Default Initialization Files

When a user logs in to the system, the user's login shell is invoked. The shell program looks for its initialization files in the correct order for the shell. The shell program then executes the commands contained in each file and, when it is finished, displays the shell prompt on the user's screen.

Default user initialization files (such as .cshrc, .profile, and .login) are created automatically in the user's home directory when a new user account is added. You can predefine the contents of these files, or you can choose to use the system default files. Oracle Solaris provides default user initialization files for each shell in the /etc/skel directory on each system. These files are listed in Table 7-9.

Table 7-9 Default Initialization Files

Filename	Description
local.cshrc	The default .cshrc file for the C shell
local.login	The default .login file for the C shell
local.profile	The default .profile file for the Bourne and Korn shells

You can use these initialization files as a starting point and modify them to create a standard set of files that provide a work environment that is common to all users. You can also modify them to provide a working environment for different types of users.

Customizing User Initialization Files

When a user logs in to a system, the shell initialization files determine the work environment. The shell startup scripts can be modified to set environment variables and directory paths that are needed by a specific user or a group of users. These shell startup scripts are located in the `/etc` directory and in the user's home directory.

Each shell has a globally distributed user initialization file called a "site initialization file." With this file, you can continually introduce new functionality to all the user work environments by editing one initialization file. This file is located in the `/etc` directory and is described in the previous sections for each shell. It's the first initialization file to be read when the user initially logs in.

When you are setting up user initialization files, it might be important to allow the users to customize their own initialization files. The local initialization file, located in the user's home directory, allows user-specific configuration. A local initialization file lets users further customize their own work environment.

Site initialization files are located in the `/etc` directory and can be edited only by root. They are designed to distribute site-wide changes to all user work environments. Individual user initialization files are located in each user's home directory and can be customized by the owner of the directory. When a user logs in, the site initialization file is run first, and then the initialization file located in the user's home directory is run.

Site-wide Shell Initialization Files

You should not use system initialization files located in the `/etc` directory (`/etc/profile`, `/etc/.login`) to manage an individual user's work environment. Files in that folder are site initialization files, which are considered to be global files and are meant to be generic and used to set work environments for all users. The system runs these startup files first and then runs each user's startup files, located in the home directories.

The most commonly customized aspects of shell startup scripts are environment variables. Table 7-10 describes the most common environment and shell variables, including some that you might want to customize in user initialization files.

Modifying the Shell Prompt

Some users find it helpful to make their login name, the hostname, and the current directory part of the prompt. Here's how you set it up in the Korn and Bash shell:

```
PS1="$(whoami)@$(hostname) [\$PWD] #"
```

Table 7-10 Shell and Environment Variables

Variable	Description
LOGNAME	This variable defines the user's login name. It is set by the login program and wouldn't normally be modified.
HOME	This variable defines the path to the user's home directory. The cd command uses this variable when an argument is not specified. This variable is set by the login program and wouldn't normally be modified.
SHELL	SHELL defines the path to the default shell. This variable normally isn't modified manually by the user.
LPDEST	This variable sets the user's default printer.
PWD	PWD is set to the current working directory. This variable changes automatically each time the user changes directories. This variable isn't modified manually by the user.
PS1	This variable defines the shell prompts for the Bourne, Korn, and Bash shells.
PATH (or path in the C shell)	This variable lists, in order, the directories that the shell searches to find the program to run when the user enters a command. If the directory is not in the search path, users must enter the complete pathname of a command. The default PATH variable is automatically defined in .profile (Bourne, Korn, or Bash shell) or .cshrc (C shell) as part of the login process. The order of the search path is important. When identical commands exist in different locations, the first command found with that name is used. For example, suppose PATH is defined (in Bourne and Bash shell syntax) as PATH=/bin:/usr/bin:/usr/sbin:$HOME/bin, and a file named sample resides in both /usr/bin and $HOME/bin. If the user enters the command sample without specifying its full pathname, the version found in /usr/bin is used.
prompt	prompt defines the shell prompt for the C shell.
TERM (or term in the C shell)	This variable defines the terminal. This variable should be reset in /etc/profile or /etc/.login. When the user invokes a program that uses advanced terminal properties such as an editor, the system looks for a file with the same name as the definition of this environment variable. The system searches the directory /usr/share/lib/terminfo to determine the terminal characteristics.
MAIL	This variable sets the path to the user's mailbox.
MANPATH	MANPATH sets the search path for system man pages.
umask	Sets the default user mask. Although umask is a command and not a variable, it is used to set the file-mode creation mask of the current shell execution environment, as described in the section titled "The Default User Mask" later in this chapter.

The resulting prompt looks like this:

```
root@Sunfire1 [/usr/bin] #
```

The following steps show how to modify the shell environment by changing some of the variables in the shell startup file. It suggests some changes and shows the shell-specific syntax to use.

1. Log in as the user. This enables you to see the user's environment as the user would see it. You can use `su - <username>` to achieve this.
2. Set the user's default path to include the home directory as well as directories or mountpoints for the user's windowing environment and applications. To change the path setting, add or modify the line for `PATH`. For the Bourne or Korn shell, this is the syntax:

   ```
   $ PATH=/<dirname1>:/<dirname2>:/<dirname3>:.; export PATH<cr>
   ```

   For example, you could enter the following line in the user's `$HOME/.profile` file:

   ```
   $ PATH=$PATH:/usr/bin:/$HOME/bin:/net/glrr/files1/bin:.;export PATH<cr>
   ```

   For the C shell, notice that in the syntax, the colons are replaced with spaces:

   ```
   $ set path =(/<dirname1> /<dirname2> /<dirname3> .)<cr>
   ```

   For example, you could enter the following line in the user's `$HOME/.cshrc` file:

   ```
   $ set path=($path /usr/bin $HOME/bin /net/glrr/files1/bin .)<cr>
   ```

Modifying the PATH Variable

Prefixing `$PATH` (Korn and Bash shell) or `$path` (C shell) appends changes to the user's path settings that are already set by the site initialization file. When you set the `PATH` variable with this procedure, initial path settings are not overwritten and are not lost. Also note the dot (.) at the end of the list to denote the current working directory. The dot should always be at the end of the path for users and should not be used in the path for root, as discussed in the section titled "Setting the Correct Path" later in this chapter.

3. Make sure the environment variables are set to the correct directories for the user's windowing environments and third-party applications. To do so, enter `env`, and you see the following:

```
$ env<cr>
HOME=/export/home/bill
HZ=100
LOGNAME=bill
MAIL=/var/mail/bill
PATH=/usr/bin:/usr/sbin
SHELL=/usr/bin/bash
TERM=xterm
```

4. Add or change the settings of environment variables. For the Bourne or Korn shell, the syntax is as follows:

```
VARIABLE=<value>;export VARIABLE
```

The following example sets the user's default mail directory:

```
MAIL=/var/mail/bcalkins;export MAIL
```

For the C shell, the syntax for setting the local `history` variable and then exporting it is as follows:

```
setenv VARIABLE <value>
```

The following example sets the local `history` variable to `100`. The `set` command does not export the variable like the `setenv` command. The following example sets the C-shell to record the last 100 commands in the local shell only:

```
$ set history = 100<cr>
```

The Home Directory

The home directory is the portion of a file system that is allocated to a user for storing private files. The amount of space you allocate for home directories depends on the kinds of files the user creates and the type of work performed. An entire file system is usually allocated specifically for home directories, and the users all share this space. As the system administrator, you need to monitor user home directories so that one user does not use more than his or her fair share of space. You can set up a separate ZFS file system for each user and set the `quota`, `userquota`, or `groupquota` property to control the amount of disk space a user can occupy. (Disk quotas are discussed in Chapter 5, "Administering ZFS File Systems.")

Note

Previous versions of Oracle Solaris placed the root user's home directory in /. In Oracle Solaris 11, root's home directory is located in /root. No other user should have his or her home directory located in the root file system.

A home directory can be located either on the user's local system or on a remote file server. Although any directory name can be used for a home directory, it is customary that home directories are named using this convention: /export/home/<*username*>. When you put the home directory in /export/home, automounter can make it available across the network in case the user logs in from several different systems. For a large site, you should store home directories on a central server.

Regardless of where their home directories are located, users usually access them through a mountpoint named /home/<*username*>. When AutoFS is used to mount home directories, you are not permitted to create any directories under the /home mountpoint on any system. The system recognizes the special status of /home when AutoFS is active. NFS and AutoFS are covered in Chapter 9, "The Oracle Solaris Network Environment."

To access a home directory anywhere on the network, a user should always refer to it as $HOME, not as /export/home/<*username*>. The latter is machine specific, and its use should be discouraged. In addition, any symbolic links created in a user's home directory should use relative paths (for example, ../../../x/y/x) so that the links will be valid no matter where the home directory is mounted. The location of user home directories might change. By not using machine-specific names, you maintain consistency and reduce system administration.

Projects

Projects allow the tracking of resources and usage. The project concept is extremely useful when multiple projects use the same system and are charged for their usage of the system. With projects, it is now simple to identify and subsequently charge each project based on the resources used. In addition, a system administrator supporting multiple projects can perform duties associated with those projects so that his or her time is also booked to the project requesting the service. The system administrator would do this by using the newtask command. (See the newtask man page for further details about this command.)

You establish projects by using the configuration file /etc/project. The following example shows the standard /etc/project file:

```
system:0::::
user.root:1::::
```

```
noproject:2::::
default:3::::
group.staff:10::::
```

As you can see from this example, all members of the `staff` group (GID 10) belong to the project group `staff`.

You can edit this file to create new projects and assign users and groups of users to the projects. Accounting software can produce reports on usage based on the projects specified in the `/etc/project` file.

For further information on projects, see the man page entry for `project(4)` as well as the entry for the `projects(1)` command, which lists the projects a user or group belongs to.

Name Services

If you are managing user accounts for a large site, you might want to consider using a name service such as Lightweight Directory Access Protocol (LDAP) or NIS. A name service lets you store user account information in a centralized manner instead of storing it in every system's `/etc` files. When you use a name service for user accounts, users can move from system to system, using the same user account without having site-wide user account information duplicated in every system's `/etc` files. Using a name service also promotes centralized and consistent user account information.

System Security

In addition to setting up user accounts, keeping the system's information secure is one of a system administrator's primary tasks. System security involves protecting data against loss due to a disaster or system failure. In addition, the system administrator must protect systems from the threat of unauthorized access and protect data on the system from unauthorized users. Disastrous scenarios often come from authorized personnel—even system administrators—destroying data unintentionally. Therefore, the system administrator is presented with two levels of security: protecting data from accidental loss and securing the system against intrusion or unauthorized access.

The first scenario—protecting data from accidental loss—is easy to achieve with a full system backup scheme that you run regularly. Regular backups provide protection in the event of a disaster. If a user accidentally destroys data, if the hardware malfunctions, or if a computer program simply corrupts data, you can restore files from the backup media.

The second form of security—securing the system against intrusion or unauthorized access—is more complex. This book cannot cover every security hole or threat, but it does discuss security fundamentals. Protection against intruders involves the following:

- Controlling physical security: You need to limit physical access to the computer equipment.
- Controlling system access: You need to limit user access via passwords and permissions.
- Controlling file access: You need to limit access to data by assigning file access permissions.
- Auditing users: You need to monitor user activities to detect a threat before damage occurs.
- Controlling network security: You need to protect against access through phone lines, serial lines, or the network.
- Securing superuser access: You need to reserve superuser access for system administrator use only.

The following sections describe these facets of security.

Controlling Physical Security

Physical security is simple: You need to lock the door to the server room. You should limit who has physical access to the computer equipment to prevent theft or vandalism. In addition, you should limit access to the system console. This can be more difficult because modern systems use network-based consoles. The console may not necessarily be locked in the computer room with the server. Anyone who has access to the console ultimately has access to the data. If the computer contains sensitive data, you need to keep it locked in a controlled environment with filtered power and adequate protection against fire, lightning, flood, and other disasters. You should restrict access to protect against tampering with the system and its backups. Anyone with access to the backup media could steal it and access the data. Furthermore, if a system is logged in and left unattended, anyone who can use that system can gain access to the OS and the network. You need to make sure your users log out or lock their screens before walking away. In summary, you need to be aware of your users' computer surroundings, and you need to physically protect them from unauthorized access.

Controlling System Access

Controlling access to systems involves using passwords and appropriate file permissions. To control access, all logins must have passwords, and those passwords must be changed frequently. Password aging is a system parameter that you set to require users to change their passwords after a certain number of days. Password aging lets you force users to change their passwords periodically or prevent users from changing their passwords before a specified interval. You can set an expiration date for a user account to prevent an intruder from gaining undetected access to the system through an old and inactive account. For a high level of security, you should require users to change their passwords periodically (for example, every six weeks or every three months for lower levels of security). You should change system administration passwords (such as root and any other user who has administrative privileges through an RBAC account) monthly or whenever a person who knows the root password leaves the company or is reassigned. Each user should have his or her own account, and no user should disclose his or her password to anyone else.

Several files that control default system access are stored in the `/etc/default` directory. Table 7-11 describes a few of the files in the `/etc/default` directory.

You can set default values in the `/etc/default/passwd` file to control user passwords. Table 7-12 lists the options that can be controlled through the `/etc/default/passwd` file.

Complexity of the password can be controlled using the following parameters:

`MINDIFF=3` The old and new passwords must differ by at least the `MINDIFF` value.

`MINALPHA=2` Password must contain at least this number of alpha characters.

`MINUPPER=0` Password must contain at least this number of uppercase characters.

`MINLOWER=0` Password must contain at least this number of lowercase characters.

`MAXREPEATS=0` The password must not contain more consecutively repeating characters than specified by the `MAXREPEATS` value.

Table 7-11 Files in the `/etc/default` Directory

Filename	Description
`/etc/default/passwd`	This file controls the default policy on password aging.
`/etc/default/login`	This file controls system login policies, including the policy on root access. The default is to limit root access to the console.
`/etc/default/su`	This file specifies where attempts to use `su` to become root are logged and where those log files are located. This file also specifies whether attempts to use `su` to become root are displayed on a named device (such as a system console).

Table 7-12 Flags in /etc/default/passwd

Flag	Description
MAXWEEKS	Specifies the maximum time period for which a password is valid. The MAXWEEKS value can be overridden by entries in the /etc/shadow file.
MINWEEKS	Specifies the minimum time period before the password can be changed. The MINWEEKS value can be overridden by entries in the /etc/shadow file.
PASSLENGTH	Specifies a minimum password length for all regular users. Refer to the "Password Encryption" section in this chapter for information on the maximum password length.
WARNWEEKS	Specifies a time period after which the system warns of the password's expiration date. This entry does not exist in the file by default, but it can be added. The WARNWEEKS value can be overridden by entries in the /etc/shadow file.
NAMECHECK=NO	Sets the password controls to verify that the user is not using the login name as a component of the password.
HISTORY=0	HISTORY can have a value from 0 to 26. Setting a value higher than 0 forces the passwd program to log up to 26 changes to the user's password. The value entered specifies the number of changes to log preventing a user from reusing the same password for up to 26 changes. When the HISTORY value is set to zero (0), the password log for all users will be removed the next time a user changes his password. No password history will be checked if the flag is not present or has zero value.
DICTIONLIST=	Causes the passwd program to perform dictionary word lookups.
DICTIONDBDIR= /var/passwd	The location of the dictionary where the generated dictionary databases reside. This directory must be created manually.
MINSPECIAL=0	Password must contain at least this number of special characters.
MINDIGIT=0	Password must contain at least this number of digits.
MINNONALPHA=1	Describes the same character classes as MINDIGIT and MINSPECIAL combined; therefore you cannot specify both MINNONALPHA and MINSPECIAL (or MINDIGIT). You must choose which of the two options to use.
WHITESPACE= YES	Determines whether white-space characters are allowed.

Note

Privileged users, such as root, are not forced to comply with password aging and password construction requirements. A privileged user can create a null password by entering a carriage return in response to the prompt for a new password. Therefore privileged users should be extra vigilant not to use bad (that is, easy to guess) passwords.

As a system administrator, your job is to ensure that all users have secure passwords. A system cracker can break weak passwords and put an entire system at risk. You should develop and enforce a strong password policy within your organization.

You might also want to lock a user's account after a specified number of failed logins. You can accomplish this by uncommenting the following line in the `/etc/security/policy.conf` file:

```
LOCK_AFTER_RETRIES=YES
```

If a user fails to enter the correct password after the number of retries, as specified in the `/etc/default/login` file, the account is locked.

Password Encryption

The default password hashing algorithm has been changed to SHA256. As a result, there is no longer an eight-character limitation for user passwords as in previous Oracle Solaris releases. The eight-character limitation only applies to passwords that use the older `crypts_unix(5)` algorithm, which has been preserved for backwards compatibility with any existing `/etc/passwd` file entries and NIS maps.

Passwords are now encoded by using one of the other `crypt(3c)` algorithms, including the SHA256 algorithm that is the default in the Oracle Solaris 11 `/etc/security/policy.conf` file. Thus, passwords can now be much longer than eight characters.

The `/etc/security/crypt.conf` file contains identifier-algorithm mapping. The identifiers and their descriptions are as follows:

- 1: The MD5 algorithm that is compatible with the MD5 algorithms on Berkeley Software Distribution (BSD) and Linux systems. For more information, see the `crypt_bsdmd5(5)` man page.
- 2a: The Blowfish algorithm that is compatible with the Blowfish algorithm on BSD systems. For more information, see the `crypt_bsdbf(5)` man page.
- Md5: The Sun MD5 algorithm, which is considered stronger than the BSD and Linux versions of MD5. For more information, see the `crypt_sunmd5(5)` man page.
- 5: The SHA256 algorithm. SHA stands for Secure Hash Algorithm. This algorithm is a member of the SHA-2 family. SHA256 supports 255-character passwords. For more information, see the `crypt_sha256(5)` man page.

- 6: The SHA512 algorithm. For more information, see the `crypt_sha512(5)` man page.
- __unix__: The traditional UNIX encryption algorithm. For more information, see the `crypt_unix(5)` man page.

Verify the password algorithm used by viewing the entry in the `/etc/shadow` file:

```
bcalkins:$5$0kY5sMim$sK4.dJMB0BdC8FNrHaB1o/9b.2LTy81NTp3qHKC8cYB:15593::::15993:
```

In the password field (second field), the second character in the encrypted password specifies the algorithm being used. In this case, the `5` indicates that the SHA256 algorithm is used.

Where User Account Information Is Stored

When no network name service is used, user account and group information is stored in files located in the `/etc` directory. Even when you're using a name service, these local files still exist in the `/etc` directory, but most of the account information is stored in the name server's database.

/etc/passwd

Most user account information is stored in the `/etc/passwd` file; however, password encryption and password-aging details are stored in the `/etc/shadow` file. Only root can view the `/etc/shadow` file. Group information is stored in the `/etc/group` file. Users are put together into groups based on their file access needs; for example, the `acctng` group might be users in the Accounting Department.

Each line in the `/etc/passwd` file contains several fields separated by colons (`:`), and each line is formatted as follows:

```
<username>:<password>:<uid>:<gid>:<comment>:<home-directory>:<login-shell>
```

Table 7-13 defines the fields in the `/etc/passwd` file.

/etc/shadow

Each line in the `/etc/shadow` file contains several fields, separated by colons (`:`). The lines in the `/etc/shadow` file have the following syntax:

```
<username>:<password>:<lastchg>:<min>:<max>:<warn>:<inactive>:<expire>:
```

Table 7-13 Fields in the `/etc/passwd` File

Field	Description
<username>	This field contains the user or login name. A username should be unique and should consist of one to eight letters (A–Z, a–z) and numerals (0–9), but no underscores or spaces. The first character must be a letter, and at least one character must be a lowercase letter.
<password>	The *<password>* field contains an `x`, which is a placeholder for the encrypted password that is stored in the `/etc/shadow` file and that is used by the `pwconv` command, which is described later in this section.
<uid>	This field contains a UID number that identifies the user to the system. UID numbers for regular users should range from 100 to 60,000, but they can be as high as 2,147,483,647. All UID numbers should be unique. UIDs lower than 100 are reserved. To minimize security risks, you should avoid reusing UIDs from deleted accounts.
<gid>	This field contains a GID number that identifies the user's primary group. Each GID number must be a whole number between 0 and 60,000 (60,001 and 60,002 are assigned to nobody and noaccess, respectively). GIDs can go as high as 2,147,483,647, but GIDs higher than 60,002 might not be supported across other UNIX platforms. GID numbers lower than 100 are reserved for system default group accounts.
<comment>	The *<comment>* field usually contains the user's full name.
<home-directory>	This field contains the user's home directory pathname.
<login-shell>	This field contains the user's default login shell.

Table 7-14 defines the fields in the `/etc/shadow` file.

Entries made in the `/etc/shadow` file are made using the `usermod` and `passwd` commands, which were described earlier in this chapter.

You should refrain from editing the `/etc/passwd` file directly, and you should never edit the `/etc/shadow` file directly. Any incorrect entry can prevent you from logging in to the system. These files are updated automatically, using one of the Oracle Solaris account administration commands described earlier in this chapter. For example, the current entry for `bcalkins` exists in the `/etc/shadow` file:

```
bcalkins:$5$A6BCoXDa$VsORo.OlvLvCil4iX5qsnCL9IKdm7l5HeJtSpIdZxr.:15734::::::15328
```

Table 7-14 Fields in the /etc/shadow File

Field	Description
<username>	This field specifies the user or login name.
<password>	This field might contain one of the following entries: an encrypted user password; the string *LK*, which indicates an inaccessible (locked) account; the string NP, which indicates no valid password exists for the account and you cannot log in directly to this account; the string UP, which indicates that this account has not yet been activated; or NL, which means this account is a no-login account.
<lastchg>	The *<lastchg>* field indicates the number of days between January 1, 1970, and the last password modification date.
<min>	This field specifies the minimum number of days required between password changes.
<max>	This field specifies the maximum number of days the password is valid before the user is prompted to specify a new password.
<warn>	The *<warn>* field indicates the number of days before the password expiration that the user is warned.
<inactive>	This field specifies the number of days that a user account can be inactive before it is locked.
<expire>	The *<expire>* field specifies an absolute date expressed as the number of days since the UNIX epoch (January 1, 1970). Past this date, the login can no longer be used.
<flag>	This field indicates a failed login count.

After issuing the passwd -f bcalkins command to force the user to change the password at the next login, the /etc/shadow entry now looks like this:

```
bcalkins: $5$A6BCoXDa$VsORo.OlvLvCil4iX5qsnCL9IKdm7l5HeJtSpIdZxr.:0:::::
```

The third field has changed to a 0, indicating that the password has expired.

The passwd -l bcalkins command locks the user account, and the entry now shows *LK* in the second column:

```
bcalkins:*LK*$5$0kY5sMim$sK4.dJMB0BdC8FNrHaB1o/9b.2LTy81NTp3qHKC8cYB:15593::::15993
```

Notice how the password is preserved; it is only prefixed with the *LK*. That way, when the lock is removed, the old password is still intact. Unlock the account by issuing the passwd -u command.

If you must edit the /etc/passwd file manually, you should use the pwck command to check the file. The pwck command scans the password file and notes any inconsistencies. The checks include validation of the number of fields, login name, UID, GID, and whether the login directory and the program to use as shell exist.

Some experienced system administrators edit the /etc/passwd file directly for various reasons, but only after creating a backup copy of the original /etc/passwd file. For example, you might want to restore the /etc/passwd file from backup—perhaps because the original was corrupted or was incorrectly modified.

After modifying the /etc/passwd file, run the pwconv command. This command updates the /etc/shadow file with information from the /etc/passwd file.

The pwconv command relies on the special value of x in the password field of the /etc/passwd file. The x indicates that the password for the user already exists in the /etc/shadow file. If the /etc/shadow file does not exist, pwconv re-creates everything in it from information found in the /etc/passwd file.

/etc/group

Each line in the /etc/group file contains several fields, separated by colons (:). The lines in the /etc/group file have the following syntax:

```
<group-name>:<group-password>:<gid>:<user-list>
```

Table 7-15 defines the fields in the /etc/group file.

Table 7-15 Fields in the /etc/group File

Field	Description
<group-name>	This field contains the name assigned to the group. For example, members of the Accounting Department group might be called acct. A group name can have a maximum of eight characters.
<group-password>	This field usually contains an asterisk or is empty. See the information on the newgrp command in the section titled "Effective UIDs and GIDs" later in this chapter.
<gid>	The *<gid>* field contains the group's GID number, which must be unique on the local system and should be unique across the entire organization. Each GID number must be a whole number between 0 and 60,002, but it can be as high as 2,147,483,647. However, GIDs above 60,002 might not be supported on some UNIX platforms. Numbers lower than 100 are reserved for system default group accounts, so don't use them. User-defined groups can range from 100 to 60,000 (60,001 and 60,002 are reserved and assigned to nobody and noaccess, respectively).
<user-list>	This field contains a list of groups and a comma-separated list of usernames that represent the user's secondary group memberships. Each user can belong to a maximum of 1,024 secondary groups.

By default, all Oracle Solaris systems have default groups already defined in the /etc/group file. These groups should not be modified or deleted. Other than the staff group, you should not use these groups for users. Also, some system processes and applications might rely on these groups, so you should not change the GIDs or remove these groups from the /etc/group file unless you are absolutely sure of the effect on the system.

If you edit the /etc/group file manually, you should use the grpck command to verify all entries in the group file. This verification includes a check of the number of fields, the group name, and the GID, as well as a check to ensure that all login names appear in the password file.

A user can display the list of groups to which he or she belongs by typing the groups command as follows:

```
# groups<cr>
```

The primary and secondary groups are listed as follows:

```
root other bin sys adm uucp mail tty lp nuucp daemon
```

A user can change his or her primary group using the newgrp command as follows:

```
# newgrp other<cr>
```

The root user has changed his or her primary group from root to other as displayed by the id command:

```
# id<cr>
uid=0(root) gid=1(other)
```

Restricted Shells

System administrators can use restricted versions of the Korn shell (rksh) and the Bourne shell (rsh) to limit the operations allowed for a particular user account. Restricted shells are especially useful for ensuring that time-sharing users and users' guests on a system have restricted permissions during login sessions. When an account is set up with a restricted shell, users cannot do the following:

- Change directories to a directory above their home directory.
- Set the $PATH variable.

- Specify path or command names that begin with "/".
- Redirect output.

You can also provide users with shell procedures that have access to the full power of the standard shell but impose a limited menu of commands.

Don't Confuse `rsh`

You should not confuse the restricted shell `/usr/lib/rsh` with the remote shell `/usr/bin/rsh`. When you specify a restricted shell, you should not include the following directories in the user's path—`/bin`, `/sbin`, or `/usr/bin`. Doing so allows the user to start another shell (a nonrestricted shell).

RBAC

Granting superuser access to nonroot users has always been an issue in UNIX systems. In the past, you had to rely on a third-party package, such as `sudo`, to provide this functionality. `sudo(1m)` is now included with Oracle Solaris 11 for those system administrators that prefer to use it; however, Oracle prefers administrators to use RBAC over `sudo` because RBAC is much more integrated with the Oracle Solaris OS. In fact, whether you choose to embrace it or not, the OS is always using RBAC, and RBAC cannot be turned off. The kernel is always checking privileges, even when logged in as root. In ZFS, for example, the operations performed by the `zfs(1M)` command first check whether the user has an "allow" delegation and then checks privileges, even if the user is logged in as root. Furthermore, RBAC is documented, updated, and integrated throughout each release of Oracle Solaris, which makes it more stable and reliable. RBAC isn't a feature found only in Oracle Solaris; RBAC has also been deployed on other most other major platforms such as HP-UX, IBM AIX, and Linux.

RBAC uses the principle of "least privilege." This means that a user has precisely the amount of privilege that is necessary to perform a task—no more and no less. Anything required beyond the normal daily tasks are grouped into a rights profile. Users that are expected to perform a task that requires some sort of root privilege will be assigned the appropriate right to perform that task. These rights profiles are described in the section titled "Create a Role Using a Profile." But, first we need to discuss authorizations, because rights profiles are made up of authorizations.

Create a Role Using Authorizations

To better describe RBAC, it's easier to first describe how a system administrator would use RBAC to delegate an administrative task to a nonroot user in a fictional setting at Acme Corp.

At Acme Corp., the system administrator is overwhelmed with tasks. He decides to delegate some of his responsibility to Neil, a user from the engineering department who helps out sometimes with system administration tasks.

The system administrator first needs to define which tasks he wants Neil to help perform. He has identified two tasks:

- Manage user accounts.
- Manage the `svc:/network/smb:default` service in SMF.

In RBAC, when we speak of delegating administrative tasks, it is referred to as a "role" account. A role account is a special type of user account that is intended for performing a set of administrative tasks. It is like a normal user account in most respects except that users can gain access to it only through the `su` command after they have logged in to the system with their normal login account. The role also uses a special shell called the "profile shell."

Profile Shell

A profile shell is a special shell that recognizes the security attributes that are included in a rights profile. The profile shell sets a flag that enables checking privileges. Administrators can assign a profile shell to a specific user as a login shell, or the profile shell is started when that user runs the `su` command to assume a role. In Oracle Solaris, every shell has a profile shell counterpart. For example, the profile shells that are counterpart to the Bourne shell (`sh`), Bash shell (`bash`), and Korn shell (`ksh`) are the `pfsh`, `pfbash`, and `pfksh` shells, respectively. For the list of profile shells, see the `pfexec(1)` man page. All commands that are executed in a profile shell can be audited.

From a role account, a user can access commands with special attributes, typically the superuser privilege, which are unavailable to users with normal accounts.

Root as a Role

Beginning with Oracle Solaris 11, root is a role by default when the OS is installed using the Live Media installer. When root is a role, a user must first log in using his or her assigned login account and then use the `su` command to switch to the root role when root privileges are needed. This behavior can be changed by switching the root account from a role to a normal account as follows: `rolemod -K type=normal root`.

To switch root back to a role account, type `usermod -K type=role root`.

Refer to the section titled "Create a Role Using a Profile" later in this chapter for a description of the `System Administrator` profile and how the root role is assigned to a user account during the installation.

At Acme Corp., the system administrator needs to define a role username for the tasks he wants to delegate. Let's use the role username "`adminusr`." After Neil logs in with his normal login name of `neil`, he then needs to issue the `su` command and switch to `adminusr` whenever he wants to perform administrative tasks. In this section, you learn how to create a role account using the command line interface.

User Management GUI

The User Management GUI can also be used to create roles. The GUI is more user-friendly than the command line but does not provide the flexibility that the command line provides. The GUI requires a graphical desktop environment such as GNOME or X Window System and can be started using one of the following methods:

- From the desktop, choose System → Administration → User Manager.
- Start the User Manager GUI from the command line by typing: `vp usermgr &`.

The examples in this book will use the command line to create a role.

Configuring RBAC from the Command Line

So far we have determined that we want to name the role account `adminusr`. The system administrator creates the role account using the `roleadd` command. The `roleadd` command adds a role account to the `/etc/passwd`, `/etc/shadow`, and `/etc/user_attr` files. The syntax for the `roleadd` command is as follows:

```
roleadd [-c comment] [-d dir] [-e expire] [-f inactive] [-g group] \
[-G group] [-m] [-k skel_dir] [-u uid [-o]] [-s shell] [-A authorization] \
[-P profile ] [-S repository] <role username>
```

You'll notice that `roleadd` looks a great deal like the `useradd` command. Table 7-16 describes the options for the `roleadd` command.

The <*role username*> supplied to the `roleadm` command is a string of no more than eight bytes consisting of alphanumeric characters, period (.), underscore (_), and hyphen (-). The first character should be alphabetic, and the field should contain at least one lowercase alphabetic character.

When creating a role account with the `roleadd` command, you need to specify an authorization or profile to the role. An authorization is a user right that grants access to a restricted function. It is a unique string that identifies what is being authorized as well as who created the authorization.

Certain privileged programs check the authorizations to determine whether users can execute restricted functionality. Following are two predefined authorizations from the `auth_attr` database:

```
solaris.user.manage:RO::Manage user accounts::help=UserManage.html
solaris.smf.manage.smb:RO::Manage SMB Service \
States::help=SmfSMBStates.html
```

Table 7-16 roleadd Options

Option	Description
-A *<authorization>*	Assign one or more authorizations to the role. Separate multiple authorizations with a comma.
-b	The default base directory if -d is not specified.
-c *<comment>*	Any text string to provide a brief description of the role.
-d *<dir>*	The home directory of the new role account.
-D	Display the default values for the account.
-m	Creates the new role's home directory if it does not already exist.
-e *<expire>*	Specifies the expiration date for a role. After this date, no user can access this role. The *<expire>* option argument is a date entered using one of the date formats included in the template file /etc/datemsk. For example, you can enter 10/30/12 or October 30, 2012. A value of " " defeats the status of the expired date.
-f *<inactive>*	Specifies the maximum number of days allowed between uses of a login ID before that login ID is declared invalid. Normal values are positive integers.
-g *<group>*	Specifies an existing group's integer ID or character-string name. It redefines the role's primary group membership.
-G *<group>*	Specifies an existing group's integer ID or character string name. It redefines the role's supplementary group membership. Duplicates between groups with the -g and -G options are ignored.
-k *<skeldir>*	A directory that contains skeleton information (such as .profile) that can be copied into a new role's home directory. This directory must already exist. The system provides the /etc/skel directory that can be used for this purpose.
-o	Allows a UID to be duplicated.
-s *<shell>*	Specifies the user's shell on login. The default is /bin/pfsh.
-P *<profile>*	Assign one or more profiles to the role. Separate multiple profiles with a comma.
-u *<uid>*	Specifies a UID for the new role. It must be a nonnegative decimal integer. The UID associated with the role's home directory is not modified with this option; a role does not have access to its home directory until the UID is manually reassigned using the chown command.
-S *<repository>*	Specifies the repository: files or ldap.

All authorizations are stored in the auth_attr database. If you are not using a name service, this database is a file named /etc/security/auth_attr.d/core-os. The system administrator needs to use one or more of the authorizations that are stored in that file. For the Acme Corp. example, the system administrator needs to specify the authorizations shown here:

```
solaris.user.manage
```

This authorization allows an administrator to set the username, uid, gecos-field, home-dir, and login-shell for users.

```
solaris.smf.manage.smb
```

This authorization allows an administrator to enable, disable, and restart the svc:/network/smb:default service.

The system administrator would therefore issue the roleadd command as follows:

```
# roleadd -m -d /export/home/adminusr -c "Admin Assistant" \
-A solaris.user.manage,solaris.smf.manage.smb adminusr<cr>
```

A role account named adminusr with the required directory structures has been created. The next step is to set the password for the adminusr role account by typing the following:

```
# passwd adminusr<cr>
New Password:
Re-enter new Password:
passwd: password successfully changed for adminusr
```

You are prompted to type the new password twice.

Now we need to set up Neil's account so he can access the new role account named adminusr. With the usermod command, assign the role to the user account using the -R option:

```
# usermod -R adminusr neil<cr>
```

There is no need to be logged out. Previously, you needed to ensure that the user was not logged in at the time of assigning a role; otherwise, you received an error message and the role was not assigned. This is no longer the case. A role can be assigned to a user while the user is still logged in.

When the system administrator created the role with the `roleadd` command, the system made the following entry in the `/etc/user_attr` database:

```
adminusr::::type=role;auths=solaris.smf.manage.smb,solaris.user.manage;\
profiles=All;roleauth=role
```

The `/etc/user_attr` file is a local file consisting of a single line with five fields separated by colons (:).

It also made the following entry in the `/etc/passwd` file:

```
adminusr:x:103:10:Admin Assistant:/export/home/adminusr:/usr/bin/pfbash
```

Notice that the shell is the `/usr/bin/pfbash` shell, the profile shell for `bash`.

Finally, after creating the password, the following entry is in the `/etc/shadow` file:

```
adminusr:$5$g1YAB2dn$tyhN7kz69gL9bWgBBPYkUUDp0Mvm4sZGQbVWKKjnfK1:15645::::::1936
```

When the system administrator used the `usermod` command to add the role to the user `neil`, the following entry was made in the `/etc/user_attr` file:

```
neil::::roles=adminusr
```

To access the administrative functions, Neil needs to first log in using his regular user account - `neil`. Neil can check which roles he has been granted by typing the `roles` command at the command line:

```
$ roles<cr>
```

The system responds with the roles that have been granted to the user account `neil`:

```
adminusr
```

Neil then needs to `su` to the `adminusr` account by typing the following:

```
$ su adminusr<cr>
```

Neil is prompted to type the password for the role account.

Now Neil can modify user accounts (except passwords) and enable, disable, and restart the `smb` service. Any other user trying to `su` to the `adminusr` account gets this message:

```
$ su adminusr<cr>
Password:
Roles can only be assumed by authorized users
su: Sorry
```

Neil can also list his authorizations by typing

```
# auths<cr>
solaris.admin.wusb.read,solaris.mail.mailq,solaris.network.autoconf.read,\
solaris.smf.manage.smb,solaris.user.manage
```

If the system administrator later wants to assign additional authorizations to the role account named `adminusr`, he would do so using the `rolemod` command. The `rolemod` command modifies a role's login information on the system. The syntax for the `rolemod` command is as follows:

```
rolemod [-u uid] [-o] [-g group] [-G group] [-d dir] [-m] [-s shell]\
[-c comment] [-l new_name] [-f inactive] [-e expire] [-A Authorization]\
[-P profile] [-S repository] <role account>
```

If you want to remove a role account, use the `roledel` command:

```
roledel [-r] <role account name>
```

The `-r` option removes the role's home directory from the system. For example, to remove the `adminusr` role account and remove the home directory, issue the following command:

```
# roledel -r adminusr<cr>
```

Create a Role Using a Profile

I referred to "rights profiles," or simply "profiles," earlier in this chapter. Defining a role account that has several authorizations can be tedious. In this case, it's better to define a profile, which is several authorizations bundled together under one name called a "profile name." The definition of the profile is stored in the `prof_attr` database (/etc/security/prof_attr.d/core-os). Following is an example of a profile named User Management, which is in the default prof_attr database. If you are not using a name service, the prof_attr file is located in the /etc/security/prof_attr.d directory. The following is the section from the /etc/security/prof_attr.d/core-os file, which defines the User Management profile:

```
User Management:RO::\
Manage users and roles, groups, home directory:\
auths=solaris.user.manage,\
solaris.role.manage,\
solaris.group.manage,\
solaris.project.delegate;\
help=RtUserMngmnt.html
```

Several other profiles are defined in the prof_attr database. For example, the System Administrator profile is also defined as follows:

```
System Administrator:RO::\
Can perform most non-security administrative tasks:\
profiles=Audit Review,\
Extended Accounting Flow Management,\
Extended Accounting Net Management,\
Extended Accounting Process Management,\
Extended Accounting Task Management,\
Printer Management,\
Cron Management,\
Device Management,\
File System Management,\
Log Management,\
Mail Management,\
Maintenance and Repair,\
Media Backup,\
Media Catalog,\
Media Restore,\
Name Service Management,\
Network Management,\
Object Access Management,\
Process Management,\
Project Management,\
RAD Management,\
Service Operator,\
Shadow Migration Monitor,\
Software Installation,\
System Configuration,\
User Management,\
ZFS Storage Management;\
help=RtSysAdmin.html
```

This System Administrator profile automatically gets assigned to the first user account that is specified during the Oracle Solaris installation. In Chapter 1, "Installing Oracle Solaris 11," when I created the user bcalkins during the Live Media installation, the System Administrator profile was assigned to bcalkins. In addition, the root role was also assigned to the bcalkins user account. When bcalkins wants full root privileges, he switches to the root role and enters the root password as follows:

```
bcalkins@solaris:~$ su root<cr>
Password:
root@solaris:~#
```

Caution

Never remove the entire root account from the system.

Other users will not be able to switch to the root role because the role has not been assigned to their account. For example, `neil` has the following roles assigned to his account:

```
$ roles<cr>
adminusr
```

When `neil` tries to `su` to the root role, he receives an error as follows:

```
neil@solaris:/$ su root<cr>
Password:
Roles can only be assumed by authorized users
su: Sorry
```

You could remove the password for the root account (`passwd -N root`) to further protect root access. You would then enable `bcalkins` to access the root role using the `bcalkins` password and not the root password. Refer to the `roleauth=user` key that is set using `rolemod -K` in the `user_attr(4)` man page for more information.

Profiles Utility

The `profiles` utility is provided in Oracle Solaris 11 to help manage the rights profiles. In previous versions of Oracle Solaris, the system administrator had to manually edit the `prof_attr` database file. The `profiles` command will make the necessary entries in the `prof_attr` database. This section describes how to manage profiles using the `profiles` command.

List all of the rights profiles in the system repository by using the `profiles(1)` command as follows:

```
$ profiles -a<cr>
        OpenLDAP Server Administration
        TPM Administration
        CUPS Administration
        D-BUS Management
        DTrace Toolkit
```

continues

```
        Software Installation
        NTP Management
        All
        Administrator Message Edit
        Audit Configuration
        Audit Control
        Audit Review
        Console User
        Contract Observer
        Device Management
        Cron Management
        Printer Management
        Log Management
        Basic Solaris User
        . . .<output has been truncated>. . .
```

Each new user created on the system automatically gets a set of default rights profiles when the user account is created. For example, `neil` can view his default rights profile and privileges using the `profiles` command as follows:

```
$ profiles<cr>
          Console User
          Suspend To RAM
          Suspend To Disk
          Brightness
          CPU Power Management
          Network Autoconf User
          Desktop Removable Media User
          Basic Solaris User
          All
```

Use the `-l` option to display more information about each default rights profile:

```
$ profiles -l<cr>
  Console User
     auths=solaris.system.shutdown,solaris.device.cdrw,solaris.device.mount.
     removable,solaris.smf.manage.vbiosd,solaris.smf.value.vbiosd
     profiles=Suspend To RAM,Suspend To Disk,Brightness,CPU Power Management,Network
     Autoconf User,Desktop Removable Media User
  Suspend To RAM
     auths=solaris.system.power.suspend.ram
  Suspend To Disk
     auths=solaris.system.power.suspend.disk
  Brightness
     auths=solaris.system.power.brightness
  CPU Power Management
     auths=solaris.system.power.cpu
  Network Autoconf User
     auths=solaris.network.autoconf.read,solaris.network.autoconf.select,solaris.
     network.autoconf.wlan
  Desktop Removable Media User
          /usr/bin/sound-juicer    privs=sys_devices
          /usr/bin/brasero         privs=sys_devices
  Basic Solaris User
     auths=solaris.mail.mailq,solaris.network.autoconf.read,solaris.admin.wusb.read
     profiles=All
```

```
        /usr/bin/cdrecord.bin
    privs=file_dac_read,sys_devices,proc_lock_memory,proc_priocntl,net_privaddr
        /usr/bin/readcd.bin
    privs=file_dac_read,sys_devices,net_privaddr
        /usr/bin/cdda2wav.bin
    privs=file_dac_read,sys_devices,proc_priocntl,net_privaddr
```

Perhaps the system administrator wants to create a new role account and delegate the task of `User Management`. He could look through the `auth_attr` file for each authorization and assign each one to the new role account using the `roleadd -A` command as described earlier. Or, he could use the `User Management` rights profile currently defined in the `prof_attr` database, which looks like this:

```
User Management:RO::\
Manage users and roles, groups, home directory:\
auths=solaris.user.manage,\
solaris.role.manage,\
solaris.group.manage,\
solaris.project.delegate;\
help=RtUserMngmnt.html
```

`User Management` has the following authorizations assigned to it:

```
solaris.user.manage
solaris.role.manage
solaris.group.manage
solaris.project.delegate
```

When you look at these three authorizations in the `auth_attr` database, you see the following entries:

```
solaris.user.manage:RO::Manage user accounts::help=UserManage.html
solaris.role.manage:RO::Manage Roles::help=RoleManage.html
solaris.group.manage:RO::Manage groups::help=GroupManage.html
solaris.project.delegate:RO::Assign owned projects::help=ProjectDelegate.html
```

Assigning the `User Management` rights profile is the same as assigning the four authorizations listed.

The `profiles` utility is available to help the system administrator manage the rights profiles and make the job of assigning authorizations easier. For example, to view the privileges associated with the `User Management` rights profile, use the `profiles` utility with the `-p` option to invoke the utility in an interactive mode as follows:

```
$ profiles -p "User Management"<cr>
profiles:User Management>
```

Once inside the `profiles` utility, list the available subcommands by typing

```
profiles:User Management> help subcommands<cr>
Subcommands:
    add <property-name>=<property-value>
    cancel
    clear <property-name>
    commit
    delete [-F]
    end
    exit [-F]
    export [-f output-file]
    help [usage] [subcommands] [properties] [<subcommand>] [<property>]
    info [<property-value>]
    remove [-F] <property-name>[=<property-value>]
    revert [-F]
    select cmd=<path>
    set <property-name>=<property-value>
    verify
profiles:User Management>
```

Display information about the `User Management` rights profile and the authorizations associated with that profile by typing

```
profiles:User Management> info auths<cr>
auths=solaris.user.manage,solaris.role.manage,solaris.group.manage,solaris.project.
delegate
```

Notice that the four authorizations that I described earlier are listed in this profile; they make up the `User Management` rights profile.

You can also view the commands that will be allowed as part of this `User Management` profile:

```
profiles:User Management> info<cr>
    name=User Management
    desc=Manage users and roles, groups, home directory
    auths=solaris.user.manage,solaris.role.manage,solaris.group.manage,\
    solaris.project.delegate
    help=RtUserMngmnt.html
    cmd=/usr/sbin/grpck
    cmd=/usr/sbin/pwck
    cmd=/usr/sbin/useradd
    cmd=/usr/sbin/userdel
    cmd=/usr/sbin/usermod
    cmd=/usr/sbin/roleadd
    cmd=/usr/sbin/roledel
    cmd=/usr/sbin/rolemod
    cmd=/usr/sbin/groupadd
    cmd=/usr/sbin/groupdel
    cmd=/usr/sbin/groupmod
    cmd=/usr/bin/passwd
```

Note

You can also get the same information directly from the command line by typing

```
# profiles -p "User Management" info<cr>
```

The `All` rights profile grants the right for a role account to use any command when working in an administrator's shell and is typically also included in every role. The `All` profile provides access to all commands that are not explicitly assigned in other rights profiles. The profile shells can only execute commands that have been explicitly assigned to a role account through granted rights. Therefore, if the `All` profile is not specified, many of the basic commands will not be available in the role.

To create a new role account named `admin2` specifying only the `User Management` profile, use the `roleadd` command with the `-P` option:

```
# roleadd -d /export/home/admin2 -m -c "Admin Assist" -P "User Management" admin2<cr>
80 blocks
```

The following entry is added to the `user_attr` (`/etc/user_attr`) database:

```
admin2::::type=role;profiles=User Management;roleauth=role
```

Assign the new role to a user as follows:

```
# usermod -R admin2 neil<cr>
```

Assign a password to the `admin2` account:

```
# passwd admin2<cr>
```

At any time, users can check which roles have been granted to them with the `roles` command:

```
$ roles<cr>
```

The system lists the roles that have been granted to that particular user account:

```
admin2
```

The user `neil` can now create user accounts when logging in to the `admin2` role. When `neil` switches to the `admin2` role, he can view the profiles assigned to this role by using the `profiles` command as follows:

```
neil@solaris:~$ su admin2<cr>
Password:<enter password>
admin2@solaris:~$ profiles<cr>
          User Management
          Basic Solaris User
          All
```

The root user can view the contents of the rights profiles that have been assigned to a role as follows:

```
# profiles -l admin2<cr>
admin2:
  User Management
      auths=solaris.user.manage,solaris.role.manage,solaris.group.manage,solaris.
      project.delegate
          /usr/sbin/grpck              euid=0
          /usr/sbin/pwck               euid=0
          /usr/sbin/useradd            euid=0
          /usr/sbin/userdel            euid=0
          /usr/sbin/usermod            euid=0
          /usr/sbin/roleadd            euid=0
          /usr/sbin/roledel            euid=0
          /usr/sbin/rolemod            euid=0
          /usr/sbin/groupadd           euid=0
          /usr/sbin/groupdel           euid=0
          /usr/sbin/groupmod           euid=0
          /usr/bin/passwd              euid=0
  Basic Solaris User
    auths=solaris.mail.mailq,solaris.network.autoconf.read,solaris.admin.wusb.read
    profiles=All
        /usr/bin/cdrecord.bin
    privs=file_dac_read,sys_devices,proc_lock_memory,proc_priocntl,net_privaddr
        /usr/bin/readcd.bin
    privs=file_dac_read,sys_devices,net_privaddr
        /usr/bin/cdda2wav.bin
    privs=file_dac_read,sys_devices,proc_priocntl,net_privaddr
  All
    *
```

Delegating Zone Management

Rights profiles and authorizations can also be applied directly to a user account as long as the user account is using a profile shell. That way, a user can log in and have the rights profiles and authorizations granted immediately. However, this can also be a risk if the user is not careful with these authorizations. Using a role is more secure because it requires the user to make a conscious effort to gain access to the role before executing a privileged command.

In the following example, I will grant the `Zone Management` rights profile directly to the user account to allow the user to log in and manage zones. By “manage zones” I mean that the user will be able to start, stop, and reboot zones. To view the commands available with the `Zone Management` rights profile, type

```
# profiles -p "Zone Management" info<cr>
      name=Zone Management
      desc=Zones Virtual Application Environment Administration
      help=RtZoneMngmnt.html
      cmd=/usr/sbin/zoneadm
      cmd=/usr/sbin/zlogin
```

The output indicates that the user has authorization to use the /usr/bin/zoneadm and /usr/bin/zlogin commands. The profile does not allow the user to configure, install, or remove a zone; those functions require the Zone Security rights profile.

The zlogin(1M) man page specifies that the solaris.zone.manage/<*zonename*> authorization is required to use the -C (connect to zone console) option. Also, the zoneadm(1M) man page states that the user must also be authorized to execute specific subcommands using the solaris.zone.manage/<*zonename*> authorization. Therefore, assigning the Zone Management rights profile is not enough. The system administrator must also assign the authorizations as shown in the next example:

```
# usermod -P +"Zone Management" -A +solaris.zone.manage,solaris.zone.login neil<cr>
```

This rights profile and authorizations allow neil to boot, halt, reboot, and create a console login for every zone on the system. To limit neil to only managing zoneA, but to allow him to log in to the console of every zone, the system administrator needs to modify the solaris.zone.manage authorization and limit the authorization to zoneA only. To do this, the solaris.zones.manage authorization is removed as follows:

```
# usermod -A -solaris.zone.manage neil<cr>
```

Then the solaris.zones.authorization authorization is added with the /zoneA suffix as follows:

```
# usermod -A +solaris.zone.manage/zoneA neil<cr>
```

The system administrator limited the user neil by adding to the solaris.zone.manage/zoneA authorization. Otherwise, neil would be able to manage every zone on the system. However, because he did not limit the solaris.zone.login authorization, neil will still be able to use the zlogin command to connect to any zone console. The system administrator could limit neil so that he can only access the zoneA console as follows:

```
# usermod -A +solaris.zone.login/zoneA neil<cr>
```

With this authorization, neil can only manage zoneA and can only log in to zoneA's console.

User Must Have a Profile Shell

A common mistake is to grant a rights profile and authorizations to a user that does not have a profile shell (i.e., /usr/bin/bash or /usr/bin/ksh). When this happens, the authorizations do not function as anticipated. Make sure the user account uses a profile shell.

When configuring the zone with the zonecfg command, you can assign the Zone Management profile and the authorizations automatically to neil by specifying the following when configuring the zone:

```
# zonecfg -z zoneA<cr>
zonecfg:zoneA> add admin<cr>
zonecfg:zoneA:admin> set user=neil<cr>
zonecfg:zoneA:admin> set auths=login,manage<cr>
zonecfg:zoneA:admin> end<cr>
zonecfg:zoneA> verify<cr>
zonecfg:zoneA> commit<cr>
UX: /usr/sbin/usermod: neil is currently logged in, some changes may not take effect
until next login.
zonecfg:zoneA>exit<cr>
```

zonecfg automatically updates the /etc/user_attr file and assigns the profile and authorizations for zoneA to neil as follows:

```
neil::::auths=solaris.zone.login/zoneA,solaris.zone.manage/zoneA;profiles=Zone
Management;roles=admin2
```

Create a Custom Rights Profile

Use the profiles command to create a custom rights profile with authorizations. In previous versions of Oracle Solaris, we had to use the vi editor to manually create these profiles in the prof_attr database. The profiles command will do this for us.

Earlier I described how to add an authorization to the neil account so that he can manage and log in to the console for zoneA. If I had a number of users to which I needed to add this profile, it might be easier to create a rights profile and then assign that profile to each user. I can create the rights profile as follows:

```
# profiles -p "Zone A Admin"<cr>
profiles:Zone A Admin> set desc="Zone A Administration"<cr>
profiles:Zone A Admin> add profiles="Zone Management"<cr>
profiles:Zone A Admin> add auths=solaris.zone.manage/zoneA<cr>
profiles:Zone A Admin> add auths=solaris.zone.login/zoneA<cr>
profiles:Zone A Admin> verify<cr>
profiles:Zone A Admin> commit<cr>
profiles:Zone A Admin> exit<cr>
```

Grant the `Zone A Admin` profile to `neil` as follows:

```
# usermod -P +"Zone A Admin" neil<cr>
```

Controlling File Access

After you have established login restrictions, you need to control access to the data on the system. Some users only need to look at files; others need the ability to change or delete files. You might have data that you do not want anyone else to see. You can control data access by assigning permission levels to a file or directory.

Three levels of access permission are assigned to a UNIX file to control access by the owner, the group, and all others. You can display permissions by using the `ls -la` command. The following example shows the use of the `ls -la` command to display permissions on files in the `/users` directory:

```
# ls -la /users<cr>
```

The system responds with this:

```
drwxr-xr-x  2  bill  staff  512   Sep 23 07:02     .
drwxr-xr-x  3  root  other  512   Sep 23 07:02     ..
-rw-r--r--  1  bill  staff  124   Sep 23 07:02     .cshrc
-rw-r--r--  1  bill  staff  575   Sep 23 07:02     .login
```

The first column of information displays the type of file and its access permissions for the user, group, and others. The `r`, `w`, `x`, and `-` symbols are described in Table 7-17. The third column displays the owner of the file—usually the user who created the file. The owner of a file (and the superuser) can decide who has the right to read it, to

Table 7-17 File Access Permissions

Symbol	Permission	Means That Designated Users. . .
`r`	Read	Can open and read the contents of a file
`w`	Write	Can write to the file (that is, modify its contents), add to it, or delete it
`x`	Execute	Can execute the file (if it is a program or shell script)
`-`	Denied	Cannot read, write to, or execute the file

write to it, and—if it is a command—to execute it. The fourth column displays the group to which this file belongs—normally the owner's primary group.

When you list the permissions on a directory, all columns of information are the same as for a file, with one exception. The r, w, x, and - found in the first column are treated slightly differently for a directory than for a file, as described in Table 7-18.

You can use the commands listed in Table 7-19 to modify file access permissions and ownership, but you need to remember that only the owner of the file or root can assign or modify these values.

Use the chmod command to change the permissions on a file to rwxrwxrwx as follows:

```
# chmod 777 <filename><cr>
```

Use the chown command to change the ownership on a file to bcalkins as follows:

```
# chown bcalkins <filename><cr>
```

Table 7-18 Directory Access Permissions

Symbol	Permission	Means That Designated Users. . .
r	Read	Can list files in the directory
w	Write	Can add files or links to or remove files or links from the directory
x	Execute	Can open or execute files in the directory and can make the directory and the directories beneath it current
-	Denied	Cannot read, write, or execute

Table 7-19 File Access Commands

Command	Description
chmod	Changes access permissions on a file; you can use either symbolic mode (letters and symbols) or absolute mode (octal numbers) to change permissions on a file.
chown	Changes the ownership and optionally the group ownership of a file.
chgrp	Changes the group ownership of a file.

Use the chgrp command to change group ownership of a file to engrg as follows:

```
# chgrp engrg <filename><cr>
```

The chown command can be used to change both the user and group ownership of a file as follows:

```
# chown bcalkins:engrg <filename><cr>
```

Sometimes you don't have access to a file or directory if you use your current login and you want to switch from one login ID to another. As long as you know the login name and password, you can quickly switch to that login by using the su command, which is described in the following section.

Effective UIDs and GIDs

The su (switch user) command enables a user to become another user without logging off the system. To use the su command, you must supply the password for the user you are attempting to log in as. The root user can run su to any account without being prompted for passwords.

System administrators often use the su command. For example, as a safety precaution, rather than using the root account as a regular login, you might use a regular, nonroot login whenever you are not performing administration functions. When root access is required, you can quickly become the superuser by using the su command. When you are finished performing the task, you can exit the superuser account and continue working using your normal, nonroot account.

Root as a Role

When root is set up as a role, that role needs to be assigned to the user account before the user can assume the root role using the su command. Refer to the "RBAC" section in this chapter for more information on roles.

If the user enters the correct password, su creates a new shell process, as specified in the shell field of the /etc/passwd file for that particular user. In the following example, user1 runs the su command to become user2:

```
# su user2<cr>
```

An option to the su command is -. This option specifies a complete login. The specified user's .profile file is run, and the environment is changed to what would be expected if the user actually logged in as the specified user.

Without the - option, the environment is passed along from the original login, with the exception of $PATH, which is controlled by PATH and SUPATH in the /etc/default/su file (which is described later in this chapter). When the administrator uses su to access the root account from an untrusted user's account, the - option should always be used. If it is not used, the administrator is logged in as root, using a PATH variable defined for a nonroot user. This could result in the administrator inadvertently running commands specified in the user's PATH variable.

A user can also switch his or her primary group by using the newgrp command. The newgrp command logs in a user to a new group by changing a user's real and effective GIDs. The user remains logged in, and the current directory is unchanged. The execution of su and newgrp always replaces the current shell with a new shell. The execution of newgrp always replaces the current shell with a new shell, even if the command terminates with an error (unknown group). Any variable that is not exported is reset to null or its default value. Exported variables retain their values.

With no operands and options, newgrp changes the user's real and effective GIDs back to the primary group specified in the user's password file entry.

A password is demanded if the group has a password (in the second field of the /etc/group file), the user is not listed in /etc/group as being a member of that group, and the group is not the user's primary group. The only way to create a password for a group is to use the passwd command and then cut and paste the password from /etc/shadow to /etc/group. Group passwords are antiquated and not often used.

The Default User Mask

When a user creates a file or directory, the "user mask" controls the default file permissions assigned to the file or directory. The umask command should set the user mask in the /etc/default/login file or a user initialization file, such as /etc/profile or .cshrc. You can display the current value of the user mask by typing "umask" and pressing *Enter*.

The user mask is set with a three-digit octal value, such as 022. The first digit of this value sets permissions for the user, the second sets permissions for the group, and the third sets permissions for others. To set the user mask to 022, type the following:

```
# umask 022<cr>
```

By default, the system sets the permissions on a file to 666, granting read and write permission to the user, group, and others. The system sets the default permissions on a directory or executable file to 777, or rwxrwxrwx. The value assigned by umask is subtracted from the default. To determine what umask value you want to set, you subtract the value of the permissions you want from 666 (for a file) or 777 (for a directory). The remainder is the value to use with the umask command. For example, suppose you want to change the default mode for files to 644 (rw-r--r--). The difference between 666 and 644 is 022, so you would use this value as an argument to the umask command.

Setting the umask value has the effect of granting or denying permissions in the same way that chmod grants them. For example, the command chmod 644 denies write permission to the group and others. Setting the umask to 022 also denies write permission to the group and others.

The "sticky bit" is a permission bit that protects the files within a directory. If the directory has the sticky bit set, a file can be deleted only by the owner of the file, the owner of the directory, or root. This prevents a user from deleting other users' files from public directories. A t or T in the access permissions column of a directory listing indicates that the sticky bit has been set, as shown here:

```
drwxrwxrwt  5 root  sys     458 Oct 17 23:04 /tmp
```

You use the chmod command to set the sticky bit as follows:

```
# chmod +t /export/home/bcalkins/public<cr>
```

where the "t" option toggles the sticky bit on. Or, the sticky bit can be set by specifying the octal value as follows:

```
# chmod 1755 /export/home/bcalkins/public<cr>
```

If the sticky bit is set on a file or directory without the execution bit set for the others category (non-user-owner and non-group-owner), it is indicated with a capital T.

ACLs

ACLs (pronounced "ackls") can provide greater control over file permissions when the traditional UNIX file protection in the Oracle Solaris OS is not enough. The traditional UNIX file protection provides read, write, and execute permissions for the three user classes: owner, group, and other. An ACL provides better file security by allowing you to define file permissions for the owner, owner's group, others, and specific users and groups, and it allows you to set default permissions for each of these categories.

For example, assume you have a file you want everyone in a group to be able to read. To give everyone access, you would give "group" read permissions on that file. Now, assume you want only one person in the group to be able to write to that file. Standard UNIX doesn't let you set that up; however, you can set up an ACL to give only one person in the group write permissions on the file. Think of ACL entries as an extension to regular UNIX permissions.

ACL entries are the way to define an ACL on a file, and they are set through the ACL commands. ACL entries consist of the following fields, separated by colons:

```
entry_type:uid|gid:perms
```

Table 7-20 defines ACL entries.

Setting ACL Entries

Set ACL entries on a file or directory by using the `setfacl` command:

```
$ setfacl -s user::perms,group::perms,other:perms,mask:perms,\
acl_entry_list filename . . .<cr>
```

Setting Versus Modifying an ACL

The `-s` option sets a new ACL but also replaces an entire existing ACL with the new ACL entries. You should read any exam questions on this topic very carefully because this option can be easily confused with the `-m` option, which is used to modify an existing ACL.

The ACL entries that can be specified with the `setfacl` command are described in Table 7-21.

Table 7-20 ACL Entries

ACL Field	Description
`entry_type`	The type of ACL entry on which to set file permissions: For example, `entry_type` can be user (the owner of a file) or mask (the ACL mask).
`uid`	The username or identification number.
`gid`	The group name or identification number.
`perms`	The permissions set on `entry_type`: Permissions are indicated by the symbolic characters `rwx` or an octal number, as used with the `chmod` command.

Table 7-21 ACL Entries for Files and Directories

ACL Entry	Description
u[ser]::*<perms>*	File owner permissions.
g[roup]::*<perms>*	File group permissions.
o[ther]:*<perms>*	Permissions for users other than the file owner or members of the file group.
m[ask]:*<perms>*	The ACL mask: The mask entry indicates the maximum permissions allowed for users (other than the owner) and for groups. The mask is a quick way to change permissions on all the users and groups. For example, the mask:r-- mask entry indicates that users and groups cannot have more than read permissions, even though they might have write/execute permissions. The mask permission will override any specific user or group permissions.
u[ser]:*<uid>*:*<perms>*	Permissions for a specific user; for *<uid>*, you can specify either a username or a numeric UID.
g[roup]:*<gid>*:*<perms>*	Permissions for a specific group; for *<gid>*, you can specify either a group name or a numeric GID.
d[efault]:u[ser]::*<perms>*	Default file owner permissions.
d[efault]:g[roup]::*<perms>*	Default file group owner permissions.
d[efault]:o[ther]:*<perms>*	Default permissions for users other than the file owner or members of the file group.
d[efault]:m[ask]:*<perms>*	Default ACL mask.
d[efault]:u[ser]:*<uid>*:*<perms>*	Default permissions for a specific user; for *<uid>*, you can specify either a username or a numeric UID.
d[efault]:g[roup]:*<gid>*:*<perms>*	Default permissions for a specific group; for *<gid>*, you can specify either a group name or a numeric GID.

The following example sets the user permissions to read/write, sets the group permissions to read-only, and sets other permissions to "none" on the txt1.doc file. In addition, the user bill is given read/write permissions on the file, and the ACL mask permissions are set to read/write, which means that no user or group can have execute permissions.

```
$ setfacl -s user::rw-,group::r--,other:---,mask:rw-,user:bill:rw- txt1.doc<cr>
```

In addition to the ACL entries for files, you can set default ACL entries on a directory that apply to files created within the directory. For example, I'll use the setfacl command to add execute privileges on the /export/home/bholzgen directory for user bcalkins. This privilege on a directory allows the user bcalkins to change to that directory and do a long listing with the ls -l command to display the files in the directory. Before I set the ACL on this directory, let's look at the default permission that currently exists on this directory:

```
# ls -ld /export/home/bholzgen<cr>
drwxr-xr-x  2 bholzgen  staff  512 Jul 30 12:41 bholzgen
```

Now, issue the command to set the default ACL privileges:

```
# setfacl -s user::rwx,g::r--,o:---,d:user::rwx,d:group::r--,d:o:---\
,d:m:r-x,d:user:bcalkins:r-x /export/home/bholzgen<cr>
```

Default ACL Entries

When you set default ACL entries for specific users and groups on a directory for the first time, you must also set default ACL entries for the file owner, file group, others, and the ACL mask.

Use the getfacl command with the -d switch to display the default ACL entries for the /export/home/bholzgen directory as follows:

```
# getfacl -d /export/home/bholzgen<cr>
```

The system responds with the following:

```
# file: /export/home/bholzgen
# owner: bholzgen
# group: staff
default:user::rwx
default:user:bcalkins:rwx     #effective:rwx
default:group::r--            #effective:r--
default:mask:rwx
default:other:---
```

Now, the only people allowed to change to the /export/home/bholzgen directory are bholzgen and bcalkins. No other members, except root, will be able to access this directory—not even members of the same group.

Checking the New File Permissions

Check the new file permissions with the ls -l command. The plus sign (+) to the right of the mode field indicates that the file has an ACL:

```
$ ls -l<cr>
 total 210
 -rw-r-----+  1 mike  sysadmin  32100  Sep 11 13:11 txt1.doc
 -rw-r--r--   1 mike  sysadmin  1410   Sep 11 13:11 txt2.doc
 -rw-r--r--   1 mike  sysadmin  1700   Sep 11 13:11 labnotes
```

Verifying ACL Entries

To verify which ACL entries were set on the file, use the `getfacl` command:

```
$ getfacl txt1.doc<cr>
```

The system responds with this:

```
# file: txt1.doc
# owner: mike
# group: sysadmin
user::rw-
user:bill:rw-    #effective:rw-
group::r--       #effective:r--
mask:rw-
other:---
```

Copying a File's ACL to Another File

Copy a file's ACL to another file by redirecting the `getfacl` output as follows:

```
getfacl <filename1> | setfacl  -f  -  <filename2>
```

The following example copies the ACL from file1 to file2:

```
# getfacl file1 | setfacl -f - file2<cr>
```

Issuing the `getfacl` command, you can verify that the change has been made:

```
# getfacl file*<cr>

# file: file1
# owner: root
# group: other
user::rw-
user:bcalkins:rw-    #effective:rw-
group::r--           #effective:r--
mask:rw-
other:---
```

continues

```
# file: file2
# owner: root
# group: other
user::rw-
user:bcalkins:rw-          #effective:rw-
group::r--                 #effective:r--
mask:rw-
other:---
```

Modifying ACL Entries on a File

Modify ACL entries on a file by using the `setfacl` command:

```
setfacl -m <acl_entry_list> <filename1> [filename2 . . .]
```

Table 7-22 describes the arguments for the `setfacl` command.

Deleting ACL Entries from a File

To delete an ACL entry from a file, use the `setfacl -d` *`<acl_entry_list>`* command. The following example illustrates how to remove an ACL entry for user `bcalkins` on `file1` and `file2`:

```
# setfacl -d u:bcalkins file1 file2<cr>
```

Use the `getfacl` command, described earlier, to verify that the entries have been deleted.

Setting the Correct Path

Setting your path variable (`$PATH`) correctly is important; if you do not set it correctly, you might accidentally run a program introduced by someone else that

Table 7-22 `setfacl` **Arguments**

Argument	Description
`-m`	Modifies the existing ACL entry.
`<acl_entry_list>`	Specifies the list of one or more ACL entries to modify on the file or directory; you can also modify default ACL entries on a directory. (See Table 7-21 for the list of ACL entries.)
`<filename>`	Specifies the file or directory.

harms the data or your system. That kind of program, which creates a security hazard, is called a "Trojan horse." For example, a substitute su program could be placed in a public directory where you, as system administrator, might run it. Such a script would look just like the regular su command. The script would remove itself after execution, and you would have trouble knowing that you actually ran a Trojan horse.

The path variable is automatically set at login time through the /etc/default/login file and the shell initialization files .login, .profile, and/or .cshrc. Setting up the user search path so that the current directory (.) comes last prevents you and your users from running a Trojan horse. The path variable for superuser should not include the current directory (.).

The setuid and setgid Programs

When the set-user identification (setuid) permission is set on an executable file, a process that runs the file is granted access based on the file's owner (usually root) rather than on the user who created the process. This enables a user to access files and directories that are normally available only to the owner. For example, the setuid permission on the passwd command makes it possible for a user to modify the /etc/passwd file to change passwords. When a user executes the passwd command, that user assumes the privileges of the root ID, which is UID 0. The setuid permission can be identified by using the ls -l command. The s in the permissions field of the following example indicates the use of setuid, and the second s indicates the use of setgid:

```
# ls -l /usr/bin/passwd<cr>
  -r-sr-sr-x   1 root      sys      10332 May  3 08:23 /usr/bin/passwd
```

Many executable programs must be run by root (that is, by the superuser) in order to work properly. These executable programs run with the UID set to 0 (setuid=0). Anyone running these programs runs them with the root ID, which creates a potential security problem if the programs are not written with security in mind.

On the other hand, the use of setuid on an executable program presents a security risk. A determined user can usually find a way to maintain the permissions granted to him or her by the setuid process, even after the process has finished executing. For example, a particular command might grant root privileges through setuid. If a user could break out of this command, he or she could still have the root privileges granted by setuid on that file. An intruder who accesses a system will look for any files that have the setuid bit enabled.

Except for the executables shipped with Oracle Solaris that have setuid set to root, you should disallow the use of setuid programs—or at least restrict and keep them to a minimum. A good alternative to using setuid on programs is to use an

RBAC account where specific authorizations can be assigned to provide access to administrative functions without using the root account or changing permissions on Oracle Solaris executables. RBAC was covered earlier in this chapter.

The set-group identification (`setgid`) permission is similar to that of `setuid`, except that with `setgid` the process's effective GID is changed to the group owner of the file, and a user is granted access based on permissions granted to that group. By using the `ls -l` command, you can see that the file `/usr/bin/mail` has `setgid` permissions:

```
# ls -l /usr/bin/mail<cr>
-r-x--s--x    1 bin  mail    74792 Oct 20  2011 /usr/bin/mail
```

The following example illustrates how to set the UID on an executable file named `myprog1`:

```
# chmod 4711  myprog1<cr>
```

You can verify the change by entering the following:

```
# ls -l myprog1<cr>
```

The system responds with this:

```
-rws--x--x    1    root    other    25    Mar    6    11:52    myprog1
```

The following example illustrates how to set the GID on an executable file named `myprog1`:

```
# chmod 2751 myprog1<cr>
```

You can verify the change by entering the following:

```
# ls -l myprog1<cr>
```

The system responds with this:

```
-rwxr-s--x    1    root    other    25    Mar    6    11:58    myprog1
```

A user can set the UID or GID permission for any file he or she owns.

Auditing Users

The following sections describe a few of the commands used to view information about users who have logged in to the system.

Monitoring Users and System Usage

As a system administrator, you need to monitor system resources and watch for unusual activity. Having a method to monitor the system is useful, especially when you suspect a breach in security. For example, you might want to monitor the login status of a particular user. In that case, you could use the `logins` command to monitor a particular user's activities, as described in in the following steps:

1. Become the superuser.
2. Display a user's login status by using the `logins` command:

```
# logins -x -l <username><cr>
```

For example, to monitor login status for the user `calkins`, enter the following:

```
# logins -x -l calkins<cr>
```

The system displays the following information:

```
calkins     200     staff          10    Bill S. Calkins
                    /home/calkins
                    /usr/bin/bash
                    PS 060508 10 7 -1
```

Table 7-23 lists the information displayed in the output of the `logins` command.

You should monitor user logins to ensure that their passwords are secure. A potential security problem is for users to use blank passwords (that is, users using carriage returns for passwords) or no password at all. When an account does not have a password, the password prompt will not be presented at login. Simply enter the

Table 7-23 `logins` **Command Output**

Field	Description
`calkins`	The login name
`200`	The UID
`staff`	The primary group
`10`	The GID
`Bill S. Calkins`	The comment field of the `/etc/passwd` file
`/home/calkins`	The user's home directory
`/usr/bin/bash`	The user's default login shell
`PS 060513 10 7 -1`	The password aging information: the last date the password was changed, the number of days required between changes, the number of days allowed before a change is required, and the warning period

username, and you are in. You can periodically check user logins by using the method described in the next steps.

1. Become the superuser.
2. Display users who have no passwords by using the `logins` command:

   ```
   # logins -p<cr>
   ```

   The system responds with a list of users who do not have passwords.

Another good idea is to watch anyone who has tried to access the system but failed. You can save failed login attempts by creating the `/var/adm/loginlog` file with read and write permission for root only. After you create the `loginlog` file, all failed login activity is automatically written to this file after five failed attempts. This file does not exist by default; you, as the system administrator, must create it. To enable logging to this file as root, you can create the file as follows:

```
# touch /var/adm/loginlog<cr>
```

Then set the permission on the file to 600:

```
# chmod 600 /var/adm/loginlog<cr>
```

The loginlog file contains one entry for each failed attempt. Each entry contains the user's login name, the tty device, and the time of the failed attempt. If a person makes fewer than five unsuccessful attempts, none of the attempts is logged.

The following is an example of an entry in which someone tried to log in as root but failed:

```
# more /var/adm/loginlog<cr>
root:/dev/pts/5:Fri Feb 1 11:36:40 2013
root:/dev/pts/5:Fri Feb 1 11:36:47 2013
root:/dev/pts/5:Fri Feb 1 11:36:54 2013
root:/dev/pts/5:Fri Feb 1 11:37:02 2013
```

The loginlog file might grow quickly. To use the information in this file and to prevent the file from getting too large, you must check it and clear its contents occasionally. If this file shows a lot of activity, someone might be attempting to break in to the computer system.

Checking Who Is Logged In

You use the who command to find out who is logged in to a system. To obtain the information it gives you, the who command examines the /var/adm/utmpx and /var/adm/wtmpx files. The utmpx file contains user access and accounting information for the who command (as well as for the write and login commands). The wtmpx file contains the history of user access and accounting information for the utmpx file.

Without arguments, the who command lists the login account name, terminal device, login date and time, and location where the user logged in. Here is an example:

```
# who<cr>
root       pts/3        Jan 11 14:47       (10.64.178.2)
root       pts/1        Jan 10 15:42       (sparc1.PDESIGNINC.COM)
root       pts/2        Jan 10 15:53       (sparc1.PDESIGNINC.COM)
root       pts/4        Jan 11 14:48       (pluto)
```

Table 7-24 lists some of the most common options used with the who command.

The rusers command is similar to the who command, but it can be used to list users logged in on a remote host. To use rusers, the rpc.rusers daemon must be running. Check whether the rpc.rusers daemon is running by typing

```
# svcs rusers<cr>
```

For more information on the svcs command, refer to Chapter 3, “Boot and Shutdown Procedures for SPARC and x86-Based Systems.”

Table 7-24 Common Options Used with the `who` Command

Options	Description
`-a`	Processes `/var/adm/utmpx` or the named file with `-b`, `-d`, `-l`, `-p`, `-r`, `-t`, `-T`, and `-u` options turned on.

`-b`	Indicates the time and date of the last reboot, as shown in the following example:
	`$ who -b<cr>`
	`   .       system boot  Feb  1 04:27`

`-m`	Outputs only information about the current terminal. Here's an example:
	`$ who -m<cr>`
	`bcalkins        pts/1              Feb  1 09:28         (:0.0)`

`-n <x>`	Takes a numeric argument, <x>, which specifies the number of users to display per line. <x> must be at least 1. The `-n` option can be used only with the `-q` option.

`-q`	Displays only the names and the number of users currently logged on. When this option, which stands for quick `who`, is used, all other options are ignored. The following is an example of the `-q` and `-n` options being used together:
	`$ who -q -n2<cr>`
	`bcalkins   bcalkins`
	`# users=2`

	The system responds with this:
	`root      bcalkins`
	`sburge     czimmerman`
	`# users=4`

`-r`	Indicates the current run level of the `init` process. Here's an example of the output returned by
	`$ who -r<cr>`
	`   .       run-level 3  Oct 18 09:02      3     0  S`

`-s`	Lists only the name, line, and time fields. This is the default when no options are specified as follows:
	`$ who -s<cr>`
	`bcalkins   vt/7     Feb  1 09:28       (:0)`
	`bcalkins   pts/1    Feb  1 09:28       (:0.0)`

To list users logged in to other systems on your network, use the `rusers` command as follows:

```
# rusers -l<cr>
Sending broadcast for rusersd protocol version 3. . .
root        smokey:pts/1        Aug 12 10:07        29 (192.168.1.87)
root        ultra5:pts/1        Aug 12 17:33        (billsgateway.wca)
Sending broadcast for rusersd protocol version 2. . .
#
```

The `whoami` Command

The command `whoami` displays the effective current username. It is a lot like the `who` command used with the `am` and `i` options. These two options to the `who` command limit the output to describing the invoking user, which is equivalent to the `-m` option. `am` and `i` must be separate arguments.

`whoami` is a carryover from BSD UNIX. This old BSD command is now found under the `/usr/bin` directory. `/usr/bin/whoami` displays the login name that corresponds to the current effective UID. If you have used `su` to temporarily change to another user, `/usr/bin/whoami` reports the login name associated with that user ID, where the `who` command reports the original login ID. For example, suppose you are logged in as `bcalkins` and issue the following `su` command to become `root`:

```
# su - root<cr>
```

Now issue the `who am i` command:

```
# who am i<cr>
```

The system reports that you are logged in as `bcalkins`. The `who am i` command looks up the entry for your current `tty` in the `utmpx` file:

```
bcalkins  pts/7       Feb 1 19:08
```

Next, you can issue the `whoami` command:

```
# /usr/ucb/whoami<cr>
```

The system reports your current effective UID as follows:

```
root
```

id Command

The `id -un` command also provides the effective current name.

The whodo Command

The `whodo` command produces formatted and dated output from information in the `/var/adm/utmpx`, `/tmp/ps_data`, and `/proc/pid` files. It displays each user logged in and the active processes owned by that user. The output of the `whodo` command shows the date, time, and machine name. For each user who is logged in, the system displays the device name, UID, and login time, followed by a list of active processes associated with the UID. The process list includes the device name, process ID, CPU minutes and seconds used, and process name. You issue the `whodo` command as follows:

```
# whodo<cr>
```

The system responds with this:

```
Friday, February  1, 2013 09:44:33 AM EST
solaris

console    root       15:58
     console      1074      0:00 bash
     console      2359      0:00 su
     console      2360      0:00 bash
     console      2364      0:00 whodo
```

You use the `-l` option with the `whodo` command to get a long listing:

```
# whodo -l<cr>
```

The system responds with this:

```
  8:37am  up 2 day(s), 16 hr(s), 44 min(s)  1 user(s)
User     tty            login@  idle    JCPU   PCPU  what
root     console        Tue 3pm            10          whodo -l
```

The fields displayed are the user's login name; the name of the `tty` the user is on; the time of day the user logged in; the idle time (which is the time since the user last typed anything in *hours:minutes*); the CPU time used by all processes and their children on that terminal (in *minutes:seconds*); the CPU time used by the currently active processes (in *minutes:seconds*); and the name and arguments of the current process.

The `last` Command

The `last` command looks in the `/var/adm/wtmpx` file for information about users who have logged in to the system. The `last` command displays the sessions of the specified users and terminals in reverse chronological order, displaying the most recent login first. For each user, `last` displays the time when the session began, the duration of the session, and the terminal where the session took place. The `last` command also indicates whether the session is still active or was terminated by a reboot.

For example, the command `last root console` lists all of root's sessions, as well as all sessions on the console terminal:

```
# last root console |more<cr>
```

The system responds with this:

```
. . .<output has been truncated> . . .
root          console                          Wed Dec 12 08:54 - down    (19:33)
root          console                          Wed Dec 12 03:39 - down    (05:13)
root          console                          Tue Dec 11 06:47 - down    (20:49)
root          console                          Fri Dec  7 07:56 - down  (3+22:50)
root          console                          Fri Dec  7 06:39 - down    (01:15)
wtmp begins Fri Dec  7 06:37
```

Use the `last reboot` command to display an approximate record of when the OS instance was shut down and when it was rebooted as follows:

```
# last reboot<cr>
. . .<output has been truncated> . . .
reboot        system down                      Fri Dec  7 07:59
reboot        system boot                      Fri Dec  7 07:55
reboot        system down                      Fri Dec  7 07:54
reboot        system boot                      Fri Dec  7 06:37

wtmp begins Fri Dec  7 06:37
```

The `uptime` Command

Use the `uptime` command to show how long the system has been up:

```
# uptime<cr>
  9:04am  up 1 day(s),  5:46,  1 user,  load average: 0.02, 0.03, 0.03
```

Controlling Network Security

The most difficult system administration issue to address is network security. When you connect your computer to the rest of the world via a network such as the Internet, someone can find an opening and breach your security. The following sections describe a few fundamental recommendations for tightening up a system in a networked environment.

Securing Network Services

Oracle Solaris is a powerful OS that executes many useful services such as FTP and HTTP services. However, some of the services aren't needed and can pose potential security risks, especially for a system that is connected to the Internet. The first place to start tightening up a system is by disabling unneeded network services.

The `inetd` daemon is the delegated restarter for Internet services for SMF. `inetd` is responsible for managing service states in response to administrative requests, system failures, and service failures. It's a network listener, listening for network requests for services. You can list all of the network services that `inetd` manages and view their state with the `inetadm` command as follows:

```
# inetadm<cr>
ENABLED   STATE          FMRI
disabled  disabled       svc:/application/cups/in-lpd:default
disabled  disabled       svc:/application/x11/xfs:default
disabled  disabled       svc:/application/x11/xvnc-inetd:default
enabled   online         svc:/network/rpc/smserver:default
enabled   online         svc:/network/rpc/gss:default
disabled  disabled       svc:/network/rpc/rex:default
disabled  disabled       svc:/network/rpc/spray:default
disabled  disabled       svc:/network/stlisten:default
disabled  disabled       svc:/network/nfs/rquota:default
disabled  disabled       svc:/network/stdiscover:default
disabled  disabled       svc:/network/comsat:default
enabled   online         svc:/network/security/ktkt_warn:default
```

The previous command was run on a desktop. On an Oracle Solaris server, you will see many more network services listed as follows:

```
# inetadm<cr>
ENABLED   STATE          FMRI
disabled  disabled       svc:/application/cups/in-lpd:default
disabled  disabled       svc:/network/time:dgram
disabled  disabled       svc:/network/time:stream
enabled   online         svc:/network/rpc/smserver:default
disabled  disabled       svc:/network/rpc/rstat:default
disabled  disabled       svc:/network/rpc/rusers:default
disabled  disabled       svc:/network/rpc/wall:default
```

```
disabled  disabled     svc:/network/rpc/rex:default
enabled   online       svc:/network/rpc/gss:default
disabled  disabled     svc:/network/rpc/spray:default
disabled  disabled     svc:/network/shell:default
disabled  disabled     svc:/network/shell:kshell
enabled   online       svc:/network/security/ktkt_warn:default
disabled  disabled     svc:/network/echo:dgram
disabled  disabled     svc:/network/echo:stream
disabled  disabled     svc:/network/comsat:default
disabled  disabled     svc:/network/stlisten:default
disabled  disabled     svc:/network/daytime:dgram
disabled  disabled     svc:/network/daytime:stream
disabled  disabled     svc:/network/nfs/rquota:default
disabled  disabled     svc:/network/telnet:default
disabled  disabled     svc:/network/discard:dgram
disabled  disabled     svc:/network/discard:stream
disabled  disabled     svc:/network/chargen:dgram
disabled  disabled     svc:/network/chargen:stream
disabled  disabled     svc:/network/finger:default
disabled  disabled     svc:/network/login:eklogin
disabled  disabled     svc:/network/login:klogin
disabled  disabled     svc:/network/login:rlogin
disabled  disabled     svc:/network/stdiscover:default
disabled  disabled     svc:/network/rexec:default
disabled  disabled     svc:/network/tftp/udp6:default
disabled  disabled     svc:/network/talk:default
```

The `inetadm` command is described in Chapter 9. Most network services are already disabled by default. Chapter 3 described hardening the system by disabling many unneeded network services. You can individually deactivate unnecessary network services by disabling them using the `svcadm disable` command described in Chapter 3 or by using the `inetadm` command described in this section.

In addition, many of the properties for the services managed by `inetd` can be configured using the `inetadm` command to make the service more secure. Many properties are taken from the set of default values present in the default property group of the `inetd` service. List all of the default `inetd` property values as follows:

```
$ inetadm -p<cr>
NAME=VALUE
bind_addr=""
bind_fail_max=-1
bind_fail_interval=-1
max_con_rate=-1
max_copies=-1
con_rate_offline=-1
failrate_cnt=40
failrate_interval=60
inherit_env=TRUE
tcp_trace=FALSE
tcp_wrappers=FALSE
connection_backlog=10
tcp_keepalive=FALSE
```

For example, many network services use the `tcp_trace` property that is configured for `inetd`. When `tcp_trace` is set to `TRUE`, `inetd` logs the IP address and TCP port number for each client's incoming connection to `syslogd`.

One of the inetd services is svc:/network/telnet:default. View the telnet service properties as follows:

```
# inetadm -l telnet<cr>
SCOPE    NAME=VALUE
         name="telnet"
         endpoint_type="stream"
         proto="tcp6"
         isrpc=FALSE
         wait=FALSE
         exec="/usr/sbin/in.telnetd"
         user="root"
default  bind_addr=""
default  bind_fail_max=-1
default  bind_fail_interval=-1
default  max_con_rate=-1
default  max_copies=-1
default  con_rate_offline=-1
default  failrate_cnt=40
default  failrate_interval=60
default  inherit_env=TRUE
default  tcp_trace=FALSE
default  tcp_wrappers=FALSE
default  connection_backlog=10
default  tcp_keepalive=FALSE
```

Change the default inetd property value for tcp_trace to TRUE as follows:

```
# inetadm -M tcp_trace=TRUE<cr>
```

When listing the properties for the telnet service, the tcp_trace property has also been set to TRUE:

```
# inetadm -l telnet|grep tcp_trace<cr>
default  tcp_trace=TRUE
```

To disallow telnet connections to the system, disable the telnet service as follows:

```
# inetadm -d telnet<cr>
```

To allow telnet connections, enable the service as follows:

```
# inetadm -e telnet<cr>
```

You can enable or disable all other inetd managed services in a similar manner.

Verify the state of the service using either svcs:

```
# svcs -a |grep telnet<cr>
disabled        3:58:24  svc:/network/telnet:default
```

or the inetadm command:

```
# inetadm |grep telnet<cr>
disabled  disabled       svc:/network/telnet:default
```

It is critical that you keep all unneeded network services disabled because many of the services that are run by inetd, such as rexd, pose serious security vulnerabilities. rexd is a daemon that is responsible for remote program execution. On a system that is connected to the rest of the world via the Internet, this could create a potential entry point for a hacker. You should absolutely disable Trivial File Transfer Protocol (TFTP) unless it's required. TFTP is managed by SMF, under the service identifier svc:/network/tftp/udp6:default. Administrative actions on this service, such as enabling, disabling, or requesting restart, can be performed using svcadm. Responsibility for initiating and restarting this service is delegated to inetd. Use inetadm to make configuration changes and to view configuration information for this service. The service status can be queried using the svcs command.

The /etc/default/login File

One way to protect your system from unauthorized access—regardless of whether it's on the Internet or not —is via the /etc/default/login file. You need to make sure the following line is not commented:

```
CONSOLE=/dev/console
```

With this entry, root is allowed to log in only from the secure system console and not via the network by using telnet or rlogin. However, when root is not set up as a role, this entry does not disallow a user from using the su command to switch to root after logging in as a regular user if he or she knows the root password. When root is set up as a role, no user can assume the root role, even if they know the root password, unless the root role has been assigned to the user account. The following message will be displayed when an unauthorized user tries to su to the root account:

```
$ su root<cr>
Password:
Roles can only be assumed by authorized users
```

Trusted Hosts

Along with protecting passwords, you need to protect your system from a root user coming in from across the network. For example, say `systemA` is a trusted host from which a user can log in without being required to enter a password. A user who has root access on `systemA` could access the root login on `systemB` simply by logging in across the network, if `systemA` is set up as a trusted host on `systemB`. When `systemB` attempts to authenticate root from `systemA`, it relies on information in its local files—specifically, `/etc/hosts.equiv` and `/root/.rhosts`. Because of the many risks posed by `rlogin` and other `r` commands, you should not use them. Instead, you should use the SSH commands, which are described in the section titled "The Secure Shell (`ssh`)," later in this chapter.

The `/etc/hosts.equiv` File

The `/etc/hosts.equiv` file contains a list of trusted hosts for a remote system, one per line. An `/etc/hosts.equiv` file has the following structure:

```
system1
system2 user_a
```

If a user attempts to log in remotely by using `rlogin` from one of the hosts listed in this file, and if the remote system can access the user's password entry, the remote system enables the user to log in without a password.

When an entry for a host is made in `/etc/hosts.equiv` (for example, the sample entry for `system1` shown earlier), the host is trusted and so is any user at that machine. If the username is also mentioned, as in the second entry shown in the previous example, the host is trusted only if the specified user is attempting access. A single line of "+" in the `/etc/hosts.equiv` file indicates that any host is trusted.

Don't Trust Everyone

Using a "+" in the `hosts.equiv` or `.rhosts` file is bad practice and could pose a serious security problem because it specifies that all systems are trusted. You should get into the habit of listing the trusted systems and not using the "+" sign. Better yet, you should use a more secure alternative to `rlogin`, such as SSH.

Security and the /etc/hosts.equiv File

The `/etc/hosts.equiv` file presents a security risk. If you maintain an `/etc/hosts.equiv` file on your system, this file should include only trusted hosts in your network. The file should not include any host that belongs to a different network or any machines that are in public areas. Also, you should never put a system name into the `/etc/hosts.equiv` file without a username or several names after it.

The .rhosts File

The .rhosts file is the user equivalent of the /etc/hosts.equiv file. It contains a list of hosts and users. If a host/user combination is listed in this file, the specified user is granted permission to log in remotely from the specified host without having to supply a password. Note that a .rhosts file must reside at the top level of a user's home directory because .rhosts files located in subdirectories are not consulted. Users can create .rhosts files in their home directories; this is another way to allow trusted access between their own accounts on different systems without using the /etc/hosts.equiv file.

The .rhosts file presents a major security problem. Although the /etc/hosts.equiv file is under the system administrator's control and can be managed effectively, any user can create a .rhosts file that grants access to whomever the user chooses—without the system administrator's knowledge.

Disabling .rhosts and hosts.equiv Files

To disable .rhosts and /etc/hosts.equiv access altogether while still allowing the rlogin protocol, comment the lines that reference pam_rhosts_auth.so.1 from /etc/pam.conf. This forces rlogin to use a password during authentication and effectively disables in.rshd and in.rexecd.

The only secure way to manage .rhosts files is to completely disallow them.

Restricting FTP

FTP is a common tool for transferring files across a network. Oracle Solaris 11 uses ProFTPD as the server side FTP protocol. Check to see whether FTP is installed on your system by typing

```
# pkg list ftp<cr>
NAME (PUBLISHER)                    VERSION                    IFO
network/ftp                         0.5.11-0.175.1.0.0.24.2    i--
```

If only network/ftp is displayed as shown, the FTP server is not installed. You can install ProFTPD as follows:

```
# pkg install pkg:/service/network/ftp<cr>
```

Both services should now be listed:

```
# pkg list ftp<cr>
NAME (PUBLISHER)                    VERSION                    IFO
network/ftp                         0.5.11-0.175.1.0.0.24.2    i--
service/network/ftp                 1.3.3.0.7-0.175.1.0.0.24.0 i--
```

The following user account is also created in the /etc/passwd file:

```
ftp:x:21:21:FTPD Reserved UID:/:
```

A group is created in the /etc/group file:

```
ftp::21:
```

Check the version of ProFTPD by typing

```
# /usr/lib/inet/proftpd -v<cr>
ProFTPD Version 1.3.3g
```

Although many sites leave FTP enabled, you need to limit who can use it. To disable FTP, type

```
# svcadm disable network/ftp<cr>
```

Enable the FTP server by typing

```
# svcadm enable network/ftp<cr>
```

ProFTPD uses various configuration files, which are described in Table 7-25.

In addition, the commands listed in Table 7-26 are provided by ProFTPD.

Entries in the file named /etc/ftpd/ftpusers are used to restrict access via FTP. The /etc/ftpd/ftpusers file contains a list of login names that are prohibited from running an FTP login on the system.

Table 7-25 ProFTPD Files

Option	Description
/etc/proftpd.conf	Contains most of the configuration parameters that need to be defined for the ProFTPD service to function
/etc/shutmsg	Contains information used by the ftpshut command
/etc/ftpd/ftpusers	Lists the users to be disallowed FTP login privileges
/var/log/xferlog	Lists log information for ProFTPD
/var/run/proftpd.scoreboard	Provides tracking information for each current session

Table 7-26 ProFTPD Commands

Option	Description
/usr/bin/ftp	Provides the user interface to the ProFTPD service
/usr/bin/ftpcount	Shows the current number of connections per server
/usr/bin/ftpdctl	Controls the proftpd service daemon
/usr/bin/ftptop	Displays the current status of FTP sessions in a continuously updating format
/usr/bin/ftpwho	Shows process information for all active proftpd connections and a count of all connected users to each server
/usr/sbin/ftprestart	Restarts FTP connections by using the ftpshut -R command
/usr/sbin/ftpscrub	Removes processes that are no longer live from the scoreboard file on demand
/usr/sbin/ftpshut	Shuts down FTP connections
/usr/lib/inet/proftpd	Provides the FTP services

The following is an example of a default /etc/ftpd/ftpusers file:

```
# more /etc/ftpd/ftpusers<cr>
#
# List of users denied access to the FTP server, see ftpusers(4).
#
root
daemon
bin
sys
adm
lp
uucp
nuucp
dladm
netadm
netcfg
smmsp
gdm
xvm
mysql
openldap
webservd
nobody
noaccess
nobody4
aiuser
unknown
ftp
dhcpserv
```

Names in the /etc/ftpd/ftpusers file must match login names in the /etc/passwd file.

Root Access to FTP

The default is to not allow FTP logins by root. It is dangerous to allow root access via FTP because that would allow anyone who knows the root password to have access to the entire system.

The FTP server `proftpd` reads the `/etc/ftpd/ftpusers` file each time an FTP session is invoked. If the login name of the user trying to gain access matches a name in the `/etc/ftpd/ftpusers` file, access is denied.

Use the `ftpshut` command to close down the FTP server without stopping the FTP daemon. The `ftpshut` command will block connections and stop the current connection but will not shut down the FTP server daemon. The syntax for the `ftpshut` command is as follows:

```
ftpshut [ -R ] [ -l min ] [ -d min ] time [  warning-message ]
```

The options for the `ftpshut` command are described in Table 7-27.

To close down the FTP server in 15 minutes, type the following command:

```
# ftpshut +15<cr>
```

Restore access to the FTP server as follows:

```
# ftprestart<cr>
```

The `/etc/shells` file contains a list of the shells on a system. Whereas the `/etc/ftpd/ftpusers` file contains a list of users not allowed to use FTP, the `/etc/shells` file enables FTP connections only to those users running shells that are

Table 7-27 `ftpshut` Options

Option	Description
`time`	The time at which the FTP server will be brought down.
`-R`	Removes the `/etc/shutmsg` file and restores `proftpd` to its normal service.
`-l` *<minutes>*	Specifies the number of minutes before shut down that the new FTP access will be disabled; default is 10 minutes.
`-d` *<minutes>*	Specifies the number of minutes before shut down that existing FTP connections will be disconnected; default is 5 minutes.
`warning-message`	Provides a message to be sent to new connections if denied and existing connections before being disconnected.

defined in this file. If this file exists and an entry for a shell does not exist in this file, any user running the undefined shell is not allowed FTP connections to this system.

The `/etc/shells` file does not exist by default. If the file does not exist, the system default shells are used. For a list of the default shells, refer to the `shells(4)` man page.

You can create the `/etc/shells` file by using the `vi` editor and listing each shell that you want to be recognized by the system. The following is an example `/etc/shells` file:

```
# more /etc/shells<cr>
        /sbin/sh
        /bin/sh
        /bin/ksh
        /bin/bash
```

`/etc/shells` May Deny Access

If you don't list all the default shells in the `/etc/shells` file, as done in the previous example, users who are using those shells are not allowed access.

Securing Superuser Access

The superuser (root) is immune from restrictions placed on other users of the system. Any Oracle Solaris account with a UID of `0` is the superuser. All UNIX systems have a default superuser login named "root." The user of this account can access any file and run any command. This login is valuable because any user who might have gotten himself or herself into trouble by removing access permissions, forgetting his or her password, or simply needing a file from an area to which he or she doesn't have access can be helped by root.

However, root access can be dangerous. Root can delete anything, including the OS. The root login is both dangerous and necessary. System administrators must not give the root password to anyone and should use it themselves only when required. If it becomes necessary to grant superuser privileges to non-root users, you should use RBAC.

Restricting Root Access

Root access needs to be safeguarded against unauthorized use. You should assume that any intruder is looking for root access. You can protect the superuser account on a system by restricting access to a specific device through the `/etc/default/login` file. For example, if superuser access is restricted to the console, the superuser can log in only at the console, which should be in a locked room. Anybody who remotely logs in to the system to perform an administrative function must first log in with his or her login and then use the `su` command to become superuser.

The following steps describe the procedure for restricting root from logging in to the system console from a remote system.

1. Become the superuser.
2. Edit the /etc/default/login file and uncomment the following line:

```
CONSOLE=/dev/console
```

You have set the variable CONSOLE to /dev/console. If the variable CONSOLE were set as follows with no value defined, root could not log in from anywhere, not even from the console:

```
CONSOLE=
```

With the CONSOLE value set to nothing, the only way to get into the system as root is to first log in as a regular user and then become root by issuing the su command. If the system console is not in a controlled environment, the option of not being able to log in to the console as root might be useful.

Monitoring Superuser Access

Oracle Solaris can be set up to log all attempts to become the superuser. The logs that contain this information are useful when you're trying to track down unauthorized activity. Whenever someone issues the su command to switch from being a user to being root, this activity is logged in the file /var/adm/sulog. The sulog file lists all uses of the su command—not only those used to switch from being a user to being the superuser. The entries in the sulog file show the date and time the command was entered, whether the command was successful, the port from which the command was issued, and the name of the user and the switched identity.

To monitor who is using the su command, the sulog logging utility must be turned on in the /etc/default/su file. By default, su logging is enabled. The following steps describe how to turn on logging of the su command if it has been disabled.

1. Become the superuser.
2. Edit the /etc/default/su file and uncomment the following line:

```
SULOG=/var/adm/sulog
```

Through the /etc/default/su file, you can also set up the system to display a message on the console each time an attempt is made to use the su command to gain superuser access from a remote system. This is a good way to immediately detect when someone is trying to gain superuser access to the system on which you are working. The following steps describe how to display root access attempts to the console.

1. Become the superuser.
2. Edit the `/etc/default/su` file and uncomment the following line:

```
CONSOLE=/dev/console
```

3. Use the `su` command to become root. Verify that a message is printed on the system console.

Root as a Role

For maximum security, root should be set up as a role account and not as a normal login account. Refer to the section titled "RBAC" for information on how to set up root as a role.

The Secure Shell (ssh)

SSH enables users to securely access a remote system over an insecure network. You can use SSH to do the following:

- Log in to a remote system (by using `ssh`).
- Copy files over the network between hosts (by using `scp` or `sftp`).
- Use as an on-demand virtual private network (VPN).
- Use to forward X Window System traffic between two machines.

Before SSH was available, remote connections were—and still can be—handled via `telnet`, `rlogin`, `rsh`, and `rcp`. These commands create insecure connections and are prone to security risks. One main problem is that the login credentials and data pass over the network unencrypted. On an insecure network, your data could be intercepted or stolen by an intruder.

Oracle Solaris 11 supports both version 1 and version 2 of SSH protocol. Version 1 has inherent security weaknesses, so you are encouraged to use only version 2. Secure shell protocol version 2 has three parts:

1. SSH transfer protocol: Used for server authentication, negotiates the algorithm and key exchange, and establishes the encrypted communication channel between the server and the client

2. SSH authentication protocol: Used to verify the identity of the user that runs the SSH client
3. SSH channel protocol: Multiplexes the encrypted channel and logical connections such as for a shell session, port forwarding, or X11 forwarding session

The following are the SSH defaults:

- Logins and passwords are secure.
- Only protocol version 2 is in effect.
- Port forwarding is disabled on both the server and the client.
- X11 forwarding is disabled on the server side and enabled on the client side.
- All authentication methods are enabled. If Kerberos is configured, SSH uses it out-of-the-box.

With SSH, you establish secure communication between two hosts on an insecure network. The two hosts are referred to as the client (that is, the host that requests the connection) and the server (that is, the host being connected to). The SSH daemon, `sshd`, starts up on each host at system boot, when the `svc:/network/ssh:default` service has been enabled by SMF. The `sshd` daemon listens for connections, and it handles the encrypted authentication exchange between the hosts. Authentication is provided by the use of passwords, public keys, or both. When authentication is complete, the user can execute commands and copy files remotely.

The `ssh` on the client side is controlled by the `/etc/ssh/ssh_config` file and by `ssh` command line options. The `ssh_config` file controls which types of authentication are permitted for accessing the server. Optionally, a user can also provide `ssh` settings in his or her own `$HOME/.ssh/config` file.

The `sshd` on the server side is controlled by the `/etc/ssh/sshd_config` file, which is controlled by the system administrator.

Normally, each user wanting to use SSH with authentication runs the `ssh-keygen` command once to create the authentication key in `$HOME/.ssh/identity`, `$HOME/.ssh/id_dsa`, or `$HOME/.ssh/id_rsa`. The client maintains the private key, and the server is provided with the public key that is needed to complete authentication. Public-key authentication is a stronger type of authentication than typical password authentication because the private key never travels over the network. To create a public/private key for public-key authentication, follow the steps outlined next.

In the following example, you'll set up public-key authentication so that `bcalkins` can log in to a remote host using `ssh`. For these steps, you'll need two systems. One will be the client, and the other will be the remote host.

1. Make sure both systems have a user account named bcalkins, a password assigned to the account, and an established home directory named /export/home/bcalkins.
2. Make sure each account has a .ssh directory in the /export/home/bcalkins home directory. If not, you can create the .ssh directory by running the ssh-keygen command described in step 7.
3. As root, enable host-based authentication on the client by adding the following line to the /etc/ssh/ssh_config file:

```
HostbasedAuthentication yes
```

4. On the remote host, enable host-based authentication by adding the following line to the /etc/ssh/sshd_config file:

```
HostbasedAuthentication yes
```

5. Start up sshd on the remote host if it is not currently running by typing

```
# svcadm enable svc:/network/ssh<cr>
```

   If the ssh service is already running, restart it as follows:

```
# svcadm restart svc:/network/ssh<cr>
```

6. On the remote host, ensure that the sshd daemon can access the list of trusted hosts by setting IgnoreRhosts to no in the /etc/ssh/sshd_config file as follows:

```
IgnoreRhosts no
```

7. On the client, log in as bcalkins and create the client's public key. To generate the public key on the client, issue the following command:

```
# ssh-keygen -t rsa<cr>
```

Use the -t option to specify the type of algorithm: rsa, dsa, or rsa1. The system responds with the following:

```
Generating public/private rsa key pair.
Enter file in which to save the key (//.ssh/id_rsa):<cr>
```

When you press *Enter*, the system responds with

```
Created directory '/export/home/bcalkins/.ssh'.
Enter passphrase(empty for no passphrase):
```

The passphrase is used for encrypting the private key. A good passphrase is 10 to 30 characters long, mixes alphabetic and numeric characters, and avoids simple English prose and English names. A carriage return entry means that no passphrase is used; this type of blank passphrase is strongly discouraged for user accounts. The passphrase is not displayed when you type it in, as shown here:

```
Enter same passphrase again:
```

Enter the passphrase again to confirm it. The system responds with

```
Your identification has been saved in /export/home/bcalkins/.ssh/id_rsa.
Your public key has been saved in /export/home/bcalkins/.ssh/id_rsa.pub.
The key fingerprint is:
c9:8e:d8:f9:69:6e:01:e7:c4:82:05:8a:8e:d3:03:56 bcalkins@solaris
```

8. The key fingerprint is displayed as a colon-separated series of two-digit hexadecimal values. You should check to make sure the path to the key is correct. In this example, the path is /export/home/bcalkins/.ssh/id_rsa.pub. At this point, you have created a public/private key pair. Now, copy the public key from the client and append the key to the $HOME/.ssh/authorized_keys file in your home directory on the remote host.
9. When the public key has been created on the client and copied to the remote host, you can start using SSH to log in to the remote system by typing this line, where <*hostname*> is the name of the remote host to which you want to connect:

```
$ ssh <hostname><cr>
```

The first time you run `ssh`

```
$ ssh 192.168.0.252<cr>
```

you're prompted with questions regarding the authenticity of the remote host as follows:

```
The authenticity of host '192.168.0.252' can't be established.
 RSA key fingerprint in is: \
78:28:11:cb:41:81:a2:73:50:5a:d4:49:bb:12:85:03
 Are you sure you want to continue connecting(yes/no)? yes<cr>
```

This is a normal message for initial connections to the remote host. If you enter "yes," the system responds with

```
Warning: Permanently added '192.168.0.252' (RSA) to the list of known hosts.
Enter passphrase for key '/export/home/bcalkins/.ssh/id_rsa':
```

After you enter your passphrase, the system will log you in to the remote host.

```
Last login: Fri Feb  1 04:48:31 2013 from 192.168.1.220
Oracle Corporation      SunOS 5.11      11.1    September 2012
```

To copy files using SSH, you start the secure copy program by typing the `scp` command, using the following syntax:

```
# scp <sourcefile> <username>@<hostname>:</destinationdir><cr>
```

Table 7-28 describes the arguments to the `scp` command.

Table 7-28 `scp` Command Arguments

Argument	Description
<sourcefile>	The name of the local file that you want to copy
<username>	The username on the remote host to which you want to connect
<hostname>	The name of the remote system to which the file will be copied
<destinationdir>	The name of the directory on the remote host to which you will copy the file

You should type the secure passphrase when prompted. The system responds by displaying the following:

- The filename
- The percentage of the file transferred as it is being copied
- The quantity of data transferred as it is being transferred
- The estimated time of arrival when the entire file will be copied to the remote directory

This example copies the file named file1 to the home directory of bcalkins on the remote host:

```
# scp file1 bcalkins@remote:~<cr>
```

The system responds with this:

```
Password:
```

If you enter the user login password, you are then logged in to the remote host:

```
file1  100%  |*************************************| 12540  0:00
```

For more information on using SSH, refer to the ssh(1) and sshd(1M) man pages.

Common-Sense Security Techniques

A system administrator can have the best system security measures in place, but without the users' cooperation, system security may be compromised. The system administrator must teach common-sense rules regarding system security, such as the following:

- Use proper passwords. Countless sites use weak passwords such as admin or supervisor for their root accounts.
- Don't give your password to anyone, no matter who the person says he or she is. One of the best system crackers of our time said that he would simply pose as a system support person, ask a user for a password, and get free reign with the system.

- Only give out a password to a known, trusted person. Users should know that no one trustworthy would ever e-mail or call asking for the password.
- If you walk away from a system, log out or lock the screen.

Summary

This chapter described how to add, modify, and remove user accounts from the command line. It discussed the commands to use and the files that are modified as a result of running these commands.

This chapter also described the user shell initialization files. It outlined how to use these files to customize the user work environment. In addition, this chapter detailed many of the default shell environment variables that control the user shell environment.

This chapter also discussed fundamental concepts in system security. When you're considering security, you need to begin by securing the hardware in a safe location. Remember that anyone who has physical access to a computer can access the OS and data, regardless of how secure you've made everything else.

Keep your data secure by controlling the user logins on the system. You should make sure that users have secure passwords and are not making their logins and passwords public. You should implement password aging and restricted shells where they make sense.

You should set up file and directory permissions to ensure that users have access to only the data that they are authorized to see. You should use secure `umask` values and, if necessary, ACLs. You should monitor all user activities using the utilities described in this chapter. Finally, you should not set `setuid` and `setgid` permissions unless absolutely necessary.

If your system is on a network, you should implement the network security measures that are described in this chapter. You should turn off unneeded services, using the "deny first, then allow" rule. In other words, you should turn off as many services and applications as possible, and then you should selectively turn on those that are essential. You should use trusted systems carefully. Also, you should keep your OS up-to-date with security updates. As new threats are discovered, you should quickly fix them by installing security updates as they become available. Chapter 2, "Managing and Updating Software with IPS," described the process of obtaining and installing software updates.

In this chapter you learned about securing the superuser password. You need to keep it under tight control and make sure that it is never made available to anyone except those who are authorized. You should limit using the superuser login unless the task to be performed requires root privileges. Instead of giving users the root password, you should create roles for users that require special privileges and use RBAC rights profiles and authorizations to grant those privileges.

8

Managing System Processes

This chapter covers Oracle Solaris processes: how to view processes, how to understand the effects that signals have on processes, and how to manage processes.

Oracle Solaris is a multitasking environment in which a number of programs run at the same time. This means that many users can be active on the system at the same time, running many jobs (processes) simultaneously. Each program can start and stop multiple processes while it is running, but only one job is active per processor at any given time while the other jobs wait in a job queue. Because each process takes its turn running in very short time slices (much less than a second each), multitasking OSs give the appearance that multiple processes are running at the same time. A parent process forks a child process, which in turn can fork other processes.

Forks

The term "fork" is used to describe a process started from another process. As with a fork in the road, one process turns into two. You'll also see the term "spawn" used—the two words are interchangeable for the purposes of this subject.

A program can be made up of many processes. A "process" is part of a program running in its own address space. A process under Oracle Solaris consists of an "address space" and a set of data structures in the "kernel" to keep track of that process. The address space is divided into various sections that include the instructions that the process may execute, memory allocated during the execution of the process, the "stack," and memory-mapped files. The kernel must keep track of the following data for each process on the system:

- Address space
- Current status of the process
- Execution priority of the process
- Resource usage of the process
- Current signal mask
- Ownership of the process

A process is distinct from a job, command, or program that can be composed of many processes working together to perform a specific task. For example, a computer-aided design application is a single program. When this program starts, it spawns other processes as it runs. When a user logs in to the program, it spawns even more processes. Each process has a process ID associated with it and is referred to as a "PID." You can monitor processes that are currently executing by using one of the commands listed in Table 8-1.

Table 8-1 Commands to Display Processes

Command	Description
`mpstat`	Executed from the command line, `mpstat` reports processor statistics in tabular form. Each row of the table represents the activity of one processor or each virtual processor when the server has multiple physical processors with multiple cores.
`ps`	`ps` is executed from the command line to display information about active processes.
`pgrep`	`pgrep` is executed from the command line to find processes by a specific name or attribute.
`prstat`	This command is executed from the command line to display information about active processes on the system.
`ptree`	This command prints the process trees containing the specified PIDs or users, with child processes indented from their respective parent processes.
`svcs`	With the `-p` option, this SMF command will list processes associated with each service instance.
`time`	This command displays the time that the system has spent executing a command.
`top`	`top` displays and updates information about the top CPU processes.

Before getting into the commands used to monitor processes, you first need to become familiar with process attributes. A process has certain attributes that directly affect execution. These are listed in Table 8-2.

ps

Use the `ps` command to view processes currently running on the system. Use the `ps` command when you're on a character-based terminal and don't have access to a graphical display. Adding the `-l` option to the `ps` command displays a variety of other information about the processes currently running, including the state of each process (listed under `S`). The codes used to show the various process states are listed in Table 8-3.

Table 8-2 Process Attributes

Attribute	Description
PID	The process identification (a unique number that defines the process within the kernel)
PPID	The parent PID (the parent of the process)
UID	The user ID number of the user who owns the process
EUID	The effective user ID of the process
GID	The group ID of the user who owns the process
EGID	The effective group ID of the user who owns the process
Priority	The priority at which the process runs

Table 8-3 Process States

Code	Process State	Description
`O`	Running	The process is running on a processor.
`S`	Sleeping	The process is waiting for an event to complete.
`R`	Runnable	The process is on the run queue.
`Z`	Zombie	The process was terminated and the parent is not waiting.
`T`	Traced	The process was stopped by a signal because the parent is tracing it.
`W`	Waiting	The process is waiting for CPU usage to drop to the CPU-caps enforced limits.

To see all of the processes that are running on a system, type the following:

```
# ps -el<cr>
```

The system responds with the following output:

```
# ps -el<cr>
 F S    UID  PID  PPID  C PRI NI    ADDR    SZ    WCHAN TTY       TIME CMD
 1 T      0    0     0  0   0 SY       ?     0            ?       0:04 sched
 1 S      0    5     0  0   0 SD       ?     0          ? ?       0:03 zpool-r
 1 S      0    6     0  0   0 SD       ?     0          ? ?       0:00 kmem_tas
 0 S      0    1     0  0  40 20       ?   718          ? ?       0:00 init
 1 S      0    2     0  0   0 SY       ?     0          ? ?       0:00 pageout
 1 S      0    3     0  0   0 SY       ?     0          ? ?       0:01 fsflush

..<output has been truncated>....
```

The manual page for the ps command describes all the fields displayed with the ps command, as well as all the command options. Table 8-4 lists some important fields.

Table 8-4 Process Fields

Field	Description
F	Flags associated with the process.
S	The state of the process.
UID	The user ID of the process owner: For many processes, this is 0 because they run setuid.
PID	The process ID of each process: This value should be unique. Generally, PIDs are allocated lowest to highest, but they wrap at some point. This value is necessary for you to send a signal, such as the kill signal, to a process.
PPID	The parent process ID: This identifies the parent process that started the process. Using the PPID enables you to trace the sequence of process creation that took place.
PRI	The priority of the process: Without the -c option, higher numbers mean lower priority. With the -c option, higher numbers mean higher priority.
NI	The nice value, used in priority computation: This is not printed when the -c option is used. The process's nice number contributes to its scheduling priority. Making a process nicer means lowering its priority.
ADDR	The memory address of the process.

Field	Description
SZ	The SIZE field: This is the total number of pages in the process. Page sizes are 8,192 bytes on sun4v systems but vary on different hardware platforms. Issue the `/usr/bin/pagesize` command to display the page size on your system.
WCHAN	The address of an event for which the process is sleeping (if it's `-`, the process is running).
STIME	The starting time of the process (in hours, minutes, and seconds).
TTY	The terminal assigned to your process.
TIME	The cumulative CPU time used by the process, in minutes and seconds.
CMD	The command name and its arguments.
LWP	The LWP ID of the LWP being reported.

You often want to look at all processes. You can do this using the command `ps -el`. A number of options are available with the `ps` command to control what information gets printed. A few of them are listed in Table 8-5.

Table 8-5 `ps` Command Options

Option	Description
`-A`	This option lists information for all processes. It is identical to the `-e` option.
`-a`	The `-a` option lists information about all of the most frequently requested processes. Processes not associated with a terminal will not be listed.
`-e`	This option lists information about every process on the system.
`-f`	`-f` generates a full listing.
`-l`	`-l` generates a long listing.
`-P`	This option prints the number of the processor to which the process is bound, if any, under an additional column header PSR. This is a useful option on systems that have multiple processors.
`-u` *<username>*	This option lists only process data for a particular user. In the listing, the numerical user ID is printed unless you give the `-f` option, which prints the login name.
`-o`	`-o` provides options to specify the information to be displayed (see example).

For a complete list of options to the ps(1) command, refer to the Oracle Solaris online manual pages.

Customize the output from the ps command by using the -o option followed by the columns of information you'd like to display. The information that can be specified after the -o is described in Table 8-6.

For a complete listing of format options, refer to the "Display Formats" section of the ps(1) man page or type

```
# ps -o<cr>
```

Table 8-6 ps Format Options

Format Option	Description
user	The effective user ID of the process
comm	The name of the command being executed
pid	The decimal value of the process ID
ppid	The decimal value of the parent process ID
vsz	The total size of the process in virtual memory, in kilobytes
time	The cumulative CPU time of the process
etime	The elapsed time since the process was started
tty	The name of the controlling terminal of the process
args	The command with all its arguments as a string
lwp	The decimal value of the LWP ID
project	The project ID of the process
zoneid	The zone ID number of the process as a decimal integer
zone	The zone ID of the process as a textual value if that value can be obtained
nwlp	The number of LWPs in the process
psr	The number of the processor to which the process or LWP is bound
pset	The ID of the processor set to which the process or LWP is bound
osz	The total size of the process in virtual memory, in pages
rss	The resident set size of the process, in kilobytes (estimated)

The system will display the command usage and the list of selectable options and fields as follows:

```
usage: ps [ -aAdefHlcjLPyZ ] [ -o format ] [ -t termlist ]
        [ -u userlist ] [ -U userlist ] [ -G grouplist ]
        [ -p proclist ] [ -g pgrplist ] [ -s sidlist ] [ -z zonelist ] [-h lgrplist]
'format' is one or more of:
user ruser group rgroup uid ruid gid rgid pid ppid pgid sid taskid ctid
pri opri pcpu pmem vsz rss osz nice class time etime stime zone zoneid
f s c lwp nlwp psr tty addr wchan fname comm args projid project pset lgrp
```

The following example demonstrates the use of the -o option followed by format options to customize the output of the ps command:

```
# ps -eo user,pid,pcpu,pmem,vsz,rss,tty,s,stime,time,nlwp,com<cr>
USER   PID %CPU %MEM   VSZ  RSS TT     S    STIME       TIME NLWP  COMMAND
root     0  0.0  0.0     0    0 ?      T  04:29:34     00:04    1  sched
root     5  0.0  0.0     0    0 ?      S  04:29:30     00:05  142  zpool-rpool
root     6  0.0  0.0     0    0 ?      S  04:29:35     00:00    1  kmem_task
root     1  0.0  0.1  2872 1448 ?      S  04:29:35     00:00    1  /usr/sbin/init

... <output is truncated>...
```

sort Command

The sort command is useful when you're looking at system processes. Use the sort command as the pipe output to sort by size or PID. For example, to sort by the SZ field, use the command ps -el | sort +9 (remember, sort starts numbering fields with 0).

pgrep

The pgrep command replaces the combination of the ps, grep, egrep, and awk commands that were used to manage processes in earlier releases of Oracle Solaris. The pgrep command examines the active processes on the system and reports the PIDs of the processes with attributes that match the criteria you specify on the command line. The command syntax for the pgrep command is shown here:

```
pgrep <options> <pattern>
```

pgrep options are described in Table 8-7.

Table 8-7 `pgrep` Options

Option	Description
`-d` *<delim>*	This option specifies the output delimiter string to be printed between each matching PID. If no `-d` option is specified, the default is a newline character.
`-f`	The regular expression pattern should be matched against the full process argument string. If no `-f` option is specified, the expression is matched only against the name of the executable file.
`-g` *<pgrplist>*	This option matches only processes whose process group ID is in the given list.
`-G` *<gidlist>*	This option matches only processes whose real group ID is in the given list. Each group ID may be specified as either a group name or a numerical group ID.
`-l`	`-l` specifies long output format. This option prints the process name along with the PID of each matching process.
`-n`	`-n` matches only the newest (most recently created) process that meets all other specified matching criteria.
`-P` *<ppidlist>*	This option matches only processes whose parent PID is in the given list.
`-s` *<sidlist>*	This option matches only processes whose process session ID is in the given list.
`-t` *<termlist>*	This option matches only processes that are associated with a terminal in the given list. Each terminal is specified as the suffix following `/dev/` of the terminal's device pathname in `/dev` (for example, `term/a` or `pts/0`).
`-u` *<euidlist>*	This option matches only processes whose effective user ID is in the given list. Each user ID may be specified as either a login name or a numerical user ID.
`-U` *<uidlist>*	This option matches only processes whose real user ID is in the given list. Each user ID may be specified as either a login name or a numerical user ID.
`-v`	`-v` matches all processes except those that meet the specified matching criteria.
`-x`	The `-x` option considers only processes whose argument string or executable filename exactly matches the specified pattern.
<pattern>	This option specifies a pattern to match against either the executable filename or full process argument string.

For example, the following pgrep command finds all processes that have "gnome" in the process argument string:

```
# pgrep -l -f "gnome"<cr>
```

The system responds with this:

```
2106 /usr/bin/gnome-terminal -x /bin/sh -c cd '/root' && exec $SHELL
 2011 /usr/bin/gnome-keyring-daemon --start --components=secrets
 1994 /usr/bin/ssh-agent -- gnome-session
 1869 /usr/lib/gdm-simple-slave --display-id /org/gnome/DisplayManager/Display2
 2043 gnome-power-manager
 1953 gnome-session
 2017 gnome-panel
 2013 /usr/lib/gnome-settings-daemon
 2107 gnome-pty-helper
```

To find the PID for the svc.startd process, issue this command:

```
# pgrep -l startd<cr>
```

The system responds with this:

```
11 svc.startd
```

prstat

Use the prstat command from the command line to dynamically monitor system processes. Again, like the ps command, it provides information on active processes. The difference is that you can specify whether you want information on specific processes, UIDs, CPU IDs, or processor sets. By default, prstat displays information about all processes sorted by CPU usage. Another nice feature with prstat is that the information remains on the screen and is updated periodically. The information displayed by the prstat command is described in Table 8-8.

This section will introduce some new terminology, so Table 8-9 defines a few terms related to processing in general.

Table 8-8 Column Headings for the `prstat` Command

Attribute	Description
PID	The process identification (a unique number that defines the process within the kernel).
USERNAME	The login ID name of the owner of the process.
SIZE	The total virtual memory size of the process in kilobytes (K), megabytes (M), or gigabytes (G).
RSS	The resident set size of the process in kilobytes, megabytes, or gigabytes.
STATE	The state of the process: `cpu`<*n*>—Process is running on CPU. `sleep`—Process is waiting for an event to complete. `run`—Process is in the run queue. `zombie`—Process has terminated and parent is not waiting. `stop`—Process is stopped.
PRI	The priority of the process.
NICE	The value used in priority computation.
TIME	The cumulative execution time for the process.
CPU	The percentage of recent CPU time used by the process.
PROCESS	The name of the process.
NLWP	The number of LWPs in the process.

Table 8-9 Process Terminology

Term	Description
Multitasking	This technique is used in an OS for sharing a single processor among several independent jobs. Multitasking introduces overhead because the processor spends some time choosing the next job to run and saving and restoring tasks' state. However, it reduces the worst-case time from job submission to completion compared with a simple batch system, in which each job must finish before the next one starts. Multitasking also means that while one task is waiting for some external event, the CPU is free to do useful work on other tasks. A multitasking OS should provide some degree of protection of one task from another to prevent tasks from interacting in unexpected ways, such as accidentally modifying the contents of each other's memory areas.

Term	Description
	The jobs in a multitasking system may belong to one or many users. This is distinct from parallel processing, in which one user runs several tasks on several processors. Time sharing is almost synonymous with multitasking, but it implies that there is more than one user.
Parallel processing	This is the simultaneous use of more than one CPU to solve a problem. The processors either may communicate to cooperate in solving a problem or may run completely independently, possibly under the control of another processor that distributes work to the others and collects results from them.
Multithreaded	Multithreaded is a process that has multiple flows (threads) of control. The traditional UNIX process contained, and still contains, a single thread of control. Multithreading separates a process into many execution threads, each of which runs independently. For more information, see the Multithreaded Programming Guide at `http://docs.sun.com/`, part number 816-5137-10.
Lightweight process	A single-threaded subprocess. LWPs are scheduled by the kernel to use available CPU resources and are allocated based on their scheduling class and priority. LWPs include a kernel thread, which contains information that must be in memory all the time, and an LWP, which contains information that is swappable. A process can consist of multiple LWPs and multiple application threads. An LWP is somewhere between a thread and a full process.
Application thread	This is a series of instructions with a separate stack that can execute independently in a user's address space. The threads can be multiplexed on top of LWPs.
Address space	This is the range of addresses that a processor or process can access or at which a device can be accessed. The term may refer to either a physical address or a virtual address. The size of a processor's address space depends on the width of the processor's address bus and address registers. Processes running in 32-bit mode have a 4GB address space (2^{32} bytes), and processes running in 64-bit mode have a 16TB (2^{64} bytes) address space.
Shared memory	This term usually refers to RAM, which can be accessed by more than one process in a multitasking OS with memory protection.

The syntax for the `prstat` command is as follows:

```
prstat [options] <count> <interval>
```

Table 8-10 describes a few of the `prstat` command options and arguments.

Table 8-10 `prstat` **Options and Arguments**

Option	Description
`prstat` Options	
`-a`	Displays separate reports about processes and users at the same time.
`-c`	Continuously prints new reports beneath previous reports instead of overwriting them.
`-C` *<psrsetlist>*	Reports only processes or LWPs that are bound to processor sets in the given list.
`-j` *<projlist>*	Reports only processes or LWPs whose project ID is in the given list: Each project ID can be specified as either a project name or a numerical project ID.
`-J`	Reports information about processes and projects.
`-k` *<tasklist>*	Reports only processes or LWPs whose task ID is in tasklist.
`-h` *<lgrplist>*	Reports only processes or LWPs whose home lgroup is in the given list of lgroups; no processes or LWPs will be listed for invalid lgroups.
`-m`	Reports microstate process accounting information: In addition to all fields listed in `-v` mode, this mode also includes the percentage of time the process has spent processing system traps, text page faults, and data page faults, and waiting for user locks and waiting for CPU (latency time).
`-n` *<nproc>*	Restricts the number of output lines: The *<nproc>* argument specifies how many lines of process or LWP statistics are reported.
`-p` *<pidlist>*	Reports only processes that have a PID in the given list.
`-P` *<cpulist>*	Reports only processes or LWPs that have most recently executed on a CPU in the given list: The *<cpulist>* argument identifies each CPU by an integer as reported by `psrinfo`.
`-S` *<key>*	This option sorts output lines by *<key>* in ascending order. Values for *<key>* can be `cpu`—Sorts by process CPU usage; this is the default. `time`—Sorts by process execution time. `size`—Sorts by size of process image. `rss`—Sorts by resident set size. `pri`—Sorts by process priority.

Option	Description
-s <*key*>	Sorts output lines by <*key*> in descending order; see the -S option for a list of valid *keys* to use.
-t	Reports total usage summary for each user.
-u <*uidlist*>	Reports only processes whose effective user ID is in the given list; the value for <*uidlist*> may be specified as either a login name or a numerical user ID.
-U <*uidlist*>	Reports only processes whose real user ID is in the given list; the value for <*uidlist*> may be specified as either a login name or a numerical user ID.
-z <*zoneidlist*>	Reports only processes or LWPs whose zone ID is in the given list; each zone ID can be specified as either a zone name or a numerical zone ID.
-Z	Reports information about processes and zones.
prstat Arguments	
<*count*>	Specifies the number of times that the statistics are repeated; by default, prstat reports statistics until a termination signal is received.
<*interval*>	Specifies the sampling interval in seconds; the default interval is 5 seconds.

psrinfo Command

psrinfo displays one line for each configured processor, displaying whether it is online, non-interruptible, offline, or powered off, as well as when that status last changed as follows:

```
$ psrinfo -pv<cr>
The physical processor has 4 cores and 16 virtual processors (0-15)
  The core has 4 virtual processors (0-3)
  The core has 4 virtual processors (4-7)
  The core has 4 virtual processors (8-11)
  The core has 4 virtual processors (12-15)
    UltraSPARC-T1 (chipid 0, clock 1000 MHz)
```

The following example uses the prstat command to view the four most active root processes running. The -n option is used here to restrict the output to the top four processes. The next number, 5, specifies the sampling interval in seconds, and the last number, 3, runs the command three times:

```
# prstat -u root -n 4 5 3<cr>
```

The system displays the following output:

```
  PID USERNAME  SIZE   RSS    STATE  PRI NICE     TIME  CPU   PROCESS/NLWP
  1312 root      31M 7504K   sleep   59     0  0:00:11  0.1%  pkg.depotd/64
  2106 root     121M   17M   sleep   59     0  0:00:04  0.1%  gnome-terminal/2
  2025 root     180M  126M   sleep   59     0  0:00:14  0.0%  java/25
  1870 root      61M   48M   sleep   59     0  0:00:04  0.0%  Xorg/3
Total: 94 processes, 933 lwps, load averages:  0.02, 0.02,  0.02
```

The output updates on your display five times every three seconds and then returns to the command prompt after the last sample is displayed.

The total line below the list of processes identifies the total number of processes, the total number of LWPs, and the CPU load averages. The averages are based on 1-, 5-, and 15-minute intervals (the same information reported by the `uptime` command).

The `prstat` command is also useful for monitoring the memory statistics of a process. The `SIZE` column reports the total virtual memory size of the process, and the `RSS` column reports the physical memory being used by the process.

You can also use the `prstat` command to target specific statistical information, such as which process has the highest CPU usage, by using the `-s` option as follows:

```
# prstat -s cpu 5 3<cr>
   PID USERNAME  SIZE    RSS  STATE  PRI NICE      TIME   CPU    PROCESS/NLWP
  1312  root      31M  7504K  sleep   59    0   0:00:16  0.1%    pkg.depotd/64
  2025  root     180M   126M  sleep   59    0   0:00:19  0.1%    java/25
  2106  root     121M    17M  sleep   59    0   0:00:06  0.0%    gnome-terminal/2
  2018  root     141M    32M  sleep   49    0   0:00:00  0.0%    nautilus/1
  2193  root    4400K  2508K  sleep   59    0   0:00:00  0.0%    top/1
  2210  root    4412K  3104K  cpu0    59    0   0:00:00  0.0%    prstat/1
  1870  root      61M    48M  sleep   59    0   0:00:06  0.0%    Xorg/3
  2057  root    6920K  4460K  sleep   59    0   0:00:00  0.0%    xscreensaver/1
  2016  root      24M    14M  sleep   59    0   0:00:00  0.0%    metacity/1
    48  netcfg  3844K  2596K  sleep   59    0   0:00:00  0.0%    netcfgd/4
   520  daemon  3336K  1032K  sleep   59    0   0:00:00  0.0%    rpcbind/1
 Total: 110 processes, 1057 lwps, load averages:  0.02,  0.02,   0.02
```

To display processes using the most memory, sort by the RSS column as follows:

```
# prstat -s rss 5 3<cr>
   PID USERNAME  SIZE    RSS  STATE  PRI NICE      TIME   CPU    PROCESS/NLWP
  2025  root     180M   126M  sleep   59    0   0:00:20  0.1%    java/25
  2017  root     158M    49M  sleep   59    0   0:00:00  0.0%    gnome-panel/1
  1870  root      61M    48M  sleep   59    0   0:00:07  0.0%    Xorg/3
  2018  root     141M    32M  sleep   49    0   0:00:00  0.0%    nautilus/1
  2024  root      50M    30M  sleep   12   19   0:00:00  0.0%    updatemanagerno/1
    13  root      22M    21M  sleep   59    0   0:00:13  0.0%    svc.configd/19
  2052  root     125M    18M  sleep   59    0   0:00:00  0.0%    isapython2.6/1
  2022  root      30M    18M  sleep   59    0   0:00:00  0.0%    isapython2.6/1
  2106  root     121M    17M  sleep   59    0   0:00:07  0.1%    gnome-terminal/2
  2013  root     123M    16M  sleep   59    0   0:00:00  0.0%    gnome-settings-/1
  2074  root     123M    16M  sleep   59    0   0:00:00  0.0%    mixer_applet2/2
 Total: 110 processes, 1057 lwps, load averages:  0.02,  0.02,   0.02
```

Adding the -a option to the prstat command will identify how many processes each user is using, what percentage of the CPUs each user is using, and how much memory they are using on the system. The following command asks for the top eight processes consuming the CPU and a list of resource consumption statistics for each user:

```
# prstat -s cpu -a -n 8<cr>
   PID USERNAME  SIZE   RSS STATE  PRI NICE      TIME  CPU  PROCESS/NLWP
  1086 bcalkins 3472K 2896K sleep   59    0   0:00:00 0.0%  su/1
  1088 root       11M 4144K cpu2    49    0   0:00:00 0.0%  prstat/1
  1087 root       10M 7184K sleep   49    0   0:00:00 0.0%  bash/1
     5 root        0K    0K sleep   99  -20   0:00:04 0.0%  zpool-rpool/166
    13 root       21M   20M sleep   59    0   0:01:30 0.0%  svc.configd/22
    11 root       21M   15M sleep   59    0   0:00:15 0.0%  svc.startd/13
    42 root     4464K 3416K sleep   59    0   0:00:00 0.0%  dlmgmtd/7
     8 root        0K    0K sleep   99  -20   0:00:01 0.0%  vmtasks/16
 NPROC USERNAME  SWAP   RSS MEMORY      TIME  CPU
    47  root      372M  228M   5.9%  0:02:02 0.0%
     2  bcalkins   13M   10M   0.3%  0:00:00 0.0%
     3  daemon     30M   19M   0.5%  0:00:00 0.0%
     1  netcfg   4368K 3784K   0.1%  0:00:00 0.0%
     2  netadm     19M   14M   0.4%  0:00:01 0.0%
Total: 58 processes, 599 lwps, load averages:  0.01, 0.05, 0.12
```

Use the -L option to display one thread per line instead of one process per line as follows:

```
# prstat -L<cr>
   PID USERNAME  SIZE   RSS STATE  PRI NICE      TIME  CPU  PROCESS/LWPID
  1137 root       11M 4848K cpu14    2    0   0:00:00 0.2%  prstat/1
   546 root       14M 9400K sleep   49    0   0:00:00 0.0%  nscd/6
  1108 root     3056K 2576K sleep   59    0   0:00:00 0.0%  telnet/1
     5 root        0K    0K sleep   99  -20   0:00:00 0.0%  zpool-rpool/15
     5 root        0K    0K sleep   99  -20   0:00:00 0.0%  zpool-rpool/14
     5 root        0K    0K sleep   99  -20   0:00:00 0.0%  zpool-rpool/13
     5 root        0K    0K sleep   99  -20   0:00:00 0.0%  zpool-rpool/12
     5 root        0K    0K sleep   99  -20   0:00:00 0.0%  zpool-rpool/11
     5 root        0K    0K sleep   99  -20   0:00:00 0.0%  zpool-rpool/10
     5 root        0K    0K sleep   99  -20   0:00:00 0.0%  zpool-rpool/9
     5 root        0K    0K sleep   99  -20   0:00:00 0.0%  zpool-rpool/8
     5 root        0K    0K sleep   99  -20   0:00:00 0.0%  zpool-rpool/7
     5 root        0K    0K sleep   99  -20   0:00:00 0.0%  zpool-rpool/6
     5 root        0K    0K sleep   99  -20   0:00:00 0.0%  zpool-rpool/5
     5 root        0K    0K sleep   99  -20   0:00:00 0.0%  zpool-rpool/4
Total: 62 processes, 603 lwps, load averages: 0.00, 0.00, 0.00
```

The last column is represented by the process name and thread number.

Finally, use the -Z option to provide a per-zone summary on a system running Oracle Solaris zones as follows:

```
# prstat -Z<cr>
   PID USERNAME  SIZE   RSS  STATE  PRI  NICE     TIME     CPU   PROCESS/NLWP
  1553     root 2628K 1460K  sleep   59     0   0:00:00    2.1%   zoneproxyd/9
  2106     root  122M   18M  sleep   59     0   0:00:13    0.1%   gnome-terminal/2
  1312     root   31M 7504K  sleep   59     0   0:00:41    0.1%   pkg.depotd/64
```

continues

```
      5        root     0K      0K  sleep   99   -20   0:00:03    0.0%    zpool-rpool/142
   2025        root  176M    130M  sleep   59     0   0:00:48    0.0%    java/25
   3288        root   17M     16M  sleep   59     0   0:00:06    0.0%    svc.configd/24
   2057        root 7572K  5092K  sleep   59     0   0:00:02    0.0%    xscreensaver/1
   3312        root 4604K  3340K   cpu3   59     0   0:00:00    0.0%    prstat/1
   1870        root   61M     48M  sleep   59     0   0:00:12    0.0%    Xorg/4
ZONEID     NPROC   SWAP    RSS  MEMORY            TIME     CPU      ZONE
     0       113  2204M   760M     24%         0:02:23    2.4%  global
     1        31   138M    77M    2.5%         0:00:07    0.0%    sol11
Total: 144 processes, 1228 lwps, load averages:   0.20,    0.07, 0.04
```

In Chapter 7, "User and Security Administration," I described projects in which user accounts can be assigned to project groups. These projects can also be used to label workloads.

The project provides a network-wide administrative identifier for related work. Projects are simply collections of tasks or processes grouped into a manageable entity and defined by the system administrator. A project might have one or more tasks associated with it that represent a workload, and a task may have one or more processes associated with it.

You can use the `prstat` command with the `-J` option to monitor the CPU usage of projects and the `-k` option to monitor tasks across your system. Therefore, you can have `prstat` report on the processes related to a project rather than just list all system processes. In addition, the system administrator can set processing limits on the project, such as setting a limit on the total amount of physical memory, in bytes, that is available to processes in the project. For more information on projects and resource capping, read the man pages on the following commands: `rcapd(1M)`, `project(4)`, `rcapstat(1)`, and `rcapadm(1M)`.

top

The `top` command is similar to the `prstat` command and is used to display and update information on the top CPU processes currently running on the system (similar to the `prstat -m` command). Like `prstat`, the `top` command updates the process information dynamically. The raw CPU percentage is used to rank processes. The following is an example of the `top` command:

```
# top<cr>
```

The system displays:

```
last pid:  2222;  load avg:  0.03,  0.02,  0.02;  up 0+01:30:27     05:59:34
104 processes: 103 sleeping, 1 on cpu
CPU states: 99.3% idle,  0.2% user,  0.5% kernel,  0.0% iowait,  0.0% swap
Kernel: 525 ctxsw, 27 trap, 748 intr, 1416 syscall, 26 flt
Memory: 3096M phys mem, 1522M free mem, 1024M total swap, 1024M free swap
 This terminal can only display 16 processes
   PID USERNAME  NLWP  PRI  NICE  SIZE   RES STATE  TIME    CPU COMMAND
  2025 root        25   59     0  180M  126M sleep  0:20  0.10% java
  2106 root         2   59     0  121M   17M sleep  0:07  0.09% gnome-terminal
  1312 root        64   59     0   31M 7504K sleep  0:17  0.08% pkg.depotd
  1870 root         3   59     0   61M   48M sleep  0:07  0.07% Xorg
  2221 root         1   59     0 4216K 2296K cpu/0  0:00  0.05% top
  2057 root         1   59     0 6920K 4460K sleep  0:00  0.01% xscreensaver
... <output has been truncated>...
```

The information displayed by the `top` command is as follows:

- The top lines of the display show general information about the state of the system. The last PID assigned to a process is displayed first, followed by the three load averages, the system uptime, and the current time.
- The second line displays the total number of processes followed by the number of processes in a particular state. The example shows 103 processes in the sleep state.
- The third line displays the percentage of time spent in each of the processor states: idle, user, kernel, iowait, and swap.
- The fourth line shows kernel-related activity.
- The fifth line shows a summary of memory and swap activity.
- The remainder of the screen displays dynamic information about individual processes.

For more information on all of the options available with the `top` command, refer to the `top(1)` man page.

mpstat

Use the `mpstat` command to report processor statistics on a multiprocessor system for each processor. When executing the `mpstat` command, we'll usually want to see more than one result, so we specify the number of seconds between each `mpstat` sample as follows:

```
# mpstat 15<cr>
```

The argument `15` specifies that I want to get a report every 15 seconds. The system displays the following information every 15 seconds:

```
CPU minf mjf xcal  intr ithr  csw icsw migr smtx  srw syscl  usr sys  wt idl
  0    0   0   59   223    3   65    0    5   18    0   127    1   4   0  95
  1    0   0  216    71   21  370    1   32   45    0   942    3   3   0  94
  2    0   0   94    40    2  176    1   12   21    0   651    3   2   0  95
  3    0   0   77    37    1   63    0    6   15    0   124    0   1   0  99
  4    0   0   63    37    0   38    0    4    8    0    63    3   0   0  97
  5    0   0   80    35    1   74    0    6   10    0   205    1   1   0  99
  6    0   0  211    43    1  487    1   35   41    0  1347   11   3   0  85
  7    0   0  196    38    0  103    0   11   25    0   372    3   1   0  96
  8    0   0  147    48    4  262    0   14   18    0   561    1   1   0  97
  9    0   0   58    45    2  144    0    7   11    0   551    2   1   0  97
 10    0   0   54    43    0  111    0   10   14    0   178    0   1   0  99
 11    0   0  302    57    1  255    1   17   59    0   952    3   2   0  95
 12    0   0  178    49    1  282    1   23   29    0   782    3   2   0  95
 13    0   0  114    44    1  175    1   13   26    0   446    3   1   0  96
 14    0   0   61    33    1   40    0    4   11    0   364    3   1   0  96
 15    0   0  261    52    7   60    0    6   10    0    90    0   1   0  99
```

The results are from a system with 4 cores and 4 threads per core (16 virtual processors). Typically, a system administrator will use the `mpstat` command to check CPU use. In this example, I look at the `idl` column (percent idle time) and see that the server's CPUs are approximately 99% idle.

Use the `mpstat` command to look for load imbalances between processors.

The fields displayed by the `mpstat` command are as follows:

- `CPU`: Displays the processor ID
- `minf`: Displays the number of minor faults in the system
- `mjf`: Displays the number of major faults in the system
- `xcal`: Displays the number of interprocessor cross-calls
- `intr`: Displays the number of interrupts in the system
- `ithr`: Displays the number of thread interrupts, excluding the clock interrupt
- `csw`: Displays the number of context switches
- `icsw`: Displays the number of involuntary context switches
- `migr`: Displays the number of thread migrations to another processor
- `smtx`: Displays the number of spins on mutual exclusion locks that fail on the first try and the number of times the CPU fails to obtain a mutex immediately
- `srw`: Displays the number of spins on reader and writer locks that fail on the first try
- `syscl`: Displays the number of system calls

- usr: Displays the percentage of user time
- sys: Displays the percentage of system time
- wt: Displays the percentage of wait time
- idl: Displays the percentage of idle time

For more information on the other columns of information, refer to the mpstat(1M) man pages.

ptree

The ptree command will display the process tree. The parent process is displayed with the respective child processes indented beneath it. Here is an example showing the processes that belong to the ssh process (PID 4681):

```
$ ptree 4681<cr>
4670  /usr/bin/gnome-terminal -x /bin/sh -c cd '/home/train' && exec $SHELL
  4673  /usr/bin/bash
    4681  ssh 192.168.1.221
```

With no arguments, the ptree command will display every process along with the associated child processes.

time

The time command is used to display the time that the system has spent executing a command. It's a useful command for benchmarking performance. Use this command to time a command on a particular system configuration and compare to another system. In the following example, I'll check the system processing time for a script I wrote named "longtime":

```
# time ./longtime<cr>
```

The system displays

```
real    14.7
user     9.9
sys      2.3
```

The `real` time is the total time that has elapsed between invoking the script and its termination. The `user` time is the time the processor spends executing your user code. Finally, the `system` time is the time the processor spends executing OS code on behalf of your process.

svcs

SMF was described in Chapter 3, "Boot and Shutdown Procedures for SPARC and x86-Based Systems," so I won't be redundant by describing it again here. However, this is just a reminder that you can use the `svcs` command with the `-p` option to list all processes associated with each service instance.

Proc Tools and /proc

Oracle Solaris process tools, called "proc tools," are a set of tools (utilities) that exercise features of `proc(4)`. `/proc` is a file system that provides access to the state of each process and LWP in the system. Images of active processes are stored in the `/proc` file system by their PID. You can display detailed information about processes that are listed in the `/proc` directory by using the proc tools. To read more on the `/proc` file system, refer to the `proc(4)` man pages. Table 8-11 lists the proc tools available in Oracle Solaris.

Table 8-11 Proc Tools

Command	Description
`pstop`	Freezes a process
`prun`	Continues a process
`preap`	Reaps zombie (defunct) processes
`pstack`	Inspects stack backtraces for each process or specified LWPs
`pmap`	Views information about the address space for a process
`pfiles`	Lists file descriptor and open file details in each process
`ptime`	Times a command; similar to `time(1)`
`psig`	Lists signal actions and handlers of each process
`pldd`	Lists dynamic libraries linked to each process
`pflags`	Lists the `/proc` tracing flags linked into each process
`pcred`	Lists process credentials

Command	Description
pargs	Lists arguments and environment variables for a process
pwdx	Lists the current working directory for a process
plockstat	Observes lock activity
truss	Traces system calls and signals for a process
dtrace	Safely traces any process activity, with minimal effect on the process and system

The commands I've described so far in this chapter are mainly process status tools. The additional proc tools in this section are classified as control tools, inspection tools, activity examination tools, and tracing tools. These tools read their statistics from the /proc file system.

Each proc tool typically uses a PID as an argument. The following example uses the pstop command to freeze PID 1112:

```
# pstop 1112<cr>
```

The pfiles command is useful for determining operational dependencies between data files and applications. The next example uses the pfiles command to list the file descriptors and open files associated with PID 3556 (cron):

```
# pfiles 3556<cr>
3556:  /usr/sbin/cron
  Current rlimit: 256 file descriptors
   0: S_IFCHR mode:0666 dev:542,1 ino:913901477 uid:0 gid:3 rdev:165,2
      O_RDONLY|O_LARGEFILE
      /rpool/z1/root/dev/null
      offset:0
   1: S_IFREG mode:0600 dev:195,65555 ino:4239 uid:0 gid:0 size:397
      O_WRONLY|O_APPEND|O_CREAT|O_LARGEFILE
      /rpool/z1/root/var/cron/log
      offset:397
   2: S_IFREG mode:0600 dev:195,65555 ino:4239 uid:0 gid:0 size:397
      O_WRONLY|O_APPEND|O_CREAT|O_LARGEFILE
      /rpool/z1/root/var/cron/log
     offset:397
   3: S_IFIFO mode:0600 dev:547,3 ino:915284190 uid:0 gid:0 size:0
      O_RDWR|O_LARGEFILE
      /rpool/z1/root/system/volatile/cronfifo
```

The pstack command will print a hexadecimal format stack trace for the LWPs, much like the truss command. The pstack command can be beneficial in finding where a process may be spending a majority of its time. In this next example, I'll use the `pstack` command on process 3556:

```
# pstack 3556<cr>
3556:  /usr/sbin/cron
 feed8305 pollsys (8047b60, 1, 8047bf8, 806e058)
 fee82e18 pselect (4, 8047c00, 0, 0, 8047bf8, 806e058) + 190
 08057e62 msg_wait(10ee0, 806e690, feed78d5, 80716d8) + 8e
 08057987 idle    (10ee0, 504dd4e8, 8047dc8, 8053ab7) + 23
 08053ad8 main    (1, 8047df4, 8047dfc, 80536bf) + 31c
 0805371d _start  (1, 8047eb0, 0, 8047ebf, 8047ed6, 8047edd) + 7d
```

Use the `psig` command to list the signal handlers of a process. In this example, I'll list how PID 3556 handles signals (signals are covered in the "Using Signals" section later in this chapter):

```
# psig 3556<cr>
3556:   /usr/sbin/cron
HUP     ignored
INT     ignored
QUIT    ignored
ILL     default
TRAP    default
ABRT    default
EMT     default
FPE     default
...<output has been truncated>...
```

Print out the credentials of a process using the `pcred` command as follows:

```
# pcred 3556<cr>
3556:  e/r/suid=0  e/r/sgid=0
       groups: 0 1 2 3 4 5 6 7 8 9 12
```

Finally, view which libraries are loaded when a process is executed by using the `pldd` command as follows:

```
# pldd 3556<cr>
3556:    /usr/sbin/cron
/rpool/z1/root/usr/lib/libc/libc_hwcap1.so.1
/rpool/z1/root/lib/libbsm.so.1
/rpool/z1/root/lib/libcontract.so.1
```

Process Types

When sitting at a terminal and typing in commands, the user is typically executing "foreground processes." Commands such as `vi` are foreground processes—they read input from the keyboard and display output to the terminal. Foreground processes maintain control of the terminal, and the user cannot do anything else in that terminal window until the execution of that command is complete.

Some processes are not interactive and don't need to run in the foreground. These are referred to as "background processes" or "jobs." A background process gets detached from the terminal, freeing up the terminal while it is running. When a user decides to run a process in the background, you must arrange for the process to get its input from another source. In addition, you need to arrange for the process to output to a device other than the terminal, such as a file.

To run a process in the background, enter an & (ampersand) after the command:

```
# find . -name core -print &<cr>
```

After typing in this command, you're returned to a command prompt. The `find` command executes in the background. One problem, however, is that the standard output is still on your terminal. In other words, as the `find` command executes, the results are still displayed on your screen, which can become quite annoying. It's best to redirect the output to a file, as follows:

```
# find . -name core -print  > /tmp/results &<cr>
```

After you put the `find` command in the background, the system displays two numbers associated with that process—the job number and the PID as follows:

```
[1]  14919
```

You use this job number to control background processes.

No Job Control in the `sh` shell

The Bourne shell does not provide job control. Job control enables you to check and manage your background jobs. Thus, with the Bourne shell, you can submit jobs to the background, but you cannot manage them. Use `jsh` (job shell), which provides all the functionality of `sh` and enables job control. The Korn shell (`ksh`), Bash shell, and the C shell (`csh`) all allow for job control.

The shell maintains a table containing information about processes that are currently in the background. This is referred to as the "jobs table." The jobs table is unique to the user, and each user has his or her own jobs table. Furthermore, the jobs table contains only entries for jobs that are running in your current shell.

If you start a new shell, the jobs table for the new shell is empty. Each job in the table is assigned a number that is unique to that user only. In other words, two users can each have a job numbered 1. Don't confuse this job number with a PID; remember, PIDs are unique, and no two share the same number. Any jobs that the user has placed in the background are displayed here by typing in the `jobs` command, as follows:

```
# jobs<cr>
```

The system responds with this:

```
[3] +  Running  find / -name bill -print > /tmp/results3 &
[2] -  Running  find / -name junk -print > /tmp/results2 &
[1]    Running  find / -name core -print > /tmp/results1 &
```

The jobs table contains the following information:

- A numeric value for each job
- A plus (+) symbol to designate the current job on which user commands will operate
- A minus (–) symbol to designate the next job on which the user commands will operate
- The status of the job
- The name of the job

Each job in the jobs table has one of the following states:

- `Running`—An active job
- `Stopped`—A job that has been suspended
- `Terminated`—A job that has been killed
- `Done`—A completed job

When the job finishes, the following is displayed on your terminal:

```
[1] +  Done    find / -name core -print > /tmp/results &
```

Note the job number of `1` and the status of `Done`.

If you want to terminate a job, use the `kill` command followed by a percent sign (`%`) and then the job number, as follows:

```
# kill %1<cr>
```

Note

Pay special attention to the use of the percent (%) symbol—it's absolutely required. Without it, you could kill a process and not a job and potentially crash the system. Get familiar with the `kill` command (in the next section of this chapter) before you use it.

If you do not enter a number following the `%` sign, the command acts upon the current job entry listed in the jobs table. For this example, you are going to kill job number 1, as follows:

```
# kill %<cr>
```

The following message is displayed, indicating successful termination:

```
[1] + Terminated  find / -name core -print > /tmp/results &
```

You can also bring a job back into the foreground with the `fg` command. Typing `fg` with no arguments brings the current job (the job with the + sign next to it in the jobs table) into the foreground. You can also specify the job by typing `fg %`<*`job number`*>, as follows:

```
# fg %2<cr>
```

This brings job 2 back into the foreground on your terminal.

In a windowing environment such as Java Desktop System, placing jobs in the background is not an issue. Typically, you start a job in one window and open another window to continue working. Therefore, placing jobs into the background has all but disappeared unless you are working on a character-based terminal or a system console.

Using Signals

Oracle Solaris supports the concept of sending software signals to a process. These signals are ways for other processes to interact with a running process outside the context of the hardware. The `kill` command is used to send a signal to a process. System administrators most often use the signals `SIGHUP`, `SIGKILL`, `SIGSTOP`, and `SIGTERM`. The `SIGHUP` signal is used by some utilities as a way to notify the process to do something, such as re-read its configuration file. The `SIGHUP` signal is also sent to a process if the remote connection is lost or hangs up. The `SIGKILL` signal is used to abort a process, and the `SIGSTOP` signal is used to pause a process. The `SIGTERM` signal is the default signal sent to processes by commands such as `kill` and `pkill` when no signal is specified. List all of the signals available in Oracle Solaris by typing:

```
# kill -l<cr>
```

The signals will be listed as follows:

```
 1) SIGHUP         2) SIGINT         3) SIGQUIT        4) SIGILL         5) SIGTRAP
 6) SIGABRT        7) SIGEMT         8) SIGFPE         9) SIGKILL       10) SIGBUS
11) SIGSEGV       12) SIGSYS        13) SIGPIPE       14) SIGALRM       15) SIGTERM
16) SIGUSR1       17) SIGUSR2       18) SIGCHLD       19) SIGPWR        20) SIGWINCH
21) SIGURG        22) SIGIO         23) SIGSTOP       24) SIGTSTP       25) SIGCONT
26) SIGTTIN       27) SIGTTOU       28) SIGVTALRM     29) SIGPROF       30) SIGXCPU
31) SIGXFSZ       32) SIGWAITING    33) SIGLWP        34) SIGFREEZE     35) SIGTHAW
36) SIGCANCEL     37) SIGLOST       38) SIGXRES       39) SIGJVM1       40) SIGJVM2
41) SIGRTMIN      42) SIGRTMIN+1    43) SIGRTMIN+2    44) SIGRTMIN+3    45) SIGRTMIN+4
46) SIGRTMIN+5    47) SIGRTMIN+6    48) SIGRTMIN+7    49) SIGRTMIN+8    50) SIGRTMIN+9
51) SIGRTMIN+10   52) SIGRTMIN+11   53) SIGRTMIN+12   54) SIGRTMIN+13   55) SIGRTMIN+14
56) SIGRTMIN+15   57) SIGRTMAX-15   58) SIGRTMAX-14   59) SIGRTMAX-13   60) SIGRTMAX-12
61) SIGRTMAX-11   62) SIGRTMAX-10   63) SIGRTMAX-9    64) SIGRTMAX-8    65) SIGRTMAX-7
66) SIGRTMAX-6    67) SIGRTMAX-5    68) SIGRTMAX-4    69) SIGRTMAX-3    70) SIGRTMAX-2
71) SIGRTMAX-1    72) SIGRTMAX
```

For a complete description of signals, refer to the `signal(3HEAD)` man pages as follows:

```
# man -s3head signal<cr>
```

You can write a signal handler, or trap, in a program to respond to a signal being sent. For example, many system programs, such as the name server daemon, respond to the `SIGHUP` signal by re-reading their configuration files. This signal can then be used to update the process while running, without having to terminate and restart the process. Signal handlers cannot be installed for `SIGSTOP` (23) or `SIGKILL` (9). Because the process cannot install a signal handler for signal 9, an otherwise well-behaved process may leave temporary files around or may not be able to finish critical operations that it is in the middle of performing. Thus, `kill -9` invites corruption of application data files and should only be used as a last resort.

Here's an example of how to trap a signal in a script:

```
trap '/bin/rm tmp$$;exit 1' 1 2 3 15
```

As the name suggests, `trap` traps system interrupt until some command can be executed. The previous example traps the signals 1, 2, 3, and 15 and executes the `/bin/rm tmp$$` command before exiting the program. The example deletes all `tmp` files even if the program terminates abnormally.

Review all of the signal handles (traps) for a process by issuing the `psig` command. For example, to review the signal actions and handlers for PID 3556 (`cron`), type the following:

```
# psig 3556<cr>
3556:   /usr/sbin/cron
HUP     ignored
INT     ignored
QUIT    ignored
ILL     default
TRAP    default
ABRT    default
EMT     default
FPE     default
KILL    default
BUS     default
SEGV    default
SYS     default
PIPE    default
ALRM    default
TERM    caught      cronend  RESETHAND,NODEFER
USR1    default
USR2    default
CLD     caught      child_handler   0         CLD
PWR     default
WINCH   default
URG     default
POLL    default
STOP    default
TSTP    ignored
CONT    default
...<output is truncated>...
```

The `kill` command sends a terminate signal (signal 15) to the process, and the process is terminated. Signal 15, which is the default when no options are used with the `kill` command, is a gentle kill that allows a process to perform cleanup work before terminating. Signal 9, on the other hand, is called a sure, unconditional kill because it cannot be caught or ignored by a process. If the process is still around after a `kill -9`, either it is hung up in the UNIX kernel, waiting for an event such as disk I/O to complete, or you are not the owner of the process.

The `kill` command is routinely used to send signals to a process. You can kill any process you own, and the superuser can kill all processes in the system except those that have PIDs 0, 1, 2, 3, and 4. The kill command is poorly named because not every signal sent by it is used to kill a process. This command gets its name from its most common use—terminating a process with the kill -15 signal.

Forking Problem

A common problem occurs when a process continually starts up new copies of itself—this is referred to as forking or spawning. Users have a limit on the number of new processes they can fork. This limit is set in the kernel with the MAXUP (maximum number of user processes) value. Sometimes, through user error, a process keeps forking new copies of itself until the user hits the MAXUP limit. As a user reaches this limit, the system appears to be waiting. If you kill some of the user's processes, the system resumes creating new processes on behalf of the user. It can be a no-win situation. The best way to handle these runaway processes is to send the STOP signal to all of the runaway processes to suspend the processes and then send a KILL signal to terminate the processes. Because the processes were first suspended, they can't create new ones as you kill them off.

You can send a signal to a process you own with the kill command. Many signals are available, as listed with the kill -l command. To send a signal to a process, first use the ps command to find the PID. For example, type ps -ef to list all processes and find the PID of the process you want to terminate:

```
# ps -ef<cr>
  UID   PID    PPID          C        TIME  TTY    TIME CMD
  root    0       0          0   04:29:34    ?     0:04 sched
  root    5       0          0   04:29:30    ?     0:05 zpool-rpool
  root    6       0          0   04:29:35    ?     0:00 kmem_task
  root    1       0          0   04:29:35    ?     0:00 /usr/sbin/init
  root    2       0          0   04:29:35    ?     0:00 pageout
  root    3       0          0   04:29:35    ?     0:07 fsflush
  root    7       0          0   04:29:35    ?     0:00 intrd
...<Output has been truncated>...
```

To kill the process with a PID number of 3556, type this:

```
# kill 3556<cr>
```

Another way to kill a process is to use the pkill command. pkill functions identically to pgrep, which was described earlier, except that instead of displaying information about each process, the process is terminated. A signal name or number may be specified as the first command-line option to pkill. The value for the signal can be any value displayed by the kill -l command. For example, to kill the process named psef with a SIGKILL signal, issue the following command:

```
# pkill -9 psef<cr>
```

Killing a Process

If no signal is specified, `SIGTERM` (15) is sent by default. This is the preferred signal to send when trying to kill a process. Only when a `SIGTERM` fails should you send a `SIGKILL` (9) signal to a process. As stated earlier in this section, a process cannot install a signal handler for `SIGKILL`. A `SIGKILL` could cause an otherwise well-behaved process to leave temporary files around or interrupt critical operations that the process may be performing.

The `preap` command is a process-control tool that forces the killing of a defunct process, known as a "zombie." In previous Oracle Solaris releases, zombie processes that could not be killed off remained until the next system reboot. Defunct processes do not normally affect system operation; however, they do consume a small amount of system memory. See the `preap(1)` manual page for further details of this command.

Scheduling Processes

Processes compete for execution time. Scheduling, one of the key elements in a time-sharing system, determines which of the processes executes next. Although hundreds of processes might be present on the system, only one actually uses a given CPU at any given time. Time sharing on a CPU involves suspending a process and then restarting it later. Because the suspension and resumption of active processes occurs many times each second, it appears to the user that the system is performing many tasks simultaneously.

UNIX attempts to manage the priorities of processes by giving a higher priority to those that have used the least amount of CPU time. In addition, processes that are waiting on an event, such as a keyboard press, get higher priority than processes that are purely CPU driven.

On any large system with a number of competing user groups, the task of managing resources falls to the system administrator. This task is both technical and political. As a system administrator, you must understand your company goals to manage this task successfully. When you understand the political implications of who should get priority, you are ready to manage the technical details. As root, you can change the priority of any process on the system by using the `nice` or `priocntl` commands. Before you do this, you must understand how priorities work.

Scheduling Priorities

All processes have assigned to them an execution priority—an integer value that is dynamically computed and updated on the basis of several different factors. Whenever the CPU is free, the scheduler selects the most favored process to resume executing. The process selected is the one with the lowest-priority number because lower numbers are defined as more favored than higher ones. Multiple processes at the same priority level are placed in the run queue for that priority level. Whenever the CPU is free, the scheduler starts the processes at the head of the lowest-numbered nonempty run queue. When the process at the top of a run queue stops executing, it goes to the end of the line and the next process moves up to the front. After a process begins to run, it continues to execute until it needs to wait for an I/O operation to complete, receives an interrupt signal, or exhausts the maximum execution time slice defined on that system. A typical time slice is 10 milliseconds.

A UNIX process has two priority numbers associated with it. One of the priority numbers is its requested execution priority with respect to other processes. This value (its `nice` number) is set by the process's owner and by root; it appears in the `NI` column in a `ps -l` listing. The other priority assigned to a process is the execution priority. This priority is computed and updated dynamically by the OS, taking into account such factors as the process's `nice` number, how much CPU time it has had recently, and other processes that are running and their priorities. The execution priority value appears in the `PRI` column on a `ps -l` listing.

Although the CPU is the most-watched resource on a system, it is not the only one. Memory use, disk use, I/O activity, and the number of processes all tie together in determining the computer's throughput. For example, suppose you have two groups, A and B. Both groups require large amounts of memory—more than is available when both are running simultaneously. Raising the priority of Group A over Group B might not help if Group B does not fully relinquish the memory it is using. Although the paging system does this over time, the process of swapping a process out to disk can be intensive and can greatly reduce performance. A better alternative might be to completely stop Group B with a signal and then continue it later, when Group A has finished.

Changing the Priority of a Time-Sharing Process with `nice`

The `nice` command is supported only for backward compatibility with previous Oracle Solaris releases. The `priocntl` command provides more flexibility in managing processes. The priority of a process is determined by the policies of its scheduling class and by its `nice` number. Each time-sharing process has a global priority that is calculated by adding the user-supplied priority, which can be influenced by the `nice` or `priocntl` commands and the system-calculated priority.

The execution priority number of a process is assigned by the OS and is determined by several factors, including its schedule class, how much CPU time it has used, and its `nice` number. Each time-sharing process starts with a default `nice` number, which it inherits from its parent process. The `nice` number is shown in the `NI` column of the `ps` report.

A user can lower the priority of a process by increasing its user-supplied priority number. Only the superuser can increase the priority of a process by lowering its nice value. This prevents users from increasing the priorities of their own processes, thereby monopolizing a greater share of the CPU.

Two versions of the nice command are available: the standard version, /usr/bin/nice, and a version that is integrated into the C shell as a C-shell built-in. /usr/bin/nice numbers range from 0 to +39 and the default value is 20, while the C-shell built-in version of nice has values that range from –20 to +20. The lower the number, the higher the priority and the faster the process runs.

Use the /usr/bin/nice command as described in Table 8-12 when submitting a program or command.

Note

Root may run commands with a priority higher than normal by using a negative increment, such as –10. A negative increment assigned by an unprivileged user is ignored.

As a system administrator, you can use the renice command to change the priority of a process after it has been submitted. The renice command has the following form:

```
renice priority -n <value> -p <pid>
```

Use the ps -elf command to find the PID of the process for which you want to change the priority. The process that you want to change in the following example is named "largejob":

```
# ps -elf|grep largejob<cr>
9 S  0  8200  4100  0  84  20  f0274e38  193      Jun 04 ?  0:00 largejob
```

Table 8-12 Setting Priorities with nice

Command	Description
Lowering the Priority of a Process Using /usr/bin/nice	
nice *<process_name>*	Increases the nice number by 4 units (the default)
nice -4 *<process_name>*	Increases the nice number by 4 units
nice -10 *<process_name>*	Increases the nice number by 10 units
Increasing the Priority of a Process	
nice -n -10 *<process_name>*	Raises the priority of the command by lowering the nice number

Issue the following command to increase the priority of PID 8200:

```
renice -n -4 -p 8200
```

Issuing the `ps -elf` command again shows the process with a higher priority:

```
# ps -elf|grep largejob<cr>
9 S  0  8200  4100  0  60  16  f0274e38  193    Jun 04  ?  0:00  largejob
```

Process Scheduler

Although system performance tuning is not the objective of this book, I feel it's necessary to describe how processes are scheduled in Oracle Solaris. It is the system administrator's responsibility to prioritize the processes and control their load distribution across all of the system's resources such as the CPUs, memory, and the network. The function of the OS's kernel is to allocate these processes across the system resources using the process scheduler, also called the "dispatcher." The process scheduler is managed by the SMF service `svc:/system/scheduler:default`. The process scheduler supports the concept of scheduling classes. Each class defines a scheduling policy that is used to schedule processes within the class. The scheduling policy of a process determines its priority in the queue.

Oracle Solaris supports several process-scheduling classes that can be configured on the system. It's the system administrator's responsibility to choose the proper scheduling class for a project. The possible process scheduling classes in Oracle Solaris are as follows:

- Fair share (FSS)
- Fixed (FX)
- System (SYS)
- Interactive (IA)
- Real-time (RT)
- Time-sharing (TS)

By default, Oracle Solaris uses the time-sharing (TS) scheduling class for conventional work. Priorities in this class are dynamically adjusted in an attempt to allocate processor resources evenly. An enhanced version of the TS scheduling class is the interactive (IA) class.

Oracle Solaris also offers the real-time (RT) scheduling class, which implements a weighted scheduling policy to ensure that specific workloads or processes get immediate access to the processor. Threads running in the RT class are of fixed priority with a fixed-time duration called “quantum.” Oracle Solaris Resource Manager has no control over any process running in the RT class.

FSS

FSS is a share-based rather than a priority-based scheduler. Although the TS scheduler is the default, The FSS is the preferred scheduler. Threads managed by FSS are scheduled based on their associated shares and the processor use. The FSS allows the system administrator to specify that certain processes should be given more resources than others. This can be beneficial when trying to balance workloads for multiple projects in non-global zones.

The FSS scheduler limits CPU usage only if there is competition for CPU resources between projects. Projects were described earlier in the “`prstat`” section of this chapter and also in Chapter 7. When competition is low, FSS allows a single active project to consume 100% of the CPU, irrespective of the number of shares that were allocated. When a project is not using all of the CPU resources to which it is entitled, the remaining CPU resources are distributed between other active processes.

The scheduling priority of a process is the priority assigned by the process scheduler. Use the process scheduler administration command, `dispadmin`, to list the default scheduling policies as follows:

```
# dispadmin -d<cr>
dispadmin: Default scheduling class is not set
```

The `-d` option is used to display the name of the default scheduling class to be used on reboot or when starting the `svc:/system/scheduler:default` service. If a class name is not specified with the `dispadmin -d` command, as in the previous example, the name and description of the current default scheduling class is displayed. In the previous example, a scheduling class is not been set.

Furthermore, the `priocntl` command can also be used to display process scheduling classes and priority ranges as follows:

```
# priocntl -l<cr>
CONFIGURED CLASSES
==================
SYS (System Class)
TS (Time Sharing)
      Configured TS User Priority Range: -60 through 60
SDC (System Duty-Cycle Class)
FX (Fixed priority)
       Configured FX User Priority Range: 0 through 60
```

To set the scheduling class to the FSS, type the following:

```
# dispadmin -d FSS<cr>
#
```

Now the default scheduler is set to the FSS. Restart the `svc:/system/scheduler:default` service to put the scheduler into effect as follows:

```
# svcadm restart svc:/system/scheduler:default<cr>
```

Verify the default scheduler as follows:

```
# dispadmin -d<cr>
FSS  (Fair Share)
```

The `priocntl` command also shows the change:

```
# priocntl -l<cr>
CONFIGURED CLASSES
==================
SYS (System Class)
TS (Time Sharing)
        Configured TS User Priority Range: -60 through 60
SDC (System Duty-Cycle Class)
FX (Fixed priority)
        Configured FX User Priority Range: 0 through 60
IA (Interactive)
        Configured IA User Priority Range: -60 through 60
FSS (Fair Share)
        Configured FSS User Priority Range: -60 through 60
```

The scheduling classes, along with their priority ranges, are displayed for each class. You need to know these ranges when you designate a priority of a process using the `priocntl` command.

The `-c` option to the `ps` command can be used to display information about scheduler properties for processes. Display the priority of a process using the `ps` command as follows:

```
# ps -ecl|more<cr>
 F S   UID   PID   PPID    CLS   PRI   ADDR     SZ   WCHAN TTY      TIME CMD
 1 T     0     0      0    SYS    96      ?      0         ?        0:04 sched
 1 S     0     5      0    SDC    99      ?      0       ? ?        0:02 zpool-rp
 1 S     0     6      0    SDC    99      ?      0       ? ?        0:00 kmem_tas
 0 S     0     1      0    FSS    29      ?    718       ? ?        0:00 init
 1 S     0     2      0    SYS    98      ?      0       ? ?        0:00 pageout
 1 S     0     3      0    SYS    60      ?      0       ? ?        0:00 fsflush
 1 S     0     7      0    SYS    60      ?      0       ? ?        0:00 intrd
 1 S     0     8      0    SDC    99      ?      0       ? ?        0:00 vmtasks
 0 S     0   187      1    FSS    29      ?    442       ? ?        0:00 utmpd
 0 S     0    11      1    FSS    29      ?   4434       ? ?        0:03 svc.star
...<output has been truncated>...
 0 S     0  1767      1    FSS    29      ?   1439       ? ?        0:00 gvfsd-me
 0 S     0  1769      1    FSS    29      ?  30938       ? ?        0:01 gnome-te
 0 S     0  1771   1769    FSS    29      ?    596       ? ?        0:00 gnome-pt
 0 S     0  1772   1769    FSS     1      ?    849       ? pts/1    0:00 bash
```

The `zpool-rp` process has one of the highest priorities, showing a PRI value of 99, whereas the `bash` process has the lowest priority of 1.

As described earlier, I can use the `priocntl` command to display or set scheduling parameters for a specified process. You can even use this command to move processes to another scheduling class without rebooting. `priocntl` can be used to display the current configuration information for the system's process scheduler, as shown earlier, or it can be used to execute a command with the specified scheduling (`-c` option) and priority (`-p`) value.

Using the Oracle Solaris Batch-Processing Facility

A way to divide processes on a busy system is to schedule jobs so that they run at different times. A large job, for example, could be scheduled to run at 2:00 AM, when the system would normally be idle. Oracle Solaris supports two methods of batch processing: the `crontab` and `at` commands. The `crontab` command schedules multiple system events at regular intervals, and the `at` command schedules a single system event.

Configure `crontab`

`cron(1M)` is an Oracle Solaris utility named after Chronos, the ancient Greek god of time. It enables you to execute commands automatically according to a schedule you define. The `/usr/sbin/cron` daemon schedules system events according to commands found in each `crontab` file. A `crontab` file consists of commands, one per line, that will be executed at regular intervals. The beginning of each line contains five date and time fields that tell the `cron` daemon when to execute the command. The sixth field is the full pathname of the program you want to run. These fields, described in Table 8-13, are separated by spaces.

Table 8-13 The `crontab` File

Field	Description	Values
1	Minute	0 to 59: A * in this field means every minute.
2	Hour	0 to 23: A * in this field means every hour.
3	Day of month	1 to 31: A * in this field means every day of the month.
4	Month	1 to 12: A * in this field means every month.
5	Day of week	0 to 6: A * in this field means every day of the week (0 = Sunday).
6	Command	Enter the command to be run.

Follow these guidelines when making entries in the crontab file:

- Use a space to separate fields.
- Use a comma to separate multiple values in any of the date or time fields.
- Use a hyphen to designate a range of values in any of the date or time fields.
- Use an asterisk as a wildcard to include all possible values in any of the date or time fields. For example, an asterisk (*) can be used in the first five fields (time fields) to mean all legal values.
- Use a comment mark (#) at the beginning of a line to indicate a comment or a blank line.
- Each command within a crontab file must consist of one line, even if it is very long, because crontab does not recognize extra carriage returns.
- There can be no blank lines in the crontab file. Although this is not documented well, and some crontab files I've seen contain blank lines, the system will generate an e-mail to root with a message that "there is an error in your crontab file."

The following sample crontab command entry displays a reminder in the user's console window at 5:00 PM on the 1st and 15th of every month:

```
0 17 1,15 * * echo Hand in Timesheet > /dev/console
```

crontab files are found in the /var/spool/cron/crontabs directory. Several crontab files besides root are provided during the SunOS software installation process; they are also located in this directory. Other crontab files are named after the user accounts for which they are created, such as bill, glenda, calvin, or nicole. They also are located in the /var/spool/cron/crontabs directory. For example, a crontab file named "root" is supplied during software installation. Its contents include these lines:

```
10 3 * * * /usr/sbin/logadm
15 3 * * 0 /usr/lib/fs/nfs/nfsfind && /usr/lib/fs/nfs/nfsfind
30 3 * * * [ -x /usr/lib/gss/gsscred_clean ] && /usr/lib/gss/gsscred_clean
```

The first command line instructs the system to run /usr/sbin/logadmin at 3:10 AM every day of the week. The second command line orders the system to execute nfsfind on Sunday at 3:15 AM. The third command line runs each night at 3:30 AM and executes the gsscred command. The cron daemon never exits and is started via the svc:/system/cron:default service. The /etc/cron.d/FIFO file is used as a lock file to prevent running more than one instance of cron.

Creating and Editing a `crontab` File

Creating an entry in the `crontab` file is as easy as editing a text file using your favorite editor. Use the steps described next to edit this file; otherwise, your changes are not recognized until the next time the `cron` daemon starts up. `cron` examines `crontab` configuration files only during its own process-initialization phase or when the `crontab` command is run. This reduces the overhead of checking for new or changed files at regularly scheduled intervals. The following steps describe how to create or edit a `crontab` file.

1. To create or edit a `crontab` file belonging to root or another user, become the superuser.
2. Create a new `crontab` file or edit an existing one by typing the following:

```
# crontab -e<cr>
```

`crontab` Default Editor

The `crontab` command chooses the system default editor, which is `ed`, unless you've set the `VISUAL` or `EDITOR` variable to `vi` (or another editor), as follows:

```
# EDITOR=vi;export EDITOR<cr>
```

3. Add command lines to the file following the syntax described in Table 8-13. Because `cron` jobs do not inherit the user's environment, such as `PATH`, you should specify the full pathname for commands.
4. Save the changes and exit the file. The `crontab` file is placed in the `/var/spool/cron/crontabs` directory.
5. Verify the `crontab` file by typing the following:

```
# crontab -l<cr>
```

The system responds by listing the contents of the `crontab` file.

Control Access to `crontab`

You can control access to `crontab` by modifying two files in the `/etc/cron.d` directory: `cron.deny` and `cron.allow`. These files permit only specified users to perform `crontab` tasks such as creating, editing, displaying, and removing their own crontab files. The cron.deny and cron.allow files consist of a list of usernames, one per line. These access control files work together in the following manner:

- If cron.allow exists, only the users listed in this file can create, edit, display, and remove crontab files.
- If cron.allow doesn't exist, all users may submit crontab files, except for users listed in cron.deny.
- If neither cron.allow nor cron.deny exists, superuser privileges are required to run crontab.

Superuser privileges are required to edit or create cron.deny and cron.allow.

During the Oracle Solaris software installation process, a default /etc/cron.d/cron.deny file is provided. It contains the following entries:

- daemon
- bin
- nuucp

None of the users listed in the cron.deny file can access crontab commands. The system administrator can edit this file to add other users who are denied access to the crontab command. No default cron.allow file is supplied. This means that, after the Oracle Solaris software installation, all users (except the ones listed in the default cron.deny file) can access crontab. If you create a cron.allow file, only those users can access crontab commands.

Scheduling a Single System Event (at)

The at(1) command is used to schedule jobs for execution at a later time. Unlike crontab, which schedules a job to happen at regular intervals, a job submitted with at executes once, at the designated time.

To submit an at job, type at followed by the time that you would like the program to execute. You'll see the at> prompt displayed, and it's here that you enter the at command. When you are finished entering the at command, press *Ctrl+D* to exit the at prompt and submit the job as shown in the following example:

```
# at 07:45am today<cr>
at> who > /tmp/log<cr>
at> <Press Control+d>
job 912687240.a at Thu Jun 6 07:14:00
```

When you submit an at job, it is assigned a job identification number, which becomes its filename along with the .a extension. The file is stored in the /var/

spool/cron/atjobs directory. In much the same way as it schedules crontab jobs, the cron daemon controls the scheduling of at files.

The command syntax for at is shown here:

```
# at [-m -l -r] <time> <date>
```

The at command is described in Table 8-14.

You can set up a file to control access to the at command, permitting only specified users to create, remove, or display queue information about their at jobs. The file that controls access to at is /etc/cron.d/at.deny. It consists of a list of usernames, one per line. The users listed in this file cannot access at commands. The default at.deny file, created during the SunOS software installation, contains the following usernames:

- daemon
- bin
- nuucp

Table 8-14 at Command Syntax

Option	Description
-m	Sends you mail after the job is completed.
-c	Executes the job in the C-shell.
-k	Executes the job in the Korn shell.
-s	Executes the job in the Bourne shell.
-f <*file*>	Specifies the path to a file to be used as the source of the at job.
-l	Reports all jobs for the user.
-p <*project*>	Specifies under which project the at or batch job is run.
-q <*queuename*>	Specifies in which queue to schedule a job.
-r <*jobID*>	Removes a specified job.
-t <*time*>	Submits the job to be run at the time specified; the time option must have the format as specified by the touch(1) command.
<*time*>	The hour when you want to schedule the job; add AM or PM if you do not specify the hours according to a 24-hour clock (midnight, noon, and now are acceptable keywords; minutes are optional).
<*date*>	The first three or more letters of a month, a day of the week, or the keywords "today" or "tomorrow".

With superuser privileges, you can edit this file to add other usernames whose `at` access you want to restrict.

Checking Jobs in Queue (`atq` and `at -l`)

To check your jobs that are waiting in the `at` queue, use the `atq(1)` command. This command displays status information about the `at` jobs you created. Use the `atq` command to verify that you have created an `at` job. The `atq` command confirms that `at` jobs have been submitted to the queue, as shown in the following example:

```
# atq<cr>
```

The system responds with this:

```
Rank  Execution Date Owner  Job          Queue    Job Name
1st   Jun   6, 08:00  root   912690000.a    a      stdin
2nd   Jun   6, 08:05  root   912690300.a    a      stdin
```

Another way to check an `at` job is to issue the `at -l` command. This command shows the status information on all jobs submitted by a user, as shown in this example:

```
# at -l<cr>
```

The system responds with this:

```
user = root  912690000.a  Thu Jun  6 08:00:00
user = root  912690300.a  Thu Jun  6 08:05:00
```

Removing and Verifying Removal of `at` Jobs

To remove the `at` job from the queue before it is executed, type this:

```
# at -r [job-id]
```

`job-id` is the identification number of the job you want to remove.

Verify that the `at` job has been removed by using the `at -l` (or `atq`) command to display the jobs remaining in the `at` queue. The job whose identification number you specified should not appear. In the following example, you'll remove an `at` job that was scheduled to execute at 8:00 AM on June 6. First, check the at queue to locate the job identification number:

```
# at -l<cr>
```

The system responds with this:

```
user = root  912690000.a  Thu Jun  6 08:00:00
user = root  912690300.a  Thu Jun  6 08:05:00
```

Next, remove the job from the at queue:

```
# at -r 912690000.a<cr>
```

Finally, verify that this job has been removed from the queue:

```
# at -l<cr>
```

The system responds with this:

```
user = root  912690300.a  Thu Jun  6 08:05:00
```

Configure System Core Files

Process core files are created when a program or application terminates abnormally. Not only can software problems cause core dumps, but so can hardware problems. The default location for a core file to be written is the current working directory. However, as the system administrator, you might want to configure the system so that all core files are written to a central location. This would make administration and management of core files much easier because core files can sometimes take up a significant amount of disk space.

You manage core files by using the coreadm command:

```
coreadm  [-g <pattern>] [-G <content>] [-i <pattern>] [-I <content>] \
[-d <option>...]  [-e <option>...]
coreadm  [-p <pattern>] [-P <content>] [pid]
coreadm -u
```

The options for the coreadm command are described in Table 8-15.

Running `coreadm` with no options displays the current core file configuration. When you use the `coreadm` command to modify the default `coreadm` configuration, the `/etc/coreadm.conf` file is created and contains the current core configuration.

A core file name pattern consists of a file system pathname, along with embedded variables. These variables are specified with a leading `%` character. The values are then expanded when a core file is created. Valid pattern variables are described in Table 8-16.

Table 8-15 `coreadm` Command Options

Option	Description
`-g` *<pattern>*	Sets the global core file name pattern
`-G` *<content>*	Sets the global core file content using one of the description tokens
`-i` *<pattern>*	Sets the per-process core file name pattern
`-I` *<content>*	Sets the per-process core file name to content
`-d` *<option>*	Disables the specified core file option
`-e` *<option>*	Enables the specified core file option
`-p` *<pattern>*	Sets the per-process core filename pattern for each of the specified PIDs
`-P` *<content>*	Sets the per-process core file content to content
`-u`	Updates the system-wide core file options from the configuration file `/etc/coreadm.conf`

Table 8-16 `coreadm` Patterns

Pattern	Description
`%p`	Specifies the PID.
`%u`	Specifies the effective user ID.
`%g`	Specifies the effective group ID.
`%d`	Specifies the executable file directory name.
`%f`	Specifies the executable filename.
`%n`	Specifies the system node name; this is the same as running `uname -n`.
`%m`	Specifies the machine name; this is the same as running `uname -m`.
`%t`	Specifies the decimal value of time, as the number of seconds since 00:00:00 January 1, 1970.
`%z`	Specifies the name of the zone in which the process is executed (zonename).
`%%`	Specifies the literal "%" character.

Table 8-17 `coreadm -d` and `-e` Flag Options

Option	Description
global	Allows core dumps, using the global core pattern
process	Allows core dumps, using the per-process core pattern
global-setid	Allows setid core dumps, using the global core pattern
proc-setid	Allows setid core dumps, using the per-process core pattern
log	Produces a syslog message when an attempt is made to generate a global core file

The -d and -e flags of the coreadm command can take several options. These options are listed in Table 8-17.

To configure the system's core configuration to send a message to the syslogd daemon when a core file has been created, issue the following command:

```
# coreadm -e log<cr>
```

The next steps describe how to modify the core file configuration so that all files are dumped into the directory /cores and named core, followed by the system name and then the name of the program being run.

1. As root, use the coreadm command to display the current coreadm configuration:

```
# coreadm<cr>
     global core file pattern:
     global core file content: default
       init core file pattern: core
            init core file content: default
            global core dumps: disabled
      per-process core dumps: enabled
     global setid core dumps: disabled
per-process setid core dumps: disabled
    global core dump logging: disabled
```

2. As root, issue the following command to change the core file setup:

```
# coreadm -i /cores/core.%n.%f<cr>
```

3. Run coreadm again to verify that the change has been made permanent:

```
# coreadm<cr>
global core file pattern:
global core file content: default
       init core file pattern: /cores/core.%n.%f
       init core file content: default
            global core dumps: disabled
       per-process core dumps: enabled
      global setid core dumps: disabled
 per-process setid core dumps: disabled
     global core dump logging: disabled
```

Use the gcore command to manually generate a core dump of a process. This is useful for verifying your coreadm settings or if you need to generate a core dump for analysis purposes. For example, to create a per-process core image of the current shell, type

```
# gcore -p -g $$<cr>
```

The system responds with this:

```
gcore: /cores/core.sunfire.sh dumped
```

The -p option produces per-process specific content, and the -g option produces a global core file. Various commands such as dbx, mdb, and pstack can be used to analyze a core dump file, but those commands are beyond the scope of this book.

The coreadm process is configured by SMF at system boot time. Use the svcs command to check its status. The service name for this process is svc:/system/coreadm:default.

Configure System Crash Dumps

When a serious error is encountered, the system displays an error message on the console, dumps the entire contents of physical memory to the disk, and then reboots the system. A crash dump is a snapshot of the physical memory, saved on disk, at the time a fatal system error occurs.

Normally, crash dumps are configured to use the swap partition to write the contents of memory. The savecore program runs when the system reboots and saves the image in a predefined location, /var/crash/.

You configure crash dump files by using the dumpadm command. Running this command with no options displays the current configuration, which is obtained from the file /etc/dumpadm.conf:

```
# dumpadm<cr>
```

The system responds with this:

```
Dump content: kernel pages
Dump device: /dev/zvol/dsk/rpool/dump (dedicated)
Savecore directory: /var/crash
  Savecore enabled: yes
  Save compressed: on
```

The following is the syntax of the dumpadm command:

```
/usr/sbin/dumpadm [-nuy] [-c <content-type>] [-d <dump-device>]\
[-m <mink> | <minm> | <min%>]  [-s <savecore-dir>] [-r <root-dir>] [-z <on|off>]
```

The options for the dumpadm command are described in Table 8-18.

Table 8-18 dumpadm Command Syntax

<table>
<tr><th>Option</th><th>Description</th></tr>
<tr><td>-c <content-type></td><td>This option modifies crash dump content. Valid values are kernel (just kernel pages), all (all memory pages), and curproc (kernel pages and currently executing process pages).</td></tr>
<tr><td>-d <dump-device></td><td>This option modifies the dump device. This can be specified either as an absolute pathname (such as dev/zvol/dsk/rpool/dump) or the word swap, in which case the system identifies the best swap area to use.</td></tr>
<tr><td>-m <mink> |</td><td>This option maintains minimum free space in the current savecore directory, <minm> | <min%>

It is specified either in kilobytes, megabytes, or a percentage of the total current size of the directory.</td></tr>
<tr><td>-n</td><td>-n disables savecore from running on reboot. This is not recommended because, with it, any crash dumps would be lost.</td></tr>
<tr><td>-s <savecore-dir></td><td>This option specifies a savecore directory other than the default /var/crash.</td></tr>
</table>

(continues)

Table 8-18 dumpadm Command Syntax (*Continued*)

Option	Description
-u	-u forcibly updates the kernel dump configuration based on the contents of /etc/dumpadm.conf.
-r *<root-dir>*	This option specifies a different root directory. If this option is not used, the default / is used.
-y	The -y option enables savecore to run on the next reboot. This setting is used by default.
-z *<on|off>*	This option modifies the dump configuration to control the operation of savecore on reboot. Use on, to enable saving core files in a compressed format, and off, to automatically uncompress the crash dump file. The default is on.

To change the dedicated ZFS volume for crash dumps, issue the following command:

```
# dumpadm -d dev/zvol/dsk/pool1/dump<cr>
```

The entire ZFS volume is used for a crash dump. The system responds with this:

```
Dump content: kernel pages
Dump device: / dev/zvol/dsk/pool1/dump (dedicated)
Savecore directory: /var/crash
  Savecore enabled: yes
  Save compressed: on
```

For testing purposes, you may want to generate a system crash dump. You can do this by issuing the reboot -d command or by using the savecore -L command to create a live OS core dump. To use the savecore command, you must first use dumpadm to set a nonswap device as the dump device. Another method is to press *Stop+A* to get to the OpenBoot PROM and then type the OBP command sync to force a crash dump.

The dumpadm process is now configured by SMF at system boot time. Use the svcs command to check its status. The service name for this process is svc:/system/dumpadm:default.

Summary

This chapter discussed Oracle Solaris processes and the various utilities available to monitor them. Using commands such as `ps` and `prstat`, you can view all of the attributes associated with a process. In addition, I described foreground and background jobs.

The concept of sending signals to a process was outlined. A signal is a message sent to a process to interrupt it and cause a response or action. You also learned how to send signals to processes to cause a response such as terminating a process.

Setting process priorities was described. I also discussed the concept of projects and tasks along with administrative commands used to manage them. The various commands, such as `nice` and `priocntl`, that are used to set and change process priorities were described. You learned about system scheduling classes and how to set scheduling classes. In addition, you learned how to use the `crontab` and `at` facilities. You can use these facilities to submit batch jobs and schedule processes to run when the system is less busy, to reduce the demand on resources such as the CPU and disks. Last, I described how to manage core files and crash dumps on your system.

The system administrator needs to be aware of the processes that belong to each application. As users report problems, the system administrator can quickly locate the processes being used and look for irregularities. By keeping a close watch on system messages and processes, you'll become familiar with what is normal and what is abnormal. Don't wait for problems to happen—watch system messages and processes daily. Create shell scripts to watch processes for you and to look for irregularities in the system log files. By taking a proactive approach to system administration, you'll find problems before they affect the users.

9

The Oracle Solaris Network Environment

This chapter covers the basics of the Oracle Solaris network environment. It provides you with the fundamental information you need to get started managing an Oracle Solaris system in a networked environment. The topics discussed here include an overview of the client/server model and information on setting up the network interfaces, managing network services, and configuring the services that are started automatically at boot time.

Client/Server Model

The client/server model describes the communication process between computers or programs. When the client makes a service request to the server, the server fulfills that request. Although a system can be both a server and a client, the model is more widely used across a network.

Typical examples of client/server relationships are with DNS and NFS. Both of these topics are described later in this book.

A client is a host or process that uses services from another host or program. A client can also provide services to other client applications.

A server can provide and manage many different services for the client. It is a host or process that provides services to a client. For example, it may provide disk space, windowing, or Web services to a client. The later section titled "RPC Services" describes specifically how the server responds to a client's request for services.

Hosts

If you are an experienced UNIX/Oracle Solaris user, you are no doubt familiar with the term "host," which is often used as a synonym for computer or machine. In Oracle Solaris, you'll also see a computer machine referred to as a "node."

A server and client are both hosts, or nodes, on the network, and each has a hostname (also called a "nodename"). Every system on the network usually has a unique hostname. Hostnames let users refer to any computer on the network by using a short, easily remembered name rather than the host's network IP address.

From a TCP/IP perspective, only two types of entities exist on a network: routers and hosts. When a host initiates communication, it is called a "sending host," or "sender." For example, a host initiates communications when the user uses `ping` or sends an e-mail message to another user. The host that is the target of the communication is called the "receiving host" or "recipient."

Each host has an Internet address and a hardware address that identify it to its peers on the network, and it usually has a hostname. These are described in Table 9-1.

Oracle Solaris TCP/IP

The International Organization for Standardization (ISO) describes the Open Systems Interconnection (OSI) Reference Model as seven layers through which data must travel from one device to another over the network. These layers are also

Table 9-1 Host Information

Identity	Description
Hostname	Every system on the network usually has a unique hostname. Hostnames let users refer to any computer on the network by using a short, easily remembered name rather than the host's network IP address.
Internet address	Each machine on a TCP/IP network has a 32-bit Internet address (or IP address) that identifies the machine to its peers on the network. This address must be unique on the network.
Hardware address	Each host on a network has a unique Ethernet address, also referred to as the media access control (MAC) address. The manufacturer physically assigns this address to the machine's network interface card(s). This address is unique worldwide—not just for the network to which it is connected.

referred to as the "network stack." These structured layers of network activity as described in Table 9-2.

The Internet protocol suite TCP/IP can also be viewed as a network stack in which each layer describes the transmission of data from one device to another over the network. The TCP/IP model has only four layers, whereas the OSI model has seven layers. The TCP/IP model also differs from the OSI Reference Model as follows:

- TCP/IP combines the session and presentation layers into the application layer.
- TCP/IP combines the physical and data-link layers into the network access layer.
- Layer 3 is referred to as the "Internet layer" (also called "network layer" or "IP layer").

The Oracle Solaris implementation of TCP/IP is slightly different from the typical TCP/IP model in that layers 1 and 2 are not combined, as described in Table 9-3.

Table 9-2 OSI Reference Model

Layer	Description
1	Physical
2	Data link
3	Network
4	Transport
5	Session
6	Presentation
7	Application

Table 9-3 Oracle Solaris TCP/IP Model

Layer	Description
1	Physical
2	Data link
3	Internet
4	Transport
5, 6, 7	Session, presentation, application

Network Interface

An Oracle Solaris system normally contains at least one NIC to allow it to participate in a network environment. Each NIC will be given its own unique IP address. When installing the OS, you'll be given the opportunity to configure one NIC as the primary network interface. Any additional interfaces can be configured manually after the installation completes.

If you're familiar with previous versions of Oracle Solaris, you will recognize that network administration has been redesigned in Oracle Solaris 11. Oracle Solaris 11 now provides two options for configuring the network: manual and automatic. You can manually configure the network using the `dladm` and `ipadm` commands from the command line. You can also use the automated feature called "reactive network configuration" (formerly known as "Network Auto-Magic" [NWAM]), which automates and simplifies the network configuration. I'll begin this chapter by describing the manual option and then describe reactive network configuration later in the chapter.

Fixed Network Configuration

The manual administration of the network interface in Oracle Solaris 11 has changed from previous versions of the OS. Network administration is performed by administering the data link using the `dladm` administration command. In addition, you will also need to create and configure an IP interface using the `ipadm` command. The network configuration is now managed entirely through SMF, and the following network configuration files are no longer used in Oracle Solaris 11:

- `/etc/defaultdomain`
- `/etc/dhcp.*`
- `/etc/hostname.*`
- `/etc/hostname.ip*.tun*`
- `/etc/nodename`
- `/etc/nsswitch.conf`

The method used to install the OS on your system will determine the default network settings configured on your system. For example, when installing the OS using the Live Media (GUI) installation, the network is configured to use the automatic network configuration option called reactive network configuration.

For a text installation, you are able to choose which network configuration option to use:

- Automatic
- Manual
- None

Before configuring your network, you should determine which network configuration option your system is currently using by typing the `netadm list` command as follows:

```
# netadm list<cr>
The following output is displayed:

TYPE        PROFILE         STATE
ncp         Automatic       disabled
ncp         DefaultFixed    online
loc         Automatic       offline
loc         NoNet           offline
loc         DefaultFixed    online
```

The `Automatic` profile is disabled and the `DefaultFixed` profile is online, indicating that the reactive network configuration is disabled on this system and this system is using a fixed network configuration. For more information on reactive network configuration and network profiles, refer to the section titled "Reactive Network Configuration" later in this chapter.

Fixed network configuration is much like the manual configuration method that was used on previous versions of Oracle Solaris. But, do not confuse fixed network configuration with simply configuring static IP addresses. In a fixed network configuration, you can assign a DHCP address to an interface. Also, in a fixed configuration, the network configuration remains unchanged regardless of changes in the system's network environment. If changes in that environment occur, such as adding more network interfaces, the system administrator must manually reconfigure the system's network setup to have the system adapt to the new environment.

If the system returns the following list of profiles, where the `Automatic` profile is `online`, your system is using the automatic network configuration option:

```
# netadm list<cr>

TYPE        PROFILE         STATE
ncp         Automatic       online
ncu:phys    net0            online
ncu:ip      net0            online
ncp         DefaultFixed    disabled
loc         Automatic       online
loc         NoNet           offline
```

You should also see the `network/physical:default` service online as follows:

```
# svcs network/physical<cr>
STATE          STIME    FMRI
online          4:11:55  svc:/network/physical:upgrade
online          4:23:29  svc:/network/physical:default
```

Before proceeding with the manual method of configuring your network, ensure that your system is using the manual network configuration method by issuing the following commands:

```
# netadm enable -p ncp DefaultFixed<cr>
```

I describe this command later in the chapter. For a complete description of how to disable the reactive network configuration option, refer to the section titled "Disable the Reactive Network Configuration."

Identifying the Physical Network Interface

When configuring a NIC manually, we begin by identifying the physical NICs that are installed in the system. Use the `dladm show-link` command to identify the network interfaces currently available on the system as follows:

```
# dladm show-link<cr>
LINK                CLASS       MTU      STATE     OVER
net1                phys        1500     down      --
net2                phys        1500     down      --
net0                phys        1500     up        --
net3                phys        1500     down      --
```

Every network interface has a link name that is displayed in the first column, and I'll describe that later. In addition, the CLASS of each link is displayed. The class can be `phys`, `vlan`, `bridge`, `aggr`, etc. In the example, the links are all of the `phys` class. Display more information about the physical links using the `dladm show-phys` command as follows:

```
# dladm show-phys<cr>
LINK              MEDIA          STATE    SPEED    DUPLEX     DEVICE
net1              Ethernet       down     0        unknown    e1000g1
net2              Ethernet       down     0        unknown    e1000g2
net0              Ethernet       up       1000     full       e1000g0
net3              Ethernet       down     0        unknown    e1000g3
```

The physical links (LINK column) are directly associated with a device and possess a device name (DEVICE column), also called the device instance name. The instance name is composed of the driver name (e1000g) and the device instance number (0-n). Typical driver names are nge, nxge, bge, and e1000g. Each link is assigned a device instance number with a value 0 through "n," where "n" is the number of interfaces of that driver type installed on the system. Therefore, in the example, four device instances of the device type e1000g are identified: e1000g0, e1000g1, e1000g2, and e1000g3. This particular system has a four-port NIC installed.

Data Link

The NIC provides the connection between the system and the network. This controller is configured over a data link. A data link corresponds to a device instance. This link name represents the data-link object in the second layer of the TCP/IP model and is used for administrative purposes.

Each hardware device instance in the hardware layer has a corresponding data link on the data-link layer and a configured interface on the interface layer. For example, a hardware device instance (e.g., e1000g0) in the hardware layer has a corresponding link on the data-link layer (e.g., net0) and a configured interface on the interface layer (e.g., net0).

Data-Link Names

Oracle Solaris uses net as a default naming scheme for the data link and IP interface, but this name can be customized. It's common to use the same name as the underlying hardware (e.g., e1000g).

Figure 9-1 illustrates the one-to-one relationship between the network device, its device instance, its data link, and the IP interface.

Figure 9-1 illustrates a four-port Ethernet interface installed on a system where

- One NIC (e1000g) is on the hardware layer.
- There are four instances of the device (e1000g0-3) on the device layer.
- e1000g0 is configured and has a corresponding data link (net0) on the data-link layer.
- The IP interface uses the default Oracle Solaris name (net0) and is configured with an IPv4 or IPv6 address.

dladm: *Administer Data Links*

Use the dladm command to administer data links. dladm is used with one of its many subcommands to administer the data link at each layer of the TCP/IP network stack. The common subcommands used with the dladm command are described in Table 9-4:

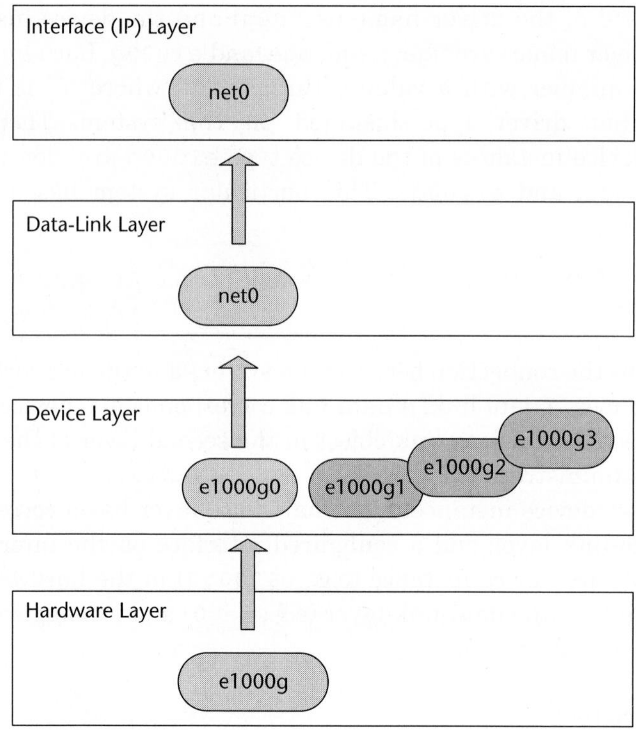

Figure 9-1 Oracle Solaris network stack

Table 9-4 `dladm` Subcommands

Subcommand	Description
`show-link`	Displays information about links on the data-link layer
`show-phys`	Shows the physical device and attributes of all physical links
`delete-phys`	Deletes the configuration of a link
`show-linkprop`	Shows the current value for one or more properties of either for all, or for the specified data link
`set-linkprop`	Sets the values of one or more properties on the link specified
`reset-linkprop`	Resets one or more properties to their initial startup values on the link specified

Figure 9-2 illustrates where to use each subcommand to display information on each layer of the TCP/IP network stack.

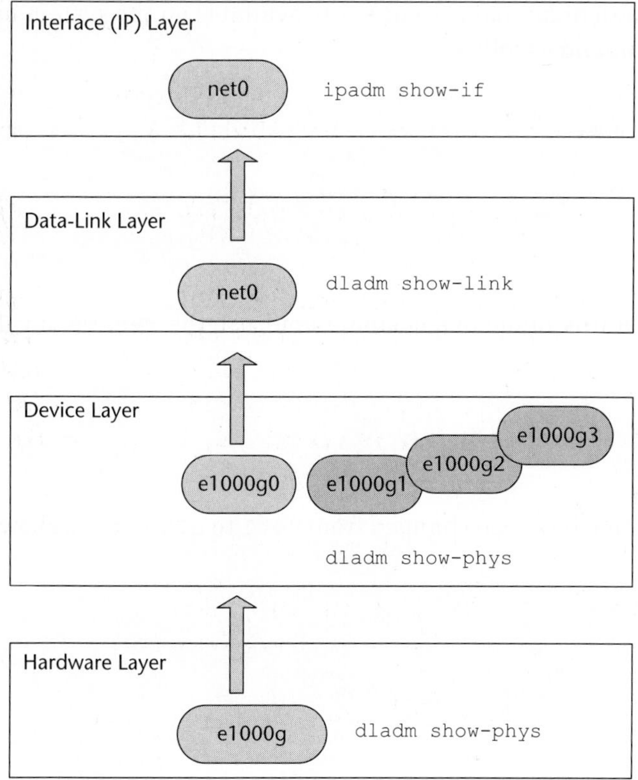

Figure 9-2 Oracle Solaris network administration commands

Display the NICs connected to your system along with the physical attributes of the corresponding data links using the `dladm show-phys` command as follows:

```
# dladm show-phys<cr>
LINK            MEDIA        STATE    SPEED    DUPLEX     DEVICE
net1            Ethernet     down     0        unknown    e1000g1
net2            Ethernet     down     0        unknown    e1000g2
net0            Ethernet     up       1000     full       e1000g0
net3            Ethernet     down     0        unknown    e1000g3
```

The first column of information displays the link name. The system has four physical links named `net0` through `net3`. The STATE of `net0` is `up`, while the STATE for the other links is `down`. `net0` is the only link configured on this system. The other links are down because they are not configured. The speed of `net0` is 1,000Mb per second, full duplex, and the device instance name is `e1000g0`.

Display the data links that are currently available on the system using the `dladm show-link` command as follows:

```
# dladm show-link<cr>
LINK            CLASS       MTU      STATE     OVER
net1            phys        1500     down      --
net2            phys        1500     down      --
net0            phys        1500     up        --
net3            phys        1500     down      --
```

To change a data-link name to a custom name, use the `rename-link` subcommand as follows:

```
# dladm rename-link net1 e1000g1<cr>
```

The data-link name has been changed from `net1` to `e1000g1` as shown:

```
# dladm show-link<cr>
LINK            CLASS       MTU      STATE     OVER
e1000g1         phys        1500     down      --
net2            phys        1500     down      --
net0            phys        1500     up        --
net3            phys        1500     down      --
```

`ipadm`: Administer the IP Interface

The `ipadm` command is used to administer the network IP interfaces and TCP/IP tunables. The common subcommands used with the `ipadm` command are described in Table 9-5.

Table 9-5 `ipadm` Subcommands

Subcommand	Description
`create-ip`	Creates an IP interface
`delete-ip`	Deletes an IP interface
`show-if`	Shows network interface configuration information
`create-addr`	Creates a static IPv4 or IPv6 address on the interface
`delete-addr`	Deletes all addresses on the specified interface
`show-addr`	Shows address information

ifconfig

For those system administrators with experience on previous versions of Oracle Solaris, the `ifconfig` command is still available to display the IP interface configuration on the interface layer. The `ipadm` command will eventually replace the `ifconfig` command for interface configuration. The command also replaces the `ndd` command to configure protocol properties.

To display information about the current IP interface configuration, use the `ipadm show-if` command as follows:

```
# ipadm show-if<cr>
IFNAME     CLASS      STATE   ACTIVE  OVER
lo0        loopback   ok      yes     --
net0       ip         ok      yes     --
```

Display the address associated with the IP interface using the `show-addr` subcommand as follows:

```
# ipadm show-addr<cr>
ADDROBJ          TYPE         STATE   ADDR
lo0/v4           static       ok      127.0.0.1/8
net0/v4          dhcp         ok      192.168.1.39/24
lo0/v6           static       ok      ::1/128
net0/v6          addrconf     ok      fe80::221:28ff:fe10:e818/10
```

Configure an IP Interface

To configure an additional IP interface on your system, you need to

1. Identify all of the data links currently configured on your system. You can also rename the data link if necessary using the `dladm rename-link` command.
2. Display the network interface IP address for all data links.
3. Create an IP network interface.
4. Assign an IP address to the IP interface.
5. Verify the IP address.

Configure the network interface using the `dladm` and `ipadm` commands. The network interfaces are automatically started by SMF through the `svcs:/network/physical` service when the system boots, so make sure that this service is online. It is not necessary to modify configuration files to make the network configuration persist across reboots.

The following steps illustrate the process of creating an IP interface and assigning an IP address to the IP interface.

1. Identify all of the links configured on the system:

```
# dladm show-phys<cr>
LINK      MEDIA        STATE    SPEED    DUPLEX     DEVICE
net1      Ethernet     down     0        unknown    e1000g1
net2      Ethernet     down     0        unknown    e1000g2
net0      Ethernet     up       1000     full       e1000g0
net3      Ethernet     down     0        unknown    e1000g3
```

2. Check the MAC address of all interfaces on the system to make sure that each interface has a unique MAC address. I'll use the `show-linkprop -p mac-address` command to display the MAC address for each interface as follows:

```
# dladm show-linkprop -p mac-address<cr>
LINK      PROPERTY      PERM  VALUE               DEFAULT             POSSIBLE
net1      mac-address   rw    0:21:28:10:e8:19 0:21:28:10:e8:19   --
net2      mac-address   rw    0:21:28:10:e8:1a 0:21:28:10:e8:1a   --
net0      mac-address   rw    0:21:28:10:e8:18 0:21:28:10:e8:18   --
net3      mac-address   rw    0:21:28:10:e8:1b 0:21:28:10:e8:1b   --
```

I've identified the data link that I want to configure: `net1`.

3. I'll rename the data link from `net1` to `e1000g1` to reflect the actual device instance name of the NIC. Use the `rename-link` subcommand to rename a data link as follows:

```
# dladm rename-link net1 e1000g1<cr>
```

Verify the name change as follows:

```
# dladm show-link<cr>
LINK          CLASS       MTU       STATE       OVER
net0          phys        1500      up          --
e1000g1       phys        1500      unknown     --
net2          phys        1500      down        --
net3          phys        1500      down        --
```

4. Display the current network IP address information on your system as follows:

```
# ipadm show-addr<cr>
ADDROBJ          TYPE        STATE      ADDR
lo0/v4           static      ok         127.0.0.1/8
net0/v4          dhcp        ok         192.168.1.39/24
lo0/v6           static      ok         ::1/128
net0/v6          addrconf    ok         fe80::221:28ff:fe10:e818/10
```

5. Create the IP interface for the e1000g1 data link as follows:

```
# ipadm create-ip e1000g1<cr>
```

The create-ip subcommand creates an IP interface that handles both IPv4 and IPv6 packets. This IP interface will persist across reboots.

6. Display the IP interface as follows:

```
# ipadm show-if<cr>
IFNAME         CLASS          STATE          ACTIVE         OVER
lo0            loopback       ok             yes            --
net0           ip             ok             yes            --
e1000g1        ip             down           no             --
```

7. Configure the IP interface with a valid IP address as follows:

```
# ipadm create-addr -T static -a 192.168.1.40/24 e1000g1/v4<cr>
```

The -T option specifies the type of IP address that is assigned to the interface. In this case, I specified static to assign a static IP address.

The -a option specifies the IP address to configure on the interface. The IP address is 192.168.1.40, and 24 is the prefix length.

The prefix length uses Classless Inter-Domain Routing (CIDR) notation and is used to specify the length of the network ID (subnet mask) that is part of the IPv4 address. It indicates how many IPv4 addresses are available for the hosts on your network. If you do not include the prefix length value, then the netmask is computed according to the sequence listed for netmask in the name-service switch service.

I specify the interface object name as two parts separated by a "/." This interface object name is an identifier for the unique IP address. The first part refers to the IP interface to which the address is assigned. This interface name must reflect the name of the data link on which the IP interface is configured. I specified e1000g1. The second part after the "/" is a user-specified string. This string consists of alphanumeric characters that begin with an alphabetic letter and has a maximum of 32 characters. I specified "v4."

8. Verify the IP interface and address with the show-addr command as follows:

```
# ipadm show-addr<cr>
ADDROBJ          TYPE          STATE     ADDR
lo0/v4           static        ok        127.0.0.1/8
net0/v4          dhcp          ok        192.168.1.39/24
e1000g1/v4       static        ok        192.168.1.40/24
lo0/v6           static        ok        ::1/128
net0/v6          addrconf      ok        fe80::a00:27ff:fe3f:5d8c/10
```

Configure an IP Interface to Use `dhcp`

This next example will show how to change the network interface to obtain an IP address using DHCP rather than using a static IP address.

1. Display the current IP configuration as follows:

```
# ipadm show-addr<cr>
ADDROBJ           TYPE         STATE      ADDR
lo0/v4            static       ok         127.0.0.1/8
net0/v4           dhcp         ok         10.0.2.15/24
e1000g1/v4        static       ok         192.168.1.40/24
lo0/v6            static       ok         ::1/128
net0/v6           addrconf     ok         fe80::a00:27ff:fe3f:5d8c/10
```

   Notice that `e1000g1/v4` has a static IP address as displayed in the TYPE column.

2. Delete the static IP address for `e1000g1/v4` as follows:

```
# ipadm delete-addr e1000g1/v4<cr>
```

   Verify the IP interface as follows:

```
# ipadm show-addr<cr>
ADDROBJ           TYPE         STATE      ADDR
lo0/v4            static       ok         127.0.0.1/8
net0/v4           dhcp         ok         10.0.2.15/24
lo0/v6            static       ok         ::1/128
net0/v6           addrconf     ok         fe80::a00:27ff:fe3f:5d8c/10
```

3. Configure DHCP on the interface as follows:

```
# ipadm create-addr -T dhcp e1000g1/v4<cr>
```

4. Verify the configuration as follows:

```
# ipadm show-addr<cr>
ADDROBJ           TYPE         STATE      ADDR
lo0/v4            static       ok         127.0.0.1/8
net0/_b           dhcp         ok         10.0.2.15/24
e1000g1/v4        dhcp         ok         10.0.3.15/24
lo0/v6            static       ok         ::1/128
net0/_a           addrconf     ok         fe80::a00:27ff:fe3f:5d8c/10
```

   The TYPE column now describes `e1000g1/v4` as using `dhcp`.

Administering the Network IP Interface

Administer the network IP interface using the `ipadm` command that was described in the previous section. Administration tasks may involve

- Taking down the IP interface
- Bringing up an IP interface
- Deleting an IP address for an IP interface
- Examining the status of an IP interface
- Deleting an IP interface

Bring Down an IP Interface

In the previous section, I configured the `e1000g1/v4` IP interface with a static IP address as displayed by the following `show-addr` command:

```
# ipadm show-addr e1000g1/v4<cr>
ADDROBJ            TYPE      STATE    ADDR
e1000g1/v4         static    ok       192.168.1.40/24
```

To take the `e1000g1/v4` IP interface out of service, use the `ipadm down-addr` command to take down the interface as follows:

```
# ipadm down-addr e1000g1/v4<cr>
```

Verify that the IP interface has been brought down by running the `ipadm show-addr` command as follows:

```
# ipadm show-addr e1000g1/v4<cr>
ADDROBJ            TYPE      STATE     ADDR
e1000g1/v4         static    down      192.168.1.40/24
```

Bring Up an IP Interface

To bring the IP interface back up, use the `ipadm up-addr` command as follows:

```
# ipadm up-addr e1000g1/v4<cr>
```

Verify that the network interface has been brought up:

```
# ipadm show-addr e1000g1/v4<cr>
ADDROBJ            TYPE      STATE     ADDR
e1000g1/v4         static    ok        192.168.1.40/24
```

Delete an IP Address

Delete an IP address that is assigned to an IP interface using the `ipadm delete-addr` command. Delete the IP address assigned to the `e1000g1/v4` IP interface as follows:

```
# ipadm delete-addr e1000g1/v4<cr>
```

Verify that the address has been deleted by issuing the `ipadm show-addr` command as follows:

```
# ipadm show-addr e1000g1/v4<cr>
ipadm: address object not found
```

Examine the Status of an IP Interface

Up to this point, I've been displaying the IP interface address using the `ipadm show-addr` command. This command displays all of the network interfaces, their IP addresses, and their status.

I can also display the IP interface configuration information by issuing the `ipadm show-if` command as follows:

```
# ipadm show-if<cr>
IFNAME     CLASS        STATE    ACTIVE   OVER
lo0        loopback     ok       yes      --
net0       ip           ok       yes      --
e1000g1    ip           down     no       --
```

When the IP address was deleted earlier, the network interface is no longer configured and is in the down state. Assign a new IP address to the interface as follows:

```
# ipadm create-addr -T static -a 192.168.1.40/24 e1000g1/v4<cr>
```

Issue the `ipadm show-if` command again to display the new configuration as follows:

```
# ipadm show-if<cr>
IFNAME     CLASS        STATE    ACTIVE   OVER
lo0        loopback     ok       yes      --
net0       ip           ok       yes      --
e1000g1    ip           ok       yes      --
```

You can also display a specific interface by specifying the interface name as an argument as follows:

```
# ipadm show-if e1000g1<cr>
IFNAME     CLASS    STATE     ACTIVE    OVER
e1000g1    ip       ok        yes       --
```

Display the properties for an IP interface using the `ipadm show-ifprop` command as follows:

```
# ipadm show-ifprop<cr>
IFNAME    PROPERTY      PROTO   PERM    CURRENT    PERSISTENT    DEFAULT    POSSIBLE
lo0       arp           ipv4    rw      on         --            on         on,off
lo0       forwarding    ipv4    rw      off        --            off        on,off
lo0       metric        ipv4    rw      0          --            0          --
lo0       mtu           ipv4    rw      8232       --            8232       68-8232
```

List the properties for an IP address using the `ipadm show-addrprop` command as follows:

```
# ipadm show-addrprop e1000g1/v4<cr>
ADDROBJ      PROPERTY    PERM CURRENT          PERSISTENT    DEFAULT          POSSIBLE
e1000g1/v4   broadcast   r-   192.168.1.255    --            192.168.1.255    --
e1000g1/v4   deprecated rw    off              --            off              on,off
e1000g1/v4   prefixlen   rw   24               24            24               1-30,32
e1000g1/v4   private     rw   off              --            off              on,off
e1000g1/v4   reqhost     r-   --               --            --               --
e1000g1/v4   transmit    rw   on               --            on               on,off
e1000g1/v4   zone        rw   global           --            global           --
...<output has been truncated>...
```

Delete an IP Interface

When the IP interface is no longer needed, it can be deleted using the `ipadm delete-ip` command. To permanently delete the `e1000g1/v4` IP interface, issue the following command:

```
# ipadm delete-ip e1000g1/v4<cr>
```

Verify that the IP interface has been deleted by issuing the `ipadm show-if` command as follows:

```
# ipadm show-if<cr>
IFNAME     CLASS       STATE    ACTIVE    OVER
lo0        loopback    ok       yes       --
net0       ip          ok       yes       --
```

The `e1000g1` interface is no longer listed.

Reactive Network Configuration

Reactive network configuration (formerly called Network Auto-Magic) provides an automated method of configuring the network and is designed to simplify network administration in Oracle Solaris 11. This feature was not available in previous versions of Oracle Solaris.

In a reactive network configuration, the system automatically adapts to any change in the network condition without requiring manual reconfiguration. The reactive network configuration is used mainly on laptops and desktops, whereas the fixed network configuration is used on servers.

If the OS is installed using the Live Media installer, the network is automatically configured using the reactive network configuration. If the OS is installed using the text installer, you are given the option of selecting either an automatic or manual configuration. For more information on the methods of installing, please refer to Chapter 1, "Installing Oracle Solaris 11."

The reactive network configuration consists of the following network configuration components:

- Network configuration profiles (NCPs)
- `Location` profile
- Network configuration units
- External network modifiers
- Known wireless local area networks (WLANs)

A system's network configuration is managed by a specific NCP and a corresponding `Location` profile. Only one pair of NCP and `Location` profiles can be active at one time to manage a system's network configuration. All other NCPs on the system are not operational. The active NCP can be either reactive or fixed. With a reactive profile, the system monitors the network configuration to adapt to changes in the system's network environment. With a fixed profile, the network configuration is instantiated but not monitored.

The NCP specifies the configuration of the network data links and IP interfaces. The default NCP used for the reactive network configuration is the `Automatic` NCP. Additionally, there can also be user-defined NCPs.

Network configuration units are containers that store all of the individual configuration objects that make up an NCP. An object is a network data link or IP interface.

A `Location` profile specifies the system-wide network configuration including the name services, domain, IP filter, and IPsec configuration. This profile contains a set of properties that define the system-wide network configuration.

External network modifiers are profiles that are used to manage applications that are external to the reactive network, such as a VPN application.

WLANs are configuration objects that a reactive network uses to monitor and store information about wireless networks that are available. The reactive network maintains a list of all of the wireless networks and refers to this list to determine the order in which the wireless connections are attempted.

Network Configuration Profiles

A reactive network automatically manages a network configuration by using the network configuration information defined in an NCP. When the automatic network configuration is selected during the installation, a default NCP called `Automatic` is selected. There can be any number of custom NCPs configured on a system, but only one may be active at one time.

The `Automatic` NCP is a system-defined profile that cannot be modified or deleted. The `Automatic` NCP represents all of the data links and IP interfaces that are currently available on the system. As network devices are added or removed, the `Automatic` NCP is updated. This profile cannot be edited. The `Automatic` profile uses DHCP and address autoconfiguration to make it possible to obtain IP addresses from a DHCP server. This profile also autoselects a data link. A reactive network will favor a wired link over a wireless link.

NCPs are created and modified using the `netcfg` command. List the NCPs on your system using the `netcfg list` command as follows:

```
# netcfg list<cr>
NCPs:
        Automatic
        DefaultFixed
Locations:
        Automatic
        NoNet
        DefaultFixed
```

All of the default top-level configuration profiles are listed.

Use the `netcfg` command to create a configuration profile. Creating a configuration profile requires an advanced knowledge of Oracle Solaris network administration and is outside the scope of this chapter. For more information on creating network configuration profiles, refer to the `netcfg(1M)` man page.

Reactive Network Services

At any given time, for the network to function, the `svc:/network/physical:default` service must be enabled on the system. The `svc:/network/physical:`

default service manages the physical network interface configuration according to the policy that is specified by the profiles that are enabled on the system.

> **Network Auto-Magic (NWAM)**
>
> The reactive network configuration was called Network Auto-Magic (NWAM) in earlier versions of Oracle Solaris 11 (prior to version 11.1). Prior to Oracle Solaris 11.1, there was also a service named svc:/network/physical:nwam that managed NWAM. This service is no longer available, and the nwamd daemon is now managed by the svc:/network/physical:default service.

Use the netadm command to administer the reactive network profiles and the nwamd daemon. The nwamd daemon is a system daemon, started by the svc:/network/physical:default service, and it manages all of the network interfaces. Use the netadm list command to list all of the NCPs on the system and their current state as follows:

```
# netadm list<cr>
TYPE        PROFILE        STATE
ncp         Automatic      online
ncu:phys    e1000g1        online
ncu:ip      e1000g1        online
ncp         DefaultFixed   disabled
loc         Automatic      online
loc         NoNet          offline
```

The output indicates that the reactive network configuration is enabled and active.

Disable the Reactive Network Configuration

A reactive network configuration works well for environments running Oracle Solaris on a laptop because the reactive network will automatically connect to networks in a variety of settings where there are frequent changes in the network environment. However, for a server environment, you will probably disable the reactive network and enable the fixed network configuration so that you can configure the network manually as described earlier in this chapter. You also need to disable the reactive network if you need to configure IP Multipathing, virtual networks, or bridging, and when the server is running a shared stack non-global zone.

To disable the reactive network, you will need to make the DefaultFixed NCP active as follows:

```
# netadm enable -p ncp DefaultFixed<cr>
Enabling ncp 'DefaultFixed'
```

Also, make sure that the svc:/network/physical:default service is online as follows:

```
# svcadm enable network/physical:default<cr>
```

Verify that the services are online as follows:

```
# svcs network/physical<cr>
STATE          STIME    FMRI
online         Sep_10   svc:/network/physical:upgrade
online         Sep_10   svc:/network/physical:default
```

Verify that the `DefaultFixed` NCP is active. When the `DefaultFixed` NCP is active, the `netadm list` command displays the following output:

```
# netadm list<cr>
TYPE        PROFILE         STATE
ncp         Automatic       disabled
ncp         DefaultFixed    online
loc         Automatic       offline
loc         NoNet           offline
loc         DefaultFixed    online
```

Enable the Reactive Network Configuration

To enable the reactive network configuration, you will need to make the `Automatic` profile active again. To enable the reactive network, type

```
# netadm enable -p ncp Automatic<cr>
Enabling ncp 'Automatic'
```

When the `Automatic` NCP is active, the `netadm list` command will list the NCPs as follows:

```
# netadm list<cr>
TYPE        PROFILE         STATE
ncp         Automatic       online
ncu:phys    e1000g1         online
ncu:ip      e1000g1         online
ncp         DefaultFixed    disabled
loc         Automatic       online
loc         NoNet           offline
```

Configuring Additional Network Services

To complete the network connectivity for your system, you may need to configure the client for a name service, configure the default route, or set the default domain. The procedure to set each of these was changed in Oracle Solaris 11 from previous versions of the OS.

Configure and Activate DNS

Before configuring DNS, make sure that the reactive network is disabled and the fixed network configuration is enabled. As described earlier in this chapter, you can do this by verifying that the `network/physical:default` service is `online` as follows:

```
# svcs network/physical<cr>
STATE          STIME    FMRI
online          4:11:55 svc:/network/physical:upgrade
online          4:23:29 svc:/network/physical:default
```

Also, verify that the `DefaultFixed` profile is active as follows:

```
# netadm list<cr>
TYPE         PROFILE          STATE
ncp          Automatic        disabled
ncp          DefaultFixed     online
loc          Automatic        offline
loc          NoNet            offline
loc          DefaultFixed     online
```

The `svc:/network/dns/client:default` service manages the DNS configuration in Oracle Solaris 11. In previous versions of Oracle Solaris, DNS was configured by editing the `/etc/resolv.conf` file. In Oracle Solaris 11, the `svc:/network/dns/client:default` service will automatically populate the `/etc/resolv.conf` file. This file is provided for backward compatibility and should not be manually edited.

View the existing DNS client configuration as follows:

```
# svccfg -s network/dns/client listprop config<cr>
config                          application
config/value_authorization astring      solaris.smf.value.name-\
service.dns.client
config/nameserver              net_address 192.168.1.252 8.8.8.8
config/search                  astring     unixed.local
```

Configure DNS settings on a client by modifying the properties for the `svc:/network/dns/client:default` service. Use the `svccfg` command described in Chapter 3, "Boot and Shutdown Procedures for SPARC and x86-Based Systems," to change these properties as follows:

```
# svccfg -s dns/client<cr>
```

Define the name server by setting the `config/nameserver` property. This will automatically update the `/etc/resolv.conf` file:

```
svc:/network/dns/client> setprop config/nameserver = net_address:\
(192.168.1.251 192.168.1.252)<cr>
```

Define the domain by setting the `config/domain` property as follows:

```
svc:/network/dns/client> setprop config/domain = astring: "unixed.local"<cr>
```

Exit the service configuration utility:

```
svc:/network/dns/client> exit<cr>
```

Verify the DNS client configuration as follows:

```
# svccfg -s network/dns/client listprop config<cr>
config                       application
config/value_authorization astring      solaris.smf.value.name-service.dns.client
config/nameserver           net_address 192.168.1.251 192.168.1.252
config/search               astring     unixed.local
```

Configure the Name Service Switch

The name service switch controls how a client machine (or application) obtains network information. The name service switch file coordinates the usage of the different naming services and has the following roles:

- It contains the information that the client system needs to locate user authorizations and profiles.
- It determines which sources will be used to resolve the names of other hosts on the network. This can be a single source or multiple sources. All sources are searched until the information is found.
- It is used to determine how user logins and passwords are resolved at login.

The name service switch is often simply referred to as "the switch." The switch determines which naming services an application uses to obtain naming information, and in what order.

The configuration of the name service switch is performed by setting the `config` group properties in the `svc:/system/nameservice/switch` service. Define the name resolution order for "hosts" by selecting the `name-service/switch` and setting the `config/host` property as follows:

```
svc:/network/dns/client> select name-service/switch<cr>
svc:/system/name-service/switch> setprop config/host = astring: "files dns"<cr>
```

Previous versions of Oracle Solaris used the `/etc/nsswitch.conf` file for setting the name service. In Oracle Solaris 11, the `config` property group for the `name-service/switch` service contains all of the configuration information for the `nsswitch.conf` file and will automatically make the entries in the `/etc/nsswitch.conf` file. It is no longer necessary to manually edit the `/etc/nsswitch.conf` file. The file is still provided in Oracle Solaris 11 for backward compatibility.

Finally, review the `config` property group settings as follows:

```
svc:/network/dns/client> listprop config<cr>
config                        application
config/value_authorization astring    solaris.smf.value.name-service.dns.client
config/nameserver             net_address 192.168.1.251 192.168.1.252
config/domain                 astring    unixed.local
config/host                   astring    "files dns"
```

Exit the configuration utility:

```
svc:/network/dns/client> exit<cr>
```

Activate DNS as follows:

```
# svcadm enable dns/client<cr>
```

Refresh the `name-service/switch` service to reflect the changes made to the service properties as follows:

```
# svcadm refresh name-service/switch<cr>
```

Configure the Default Route

Configure the default route on your system using the `route` command as follows:

```
# route -p add default 192.168.1.1<cr>
```

This default route will persist across reboots. Verify the default route:

```
# netstat -r<cr>

Routing Table: IPv4
Destination              Gateway           Flags       Ref    Use     Interface
-------------------- -------------------- ----- ----- ---------- ---------
default              192.168.1.1          UG          2          2
solaris              solaris              UH          2          0 lo0
192.168.1.0          192.168.1.40         U           4        282 e1000g1

Routing Table: IPv6
Destination/Mask              Gateway                   Flags  Ref     Use    If
--------------------------- --------------------------- ------ --- --------- ---
solaris                       solaris                   UH       2        14 lo0
```

Previous versions of Oracle Solaris used the `/etc/defaultrouter` file for setting the name of the system's default router. This file is obsolete, and it is no longer necessary to manually edit the `/etc/defaultrouter` file. However, the file is still provided in Oracle Solaris 11 for backward compatibility. Default routes will be created for any router addresses specified in the `/etc/defaultrouter` file, but they will not change when the underlying NCP changes or when the default route is changed with the `netstat` command.

Reset the Name Service Switch

If you wish to disable DNS and put the name service switch back to "`files only`," issue the following command:

```
# /usr/sbin/nscfg unconfig name-service/switch<cr>
```

Refresh the `name-service` switch service for the changes to take effect as follows:

```
# svcadm refresh name-service/switch<cr>
```

The `nscfg unconfig` command resets the SMF configuration only. You can also use the `sysconfig` command that was described in Chapter 1 to reset SMF services to their original state.

The System Hostname

The system hostname is managed by SMF through the `svc:/system/identity:node` service. The `svc:/system/identity:node` service has a property, `config/nodename`, used for setting the hostname. To determine the current system hostname, type

```
# hostname<cr>
```

The system returns the system name:

```
solaris
```

The service property can only be set if the DHCP server does not provide a value for the nodename. To set or change the system hostname, set the config/nodename property value as follows:

```
# svccfg -s svc:/system/identity:node setprop config/nodename = "systemb"<cr>
```

Refresh and restart the service as follows:

```
# svcadm refresh svc:/system/identity:node<cr>
# svcadm restart svc:/system/identity:node<cr>
```

Verify the new hostname by typing

```
# hostname<cr>
systemb
```

or by typing

```
# uname -n<cr>
systemb
```

You can also change the hostname temporarily using the uname -S command as follows:

```
# uname -S systemb<cr>
```

When changing the hostname with uname -S, the change will not persist across reboots.

For those system administrators with experience in previous versions of Oracle Solaris, the hostname was set in the /etc/nodename file. In Oracle Solaris 11, if the /etc/nodename file is present and the svc:/system/identity:node service property is not set, the SMF service reads the /etc/nodename file and populates the property. However, once the service property has been set, the /etc/nodename file is removed.

When the system's network configuration is set by the DHCP protocol, the SMF service property is used only if the DHCP server does not provide a hostname.

Use the `svcprop` command to display the `config/nodename` property for the `system/identity:node` service as follows:

```
# svcprop -p config node<cr>
config/nodename astring solaris
config/loopback astring solaris
```

Virtual Networking

A virtual network (VNIC) is a pseudo-interface created on a data link. This data link can be a physical NIC or an etherstub (described later).

The VNIC looks and acts like a physical network interface with the same data-link functionality as a physical interface. It has its own MAC address and IP address. The `dladm` command is used to create a VNIC, and the `ipadm` is used to configure the IP interface on the VNIC, just like we did earlier in this chapter when manually configuring a network interface.

The purpose of network virtualization is to allow sharing of network resources in an efficient, controlled, and secure way. A single physical network can be partitioned into several virtual interfaces and shared between multiple zones running on the same machine. In addition, network virtualization allows the system administrator to manage the network resources more efficiently, such as by setting network bandwidth limits on each virtual interface. The end product of creating VNICs and linking them together with a virtual switch is the simple virtual network, as shown in Figure 9-3.

Configure a Simple Virtual Network

One use of virtual networks is to support non-global zones. The non-global zones are all sharing the same physical NIC. When creating two or more VNICs on the same physical NIC (`net0`), as shown in Figure 9-3, a virtual switch is created. Traffic

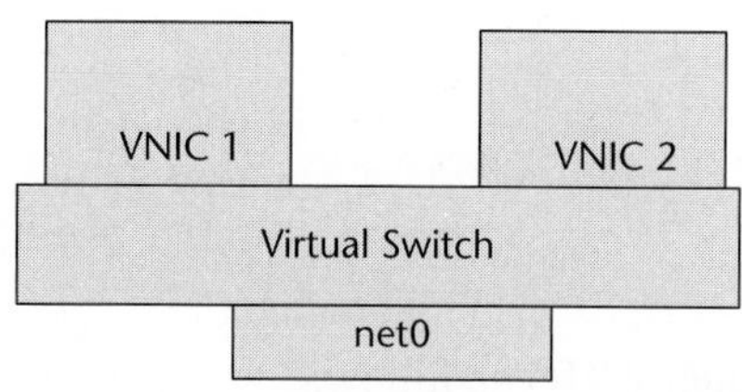

Figure 9-3 Simple virtual network

between VNIC1 and VNIC2 will be managed via this virtual switch. The following steps describe how to create VNIC1 and VNIC2:

The following physical NICs are available:

```
# dladm show-link<cr>
LINK           CLASS     MTU      STATE      OVER
net0           phys      1500     unknown    --
e1000g1        phys      1500     up         --
net2           phys      1500     unknown    --
net3           phys      1500     unknown    --
```

Use the `dladm create-vnic` command to create two VNICs on `net0`, as follows:

```
# dladm create-vnic -l net0 vnic1<cr>
# dladm create-vnic -l net0 vnic2<cr>
```

The `-l` option is followed by the link name: `net0`

View the new VNICs as follows:

```
# dladm show-link<cr>
LINK           CLASS     MTU      STATE      OVER
net0           phys      1500     down       --
e1000g1        phys      1500     up         --
net2           phys      1500     unknown    --
net3           phys      1500     unknown    --
vnic1          vnic      1500     up         net0
vnic2          vnic      1500     up         net0
```

I can list only the VNICs by using the `dladm show-vnic` command as follows:

```
# dladm show-vnic<cr>
LINK       OVER     SPEED    MACADDRESS           MACADDRTYPE    VID
vnic1      net0     0        2:8:20:3b:13:7c      random         0
vnic2      net0     0        2:8:20:2c:5b:12      random         0
```

The data links exist, but the IP interface has not been created yet, as shown with the `ipadm show-if` command:

```
# ipadm show-if<cr>
IFNAME     CLASS      STATE   ACTIVE   OVER
lo0        loopback   ok      yes      --
e1000g1    ip         ok      yes      --
```

Create the IP interfaces on each VNIC as follows:

```
# ipadm create-ip vnic1<cr>
# ipadm create-ip vnic2<cr>
```

Display the new IP interfaces as follows:

```
# ipadm show-if<cr>
IFNAME     CLASS      STATE   ACTIVE  OVER
lo0        loopback   ok      yes     --
e1000g1    ip         ok      yes     --
vnic1      ip         down    no      --
vnic2      ip         down    no      --
```

The VNIC IP interface can be managed using the `ipadm` command as I described earlier when managing a physical NIC. For example, set the IP interface to use a static IP address as follows:

```
# ipadm create-addr -T static -a 192.168.1.200/24 vnic1/v4<cr>
```

Verify the settings on the IP interface as follows:

```
# ipadm show-addr<cr>
ADDROBJ          TYPE      STATE   ADDR
lo0/v4           static    ok      127.0.0.1/8
e1000g1/v4       static    ok      192.168.1.40/24
vnic1/v4         static    ok      192.168.1.200/24
lo0/v6           static    ok      ::1/128
```

A `ping` to the VNIC IP interface shows that the interface is fully functional:

```
# ping 192.168.1.200<cr>
192.168.1.200 is alive
```

The etherstub

The etherstub is also a type of VNIC. Think of it as a virtual switch, too. The etherstub is a pseudo-network interface that provides an unmanaged virtual Ethernet switch for virtual interfaces. Use the etherstub to isolate the virtual

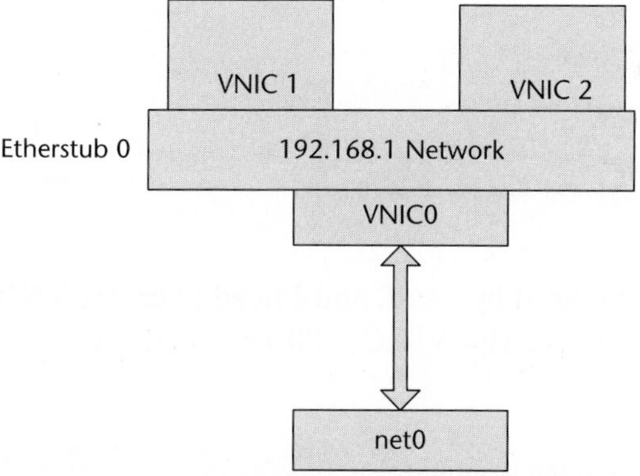

Figure 9-4 Private virtual network

network from the rest of the virtual networks on the system as well as from the external network. Network traffic originating from the VNIC connected to the etherstub is directed to other VNICs connected to the same etherstub.

Use the etherstub to create a private virtual network and isolate one virtual network from other virtual networks on the same system as shown in Figure 9-4.

Create a Private Virtual Network between Zones

In the previous section, I created a simple virtual network. Next, I'll create a second private network on the `net2` data link. I'll then use this private virtual network to connect two non-global zones. The current configuration is as follows:

```
# dladm show-link<cr>
LINK            CLASS    MTU      STATE        OVER
net0            phys     1500     up           --
net1            phys     1500     unknown      --
net2            phys     1500     unknown      --
net3            phys     1500     unknown      --

# ipadm show-addr<cr>
ADDROBJ         TYPE     STATE    ADDR
lo0/v4          static   ok       127.0.0.1/8
net0/v4         static   ok       192.168.0.10/24
lo0/v6          static   ok       ::1/128
```

`net0` is configured and has an IP address of 192.168.0.10. The system has a public network configured: 192.168.0. I want to create a private virtual network, 192.168.1, as shown in Figure 9-4. I'll first create an etherstub named `stub0` as follows:

```
# dladm create-etherstub stub0<cr>
```

Verify that the etherstub has been created as follows:

```
# dladm show-link<cr>
LINK              CLASS          MTU     STATE      OVER
net0              phys           1500    up         --
net1              phys           1500    unknown    --
net2              phys           1500    unknown    --
net3              phys           1500    unknown    --
stub0             etherstub      9000    unknown    --
```

An etherstub cannot be used by itself, and I need to create VNICs on this etherstub. The etherstub will connect the VNICs. I'll create the first VNIC (`vnic1`) on the etherstub as follows:

```
# dladm create-vnic -l stub0 vnic1<cr>
```

I'll create a second VNIC (`vnic2`) on the private network as follows:

```
# dladm create-vnic -l stub0 vnic2<cr>
```

Display the virtual network configuration using the `dladm show-vnic` command as follows:

```
# dladm show-vnic<cr>
LINK            OVER     SPEED    MACADDRESS          MACADDRTYPE    VID
vnic1           stub0    0        2:8:20:6b:fe:56     random         0
vnic2           stub0    0        2:8:20:e3:4e:b4     random         0
```

No data is passing over the links yet, so no speed is being recorded. Each VNIC has a random MAC address assigned. The VLAN ID is 0.

Now create two non-global zones and allocate `vnic1` to the first zone and `vnic2` to the second zone. For more information on creating an exclusive IP zone, refer to Chapter 6, "Administering Zones."

The zones will communicate over the virtual network. When I create each zone, I'll configure them as exclusive IP zones. To use VNICs, the zones must be configured as exclusive IP zones, which is the default.

Because I already have an exclusive IP zone named `sol11_zone`, I'll add the VNIC to the zone as follows:

```
# zonecfg -z sol11_zone<cr>
zonecfg:sol11_zone> add net<cr>
zonecfg:sol11_zone:net> set physical=vnic1<cr>
zonecfg:sol11_zone:net> end<cr>
zonecfg:sol11_zone > exit<cr>
```

Display the zone configuration to verify the settings as follows:

```
# zonecfg -z sol11_zone info<cr>
zonename: sol11_zone
zonepath: /rpool/z1
brand: solaris
autoboot: false
bootargs:
file-mac-profile:
pool:
limitpriv:
scheduling-class:
ip-type: exclusive
hostid:
fs-allowed:
net:
        address not specified
        allowed-address not specified
        configure-allowed-address: true
        physical: vnic1
        defrouter not specified
```

After booting the zone, I'll log in to the zone and display the data links available in that zone as follows:

```
sol11_zone:~# dladm show-link<cr>
LINK                CLASS      MTU     STATE      OVER
vnic1               vnic       9000    up         ?
```

`vnic1` is now visible in the zone. Create the IP interface in the zone as follows:

```
sol11_zone:~# ipadm create-ip vnic1<cr>
```

Set the IP address as follows:

```
sol11_zone:~# ipadm create-addr -T static -a local=192.168.1.10/24 vnic1/v4<cr>
```

Verify that the zone's IP interface has an IP address and that the interface is up as follows:

```
# ipadm show-addr<cr>
ADDROBJ            TYPE      STATE      ADDR
lo0/v4             static    ok         127.0.0.1/8
vnic1/v4           static    ok         192.168.1.10/24
lo0/v6             static    ok         ::1/128
```

From the global zone, you can view the configured data link as follows:

```
# dladm show-link<cr>
LINK                CLASS         MTU      STATE      OVER
net0                phys          1500     up         --
net1                phys          1500     unknown    --
net2                phys          1500     unknown    --
net3                phys          1500     unknown    --
stub0               etherstub     9000     unknown    --
vnic0               vnic          9000     up         stub0
vnic1               vnic          9000     up         stub0
sol11/vnic1         vnic          9000     up         stub0
vnic2               vnic          9000     up         stub0
```

Continue by assigning `vnic2` to the second non-global zone, configuring the IP interface, and setting an IP address for the zone. For the second zone, I'll use a `solaris10` brand zone. As described in Chapter 6, a `solaris10` brand zone runs the Oracle Solaris 10 operating environment. In Oracle Solaris 10, the network environment is configured much differently using the `ifconfig` command. If you're not familiar with how to configure the network on an Oracle Solaris 10 system, refer to Chapter 1 in *Solaris 10 System Administration Exam Prep (Exam CX-310-202), Part II,* ISBN 978-0-7897-3817-2, written by Bill Calkins and published by QUE Publishing.

The second zone is named sol10. It is already configured as an exclusive IP zone, and I simply add vnic2 to the zone configuration as follows:

```
zonecfg:sol10> add net<cr>
zonecfg:sol10:net> set physical=vnic2<cr>
zonecfg:sol10> end<cr>
zonecfg:sol10> exit<cr>
```

Display the solaris10 brand zone configuration as follows:

```
# zonecfg -z sol10 info<cr>
zonename: sol10
zonepath: /zone/sol10
brand: solaris10
autoboot: false
bootargs:
file-mac-profile:
pool:
limitpriv:
scheduling-class:
ip-type: exclusive
hostid:
fs-allowed:
net:
        address not specified
        allowed-address not specified
        configure-allowed-address: true
        physical: vnic2
        defrouter not specified
```

I'll boot the zone and log in to the zone. I'll plumb the interface, assign an IP address, and bring up the interface as follows:

```
# ifconfig vnic2 plumb 192.168.1.11 up<cr>
```

When both zones are booted, verify that the virtual network is operational by using the ping command. From one zone, you should be able to ping the IP address of the other zone. The ping command is described in the next section.

Checking the Network

Oracle Solaris provides several network commands that you can use to check and troubleshoot a network:

- ping: ping stands for packet Internet groper. The ping command sends an ICMP packet to another host to test its network status. The remote system sends an ICMP packet back to the originating host if the ping command succeeds. If no packet is received from the remote system, it is deemed to be down, and a message is returned to the calling host. The options to the command allow continuous packets or a specified number of packets to be sent as well as different sizes of packets.

- `snoop`: The `snoop` command captures and inspects network packets. Captured packets can be displayed as they are received or saved into a file to be analyzed later. `snoop` can produce large amounts of information, with each entry being displayed in single-line summary form or multiline verbose form.
- `netstat`: The `netstat` command displays network status information. You can see the status of the network interface, monitor how many packets are passing through the interface, and monitor how many errors are occurring. This command is used extensively in identifying overloaded networks where the packet collision rate would be much higher than expected.

Each of the commands listed here is demonstrated in the next set of steps.

1. Check the network connection to another system by typing the following:

```
# ping <options> <ip-address><cr>
```

For example, to check the network between `systemA` and `systemB`, type `ping systemB` from `systemA`. If the check is successful, the remote system replies with the following:

```
systemB is alive
```

If the network is not active, you get this message:

```
no answer from systemB
```

If you get this negative response, check your cable and make sure that both the local system and the remote system are configured properly.
It could also be that the network interface is not marked as `up`. The `ipadm show-if` command can be used as described earlier to check the status of the network interface.

2. Use the `snoop` utility to determine what information is flowing between systems. The `snoop` utility can show what actually happens when one system sends a `ping` to another system. The following example shows network traffic

being monitored between two hosts, namely `192.168.1.230` and `192.168.1.221`:

```
# snoop 192.168.1.230 192.168.1.221<cr>
```

The system responds with one line of output for each packet on the network:

```
Using device net0 (promiscuous mode)
192.168.1.221 -> solaris       ICMP Echo request (ID: 3313 Sequence number: 0)
      solaris -> 192.168.1.221 ICMP Echo reply (ID: 3313 Sequence number: 0)
```

When you are finished viewing information from `snoop`, press *Ctrl+C* to quit.

The `-d` Option

On a system with multiple network interfaces, use the `-d` option with `snoop` to specify the network device you want to watch. For example, to watch the `e1000g0` interface only, type

```
# snoop -d e1000g0 192.168.1.230 192.168.1.221<cr>
```

3. Check for network traffic by typing the following:

```
# netstat -i 5<cr>
```

The system responds with the following:

```
input    net0              output           input      (Total)     output
packets  errs     packets  errs     colls   packets    errs     packets   errs  colls
95218    49983    189      1        0       218706     49983    123677    1     0
0        0        0        0        0       3          0        3         0     0
0        0        0        0        0       4          0        4         0     0
1        1        0        0        0       144        1        143       0     0
0        0        0        0        0       256        0        256       0     0
0        0        0        0        0       95         0        95        0     0
0        0        0        0        0       1171       0        1171      0     0
```

The `netstat` command is used to monitor the system's TCP/IP network activity. `netstat` can provide some basic data about how much and what kind of network activity is happening. You should ignore the first line of output, as this shows the overall activity since the system was last booted. The `-i` option shows the state of the network interface used for TCP/IP traffic. The last option, `5`, reissues the `netstat` command every five seconds to get a good sampling of network activity, with each line showing the activity since the last display, in this case five seconds. You can press *Ctrl+C* to break out of the `netstat` command.

To check the status on a particular interface, type `netstat -I` *<interfacename>* followed by the interval as follows:

```
# netstat -I e1000g1 5<cr>
```

4. Look in the `colls` column to see whether a large number of collisions occurred. To calculate the network collision rate, divide the number of output collisions (`output colls`) by the number of output packets. A network-wide collision rate greater than 10% can indicate an overloaded network, a poorly configured network, or hardware problems.
5. Examine the `errs` column to see whether a large number of errors occurred. To calculate the input packet error rate, divide the number of input errors by the total number of input packets. If the input error rate is high—more than 25%—the host might be dropping packets because of transmission problems. Transmission problems can be caused by other hardware on the network, heavy traffic, and low-level hardware problems. Routers can drop packets, forcing retransmissions and causing degraded performance.
6. Type `ping -sRv` *<hostname>* from the client to determine how long it takes a packet to make a round trip on the network. If the round trip takes more than a few milliseconds, the routers on the network are slow or the network is very busy. Issue the `ping` command twice, and ignore the first set of results. The `ping -sRv` command also displays packet losses. If you suspect a physical problem, you can use `ping -sRv` to find the response times of several hosts on the network. If the response time (in milliseconds) from one host is not what you expect, you should investigate that host.

Network Services

In previous releases of Oracle Solaris, the `inetd` network daemon was responsible for running network services on demand and was configured by editing the file, `/etc/inetd.conf`. This has all changed. The services that were previously configured using this file are now configured and managed by SMF. This topic is described fully in Chapter 3. The `inetd` daemon is still active, `inetd` is the SMF-delegated restarter for Internet services. Its job is to manage service states in response to administrative requests, system failures, and service failures. It listens for network requests for services.

The inetadm command is used to observe or configure inetd controlled services and to carry out the management of these network services. The inetadm command is used to

- List inetd controlled services.
- List the inetd service properties and values.
- Enable and disable inetd controlled services.
- Modify the inetd service property values.

To list the network services being managed by SMF on a server, enter the inetadm command with no options:

```
# inetadm<cr>
ENABLED   STATE          FMRI
disabled  disabled       svc:/application/cups/in-lpd:default
disabled  disabled       svc:/network/tftp/udp6:default
disabled  disabled       svc:/network/time:dgram
disabled  disabled       svc:/network/time:stream
enabled   online         svc:/network/security/ktkt_warn:default
disabled  disabled       svc:/network/echo:dgram
disabled  disabled       svc:/network/echo:stream
disabled  disabled       svc:/network/nfs/rquota:default
disabled  disabled       svc:/network/rexec:default
enabled   online         svc:/network/rpc/smserver:default
enabled   online         svc:/network/rpc/gss:default
disabled  disabled       svc:/network/rpc/rex:default
disabled  disabled       svc:/network/rpc/rstat:default
disabled  disabled       svc:/network/rpc/wall:default
disabled  disabled       svc:/network/rpc/rusers:default
disabled  disabled       svc:/network/rpc/spray:default
disabled  disabled       svc:/network/login:eklogin
disabled  disabled       svc:/network/login:klogin
disabled  disabled       svc:/network/login:rlogin
disabled  disabled       svc:/network/chargen:dgram
disabled  disabled       svc:/network/chargen:stream
disabled  disabled       svc:/network/comsat:default
disabled  disabled       svc:/network/discard:dgram
disabled  disabled       svc:/network/discard:stream
disabled  disabled       svc:/network/stdiscover:default
disabled  disabled       svc:/network/finger:default
disabled  disabled       svc:/network/daytime:dgram
disabled  disabled       svc:/network/daytime:stream
disabled  disabled       svc:/network/telnet:default
disabled  disabled       svc:/network/stlisten:default
disabled  disabled       svc:/network/talk:default
disabled  disabled       svc:/network/shell:default
disabled  disabled       svc:/network/shell:kshell
```

The preceding code shows, for example, that the network/rpc/spray service is in the disabled state. To enable this service, use the inetadm command with the -e option:

```
# inetadm -e spray<cr>
```

Now you can see that the service has been enabled and is available for use:

```
# inetadm | grep spray<cr>
enabled   online         svc:/network/rpc/spray:default
```

To disable the spray service, use the inetadm command with the -d option:

```
# inetadm -d spray<cr>
```

Check again to verify that the service is now disabled:

```
# inetadm | grep spray<cr>
disabled disabled    svc:/network/rpc/spray:default
```

Note

Other commands work, too. You are not limited to the inetadm command to view and control legacy network services. The svcs -a command can also be used to view the status, and the svcadm command can control legacy network services as well.

You can also use the svcadm command to disable network services. For example, you could disable spray by typing svcadm disable svc:/network/rpc/spray:default.

You can also list the properties and values of a selected network service using the -l option to the inetadm command. The following code lists the properties of the spray service:

```
# inetadm -l spray<cr>
SCOPE    NAME=VALUE
         name="sprayd"
         endpoint_type="tli"
         proto="datagram_v"
         isrpc=TRUE
         rpc_low_version=1
         rpc_high_version=1
         wait=TRUE
         exec="/usr/lib/netsvc/spray/rpc.sprayd"
         user="root"
default  bind_addr=""
default  bind_fail_max=-1
default  bind_fail_interval=-1
default  max_con_rate=-1
default  max_copies=-1
default  con_rate_offline=-1
default  failrate_cnt=40
default  failrate_interval=60
default  inherit_env=TRUE
default  tcp_trace=FALSE
```

```
default  tcp_wrappers=FALSE
default  connection_backlog=10
default  tcp_keepalive=FALSE
```

Each network service uses a port that represents an address space and is reserved for that service. Systems communicate with each other through these ports. Well-known ports are listed in the `/etc/services` file, which is a symbolic link to `/etc/inet/services`. The following are a few entries from the `/etc/services` file:

```
chargen     19/tcp      ttytst source
chargen     19/udp      ttytst source
ftp-data    20/tcp
ftp         21/tcp
```

From these entries, you can see that the `chargen` service uses port 19 and uses both TCP and User Datagram Protocol (UDP). It also has aliases assigned.

Each network service uses a well-known port number that is used by all the hosts on the network. Keeping track of these ports can be difficult, especially on a network that supports several network services.

RPC Services

Oracle Solaris uses a client/server model known as remote procedure call (RPC). With an RPC service, a client connects to a special server process, `rpcbind`, which is a "well-known service." When you boot the Oracle Solaris 11 OS, the `/lib/svc/method/rpc-bind` startup script initializes the `rpcbind` service. The port number used by the `rpcbind` daemon is listed in the `/etc/inet/services` file. After the system starts up, the `rpcbind` daemon starts listening at port 111.

RPC services are developed using a set of utilities developed by Sun Microsystems, Inc. The developer assigns a unique program number to them when they are written; typically they are not assigned to well-known ports. There are two types of RPC services:

1. Services that start by default at system boot time (such as `mountd`)
2. Services that do not start automatically at boot and must start on demand (such as `sprayd`)

RPC services that are started at bootup are started via their individual startup scripts. An example of an RPC service is the `mountd` daemon, which is started automatically by the `svc:/network/nfs/server` service. RPC services are started on available ports above 32768.

Some RPC services are started on demand. When a client requests a service, the process returns the port number of the requested service to the client. The client then generates a new request using the port number it just received for the requested service. Here's how the process takes place:

1. The `rpcbind` daemon is started via its startup script. The `sprayd` service is listed in the `/etc/rpc` file. It registers its current port assignment and program number with the `rpcbind` process during boot.
2. A user on a remote system, sysA (the client), issues a `spray` command to sysB (the server). The `spray` request is initially addressed to port 111 and contains the program number of the `sprayd` service. When a remote system (client) makes an RPC call to a given program number on a server, it must first contact the `rpcbind` service on the server to obtain the port address. The client must do this before it can send the RPC requests.
3. The `rpcbind` daemon on sysB reads the program number and determines that the request is for the `sprayd` service. The `rpcbind` daemon returns the current port number of the `sprayd` service to sysA.
4. sysA sends a second request to the port number of the `sprayd` service on sysB. The `inetd` daemon receives the request.
5. This `rpc.sprayd` daemon takes over the `spray` session's communication.

`rpcbind` registers port numbers associated with each RPC service listed in the `/etc/rpc` file. The `rpcbind` process receives all RPC-based client application connection requests and sends the appropriate server port number to the client. For example, `mountd` is listed in the `/etc/rpc` file as follows:

```
mountd      100005  mount showmount
```

The `mountd` daemon has a program number of `100005` and is also known as `mount` and `showmount`.

You use the `rpcinfo` utility with the `-p` option to list registered RPC programs running on a system. For example, you can check on processes on another system like this:

```
# rpcinfo -p 192.168.1.21<cr>
```

The system responds with a list of all the registered RPC services found running on that system:

```
program  vers  proto  port    service
100005    1     udp    32784   mountd
. . .<output has been truncated>. . .
```

The output displays the program number, version, protocol, port, and service name. One of them in this example is the `mountd` service.

You can also use `rpcinfo` to unregister an RPC program. When you use `rpcinfo` with the `-d` option, you can delete registration for a service. For example, if `sprayd` is running on the local system, you can unregister and disable it:

```
# rpcinfo -d sprayd 1<cr>
```

The `sprayd` service would be unregistered from RPC. You could restart the `sprayd` service by issuing a restart command using the `svcadm` command:

```
# svcadm restart spray<cr>
```

This causes the `spray` service to restart and automatically re-register the RPC program associated with the `spray` service.

Summary

Although networking is a topic that could consume many chapters in this book, the fundamentals that you need to know to be able to manage an Oracle Solaris system on the network are described here.

After reading this chapter, you should understand how to configure and manage network services in Oracle Solaris 11. Some new commands were introduced—specifically, `dladm` and `ipadm`.

I described how to configure a network interface manually and automatically using NWAM. I also detailed how to create virtual network interfaces and a virtual network and how to configure non-global zones to communicate over a private virtual network.

In addition, this chapter discussed some of the network-related commands and utilities that you can use for monitoring and maintaining the network. In a networked environment, system performance depends on how well you've maintained your network. An overloaded network can disguise itself as a slow system and can even cause downtime. You should monitor your network continuously. You need to know how the network looks when things are running well so that you know what to look for when the network is performing poorly. The network commands described in this chapter only report numbers. You're the one who decides whether these numbers are acceptable for your environment. As stated earlier, practice and experience will help you excel at system administration. The same holds true for network administration.

10

Network File Systems

Previous chapters in this book described how to install the OS, create file systems, and configure the network. Since the early days of Oracle Solaris, when it was still called SunOS, the mantra was: "The network is the computer." SunOS began in an era when distributed computing was in its early stages. Multiple standalone servers, each running separate applications and all creating their own data, were configured in an environment to all work together. Although each server ran processes and stored data independently on its own disks, from the user's perspective, everything was on a single computer. Data was spread across multiple servers, and regardless of where it was located, it could all be accessed instantly.

Although hardware and technology have come a long way, accessing data on remote systems is still very much the same. This chapter describes how to access remote file systems on other systems using NFS. NFS is used to share data with other UNIX file systems as well as other OSs running the NFS protocol. The Common Internet File System (CIFS) is also available on Oracle Solaris and is used to share data with Microsoft Windows–based systems. Both are considered distributed file systems, and NFS and CIFS are used to share data between systems across the network.

NFS Overview

The NFS service lets computers of different architectures, running different OSs, share file systems across a network. Just as the `mount` command lets you mount a file system on a local disk, NFS lets you mount a file system that is located on another system anywhere on the network. Furthermore, NFS support has been implemented on many platforms, ranging from Microsoft Windows Server to mainframe OSs, such as Multiprogramming with Virtual Storage (MVS). Each OS applies the NFS model to its file system semantics. For example, an Oracle Solaris system can mount the file system from a Microsoft Windows or Linux system. File system operations, such as reading and writing, function as though they are occurring on local files. Response time might be slower when a file system is physically located on a remote system, but the connection is transparent to the user regardless of the hardware or OS.

The NFS service provides the following benefits:

- It allows multiple computers to use the same files so that everyone on the network can access the same data. This eliminates the need to have redundant data on several systems.
- NFS reduces storage costs by having computers share applications and data.
- The service provides data consistency and reliability because all users access the same data.
- It makes mounting of file systems transparent to users.
- NFS makes accessing remote files transparent to users.
- The service supports heterogeneous environments.
- It reduces system administration overhead.

The NFS service makes the physical location of the file system irrelevant to the user. You can use NFS to allow users to see all of the data, regardless of location. With NFS, instead of placing copies of commonly used files on every system, you can place one copy on one computer's disk and have all other systems across the network access it. This file system that is made accessible to systems across the network is referred to as an NFS "shared resource." Under NFS operation, remote file systems are almost indistinguishable from local ones.

NFS Version 4

NFS version 4 is the default version of NFS that is used in Oracle Solaris 11. Oracle Solaris 10 introduced a new version of the NFS protocol, version 4, which had many enhancements over the version 3 protocol. I describe those enhancements in my book *Solaris 10 System Administration Exam Prep* and will not cover them again here.

Oracle Solaris 11 Enhancements to NFS v4

Oracle Solaris 11 has added enhancements to the version 4 protocol. For those of you with experience in previous versions of the OS, you may be familiar with setting NFS parameters in the `/etc/default/autofs` and `/etc/default/nfs` configuration files. In Oracle Solaris 11, all of the NFS parameters are now set through SMF service properties. Therefore, the NFS daemons that used these files also now reference the SMF service properties.

NFS provides support for mirror mounts, which is similar to AutoFS but offers advantages that I'll explain later in this chapter.

Servers and Clients

With NFS, systems have a client/server relationship. The NFS server is where the file system resides. Any system with a local file system can be an NFS server. As described later in this chapter in the section titled "Sharing a File System" you can configure the NFS server to make file systems available to other systems and users. The system administrator has complete control over which file systems can be mounted and who can mount them.

An NFS client is a system that mounts a remote file system from an NFS server. You'll learn later in this chapter in the section titled "Mounting a Remote File System" how you can create a local directory and mount the file system. As you will see, a system can be both an NFS server and an NFS client.

NFS Daemons

NFS uses a number of daemons to handle its services. These daemons are initialized at startup by SMF. The most important NFS daemons are described in Table 10-1.

NFS Services

NFS is controlled by several SMF services, which are described in Table 10-2.

Before any NFS shares are created, the default status of these services is disabled as follows:

```
disabled        5:37:49 svc:/network/nfs/status:default
disabled        5:37:49 svc:/network/nfs/nlockmgr:default
disabled        5:37:49 svc:/network/nfs/cbd:default
disabled        5:37:49 svc:/network/nfs/client:default
disabled        5:37:50 svc:/network/nfs/server:default
disabled        9:38:26 svc:/network/nfs/rquota:default
disabled        9:38:25 svc:/network/nfs/mapid:default
disabled        9:38:24 svc:/network/rpc/bind:default
```

Table 10-1 NFS Daemons

Daemon	Description
`nfsd`	This NFS server daemon handles file system exporting and file access requests from remote systems. An NFS server runs multiple instances of this daemon. This daemon is usually invoked at the multi-user-server milestone and is started by the `svc:/network/nfs/server:default` service identifier.
`mountd`	This NFS server daemon handles mount requests from NFS clients. This daemon provides information about which file systems are mounted by which clients. Use the `showmount` command, described later in this chapter, to view this information. This daemon is usually invoked at the multi-user-server milestone and is started by the `svc:/network/nfs/server:default` service identifier. This daemon is not used in NFS version 4, but you may still find it running to support the version 3 protocol.
`lockd`	This daemon runs on the NFS server and NFS client and provides file-locking services in NFS. This daemon is started by the `svc:/network/nfs/client` service identifier at the multi-user milestone. This daemon is not used in NFS version 4, but you may still find it running to support the version 3 protocol.
`statd`	This daemon runs on the NFS server and NFS client and interacts with `lockd` to provide the crash and recovery functions for the locking services on NFS. This daemon is started by the `svc:/network/nfs/client` service identifier at the multi-user milestone. This daemon is not used in NFS version 4, but you may still find it running to support the version 3 protocol.
`rpcbind`	This daemon facilitates the initial connection between the client and the server.
`rquotad`	`rquotad` is used to display user quotas for remote file systems.
`nfsmapid`	This new daemon maps to and from NFS v4 owner and group identification and UID and GID numbers. It uses entries in the `passwd` and `group` files to carry out the mapping and also references `/etc/nsswitch.conf` to determine the order of access.
`nfs4cbd`	This new client side daemon listens on each transport and manages the callback functions to the NFS server.
`nfslogd`	This daemon provides operational logging to the Oracle Solaris NFS server. The `nfslogd` daemon is not used in NFS version 4, but you may still find it running to support the version 3 protocol.

The `svc:/network/nfs/server:default` service is used to enable or disable the NFS server. Enabling the `svc:/network/nfs/server:default` service starts all of the required services. Enable the service as follows:

```
# svcadm enable network/nfs/server<cr>
```

Table 10-2 NFS Services

Daemon	Description
`svc:/network/nfs/status:default`	Manages the `statd` daemon
`svc:/network/nfs/nlockmgr:default`	Manages the `lockd` service
`svc:/network/nfs/cbd:default`	Manages the `nfs4cbd` daemon
`svc:/network/nfs/client:default`	Manages the NFS client services
`svc:/network/nfs/server:default`	Starts and stops all of the required NFS services on an NFS server
`svc:/network/nfs/rquota:default`	Manages the `rquotad` daemon
`svc:/network/nfs/mapid:default`	Manages the `nfsmapid` daemon
`svc:/network/rpc/bind:default`	Manages the `rpcbind` server

Check the status of the NFS services as follows:

```
# svcs -a |grep nfs<cr>
disabled        5:37:49 svc:/network/nfs/status:default
disabled        5:37:49 svc:/network/nfs/nlockmgr:default
disabled        5:37:49 svc:/network/nfs/cbd:default
disabled        5:37:49 svc:/network/nfs/client:default
disabled        9:38:26 svc:/network/nfs/rquota:default
online          9:38:25 svc:/network/nfs/mapid:default
offline         9:59:46 svc:/network/nfs/server:default
```

Simply enabling the `svc:/network/nfs/server:default` service is not enough because there are no NFS shares on this server. There must be at least one NFS share created before all of the required NFS server services will start. I describe how to create an NFS share in the next section.

Sharing a File System

Servers let other systems access their file systems by sharing them over the NFS environment. A shared file system is referred to as a "shared resource," or simply a "share." Other systems will access this shared resource by mounting this shared resource. A ZFS file system is shared by creating the share with the `zfs set share` command and then publishing the share by setting the ZFS `sharenfs` property to `on`.

The next sections describe the process of sharing a ZFS file system. I've included two different sections describing how to share a ZFS file system. The first section is for sharing file systems in Oracle Solaris 11 11/11 (ZFS pool version 33). The second section describes a new procedure that has been implemented in Oracle Solaris 11.1 (ZFS pool version 34 or higher). If you are using Oracle Solaris 11.1 or newer, proceed to the section titled "Sharing a ZFS File System: Oracle Solaris 11.1."

Sharing a ZFS File System: Oracle Solaris 11 11/11

This section describes how to share a ZFS file system in Oracle Solaris 11 11/11 (ZFS pool version 33). Although this procedure can be used to share a file system in Oracle Solaris 11.1, the process has been improved in Oracle Solaris 11.1 and is now much easier. I describe the new procedure in the section titled "Sharing a ZFS File System: Oracle Solaris 11.1."

The following file system is available on the system:

```
NAME            USED   AVAIL  REFER  MOUNTPOINT
pool1/data      31.5K  15.6G  31.5K  /data
```

Use the following method to share the ZFS file system:

1. Use the `zfs set share` command to create the NFS shared resource as follows:

   ```
   # zfs set share=name=data,path=/data,prot=nfs pool1/data<cr>
   ```

   The system responds with

   ```
   name=data,path=/data,prot=nfs
   ```

   The `zfs set share` syntax is described later in this section. Do not confuse the `zfs set share` command with the `zfs share` command. `zfs set share` is used to create an NFS share, whereas `zfs share` is used to publish an NFS share.

   #### The `share` Command is Deprecated

   In Oracle Solaris 11 11/11, using the `share` command or the `sharenfs` property to define and publish an NFS share of a ZFS file system is considered a legacy operation. Although the `share` command is still available in this version of Oracle Solaris 11, you should start using the `zfs set share.nfs` command described in the upcoming section titled "Sharing a ZFS File System: Oracle Solaris 11.1."

2. The share is not published until the `sharenfs` property is set to `on`. Set the `sharenfs` property on the ZFS file system as follows:

   ```
   # zfs set sharenfs=on pool1/data<cr>
   ```

   Notice that I used the dataset name, `pool1/data`, not the file system mountpoint, `/data`.

3. Verify that the `sharenfs` property is set as follows:

```
# zfs get sharenfs pool1/data<cr>
NAME          PROPERTY    VALUE    SOURCE
pool1/data    sharenfs    on       local
```

`/etc/dfs/dfstab` File

The `/etc/dfs/dfstab` file is no longer used in Oracle Solaris 11 to share file systems. SMF will automatically share the file system at bootup when the `sharenfs` property is set to `on`.

As described in the previous steps, the `set zfs share` command is used to create a new NFS share in Oracle Solaris 11 11/11.

The syntax for the `zfs set share` command is as follows (refer to the `zfs_share(1M)` man page for more information):

```
zfs set share=name=<sharename>,path=<pathname>,desc=<description>,prot=<protocol>
nfs[,property=value] <pool/filesystem>
```

where *<pool/filesystem>* is the name of the ZFS file system to be shared. Table 10-3 describes each of the options.

Table 10-3 `zfs set share` Options (NFS)

Option	Description
`name=`*<sharename>*	This option identifies a name for your share. The maximum size for a share name is 80 characters.
`path=`*<pathname>*	This option identifies a path for your NFS share that must exist within the file system or directory to be shared. This would be the mountpoint on a mounted file system.
`prot=`*<protocol>*	This option identifies the protocol as either `nfs` or `smb`.
`pool/filesystem`	This option identifies the ZFS file system to be shared.
`description="string"`	This option provides text that describes and helps to identify the share. Spaces or commas in the description must be enclosed in quote marks (" ").
`rw=`	`rw=` identifies whether the share is available as read/write to all clients. You can also specify a colon-separated list that includes hostnames, IP addresses, or a netgroup.
`ro=`	This option identifies whether the share is available as read-only to all clients. You can also specify a colon-separated list that includes hostnames, IP addresses, or a netgroup.
`root=`	`root=` identifies a root user from a specified host or list of hosts that have root access. By default, no host has root access.
`sec=`	`sec=` identifies a NFS server security mode.

Display the options used for a shared ZFS file system as follows:

```
# zfs get share pool1/data<cr>
```

The system displays the following information:

```
NAME        PROPERTY  VALUE                                              SOURCE
pool1/data  share     name=data,desc=shared data,path=/data,prot=nfs  local
```

The `zfs set share` property and options are not inherited from a parent to a descendant file system. However, the `sharenfs` property is inherited from a parent to the descendant.

An existing share can be changed by reissuing the `zfs set share` command. For example, if I want to change the description for the `data` share that I created earlier, I would issue the following command:

```
# zfs set share=name=data,desc="public data" pool1/data<cr>
name=data,desc=public data,path=/data,prot=nfs
```

I changed the description from "shared data" to "public data."

When the share is created, it is stored in a file in the `.zfs/shares` directory as follows:

```
# ls -l /data/.zfs/shares<cr>
total 2
-rwxrwxrwx+  1 root     root          160 Oct 12 12:41 data
```

The following example creates a new read-only share:

```
# zfs set share=name=data,path=/data,prot=nfs,ro=* pool1/data<cr>
name=data,desc=public data,path=/data,prot=nfs,sec=sys,ro=*
```

Root Squash

Root squash means that root will not have write access to an NFS share when accessing the share from an NFS client. Root is mapped to the `nobody` account. Root squash is the default behavior for NFS shared resources in Oracle Solaris. The alternative is to give root write access from a particular NFS client using the `root=` option as shown in the next example.

The next example creates a share that is writable by root from a remote client named "`sysa`." It disables root squash when accessing the shared resource from `sysa`.

```
# zfs set share=name=data,path=/data,prot=nfs,rw=*,root=sysa pool1/data<cr>
name=data,path=/data,prot=nfs,sec=sys,rw=*,root=sysa
```

After creating the share, don't forget to set the `sharenfs` property to publish the share as follows:

```
# zfs set sharenfs=on pool1/data<cr>
```

Finally, verify that the NFS services are online as follows:

```
# svcs -a |grep nfs<cr>
disabled        5:37:49 svc:/network/nfs/cbd:default
disabled        5:37:49 svc:/network/nfs/client:default
online          9:38:25 svc:/network/nfs/mapid:default
online         10:04:24 svc:/network/nfs/rquota:default
online         10:04:25 svc:/network/nfs/status:default
online         10:04:25 svc:/network/nfs/nlockmgr:default
online         10:04:25 svc:/network/nfs/server:default
```

The `svc:/network/nfs/cbd:default` and `svc:/network/nfs/client: default` services do not need to be running, but the other NFS services should be online.

Remove an NFS Share

Use the `zfs set -c` command to remove an NFS share. For example, to remove the `data` share that was created in the previous section, type

```
# zfs set -c share=name=data pool1/data<cr>
share 'data' was removed.
```

Verify that the share has been removed as follows:

```
# zfs get share pool1/data<cr>
```

Share and Unshare an NFS Share

As long as the `sharenfs` property is set to `on`, the file system will be shared automatically at bootup. There is no need to edit the `/etc/dfs/dfstab` file to record the information for subsequent reboots. However, you can temporarily unshare a file system using the `zfs unshare` command. For example, to unshare the data share that was created earlier, type

```
# zfs unshare pool1/data<cr>
```

To share it again, type

```
# zfs share pool1/data<cr>
```

Sharing a ZFS File System: Oracle Solaris 11.1

Oracle Solaris 11.1 (ZFS pool version 34 or higher) improves the ability to share ZFS file systems. The primary change has been the addition of new ZFS properties named `share.nfs` and `share.smb`. This section will describe the `share.nfs` property used for setting up an NFS share.

The `share.smb` property is used for sharing a file system over the SMB protocol for integration within an existing Microsoft Windows environment. You'll see "CIFS" and "SMB" used interchangeably even though, technically, CIFS is an enhanced version of the SMB protocol. Configuring the SMB server involves configuring identity mapping between the Windows and Oracle Solaris environments and is beyond the scope of this chapter. In previous versions of Oracle Solaris 11, the system administrator configured the Samba server. In Oracle Solaris 11.1, you will configure the SMB server. Samba and SMB servers cannot be used simultaneously on a single Oracle Solaris system. The Samba server must be disabled in order to run the SMB server. For more information, refer to "Managing SMB File Sharing and Windows Interoperability in Oracle Solaris 11.1," part number E29004-01, available from the Oracle Technical Library.

Setting the `share.nfs` property to `on` shares the ZFS file system and its descendants. For example, the following file system is available on the system:

```
NAME           USED   AVAIL  REFER  MOUNTPOINT
pool1/data     31.5K  15.6G  31.5K  /data
```

To share the `pool1/data` file system, type

```
# zfs set share.nfs=on pool1/data<cr>
```

Setting the share.nfs property to on creates the share and also publishes the share. This is referred to as an "automatic share." In the previous release of Oracle Solaris 11, this was a two-step process. In Oracle Solaris 11.1, the sharenfs property still exists, but it is simply an alias for the share.nfs property.

/etc/dfs/dfstab File

The /etc/dfs/dfstab file is no longer used in Oracle Solaris 11 to share file systems. SMF will automatically share the file system at bootup when the sharenfs property is set to on.

Display the shared file system by typing share as follows:

```
# share<cr>
pool1_data      /pool1/data      nfs      sec=sys,rw
```

The published share name is pool1_data. The share command simply displays the file system's share property.

To unpublish the share, type

```
# zfs unshare pool1/data<cr>
```

Unpublishing a share does not remove the share. It can be republished by typing:

```
# zfs share pool1/data<cr>
```

To remove the share, type

```
# zfs set share.nfs=off pool1/data<cr>
```

Additional NFS share properties can also be set on the share. These properties can be listed using the following command:

```
# zfs help -l properties|grep share.nfs<cr>
share.nfs                          YES      YES     on | off
share.nfs.aclok                    YES      YES     on | off
share.nfs.anon                     YES      YES     <uid>
share.nfs.charset.euc-cn           YES      YES     <access list>
share.nfs.charset.euc-jp           YES      YES     <access list>
...<list has been truncated to save space>...
```

These properties represent NFS share options that can be set when sharing the file system and are described in the `zfs_share(1M)` man page in the section titled "Global Share Property Descriptions." Use the `zfs share -o` command to create and publish a share using these options. For example, to share `pool1/data` with a share name of `mydata`, type

```
# zfs share -o share.nfs=on pool1/data%mydata<cr>
```

Display the share as follows:

```
# share<cr>
mydata      /pool1/data      nfs      sec=sys,rw
```

Set multiple options when creating the share as follows:

```
# zfs set share.nfs.nosuid=on -o share.nfs=on pool1/data%mydata<cr>
```

Rename the share named `mydata` to `public` as follows:

```
# zfs rename pool1/data%mydata pool1/data%public<cr>
```

Root Squash

Root squash means that root will not have write access to an NFS share when accessing the share from an NFS client. Root is mapped to the `nobody` account. Root squash is the default behavior for NFS shared resources in Oracle Solaris. The alternative is to give root write access from a particular NFS client by setting the `share.nfs.sec.default.root=` property as shown in the next example.

Change the share so that root has read-write access from the remote system named `hosta` as follows:

```
# zfs set share.nfs.sec.default.root=hosta pool1/data<cr>
```

Verify all of the NFS share property values as follows:

```
# zfs get share.nfs.all pool1/data<cr>
NAME         PROPERTY            VALUE  SOURCE
pool1/data   share.nfs.aclok     off    default
```

```
pool1/data   share.nfs.anon                  default
pool1/data   share.nfs.charset.*  ...        default
pool1/data   share.nfs.cksum                 default
pool1/data   share.nfs.index                 default
pool1/data   share.nfs.log                   default
pool1/data   share.nfs.noaclfab   off        default
pool1/data   share.nfs.nosub      off        default
pool1/data   share.nfs.nosuid     on         default
pool1/data   share.nfs.sec                   default
pool1/data   share.nfs.sec.*      ...        default
```

Another option is to list only the properties that have had their default values changed as follows:

```
# zfs get -e -s local,received,inherited share.all pool1/data<cr>
NAME        PROPERTY                      VALUE  SOURCE
pool1/data  share.nfs                     off    local
pool1/data  share.nfs.nosuid              on     local
pool1/data  share.nfs.sec.default.root    hosta  local
```

The `listshares` pool property is used to determine whether share information is displayed when the `zfs list` command is executed. By default, `listshares` is set to `off`. When I list the ZFS file system, I do not see the shares listed. However, when I set the value of `listshares` to `on` as follows:

```
# zpool set listshares=on pool1<cr>
```

then the `zfs list` command displays the shares:

```
# zfs list<cr>
NAME                    USED  AVAIL  REFER  MOUNTPOINT
pool1                   180K  35.2G    33K  /pool1
pool1/data               31K  35.2G    31K  /pool1/data
pool1/data%public          -      -      -  /pool1/data
pool1/data2              31K  35.2G    31K  /pool1/data2
pool1/data2%               -      -      -  /pool1/data2
...<output has been truncated>...
```

ZFS Sharing within a Non-Global Zone

Previous versions of Oracle Solaris did not allow a non-global zone to be an NFS server or to share NFS resources. In Oracle Solaris 11, you can create and publish NFS shares within the non-global zone. When sharing a ZFS file system, create the share in the non-global zone using the methods described earlier. If a ZFS file system's `mountpoint` property is set to legacy, the file system can be shared using the legacy `share` command within the non-global zone.

Mounting a Remote File System

On the NFS client, use the `mount` command to mount a shared NFS file system on a remote host. Here is the syntax for mounting NFS file systems:

```
mount -F nfs <options> <-o specific-options> <-O> <server>:<file-system> <mount-point>
```

In this syntax, *<server>* is the name (or IP address) of the NFS server on which the file system is located, *<file-system>* is the name of the shared file system on the NFS server, and *<mount-point>* is the name of the local directory that serves as the mountpoint. As you can see, this is similar to mounting a local legacy file system. The options for the `mount` command are described in Table 10-4.

Table 10-4 NFS `mount` Command Syntax

Option	Description
`-F nfs`	This option specifies the `FSType` on which to operate. In this case, the value is `NFS`.
`-r`	`-r` mounts the specified file system as read-only.
`-m`	`-m` does not append an entry to the `/etc/mnttab` table of the mounted file systems.
`-o` *<specific options>*	This option can be any of the following options, separated by commas: `rw` | `ro`: The resource is mounted read-write or read-only. The default is `rw`. `acdirmax=`*<n>*: This option designates the maximum time that cached attributes are held after directory update. The default is 60 seconds. `acdirmin=`*<n>*: This option designates the minimum time that cached attributes are held after directory update. The default is 30 seconds. `acregmax=`*<n>*: This option designates the maximum time that cached attributes are held after file modification. The default is 60 seconds. `acregmin=`*<n>*: This option designates the minimum time that cached attributes are held after file modification. The default is 3 seconds. `actimeo=`*<n>*: This option sets the minimum and maximum times for directories and regular files, in seconds. `forcedirectio` | `noforcedirectio`: If the file system is mounted with `forcedirectio`, data is transferred directly between client and server, with no buffering on the client. Using `noforcedirectio` causes buffering to be done on the client.

Option	Description
	`grpid`: The GID of a new file is unconditionally inherited from that of the parent directory, overriding any set-GID options. `noac`: This option suppresses data and attribute caching. `nocto`: Do not perform the normal close-to-open consistency. This option can be used when only one client is accessing a specified file system. In this case, performance may be improved, but it should be used with caution. `suid` | `nosuid`: `setuid` execution is enabled or disabled. The default is `suid`. `remount`: If a file system is mounted as read-only, this option remounts it as read-write. `bg` | `fg`: If the first attempt to mount the remote file system fails, this option retries it in the background (`bg`) or in the foreground (`fg`). The default is `fg`. `quota`: This option checks whether the user is over the quota on this file system. If the file system has quotas enabled on the server, quotas are still checked for operations on this file system. `noquota`: This option prevents `quota` from checking whether the user has exceeded the quota on this file system. If the file system has quotas enabled on the server, quotas are still checked for operations on this file system. retry=<*n*>: This option specifies the number of times to retry the mount operation. The default is `10000`. vers=<*NFS-version-number*>: By default, the version of NFS protocol used between the client and the server is the highest one available on both systems. If the NFS server does not support the NFS 4 protocol, the NFS mount uses version 2 or 3. port=<*n*>: This option specifies the server IP port number. The default is `NFS_PORT`. `proto=netid` | `rdma`: The default transport is the first `rdma` protocol supported by both client and server. If no `rdma`, TCP is used and, failing that, UDP. Note that NFS version 4 does not use UDP, so if you specify `proto=udp`, NFS version 4 is not used. `public`: This option forces the use of the public file handle when connecting to the NFS server. `sec=mode[:mode]`: This option publishes a share by using one or more of the specified security modes. The mode in the `sec=mode` option must be a node name supported on the client. If the `sec=` option is not specified, the default security mode used is AUTH_SYS. Multiple `sec=` options can be specified on the command line, although each mode can appear only once. The security modes are defined in `nfssec(5)`.

(*continues*)

Table 10-4 NFS `mount` Command Syntax (*Continued*)

Option	Description
`-O` *<specific options>*	`rsize=`*<n>*: This option sets the read buffer size to *<n>* bytes. The default value is `32768` with version 3 or 4 of the NFS protocol. The default can be negotiated down if the server prefers a smaller transfer size. With NFS version 2, the default value is `8192`. `wsize=`*<n>*: This option sets the write buffer size to *<n>* bytes. The default value is `32768` with version 3 or 4 of the NFS protocol. The default can be negotiated down if the server prefers a smaller transfer size. With version 2, the default value is `8192`. `timeo=`*<n>*: This option sets the NFS timeout to *<n>* tenths of a second. The default value is 11 tenths of a second for connectionless transports and 600 tenths of a second for connection-oriented transports. `retrans=`*<n>*: This option sets the number of NFS retransmissions to *<n>*; the default value is `5`. For connection-oriented transports, this option has no effect because it is assumed that the transport will perform retransmissions on behalf of NFS. `soft` | `hard`: This option returns an error if the server does not respond (`soft`), or it continues the retry request until the server responds (`hard`). If you're using `hard`, the system appears to hang until the NFS server responds. The default value is `hard`. `intr` | `nointr`: This option enables or does not enable keyboard interrupts to kill a process that hangs while waiting for a response on a hard-mounted file system. The default is `intr`, which makes it possible for clients to interrupt applications that might be waiting for an NFS server to respond. `xattr` | `noxattr`: This option allows or disallows the creation of extended attributes. The default is `xattr` (allow extended attributes). `-O`: The overlay mount lets the file system be mounted over an existing mountpoint, making the underlying file system inaccessible. If a mount is attempted on a preexisting mountpoint and this flag is not set, the mount fails, producing the "device busy" error.

The following example describes how to mount an NFS file system named `/data`, located on the remote server named `sysa`, and mounting it on the local mountpoint named `/mnt` using default options:

```
# mount -F nfs sysa:/data /mnt<cr>
```

An optional method is to mount the NFS file system using an NFS URL as follows:

```
# mount -F nfs nfs://sysa:/data /mnt<cr>
```

File systems mounted with the bg option indicate that mount is to retry in the background if the server's mount daemon (mountd) does not respond when, for example, the NFS server is restarted. From the NFS client, mount retries the request up to the count specified in the retry=<*n*> option. After the file system is mounted, each NFS request made in the kernel waits a specified number of seconds for a response (specified with the timeo=<*n*> option). If no response arrives, the timeout is multiplied by 2, and the request is retransmitted. If the number of retransmissions has reached the number specified in the retrans=<*n*> option, a file system mounted with the soft option returns an error, and the file system mounted with the hard option prints a warning message and continues to retry the request. Oracle recommends that file systems mounted as read-write or containing executable files should always be mounted with the hard option. If you use soft-mounted file systems, unexpected I/O errors can occur. For example, consider a write request: If the NFS server goes down, the pending write request simply gives up, resulting in a corrupted file on the remote file system. A read-write file system should always be mounted with the specified hard and intr options. This lets users make their own decisions about killing hung processes. You use the following to mount a file system named /data located on a host named thor with the hard and intr options:

```
# mount -F nfs -o hard,intr thor:/data /data<cr>
```

If a file system is mounted hard and the intr option is not specified, the process hangs when the NFS server goes down or the network connection is lost. The process continues to hang until the NFS server or network connection becomes operational. For a terminal process, this can be annoying. If intr is specified, sending an interrupt signal to the process kills it. For a terminal process, you can do this by pressing *Ctrl+C*. For a background process, sending an INT or QUIT signal usually works:

```
# kill -QUIT 3421<cr>
```

Overkill Won't Work

Sending a kill signal -9 does not terminate a hung NFS process.

To mount a file system called /data that is located on an NFS server called thor, you issue the following command, as root, from the NFS client:

```
# mount -F nfs -o ro thor:/data /thor_data<cr>
```

In this case, the /data file system from the server thor is mounted read-only on /thor_data on the local system. Mounting from the command line enables temporary viewing of the file system. If the umount command is issued or the client is restarted, the mount is lost. If you would like this file system to be mounted automatically at every startup, you can add the following line to the /etc/vfstab file:

```
thor:/data - /thor_data nfs - yes ro
```

Sometimes you rely on NFS mountpoints for critical information. If the NFS server were to go down unexpectedly, you would lose the information contained at that mountpoint. You can address this issue by using client-side failover. With client-side failover, you specify an alternative host to use in case the primary host fails. The primary and alternative hosts should contain equivalent directory structures and identical files. This option is available only on read-only file systems.

To set up client-side failover, on the NFS client, mount the file system using the -ro option. You can do this from the command line or by adding an entry to the /etc/vfstab file that looks like the following:

```
zeus,thor:/data - /remote_data nfs - no ro
```

If multiple file systems are named and the first server in the list is down, failover uses the next alternative server to access files. To mount a replicated set of NFS file systems, which might have different paths to the file system, you use the following mount command with a comma separated list of <*server*>:<*filesystem*> paths as follows:

```
# mount -F nfs -o ro zeus:/usr/local/data,thor:/home/data /usr/local/data<cr>
```

Replication is discussed further in the "AutoFS" section later in this chapter.

Verify the mounted NFS file system as follows:

```
# nfsstat -m<cr>
/mnt from sysa:/data
 Flags:
         vers=4,proto=tcp,sec=sys,hard,intr,link,symlink,acl,rsize=1048576,wsize=1048576,
retrans=5,timeo=600
 Attr cache:      acregmin=3,acregmax=60,acdirmin=30,acdirmax=60
```

Each mounted NFS file system is listed along with the options used to mount each file system. The NFS protocol used is also displayed.

It's important to know which systems have mounted a shared resource on an NFS server. For instance, if you reboot the NFS server, several NFS clients might be affected. Previous versions of Oracle Solaris had the `showmount` and `dfmounts` commands that would display this client information on the server. These commands do not work on NFS version 4 and, as of this writing, no replacement has been implemented.

Changing the NFS Version

You may want to change the NFS version that is used by default on your system. Oracle Solaris 11 uses NFS v4 by default, but this can be changed by using the `sharectl` command. For example, if you have an NFS client running Oracle Solaris 11 and if you will be accessing NFS shares located on an Oracle Solaris 9 server, the client will automatically negotiate with the server and connect using the highest available version. On Oracle Solaris 9, that version would be v3. You may want to make v3 the default on the client. Do this as follows:

```
# sharectl set -p client_versmax=3 nfs<cr>
```

You can also specify that you do not want the client to ever negotiate down to version 2. Do this as follows:

```
# sharectl set -p client_versmin=3 nfs<cr>
```

Both commands could be used together, setting the min and max, to limit the client to only version 3.

The system administrator can also specify the version of NFS to be used when mounting the remote NFS share. In the following example, the `vers` option to the `mount` command is used to mount the `/data` file system on `sysa` using NFS version 4:

```
# mount -F nfs -o vers=4 sysa:/data /mnt<cr>
```

Use the nfsstat command to verify which version of NFS the server and client are using. The nfsstat command will display statistical information about NFS and RPC. In the following example, I'll check the NFS statistics for the NFS mountpoint named /net/sysa/data:

```
# nfsstat -m /net/sysa/data<cr>
/net/sysa/data from sysa:/data
 Flags:
         vers=4,proto=tcp,sec=sys,hard,intr,link,symlink,acl,mirrormount,rsize=1048576,
wsize=1048576,retrans=5,timeo=600
 Attr cache:    acregmin=3,acregmax=60,acdirmin=30,acdirmax=60
```

The -m option displays statistics for the NFS-mounted file system specified. Notice that version 4 is being used.

AutoFS

When a network contains even a moderate number of systems all trying to mount file systems from each other, managing NFS can quickly become a nightmare. The AutoFS facility, also called the "automounter," is designed to handle such situations by providing a method by which remote directories are mounted automatically, only when they are being used. AutoFS, a client-side service, is a file system structure that provides automatic mounting.

When a user or an application accesses an NFS mountpoint, the mount is established. When the file system is no longer needed or has not been accessed for a certain period, the file system is automatically unmounted. As a result, network overhead is lower, the system boots faster because NFS mounts are done later, and systems can be shut down with fewer ill effects and hung processes.

File systems shared through the NFS service can be mounted via AutoFS. AutoFS is initialized by automount, which is run automatically when a system is started. The automount daemon, automountd, runs continuously, mounting and unmounting remote directories on an as-needed basis.

Mounting does not need to be done at system startup, and the user does not need to know the superuser password to mount a directory (normally file system mounts require superuser privilege). With AutoFS, users do not use the mount and umount commands. The AutoFS service mounts file systems as the user accesses them and unmounts file systems when they are no longer required, without any intervention on the part of the user.

However, some file systems still need to be mounted using the mount command with root privileges. For example, on a diskless computer, you must mount /, /usr, and /usr/kvm by using the mount command, and you cannot take advantage of AutoFS.

Two programs support the AutoFS service: automount and automountd. Both are run when a system is started by the svc:/system/filesystem/autofs:default service identifier.

AutoFS File System Package

The autofs package must be installed on the server. Verify that the package is installed by typing pkg info autofs<cr>.

The automount service sets up the AutoFS mountpoints and associates the information in the /etc/auto_master file with each mountpoint. The automount command, which is called at system startup time, reads the master map file /etc/auto_master to create the initial set of AutoFS mounts. These mounts are not automatically mounted at startup time. They are trigger points, also called "trigger nodes," under which file systems are mounted in the future. The following is the syntax for automount:

```
automount [-t <duration>] [-v]
```

Table 10-5 describes the syntax options for the automount command.

If it is not specifically set, the value for *<duration>* of an unused mount is set to 10 minutes. In most circumstances, this value is good; however, on systems that have many automounted file systems, you might need to decrease the *<duration>* value. In particular, if a server has many users, active checking of the automounted file systems every 10 minutes can be inefficient. Checking AutoFS every 300 seconds (5 minutes) might be better. You can edit the /etc/default/autofs script to change the default values and make them persistent across reboots.

If AutoFS receives a request to access a file system that is not currently mounted, AutoFS calls automountd, which mounts the requested file system under the trigger node.

Table 10-5 automount Command Syntax

Option	Description
-t *<duration>*	This option sets the time, in seconds, that a file system is to remain mounted if it is not being used. The default value is 600 seconds.
-v	-v selects verbose mode. Running the automount command in verbose mode allows easier troubleshooting.

The automountd daemon handles the mount and unmount requests from the AutoFS service. The syntax of this command is as follows:

```
automountd [-Tnv] [-D <name>=<value>]
```

Table 10-6 describes the syntax options for the automountd command.

The automountd daemon is completely independent from the automount command. Because of this separation, it is possible to add, delete, or change map information without first having to stop and start the automountd daemon process.

When AutoFS runs, automount and automountd initiate at startup time from the svc:/system/filesystem/autofs service identifier. If a request is made to access a file system at an AutoFS mountpoint, the system goes through the following steps:

1. AutoFS intercepts the request.
2. AutoFS sends a message to the automountd daemon for the requested file system to be mounted.
3. automountd locates the file system information in a map and performs the mount.
4. AutoFS allows the intercepted request to proceed.
5. AutoFS unmounts the file system after a period of inactivity.

Caution

Mounts managed through the AutoFS service should not be manually mounted or unmounted. Even if the operation is successful, the AutoFS service does not check that the object has been unmounted, and this can result in possible inconsistency. A restart clears all AutoFS mountpoints.

Table 10-6 automountd **Command Syntax**

Option	Description
-T	-T displays each RPC to standard output. You use this option for troubleshooting.
-n	This option disables browsing on all AutoFS nodes.
-v	-v logs all status messages to the console.
-D *<name>*=*<value>*	This option substitutes a value for the automount map variable indicated by *<name>*. The default *<value>* for the automount map is /etc/auto_master.

AutoFS Maps

The behavior of the automounter is governed by its configuration files, called "maps." AutoFS searches maps to navigate its way through the network. Map files contain information, such as the location of other maps to be searched or the location of a user's home directory, for example.

The three types of automount maps are the master map, the direct map, and the indirect map. Each is described in the following sections.

Master Maps

To start the navigation process, the `automount` command reads the master map at system startup. This map tells the automounter about map files and mountpoints. The master map lists all direct and indirect maps and their associated directories.

The master map, which is in the `/etc/auto_master` file, associates a directory with a map. The master map is a list that specifies all the maps that AutoFS should check. The following example shows what an `auto_master` file could contain:

```
# Copyright (c) 1992, 2011, Oracle and/or its affiliates. All rights reserved.
#
# Master map for automounter
#
+auto_master
/net            -hosts          -nosuid,nobrowse
/home           auto_home       -nobrowse
/nfs4           -fedfs          -ro,nosuid,nobrowse
```

This example shows the default `auto_master` file. The lines that begin with "#" are comments. The line that contains "`+auto_master`" specifies the AutoFS NIS table map. Each line thereafter in the master map, `/etc/auto_master`, has the following syntax:

```
<mount-point> <map-name> <mount-options>
```

Each of these fields is described in Table 10-7.

> **Map Format**
>
> A line that begins with a pound sign (#) is a comment, and everything that follows it until the end of the line is ignored. To split long lines into shorter ones, you can put a backslash (\) at the end of the line. The maximum number of characters in an entry is 1,024.

Table 10-7 `/etc/auto_master` **Fields**

Field	Description
<mount-point>	This is the full (absolute) pathname of a directory that is used as the mountpoint. If the directory does not exist, AutoFS creates it, if possible. If the directory does exist and is not empty, mounting it hides its contents. In that case, AutoFS issues a warning. Using the notation "/-" as a mountpoint indicates that a direct map with no particular mountpoint is associated with the map.
<map-name>	This is the map that AutoFS uses to find directions to locations or mount information. If the name is preceded by a slash (/), AutoFS interprets the name as a local file. Otherwise, AutoFS searches for the mount information by using the search specified in the name service switch configuration file (/etc/nsswitch.conf).
<mount-options>	This is an optional comma-separated list of options that apply to the mounting of the entries specified in *<map-name>*, unless the entries list other options. Options for each specific type of file system are listed in Table 10-4. For NFS-specific mountpoints, the bg (background) and fg (foreground) options do not apply.

Every Oracle Solaris installation comes with a master map, called /etc/auto_master, that has the default entries described earlier. Without any changes to the generic system setup, clients should be able to access remote file systems through the /net mountpoint. The following entry in /etc/auto_master allows this to happen:

```
/net  -hosts  -nosuid,nobrowse
```

For example, let's say that you have an NFS server named apollo that has the /export file system shared. Another system, named zeus, exists on the network. This system has the default /etc/auto_master file; by default, it has a directory named /net. If you type the following, the command comes back showing that the directory is empty—nothing is in it:

```
# ls /net<cr>
```

Now type this:

```
# ls /net/apollo<cr>
```

The system responds with this:

```
export
```

Why was the /net directory empty the first time you issued the ls command? When you issued ls /net/apollo, why did it find a subdirectory? This is the automounter in action. When you specified /net with a hostname, automountd looked at the map file—in this case, /etc/hosts—and found apollo and its IP address. It then went to apollo, found the exported file system, and created a local mountpoint for /net/apollo/export. It also added the following entry to the /etc/mnttab table:

```
-hosts  /net/apollo/export  autofs  nosuid,nobrowse,ignore,nest,dev=2b80005 941812769
```

This entry in the /etc/mnttab table is referred to as a trigger node (because, in changing to the specified directory, the mount of the file system is "triggered").

If you enter mount, you won't see anything mounted at this point:

```
# mount<cr>
```

The system responds with this:

```
/ on rpool/ROOT/solaris read/write/setuid/devices/rstchown/dev=4750002 on Wed Dec 31
19:00:00 1969
/devices on /devices read/write/setuid/devices/rstchown/dev=8880000 on Mon Feb 25
04:41:11 2013
/dev on /dev read/write/setuid/devices/rstchown/dev=88c0000 on Mon Feb 25 04:41:11 2013
/system/contract on ctfs read/write/setuid/devices/rstchown/dev=8980001 on Mon Feb 25
04:41:11 2013
/proc on proc read/write/setuid/devices/rstchown/dev=8900000 on Mon Feb 25 04:41:11 2013
/etc/mnttab on mnttab read/write/setuid/devices/rstchown/dev=89c0001 on Mon Feb 25
04:41:11 2013
/system/volatile on swap read/write/setuid/devices/rstchown/xattr/dev=8a00001 on Mon
Feb 25 04:41:11 2013
/system/object on objfs read/write/setuid/devices/rstchown/dev=8a40001 on Mon Feb 25
04:41:11 2013
/etc/dfs/sharetab on sharefs read/write/setuid/devices/rstchown/dev=8a80001 on Mon Feb
25 04:41:11 2013
/lib/libc.so.1 on /usr/lib/libc/libc_hwcap1.so.1 read/write/setuid/devices/rstchown/
dev=4750002 on Mon Feb 25 04:41:23 2013
/dev/fd on fd read/write/setuid/devices/rstchown/dev=8b80001 on Mon Feb 25 04:41:26 2013
/var on rpool/ROOT/solaris/var read/write/setuid/devices/rstchown/nonbmand/exec/xattr/
atime/dev=4750003 on Mon Feb 25 04:41:27 2013
/tmp on swap read/write/setuid/devices/rstchown/xattr/dev=8a00002 on Mon Feb 25 04:41:27 2013
/var/share on rpool/VARSHARE read/write/setuid/devices/rstchown/nonbmand/exec/xattr/
atime/dev=4750004 on Mon Feb 25 04:41:28 2013
/export on rpool/export read/write/setuid/devices/rstchown/nonbmand/exec/xattr/atime/
dev=4750005 on Mon Feb 25 04:41:45 2013
```

```
/export/home on rpool/export/home read/write/setuid/devices/rstchown/nonbmand/exec/
xattr/atime/dev=4750006 on Mon Feb 25 04:41:45 2013
/export/home/bcalkins on rpool/export/home/bcalkins read/write/setuid/devices/
rstchown/nonbmand/exec/xattr/atime/dev=4750007 on Mon Feb 25 04:41:45 2013
/rpool on rpool read/write/setuid/devices/rstchown/nonbmand/exec/xattr/atime/
dev=4750008 on Mon Feb 25 04:41:45 2013
/home/bcalkins on /export/home/bcalkins read/write/setuid/devices/rstchown/dev=4750007
on Mon Feb 25 09:42:39 2013
```

Now type this:

```
# ls /net/apollo/export<cr>
```

You should have a bit of a delay while `automountd` mounts the file system. The system responds with a list of files located on the mounted file system. For this particular system, it responds with the following:

```
files  lost+found
```

The files listed are files located on `apollo`, in the `/export` directory. If you enter `mount`, you see an NFS file system mounted on `apollo` that wasn't listed before.

The automounter automatically mounted the `/export` file system that was located on `apollo`. Now look at the `/etc/mnttab` file again, and you will see additional entries for the NFS-mounted resource.

If the `/net/apollo/export` directory is accessed, the AutoFS service completes the process, with these steps:

1. It pings the server's mount service to see whether it's alive.
2. It mounts the requested file system under `/net/apollo/export`. Now the `/etc/mnttab` file contains the new entries for the remote NFS mount.

Because the automounter lets all users mount file systems, root access is not required. AutoFS also provides for automatic unmounting of file systems, so there is no need to unmount them when you are done.

Direct Maps

A direct map lists a set of unrelated mountpoints that might be spread out across the file system. A complete path (for example, `/usr/local/bin`, `/usr/man`) is listed in the map as a mountpoint. A good example of where to use a direct mountpoint is for `/usr/man`. The `/usr` directory contains many other directories, such as

/usr/bin and /usr/local; therefore, it cannot be an indirect mountpoint. If you used an indirect map for /usr/man, the local /usr file system would be the mountpoint, and you would cover up the local /usr/bin and /usr/etc directories when you established the mount. A direct map lets the automounter complete mounts on a single directory entry such as /usr/man, and these mounts appear as links with the name of the direct mountpoint.

A direct map is specified in a configuration file called /etc/auto_direct. This file is not available by default and needs to be created. With a direct map, there is a direct association between a mountpoint on the client and a directory on the server. A direct map has a full pathname and indicates the relationship explicitly. This is a typical /etc/auto_direct map file that was created:

```
/usr/local          -ro
/share                       ivy:/export/local/share
/src                         ivy:/export/local/src
/usr/man            -ro      apollo:/usr/man zeus:/usr/man neptune:/usr/man
/usr/game           -ro      peach:/usr/games
/usr/spool/news     -ro      jupiter:/usr/spool/news saturn:/var/spool/news
```

Map Naming

The direct map name /etc/auto_direct is not a mandatory name; it is used here as an example of a direct map. The name of a direct map must be added to the /etc/auto_master file, but it can be any name you choose. It should, however, be meaningful to the system administrator.

Lines in direct maps have the following syntax:

```
<key> <mount-options> <location>
```

The fields of this syntax are described in Table 10-8.

In the previous example of the /etc/auto_direct map file, the mountpoints, /usr/man and /usr/spool/news, list more than one location:

```
/usr/man            -ro   apollo:/usr/man zeus:/usr/man neptune:/usr/man
/usr/spool/news     -ro   jupiter:/usr/spool/news saturn:/var/spool/news
```

Multiple locations, such as those shown here, are used for replication or failover. For the purposes of failover, a file system can be called a replica if each file is the same size and it is the same type of file system. Permissions, creation dates, and other file attributes are not a consideration. If the file size or the file system types are different, the remap fails and the process hangs until the old server becomes available.

Table 10-8 Direct Map Fields

Field	Description
<key>	*<key>* indicates the pathname of the mountpoint in a direct map. This pathname specifies the local directory on which to mount the automounted directory.
<mount-options>	This field indicates the options you want to apply to this particular mount. These options, which are listed in Table 10-4, are required only if they differ from the map default options specified in the `/etc/auto_master` file. There is no concatenation of options between the automounter maps. Any options added to an automounter map override all of the options listed in previously searched maps. For instance, options included in the `auto_master` map would be overwritten by corresponding entries in any other map.
<location>	This field indicates the remote location of the file system, specified as *<server:pathname>*. More than one location can be specified. *<pathname>* should not include an automounted mount point; it should be the actual absolute path to the file system. For instance, the location of a home directory should be listed as `server:/export/home/username`, not as `server:/home/username`.

Replication makes sense only if you mount a file system that is read-only because you must have some control over the locations of files that you write or modify. You don't want to modify one server's files on one occasion and, minutes later, modify the "same" file on another server. The benefit of replication is that the best available server is used automatically, without any effort required by the user.

If the file systems are configured as replicas, the clients have the advantage of using failover. Not only is the best server automatically determined, but, if that server becomes unavailable, the client automatically uses the next-best server.

An example of a good file system to configure as a replica is the manual (man) pages. In a large network, more than one server can export the current set of man pages. Which server you mount them from doesn't matter, as long as the server is running and sharing its file systems. In the previous example, multiple replicas are expressed as a list of mount locations in the map entry. With multiple mount locations specified, you could mount the man pages from the `apollo`, `zeus`, or `neptune` servers. The best server depends on a number of factors, including the number of servers supporting a particular NFS protocol level, the proximity of the server, and weighting. The process of selecting a server goes like this:

1. During the sorting process, a count of the number of servers supporting the NFS version 2, 3, and 4 protocols is done. The protocol supported on the most servers is the protocol that is supported by default. This provides the client

with the maximum number of servers to depend on. If version 3 servers are most abundant, the sorting process becomes more complex because they will be chosen as long as a version 2 server on the local subnet is not being ignored. Normally, servers on the local subnet are given preference over servers on a remote subnet. A version 2 server on the local subnet can complicate matters because it could be closer than the nearest version 3 server. If there is a version 2 server on the local subnet, and the closest version 3 server is on a remote subnet, the version 2 server is given preference. This is checked only if there are more version 3 servers than version 2 servers. If there are more version 2 servers than version 3 servers, only a version 2 server is selected.

2. After the largest subset of servers that have the same protocol version is found, that server list is sorted by proximity. Servers on the local subnet are given preference over servers on a remote subnet. The closest server is given preference, which reduces latency and network traffic. If several servers are supporting the same protocol on the local subnet, the time to connect to each server is determined, and the fastest time is used.

   You can influence the selection of servers at the same proximity level by adding a numeric weighting value in parentheses after the server name in the AutoFS map. Here's an example:

   ```
   /usr/man -ro apollo,zeus(1),neptune(2):/usr/man
   ```

   Servers without a weighting have a value of `0`, which makes them the most likely servers to be selected. The higher the weighting value is, the less chance the server has of being selected. All other server-selection factors are more important than weighting. Weighting is considered only in selections between servers with the same network proximity.

With failover, the sorting is checked once at mount time, to select one server from which to mount, and again if the mounted server becomes unavailable. Failover is particularly useful in a large network with many subnets. AutoFS chooses the nearest server and therefore confines NFS network traffic to a local network segment. In servers with multiple network interfaces, AutoFS lists the hostname associated with each network interface as if it were a separate server. It then selects the nearest interface to the client.

In the following example, you set up a direct map for `/usr/local` on `zeus`. Currently, `zeus` has a directory called `/usr/local` with the following directories:

```
# ls /usr/local<cr>
```

The following local directories are displayed:

```
bin  etc  files  programs
```

If you set up the automount direct map, you can see how the /usr/local directory is overwritten by the NFS mount. Follow the procedure shown in following steps for creating a direct map.

Creating a Direct Map

For these steps, you need two systems: a local system (client) and a remote system named zeus. It does not matter what the local (client) system is named, but if your remote system is not named zeus, be sure to substitute your system's hostname.

Perform steps 1 and 2 on the remote system, zeus:

1. Create a directory named /usr/local, and share it:

```
# mkdir /usr/local<cr>
# share -F nfs /usr/local<cr>
```

2. Create the following files and directories in the /usr/local directory:

```
# mkdir /usr/local/bin /usr/local/etc<cr>
# touch /usr/local/files /usr/local/programs<cr>
```

Perform steps 3 through 5 on the local system (client):

3. Add the following entry in the master map file called /etc/auto_master:

```
/-  /etc/auto_direct
```

4. Create the direct map file called /etc/auto_direct with the following entry:

```
/usr/local  zeus:/usr/local
```

5. Because you're modifying a direct map, run automount to reload the AutoFS tables:

```
# automount<cr>
```

If you have access to the /usr/local directory, the NFS mountpoint is established by using the direct map you have set up. The contents of /usr/local have changed because the direct map has covered up the local copy of /usr/local:

```
# ls /usr/local<cr>
```

You should see the following directories listed:

```
bin  etc  files  programs
```

Overlay Mounting

The local contents of /usr/local have not been overwritten. After the NFS mountpoint is unmounted, the original contents of /usr/local are redisplayed.

If you enter the mount command, you see that /usr/local is now mounted remotely from zeus:

```
# mount<cr>
...<output has been truncated>...
/usr/local on zeus:/usr/local remote/read/write/setuid/devices/rstchown/xattr/\
dev=8b00005 on Mon Feb 25 16:32:11 2013
```

Indirect Maps

Indirect maps are the simplest and most useful AutoFS maps. An indirect map uses a key's substitution value to establish the association between a mountpoint on the client and a directory on the server. Indirect maps are useful for accessing specific file systems, such as home directories, from anywhere on the network. The following entry in the /etc/auto_master file is an example of an indirect map:

```
/share    /etc/auto_share
```

With this entry in the /etc/auto_master file, /etc/auto_share is the name of the indirect map file for the mountpoint /share. For this entry, you need to create an indirect map file named /etc/auto_share, which would look like this:

```
# share directory map for automounter
#
ws      neptune:/export/share/ws
```

If the /share/ws directory is accessed, the AutoFS service creates a trigger node for /share/ws, and the following entry is made in the /etc/mnttab file:

```
-hosts  /share/ws  autofs nosuid,nobrowse,ignore,nest,dev=###
```

If the /share/ws directory is accessed, the AutoFS service completes the process with these steps:

1. It pings the server's mount service to see whether it's alive.
2. It mounts the requested file system under /share. Now the /etc/mnttab file contains the following entries:

```
-hosts  /share/ws  autofs  nosuid,nobrowse,ignore,nest,dev=###
neptune:/export/share/ws /share/ws  nfs  nosuid,dev=#### #####
```

Lines in indirect maps have the following syntax:

```
<key> <mount-options> <location>
```

The fields in this syntax are described in Table 10-9.

For example, say an indirect map is being used with user home directories. As users log in to several different systems, their home directories are not always local to the system. It's convenient for the users to use the automounter to access their

Table 10-9 Indirect Map Field Syntax

Field	Description
<key>	*<key>* is a simple name (with no slashes) in an indirect map.
<mount-options>	A comma separated list of options to apply to this particular mount. These options, which are described in Table 10-4, are required only if they differ from the map default options specified in the /etc/auto_master file.
<location>	*<location>* is the remote location of the file system, specified as *<server:pathname>*. More than one location can be specified. *<pathname>* should not include an automounted mountpoint; it should be the actual absolute path to the file system. For instance, the location of a directory should be listed as server:/usr/local, not as server:/net/server/usr/local.

home directories, regardless of what system they're logged in to. To accomplish this, the default /etc/auto_master map file needs to contain the following entry:

```
/home     /etc/auto_home     -nobrowse
```

/etc/auto_home is the name of the indirect map file that contains the entries to be mounted under /home. A typical /etc/auto_home map file might look like this:

```
# more /etc/auto_home<cr>
dean                      willow:/export/home/dean
william                   cypress:/export/home/william
nicole                    poplar:/export/home/nicole
glenda                    pine:/export/home/glenda
steve                     apple:/export/home/steve
burk                      ivy:/export/home/burk
neil    -rw,nosuid        peach:/export/home/neil
```

Indirect Map Names

As with direct maps, the actual name of an indirect map is up to the system administrator, but a corresponding entry must be placed in the /etc/auto_master file, and the name should be meaningful to the system administrator.

Now assume that the /etc/auto_home map is on the host oak. If user neil has an entry in the password database that specifies his home directory as /home/neil, whenever he logs in to computer oak, AutoFS mounts the directory /export/home/neil, which resides on the computer peach. Neil's home directory is mounted read-write, nosuid. Anyone, including Neil, has access to this path from any computer set up with the master map referring to the /etc/auto_home map in this example. Under these conditions, user neil can run login, or rlogin, on any computer that has the /etc/auto_home map set up, and his home directory is mounted in place for him.

Another example of when to use an indirect map is when you want to make all project-related files available under a directory called /data that is to be common across all workstations at the site. The following steps show how to set up an indirect map:

Setting Up an Indirect Map

1. Add an entry for the /data directory to the /etc/auto_master map file:

```
/data  /etc/auto_data  -nosuid
```

The auto_data map file, named /etc/auto_data, determines the contents of the /data directory.

2. Add the -nosuid option as a precaution. The -nosuid option prevents users from creating files with the setuid or setgid bit set.
3. Create the /etc/auto_data file and add entries to the auto_data map. The auto_data map is organized so that each entry describes a subproject. Edit /etc/auto_data to create a map that looks like the following:

```
compiler        apollo:/export/data/&
window          apollo:/export/data/&
files            zeus:/export/data/&
drivers         apollo:/export/data/&
man             zeus:/export/data/&
tools           zeus:/export/data/&
```

Using the Entry Key

The ampersand (&) at the end of each entry is an abbreviation for the entry key. For instance, the first entry above is equivalent to the entry: compiler apollo:/export/data/compiler.

Because the servers apollo and zeus view similar AutoFS maps locally, any users who log in to these computers find the /data file system as expected. These users are provided with direct access to local files through loopback mounts instead of NFS mounts.

4. Because you changed the /etc/auto_master map, the final step is to reload the AutoFS tables:

```
# automount<cr>
```

Now, if a user changes to the /data/compiler directory, the mountpoint to apollo:/export/data/compiler is created:

```
# cd /data/compiler<cr>
```

5. Type mount to see the mountpoint that was established:

```
# mount<cr>
```

The system shows that /data/compiler is mapped to apollo:/export/data/compiler:

```
/data/compiler on apollo:/export/data/compiler read/write/remote on Mon Feb 25
17:17:02 2013
```

If the user changes to /data/tools, the mountpoint to zeus:/export/data/tools is created under the mountpoint /data/tools.

Directory Creation

There is no need to create the directory /data/compiler to be used as the mountpoint. AutoFS creates all the necessary directories before establishing the mount.

You can modify, delete, or add entries to maps to meet the needs of the environment. As applications (and other file systems that users require) change location, the maps must reflect those changes. You can modify AutoFS maps at any time. However, changes do not take place until the file system is unmounted and remounted. If a change is made to the auto_master map or to a direct map, those changes do not take place until the AutoFS tables are reloaded:

```
# automount<cr>
```

Remember the Difference between Direct and Indirect Maps

The /- entry in /etc/auto_master signifies a direct map because no mountpoint is specified. This means that an absolute pathname is specified in the map. Indirect maps contain relative addresses, so the starting mountpoint, such as /home, appears in the /etc/auto_master entry for an indirect map.

When to Use automount

The most common and advantageous use of automount is for mounting infrequently used file systems on an NFS client, such as online reference man pages. Another common use is accessing user home directories anywhere on the network. This works well for users who do not have a dedicated system and who tend to log in from different locations. Without the AutoFS service, to permit access, a system administrator has to create home directories on every system that the user logs in to. Data has to be duplicated everywhere, and it can easily become out of sync. You certainly don't want to create permanent NFS mounts for all user home directories on each system, so mounting infrequently used file systems on an NFS client is an excellent use for `automount`.

You can also use `automount` if a read-only file system exists on more than one server. By using `automount` instead of conventional NFS mounting, you can configure the NFS client to query all the servers on which the file system exists and mount from the server that responds first.

You should avoid using `automount` to mount frequently used file systems, such as those that contain user commands or frequently used applications; conventional NFS mounting is more efficient in this situation. It is quite practical and typical to combine the use of `automount` with conventional NFS mounting on the same NFS client.

Mirror Mounts

Oracle Solaris 11 includes a new NFS feature called the "mirror mount facility," which is much easier to use than the previously described AutoFS. Mirror mounts are an enhancement that goes above and beyond AutoFS. It allows the system administrator to mount all of the server's shared NFS file systems on a client with a single mount command. For example, `sysa` has the following file systems shared:

```
# share<cr>
data        /data                      nfs    sec=sys,rw     public data
bcalkins    /export/home/bcalkins      nfs    sec=sys,rw
```

On the NFS client, I'll mount the NFS shares as follows:

```
# mount sysa:/ /mnt<cr>
```

In the NFS client's `/mnt` directory, both NFS shares are listed:

```
# ls /mnt<cr>
data  export
```

When accessing the NFS share, it is automatically mounted on the client, and both NFS file systems are now accessible from the `/mnt` directory. Furthermore, if I add a third share on the server, that mountpoint is automatically mounted on the NFS client through the same `/mnt` directory.

Mirror mounted file systems will be automatically unmounted if idle and after a certain period of inactivity. The inactivity period is set using the timeout parameter (automount -t command), which is used by the automounter for the same purpose and described earlier in this chapter.

Troubleshooting NFS Errors

After you configure NFS, it's not uncommon to encounter various NFS error messages. The following sections describe some of the common errors you may encounter while using NFS.

The Stale NFS File Handle Message

The "stale NFS file handle" message appears when a file was deleted on the NFS server and replaced with a file of the same name. In this case, the NFS server generates a new file handle for the new file. If the client is still using the old file handle, the server returns an error that the file handle is stale. If a file on the NFS server was simply renamed, the file handle remains the same.

A solution to this problem is to unmount and remount the NFS resource on the client.

The RPC: Program Not Registered Error

You may receive the "RPC: program not registered" message while trying to mount a remote NFS resource or during the boot process. This message indicates that the NFS server is not running the mountd daemon.

To solve the problem, log in to the NFS server and verify that the mountd daemon is running by issuing the following command:

```
# pgrep -fl mountd<cr>
```

If mountd is not running, verify that the file system share is created by typing

```
# zfs get share<cr>
NAME          PROPERTY    VALUE                                          SOURCE
pool1/data    share       name=data,desc=public data,path=/data,prot=nfs  local
```

Also, make sure that the sharenfs property is set to on:

```
# zfs get share.nfs pool1/data<cr>
NAME         PROPERTY    VALUE      SOURCE
pool1/data   share.nfs   on         local
```

Finally, verify that the share has been published as follows:

```
# share<cr>
data  /data  nfs  sec=sys,rw  public data
```

Verify that the NFS server services are online as follows:

```
# svcs -a|grep nfs<cr>
online          4:41:20 svc:/network/nfs/cbd:default
disabled          4:41:20 svc:/network/nfs/client:default
online            4:41:45 svc:/network/nfs/fedfs-client:default
online            9:41:52 svc:/network/nfs/mapid:default
online            9:59:32 svc:/network/nfs/status:default
online            9:59:32 svc:/network/nfs/nlockmgr:default
online            9:59:32 svc:/network/nfs/rquota:default
online            9:59:33 svc:/network/nfs/server:default
```

If the NFS services are not running, try restarting them as follows:

```
# svcadm restart svc:/network/nfs/server<cr>
```

Make sure that the `rpcbind` daemon is running on the server as follows:

```
# svcs -a|grep bind<cr>
online      10:01:23 svc:/network/rpc/bind:default
# rpcinfo -u localhost rpcbind<cr>
program 100000 version 2 ready and waiting
program 100000 version 3 ready and waiting
program 100000 version 4 ready and waiting
```

If the server is running, it prints a list of program and version numbers that are associated with the UDP protocol.

The NFS: Service Not Responding Error

The "NFS: Service not responding" error message indicates that the NFS server may not be running the required NFS server daemons.

To solve the problem, log in to the NFS server and verify that the `mountd` daemon is running by issuing the following command:

```
# pgrep -fl mountd<cr>
# rpcinfo -u localhost mountd<cr>
program 100005 version 1 ready and waiting
program 100005 version 2 ready and waiting
program 100005 version 3 ready and waiting
```

If the server is running, it prints a list of program and version numbers that are associated with UDP. If these commands fail, restart the NFS services as follows:

```
# svcadm restart svc:/network/nfs/server<cr>
```

The Server Not Responding Error

The "server not responding" message appears when the NFS server is inaccessible for some reason.

To solve the problem, verify that network connectivity exists between the client and the NFS server.

```
# ping sysa<cr>
sysa is alive
```

The RPC: Unknown Host Error

The "RPC: Unknown host" message indicates that the hostname of the NFS server is missing from the hosts table.

To solve the problem, verify that you've typed the server name correctly and that the hostname can be resolved properly as follows:

```
# getent hosts sysa<cr>
192.168.1.125  sysa
```

The No Such File or Directory Error

You may receive the "no such file or directory" message while trying to mount a remote resource or during the boot process. This error indicates that an unknown file resource is on the NFS server.

To solve the problem, make sure that you are specifying the correct share name that is shared on the server.

Summary

In this chapter, you learned what NFS is and how to share NFS resources on an NFS server. You also learned how to mount those resources on an NFS client. This chapter described AutoFS and mirror mounts and the many options that are available when you're mounting NFS resources. The goal in using these options is to minimize user downtime caused by unplanned system outages and unavailable resources.

Finally, the troubleshooting section described some of the more common problems and error messages that you may encounter while using NFS.

Index

C

J

K

L

M

O

P

Q

R

S

T

V

W

X

Z

Addison Wesley

AdobePress

ALPHA

Cisco Press

FT Press

IBM Press

Microsoft Press

New Riders

O'REILLY

Peachpit Press

PRENTICE HALL

que

Redbooks

SAMS
sas

vmware PRESS

WILEY

wrox